ENCYCLOPEDIA OF
ANTIQUES

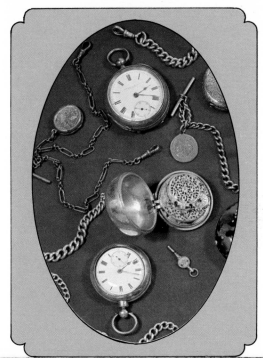

Introduction by
WENDELL GARRETT
Consultant Editor
ROSEMARY KLEIN

ENCYCLOPEDIA OF
ANTIQUES

Contributors include:
William Allan
Douglas Ash
James Ayres
Judith Banister
Lindsay Boynton
Eric Bruton
Kathryn C. Buhler
Malcolm Burgess
Ben George Burrough
Anthony Coleridge
Jeremy Cooper
Sylvia Coppen-Gardner
John Culme
John Cushion
Felice Davis
Frank Davis
Anthony Derham
Diana Dolan
Michael Eveleigh
Martha Gandy Fales
Lucinda Fletcher
Philippe Garner
Tom Milnes Gaskell
Geoffrey Godden
Ian Grant
Gabriella Gros-Galliner
Jonathan Harris
Malcolm Haslam
Charles Hay
Wendy Hefford
Oliver Hoare
G. Bernard Hughes
Graham Hughes
Therle Hughes
William Hutton
Gervase Jackson-Stops
Robert Wyse Jackson
Cedric Jagger
Madeleine Jarry
Edward T. Joy
Alison Kelly
John Kenworthy-Browne
Michael Kirkby
Ara de Korostovetz
Ralph and Terry Kovel
Peter Lazarus
Ronald A. Lee
Patricia McCawley
Katharine Morrison McClinton
Keith Middlemas
J. Jefferson Miller
Vesey Norman
Anthony Oliver
Jock Palmer
Herbert Peck
Flavia Petrie
Edward Pinto
Ada Polak
Pietro Raffo
John Raison
B. W. Robinson
Henry Sandon
Diana Scarisbrick
John Scott-Taggart
Raymond Shepherd
Simon Spero
Lynne Thornton
Kenneth Ullyett
Edmund de Unger
Shirley De Voe
J-G Watelet, S. Henrion-Giele
Geoffrey Wills
Kenneth Wilson
Nicholas Wolfers

Acknowledgments

*Cooper-Bridgeman: both pictures
this page.*
Pictor International: half-title.
*Picturepoint: endpapers and
title-spread.*

First published 1976 in the USA by
Galahad Books, a division of
A & W Promotional Book
Corporation,
95 Madison Avenue, New York,
N.Y. 10016

ISBN 0 88365 137 8

Library of Congress Catalog
Card Number 76-19199

© 1971/1976 Phoebus Publishing
Company/BPC Publishing Limited

All rights reserved

This book has been produced by
Phoebus Publishing Company in
co-operation with Octopus Books
Limited, and is published in the
USA by arrangement with Octopus
Books Limited, London, England

Produced by Mandarin Publishers
Limited
22a Westlands Road, Quarry Bay,
Hong Kong

Printed in Hong Kong

Ceramics

page 10

Ming Dynasty Porcelain, The Porcelain of Japan, Persian Potters and their Wares, The Stoneware of Germany, Italian Maiolica, French Faience, Dutch Delft, Spanish Pottery, Early American Pottery, Kaendler and Early Meissen, Mennecy and Chantilly, Early Sèvres, Chelsea Porcelain, Worcester Porcelain, Early Wedgwood, Blue and White Wares, English Lustreware, Transfer-printed Ceramics, Early American Porcelain, Staffordshire Figures, The Artist Potters, Rookwood.

Furniture

page 116

Elizabethan Oak, Early Italian Furniture, Lacquered Furniture, The Age of Walnut, Boulle and Louis XIV, William and Mary, Early American Furniture, Queen Anne, American Colonial Furniture, The Ebénistes of Louis XV, Reisener and Louis XVI, French Provincial Furniture, English Chippendale, American Chippendale, Hepplewhite, Sheraton, Early Federal Furniture, Later Federal Furniture, Consulate and Empire, Regency, Biedermeier, Shaker Furniture, Victorian Gothic, Arts and Crafts Furniture, Art Nouveau Furniture.

Glass

page 236

Venetian Glass, Early German and Bohemian Glass, Early Looking Glasses, Eighteenth-Century English Wineglasses, American Colonial Glass, Irish Glass, Later Bohemian Glass, Victorian Glass, Nineteenth-Century American Glass, French Paperweights, French Coloured Glass, English Cameo Glass, French Art Nouveau Glass, American Art Glass, Tiffany Glass.

Silver and Gold

page 306

Silver Mounted Wares, Early American Silver, German Silver, Chinoiserie Silver, Queen Anne Silver, American Colonial Silver, Paul de Lamerie, Irish Silver, Paul Revere, French Gold Boxes, French Empire Silver, Sheffield Plate, Paul Storr, Tea and Coffee Services.

Endpapers: **Chinese cabinet,** *late 17th century.*
Half-title page: **Pocket watches** *of the 19th century.*
Title spread: **Opaque twist glasses.** *Late 18th century, English.*
This page: **Gold sacred goose vessel.** *19th-century Burmese filigree work inlaid with rubies and imitation emeralds.*
(Victoria and Albert Museum, London)
Right: **Capodimonte vase** *from an 18th-century Neapolitan porcelain factory.*
(Victoria and Albert Museum)

Arts and Decoration

page 374

Ornamental Jade, Netsuke and Inro, Russian Embroidery, Persian Carpets, French Tapestry, American Coverlets, Persian Miniatures, French Fans, English Enamels, French Clocks, English Clocks, Early American Clocks, Victorian Pocket Watches, Later American Clocks and Watches, Papier-Mâché, Stevengraphs, Tunbridge Ware, Fitted Boxes, Smoking Accessories, Early Jewellery, Art Nouveau Jewellery.

Index   **page 470**

Introduction

That the collecting of antiques as well as fine arts is a 'world habit' today – practised more or less unconsciously even by the non-collectors, in overwhelming proportions and with wide-spread implications – is an observable and undisputed fact. In spite of oscillations in the world's economy and fluctuations in the tides of taste, prices in the antiques market continue to hold firm, and hardly a season passes without a number of new high records being established in the auction rooms. All of the evidence attests to a growing ascendancy of collecting, whether for profit or pleasure, by public institutions and private individuals.

It would be difficult to name a pastime that musters such singleminded devotion around the world as the collecting of antiques. Collecting is at once an art and a response to impulses of great depth. As an impulse, it is related to the life of early man in his gathering and storing of food and other elements essential to survival. As an art, it has its own long history and noble traditions. Where cultural attainments have been admired, collections of art objects have been used to gain distinction. The strong desire to preserve collections as immortal monuments to men's achievements has also been an undeniable factor. (It was the American industrialist Henry E. Huntington who said: 'The ownership of a fine library is the surest and swiftest way to immortality.') Finally men have traditionally urged upon themselves the higher search for knowledge and aesthetic satisfaction.

More specifically, the twentieth-century phenomenon of collecting antiques has grown out of a cultural homesickness for the simpler homespun ways of youth, a search for meaning amid the uncertainties and changes of the post-industrial-revolution era. When Henry Ford started his collection of Americana, he stated that he not only wished to remind people how far and how fast Americans have come since their seventeenth-century founding, but also wanted to use his restored village to 'emphasize the pioneer qualities of self-dependence and resourcefulness that carved this country out of the wilderness.' Thus Ford expressed his belief that 'the farther you look back, the farther you can look ahead.'

The collecting habit can, admittedly, become something of a mania. A beginning collector, often impelled by the valor of ignorance, is frequently unaware of the vastness of the subject and the difficulties that lie in the way of attaining any sort of supremacy in it. This is fortunate, for otherwise he might not have had the temerity to make the attempt. Yet, nearly every collector will testify to those occult forces that guide him into a shop or bring a great rarity his way. And herein lies that unique pleasure of the past. Any antiques shop or rare-book shop might place over its door the inscription on the proscenium of the old Lampson Lyceum at Yale University: 'Here we learn not studies, but life.'

Wendell D. Garrett

Ceramics

Mustard-pot and cover, Saint-Cloud, 1725–50. European potters experimented throughout the seventeenth century with ceramic methods, imitating the wares which were cheaply and abundantly imported from China. Rouen and Saint-Cloud were the principal centres of production in France. This beautiful mustard-pot and cover is an excellent example of the most popular form of enamel painting used at Saint-Cloud. Using bold, strong colours, this style is in direct imitation of the Japanese Arita porcelain decorated in the Kakiemon manner. A large number of these wares were imported into England at the time. (Musée des Arts Décoratifs, Paris.)

The first rare pieces of Chinese porcelain to reach Europe in the fourteenth century were brought back by explorers and traders of the Eastern caravan routes. By the beginning of the seventeenth century, an important export trade with China was flourishing, started by the Portuguese and continued by the newly formed Dutch East India Company. Large quantities of blue and white porcelain were brought into Amsterdam and other ports, causing a stir that was to have a far-reaching effect on the direction of European ceramics thereafter.

The making of pottery (earthenware) is one of the oldest crafts in the world. Simple, functional clay pots baked in a fire to harden have been made since prehistoric times. The advanced technology of porcelain-making, however, was developed in China sometime during the T'ang period (A.D. 618–906). The T'ang potters used richly coloured lead glazes on their stoneware horses and camels used as tomb furnishings, although their first porcelain wares were pure white.

The Chinese had an impressive knowledge of ceramics acquired over many centuries. They were skilled at making glazed stoneware, which required a much higher firing temperature than ordinary earthenwares. Thus, it was a natural step to discover how to fire the porcelain bodies at even higher temperatures. Porcelain was made of a blend of white china clay (kaolin) and felspathic rock (petuntze). A translucent glaze also derived from felspar fused with the body during firing to produce a ceramic that was hard, durable and smooth to the touch, and yet of fragile and translucent appearance.

Although true hard-paste porcelain in the Chinese manner was not made in Europe until 1708 when experiments at Meissen in Germany were finally successful, there were many other important decorative ceramics in production throughout Europe. In Germany, from the fourteenth century, Rhineland potters were turning out sturdy stonewares, often incised and carved with masks and relief designs, which were glazed by means of throwing salt into the kiln when the fire was at its most intense. The resulting glaze looked rather like the skin of an orange.

At about the same time, Italy was producing elaborately decorated Maiolica which in turn had derived from the diaper patterned and lustred Hispano-Moresque wares of Moorish Spain. Earthenware was dipped into a smooth, milky white glaze to which oxide of tin had been added. The gleaming white surface was a perfect foil for the brilliant enamelled decorations typical of the Renaissance period in Italy. The art of tin-glazing spread throughout Europe and in France was called Faience, in Holland and England, Delft.

During the Ming period (1368–1644), plain white porcelain gave way to pieces decorated under the glaze in a rich cobalt blue pigment imported from Persia. The decorative blue and white wares thus produced found immediate approval in European markets and it was the overwhelming popularity of these wares that inspired European potters to imitate the decorations on their own Delftwares and later soft-paste porcelains as the vogue for Chinese-inspired decorations (Chinoiserie) reached every aspect of the decorative arts during the eighteenth century.

Exquisite creamy-white *blanc de Chine* sculptures were cherished in seventeenth century Europe and served as inspiration for modellers at Meissen and Bow. Delicate multi-coloured enamelled decorations, notably in the *famille verte* and *famille rose* range were beginning to supplant the popularity of blue and white from Nanking.

Japan had unravelled the secrets of porcelain-making much earlier than Europe, and her Arita wares found an eager export market. Of individualistic shapes and decoration, Imari and Kakiemon porcelains were as highly prized by Europeans as the finest Chinese pieces.

The search for the secrets of porcelain's manufacture in Europe produced a delicate substitute known as 'soft paste.' (The terms 'hard' and 'soft' paste refer to the differences in firing temperature.) Soft-paste was made from a blend of white substances including clay and alabaster and a glasslike frit. Soft paste porcelain was first made in Florence about 1575 and a century later at Rouen in France. Although hard-paste porcelain was made at Meissen soon after the beginning of the eighteenth century, it was several decades before the technique became widespread, and soft-paste continued to be made throughout the century in France and in England.

Most famous of all the French soft-paste porcelains were those made at the royal manufactory of Sèvres. Started at Vincennes in 1738, the factory later moved to Sèvres and enjoyed the patronage of the French Royal family and court until the Revolution. Hard paste was made at Sèvres in the second half of the century, and the two porcelains continued to be made side by side until 1800. Early Sèvres is famous for its softly coloured background glazes in such beautiful shades as turquoise, rose pompadour and royal blue. They provided a superb background for the hand-painted and lavishly gilded decorations for which Sèvres was renowned.

In England, factories at Chelsea, Bow, and Derby made soft paste to compete with French products. Rich deposits of clay found in Staffordshire assured the success of the thriving pottery industry and the period was one of innovation and imagination. British potters, like Josiah Wedgwood, were both creative and prolific. Wedgwood is famous for the variety of his wares, notably creamy white earthenwares, Jasper ware and black basalt pieces.

The art of transferring printed patterns onto earthenware bodies was developed in the second half of the eighteenth century, thus opening the way for the mass-production of decorated pottery. In the nineteenth century, another British potter, Josiah Spode II, perfected a porcelain recipe that included bone ash which has been the basis for English bone-china ever since.

In America, early domestic pottery made by immigrant potters was simple redware, sometimes ornamented by the addition of liquid clay or slip motifs. Pennsylvania's German settlers brought with them techniques of making stonewares, using the abundant natural clay resources. These everyday wares acquired a unique flavour with the addition of simple folk art motifs in cobalt blue and occasionally brown pigments. By the nineteenth century, a rising middle class in America formed an eager market for the vast number of decorated products exported by the Staffordshire potteries. The manufacture of porcelain in America was limited until late in the century, but wealthy merchants like Elias Haskett Derby of Salem, Massachusetts, imported a good deal of the Oriental wares so fashionable in Europe.

The production of ceramics in every country was well-established and particularly in Britain, catered for every possible taste.

At the end of the nineteenth century, there was a vogue for Japonaisserie – designs inspired by Japanese culture – and it affected the decorative arts in the same way that the fashion for Chinoiserie had influenced trends in the previous century. Art potteries sprang up in Britain and America, and began making pieces that relied for their beauty on simplicity of line and textured glazes rather than on the over-elaborate ornamentation of a few decades before. Studios like Rookwood in America became famous for their elegant vases and ewers decorated with Japanese style simplicity in the fashion of the day.

In porcelain making, the quality of Chinese wares had declined from their prominence in the nineteenth century and the West was at last able to look to the superlative products of their own factories for their practical and decorative needs.

Ming Dynasty Porcelain

A. C. Cooper

2
3

Fig. 1 (Back) **Large dish** of the Cheng-te period (1506–21). Imperial yellow glazed ground, decorated with the outline of a green glazed dragon. (Front) **Small dish** of the Cheng-te period (1506–21). Plain Imperial yellow glaze, painted with the six-character mark of the Emperor. (Author's Collection.)

Fig. 2 **Fishbowl** of the Lung-ch'ing period (1567–72). Diameter 29 ins. This massively potted bowl is an example of the larger wares made during the latter part of the Ming dynasty. Infinitely more difficult to produce than thin, delicate pieces, the sides of this bowl are in many places more than an inch thick. The painting is in the best Ming tradition; it depicts five-clawed dragons about to grasp at the flaming pearls on which they feed, and rushing through cloud scrolls above great waves breaking on to rocks. (Author's Collection.)

Fig. 3 **Tou T'sai jar** of the Ch'eng-hua period (1464–87). Although this charming jar has been extensively repaired, it is an excellent example of the earliest type of enamel painting done in China. This was the last major problem to be solved in the potter's art, and the solution, using a 'muffle kiln', was discovered late in the fifteenth century. The jar is one of the now very rare pieces which are painted with the six-character mark of the emperor of the period and accepted as dating from his reign. (Author's Collection.)

Porcelain techniques, developed in China over many centuries, reached perfection in the Ming dynasty when the huge demands of the West for wares of every variety were met

Before discussing the characteristics of the ceramic art industry in China during the Ming dynasty, it is essential to put this whole group of wares into context by means of a short historical and social survey.

The Shang dynasty (1766–1122 B.C.), evolving fast from a nomadic, neolithic culture, established a sophisticated farming, ancestor-worshipping civilisation towards 1500 B.C. Of their coarse, sun-dried pottery vessels painted with bold geometric designs, those excavated seem to be predominantly funerary, although among the succeeding Chou dynasty (1027–221 B.C.) burials, a number of obviously secular shapes are found.

Although not a period of economic stability, the first great T'ang emperor, Li Shih-min (called T'ang T'ai-tsung) established the T'ang dynasty in 618 on such a firm foundation that the arts flourished; ceramic shapes and techniques of decoration, often now taken directly from shapes of vessels used by the welcomed near-Eastern trader, for the first time took on a distinctive splendour and freedom.

The potters of the succeeding Sung dynasty (A.D. 960–1279), having discovered the secret of firing a porcelain clay, pandered to the refined tastes of the aesthetic Court by producing a series of wares now usually accepted as the synthesis of the Western collector's vision of Cathay. The emphasis being purely on shape and proportion, these wares were decorated with lightly carved or finely moulded, mainly floral, motifs under the monochrome glazes: the great Kuan and Lung-ch'uan celadons, the ivory Ting yao glazes, the Ch'ing pai wares (the name refers to the colour of the sky after rain, and accurately reflects the state of mind of the patrons of this art).

In 1368, when Chu Yuang-chang (Hung-wu) established the 'brilliant' Ming dynasty at Nanking, his potters had completely mastered the manufacture of a true high-fired porcelain, translucent and with a beautiful resonance. They could execute the most delicately potted stem-cups for the finest wine, or throw massively constructed storage jars. The glaze often cracked along the joints during the firing, showing clearly how the flat base, the lower

part of the body, the wide deep shoulder (they would have been potted as bowls) and the neck were made separately, and then 'luted' together (stuck with a porcelain clay watered down to a creamy consistency, called slip) after drying, and before being decorated and glazed. Even though large cracks sometimes appeared in the base during the drying, prior to the firing, this was obviously not considered a defect serious enough to make the vase a 'waster', and that these cracks were simply filled in before the whole vase was fired is a good indication of how highly these large early pieces were valued.

They could execute delicate stem-cups as well as massive storage jars

During the short but culturally important Mongol occupation before the Ming – the Yuan dynasty (1280–1368) – the under-glaze method of painting had been developed. Consisting simply of the painting of the design on to the body after a first firing, this was obviously a major step. The early Ming decorators exploited to the full the possibilities of both the unpredictable iron red (moments of over-oxidisation in the kiln could mean that the colour would either run or turn pale greyish-green) and the costly but instantly appreciated and sought-after wares painted with cobalt blue imported from Burma.

The fourteenth-century examples of both these groups, probably most obviously characterised by the brilliantly precise painting of loosely composed decoration, were potted from finely mixed white clays, which often in the firing burnt a pale orange colour across the predominantly flat or shallowly cut bases, while the glazes tend to be thin and slightly grey in tone. Figure 5 is one of the finest 'text book' examples of fourteenth-century under-glaze blue; it is a storage jar, the construction of which is similar to those mentioned above. The shallowly domed lid was probably shaped like a lotus leaf. Clearly visible in the brush-strokes is the famous 'heaped and piled' effect produced by the slightly uneven grinding of the cobalt.

In early fifteenth-century wares, the clear glazes were often very thick, and though carefully and evenly applied and controlled, this often allowed the blue to 'bleed' or smudge very slightly into them during the firing, giving a depth and richness to the blue very characteristic of this group. Figure 7 shows not only the obvious difference between the early fifteenth-century Chinese porcelain dish and the seventeenth-century Turkish faience dish, but

13

Fig. 4 *Celadon bowl*, fifteenth century. Diameter 16½ ins. This magnificent fluted celadon glazed bowl has an applied moulded plaque in the centre of the interior. Bowls of this sort, carrying on the classic Sung tradition of celadon wares, found their greatest success at the Courts of Egypt and Persia, at the rich trading markets of the Malay Archipelago and in the ports of Burma and India. (Christie's.)

Fig. 5 *Storage jar* of the Yuan Dynasty (1280–1368), fourteenth century. Height 12 ins. This heavily potted Kuan jar is a rare example of the fine underglaze blue painting which was developed during the Mongol occupation before the Ming dynasty. The 'heaped and piled' effect produced by uneven grinding of the cobalt is visible in the brush-strokes. The jar once had a shallowly domed lid, probably shaped like a lotus leaf. (Christie's.)

4

5

illustrates the fact that in Turkey, even at such an early date, Chinese porcelain, which had been traded for several centuries, was considered the ideal and faithfully copied in a less costly ware for the home market.

The tradition which the potters of the classic Sung celadons had established continued into the Ming dynasty; but, whereas the emphasis had earlier been on exquisite proportions and fine potting – they had been admired and, to quote C. P. Fitzgerald, 'venerated as the expression of the artist's perception of truth' – during the fourteenth and fifteenth centuries the celadon wares produced were predominantly very heavily potted large plates, serving dishes and great deep bowls (Fig. 4). They also included storage jars and hanging lanterns, boldly carved or decorated with applied pre-moulded designs and thickly covered with a characteristic olive celadon glaze which pooled during the firing into the recesses of carving and around the relief of the applied moulded decoration.

While certainly used at the Chinese Court, these wares found their greatest success not only at the near-Eastern Courts of Egypt and Persia, for which they were perhaps first intended, but also on the rich trading markets of the Malay Archipelago and in the ports along the coasts of Burma and India at which the merchants had to stop during their long sea voyages. In the first early sixteenth-century inventories of the great collections of Chinese porcelains at the Topkapi Saray in Istanbul, the actual generic term for the celadon group was *Martabani*, referring to the port of Martaban in Burma from which these wares were thought to originate.

Poison was supposed to boil if it touched a dish of celadon porcelain

The reason for this great demand was not purely a question of aesthetic appreciation, or one of rarity. Although the origin of the story is lost, poisoned food was supposed to boil if it so much as touched a dish of this celadon porcelain – and it is not difficult to imagine this secret being whispered into any willing ear along the 'silk road'.

Towards the end of the fifteenth century, during the reign of Ch'eng-hua, the Imperial kilns at the now undisputed centre of porcelain manufacture, Ching-te-chen, produced the first porcelain decorated with enamel colours. Painted on to a clear glazed vessel which was then refired in a low temperature 'muffle kiln', this process was the last major problem in the potter's art to be solved. Figure 3 illustrates a small jar, one of the now very rare pieces which, although painted with the six-character mark of the emperor during whose reign the piece was made (here the characteristically thickly written and crowded mark of Ch'eng-hua) are accepted as actually dating from the period of that mark.

It is as well here to explain an aspect of peculiarly Chinese philosophy regarding the copy versus the fake. Any kiln whose potters and painters were competent enough to make a pot in a popular earlier style so well that it emerged from the kiln in every way as beautiful as the original from which it was taken, would have painted the new piece with the mark of the emperor associated with the period

during which the production of the particular ware reached its (aesthetic and technical) zenith. This was a purely honorific or dedicatory marking, and not until comparatively recently has it taken on a definitely fraudulent intent.

The reigns of the middle to late Ming emperors (Hung-chih to Wan-li), although often unstable in themselves and with strong eunuch corruption and exorbitant taxation, saw a constant increase in the importance of an export trade in porcelain to the countries beyond the established markets of South East Asia, India and the near East. Figure 9 illustrates the recurrence of a popular exported shape, the ewer. On the bottom left is the heavily potted early fifteenth-century example, perhaps taken from an Islamic metalwork prototype, the smudgy but free style of painting clearly different, under the thick eggshell glaze, from the marked eighteenth-century ewer on the right. Although a faithful copy, the technique is far more precise and controlled, with the 'heaped and piled' effect carefully imitated under a thin glassy glaze. (The bridge and base of the spout have been restored on this ewer, and the dead white of the overpainted repair contrasts with the subtle, deep white of the body, often more clearly seen on a photograph than when the piece is handled.) In the centre is a sixteenth-century version, the design only very loosely similar, and painted in a washy grey-blue typical of all but the top quality export pieces.

On 6 January, 1515, an Italian in Portuguese service, Andrea Corsali, wrote to Giuliano de' Medici that 'merchants of the land of China make voyages to Malacca across the Great Gulf (of Siam) to acquire cargoes of spices, and they bring from their own country . . . porcelain'. Although not very long after this specimens arrived in Portugal itself, it was the Dutch who, in 1595, followed the Portuguese routes

Fig. 6 *Kuan Yin, the Goddess of Mercy, in meditation,* *late Ming dynasty (early seventeenth century).* Blanc de chine porcelain. This fine figure of the Buddhist Bodhisattva, Avalokitesvara, illustrates the extraordinary technical skill of the Ming modellers. *(Author's Collection.)*

Fig. 7 (Left) *Dish, Chinese, early fifteenth century.* Blue and white porcelain, about 14 ins. diameter.
(Right) *Dish, Turkish, early seventeenth century.* Blue and white pottery. Diameter about 14 ins. Both found recently in Damascus, these dishes show the importance of Chinese porcelain to near-Eastern pottery design. The Turkish faience dish is a faithful copy of the Chinese piece.
(Author's Collection.)

Fig. 8 (Behind) *Serving-dish of the Wan-li period (1573–1620).* Kraak porselyn.
These early export wares, brought in large quantities to the West by the Dutch East India Company, derived their name from the Portuguese trading ships, the Carracas.
(Left) *'Provincial' dish, Chinese, early sixteenth century.* Probably intended for the South East Asia market, these dishes were the first mass-produced wares for everyday use.
(Right) *Ginger-jar from the reign of K'ang-hsi (1662–1722) in the Ch'ing Dynasty.*
(Christie, Manson and Woods, London.)

7

8

15

Fig. 9 *Ewers,* Chinese (from the
left) *early fifteenth, mid-sixteenth
and mid-eighteenth centuries.
The ewer was a consistently
popular form of export ware.*
(Christie's.)

around the Cape of Good Hope and established themselves at Canton with the declared aim of trading; and it was the Dutch East India Company that first brought quantities of porcelain to the appreciative European market, making porcelain wares objects of relatively expensive everyday use as opposed to the wonderful rarities of fifty years before.

These first imports, the *Kraak porselyns,* as the Dutch called them then and as they are still called, are well illustrated by the large deep serving-dish in Figure 8. They were usually thinly potted, and sand from the saggars in which they were fired was often not properly cleaned off the deep foot rims. This, together with the characteristically watered down, deep purplish-blue used in the painting of the later Ming export wares, makes this a distinctive group. The name *Kraak,* rather than referring to the crackled glaze of some pieces, comes from the Portuguese trading ships, the Carracas.

The earlier sixteenth-century 'provincial' dish in Figure 8, a very good example of the first truly mass-produced wares for day-to-day use, shows the diluted blue with which these much cheaper types were painted. Also typical of this class of ware is the very loose calligraphic style with which the predominantly mythical animal and formalised flowering branch subjects were treated.

As widely appreciated as the thinnest and most delicately conceived pieces, but infinitely more difficult to produce, were the colossal fishbowls made for the Court during the latter part of the

dynasty. Figure 2 shows such a bowl; measuring an uneven twenty-nine inches in diameter, the sides are in many places over one inch thick. Dating from the short reign of Lung-ch'ing, it is an example of the very best in Ming painting. On the outside, Imperial five-clawed dragons rush through cloud scrolls above great waves breaking on to rocks, to grasp at the flaming pearls on which they feed. Tradition has it that these bowls were declared impossible to make, until a desperate potter, sure that he would be executed because he could devise no method of firing such vast pieces, flung himself into the burning kiln, and the bowls, having been fired, emerged in every way perfect. Technically, this would be more likely to contain some element of truth were it to refer to an under-glaze red firing, since a burning human body would certainly provide the excess carbon monoxide essential to the production of this colour.

As this is essentially an outline of only the mainstream production of the Ming porcelain industry, the subsidiary tilemakers' wares, the pieces made during the Ming dynasty but following earlier traditions, the Southern Annamese export wares and the monochrome glazes are not discussed here. It must suffice to illustrate as Figure 6 a fine late Ming *blanc de chine* figure of the Buddhist Bodhisattva, Avalokitesvara, manifested in Chinese art as the Goddess of Mercy, seated in meditation on an outcrop of rock. The sheer technical skill necessary to model this figure, as to fire the fishbowl, prove that by the end of the dynasty porcelain manufacture was no longer a problem in itself. The kiln managers could then concentrate quietly on developing production techniques to cope with the opening floodgates of European demand. ⬧

9

MUSEUMS AND COLLECTIONS

Ming porcelain may be seen at the following:

CHINA
Peking: Imperial Museum
FORMOSA   Former Imperial Collections,
                      Taiwan

FRANCE
Paris: Musée Guimet
GREAT BRITAIN
London: British Museum
                      Percival David Foundation
                      Victoria and Albert Museum
Oxford: Ashmolean Museum
JAPAN
Tokyo: Tokyo National Museum
SWEDEN
Stockholm: Östasiatiska Museet
TURKEY
Istanbul: Topkapi Saray Museum
U.S.A.
Cambridge, Mass.: Fogg Art Museum
Cleveland, Ohio: Cleveland Museum of Art
Washington, D.C: Freer Gallery of Art

FURTHER READING

Ming Porcelains, Their Origins and Development by A. M. Joseph, 1971.
Ming Pottery and Porcelain by Soame Jenyns, London, 1953.
'Fourteenth-Century Blue-and-White' by John Pope in **Freer Gallery of Art Occasional Papers,** Washington, 1952.

The Porcelain of Japan

Although the first Japanese
porcelains were directly inspired
by Chinese ceramics, in a short
time they acquired a distinctly
Japanese character

Fig. 1 **Dish**, *Japanese, mid-
seventeenth century. Blue and
white. Painted in a typically free
style of brushwork, this dish
shows the blurred effect due to
the fluxing of the cobalt blue with
the glaze.*
(Author's Collection.)

Fig. 2 **Baluster jar**, *early
Kakiemon, c.1670. Decorated
with enamel colours.
This early piece is painted
boldly with a typical river and
mountain landscape.
(Christie's.)*

Fig. 3 **'Coloured Arita' plate**,
*first half of the eighteenth
century. Decorated in enamel
colours in a style inspired by
Chinese* famille verte.
*Pieces of this sort were made at
both the Kakiemon and the Arita
kilns, using a similar palette.
(Author's Collection.)*

Although China had begun producing true high-
fired porcelain in the fourteenth century, it
was not until the early seventeenth century that
the technique was mastered in feudal Japan. Prior
to this date, all porcelain had been imported from
China. It is probable that the Tokugawa Shogunate,
wishing to be free of the Chinese porcelain merchants, abducted potters from Korea. (Attacks were
made on Korea in 1592 and again in 1597.) Part of
the spoils of war were the 'potter communities' that
were brought back to Japan and settled near Arita.
But it was not until 1616 that a Korean, Rhee Sambae (in Japanese, Risampie) found porcellaneous
clay at Tegundani in Arita, thus making him the
father of Japanese porcelain. The kilns, techniques and styles of this proto-Japanese porcelain
clearly show a strong Korean affinity and can often

be mistaken for Korean by those who are not
familiar with the originals.

A popular misconception is that the name 'Imari'
indicates a kiln or factory. The name derives
from the port of Imari whence the wares were
shipped, just as 'Nanking' has become a generic
name for the Chinese export blue and white
shipped from that port. The name 'Imari' has been
adopted to describe the palette of under-glaze blue
and over-glaze iron red and gilt of the Arita export
wares. The bulk of seventeenth-century Japanese
porcelain is blue and white, and a characteristic
feature is that, due to fluxing of the cobalt with the
glaze, the blue decoration bleeds into the surrounding area causing a blurred effect (Fig. 1). It
was basically to overcome this fault that the early
workmen painted iron red and gold on to the glaze
to conceal the blurred edges.

European influence began to be felt as early as
1542 with the arrival of the Portuguese and, a little
later, of Saint Francis Xavier who preached
Catholic Christianity to great effect. So much so,
in fact, that the Shogunate, realising the disturbing

Fig. 4 *Figure, Imari, late seventeenth century. A type of figure originally made at the Kakiemon kilns.*
(Christie's.)

Fig. 5 *Dish, Imari, mid-seventeenth century. Decorated in under-glaze blue and over-glaze enamels with a Kabuki theatre scene.*
(Private Collection.)

Fig. 6 *Small hexagonal wine-cup, Nabeshima, early eighteenth century.*
(Author's Collection.)

Fig. 7 *Dish, Nabeshima, early eighteenth century. Decorated in under-glaze blue and over-glaze enamels with toadflax flowers.*
(Sotheby and Co., London.)

Fig. 8 *Dish, Ko-Kutani, first half of the seventeenth century. Decorated in bold enamels with the 'three friends' – plum, bamboo and pine.*
(Christie's.)

Fig. 9 *Dish, Nabeshima, second half of the eighteenth century. Painted in blue and white with water gushing through a weir.*
(Sotheby's.)

4

A. C. Cooper

effect it was having, ordered the expulsion of the missionaries. The Protestant Dutch, lacking missionary zeal but with good commercial instincts, were allowed to establish their warehouses on the island of Deshima, and became the only group of Europeans to carry on trade with the Japanese.

A curious feature of early Japanese porcelains is the spur marks, usually three, five or seven in number. These are marks made by the small supports used in the kilns during firing. China ceased using such spurs in the tenth or eleventh century but the practice persisted in Korea into the fifteenth and sixteenth centuries. As skill improved and purer cobalt became available, so the decoration became more controlled. Simple flowers gave way to elaborate panels enclosed by octopus scroll borders (in fact, a dissolved foliage scroll). The decorative repertoire is drawn basically from folk history and culture, and includes the 'Three Friends' motif: the plum, bamboo and pine; birds and tigers also often occur. Pieces expressly made for export were often copied from wooden models supplied by the Dutch traders and include covered jars, tankards (some especially designed for silver mounting in Europe) and large dishes, most famous of which are those bearing the 'V.O.C.' monogram of the Dutch East India Company (Vereenigde Oostindische Compagnie).

Pieces for the home market were at this date still usually made in imitation of the ware imported from China. Among these the pieces enamelled in the typical late Ming style were the most popular and it is interesting that this group is still among the most collected today. Having established a successful industry producing good quality blue and white, the kiln masters turned their attention to perfecting the technique of enamelling in colours on porcelain. Three basic types exist: coloured Imari, Kakiemon and Kutani.

The history of Kakiemon has been gleaned from the records of the family. According to tradition, Sakaida Kizai-emon, an Arita potter, made an ornament in the form of twin persimmons (*kaki*) for his feudal lord, the *daimyo* Nabeshima, who was so pleased with its artistry that he conferred on him the honorific name of Kaki-emon. Sakaida adopted this as his family name, marking his lord's favour. He worked as a foreman under a merchant named Toshima Tokuyemon, who is thought to have acquired the secret of enamelling in colours from a Chinese enameller at Nagasaki; after some false starts they mastered the art and began one of the most important ceramic productions.

In the early stage the white-glazed pieces were brought from the factories to the Kakiemon workshops for enamelling, although eventually they acquired their own kiln. Their highly distinctive designs and colour schemes made such an impact on the European market that, within a few years of the first pieces being imported, all the major porcelain factories in Europe produced pieces in direct imitation. The body of these wares is generally milky white with a matt surface showing a slightly greasy-looking sheen, while the poorer quality pieces have a coarse, almost gritty texture.

On the best pieces the enamelled designs are delicately and sensitively executed with occasional black outlines which hint at, rather than define, the decoration. The earlier pieces use a thick bright turquoise and a vibrant iron red, imitating the fiery orange-red of ripe persimmons. This colour scheme must have been taken from the Chinese Swatow porcelains imported during the sixteenth and seventeenth centuries. The additional colours which distinguish the Kakiemon enamel palette are a striking azure blue, soft orange, transparent primrose yellow, lavender blue and grass green. The use of a brownish purple occurs only on rather later pieces.

All the early Kakiemon pieces were intended for the personal use of the *daimyo* and his Court, and the decorative themes reflect a strictly Japanese taste. The first-phase work of the Kakiemons (roughly 1640–70) is confined to boldly painted designs of landscapes (Fig. 2); flowers and shrubs growing from rockwork; and birds on branches. Unlike so many decorative techniques, the Kakiemon group became more refined as time went on and, while the seventeenth-century pieces had decorations which covered large areas of the piece, in the eighteenth century the decoration becomes sparser. It is this group that shows, more than any other, the water-colour quality of the enamelling. Marks rarely appear before the eighteenth century, and those most commonly found are the *fuku* (happiness) and *kin* (gold) marks. A wide variety of shapes occur, ranging from covered baluster jars, deep, covered food bowls, ewers and bottles, to human and animal figures (Fig. 10). The influence of European designs and shapes can be seen on pieces which date from the early eighteenth century onwards, and there are a number of pieces executed exclusively for the European market.

Any successful innovation has its copyists and the neighbouring kilns at Arita soon adapted their Imari palette by adding pale yellow and green enamel to foliage, thus giving a new liveliness to their pieces; before long, something approaching the Kakiemon palette developed alongside the old Imari palette.

The problem of identification or classification of these wares as distinct from the true Kakiemon pieces is so difficult that some scholars prefer to think only in terms of 'coloured Arita' (Fig. 3), thereby avoiding any separate classification. Among the rarest coloured Imari pieces are those early pieces with designs exclusively for the Japanese market, like the *Kabuki* plate in Figure 5 which has, in addition to the Imari colours, yellow, turquoise and aubergine over-glaze enamels.

While the decoration of most Kakiemon wares was of purely Japanese inspiration, the Kutani wares represent a different tradition, being directly derived from the late Ming coloured pieces. Of all Japanese porcelains, these Kutani wares are the most highly prized, but they are also perhaps the most difficult to date. So far no positive kiln-site or reliable literary records have been traced. The early porcelains are always referred to as *Ko*-Kutani (old Kutani), to distinguish them from the *Ao*-Kutani (new Kutani) stonewares of the nineteenth-century revival wares.

Rich, harmonious colours and free, impressionistic decoration

The body of *Ko*-Kutani pieces is generally whitish grey, the glaze milky white with a subtle, velvety softness to the touch. The enamels are exceptionally rich and harmonious, varying from brilliant

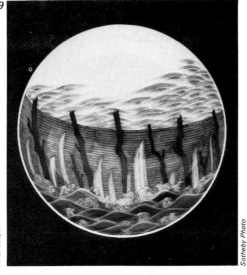

transparency to subdued opacity. Colours include a thick, vivid green, egg yellow, aubergine, Prussian blue and an iron red which ranges from cherry red to warm brown. The decoration is nearly always executed in the boldly free and impressionistic manner of the late Ming wares which inspired them (Fig. 8), frequently with birds and insects amid flowering trees and shrubs. Animals rarely feature in these decorations and the figures particularly are Chinese in conception. The true *Ko*-Kutani pieces were probably made during the last half of the seventeenth century and were again for the exclusive use of the *daimyo* and his Court. In 1816 Yoshidaya Denyemon revived the manufacture of Kutani wares, either on the original site or close to it. These kilns continued to operate until their closure between 1863 and 1869, caused by a general depression. These *Ao*-Kutani wares somehow lack the vitality of their earlier counterparts; the designs are stiff and the use of colour smudgy, even when directly copying the earlier examples. The most typical of these *yoshidaya* (revival wares) are those with heavy enamelling, green or yellow grounds and with the decoration outlined in black. These pieces frequently bear a two-character mark never seen on *Ko*-Kutani wares.

It does not seem that the volume of *Ko*-Kutani pieces claimed as genuine could have come from a small factory with a short life of about thirty years. The Arita pieces in *Ko*-Kutani style still use the same type of enamel but usually overdo the original designs and so change their essential character. It is possible that the craftsmen who worked at the early Kutani kilns moved to Arita when their own factory ceased in the late seventeenth century, and this could explain the large volume of *Ko*-Kutani style wares coming from Arita.

The kilns were moved to preserve intact the secret skills of the potters and enamellers

Of all porcelain made in Japan, the most exclusive was that produced for the *daimyo* Nabeshima. The Nabeshima family records, more reliable than usual, state that a kiln was started in 1628 to produce fine porcelains 'like the Chinese'. The first kiln lasted on the same site until about 1665 or 1660, and the wares it produced seem to have been of little significance. It is probably at the second site, until about 1675, that coloured Nabeshima was produced, and the general wares were of noticeably higher quality. These moves were occasioned by the need to preserve intact the secret skills of the potters and enamellers. It was on the final site that the finest Nabeshima pieces were produced, achieving a unique degree of technical excellence. All the pieces were made for the exclusive use of the *daimyo* Nabeshima, his family and friends, and any piece of less than perfect quality was ordered to be destroyed.

Unlike the other kilns at Arita, those of the Nabeshima family were protected from industrial uncertainty and the potters had a status superior to their counterparts working in the other kilns. There was a deliberate policy to recruit the very best artists, enamellers and potters for this kiln and, having succeeded in getting them to join the Nabeshima workshops, steps were taken to ensure that they stayed there. If for any reason a workman

19

Fig. 10 *Buddhistic Lion,
Kakiemon, second half of the
seventeenth century the base
with typical octopus scroll
decoration in association with
peony flowers.*
*(Christie, Manson and
Woods Ltd., London.)*

should leave, he was obliged to keep all that he had learnt to himself, and he was forbidden to join another kiln or set up on his own as a potter or enameller. One of the notable successes of these kilns was the mastery of painting in under-glaze blue. A high degree of skill was required and achieved, and there is a complete absence of fuzziness of the outlines of the under-glaze decoration. The colour of the blue is thin and soft (Fig. 6), lending itself admirably as a base for over-glaze enamelling in colours which achieved a high degree of excellence.

The decoration is always executed in a naturalistic manner, though some compositions are very formal. Naturalistic plum-blossom floats on formalised water, or naturalistic trees cascade on to water that resembles fish scales (Fig. 9). Whatever the subject used, be it flowers (Fig. 7), shrubs or birds, a certain balance between formality and naturalism was sought. The underside is always in a simple style, with formal flower sprays, or bundles of money joined with elaborate tassels, and a simple comb or cog-wheel pattern round the disproportionately high foot. Particularly apparent in the dishes which use designs derived from textile patterns is the technique of *tou ts'ai* enamelling copied from the Chinese.

Last of the main producers of porcelain in Japan are the kilns on Hirado, which are thought to have started in the late sixteenth century under the Koreans brought there by the *daimyo* Hideyoshi. Porcellaneous clay was found on the island and production commenced.

These early wares were mostly blue and white, and show the strong influence of a Korean heritage, but it was not until the late eighteenth century and early nineteenth century that the Hirado wares achieved recognition. They are made of the finest white porcelain and painted in a soft, slightly violet toned cobalt blue with miniaturist landscapes. These wares are mostly faceted bottles or flasks with narrow necks, although some other vases and utensils have animals or insects moulded on to the sides. The aesthetically fine earlier wares are regrettably eclipsed in sheer virtuosity by the later nineteenth-century wares which achieve a staggering mastery of the medium. Vases and incense-burners of elaborate construction have large areas of reticulated panelling and appear so frail that it seems a miracle that they even survived the kiln firings, let alone the long journeys to Europe.

While it was in feudal Japan that these first porcelain factories flourished, the appreciation of the medium is still very much present in today's affluent islands, and the porcelain produced for both home and export markets still shows a definitively original concept of handling and decoration.

10

A. C. Cooper

MUSEUMS AND COLLECTIONS
Japanese porcelain may be seen at the following:

GREAT BRITAIN
London: British Museum
                 Hampton Court Palace
                 Victoria and Albert Museum
Oxford: Ashmolean Museum

JAPAN
Tokyo: National Museum

U.S.A.
Boston, Mass.:   Boston Museum of Fine Arts
Cambridge, Mass.: Fogg Art Museum
Cleveland, Ohio: Museum of Art

THE NETHERLANDS
Amsterdam: Rijksmuseum
Leyden: Rijksmuseum voor
                 Volkenkunde

FURTHER READING

Japanese Porcelain by Soame Jenyns, London, 1965.
Porcelain and the Dutch East India Company, 1602–1682 and **The Japanese Porcelain Trade of the Dutch East India Company after 1683** by T. Volker, vols. 11 and 13 published by the Rijksmuseum voor Volkenkunde, Leyden, 1954 and 1959.

Persian Potters and their Wares

Standing at the gateway to the Orient, Persian potters were strongly influenced by the porcelain of China. Nevertheless, the indigenous Islamic tradition imbued their work with a highly individual character

The most frequently encountered types of Persian pottery of the sixteenth and seventeenth centuries are those decorated in blue on a white ground, in the Chinese style. It has been argued that the Chinese potters originally took the idea, along with the cobalt ore they imported, from Persia, where, from the early thirteenth century onwards, blue decoration, outlined in black to prevent running, was common. As black would not have withstood the high temperature in the porcelain kilns, the Chinese had to omit it, making the outlines in darker blue instead. It is not known when the Chinese blue and white porcelain first started arriving in the Middle East, but there is evidence in miniature paintings to show that it was known in the fourteenth century, and certainly it had become the prevalent fashion by the fifteenth century. It was the fourteenth- and fifteenth-century Ming porcelain which gave the main inspiration for design.

The Persians never mastered the art of making porcelain themselves, but they admired and valued it to such an extent that, as Thomas Herbert, an Englishman in Isfahan in the early seventeenth century, remarked, 'they commonly eat in earth [enware] and porcelain, not valuing silver', and the word *Chini* (Chinese) came to be used to describe anything of fine quality, regardless of the material of which it was made. Shah 'Abbas thought it sufficiently important to dedicate a collection of 1,162 pieces of Chinese porcelain to the shrine of his revered ancestor, Shaykh Safi, in 1611, of which eight hundred and five pieces remain, forming one of the world's finest collections. A curious incident is related by the official chronicler of the occasion, namely that when Shah 'Abbas entered the kitchens at Ardabil, 'the lid of a nearby saucepan lifted itself about nine inches and crashed down on the saucepan with such a noise . . . much to the astonishment of those present'. If this amazing saucepan could be found, it would no doubt be a valuable collector's item.

In 1682, the British East India Company recorded that Kirman and Meshed were the two places where really good imitations of Chinese porcelain could be obtained. The shapes, as well as the designs,

21

Museum Photo

Fig. 2 **Plate,** *Kubachi, c.1600. Sometimes plates were decorated with portraits, but it is not known if the figure here represents a specific person. (Victoria and Albert Museum.)*

followed the Chinese example – big dishes and bowls, jars, vases and bottles. Even the shape of a Chinese pouring vessel was adapted to the needs of the *qalian* (hookah), the side hole receiving the wooden mouthpiece, and the tall stem holding the tobacco cup fixed on top (Fig. 1).

The Chinese influence on Meshed and Kirman wares

Although deceptive at first, a close examination will always distinguish Persian wares. The pottery, however fine, does not have the hard, compact, vitreous quality of porcelain, and often is softer and manifestly coarser in grain. In order to achieve a similarity to porcelain, the painted decoration of the pottery was covered in a hard and brilliant transparent glaze.

The best technique was evolved in Meshed (this is a generally accepted attribution for the group rather than an established fact), where the potters employed a hard white body and a clear thin glaze. The glaze has a greenish tinge more evident where it is thicker; the designs are sharply outlined in intense black and filled in with shades of a slightly violet transparent blue. Usually on the bottom there is an attempt to imitate a Chinese mark in black, taking the form of concentric squares, which illustrates the lengths to which the Persians went in their emulation of the Chinese.

The earliest examples are extremely rare, dating from the second half of the sixteenth century and showing long-legged cranes flying among trailing clouds and delicately observed birds perched beside rather limp flowers. About 1600, the style became less individual and lasted in a similar vein until the end of the century, tending to become more and more sloppy towards 1700. Human figures sometimes appear, intended as Chinese, but somehow looking more European, and the figure of a drunken Chinaman hugging a winebottle and showing his legs seems to have been a hugely appreciated joke at this time. A bowl in the

Staatliche Museen, Berlin, is particularly interesting, showing an adaptation of a European painting of a Virgin and Child. The *qalian* base in Figure 1 has a more usual decoration of panels enclosing animals, and a relatively restricted vocabulary of floral types. Also serving as *qalian* bases are the particularly charming animal figures such as the duck in the Victoria and Albert Museum, London, complete with the legs painted underneath.

The wares attributed to Kirman have fine and relatively soft white bodies, often thickly potted, with a bright and warm blue painted under a thickish, rather uneven glaze full of tiny bubbles which tend to run into green drops. The outlines are usually executed in darker blue, rather than black as at Meshed, and frequently look blurred 'like ink lines on blotting paper', as Lane describes it in his *Later Islamic Pottery*. Again one finds imitation Chinese marks on the base, called 'tassel marks' because of their odd trailing shapes. The drawing became more Persian as the seventeenth century progressed and there was a great simplification and stylisation of Chinese designs.

Pieces from the sixteenth century are hardly known. The repertoire of shapes included the usual bowls and dishes, but also many-faceted forms such as octagonal trays and plates. Sometimes the design was a simple outline, and occasionally figurative subjects were outlined in black. A bottle of *c.*1550 in the Schloss Charlottenburg, Berlin, painted in blue and white with celadon green details and with a fantastic figure of a dragon, is worth mentioning as a splendid piece of decorative painting. The extraordinary decorative genius of the Persians which transformed all they touched is manifest here, because although the dragon closely resembles his Chinese original, he is unmistakably Persian in his placing and the power of the drawing.

More numerous than the Kirman blue and white are the polychrome pieces, although polychrome tends to be an addition to the basic blue and white scheme. The influence of Isnik pottery after 1550 is perhaps apparent in the choice of a thick tomato red slip, akin in appearance to the 'Armenian bole'. A celadon green, which turned to a *café au lait* colour when badly fired, was also used, as well as a chocolate brown, yellow and black. The blue and white decoration remains basically Chinese, but the colours are applied in a manner more characteristically Persian, with sprays of thin flowers, often contained in elegant panels, and spirals incised through bands of shiny colour. Later in the seventeenth century, moulded designs were experimented with at both Kirman and Meshed.

The development of more specifically Persian pottery

Although by no means exhaustive, the examination of the two groups above give, perhaps, an idea of Chinese-inspired pottery in Persia. These groups were the most commonly found. The Kubachi group may be taken first of the more specifically Persian types. It is a homogeneous group, so named because a large number of intact pieces were found in the remote Caucasian hill-town of Kubachi, whose inhabitants probably exchanged them for weapons, and then kept them for wall decoration,

Fig. 3 *Ewer*, late seventeenth century. Honey-coloured with a clear glaze. (Victoria and Albert Museum.)

Fig. 4 *Painted tile wall decoration* from the Chihil Sutun Palace, Isfahan, seventeenth century.
'This type of large-scale wall decoration was inspired by the frescos and wall paintings of Europe and indeed, several European painters were recorded in Persia at this period. The figures themselves, however, were inspired by the work of miniaturists such as Riza-i-'Abbasi 'whose unctuous rhythms would appear obscene even without the occasional help from the subject matter'. (Arthur Lane, Later Islamic Pottery.)

Fig. 5 *Bottle*, seventeenth century. Lustreware, height 8½ ins.
The 'leaf-specimen' treatment is very unusual in the decoration of this period.
(Christie's.)

Fig. 6 *Beaker*, late seventeenth century. Turquoise glaze.
This beaker was almost certainly designed to hold toilet accessories. The colour is opaque and very well preserved.
(Victoria and Albert Museum.)

Museum Photo

Olga Ford

piercing the bases for suspension. They may have been made in Tabriz, and have been found in widely dispersed areas. The white bodies are very soft and loose-grained, and where the glaze has not covered the entire surface they turn very dark as they are easily impregnated with dirt. The glaze is thin, and develops a wide crackle into which dirt also tends to seep, as can be seen in the marvellous portrait plate illustrated here (Fig. 2). It is in the extraordinary decorative flair that the interest of these wares lies; from the point of view of materials they are very rough. Some early pieces are decorated in the blue and white Chinese style under a clear glaze or, more rarely, under a yellow or green glaze; others have black incised panels under a turquoise glaze, such as the famous example dated 1468 with the inscription 'May this dish ever be full and surrounded by friends, may they never lack anything and eat their fill'.

A more typical polychrome decoration seems to have originated during the reign of Shah Tahmasp (1524–76) with figures of musicians and dancers in the style of the miniatures of the period enclosed in cell patterns and leaf borders. After 1550 the palette of black outlines containing a deep, runny blue came

into use with dull green, thick yellow ochre and thick brownish red. Occasionally, the yellow or a pale salmon red is used for the whole background, another Isnik-inspired trick. Tiles were decorated with portraits as on the plate illustrated in Figure 2 which has a typical narrow ring foot and flattened rim. The slightly inclined head is recognizably from the Shah 'Abbas period and the foliage has much the same Persian feel about it as already noted in the Kirman decoration. The production seems to have died out after Shah 'Abbas and was perhaps adversely affected by the move of the capital to Isfahan in 1598.

Lustring was a technique invented by the Islamic potters in Mesopotamia in the ninth century and was a jealously guarded secret brought to great fruition in Persia in the twelfth and thirteenth centuries. From the names of the potters we know of this period, it is almost as if the secret of lustreware was kept in one or two families, but it is very unlikely that the process was handed down continuously until its sudden re-emergence in the seventeenth century. The bodies of the vessels at this later period were very white, compact and rather heavy. The lustre, often of a deep brown colour, gives a range of rainbow reflections from gold to purple and ruby red, sometimes set against a deep blue ground, or, even more rarely, turquoise. Arthur Lane ingeniously suggested that the high proportion of winebottles may point to Shiraz as the centre of production because this city was so famous for its wines. The decoration is painted in silhouette showing nimble animals skipping amongst foliage and trees and is treated in a style not unrelated to Kirman. The bottle illustrated (Fig. 5) is unusual, the drawing much stronger showing two magnificent dragons, a fox and a bird and leaf shapes, and the Persian word for 'a believer' written in yellow lustre round the rim. This type is so far undocumented. Another similar piece is in the Teheran Museum, with lustre much

A. C. Cooper

K. Hoddle

A. C. Cooper

paler in colour, and the fox and bird in much more obvious relation to each other, perhaps illustrating a fable.

Monochrome wares of the Safawid period again turn to China for inspiration. Celadon greens are common and many of the articles seem to have been destined for use in the Turkish bath (*hammam*). Tile representations of bathing beauties show them sprinkling themselves with rare perfumes from beak-spouted vessels. The bowl with small birds in the bottom which can just be glimpsed in Figure 7 was almost certainly a luxury ware for use in the bath and the ewers and slender-necked vases hint at a similar destination. The potting tends to be heavy, sometimes with a glassy, honey-coloured glaze (Fig. 3) or an array of subtle greens, blues, turquoise, purple or pink. Other vessels were carved with hunting scenes (Fig. 8) or animals, and. one category has moulded panels outlined in relief containing different intense colours. Another group shows a type of monochrome ware painted with sprays of flowers which can be compared to those which are painted in white or cut through the thick monochrome ground.

A last mention should be made of a group of delicate, very fine-grained, pure white pottery covered in a shiny glaze, often incised and carved beneath the glaze or decorated with cut away monochrome slips.

Fig. 7 **Bowl,** *Meshed, first half of the seventeenth century. Diameter 13 ins. This bowl is in the Chinese manner. (Christie's.)*

Fig. 8 **Bottle,** *attributed to Isfahan, seventeenth century. Green glaze. The vessel is moulded with an elaborate animal scene. (Victoria and Albert Museum.)*

MUSEUMS AND COLLECTIONS

Persian pottery can be seen at the following:

GERMANY
Berlin: Staatliche Museen

GREAT BRITAIN
London: British Museum
               Victoria and Albert Museum

IRAN
Teheran: Iran Archaeological Museum

PORTUGAL
Lisbon: Calouste Gulbenkian Foundation

U.S.A.
New York: Metropolitan Museum of Art

FURTHER READING

Islamic Pottery by G. Fehérrára, 1973.
Iranian Ceramics by Charles K. Wilkinson, 1963.
Later Islamic Pottery by Arthur Lane, London, 1959.

K. Hoddle

The Stoneware of Germany

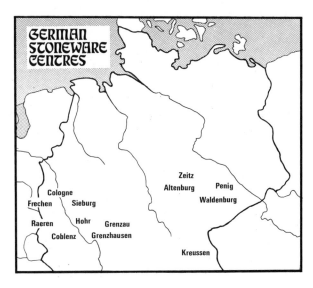

GERMAN STONEWARE CENTRES

Zeitz
Altenburg
Penig
Cologne
Waldenburg
Frechen
Sieburg
Raeren
Hohr
Grenzau
Coblenz
Grenzhausen
Kreussen

Museum Photo

Fig. 1 *Jug*, *Cologne or Frechen,*
c.1570.
*This type of mottled brown-
glazed stoneware is known as
tigerware because its appearance
resembles a tiger's coat. The jug
was mounted in England with a
silver-gilt cover, handle and base.
(Victoria and Albert Museum,
London.)*

Fig. 2 *Inkstand*, *Westerwald,*
c.1730. Height 15½ ins.
*This inkstand is typical of the
rather fanciful later wares
produced in the Westerwald.
(Fitzwilliam Museum, Glaisher
Collection.)*

Stoneware, the characteristic
pottery of the Rhineland and east
Germany, was shaped and
ornamented to suit the taste of
many export markets

Stoneware is a type of pottery made from clay,
which is fired at a high temperature to produce a
very hard material impervious to most liquids. The
kilns in which it is baked have to be raised to
between 1200° and 1400° centigrade and thus its
manufacture is dependent on ample supplies of
fuel. In Germany, the well-wooded slopes bordering
the river Rhine provided not only sufficient timber
to establish and maintain this important industry,
but also deposits of suitable clay.

Stoneware naturally has a completely matt
surface, but a finishing coat of glaze was usually
added. This was applied in spite of the fact that
stoneware vessels are watertight and it must be
assumed that it was given a shiny appearance for
reasons of decoration.

Pottery with the surface texture of the skin of an orange

The lead-based glazes normally employed on
pottery would not withstand a high temperature.
For stoneware it was discovered that common salt,
introduced into the kiln at the time of greatest heat,
resulted in a thin, colourless, even glaze. The pieces
so treated almost always have a distinctively glossy
and slightly wrinkled surface, which has the texture
of the skin of an orange.

A small range of colours was available, either
covering the whole article or emphasising some
feature, by dipping in or brushing on a mineral

Museum Photo

25

Museum Photo

Sotheby Photo

Fig. 3 **Tankard, or Schnelle,**
Raeren, c. 1570. Height 10 ins.
This tankard is coated with
a wash of brown, salt-glazed
and decorated with reliefs
depicting the story of Samson.
(Fitzwilliam Museum,
Cambridge. Glaisher Collection.)

Fig. 4 **As the old sing, so the**
young pipe *by Jacob*
Jordaens (1593–1678), Flemish.
Oil on canvas, $57\frac{1}{4}$ x $85\frac{3}{4}$ ins.
(Private Collection.)

Museum Photo

wash of iron (for brown), cobalt (for blue), or manganese (for purple or black). The most popular was an all-over brown, which sometimes resulted in the mottled skin resembling miniature animal-markings seen on tigerware (Fig. 1). Equally characteristic is a deeply toned bright blue applied in contrast to the greyish background (Fig. 7).

Further embellishment took the form of silver or silver-gilt mounts, which demonstrate how highly their original owners valued the pieces. Jugs of tigerware were especially favoured for this treatment and many surviving examples have covers and foot-rims bearing date-letters of the late sixteenth century (Fig. 1).

The stoneware industry was established in the Rhineland by the late Middle Ages and reached its peak of production there in the fifteenth and sixteenth centuries. The numerous factories were situated in an area bordering the river between Cologne and Coblenz and there were other, smaller, centres in the east of the country. Much of the considerable output was exported throughout Europe, with inscriptions and decoration to suit the market, causing confusion as to the place of its manufacture.

One of the most important centres of stoneware production was Raeren where, in the second half of the sixteenth century, Jan Emens was active. He has been described as 'perhaps the greatest figure in the history of Rhenish stoneware'. A typical example of Emens's relief designs is the tall tankard, or *Schnelle*, (Fig. 3), which bears scenes from the story of Samson – Samson carrying off the gates of Gaza, Manoah's sacrifice, and Delilah cutting off the hair of Samson. His work is often signed with his initials, I.E., and is sometimes dated.

In about 1586 Emens began to produce a series of large jugs with rounded bodies and short necks, ornamented with bands of figures. These depict biblical and mythological scenes and in designing them he made use of contemporary engravings by Hans Sebald Beham, Etienne de Laune, Adrian

Collaert and many other engravers.

Early Raeren stoneware was brown in colour and while the production of this continued, a new type, with a grey body, to which decoration in blue was added, made its appearance. The ornament on it was often of a higher quality than hitherto, with the relief modelling showing notable clarity.

In addition to those of Jan Emens, initials found on the ware include those of members of the Mennicken family, of whom Baldem Mennicken has left dated work of between 1575 and 1584. As the letters were cut with the pattern of the mould when it was first made, and the mould might have remained in use for a hundred years or more, their presence, and that of a date, is no guarantee that a piece bearing them is of early manufacture.

At Siegburg, potteries were active from at least the fourteenth century and had been formed into a guild by about 1450. The majority of their output was in a near-white material that was frequently left unglazed. Some of the early pieces show patches of reddish-brown which were acquired by accident, while others bear an all-over faint tint of pink or pale brown.

Jugs and drinking-vessels of all kinds were made, but the most typical at Siegburg was the *schnelle*. Its distinctive tall and slender form was followed in the shaping of many other pieces, both at the time and for long afterwards.

As was commonplace in other centres, the Siegburg industry was confined to a few families, and the names of the Knütgens, Symons, Flachs and Omians were prominent over the years. In 1590, Anno Knütgen, with his sons Bertram and Rütger, left Siegburg and established themselves at Höhr, in the Westerwald, where they continued their craft. Their departure anticipated the virtual extinction of potting both at Siegburg and Raeren. In the course of the Thirty Years' War, which ravaged parts of Germany between 1618 and 1648, both these towns were sacked in 1632 by the army

Museum Photo

Museum Photo

Fig. 5 **Jug,** *Bunzlau, mid-eighteenth century. Height 7¼ ins.*
This jug is decorated with reliefs of flowers and leaves and has a Prussian eagle bearing the cypher of Frederick the Great. (Fitzwilliam Museum, Glaisher Collection.)

Fig. 6 **Wine-bottle or 'Bellarmine',** *partly brown, made either in Cologne or Frechen, second half of the sixteenth century. Height 7⅝ ins. The bottle is decorated with a bearded mask at the neck and five star-like medallions enclosing the head of a Roman soldier. (Fitzwilliam Museum, Glaisher Collection.)*

Fig. 7 **Grey stoneware tankard,** *Westerwald, 1700. Height 6 ins. From the 'Land of the Pot-bakers', this grey stoneware tankard is decorated in blue and manganese. (Fitzwilliam Museum, Glaisher Collection.)*

Fig. 8 **Tankard, or Schnelle,** *bearing the initials L.W. Siegburg, c.1576. Height 9½ ins. Tankards were often decorated with religious scenes or scenes from history, like this suicide of Lucretia. (Fitzwilliam Museum, Glaisher Collection.)*

Museum Photo

of Gustavus of Sweden. Although some of the potteries were re-started, they never recovered their former prosperity.

Cologne, the important city and port on the Rhine, boasted three stoneware potteries, which were at the height of their production in the middle of the sixteenth century. All of them produced a grey-bodied material coated with a wash of brown and an overall glaze. Most examples have the speckled or mottled appearance that has earned the variety the name of tigerware.

The biggest of the potteries was situated in the Maximinenstrasse, where excavations have revealed evidence of the various types of articles that were made there. In particular, this factory was the source of many of the so-called 'Bellarmines', known also as Greybeards, *Bartmannskrüge* or *Barbmans*. They acquired the name by which they are best-known in England because of their supposed caricature-likeness to the Italian Catholic divine, Cardinal Roberto Bellarmino (1542–1621), whose publications incited anger among Protestants. The 'Bellarmine', with its bearded mask on the short neck was sometimes decorated with scrolled stems of oak leaves and roses, and occasionally patterns copied from published engravings were employed (Fig. 6).

The Komödiengasse factory, under the direction of Herman Wollters, made similar types of ware, but at a slightly later date. Excavations on the site in 1890 or 1891 laid bare a kiln and 'round about the ruins was heaped an accumulation of fragments and castaway pieces'. The third, the Eigelstein, factory differed little in its general output from the others. Some pieces bearing dates in the 1560s have been attributed to it.

The Cologne potters quarrelled for many years with the city authorities, and finally the latter triumphed. The kilns were closed and by the end of the sixteenth century the industry had been transferred to nearby Frechen.

Pottery of one kind or another was made at Frechen, about eight miles to the west of Cologne, from the Middle Ages. By the fifteenth century,

stoneware was being produced in large quantities and, following the arrival of the Cologne potters in about 1600, the town attained considerable importance. However, its reputation rests more on the quantity of goods produced than on their artistic quality.

'Eat, drink and obey the Ten Commandments'

Although many types of vessels were made there, it would seem that the larger proportion comprised 'Bellarmines'. They were frequently made more attractive for foreign buyers by the addition of armorial shields. In some instances German inscriptions were translated for the benefit of distant buyers, but perfect accuracy was not always achieved, and the carelessness or illiteracy of the potters resulted in garbled lines like the injunction 'Drinck und Eate, Got and His Commandement nic not Vergeat', a version of 'Eat, drink and obey the Ten Commandments'.

The Westerwald district, because of the number of potteries in it, was named *Kännerbackerland* (literally, 'The Land of Pot-bakers'). It lay on the Rhine, opposite Coblenz, and the most important of the group of towns in it concerned with potting were Höhr, Grenzau and Grenzhausen. The industry began to assume consequence with the arrival there from Siegburg in 1590 of Anno Knütgen and his sons, and later, members of the Mennicken family from Raeren.

The former settled at Höhr and although they began predictably, making wares of the off-white Siegburg type, they later turned to producing a grey-coloured stoneware with painted blue decoration. It was a typical manufacture of all the potteries of the area, and few examples are traceable to any particular source.

The Mennickens went to Grenzhausen and, again, made the shapes and used the patterns with which they were already familiar. The initials of Johann are said to be 'perhaps the commonest on

27

Fig. 9 **Brown-glazed jug,**
*Cologne, Maximinenstrasse
factory, c.1530. Height 4⅛ ins.
(Fitzwilliam Museum, Glaisher
Collection.)*

Museum Photo

Fig. 10 **Tankard, or
Apostolenkrüge,** *Kreussen, first
half of the seventeenth century.
Height 7⅛ ins. (Fitzwilliam
Museum, Glaisher Collection.)*

Museum Photo

all Rhenish stoneware'. They brought with them the moulds used originally by Jan Emens and other Raeren craftsmen, retaining their initials.

The use of delicate relief ornaments waned towards the close of the seventeenth century. Decoration then took the form of applied rosettes, lion masks and other devices in conjunction with bands of incised lines and raised dots, all emphasised with blue, and sometimes purple, against the grey background. The furrows restrained the colour from flowing and in addition formed part of the basic pattern. As at Cologne, much of the production was made for export, and was suitably ornamented for the intended market. For England, the initials *G.R.* for Guglielmus Rex (William III of Orange), were the same as for the three Georges, so they are no indication of date.

In the mid-eighteenth century, fanciful pieces were produced, and the inkstand shown in Fig. 2 is representative of such elaborate essays. Birds and animals were similarly rendered and standing figures of men holding small pots, probably intended for use as salt-cellars, have been recorded.

Outside the Rhineland, a distinctive stoneware was manufactured at Kreussen, near Bayreuth, in Bavaria. Long known as a source of pottery stoves (*Haffner*), stoneware became an important part of the output for most of the seventeenth century. The material is a light brown-grey, but it was invariably given a coating of colour, usually chocolate-brown but occasionally lighter in shade.

In the most distinctive articles the patterns are picked out in white and opaque colours against their sombre background. Alternatively, the designs were painted on a smooth surface, where the effect is no less telling. It has been mentioned that there is a strong resemblance between specimens of Kreussen stoneware and contemporary Bohemian glass, which was painted with enamels of the same kind. It is not unlikely that the same artists decorated both, as the glass industry was located at no great distance from the potteries.

Jugs, flasks and tankards were among the pieces made, and they were often decorated in stock patterns which have given their name to the type. They include *Planetenkrüge*, painted with figures representing the Planets; *Apostolenkrüge* (Fig. 10), with figures of the Apostles; and *Hochzeitkrüge*, with marriage scenes.

In the south and south-east of Germany were a number of potteries which made interesting stoneware from the sixteenth century onwards. At Penig, Zeitz and Waldenburg (Saxony) distinctive types were made, the latter decorating dark brown-coloured jugs with bands of incised dots and zig-zags. However, the various potteries copied one another, and precise allocation of specimens is not always possible.

At Altenburg (Thuringia) brown-surfaced pieces were also ornamented by means of a roulette, while in the Voigtland area, in the south-west corner of Saxony, coloured painting in the manner of Kreussen was used. From there also came tankards (*Perlkrüge*) decorated with simple patterns of flowers, figures and other subjects formed from small dots of clay in a contrasting colour to that of the background.

At Bunzlau, in the province of Silesia, now part of Poland, an old-established pottery produced stoneware from the eighteenth century. The grey body was disguised by a coating of coffee or rust-colour, which was often decorated with applied reliefs in a yellowish clay (Fig. 5). Sometimes painting was added, and this was further embellished with gilding.

It may be noted that some of the above mentioned potteries continued in operation, or were revived, in comparatively modern times. They made articles of traditional types, and these are not always easy to differentiate from the truly old. For instance, it is known that in the late nineteenth century, forgeries of early Siegburg pieces were made at Höhr.

FURTHER READING

World Ceramics ed. by R. J. Charleston, Chapter IV, 'Stoneware', Germany, by F. A. Dreier, London, 1968.
European Ceramic Art by W. B. Honey, 'Rhenish Stoneware', London, 1952.
The Ancient Art Stoneware of the Low Countries and Germany by M. L. E. Solon, London, 1892.

Italian Maiolica

Fig. 1 **Vase** from Deruta c.1515. Height 15⅜ ins. The shape is typical of Deruta maiolica, as is the multicoloured decoration. (Victoria and Albert Museum, London.)

J. Freeman

In the attempt to imitate Chinese porcelain and Moorish lustreware, the Italians evolved a distinctive and very beautiful form of pottery known as maiolica

Maiolica is the name given to a distinctive type of Italian pottery with painted decoration on a white glaze containing tin oxide. As early as the fourteenth century, Italian potters were making maiolica painted in a limited range of colours and by the end of the fifteenth century the vogue for these wares, chiefly as decorative objects, was well established, the chief centre of production being Faenza. At first the word maiolica was used only to describe the lustre-decorated pottery imported from Spain in the fourteenth and fifteenth centuries. This was carried in trading ships from Majorca, and the term maiolica is derived from the name of that island. It continued to be used only for lustred wares during the sixteenth century and not until much later was it generally applied to all Italian tin-glazed pottery. The technique of lustre-painting was not discovered in Italy until about 1500, when it was first used at Deruta, near Perugia.

Much of our knowledge of the technical aspects of making maiolica has been obtained from a manuscript entitled *The Three Books of the Potter's Art* (Fig. 5), written by Cipriano Piccolpasso sometime between 1556 and 1559 and now in the Victoria and Albert Museum. Piccolpasso was a native of Castel Durante, a town famous for producing fine maiolica at the beginning of the sixteenth century, but already on the decline by Piccolpasso's time. His manuscript provides not only a full account of the actual processes of manufacture, but also much information about the building of kilns and the recipes for the glazes and pigments. He even explains the best way to make brushes for the painters. Many of the expressions used to describe the manufacture and decoration of maiolica are derived from Piccolpasso, although he uses the word itself to refer to lustre.

Piccolpasso begins with advice on the collection of suitable clay and the preparation of a uniform plastic mass ready to be used by the potter. Round objects were thrown on a wheel, but, if some other shape was required, it was made by pressing slabs

29

Fig. 2 *Salt-cellar*, c.1580–1600. Height 9 ins. This appears to be a commemorative piece with the bust of a soldier painted in the well and a Latin inscription referring to his ability to defeat the foe.
(Victoria and Albert Museum.)

Fig. 3 *Dish* by Maestro Giorgio Andreoli, Gubbio, signed and dated 1527. Diameter 8 ins. The centre is decorated with the arms of Vitelli. The red is produced by the use of copper and is characteristic of pottery from Gubbio.
(Victoria and Albert Museum.)

Fig. 4 *Plate*, Cafaggiolo, c.1510. Diameter 9¼ ins. The decoration shows a maiolica painter at work with his paints beside him.
(Victoria and Albert Museum.)

2

3

J. Freeman

4

5

Art-Wood Photography.

30

of clay into a mould. Tiles and panels were made by cutting slabs of clay to the required shape and thickness. The vessel was then fired in a kiln to produce the so-called biscuit condition, which varied in colour from red to buff.

It was impossible for the painter to erase any mistakes

The next stage was the application of the tin-glaze, the *bianco*, which contained oxides of tin and lead, and *mazacotto*; this last ingredient was made by fusing a mixture of sand and wine lees. The glaze was mixed with water to a milky consistency and the vessel dipped in it. The white coat was allowed to dry and was then ready to be decorated. The surface of this unfired glaze acted rather like blotting-paper and absorbed the pigment immediately it was applied, making it impossible for the painter to erase any mistakes. But the great advantage of the tin-glaze was that it did not run during the firing.

At the end of the fifteenth century, potters were brought from Montelupo to work for a branch of the Medici family at Cafaggiolo, near Florence. The plate in Fig. 4 comes from this factory and was made there in about 1510. It is attributed to a painter who signed himself Jacopo, and it shows a maiolica painter at work. On a ledge in front of him are two finished pieces and on a bench beside him are his colours in small dishes, each with its own brushes. The maiolica painter by this time had a much wider range of colours, all derived from metallic pigments – blue, yellow, green, purple, orange and occasionally a bright red. A mixture of these produced black; white was obtained from a pigment similar to the *bianco*. By blending these colours he could increase the range.

'Prayers were offered to God with all the heart and the fires were lit'

When the pigments had dried the vessel was given a final transparent lead glaze, the *coperta*, to enhance the brilliance of the colours. The pieces were stacked into the kiln, and then, as Piccolpasso tells us, 'prayers were offered to God with all the heart and the fires were lit'.

For pieces that were to be decorated with lustre, there was still one more stage in the process. The lustre consists of a very thin layer of metal, deposited when the pigment is subjected to a reducing atmosphere in the kiln, at a much lower temperature. The two lustre pigments used in Italy contained either silver or copper. The silver lustre is a rather hard, bright yellow and is typical of Deruta pieces (Fig. 12). Copper produces a glowing ruby red which is characteristic of the pottery of Gubbio (Fig. 3). The most famous of the lustre workshops in Gubbio was that of Maestro Giorgio Andreoli, whose signature, often accompanied by the date, appears on many pieces between the years 1518 and 1541. The dish in Fig. 3 is signed by him and dated 1527 in lustre on the back.

Maiolica was used to make a wide variety of objects and lists of these appear in Piccolpasso's manuscript. Throughout the sixteenth century the emphasis was directed more and more on their decorative qualities, but at all times simple useful wares continued to be made. Among the commonest surviving shapes are plates and dishes, which provided a good surface for the painter to work on. Jugs and vases are found in different sizes and shapes and a group of very large jugs made in the early part of the century has been attributed to Cafaggiolo. The vase in Fig. 1 is a shape characteristic of Deruta and is found with both lustre and polychrome decoration. One important group of maiolica vessels is those made as storage jars for use in pharmacies. The containers for liquids are either long-necked flasks or globular jars with a spout and a handle, while dry drugs were kept in a tall narrow-waisted jar called an *albarello*. The *albarello* in Fig. 13 is attributed to Siena where maiolica was first made at the end of the fifteenth century under the influence of Faenza.

As the century progressed, shapes became more and more complicated and influenced by metal-

31

Fig. 8 **Globular jar** *from Faenza, c.1500. Height 13½ ins. Faenza was the chief centre of production of maiolica during the fifteenth century. This jar has the cherub head and wings pattern repeated around its surface divided up by varied bands of decoration on an ochre ground. The freer, more elegant manner points the way to designs used after 1500. (Gambier-Parry Collection, Courtauld Institute Galleries, London.)*

Fig. 9 **Dish depicting Horatio defending the bridge** *painted by Francesco Xanto Avelli, Urbino, 1537. Diameter 18¼ ins. (Fitzwilliam Museum.)*

Fig. 10 **Plate** *from Deruta, c.1525. Diameter 14½ ins. (Victoria and Albert Museum.)*

Fig. 11 **Dish** *from Urbino, c.1560–70. 26½ x 20¾ ins. In the centre is a scene depicting the gathering of manna while around the borders the delicately painted decoration is reminiscent of antique grotesques. (Victoria and Albert Museum.)*

Fig. 12 **Dish** *from Deruta, early sixteenth century. Diameter 15½ ins. Characteristic of Deruta maiolica decoration is the portrait bust painted in the centre of the plate. (Wallace Collection, London.)*

Fig. 13 **Albarello** *from Siena, c.1500. Height 5½ ins. Albarelli, or tall jars with nipped waists, were generally used by apothecaries to hold dry drugs. (Victoria and Albert Museum.)*

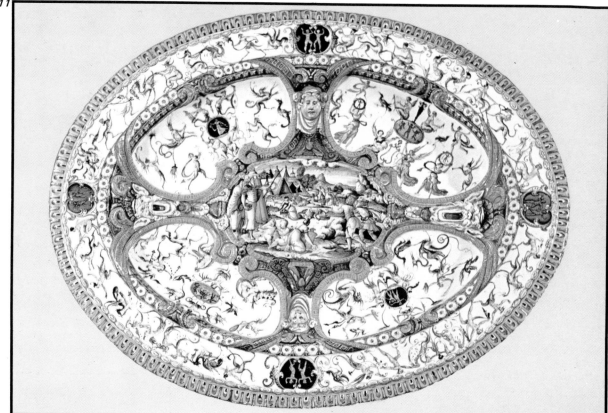

work. The Faenza dish in Fig. 14, which was made in about 1530, has gadrooning in imitation of a metal piece. At the same time, the decoration took less and less account of the shape or use of the vessel. There is a large table cistern in the Fitzwilliam Museum that is typical of the elaborate shapes of the second half of the century with no area left free of decoration. This was probably made in the Urbino workshop of the Fontana family.

Throughout the sixteenth century the fashion for a particular type of decoration, once established by one centre, was soon taken up at others. This, coupled with the fact that potters and painters moved from place to place, makes the attribution of many pieces to a particular workshop, difficult.

14

J. Freeman

Fig. 14 **Dish** *from Faenza, c.1530. Diameter 8 ins. The figure of Cupid has always been a popular motif. Here he is shown in a contemplative mood, leaning against an urn. (Victoria and Albert Museum.)*

The decoration used in the previous century was predominantly concerned with ornamental designs. These patterns based on geometric shapes and plant motifs continued to be used during the early part of the sixteenth century. The large jar attributed to Faenza (Fig. 8) and the Siena *albarello* (Fig. 13) date from about 1500. The decoration on both of them contains elements that were used in the fifteenth century combined in a freer, more elegant manner. On the jar, the decoration in the panels between the cherubs' heads especially, points the way to the designs used after 1500.

The sixteenth century is chiefly noted for the development of a pictorial style of painting known as *istoriato*, in which the decoration represented one or more episodes from a story. These were taken from a great many sources that included the Bible, the works of the writers of antiquity, like Ovid and Pliny, and Italian writers such as Ariosto. For the composition of their designs, the painters made much use of engravings; the print in some cases was copied very closely and in others elements from different prints were combined. Use was also made of woodcut illustrations from early printed books. The Castel Durante plate in Fig. 6 is painted with the story of Peleus and Thetis, adap-

ted from woodcut illustrations in an edition of Ovid's *Metamorphoses*, published in Venice in 1497. By the third decade of the century the principal engravings used were those of Marcantonio Raimondi after the works of Raphael and his School. Because of this, in the late eighteenth century this type of maiolica was associated with Raphael and the ware was called Raphaelle after him. At this time, the practice was begun of identifying the subject of the story on a dish by means of an inscription in blue on the back. This is often accompanied by the date and sometimes by the artist's signature.

The earliest *istoriato* pieces came from Faenza and Cafaggiolo, but it was at Castel Durante and later at Urbino that the style developed. One of the most distinguished of all the *istoriato* painters was Nicola Pellipario. He began his career at Castel Durante where in about 1519 he painted a service for Isabella d'Este, wife of Gianfrancesco Gonzaga, duke of Mantua (Fig. 6). By 1528 he had moved to Urbino and he continued there until the early 1540s. Another well-known painter working in Urbino at the same time was Francesco Xanto Avelli. He painted the large dish in Fig. 9 showing Horatio defending the bridge, taken from Livy's history of Rome. It is inscribed on the back with his signature and the date 1537. During the second half of the century the Fontana workshop introduced a style of decoration using grotesques, based on prints after the frescoes by Raphael in the Vatican (Fig. 11). *Istoriato* ware in the Urbino style was produced in Venice, but the characteristic maiolica of this centre has the tin-glaze stained pale blue, with painting in dark blue and white.

Reaction against this profusion of decoration led to the production of pieces painted with sketchy figures in blue, yellow and orange. Others were left white without any decoration. Both these types continued to be made into the seventeenth century.

MUSEUMS AND COLLECTIONS

Collections of Italian maiolica are represented at the following:

GREAT BRITAIN
Cambridge:	Fitzwilliam Museum
London:	Victoria and Albert Museum
	Wallace Collection
Oxford:	Ashmolean Museum

ITALY
Faenza:	Museo Internazionale delle Ceramiche
Florence:	Museo Nazionale (Bargello)
Rome:	Museo di Palazzo Venezia

U.S.A.
Cincinnati, Ohio:	Taft Museum

FURTHER READING

Maiolica, Delft and Faience by G. Scavizzi, 1970.
Five Centuries of Italian Maiolica by Guiseppe Liverani, New York, 1960.
Italian Maiolica by Bernard Rackham, London, 1952 (1964).
Catalogue of Italian Maiolica by Bernard Rackham, Victoria and Albert Museum, London, 1940.
Guide to Italian Maiolica by Bernard Rackham, Victoria and Albert Museum, London, 1933.

French Faience

Fig. 1 *Ewer*, *Rouen, early eighteenth century, like the sugar castor in Fig. 2, this ewer is of the Delft type known as* Violette *faience.* (*Victoria and Albert Museum.*)

Fig. 2 *Sugar castor*, *Rouen, early eighteenth century. Painted blue and white, this attractive sugar castor is in the manner of Delft.* (*Victoria and Albert Museum.*)

In the early sixteenth century pottery was being made in France which was comparable with the finest Italian Maiolica. By the eighteenth century even the tables of the nobility were graced with these magnificent and elaborately decorated pieces. These wares were called faience; it was pottery to rival silver

In describing French faience (tin-glazed earthenware), mention must first be made of the pottery known as St. Porchaire, which superficially resembles faience, but which was produced by a quite different technique. Because the clay was fine-grained and rich in silica, the body remained white after firing and the surface was then decorated with coloured lines, the whole being covered with a transparent lead glaze. This technique of decoration may have involved some kind of printing process. On a broken portion of a St. Porchaire plate in the Victoria and Albert Museum the decorated lines are formed by grooves filled with coloured slip, or semi-fluid clay. Underneath the rim the plate bears an indented mark. The decorative outlines on this ware were sometimes impressed on to the soft clay before firing with a stamping iron, and the colours and occasional moulded ornamentation added later.

St. Porchaire ware was made in elegant shapes and designs, and clearly intended for the nobility

St. Porchaire, otherwise known as Henri II ware, was made in the sixteenth century in the most elegant shapes and designs, often bearing coats of arms, and clearly intended for the nobility (Fig. 6). Its exact origin is a matter for dispute. The historian Filon discovered certain documents at the Castle of Oiron, near Thouars, which, he believed, proved that around 1529 some outstanding pottery was being made there by the librarian, Bernard, and his assistant, Charpentier, under the personal supervision of the lady of the castle, Countess Helen of Hangest. Filon thought that the style of decoration on the pottery was reminiscent of the tooling of leather in bookbinding (Fig. 6). Most of the known pieces of this ware have been found around Oiron and many bear the arms of noble families of the region. Nevertheless, the pottery is now more generally referred to as St. Porchaire, following the discovery of an inventory in Thouars Castle, dated 1542, in which an entry, referring to two *tazze* made of St. Porchaire clay, was found. Another theory is that the ware originated in the vicinity of Paris. Be this as it may, the existence of this fascinating style of pottery shows that the faience technique had its rivals, even in Renaissance times.

The distinctive feature of faience, as of maiolica and delft, is that the clay body is coated with an opaque white glaze made from oxide of tin, instead of with a transparent lead glaze. Opaque tin glaze was an ancient invention used by Assyrian potters in

K. Hoddle

K. Hoddle

the ninth century B.C. for covering bricks and wall tiles. The technique was rediscovered in Mesopotamia in the ninth century A.D. and used for decorative plates. From there it spread to Persia and ultimately to Europe via Islamic Spain, where the famous Hispano-Moresque style was developed. From Spain, via Majorca, the ware reached Italy where it came to be known as maiolica. Some examples of the technique may have come into France from Northern Italy, but most of the early infiltration was probably from Spain.

In the fourteenth century the Papal court at Avignon employed artists from both Spain and Italy, and tin-glazed tiles and other pottery of the period have been found in the Papal palace and other buildings in the vicinity. These early pieces were rather thin and grey and somewhat coarsely painted. The colouring, like that on early Italian maiolica, was confined to green and purple.

Towards the end of the fifteenth century in Italy, the technique was first introduced of painting ceramic colours on to a thin glaze which could withstand a high temperature. This led to the development of the famous pictorial styles in Italian maiolica. In the sixteenth and seventeenth centuries, French faience craftsmen tended to adopt the style of the Italian potters, some of whom had come into the country to build kilns at Nevers and at Lyons (Fig. 4).

The first great master of French faience was Masséot Abaquesne, who was working at Rouen by 1526 (Fig. 9). He found a ready patron in the Duc de Montmorency, who was a great lover of Italian art. In 1542 Abaquesne designed a pavement for the château of Ecouen. In 1543 he was commissioned to make three hundred and forty-six dozen drug jars for a Rouen chemist. They were probably made in the typical Italian *albarello* shape.

Another master of French faience, whose work was also essentially Italian in character, was the Huguenot, Antoine Sigalon, born near Nîmes. Although he made mainly tiles and everyday pieces, his reputation stems from his elaborately painted faience (Fig. 3). How he acquired the knowledge to produce this is a mystery, but his ware was equal to the finest Italian maiolica. But for the word Nîmes on authenticated pieces, they could be taken for good examples of Urbino or Castel Durante. Although Abaquesne and Sigalon were undoubtedly leading faience makers, their output was not very great.

In the sixteenth century, important cultural and commercial relations were being established between Italy and France. The Medici and the Sforza families established banks at Lyon. Documentary evidence shows that in 1554, the Genoese potter, Griffo, and later in 1574, two men from

K. Hoddle

Fig. 3 **Dish,** by Antoine Sigalon, Nîmes, c.1580. (Victoria and Albert Museum.)

Fig. 4 **Plate,** Lyons, second half of the sixteenth century. This plate shows Paris presenting the golden apple to Venus. (Victoria and Albert Museum.)

Fig. 5 **Basin or table cistern,** Nevers, c.1670. This piece is painted in polychrome with mythological scenes after engravings by Michel Dorigny (1617–66). (Musée de Céramique, Sèvres.)

Fig. 6 **Table Candlestick,** sixteenth century, Saint-Porchaire or Henri II ware. Contrasting coloured slips have been used on this piece which was possibly made for the King. (Petit Palais, Paris.)

Fig. 7 **Oval dish,** Nevers, 1589. The front of this dish is reminiscent of late Urbino maiolica. The blue wave decoration became a speciality of Nevers faience. (Louvre, Paris.)

Fig. 8 **Vase and cover,** Rouen, late seventeenth century. (Louvre.)

Faenza, Giulio Gambini and Domenico Tardessir, petitioned Henri III for the exclusive right to make painted maiolica in the Italian manner, which they claimed to have introduced into France.

Although its existence is proven by documentation, little is known about the nature of early Lyons faience, but there is a plate marked 'Lyons 1582' in the British Museum. The Lyons potters are known to have produced *faience blanche* which was a style fashionable in Faenza. A fine quality tin glaze was left substantially undecorated except for the central portion.

Their success was so great that Conrado was given French citizenship and raised to the nobility

Nevers was another important centre, the faience craft having been introduced there under the patronage of the Duke Luigi Gonzaga of Mantua, who became Duke of Nivernais in 1565 through his marriage to Henriette de Clèves. He was a great lover of the arts and brought from his native Italy some outstanding craftsmen, in particular Domenico Conrado and his brothers from Albissola near Savona. Their success at Nevers was so great that in 1578 Conrado was granted French citizenship, and in 1604 he was raised to the nobility. Between 1588 and 1590 his brother Augustin was in partnership with Giulio Gambini, the Italian potter from Lyon. The strong influence of Faenza discernible on the early products of Nevers was no doubt due to Gambini's presence and the partnership brought to Nevers the best of the late Urbino pictorial style. This phase lasted well into the seventeenth century, the designs including biblical and mythological subjects (Fig. 11).

Some large figures were also produced at Nevers in the seventeenth century, probably at the Conrado workshop, where the artist, Daniel Lefebvre, was employed from 1629 to 1649. Some of the large Nevers figures are marked with his initials. Antoine Conrado, son of Domenico Conrado, was made *faiencier ordinaire* to the King in 1644. The monopoly of the Conrado family lasted until about 1630 when other factories began to make their appearance.

Early Nevers faience has mythological and religious pictures copied from contemporary engravings

Nevers faience was usually painted in the style of Savona maiolica, with mythological and religious scenes copied from contemporary engravings (Fig. 5). The clay and the glaze employed at Nevers were harder than those of Savona, and the firing was done at higher temperatures. The resulting colours were of rather faded tints, the manganese pigments tending to turn pale violet and the green and yellow copper colours to lose their intensity. The Nevers potters dispensed with the use of the *coperta*, the final protective covering of thin, glassy lead glaze which is normally present on Italian maiolica.

A new technique of painting was introduced at the Conrado factory. The basic tin glaze was rendered blue by the addition of cobalt, and on to this ground designs were painted with a thick, white enamel paste. This is referred to as the Persian style, but it is more likely to have derived from Limoges enamels. In the course of time pseudo-oriental designs succeeded the Italian idiom (Fig. 10). The Nevers potters, like most French faience-makers of the day, copied the pottery imported from Holland, where Chinese porcelain styles were the dominant fashion.

Throughout the eighteenth century Nevers remained one of the great centres of French faience, but it never produced a truly French style. The first great innovators in France worked at Rouen. In 1644 Nicholas Poirel of Rouen, Sieur de Grandval and sometime usher to the Queen, applied for the sole right to make white and painted pottery in Normandy. The short-lived factory of Abaquesne from the previous century had disappeared without a trace, leaving no other potteries in the town, and Poirel readily obtained his monopoly. There are no documents extant concerning Poirel's business prior to the deed of sale of his factory and monopoly to Edmé Poterat in 1647. It appears that Poterat, whose name was to become so famous in the history of ceramics, had been making faience on the premises for some two years. He made use of workmen and equipment from Nevers, and at first produced pieces in the same Italian style. The name of Custode, a family that worked for Conrado at Nevers before setting up on their own, appears among Poterat's list of workmen.

After a time, Poterat adopted a new method of decoration that did not require great skill. This was known as *lambrequin* or *broderie*, and is seen at its best on large trays or platters, which were made for actual use, not just for display on dressers.

A. C. Cooper

Réalités: M. Nahmias

Giraudon

Connaissance des Arts: Boitier

Connaissance des Arts: Boitier

G·A·ROVEN
1542

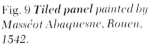

Fig. 11 **Vase**, Nevers, early eighteenth century.
Painted with an Old Testament scene, this plate is
in the colours of the Nevers palette.
(Victoria and Albert Museum.)

Fig. 9 **Tiled panel** painted by
Masséot Abaquesne, Rouen,
1542.
This panel clearly shows the
influence of Italian maiolica
from Urbino. It shows Mucius
Scaevola at the Camp of Lars
Porsena.
(Private Collection.)

Fig. 10 **Wig stand**, Nevers, late
seventeenth century.
Unusual today, the wig stand was
an everyday object in the
seventeenth century. This one is
painted in blue and white with an
oriental design, particularly
popular at Nevers.
(Victoria and Albert Museum.)

Their dimensions were given in terms of what they would hold, such as twelve to fifteen chickens, or twenty partridges.

By 1663 the faience industry of Rouen was sufficiently developed to come to the notice of the finance minister, Colbert, who was investigating the state of the industries of the kingdom. He made a proposal 'to encourage and reward the Faiencers of Rouen and the neighbourhood, to stimulate competition among them, to supply them with good designs, and to make them work for the King'. The report shows that Poterat had failed in his attempts to enforce his legal monopoly. The first potter to start up in Rouen independently was Butin, who described himself as a painter and sculptor on faience. When it was seen that Poterat's attempts to remove Butin had failed, five other kilns were set up, all in the St. Sever district.

Edmé Poterat's most able assistant was his eldest son, Louis, who like many potters of the time, was fascinated by the secret of translucent porcelain. While still working for his father, he achieved some success in making it and, in 1673, he obtained a Letter Patent from the King, granting him a thirty-year right to manufacture both porcelain and Violette faience, that is, faience painted in blue and other colours after the manner of Delft (Figs. 1 and 2).

At the beginning of the eighteenth century the faience industry entered a new period of prosperity and brilliance. Development was aided by the widespread melting down of silver wares instigated by Louis XIV, and followed by his nobles, in an attempt to save the state from financial ruin. There was a need to display something suitable on the dresser in place of the plate, with the effect that there was an immediate run on all stocks of pottery. This new demand enabled the Rouen potters to turn from the simpler and more economical decorations to more extravagant and ambitious styles suited to the aristocracy. New shapes were introduced, taken from the silver and gold tableware, and plain blue and white colours gave way to elaborate polychrome and to imitations of the famille verte and famille rose styles of Chinese porcelain. The best of the Chinese style of Rouen was produced between 1720 and 1750.

In about 1740 Rouen potters began to use rococo shapes and motifs and painted scenes similar to those of Watteau and Boucher. Thirty years later Levavasseur, in an attempt to revive the flagging interest in faience and to compete with the products of Marseilles and Strasbourg, adopted the use of enamel decoration.

MUSEUMS AND COLLECTIONS
French faience may be seen at the following:
FRANCE
Marseilles: Musée Cantini
Nevers: Musée Municipal
Paris: Louvre
Rouen: Musée des Beaux-Arts
GREAT BRITAIN
Cambridge: Fitzwilliam Museum
London: British Museum
Victoria and Albert Museum
Oxford: Ashmolean Museum

FURTHER READING
French Faience (rev. ed.) by A. Lane, London, 1970.
French Faience by J. Giacomotti, London, 1963.
Five Centuries of Italian Maiolica by G. Liverin, London, 1960.

Dutch Delft

Fig. 1 **Punch-bowl** *commemorating the Peace of Ryswyck, dated 1697. (Victoria and Albert Museum.)*

Fig. 2 **Wig stand,** *decorated in imitation of Chinese porcelain, late seventeenth century. (Victoria and Albert Museum.)*

Fig. 3 **Tea-caddy,** *mark LF or LVE, c.1700. Black enamel painted to imitate Chinese lacquer. (Victoria and Albert Museum.)*

To compete with the flood of imported Chinese porcelain, Dutch potters developed a type of faience as much appreciated today as in the seventeenth century

Into the sombre world of pewter and stoneware, wooden platters and leather mugs, Chinese porcelain made its dazzling appearance. The depth and brilliance of the blues, the sparkling white and deep reds and greens of late Ming polychrome impressed the whole of Europe. Even a hundred years later, Augustus the Strong of Saxony could talk of his '*Maladie de Porcelaine*', a disease which emptied his treasury faster than anything else. No true porcelain was made in Europe until after the discovery of the porcelain *arcanum* by Böttger at Meissen in 1708, and, in 1600, all eyes were turned to the East.

Even the stalwart Dutch felt the need to copy the hard, ringing, translucent vessels. Some of them

may have had an eye to the main chance, and speculators would certainly have put their money on the Dutch East India Company, formed in 1602. The pottery industry, however, began to apply itself to the new problems and to look for ways of competing with the flood of imports.

Maiolica had been made in innumerable small potteries all over the northern Netherlands and the potters were very experienced and ready to try, develop and perfect new techniques. Indeed, one of the most interesting aspects of seventeenth-century delft is its concentration and steady evolution. English delft never – and some would appreciate it more on this account – acquired the technical finesse of the Dutch. It was neither as elaborate nor as sophisticated, although many Dutch potters worked in England.

Delft is a decorated, tin-glazed earthenware, known elsewhere on the Continent as faience, from Faenza in Italy, the town of its origin. It appeared in the Netherlands early in the seventeenth century, when efforts were made at Delft and Haarlem to produce a finer body. There was considerable confusion between the names 'faience' and 'porcelain'

Fig. 4 **Dish**, second half of the seventeenth century. (Victoria and Albert Museum.)

Fig. 5 **Roundel**, painted by van Frijtom, c.1670. (Victoria and Albert Museum.)

Fig. 6 **Jar and cover.** Although this vase has an outline clearly derived from Chinese pieces of the period, its overall appearance is strictly European. The fluting is a Dutch feature, and the decoration, executed in the manner of one of the greatest Dutch painters, is distinctly European in flavour. (Victoria and Albert Museum.)

Fig. 7 **Apothecary jar** with peacock design. This design was introduced sometime before 1665 and was a popular surround for the cartouches of drug jars for the next hundred years. (Wellcome Museum of Medical Science, London.)

Fig. 8 **Bulb vase and cover** with polychrome decoration. Of somewhat ungainly form, this vase was designed to hold tulips in large quantities. (Victoria and Albert Museum.)

2

K. Hoddle

3

K. Hoddle

4

Museum Photo

5

Museum Photo

7

Museum Photo

8

Museum Photo

Fig. 9 **Plate**, *mark R for De Roos,
early eighteenth century.
In the characteristic blue and
white of Delft, this charming
plate depicts the biblical story
of Jacob's Dream. In contrast to
this Westernised scene, the border
imitates a sophisticated Chinese
pattern.
(Victoria and Albert Museum.)*

Fig. 10 **Panel of tiles**, *first half of
the seventeenth century.
Polychrome decoration.
This pattern of grapes and
pomegranates was one of the
earliest and most popular of floral
tile designs. It was later
superseded by blue and white
tiles with a great variety of
subjects.
(Victoria and Albert Museum.)*

K. Hoddle

Museum Photo

and in 1648 decrees were issued by the Dutch High Court to determine the name of the 'new invention'.

The painters were called *plateelschilder* and must have been very skilled; of course at that time there was an enormous amount of popular painting in Holland, and son followed father as a matter of course in a trade which supplied cheap oil-paintings to all but the poorest. It would not have been difficult to learn to reproduce genre scenes, landscapes and so on, but the painter on faience had an especially difficult task. For one thing, no corrections were possible as the brush-work was done entirely on to the powdered glaze; also, the high-temperature kilns allowed only a very restricted palette – yellow, manganese, purple, green and blue – but a skilful *plateelschilder* could vary his tones and achieve effects of shading. They used very fine brushes made of cow-bristle and, later, badger-hair. Brushes called *trekkers* were used for outlining, and a more mechanical aid was the *sponse* – a card with the design pricked through it, so that it could be laid over a piece and carbon powder blown through. The design was then traced over and filled in.

The last firing was the most important stage of

all and the kilns had to be carefully controlled, with the pieces properly stacked. The kilns were designed to allow the firing of objects at different stages of production, an aspect which was becoming more pressing as the forests of Europe were fast being depleted. Decorated faience was fired in the chamber above the hottest part of the fire and it is always possible to see the spur-marks where pieces were stacked. Exceptional pieces were fired in saggars (cases of baked fireproof clay) and thus protected from the smoke and flames, but, until the muffle-kiln was introduced, red and gold were always capricious as they were inclined to turn brown, or flake off in the kiln.

Maiolica had been predominantly multi-coloured, but delft was nearly all blue and white in imitation of Chinese porcelain. Some polychrome was made in the first half of the seventeenth century and the technique was greatly improved after the advent of the muffle-kilns, but the peak period of production was between 1670 and 1730, when all the techniques had been completely mastered.

The Dutch had already arrived in China in 1596 and porcelain of the Wan-li period (1573–1619) had

Fig. 11 **Tulip Vase**, *mark AK in
monogram, Greek A, c.1694.
This handsome vase, from a set
made for Hampton Court, is
from a design by Daniel Marot.
(Victoria and Albert Museum.)*

Fig. 12 **Milk pan**, *mark AK in
blue, Greek A, 1690-94. Blue
and white.
Probably from the set made
for the dairy at Hampton
Court, this milk pan has a
pouring lip to help with the
cream-separating process. Delft
pottery was so popular in
England that whole sets such as
this were commissioned.
(Victoria and Albert Museum.)*

been familiar in Europe since the Portuguese began to import it in the middle of the sixteenth century. In 1602, Admiral van Heemskirk seized a merchant ship loaded for her return to Spain, and the auction held in the same year at Middelburg increased the porcelain fever. The city of Delft was represented in the *collegium* of seventeen members governing the Dutch East India Company, so that the potters must always have been able to handle plenty of models. At first the copies were primitive, but gradually the potters of Delft, Haarlem and Amsterdam learned to integrate the two very different styles, so that some of the incongruities, such as religious epithets in Dutch within a Wan-li border,

white became more popular, superseding the earlier pomegranate and grape polychrome decoration (Fig. 10). Now every imaginable kind of theme appeared on tiles: land-, sea- and harbour-scapes, cities, houses, ships, biblical stories and so on. Tiles were used everywhere in the house. A painting by Pieter de Hooch in the National Gallery, London, shows an interior in which an integrated pattern of tiles surrounds a fireplace.

As the supply of Hispano-Moresque tiles dried up, the Dutch enlarged their production and increased their exports. Another aspect of tile-production was that of finely painted plaques and

Fig. 13 *Candlestick*, mark D, with a shaft and the number 24, De Dissel, c.1660. *Blue decoration in the Chinese manner.* (Gemeentemuseum, The Hague.)

Fig. 14 *Tile* after Daniel Marot. *Blue and white decoration.* (Rijksmuseum.)

Fig. 15 *Small dish* from a tiffin set from the Young Moor's Head Factory of the Hoppesteyns. *Polychrome and gold, 1680–92.* (Rijksmuseum.)

began to disappear. They copied not only the patterns, but also the shapes from Oriental models; baluster-vases, covered pots, deep bowls and plates, some of which were of immense size as the century wore on and their skill grew surer.

Side by side with the new development, the old production of apothecaries' jars and tiles of all kinds continued. Early pharmacy jars are lined with lead-glaze, the tin-glaze being confined to the outside; this gradually changed to an all-over tin-glaze and after 1630 the linear, braided decoration gave way to a cartouche, blue on white, containing the name of the medicament, surrounded by swags, *putti*, fleurs-de-lys and garlands. Very characteristic is a motif of two peacocks facing a central basket of fruit or flowers (Fig. 7). Large numbers of these peacock jars were made for about one hundred years after their introduction, sometime before 1665, and nearly all were unmarked, making attribution to any particular factory difficult.

A consignment of seven thousand tiles was sent to Nantes

Tiles were consistently made and exported throughout Europe. One consignment of seven thousand tiles sent in sixteen crates to Nantes and thence overland by way of Blois to the Château of Beauregard is recorded. The floor of tiles was laid in 1646 and is still described as 'a whole army on the march' – soldiers were a very popular subject. Tiles were still made in sets of four with an integrated corner-pattern, but in the early seventeenth century this degenerated into a flower or a shape unrelated to the central motif, whilst blue and

roundels with landscapes and other scenes, used mainly for decoration. Frederick van Frijtom, an independent master-potter and pottery painter, who was not a native of Delft although he worked there, is famous for his plaques of landscapes without a border which were clearly intended to be framed (Fig. 5). He died sometime before 1702.

Delft faience entered its finest period in the middle of the seventeenth century. In other factories in Holland, the tin-glazed wares made no substantial improvement after that date.

In 1654, the town of Delft was almost completely destroyed by the explosion of a gunpowder boat. During the reconstruction of the city, the old breweries, which had fallen into disuse, were taken over by the potters, which accounts for the bizarre names of the factories: The Three Golden Ash-Barrels, The Double Jug, for instance. The city encouraged the pottery business and the factories were owned either by syndicates or by wealthy citizens. Generally, the potters were not in control, although the Potters' Guild – The Guild of Saint Luke – decreed that no-one could be a manager who was not also a master-potter.

The Eenhoorns were the most important family of potters in Delft and they produced tin-glazed earthenware from the middle of the seventeenth century until about 1773. The founder of the business was Wouter van Eenhoorn, who acquired the factory called *De Porceleyne Fles* (The Porcelain Bottle) with Quirinus van Cleynhoven in 1655, and the brewery called *De Grieksche A* (The Greek A) in 1658. In 1674, his son Samuel took over from him. Wouter was also co-proprietor of *De Drei Vergulde Astonnekens* (The Three Golden Ash-Barrels), *Het Hooge Huys* (The Tall House)

Fig. 16 *Fluted plate with decoration in imitation of Imari ware. Mark AK. The patterns of Japanese Imari ware were much imitated in Holland.*
(Victoria and Albert Museum.)

Fig. 17 *Plate, dated 1689. Decorated in blue and white with a Chinese boy and the initials ANS.*
(Victoria and Albert Museum.)

16

Museum Photo

17

Museum Photo

and *De Paeuw* (The Peacock), a very important factory.

The question of marks inevitably arises and Dutch delft has many, most of them factory marks or marks of the owner and the potter or painter. They are useful for research, for comparison and for building up a background of knowledge of pattern and design, but they are not a good guide for investment; quality is always the first criterion in that case and it is more interesting to learn to judge style than to memorise lists of marks.

Decoration on seventeenth-century delft was almost infinite, but there was also a large production of domestic *wit goet* – white, undecorated wares such as pitchers, plates and bowls with fluted rims. Coats of arms appeared as early as 1610, but became more popular after 1650 when families ordered them; failing a coat of arms, a family would make do with a monogram. Plates were made in sets with rhyming couplets, one line on each, a practice also found in England, where it was certainly introduced by immigrant Dutch potters, not noted for their command of English spelling. William and Mary bowls and deep dishes were painted with the heads of the sovereigns within borders of oranges and foliage. Some were made in Lambeth, in London, by Dutch potters, though they can usually be distinguished. Other themes were landscapes, river scenes, portraits, interiors and scenes from rural life, especially on plaques; biblical scenes and religious inscriptions with a date; portraits of the famous – scientists, theologians and historians – copied from engravings; and, throughout the whole period, blue and white imitations of the birds and flowers on late Ming and early Ch'ing porcelain.

Delicate paintings of women and children

A type of ceremonial plate made about 1675 was given the name *Porselyn-Karakter* for the outstanding delicacy of its design and execution. This had a polygonal medallion enclosing a landscape with a background of luxurious plants and a single bird, or perhaps a stag, in the foreground. The border of repeating Wan-li symbols alternated with other Chinese symbols within small frames. The blue was dark, inclined to violet. About the same time, a characteristic of Dutch delft called *trek* was invented, probably by Samuel Eenhoorn. This was a method of outlining in black and dark blue.

Although blue and white predominated, polychrome was never abandoned and a gradual refinement of technique can be observed. Such pieces were fired in containers and then glazed with *kwaart*, which imparted a final sheen. About 1700, many new influences affected the Delft potters, and after that date a greater variety developed. In the last years of the seventeenth century, experiments were made with black, dark brown or olive grounds, possibly in imitation of Oriental lacquer, rather than the *famille noire* of K'ang-hsi, and by this time the familiar Wan-li style had been replaced by more delicate paintings of women and children.

The finest period lasted until about 1730, when Delft, in common with all the other European faience factories, began to sacrifice its vigour to the lure of enamel colours and the pretty triviality of porcelain. This brief survey, however, breaks off at the turn of the century, when the potters of Delft were still at the height of their powers.

Identifying Delft

The following are the most important Delft factories.

De Paeuw (The Peacock) 1651–1705. Various owners, the most important being Lambrecht van Cruyck, Willem Cleffius and Wouter van Eenhoorn.

Het Jonge Moriaenshooft (The Young Moor's Head) 1660–92. Owned by the Hoppesteyns, father, Jacob and son, Rochus, who was sole owner from 1664–71. Technically very important, with fine representations of Chinese porcelain in polychrome and gilding. Colours; violet, blue, green, bright red and gold; perhaps Rochus' invention.

De Grieksche A (The Greek A) 1674–1722. Founder Wouter van Eenhoorn. His son, Samuel, was owner after 1678. The painting is noted for its loose grouping of figures and detailed drawing of faces and clothes. He may have invented *trek*. The factory was acquired from Samuel's widow by Adriaen Kocks who extended and increased its reputation. A royal commission by William III for Hampton Court, between 1689 and 1694, gives the Greek A a special interest. The pieces were designed by the King's architect, Daniel Marot (Figs. 11 and 12).

De Metalen Pot (The Metal Pot) 1670–1721. Lambertus Cleffius took over the factory from Van Kessel and managed it till 1691. His mark LC may be his own signature or a factory mark. Lambert van Eenhoorn acquired the factory in 1691. There was a quarrel lasting over twenty years about his mark LVE with Victor Victorson and his son Louwys, who owned the Double Jug and signed LVF.

De Dobbelde Schenkkan (The Double Jug) 1661–1713. Founded 1661 and sold to Victorson and his son Louwys in 1688. Their ownership was the only important period. They favoured K'ang-hsi designs, especially white on blue, and made good imitations of Chinese porcelain. Fine polychrome.

De Roos (The Rose) 1662–1712. Owned by Arent Cosijn, Janson van Straten and, finally, Danmas Hofdijk. This factory had a preference for religious subjects and produced fine polychrome in the later period (Fig. 9).

MUSEUMS AND COLLECTIONS
Dutch Delft may be seen at the following:

FRANCE
Paris: Musée National de Céramique

GREAT BRITAIN
London: British Museum
 Victoria and Albert Museum

THE NETHERLANDS
Amsterdam: Rijksmuseum

FURTHER READING
Delft Ceramics by C. H. de Jonge, London, 1970.
Collecting Delft by Diana Imber, 1968.
Les Faiences de Delft by H. Fourest, Paris, 1957.
European Ceramic Art by W. B. Honey, London, 1952.

Spanish Pottery

Fig. 2 **Dish**, *Catalonia, early seventeenth century.*
Lustre pattern background painted with blue.
This fine example of Catalan painting in blue and lustre
has three radiating flowers or leaves.
(Victoria and Albert Museum.)

Fig. 1 **Dish**, *Talavera,*
seventeenth century. Painted
with blue and ochre.
Decorated with a helmeted head,
this dish is characteristic of the
bold and attractive caricature-
like painting of Talavera de la
Reina. This great pottery centre,
increasingly important as
lustreware lost its prominence,
was some eighty miles south
west of Madrid. The patterns
created there were almost wholly
figurative, ranging from
realistically detailed scenes to
powerful, sketchy caricatures
as on this dish.
(Victoria and Albert Museum,
London.)

From the rare beauty of Hispano-Moresque lustreware to the more domestic elegance of Alcora earthenware, Spanish pottery was both richly decorated and colourful

The two hundred years between 1600 and 1800 stretched from the end of the Renaissance to an utterly different, and modern, Europe. When Philip II died, Spain was the greatest power in Europe and had carved out a great empire in the New World. With the defeat of the Armada by England in 1588, Spain began to lose her position in Europe. Her century of power and expansion which began with the unification of the kingdoms of Castile and Aragon was over, but we are interested here only in the influence and repercussions of the period and the aftermath as it affected ceramic design which henceforth would owe more and more to the designers and craftsmen of other European countries.

It is impossible to discuss the first half of the subject – seventeenth-century pottery – without some reference to the classical era, in which Spanish pottery reached its zenith of originality and beauty, and which runs from about 1400 to about 1525.

The early wares of Spain were the forerunners of pottery in Europe. The fame of Spanish pottery really rests on its lustreware, often described as 'Hispano-Moresque' because the golden lustre of the decoration was the product of Moorish potters. They introduced into Spain the process of manufacture and the decorative motifs prevalent in the Arab empire.

The influence of the Moors on Spanish culture was immense and nowhere is it seen to greater advantage than in architecture and pottery. On the earlier pottery we find Arab designs such as interlacing geometric patterns, formal foliage and Arabic writing. This script was Kufic, or the later cursive Nashki, or flowery variations that are often beautiful though corrupt, illiterate and meaningless. As the Christian kingdoms subdued the Moorish states, we get an odd but decorative mixture of Muslim and Christian motifs. For more than three centuries the lustre decoration that glitters like gold, usually with a mother of pearl opalescence, appeared on the dishes and jars.

The lustreware potteries were concentrated at first in the area of Malaga in the Moorish kingdom of Granada, but most of the lustreware of the fifteenth century was made at Manises, a short distance from Valencia. Despite their religion the Moorish potters were welcomed in a Christian state. Lustred pottery of Manises was after about 1525 extensively copied in Muel (Saragossa), Teruel, Reus (Tarragona), Barcelona and most other Catalan cities. Lustreware continued to be made in

recipe of the pigment, produced a lustre which might be brown, ruby red, golden or silvery gold. Usually the metallic reflections produced a rainbow effect in certain lights.

Lustred pottery in place of gold ornaments (thought fit only for Paradise) was approved by the puritan Muslims and was developed in about the ninth century in the Middle East. Lustreware of distinction was made in Egypt, Mesopotamia and Iran. Because of its rich beauty, it provided a substitute for gold. This factor is important in studying Spanish lustreware because the development, or robbing, of new colonies in the New World

Manises in the seventeenth century.

Most Spanish pottery, including lustreware, was decorated tin-glazed earthenware. The clay pot, after being baked hard in a kiln, was given a whitewash containing tin and lead oxides. When the film of whitewash was dry the potter painted patterns on the absorbent surface. He applied a pigment which, when the pot was baked a second time at a relatively high temperature, turned to its desired colour. The colour was imprisoned in the tin oxide glaze which fused into a hard, white, shiny coating. If lustre decoration was to be applied, a separate process was involved. The potter had before him a pot coated with a hard, white, fused coating which might be plain or decorated. Using a pigment containing oxides of copper or silver, or a mixture of both; he painted the lustre decoration on the pot which was then put into a low-temperature kiln. When the pottery reached a certain temperature smoke was let into the kiln and the carbon of the smoke combined with the oxides and produced carbon dioxide gas which was carried away. The oxides were reduced, leaving a thin film of copper or silver (or a mixture) which, depending on the

resulted in great shipments of gold and silver. Lustreware potteries were then faced with competition from the real thing and at the same time with imported Italian maiolica. A good seventeenth-century Catalan example of the use of lustre and blue is shown in Figure 2, a dish with radiating flowers in blue.

Although there was a spread of lustreware manufacture in Spain after 1550, the combination of slick commercialism and change of taste led to a slide into decadence. As regards taste, people began to tire of the abstract patterns of the Muslim potters. A preference was growing for human figures and pictorial wares in general. The Moorish potters and their Christian colleagues could draw splendidly decorative eagles and beasts, but when it came to pictorial work they had no tradition and little skill. Only the influence of Italian and French artists could give a new turn to Spanish pottery design.

Increasingly the lustreware of Catalonia in the seventeenth century illustrated human heads or whole figures. The figures may represent court ladies, warriors with helmets, peasant girls or

Museum Photo

Museum Photo

Fig. 6 *Jar and cover*, Reus, Catalonia, early seventeenth century. Painted with lustre decoration and the arms of Pope Paul V (1605–21). (Hispanic Society of America.)

Fig. 7 **Wall-cistern**, Alcora, mid-eighteenth century. Delicately painted with small-scale patterns in blue and yellow on white. Far removed from the rougher products of Talavera, Alcora pottery was supremely elegant. (Victoria and Albert Museum.)

sportsmen with falcons. Unfortunately, the Catalan painters of pottery were consistently incompetent. One would like to think their clumsy figures were caricatures, but no such generosity is possible. There seems to have been almost a Spanish tradition of fumbling inadequacy in figure-drawing. Only in some eighteenth-century Alcora pottery do we get successful and realistic figure-painting (Fig. 11). This is surprising, as in Italy beautiful portrait dishes were produced at Castel Durante and Deruta (the latter in lustre) a hundred years before. Such wares were imported into Spain and in the early part of the sixteenth century, an Italian, Francisco Niculoso, was producing in Seville maiolica tile-pictures featuring well-drawn figures.

Figure 6 shows an all-lustre jar and cover bearing the coat of arms of Pope Paul V (1605–21). This elaborate Catalan pot made at Reus for the Pope does not escape the charge of being decorated with rather ludicrous figure-painting.

From lustreware, we turn to the increasingly important pottery centre of Talavera de la Reina, a town about eighty miles to the south west of Madrid. The patterns now begin to be wholly figurative. Three classes of decoration are especially characteristic: bold caricature-like heads or equally forceful portrayals of animals; realistic detailed scenes painted in the style of a canvas-painting; and sketchy genre scenes on a white background. People were favourite subjects. Whereas the earlier Hispano-Moresque painters abhorred a vacuum and filled the surface of a pot with scrolls and flourishes when all else failed, there is after 1600 an increasing use of areas of plain white in the background.

An example of the bold and attractive caricature type of painted decoration may be seen in Figure 1, a helmeted head in blue and ochre. Similar painting (sixteenth and seventeenth centuries) is seen in the striking dish from perhaps El Puente del Arzobispo, a town close to Talavera (Fig. 3). It shows a boldly drawn heraldic lion, with parti-coloured stylised vegetation on the flat rim. These designs are

8

9

orange, purple, green and brown.

By the early part of the eighteenth century, Talavera had lost importance and in 1727 the Count of Aranda, Don Bonaventura Pedro de Alcántara, established Alcora (near Castellón de la Plana in the province of Valencia) as a centre of fine ceramic manufacture. Spanish originality had by this time exhausted itself and there developed a desire to keep up with other European countries. For at least the next ten years Alcora pottery imitated the pottery of Moustiers in France. To achieve this end, the Count had the unoriginal idea of tempting away ceramic experts, including Joseph Olerys and Edouard Roux, from the French factory. The designs of Jean Bérain, father and son, were used at Moustiers and were copied at Alcora.

The designs on Alcora wares are delicate and elegant – far removed from the rougher products of Talavera. The potting and painting were technically better and more refined. Those who find the patterns repetitious, mechanical, niggly and uninspiring and the painting and surface texture suave, will find plenty of enthusiasts to rebuke them. The eighteenth century was certainly one that appreciated boudoir elegance, and such decorative pottery (and, later, porcelain) was preferred to compositions that needed looking at and looking into. An emotional impact was the last thing desired. Innumerable small-scale motifs of grotesques, garlands, sprays of flowers, cupids, urns, lace patterns, sphinxes, *chinoiserie* figures and candelabra were largely inspired by French and Dutch pottery. Figure 8 shows an Alcora tea-caddy of about 1750 painted with small patterns in blue on white. The coat of arms indicates an ecclesiastical indulgence in tea-drinking. Figure 7 shows a large wall-cistern of the same period, delicately painted in blue and yellow.

Plaques were particularly popular and two fine examples are in the Victoria and Albert Museum. These were painted in the middle of the eighteenth century. One represents a sea-nymph with attendant figures (Fig. 11). It is signed by the painter, Vicente Ferrer. The other represents a mother and child. Both these oval plaques are realistic paintings of the highest quality and are allegories of Water and Earth. The white glazed pottery surrounding the oval is moulded and provides an exuberant rococo framing which at the same time is integral with the flat painted surface. A well-painted marine scene with ships and castles appears on a plate in the British Museum (Fig. 5).

There was no class of pottery that Alcora did not make. Tile panels showing incidents in the lives of Christ, the Virgin Mary and the saints were made for the walls of churches and other religious buildings. Large serving-dishes, cups and saucers, holy-water stoups and wall-light plaques were made, and statuettes and sculptured groups were produced in tin-glazed pottery. The founder died in 1749 and was succeeded by his son, Pedro Pablo. His activities marked a further step in Spain's attempt to catch up with the rest of Europe by making porcelain with foreign assistance, while continuing to make tin-glazed pottery which included busts and statuettes after bronzes by Giovanni Bologna.

Spain, which in the fifteenth century had blazed a trail and pioneered the manufacture of fine ceramics in Europe, was now a pale shadow of her former self and of the countries that owed so much to her; she shared the fate of all pioneers in art. 🔲

original, forceful and subtle. Distortions are deliberate and not due to inadequacy of drawing.

An example of sketchy painting of a refined yet incompetent kind is found in the elegantly shaped two-handled vase in Figure 10. A couple of gentlemen of quality, dressed in contemporary costume and equipped with swords, stand in unconvincing poses. The faces are poorly drawn in outline. There is plenty of white in the background and there are delicately drawn branches with small leaves to relieve the white spaces. The painting is typical of some of the genre pottery of Talavera. Figures dance, talk, fish, listen to music or stroll around aimlessly. One gets the impression of an elegant, financially secure society, with little to do except hunt or fight duels in their elaborate costumes.

The shapes of Talavera pottery were very varied – large jars, drug-jars (Fig. 4), large hemispherical bowls painted both inside and outside, ewers, flower-pots, goblets, jars with lids, inkwells, holy-water stoups and dishes. They were painted in a great variety of colours, such as blue, yellow,

Fig. 8 **Tea-caddy.** Alcora, c.1750. Painted with small blue patterns in white and a coat of arms. (Victoria and Albert Museum.)

Fig. 9 **Drug-jar,** Seattle, eighteenth century. The background painted in blue, orange, brown and yellow, the deer in grey-blue. (Hispanic Society of America.)

Fig. 10 **Two-handled vase,** Talavera, seventeenth century. Painted in pale colours with two swordsmen.
Typical of Spanish figure painting, these two gentlemen are sketchily and incompetently depicted. Their poses are unconvincing and their faces poorly drawn in outline, but the overall effect is refined and elegant.
(Victoria and Albert Museum.)

Fig. 11 **Oval plaque** integral with rococo moulded-pattern frame, signed by Vicente Ferrer, Alcora, mid-eighteenth century. Painted in polychrome with a sea nymph and her attendants.
One of four plaques depicting the Elements, this beautiful example represents Water. Pictorial plaques were very popular in the eighteenth century and tended to be of the highest quality.
(Victoria and Albert Museum.)

K. Hoddle

K. Hoddle

MUSEUMS AND COLLECTIONS
Spanish pottery of the seventeenth and eighteenth centuries may be seen at the following:

GREAT BRITAIN
London: British Museum

SPAIN
Madrid: Instituto de Valencia de Don Juan
Museo Arqueológico Nacional

U.S.A.
New York: Hispanic Society of America

FURTHER READING
World Ceramics edited by R. J. Charleston, London, 1968.
Lustreware of Spain by Alice W. Frothingham, New York, 1951.
Talavera Pottery by Alice W. Frothingham, New York, 1944.

Early American Pottery

Pottery was such an everyday art in the Colonies that few pieces have survived from the seventeenth and eighteenth centuries, but those pieces of redware which we still have are charming in their unsophisticated simplicity

Fig. 1 **'Money Wanted'**, *American. Redware with slip motto, length 14 ins., width 10 ins.*
The unusual motto on this large dish was probably intended for display in a shop window. Money was very scarce in early America as most trade was done by barter, and the shop would have wanted to advertise its need of this precious commodity. (Shelburne Museum, Vermont.)

Fig. 2 **Oblong dish**, *American. Redware with slip decoration, length 19 ins., width 12¾ ins., depth 3¾ ins.*
Dishes of this sort were used commonly throughout the Colonies as imported English wares were very expensive. Pottery was needed to supplement local supplies of pewter and treen. (Shelburne Museum.)

Fig. 3 **Spill holder**, *American, 1789. Redware with yellow slip decoration. Height 5 ins.*
This spill holder would have hung on the wall by the fire. (American Museum in Britain, Claverton Manor, Bath.)

Fig. 4 (opposite) **Cup and dish**, *American, the cup, 1780, 4½ x 3½ x 2¾ ins.; the dish with slip decoration and glaze, diameter 6 ins. Redware. Slip was the creamy liquid clay used to decorate a great deal of early redware. It was poured from the holes in a cup like that on the right to create patterns of the type seen on the dish. The pure lead glaze used gave the slip its yellowish colour. (John Judkin Memorial, Bath.)*

The manufacture of redware, the first pottery made in the American Colonies, began in the late 1600s and continued well into the nineteenth century. From New England to Georgia, a familiar sight in Colonial towns and villages was the potshop, where the potter, alone or with the more promising village lads as apprentices, turned out redware for house and dairy.

The long list of redware includes such useful articles as dishes, bowls, cups, mugs, basins, jelly and cake moulds, herb pots, crocks, milk pans, churns and flower pots. Occasionally, especially in the Pennsylvania area, fanciful or decorative pieces were made.

In addition to the full-time potter, there was the seasonal potter, who worked at the craft when other activities, usually of attending to his all-important food crops, permitted. After enough stock was accumulated, he loaded it on to a wagon and peddled it through the countryside. As in most Colonial transactions, money rarely changed hands and payment was made by barter, acceptable items being such useful things as tobacco, meat, corn and tar.

Several factors accounted for the vast output of redware. First, the clay used was the same as that in red brick and roof tiles and a bountiful supply was available practically everywhere. Then, the potting process was so simple that almost anyone could use it for basic products. Essential equipment called for a horse-powered mill for grinding and mixing clays, a home-made potter's wheel and kiln, a few tools, inexpensive materials, and wood fuel, usually available for the taking.

Two more persuasive influences helped to boost the production of redware: it was urgently needed to supplement pewter and treen, and it was

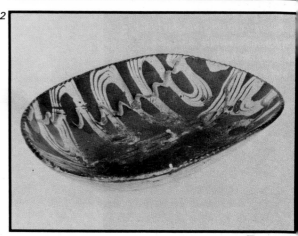

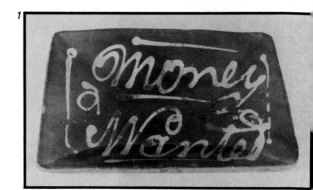

cheaper than the wares imported from England.

The basic colour of redware came from traces of iron oxide in the clay. When fired, this substance produced varying shades of red. Sometimes the red colour was retained in the finished piece by using a pure form of lead glaze – actually glass – which is transparent with a yellowish tinge. The pottery could be given other colours when something was deliberately added to the glaze. Green was produced by adding copper oxide, but the colour was costly and used sparingly. Inexpensive manganese, in varying amounts, provided tan, brown and mirror-black glazes (Fig. 6). Interesting decorative effects occurred accidentally through unsuspected impurities in the clay or unusually high temperatures in the kiln during burning. Under these conditions, pieces might develop attractive streaks or mottling in brown, green, orange or red. For intentional decoration, the potter often relied on coloured glazes, applied in an endless variety of ways, to create

unpretentious designs. The piece then received a conventional glaze before being fired. Bands of colour were a popular finish for the edges of bowls. In the heat of the kiln the decoration ran a little, producing a flowing effect (Figs. 9 and 12).

Slip, or liquid clay, offered another type of redware decoration (Fig. 4). Using a clay cup, the potter poured slip through one or several quills inserted in the liquid to make simple designs, such as scrolls, dots, or names of national heroes or the piece's intended owner (Fig. 13). Over this decoration, glaze was applied, intensifying the colours and producing a lustrous surface. Sometimes a whole redware object was immersed in cream-coloured slip (Fig. 9).

Slip had another, less obvious, use. When bright green motifs were desired, they were first executed in white slip, then covered with green glaze. If the transparent green glaze had been applied directly to the redware surface, the resulting colour would have been olive green.

6

Fig. 7 *'Apple Pie' plate,*
probably made in Pennsylvania.
Redware with slip motto.
Diameter 11 ins.
The so-called Pennsylvania
Dutch, who were actually
German settlers (Deutsch), had
two specialities: apple pie and
apple butter. Special dishes were
made for both in redware, often
identified by a motto.
(Shelburne Museum.)

Fig. 8 *Keg, American, nineteenth*
century. Redware speckled with
black, height 8½ ins.
Although redware was porous, it
was used for the short-term
storage of many things,
including liquids.
(American Museum in Britain.)

Fig. 9 *Jug, American, nineteenth*
century. Redware coated with
cream slip and decorated with
brown and green glazes.
Height 9 ins.
Entire pieces were sometimes
immersed in slip to give them a
more refined, creamy appearance.
The glazes applied as decoration
often ran in the heat of the kiln,
producing the attractive flowing
effect seen on this jug.
(American Museum in Britain.)

Fig. 10 *Water-carrier, American,*
early nineteenth century.
Height 8½ ins.
Bottles of this sort were used
by farm labourers during the
harvest. They were slung over
the men's arms to leave their
hands free for carrying tools.
(American Museum in Britain.)

11

Museum Photo

ig. 11 **Shallow bowl**, American.
edware, top diameter 17½ ins.,
ottom diameter 9¾ ins.,
epth 5½ ins.
imple wares of this sort could
e made by almost anyone with
he proper equipment. All that
as needed was a horse-powered
ill for grinding and mixing
lays, a home-made potter's
heel and kiln, a few tools,
nexpensive materials, and wood
uel, usually available for the
aking. As the necessary red clay
vas plentiful, it is not surprising
hat redware was made in large
quantities throughout the
Colonies.
Shelburne Museum.)

Little is known about the earliest potters and in many cases their work in red and other local clays has completely vanished. At the time, silversmiths had a certain prestige, but no-one attached any importance to preserving the commonplace work of the familiar potter.

The meagre records indicate, however, that pottery was made as early as 1625 at Jamestown, Virginia, the first permanent English settlement in America. Another early southern venture was undertaken by Andrew Duché (1710–78), a Huguenot who left Philadelphia to make pottery in South Carolina from 1731 to 1737. Moving on to Savannah, Georgia, and materially encouraged by General James Oglethorpe, founder of the Georgia Colony, he made pottery and experimental porcelain until 1743.

Pottery became a popular and lively trade in the Colonies

Two more efforts were launched in North Carolina. One was by a colony of Moravians, who, from 1756 to 1768, made redware, stove tiles and clay pipes in the village of Bethabara. The pottery was moved to North Salem, North Carolina, in 1768, where it continued to make wares of improved quality until about 1830.

The other North Carolina enterprise was the so-called Jugtown Pottery at Steeds, a mid-eighteenth-century settlement made up of colonists from Staffordshire. In spite of encouragement given to the pioneers, they seem to have confined their efforts to making the plainest of wares.

The number of eighteenth-century potters in the north must have been enormous. To give only one example, the small town of Peabody, Massachusetts, sent twenty-two potters to the nearby Battle of Lexington in 1775.

Because there was a lively trade in pottery among the Colonies, the place where a piece is found is not necessarily its place of origin. However, regional characteristics sometimes help to identify New England and Pennsylvania pottery. New England, mindful of its Puritan heritage, tended to produce sober, useful objects for workaday purposes. One of the only concessions to frivolity was the use of richly coloured glazes.

Often in distinct contrast was the pottery made by the Pennsylvania Dutch, who were actually *deutsch*, or German. The immigrants from the Palatinate arrived in the eighteenth century and, with Swiss Mennonites, settled in Pennsylvania's so-called 'Dutch' counties.

Redware made by these German colonists, more capable of a relaxed enjoyment of life than their New England counterparts, reflected the potters' imagination, sense of fun and love of colour. Among their products, along with the customary household and dairy items, were bird-shaped whistles, money-boxes in charming designs, and puzzle jugs. They also made articles for two typical Pennsylvania Dutch foods: flat dishes for fruit pies (Fig. 7) and pots for apple butter.

While slip decoration was used everywhere, Pennsylvania potters employed it for the superb *sgraffito*, or scratched, designs that they alone among the colonists produced. A thin slip coating on a piece was scratched through to show the redware body, the intricate designs perhaps being enhanced with additional colours.

A hundred miles of the beautiful Shenandoah Valley in Maryland and Virginia became the site of a number of late but notable potters. Most interesting was the Bell family. Peter, the founding father, worked in Hagerstown, Maryland, and Winchester, Virginia, from 1800 to 1845. His sons and grandsons carried on his work, making both redware and stoneware. Finally, the factory, which had been moved to Strasburg, Virginia, closed in 1908. In a breakaway from Pennsylvania Dutch tradition, to which they were accustomed, the Bells developed a style of their own. Their distinctive flowing designs, such as birds in browns and subdued greens, were almost Oriental in feeling. In addition to practical redware, they made appealing animal figures and other ornaments.

12

Fig. 12 *Basin, American.*
Redware coated inside with slip
and decorated with coloured
glazes, diameter 15 ins.,
depth 4½ ins.
The insides of vessels were often
coated with slip and glazed in
order to make them waterproof;
the redware itself was porous and
was eventually supplanted by
stoneware for this reason. Even
the glazes on redware were
unreliable, as can be seen by the
faults in the finish of this basin.
Its attractiveness, however, is
undeniable, and explains its
long-lasting popularity.
(Shelburne Museum.)

13

Museum Photo

Fig. 13 *Bowl, probably made in*
Pennsylvania, 1796. Redware
with slip decoration, diameter
13¼ ins.
The gaiety and lightness of touch
is characteristic of the
Pennsylvania Dutch potters. As
on the apple pie plate in Fig. 7,
the decoration is applied without
self-conscious planning,
probably through a slip cup or a
quill. The initials are probably
of the original owner.
(Shelburne Museum.)

HINTS FOR COLLECTORS

Marks or signatures on early American pottery are rare. The few seen appear on the works of master potters; no-one bothered to identify common-place pieces.

Fakes exist, particularly in redware. A few signs of age in redware (unfortunately imitated by the faker) include darkening of the piece (that is, darkening of the glaze) from acids in food and cooking heat and minute scratches made by knives. Use through the years turns the unglazed bottoms of baking dishes black. Impressed marks, which must be made while the clay is still damp, command more respect, though not always acceptance, from experts than scratched marks which can be added at any time.

It is interesting to remember that pottery, unlike antiques in many other categories, is inert. This means that if a new piece was never used but was wrapped up and put away in a trunk or drawer, it emerges, even after centuries, as fresh as on the day it left the potter's hand. A few great treasures in American redware are fine objects that have been so discovered.

MUSEUMS AND COLLECTIONS

Eighteenth-century American pottery may be seen at the following:

Dearborn, Michigan:	Henry Ford Museum
New York:	Brooklyn Museum
	New-York Historical Society
Philadelphia:	Philadelphia Museum of Art
Shelburne, Vermont:	Shelburne Museum
Sturbridge, Mass:	Old Sturbridge Village

FURTHER READING

Early American Folk Pottery by Harold F. Guillard, Philadelphia, 1971.
Early New England Potters and their Wares by Laura Woodside Watkins, Cambridge, Mass., 1950, (rev. ed.) 1968.
American Potters and Pottery by John Ramsay, Boston, Mass., 1939.
Early American Pottery and China by John Spargo, New York, 1926.
The Pottery and Porcelain of the United States by Edwin Atlee Barber, New York, 1909.

As early nineteenth-century settlers moved westward, especially into Ohio, potters travelled with them. They produced pottery blending the traditions of New England and Pennsylvania from whence these pioneers came.

With all its merits, redware also had its faults. It was brittle and chipped or broke easily. It was also porous, and therefore unsuitable for many of the items necessary in a kitchen. Even worse was the suspicion, debated at leisure in England and in the Colonies, that the lead glaze was poisonous. This fear eventually helped the introduction of stoneware at a time when redware was still able to put up a fight against it.

Kaendler and Early Meissen

Johann Joachim Kaendler was the man responsible for the triumph of Meissen. For more than fifty years the porcelain produced there was unsurpassed by the work of any other European factory

The European porcelain figure was conceived at Meissen soon after the material itself, for an inventory of 1711, the year after the factory began work, already lists several models, including a tiny but impressively baroque figure of Augustus the Strong, Elector of Saxony, King of Poland and the patron for whose satisfaction Meissen was established. Until about 1715, when it became possible to make white porcelain in some quantity, this and other models were made in the agate-hard red stoneware developed during the search for a material similar to Oriental porcelain.

The earliest figures at Meissen lacked any consistency of style, and this situation prevailed until 1727. Some are adaptations of Chinese types, while other models are related to small works in ivory, wood and metal of varied character. Generally these early figures were experiments by the factory, standing apart from the tablewares.

The Elector Augustus indulged a passion for luxury and display that achieved international repute even in an age accustomed to overweening splendour among princes. To house his immense accumulation of Oriental porcelain, he bought

Fig. 1 *Allegory of Summer by F. E. Meyer, c.1752. Painted with enamelled colours and gold, height 5½ ins.*
From a set representing The Seasons, Meyer's slender figure illustrates the light spirit of the Rococo and contrasts with the more monumental late baroque style of Eberlein's allegory in Fig. 4
(Victoria and Albert Museum.)

Fig. 2 *Shepherd with Bagpipes, possibly by J. J. Kaendler, mid-eighteenth century. Painted with enamelled colours and gold, height 10¼ ins.*
The vitality of this figure suggests that Kaendler was the modeller. It well indicates his superiority over later and lesser artists who produced so many insipid pastoral figures.
(Victoria and Albert Museum.)

K. Hoddle

Fig. 3 *Tea-urn, c.1740–45.*
The scene, probably by the
painter J. G. Heintze, shows the
town of Meissen. On the hill
above the Elbe stands the
Albrechtsburg Fortress where
the newly established factory was
first housed in 1710.
(Private Collection, London.)

⚔

Crossed swords mark adopted
1724, in blue or black enamel.

from a nobleman in 1717 a recently-built small palace across the Elbe River from his Dresden residence. It is best known as the Japanese Palace, and this was the first time that an entire building had been given over to porcelain, although richly decorated rooms designed to show off Oriental pieces had for some years been a standard feature of royal and noble houses. Augustus' programme, entirely fantastic in its scope and insensate ambition, eventually awarded the ground floor to Far Eastern wares, and the upper storey to those of Meissen. Each room was to be devoted to a separate colour of painted porcelain carefully arranged in a rich setting of stucco and carved and gilt wood.

The Elector's plans for his factory went further, encompassing a chapel with an altar, pulpit, large figures of the Apostles and even organ pipes in porcelain, and a gallery with life-sized animals and birds interspersed with huge, grotesque vases. Only parts of all this were realised, but these parts are among the prodigies of porcelain.

Shapes and designs changed with the modellers

In the 1720s, the basis for both the factory's artistic prestige and commercial success was established by J. G. Höroldt (1696–1775), who combined artistic with administrative gifts. His brilliant development of painted decoration, using *chinoiseries* of his own invention and versions of Oriental designs, was carried out on shapes offering a maximum smooth surface.

The factory's commission increasingly felt the need for tableware designs reflecting current taste, and in 1727 a young Dresden sculptor, Johann Gottlieb Kirchner (born 1706) was appointed as the factory's first trained modeller specifically to refresh the dated repertoire of forms. While he produced a few interesting pieces such as clock-cases, his work habits were too independent and after a year he was released and succeeded by the ivory carver J. C. L. Lücke, who proved even less satisfactory. For a year Meissen was without a modeller. Meanwhile the Japanese Palace was being enlarged to accommodate Augustus's plans, and in 1730 Kirchner was persuaded again to leave sculpture and return to the creation of great animals and vases in porcelain. To speed this project, another young Dresden sculptor, Johann Joachim Kaendler (1706–1775) was appointed to Meissen by Augustus whose notice he had gained while working in the Dresden Castle.

Kaendler was trained under Benjamin Thomae, one of the sculptors assisting Balthasar Permoser with the embellishment of the Zwinger (a series of linked pavilions and galleries for Saxon court festivities) where sculpture played nearly as important a role as architecture. Kaendler's adaptability to new tasks, indeed his quickness to see and exploit new possibilities for porcelain with an almost inexhaustible imagination, soon marked him as the up and coming man. Both he and Kirchner worked on the animals, but though Kirchner was made chief modeller, he was constantly at odds with the factory system and finally left Meissen in 1733. The full extent of his work is not known, for unlike Kaendler he was loath to keep records. Even so, it is clear that Kirchner, in his work at Meissen, laid the basis of a European porcelain figure-style and led the factory away from undue Oriental

influence and the realm of eccentric curiosities. Kirchner's elongated proportions and simplified modelling speak of a man who remained a sculptor at heart and they are in contrast to Kaendler's more compact modelling and agitated surfaces. Indeed, with his protean ability to adapt external ideas to his own purposes, Kaendler may well have recast some of Kirchner's models. His lovely *Virgin of the Immaculate Conception,* exceptional in that it was designed for a separate base, seems to reflect Kirchner's style (Fig. 5).

Kaendler brought to his first great task a mastery of baroque modelling and the gift of acute observation from nature. His *Goat* (Fig. 7) is one of the most impressive of the Japanese Palace animals, in which specific character was repeatedly translated into masterful sculpture. For porcelain, these figures were of enormous proportions and it proved impossible to eliminate the deep cracks caused by shrinkage in firing. In any event, Augustus's death in 1733, and subsequent shifts in direction, drew Kaendler to other tasks, though this work went on for a few more years, and from it sprang the race of smaller Meissen animals and birds which presently spread throughout Europe. The great animals are monumental achievements in every sense, and they include some of the masterpieces of animal sculpture.

Production of spectacular and ambitious dinner services was begun

Augustus the Strong was succeeded by his son, Augustus III, who fully maintained the glitter of the Dresden court, but his chief enthusiasm was for his great collection of pictures, which still testifies to his discernment. The factory's true guiding spirit now became Count Heinrich von Brühl, the new King's chief minister, and nominal director of the Meissen factory. As enlightened a patron as he was poor a statesman, Brühl recognised Kaendler's genius and promptly supported his contention that much could be done to improve tablewares with relief- and figure-modelling.

Kaendler now embarked on the great series of relief patterns that took Europe by storm with a magnificent service for Brühl's political rival Count Sulkowski, using for the dishes a wickerwork border which, with modifications, became one of the factory's most lasting patterns. While some of the Sulkowski pieces show an awareness of design in contemporary silver, no such influence is evident in the profoundly original service made for Brühl himself from 1737 to 1741, as an extended allegory on the theme of water. This was the celebrated *Swan Service,* which comprised some two thousand two hundred pieces in thirty different forms. It is the most spectacular of all porcelain services, and takes its name from the subtle swan reliefs that appear most conspicuously on the plates (Fig. 8). There were five tureen models lavishly embellished with marine deities and shell festoons, sweetmeat dishes supported by mermaids, candlesticks, platters and bowls of many types, as well as vessels for tea, coffee and chocolate. Nowhere is the beautiful porcelain material itself better displayed than in this service, where the only painting is the Brühl arms, scattered Oriental flowers and slight gilding.

Kaendler also applied his fertile imagination to

Fig. 4 *Allegory of sight by J. F. Eberlein, 1745. Painted with enamelled colours, height 8½ ins. The Five Senses are shown as standing women with appropriate attributes. Here, sight is depicted with a telescope, a mirror and an eagle. (Cecil Higgins Art Gallery, Bedford. By permission of the Trustees.)*

Fig. 5 *Virgin of the Immaculate Conception by J. J. Kaendler (1706–75), 1737. Painted with enamelled colours and gold, height 7⅝ ins. without base. This was a popular theme for religious sculpture in the eighteenth century, here rendered on a scale suited to private devotions. (Victoria and Albert Museum, London.)*

the fusion of vase forms with sculptural decoration **5** in a series of monumental vases. An ambitious *Elements* series was made for Louis XV of France in 1741–42. More restrained is the *Apollo* vase (Fig. 6), a version of one in a set of seven *Planets* vases modelled for the Empress Elizabeth of Russia in 1744. Works of this sort often had little or no painted decoration. Cultivated tastes appreciated the material for its own sake, and its glittering whiteness was an admirable foil to marble, lacquer, gilt furniture and panelling.

It is characteristic of Kaendler's capacity that while he was developing the great table services he also broke fresh ground, with profound consequences for the future with the first independent small figures, among the earliest of which are peasants playing musical instruments (Fig. 2). This was in 1736, and before the year was out he had also produced the first of his groups satirizing court manners and modes, in which the bulky crinoline skirt is often a conspicuous element; but Kaendler kept to general allusions and these are not in any way portraits. At the same time, Kaendler found perhaps his most famous theme of figure modelling in the traditional theatre of the Italian Comedy (*Commedia dell' Arte*), with its host of vivid stock characters, and his understanding of the earthy quality of their stage play inspired figures that seem to exceed the normal bounds of porcelain to convey an almost raucous vitality (Fig. 9).

Begun as an experiment, by 1740 the figures had found considerable success and, from this time on, they were central to the factory's work. A reason for their warm reception in Germany was the suitability of porcelain as table decoration, where they replaced the wax and sugar figures long customary there. Toward 1745, Kaendler used some French engravings for a series of figures which are not only picturesque, as intended, but also seem to have engaged his sympathy to an unusual degree.

In the middle of the century Meissen reached its peak, constituting Saxony's greatest source of income

The output of Kaendler and his colleagues in the 1740s was phenomenal. Besides special work for Brühl, the Court and foreign notables, they were often engaged with new relief patterns for tablewares, and there was a constant flow of figures drawn from mythology, the world of allegory, gallant pastorals, exotic peoples, peasants and gardeners. From 1735, Kaendler had a valued assistant in Johann Friedrich Eberlein (1696–1749), who helped with the *Swan Service* and also provided a series of other models of which the *Five Senses* (Fig. 4) is of particular distinction. Eberlein's work is separately recorded, but that of Peter Reinicke (at Meissen from 1743) is largely submerged by Kaendler's, who in any case 'corrected' all models before final approval.

As work records for 1749 to 1763 were lost in the Seven Years' War, we lack evidence for chronology and authorship in this period. In the early 1750s, Meissen reached its apogee of prestige and commercial success, employing nearly seven hundred people and constituting Saxony's greatest source of income. It was at this time that 'the Dresden' became generally available in England, where the

6

7

8

9

10

11

Fig. 6 *Apollo vase* by Kaendler, 1744. Unpainted, height 20⅝ ins. From the set of the seven Planets, this vase was made for the Empress Elizabeth of Russia who sent Meissen many orders. (Victoria and Albert Museum.)

Fig. 7 *Goat* by Kaendler, 1732. Unpainted, height 21⅛ ins., length 28 ins. This piece was made for Augustus's Japanese Palace, in which the King housed his vast collection of porcelain. (Victoria and Albert Museum.)

Fig. 8 *Plate from the Swan Service* by Kaendler, 1738. Painted with enamelled colours and gold, diameter 11¾ ins. This plate is completely covered with beautiful relief work from which the service takes its name. (Victoria and Albert Museum.)

Fig. 9 *Angry Harlequin* by Kaendler, c.1738. Painted with enamelled colours, height 7⅝ ins. This Harlequin was transformed from an engraved illustration in a French book on the Commedia dell' Arte, the Italian comedy which became popular throughout Europe, and particularly in France, at the end of the seventeenth century. (Fitzwilliam Museum, Cambridge.)

Fig. 10 *Potter*, probably modelled by Kaendler and P. Reinicke, c.1750. Painted with enamelled colours, height 7½ ins. This comes from a series of eighteen figures symbolising various trades. (Fitzwilliam Museum.)

Fig. 11 *Woman carrying a child* by Kaendler, 1744. Painted with enamelled colours, height 8½ ins. Here Kaendler adapted a French engraving of 1739 of a peasant woman from Savoy. (Fitzwilliam Museum.)

figures, in particular, were copied at Chelsea, Bow and Derby, and already for some years Parisian luxury merchants had mounted Meissen figures with gilt-bronze as clocks and candelabra for sale to an international clientele. One suspects that the operating pace had become so fast that the quality at Meissen suffered, and after having sustained a remarkably high creative pitch for nearly thirty years the factory's inspiration may have begun to run thin. These are the years when the proverbial 'Dresden' shepherdesses and cupids first appeared as charming novelties. Colours tend towards pale tones of yellow, mauve and turquoise patterned with Oriental flowers in place of the earlier strong colours, applied with judicious restraint.

The best work of the period is, nevertheless, of a high order. A fresh style of figure modelling, with small heads and long, slender proportions, is due to Friedrich Elias Meyer (born 1724), who joined the factory in 1748. Meyer's graceful, elegant style (Fig. 1) is more truly rococo in spirit than Kaendler's more passionate interpretations of pastoral themes (Fig. 2). A sign manual of this new direction was the introduction in about 1750 of rococo-scrolled figure bases, which were then used for new models until the rise of neo-Classicism in the 1770s.

The supremacy of Meissen was threatened and prestige was gradually lost

The years around 1750 also saw the rise of several rival factories in Germany, Italy and France which threatened Meissen's near-monopoly, and when Saxony easily fell to Frederick the Great of Prussia in 1756 the stage was set for their ascendancy, notably that of Sèvres, to whom the palm of artistic leadership now passed. Meissen destroyed its kilns in the face of the enemy, but in a few months the factory was again operating, and until 1763 Frederick acted as its last great patron.

Frederick was a lover of porcelain, with dreams of his own factory, and while he was unsuccessful in luring Kaendler to Berlin, several men, including Meyer, went to the new factory there which Frederick took over in 1763. At Meissen he not only ordered many figures and vases from existing models, but, of greater importance, commissioned six large table services. Kaendler also modelled for him a series of large mythological groups, and these ambitious tasks must have provided a welcome challenge, for he brought to the realisation of some of them, at least, his full powers of imagination and composition.

The work for Frederick was the swan-song of Meissen, for with the return of peace in 1763, the factory entered a long and uneasy period of trying to find its place in a commercial situation where its ideas now seemed dated. Meissen no longer set the pace, and it was forced to assimilate outside ideas, chiefly from France.

Kaendler lived on until 1775, but although he was respected and occasionally still received important commissions, his baroque sense was never really at home in the age of neo-Classicism. The long triumph of Meissen owed more to him than to any one other man, and for this accomplishment he ranks as an important artist in his century.

HINTS FOR DATING MEISSEN

From 1723 the Meissen factory mark was the crossed swords of Saxony in under-glaze blue. Valuable evidence for dating tablewares are the impressed symbols used by throwers and moulders in the 1730s, replaced in 1739–40 at Kaendler's insistence by impressed numerals. Under the flat bases of figures the swords mark is often faint, or burned off in firing as it was unprotected by glaze, and, for this reason, the mark was placed on the base edge from about 1745. From about 1765 to 1775, a dot was usually placed between the hilts, and then until about 1814 a star was commonly placed beneath the swords.

A large proportion of the original moulds have survived at Meissen, and from the 1850s to 1914, in particular, figures and wares taken from them formed much of the production and are often found today. The figures may be distinguished from their ancestors by the tendency to have small white surfaces exposed, by the muddy pinks, greens and browns and by the presence of such colours as chrome green and maroon which were unknown in the eighteenth century. A further aid to their recognition is the large script mould numbers incised within open glazed bases, often accompanied by impressed numbers.

MUSEUMS AND COLLECTIONS

FRANCE

| Paris: | Musée du Louvre |
| Sèvres: | Musée National de Céramique |

GERMANY

Ansbach:	Residenz
Dresden:	Porzellan-Galerie
Hamburg:	Museum für Kunst und Gewerbe
Munich:	Bayerisches Nationalmuseum

GREAT BRITAIN

Bedford:	Cecil Higgins Art Gallery
Cambridge:	Fitzwilliam Museum
London:	British Museum
	Fenton House, Hampstead
	Victoria and Albert Museum
Wiltshire:	Longleat

THE NETHERLANDS

| Amsterdam: | Rijksmuseum |

U.S.A.

| Connecticut: | Wadsworth Atheneum, Hartford |
| New York: | Metropolitan Museum of Art |

FURTHER READING

Meissen from the Beginning until 1760 by H. Morley-Fletcher, London, 1971.
German Porcelain and Faience by Siegfried Ducret, London, 1962.
Meissen and other Continental Porcelain in the Collection of Irwin Untermyer by Yvonne Hackenbroch, London, 1956.
Dresden China by W. B. Honey, London, revised 1954.
European Ceramic Art by W. B. Honey, London, 1952.
German Porcelain by W. B. Honey, London, 1947.

 # Mennecy
and Chantilly

The delicacy, plasticity and subtlety that were to make soft-paste porcelain one of the most characteristic manifestations of the rococo style were first fully realised at the factories of Chantilly and Mennecy

ig. 1 *Globular teapot,* *ennecy, mid-eighteenth* *ntury. Because of the ban on* *lding, the spout and handle* *ve been 'feathered' in blue.* *ictoria and Albert Museum.)*

ig. 2 *Sugar-bowl, stand, cover* *nd perforated spoon, Mennecy,* *id-eighteenth century with* *more highly developed* *ense of the Rococo than* *he Chantilly version in Fig. 3.* *ictoria and Albert Museum.)*

ig. 3 *Sugar-bowl, stand, cover* *nd perforated spoon, Chantilly,* *id-eighteenth century.* *ictoria and Albert Museum.)*

The first soft-paste porcelain to be manufactured in Europe, apart from a short-lived attempt in Florence in the sixteenth century, came from Rouen and St. Cloud in France at the end of the seventeenth century. These two factories produced works of great beauty using the baroque shapes and designs of contemporary faience and silverware. It was only at Chantilly and Mennecy, at the

beginning of the eighteenth century, that the possibilities of soft-paste as a medium quite different from faience were fully realised. The delicacy, plasticity and subtlety of soft-paste was from this time to be the most characteristic manifestation of the rococo movement which, with its lightness and charm, was fast ousting the baroque grandeur of a more sombre age.

The factory at Chantilly was founded in 1725 by Louis Henri de Bourbon, Prince de Condé, under the directorship of Cicaire, or Ciquaire, Cirou. The power of the Regent and his successor, the patrons of St. Cloud, was so strong that it was ten years before Cirou received a patent for his wares. At the death of the latter in 1751, the directorship passed to De Montvallier and De Roussier until 1754, and thereafter De Montvallier was sole director until 1760; then followed the directorships of Pierre Peyrard, 1760–76, Louis François Gravant, 1776–79, Dame Gravant 1779–81, and Antheaume de Surval, 1781–92. Finally, an Englishman, appropriately named Christopher Potter, acquired the factory in 1792. It eventually closed down in 1800.

The unique quality of Chantilly porcelain is in the glaze

The Prince de Condé was an avid collector of Arita porcelain imported from Japan and he set up the factory largely for the purpose of manufacturing Arita-style wares. Cirou had been employed at an offshoot of the St. Cloud factory, and the paste of Chantilly porcelain is typically made from a body of clay from Luzarches and white sand from the hills of Aumont, with potash added as a fluxing agent. The unique quality of Chantilly porcelain, however, is in the glaze, which was not the usual transparent lead glaze of soft-paste porcelains, but an opaque white tin glaze such as was used in the making of faience. This glaze prevented the use of under-glaze decoration, but, on account of its beautiful milky whiteness, was completely suitable for painting in the delicate colours of the Kakiemon style, which was the typical decoration of Arita-style wares (Fig. 3).

These Japanese designs (known inaccurately as 'à décor Coréen', since it was believed that the original pieces came from Korea), were rendered with a typically French restraint and elegance. Often they were copied from the originals, but sometimes from Meissen copies which must have been known to the Prince. The Chantilly pieces have a greater delicacy than those of Meissen, both in shape and in decoration. The Chantilly potters preferred lobed or quatrefoil shapes (Fig. 3), and their teapots were often in the form of a gourd, melon or pomegranate, usually asymmetrical in a typically rococo way, and surmounted by a knop formed, prettily but impracticably, of three flowers.

The painted decoration of this period was of superb quality. The Kakiemon colours included a brick red which tended to be matt in appearance, and a clear blue, a pale yellow and turquoise-toned greens which were perfectly fused in the soft white glaze. The subjects of the painting were usually of figures delicately outlined in black, forming designs known as 'the bursting pomegranate' (*grenade*), 'the squirrel' (*écureuil*), 'the banded hedge' (*haie fleurie*), 'the wheatsheaf' (*gerbe*), 'the

K. Hoddle

K. Hoddle

quail or partridge' (*caille* or *perdrix*), and 'the stork' (*cigogne*), all adapted from the Arita style in the most perfect taste (Fig. 6).

A typical adaptation from a Meissen original is the service decorated in the 'Prince Henri' pattern (Fig. 7), which is taken directly from the *Rote Drache* (red dragon) service made at Meissen. The original has a simple, and indeed more Oriental, round rim, whereas the Chantilly version has a shaped rim which subtly repeats the outline of the dragon motif. The motif itself, though fairly directly copied

Museum Photo

Fig. 4 **Figure of a River God by Gauron, Mennecy, 1753.** *This work shows the beauty which was achieved by French modellers, despite the unsuitability of their materials.* (Victoria and Albert Museum.)

Fig. 5 **Wine-cooler, Chantilly,** *second quarter of the eighteenth century. Painted with Kakiemon figures superior to those executed at Meissen.* (Musée des Arts Décoratifs, Paris.)

Fig. 6 **Jardinière,** *Chantilly, second quarter of the eighteenth century.* (Victoria and Albert Museum.)

Fig. 7 **Plate,** *Chantilly, second quarter of the eighteenth century. Of the 'Prince Henri' pattern, this plate is a direct copy from the 'Red Dragon' of Meissen.* (Victoria and Albert Museum.)

Fig. 8 **Sugar-bowl and cover,** *Mennecy, mid-eighteenth century. In this piece, the simple but elegant lines of Mennecy are clearly evident.* (Musée de Sceaux.)

from the Meissen service, has a restraint and elegance somehow lacking in the original, while the brilliant colours and sparse gilding of the Chantilly version are superior.

In 1751 the death of Cicaire Cirou occurred, following that of the Prince de Condé by some eleven years, and a year later a new disaster befell the factory in the shape of a royal edict which banned the manufacture of porcelain for twelve years at any factory save Vincennes, soon to become Sèvres. This occurred because Vincennes was the particular 'child' of Louis XV and Madame de Pompadour and they wished for no competition from other factories. In fact, the edict was never very strictly enforced, but the Chantilly factory now abandoned its use of tin glaze in favour of a transparent lead glaze which revealed an attractive cream-coloured body. The Kakiemon designs had been dropped after the Prince's death. Gilding, which had never been used very much, was now definitely illegal and was also dropped.

For the next few years most of the painted decoration was done in monochrome (*en camaïeu*), cupids painted in crimson after Boucher being particularly favoured, as well as figures in a slightly painted landscape. Another favourite device was the use of a border composed of diapered quatrefoils in blue enamel. Occasionally, however, polychrome pieces were made such as the vases '*à l'oreille*' in the Victoria and Albert Museum, which indicate that there was now a definite influence from Vincennes – although it has been suggested that the influence was the other way about. Naturalistic flower painting was also adapted from the German *deutsche Blumen*. As the years went by, however, the decoration and the shapes became simpler, wares decorated with 'Chantilly sprigs' in under-glaze blue being very popular, and

later, small cornflower sprigs painted in blue, green and pink enamels. These were much copied at other French and English factories. After 1780, however, nothing of good quality seems to have been made at the factory.

Although the names of some of the workers who were employed at Chantilly during the sixty-odd years of its active production are known to us, it is virtually impossible to ascribe particular works to them, and thus they remain for the most part anonymous. Many of the pieces are marked, and in the Cirou period a hunting-horn, carefully painted in red, was used (Fig. 13, below). Later pieces were marked with a blue hunting-horn, sometimes under the glaze, more carelessly drawn and often unrecognisable (Fig. 13, above). A hunting horn in gold appears on the Red Dragon service. The word 'Chantilly', accompanied by a hunting-horn in blue, is to be found on some of the wares decorated with sprigs, while *Villers Cotteret* painted in blue on a service signifies the *château* of that name for which it was made. Pieces marked 'M' were for a house in Chantilly called *Ménagerie*.

The Mennecy factory was some ten years younger than that at Chantilly. It was set up in 1734 by Louis-François de Neufville, Duc de Villeroy, under the directorship of François Barbin. The factory was first established in the rue de Charrone, Paris, where faience was produced for one year and porcelain manufactured from 1735. In 1748, the factory was removed to Mennecy. Francois Barbin was joined by his son, Jean-Baptiste, but they both died in 1765, and the following year the factory was bought by Joseph Jullien and Symphorien Jacques who worked it in conjunction with the Sceaux factory until 1772. In 1773, it was moved to Bourg-la-Reine. Jullien died in 1774, and was succeeded by his son, Joseph-Léon, while the younger Jacques joined his father in about 1790. Production continued until 1800, but by then porcelain had been abandoned for faience and cream-coloured earthenware.

The early works of this factory were derived largely from Rouen, St. Cloud and Chantilly. The shapes followed those of St. Cloud, making use of relief ornament plum blossom, as on *blanc de Chine*, spiral fluting, basket-work and so on. The decoration followed either that of Rouen and St. Cloud in the form of blue lambrequins, or that of Chantilly in the form of Kakiemon designs.

Mennecy soon, however, adopted a style of its own. Mennecy paste was an extremely beautiful dark ivory in colour, and the glaze was very wet-looking and brilliant (Fig. 4), its surface slightly wavy but without the slight pitting of St. Cloud.

Shapes and styles of Mennecy porcelain

Although the shapes of Mennecy porcelain were relatively restricted in number, they were admirably simple in form (Fig. 8). Teapots were globular, with gently curving spouts, dome lids and double-curved handles (Fig. 1). They were generally tall rather than squat. Cups and saucers were often straight-sided, tapering downwards, or pear shaped. The most characteristic pieces from the Mennecy factory were custard-cups with spiral fluting, toilet jars and sugar-bowls, often with a lid

6

7

8

Fig. 9 **Tea and coffee service,**
*Mennecy, mid-eighteenth
century.*
*One of the specialities of the
Mennecy painters was to present
vignettes of figures in a delicately
tinted landscape. The rose-bud
knop was also a favourite device.
(Private Collection.)*

Fig. 10 **Pair of figures,** *Chantilly,
eighteenth century.*
*The woman is undoubtedly
derived from a Meissen 'vintage
woman' but the man seems to be
original. Although interesting,
the figures are coarsely modelled
and somewhat wooden in
appearance.
(Private Collection.)*

Fig. 11 **Figure of a seated
Chinaman,** *Chantilly, second
quarter of the eighteenth century.*
*The painted decoration on the
robes of this charming figure
shows the influence of Meissen's
Indianische Blumen.
(Musée des Arts Décoratifs.)*

10

11

surmounted by a rose-bud (Fig. 9). One of the most
beautiful examples of French porcelain is the sugar-
bowl in Fig. 2 with its fluted stand and cover
formed by a shell-volute. This shows the different
way in which the two factories reacted to the
rococo movement. The Chantilly sugar bowl is
rococo in its elegance and restraint, its delicately
painted Kakiemon designs and its flowered knop.
The Mennecy bowl is as highly rococo in a different
way – in the swirl of its lid, which seems to have
been pulled up and twisted; a shape possible to
create only in porcelain.

The painted decoration on Mennecy porcelain is
extremely beautiful; sensitive and unassertive, it
was dominated by cool blues and pinks. Naturalistic
flower painting reached a high level of accomplishment, as did the bird-painting which recalls
that of Sceaux (Fig. 1). Landscapes with figures as
vignettes or framed in garlands of flowers have a
charm which surpasses the more elaborate
pastoral scenes of Sèvres. The Mennecy landscapes were painted in a palette of polychrome
colours dominated by earth brown and green and
are clearly influenced by Watteau and, more
particularly, Lancret (Fig. 9).

Mennecy never developed very much stylistically
and the factory continued to make mostly useful
wares (although plates are very rare) in a rococo
manner well into the 1770s, by which time the new
fashion for neo-Classicism was well entrenched.

The mark for Mennecy porcelain was 'DV', for
the Duc de Villeroy, occasionally painted in red,
or, rarely, blue, but more often incised (Fig. 14).
When the factory moved to Bourg-la-Reine, the
mark of 'BR', incised, was used.

The French soft-paste factories were considerably
less prolific in figure modelling than were their
German hard-paste counterparts. This was simply

63

Fig. 12 *A boy and a girl playing musical instruments, Mennecy, mid-eighteenth century. Groups of this sort, often of children playing musical instruments, were modelled after paintings by Boucher. Their immense charm and delicacy of modelling rank them with the foremost figures of the eighteenth century. (Victoria and Albert Museum.)*

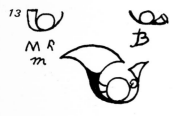

Fig. 13 *Chantilly porcelain marks. The large hunting-horn below was painted in red or occasionally in blue during the Cirou period. Later pieces were marked with carelessly drawn blue horns, sometimes under-glaze, and often almost unrecognisable, like those above.*

Fig. 14 *Mennecy porcelain marks. The Mennecy mark was 'DV' for the Duc de Villeroy, founder of the factory. It was occasionally painted in red or, more rarely, blue, as on the left; but was more often incised, as on the right. Later, 'BR' for Bourg-la-Reine was used, after the factory moved there in 1773.*

because the body of French soft-paste was less able to resist the necessary heat from the kilns. While plates, bowls, cups and so on would retain their shape, the delicately modelled free-standing figures were apt to crack or to sag; even when undamaged they lacked the crispness which only hard-paste can achieve. Nevertheless, both Chantilly and Mennecy produced figures of quality.

Figures were made at Chantilly, but some produced at Mennecy were of finer quality

The Chantilly craftsmen made several figures quite early in the history of the factory, and also toys, cane-handles, boxes, and so forth, of which there are some good examples in the Ashmolean Museum, Oxford. The pair of a 'Chinese' man and a woman is a typical example (Fig. 10). The woman is undoubtedly derived from a Meissen 'vintage-woman', but the man would seem to be original. They are interesting, but, it is thought, of little value artistically as they are rather coarsely modelled and 'wooden' in appearance. The seated chinaman in Fig. 11 has greater charm, perhaps. Later, Louis Fournier, presumably the same as the modeller of that name at Vincennes – came to work at Chantilly from 1752 to 1756 and produced some figures of good quality.

The Mennecy factory, apart from producing some delightful toys, snuff-boxes and so on, excelled in figure modelling. Some of them were rather pedestrian, and have been compared with the figures made at Bow, but others are of the finest quality. Most notable is the work of the sculptor Gauron who came to work at the factory in 1753. It was he who made the beautiful River God in the Victoria and Albert Museum (Fig. 4). It is thought that he later worked at Vincennes; he then went to Tournai and Chelsea. Perhaps the most successful of the Mennecy figures were the groups of children modelled after paintings by Boucher (Fig. 12). These are beautifully modelled and usually portray children playing on a rock-work base; they always seem to be on the point of falling off. With their delicate tinting and rococo charm, they must be among the finest figures to be produced in Europe.

During and after the 1770s, the porcelain of both the Chantilly and the Mennecy factories declined rapidly, both in quality and in quantity. For this, there are two reasons: the supremacy of the Sèvres factory, and the advent of neo-Classicism.

The Vincennes factory, which had been founded originally in 1738, was officially recognised by the Crown in 1745. It then became the plaything of Louis XV (and subsequently of Louis XVI) and had as its patroness the powerful Madame de Pompadour, who, in 1753, began her plan for its removal to her property at Sèvres. As early as 1748, the Mennecy factory had come into conflict with Vincennes, being forbidden to produce pieces in the manner of the latter factory, or to use gilding, this being the reason why Mennecy pieces are feathered in blue or pink rather than in gold. The factory promptly moved further out of Paris. The royal edict of 1752 had further hampered rival porcelain factories, and after this the monopolising influence of Sèvres increased, the smaller factories confining themselves to purely useful wares.

The properties of porcelain proved unsuited to the neo-Classical style

The seeds of neo-Classicism had been sown earlier in the century, but it was not until the 1760s that its effect on the decorative arts was felt. Porcelain, with its delicacy and plasticity, was not suited to the austerity and sobriety that neo-Classicism demanded. Sèvres, it is true, continued to flourish, producing works which exhibited a strange combination of austerely classical forms on the one hand, and lavish, even vulgar, decoration on the other. The smaller factories could make no such compromise; instead, they turned to the production of faience and the production of cream-coloured earthenware made fashionable by Wedgwood.

Nevertheless, in the previous fifty-odd years, the factories at Chantilly and Mennecy had turned the art of porcelain manufacture into the embodiment of the rococo spirit, that most decorative of all art movements.

MUSEUMS AND COLLECTIONS
Chantilly and Mennecy porcelain may be seen at the following:

FRANCE
Paris: Musée des Arts Décoratifs
Sèvres: Musée National de Céramique
GREAT BRITAIN
Cardiff: National Museum of Wales
Edinburgh: Royal Scottish Museum
London: Victoria and Albert Museum
Oxford: Ashmolean Museum

FURTHER READING
Seventeenth and Eighteenth Century French Porcelain by George Savage, London, 1960.
French Porcelain of the Eighteenth Century by W. B. Honey, London, 1950.
Histoire des Manufactures Françaises de Porcelaine by X. de Chavagnac and A. de Grollier, Paris, 1906.

Early Sèvres

Fig. 1 **Inkstand** *after a design by Duplessis* père, *marked F for 1758. In the form of a terrestrial and celestial globe on either side of the royal crown of France, this inkstand was probably a gift from the King to his daughter, Marie Adélaïde of France, whose monogram it bears. (Wallace Collection, London.)*

The exotic taste of Madame de Pompadour and the lavish extravagance of Louis XV raised the porcelain of Sèvres to new heights of fantasy and elaboration

The first fourteen years of the royal manufactory of Sèvres are considered by connoisseurs to be its greatest period. This greatness was the direct outcome of the vigour and energy generated in the project by Madame la Marquise de Pompadour, who was accepted as France's arbiter of elegance until long after her death in 1764.

The world's finest collection of Sèvres porcelain, dating from 1753, is in the possession of Her Majesty The Queen at Buckingham Palace and Windsor Castle. Displaying colour and gold with spectacular magnificence, this priceless collection was started by George III and extended by George IV during the 1820s. These monarchs acted upon expert advice from Lord Yarmouth, later Marquess of Hertford and founder of the Wallace Collection. The radiantly beautiful porcelain of Sèvres includes table centres, covered vases, many differently shaped *jardinières* and intricate baskets resembling open wickerwork in gold.

When the old Vincennes building became unsafe to carry the working load, the plant and *ateliers* were transferred at a cost of one million *livres* to palatial premises at Sèvres; near Madame de

J. Freeman

Réalites: M. Nahmias

J. Freeman

Fig. 2 *Pot-pourri, 1759. The Teniers-inspired medallion is painted with minute attention to detail.*
(Musée des Arts Décoratifs, Paris.)

Fig. 3 *Saucer painted by Vieillard, marked H for 1760.*
(Wallace Collection.)

Pompadour's Château de Bellevue, they were half-way between Paris and Versailles. Here, soft-paste porcelain continued to be made by improved formulae and processes: glazes were silky and smooth and decorations richly ornate, out-ranking the hard-paste of Germany. The porcelain could, however, be fabricated only into simple forms. The easily fusible glaze was sprayed upon the oven-fired biscuit to make it adhere firmly, a little vinegar having first been added, and proved ideal for ground colours giving to enamels a new luminous brilliance. Colours merged into this glaze in such a way that the decorated surface was as smooth as the unpainted glaze and apparently no thicker. Forgers have never succeeded in repro-ducing it.

The cost of operating the Sèvres factory, entirely financed by Louis XV, was nearly four times its income. The King is known to have sent his silver plate to the mint during periods of national financial stringency, replacing it with Sèvres porcelain. In an endeavour to liquidate rival porcelain-makers, Louis created various monopolies favouring Sèvres. For example, other factories were forbidden to paint in polychrome, to use gold, or to make sculpture, and import duties were imposed upon Meissen and other German porcelains, making it unprofitable for merchants to handle them.

Installed at Sèvres, technicians and artists scored new triumphs that became a source of national pride. Since soft-paste porcelain, when moulded into complex shapes, tended to fracture in the kiln or in use at table, Sevres specialised in gilt and painted ware for display cabinets and the luxury trade. Potential was concentrated on magnificent creations whose splendour was limited only by their cost. Throughout this period, 'bread and

butter' patterns, those intended to bring in a steady revenue, were held virtually in abeyance.

Astronomical prices resulted from financial losses due to the slow preparation processes. The ingredients for the white frit – sand from Fontaine-bleau, sea-salt, nitre, alum, alabaster and soda from Alicante – were fired for fifty hours, then ground to a fine powder for three weeks. After drying and re-crushing between rollers, the powder was mixed with clay from Argenteuil, to which soap was added to provide plasticity. The machines were operated by horse power. The resulting paste was difficult to manipulate and cracked easily during the final firings; much time was also spent in designing, colour preparation and painting. Meissen patterns were skilfully transformed into distinctly French designs: formal scrolled motifs and borders on handles and spouts are characteristic. A cabinet plate or a caudle-cup and saucer might cost, in contemporary currency, as much as three hundred and eighty-five new French francs at the factory.

To assist sales, Louis XV held annual exhibitions at the Palace of Versailles, three rooms being cleared of furniture and the porcelain displayed on tables. The King not only attended, but acted as salesman. The Marquis d'Argenson recorded in his *Mémoires* that 'every New Year's Day they bring into Versailles the newest and choicest pieces of Sèvres porcelain which the King himself distributes among his great lords for their money; he fixes the prices himself and they are not cheap'. Later, a royal shop devoted to the sale of Sèvres porcelain was opened in the rue de la Monnaie, Paris.

Ground colours became one of Sèvres' dominat-ing splendours. First came *bleu de roi*, or *bleu royale*. Decorators soon discovered that this was too intense and overpowering to use in unbroken

Fig. 4 **Breakfast-service,** *consisting of a tray, sugar-basin, cup and saucer, marked I for 1761.*
Decorated in rose Pompadour marbled with gold and blue, painted with birds and landscapes by F. Aloncle (active 1758–81).
(Wallace Collection.)

masses. Its fierce glow dazzled, making it expedient to soften its brilliance by overpainting with a pattern in gold, such as a network of fine tracery, vermiform lines or marbling. Various forms of the 'partridge eye' or *œil de perdrix*, consisted of tiny circles or double circles of dots, often found in sea-green or bright blue in which reserves are set against the monochrome or dotted ground (Fig. 7).

A jug, for instance, might be decorated with three oval reserves containing floral subjects set against a *bleu de roi* ground enriched with gilt 'partridge eyes'. Pairs of *jardinières* might be covered with fine gold vermiform reticulations which have been compared with 'grease spots floating on broth' – the decorator's term is *caillouté*, or pebble pattern.

Pinks, reds, blues and greens were enriched with gilt patterns

The enameller Xhrouet invented the *rose carné* ground colour in 1757. This was a pure opaque flesh tint difficult to achieve, for, if the firing temperature were too high, it was converted to a dirty yellow; if too low, it became brownish and mottled. This colour was soon re-named *rose Pompadour*; the finest specimens date from before 1766 (Fig. 4). Other ground colours evolved by the early Sèvres chemists were crimson, apple green, turquoise and mulberry, all enriched with gilt patterns.

Infinite care was taken with gilding throughout the royal period, when gold-enriched Sèvres porcelain was recognised as the pride of France. Honey-gilding was then virtually a new process in Europe. Pure gold-leaf, ground into honey, was laid thickly over the glaze in flat touches, fired and

then burnished with an iron nail. Often it was exquisitely chased and engraved, but might be left soft and dull.

The dearth of figure painters in France had impelled the Sèvres management to recruit fan painters into their *ateliers*. These artists treated porcelain as though it were the parchment to which they were accustomed. They painted figure subjects with heavy, pasty body colours as though they were *gouache*, betraying their ignorance of the colour changes that occurred in the muffle-kiln. By 1760, colours were laid on impasto or floated on in the manner of water-colours.

Decorators devoted their energies mainly to bird and flower painting and also achieved enormous success with delicate subjects in different shades of either crimson or blue, using fine brushstrokes, the results resembling colour sketches rather than finished paintings. Eventually, a staff of artists was trained to share in decorating the superb cabinet porcelain of Sèvres, which became the wonder of the world. The Duc de Luynes recorded that, by 1760, 'there were 60 painters in the painting room, each with a separate *atelier* . . . vases to hold flowers were sold at 20 *louis* each . . . there are now about five hundred working people'.

Flower-painters now scattered their lovely blossoms over the delicate porcelain, or arranged them in garlands. The exquisite Sèvres *rose* came into being at this time. *Chinoiserie*, Europe's interpretation of Chinese art, was designed in the Sèvres manner, particularly versions of Chinese exotic birds. Figure and landscape painters produced small, delicate pictures, of which many were signed.

Sèvres never imitated the rich relief decorations found on German hollow-ware of this period. The

9

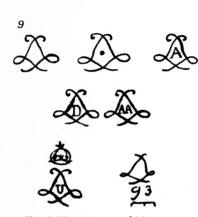

technical reason for this was that soft-paste porcelain was entirely unsuited for sharp relief work.

Table centres in a design vaguely suggesting a rigged ship, known as *vaisseau à mât* (ship with a mast), are splendid examples of early Sèvres (Fig. 5). These are in three parts: a stand with four scrolled legs supports a boat-shaped rose-water vessel decorated with monochrome paintings, the top pierced with circular holes to allow the scent to perfume the room. In the most ship-like designs there may be a Neptune or lion's head at each end with a fluted lifting-handle extending from the open mouth. The third unit, the lid, is then shaped as a central mast supporting formalised sails and rigging. Gold *fleurs-de-lis* star the white banner of France draped from the mast-top, displaying to perfection the fine translucency of the porcelain. Perforated scales on the sails contrast with the four rope ladders of blue bugles. This heraldic conceit represents the ship which is displayed in the coat of arms of Paris. An example in London at Buckingham Palace in *gros bleu* and green ground colours is decorated with gold-framed reserves containing exotic birds in landscapes. This bears the Sèvres mark containing the date-letter for 1758 and measures twenty inches in height. There are magnificent examples in the collection at Windsor, the Wallace Collection (Fig. 5) and the Victoria and Albert Museum. Queen Victoria bought a Minton reproduction in 1880.

Delicately applied miniature paintings with elaborate rococo borders

Spectacular vases painted with birds, animals, flowers, *fêtes galantes*, military scenes, *chinoiserie* and so on, displayed against beautiful ground colours, were given names associated with the designer, or with their form or salient ornamental motifs. *Le vase à tourterelles* has handles modelled as a pair of doves; *le vase à terrasse* is raised on a fretted ring of ormolu; *le vase militaire* is decorated with flags and war trophies; *le vase aux tritons* is supported by a group of young tritons modelled by Louis Felix de la Rue; *le vase ruche d'abeilles* is in the shape of a bee-skip; *le vase tête du bouc à raisins* has goat's head handles entwined with a fruiting vine.

Oval *pot-pourri* vases were constructed from four units: a stand with four scrolled legs; a canoe-shaped bowl; an elaborately pierced cover, and a conical lid decorated with a finial, hand-modelled as a cluster of flowers and painted in natural colours. The whole was raised on a glass-topped, gilt-bronze plinth with sides decorated in relief, the pedestal being designed to match the supported vase.

Many differently shaped *jardinières* were fashionable throughout the period, their sides displaying delicate miniature paintings bordered with richly tooled gilding in elaborate rococo designs. There are two identically shaped *jardinières* in the Victoria and Albert Museum, one of which has a green ground with reserves enclosing figure subjects signed by the painter and with the date-letter for 1759; the other has a *rose Pompadour* ground with cupids and flowers painted by Dubois in 1761. Some *jardinières* were raised on loose

pedestals, others were given scroll feet.

Decorative porcelain made especially for the King incorporated in its design the royal crown in some form, often embossed as a richly gilt finial. An inkstand made for Louis XV in 1758, and now in the Wallace Collection, has terrestrial and celestial globes as containers for the essential sand and lead shot positioned one on each side of an inkpot which is shaped as the crown of France resting on a cushion. This bears the cipher of his daughter Marie Adélaïde (Fig. 1).

The contours of early Sèvres tableware such as dessert- and dinner-services followed the subtle shaping and curving fashionable in contemporary table silver. Tea- and coffee-services – trays, sugar basins and milk-pots – might be of cabinet quality or virtually plain. A jug might have a long cylindrical neck or a large body with short neck and small mouth. Cups of this period were of the 'can' variety – cylindrical, with vertical sides. This shape displays painted scenes in polychrome or designs in monochrome crimson or green, in tones much softer than the contemporary German wares, and much more satisfactorily presented than on curved or fluted cups. Decorations were enclosed in frames of tooled gold. Later in the period delicate miniature paintings were fashionable. Among the wide range of small presentation pieces were tobacco and snuff-boxes, patch-boxes, watch-cases, counter-boxes, needle-cases, scent-bottles, etuis, thimbles, buttons and cane heads, all to be found with flowers or birds in full colours and often monogrammed.

In 1757, Falconet was appointed chief modeller, an appointment he held until 1766 when he left for Russia. At Sèvres he modelled such outstanding groups as *La Lanterne Magique*, 1757; *La Baigneuse*, 1759; and *Le Tourniquet*, 1760. The influence of Boucher is to be seen in some of his groups such as *La Laitière* and the important *Léda et le Cygne*, 1764. After Falconet's departure from Sèvres in 1766, sculptors of renown were commissioned to model reduced versions of their monumental works.

MUSEUMS AND COLLECTIONS
Early Sèvres porcelain may be seen at the following:

FRANCE
Paris: Musée des Arts Décoratifs
Sèvres: Musée National de céramique
GREAT BRITAIN
Aylesbury: Waddesdon Manor
London: British Museum
Victoria and Albert Museum
Wallace Collection
Wellington Museum, Apsley House
Windsor: Windsor Castle
U.S.A.
Gautier, Miss.: Gautier Plantation House
New York: Metropolitan Museum of Art

FURTHER READING
French Porcelain of the Eighteenth Century by W. B. Honey, London, rev. ed. 1972.
Sèvres by C. C. Dauterman, London, 1969.
Catalogue of the Jones Collection (in the Victoria and Albert Museum), Part II by William King, London, 1924.

6

7

Chelsea Porcelain

Fig. 1 *The Music Lesson,* *marked with a gold anchor,* *Chelsea, c.1765. Height 16 ins.* *This delightful scene is based on* *a painting by François Boucher* *called L'Agréable Leçon.* *(Victoria and Albert Museum,* *London.)*

Fig. 2 *La Nourrice, also called* *the Chellsea Nurs, marked with* *a red anchor, Chelsea, c.1755.* *Height 7½ ins.* *Derived from a sixteenth-century* *earthenware model made near* *Fontainebleau, this famous piece* *has a wonderfully tranquil charm.* *(Victoria and Albert Museum.)*

Fig. 3 *Goat and Bee Jug,* *marked with an incised triangle,* *Chelsea, c.1745. Height 4½ ins.* *This jug is based on a silver* *design of the period.* *(Cecil Higgins Art Gallery,* *Bedford, by permission of the* *Trustees.)*

Chelsea, possibly the earliest English porcelain factory, produced fine and beautifully decorated wares, largely inspired by Meissen and the Orient

Despite the long history of porcelain-making in China and Japan, it was not until the sixteenth century that an imitation was made in Europe. This so-called Medici porcelain, like the later manufacture at Rouen in the 1670s, was not the true hard-paste but a soft-paste, based primarily on glass rather than on rock. However, in the early part of the eighteenth century, J. F. Böttger at Meissen discovered how to make true, or hard-paste, porcelain. Böttger's court appointment was primarily to pursue the alchemist's dream of making gold, but from the large quantity and fine quality of porcelain produced for Augustus the Strong, it may be assumed that the latter was well pleased with the alternative discovery.

In England, the search for porcelain was backed by no such royal wealth and, indeed, the number of failures and bankruptcies among people involved in its production during the second half of the eighteenth century was distressingly large. That Chelsea in its early days may have had some sort of aristocratic backing is illustrated by the interest taken in its activities by Sir Everard Fawkener, secretary to the Duke of Cumberland (the 'Butcher of Culloden', and brother to George II). But, if this is a fact, Chelsea was alone in this among the early English factories, and any such direct support can only have been a marginal factor in its progress.

A Huguenot silversmith from Flanders, Nicholas Sprimont, provided the main inspiration for this new Chelsea factory in the 1740s, possibly aided by a chemist named Briand and a fellow Huguenot, a jeweller named Gouyn. Sprimont himself had registered his mark as a silversmith in 1742, but he turned his attentions at an early stage to the manufacture of porcelain, for his earliest dated pieces bear the date 1745. One piece even has a date which has been interpreted as 1743, but there is no agreement on this.

By about 1750, at least six soft-paste factories had sprung up in England, and of these it is not unlikely that Chelsea was the first. Certainly no other porcelain of English manufacture carries a date earlier than 1745. Equally true is that the early Chelsea porcelain was of a very attractive quality, highly translucent and based on glass ingredients. A number of pieces which were produced in this first period, the 'Triangle Period', so-called because of the frequent use of an incised triangle as a mark, bear close affinities to Sprimont's silverwork. This was of high quality, in style not at all typical of the work of other silversmiths in England, at the time, and showing a particular emphasis on scroll-work and shell motifs. These features appear in some of his porcelain pieces such as sauce-boats and salt-cellars, although the curious cream-jugs, the bottom part of which were moulded in the form of a goat and which usually have a bee above the goat's head (Fig. 3), derive from the work of other silversmiths.

The majority of the products of this period, which takes us more or less to the end of the decade, were as attractive in shape as the porcelain itself is pleasing to handle, and include salts with a cray-fish modelled across one side of them, teapots, coffee-pots and beakers, with or without handles, moulded with overlapping leaves or with a tea plant motif, and shallow strawberry dishes with applied leaves and flowers and painted with butter-flies, insects and further floral decoration. Many of

K. Hoddle

Hawtley Studio

71

Fig. 4 *Scent-Bottle, Gold Anchor Period, Chelsea, c.1760.*
Height 3⅛ ins.
Not only were scent bottles the delight of London in the latter half of the eighteenth century, they were also exported in large numbers to the Continent where the gaiety and liveliness that were such a hallmark of Chelsea made them equally popular.
(Author's Collection.)

Fig. 5 (Left) *Plate, Raised Anchor Period, Chelsea, c.1750–52. Diameter 7½ ins.*
(Right) *Plate, Chelsea, c.1752–54. Diameter 9 ins.*
The decoration on these plates is in imitation of the Kakiemon style. There are spur marks from the kiln on the bases.
(Author's Collection.)

Fig. 6 *Octagonal bowl and saucer, possibly by J. H. O'Neale, Red Anchor Period, Chelsea, c.1755. Diameter of saucer 5 ins., height of bowl 2 ins.*
O'Neale painted many animal subjects for Worcester at a later date, but never surpassed his early work at Chelsea.
(Author's Collection.)

Fig. 7 *Madonna and Child by Joseph Willems, marked with a red anchor, Chelsea, c.1755. Height 8⅛ ins.*
The probable source for this design was a painting by Van Dyck. Note the serpent emerging beside the globe.
(Cecil Higgins Art Gallery.)

Fig. 8 *Farmyard clock-case; marked with a red anchor, Chelsea, c.1755. Height 8½ ins.*
The figures of the Red Anchor Period were the glory of Chelsea porcelain. The modelling and skilful attention to detail reached a standard never surpassed in English wares. This delightful example still holds its original clock, unlike a similar case to be seen at the British Museum in London.
(Author's Collection.)

the pieces of this period are left in the white, but when enamelled the colouring and patterns are often in imitation of the prunus, bamboo and other plants normally found in decoration on the porcelain of the Kakiemon potters of Arita (Fig. 5), as well as their strange 'tygers' and weird birds.

Figures, invariably in the white, were also made during the early years, and these too derive largely from Oriental originals. Some remarkable, grotesque teapots consist of a Chinaman riding either on a parrot or on a serpent, which represents the spout. Pu-Tai, sometimes referred to as the Corpulent Monk, at other times as the God of Wealth and Contentment, is not so pleasing to Western tastes as, for instance, a fine figure of a fisherman, modelled after a painting by François Boucher. A French origin for the teapots with overlapping leaves, mentioned above, should also be noted, for soft-paste factories had been in existence for varying lengths of time at St. Cloud, Mennecy, Chantilly and Vincennes. This last, being transferred to Sèvres, became the great royal factory of France.

The trident and the anchor: both marks show an association with the sea

The ensuing period is characterised by the frequent use of a raised anchor, and in one form or another the use of an anchor as a mark was retained during and even beyond the life of Chelsea as an independent factory. Another mark, very rarely used in the Triangle Period, is a crown with a trident through it. This has, in common with the anchor, an association with the sea, but the reason for its adoption is equally obscure.

The porcelain used during the Raised Anchor Period contains less lead than the earlier creations, and in consequence is less glassy and more opaque. This change in composition was already under way during the Triangle Period, thus emphasising the fact that considerable overlapping of material, form and decoration takes place between the various periods known by their most frequently used marks. The quality of Raised Anchor products remained for the most part high, approximately covering the years 1749–53. Figure subjects include a series of birds, usually coloured, taken from the book by G. Edwards called the *Natural History of Uncommon Birds* (Fig. 9); imitations of Meissen artisan characters, such as the strongly modelled *Hurdy-Gurdy Player*; figures from the Italian Comedy, also largely inspired by Meissen; the famous *Chellsea Nurs*, or *La Nourrice* (Fig. 2), derived from a sixteenth-century pottery figure made at Fontainebleau; a pug dog, Oriental figures such as Kuan Yin, busts such as a child's head and that of the Duke of Cumberland (both in white), and a figure of a gardener's companion. Much of the decoration of these figures and of the contemporary wares appears to have been carried out in William Duesbury's London studio, prior to his becoming chief proprietor of the Derby factory.

The wares of this period continued to show strong Oriental inspiration in their decoration, but the influence of Meissen became increasingly more prominent. Certain kinds of flower decoration and landscape scenes are clearly of Meissen origin and indeed much of the Oriental type decoration had

picked up Meissen mannerisms in the process of being translated on to Chelsea porcelain.

However, the most interesting and attractive decoration is the fable painting which appears on cups, saucers, dishes, teapots and other wares. Two names in particular have been suggested as likely painters of these lively animal scenes: William Duvivier, from Tournai, and Jefferyes Hamett O'Neale, who much later did similar work on Worcester wares. If the original fable painter was indeed O'Neale, it can fairly be said that the matching of animal decoration to porcelain was never better accomplished than in his early Chelsea work (Fig. 6). Another type of decoration of purely English inspiration is known as the 'Hans Sloane plants'. These were largely taken from the drawings of Philip Miller, head gardener at the botanical gardens founded in Chelsea by Sir Hans Sloane.

The range of shapes for table wares also widened. Prominent among these are dishes in silver shapes, hexagonal bowls with everted rims, peach-shaped cups with or without stalk handles, all-white plates and beakers with prunus blossom in relief in imitation of *blanc de Chine*, hexagonal vases and other vase and bottle shapes.

During the latter part of this period the raised anchor is sometimes painted over in red, but by 1752, a red anchor, not in relief, but painted direct on to the glaze had become more common. The so-called Red Anchor Period lasted until about 1758, but its use continued occasionally for several years afterwards into the final era of Chelsea as an independent factory, namely the Gold Anchor Period of 1758–69.

Small, decorative items show skilful attention to detail

The figures of the Red Anchor Period are perhaps the chief glory of English porcelain (Fig. 8), derivative though many of them are from the work of Kaendler and Reinicke at Meissen. The Chelsea adaptations were probably created mainly by Joseph Willems from Brussels who stayed with the factory for most of its independent existence. The same Italian Comedy and artisan themes were favoured and developed, while classical, religious, animal and bird figures were also produced (Fig. 7). The modelling reached a standard never surpassed in English porcelain and the same skilful attention to detail is shown in the Red Anchor scent-bottles, in human, animal and bird form.

It may be noted in passing that scent-bottles had also been produced by the 'Girl in a Swing' factory between 1749 and 1754. The relationship between this factory and Chelsea is not clear, but it is at least possible that the bulk of the workmen employed came from Chelsea, and its guiding light was probably the jeweller Charles Gouyn. Besides the neatly made scent-bottles, there are also some much rarer figures, modelled in a unique and somewhat dainty style, as well as some still rarer wares, some of which were made for the dressing-rather than the dinner table. Formerly, these products were often attributed to Chelsea, but whatever the connection between the two factories it now seems probable that the 'Girl in a Swing' establishment was altogether separate.

To return to Chelsea proper, table-wares of the

6

7

8

Red Anchor Period continued to display Oriental, Continental and fable motifs and are often recognised by the 'moons' which can be seen in the porcelain when held up to the light, and also by the small spur marks on bases where the pieces rested in firing kilns. These features also occur in the earlier products of Chelsea, but the handsome animal and vegetable tureens with their stands are a new development. They may take the form of pineapples, melons, lemons, asparagus bundles, cauliflowers, rabbits, pigeons, ducks, swans, eels, boars and even carp or plaice.

Chelsea also produced a limited quantity of wares decorated with under-glaze blue in the Chinese style, sometimes marked with a blue anchor. Perhaps these products were not considered quite sophisticated enough for the relatively

9

Fig. 9 *Great Spotted Cuckoo, one of a pair of which one is marked with a red raised anchor, Chelsea, c.1752. Height 7½ ins. The design for this exquisite bird was taken, together with many other birds, from the* Natural History of Uncommon Birds *by George Edwards, a collection of coloured engravings which was published in London in 1743–47. The decoration was probably done by William Duesbury, who was later to become proprietor of the Derby factory. (Author's Collection.)*

A. C. Cooper

wealthy customers whom Sprimont sought to attract, and far more blue and white of this period survives from Bow and Worcester. That there was no lack of quality in the Chelsea blue and white is illustrated by the continued use today of one of their few early Chinese-style patterns.

Sprimont's declining health and his frequent absences led to a lowering of standards in some, though by no means all, respects. The Gold Anchor Period is characterised by a change of taste towards the elaborate and the opulent. The coloured grounds which Meissen and Sèvres had developed became popular, while figures were likely to stand on rococo scroll bases and to be bedecked with bocage, a background of flowers and leaves. Gold was used frequently, on wares as well as figures, but the quality of the porcelain had in fact changed during the Red Anchor Period with the introduction of bone ash, an ingredient which, although rejected by Dr. Wall and his partners at Worcester, has generally survived in use in English porcelain to this day.

The range of wares widened considerably, and shapes, in particular in the case of vases and jars for purely ornamental purposes, became highly fanci-

ful, often with flamboyant scroll handles. Sèvres became now the main influence behind these objects and much of the decoration of birds and fruit, often applied in James Giles' studio, took its inspiration from the French porcelain painters. Figure painting by John Donaldson on a number of vases derived likewise from Boucher.

Many small objects were exported to the Continent

White figures were by now very rare and the richness of colour generally used often, but by no means always, concealed less careful modelling. But the animals which adorned the fable candlesticks, for instance, were lively, if sometimes cruel, and liveliness is certainly a characteristic of the popular *Ranelagh Dancers*. Scent bottles (Fig. 4) continued to delight in London and elsewhere, and these and other small objects such as needle-cases, *bonbonnières* and seals were exported freely to the Continent.

By 1770 Chelsea had passed into the hands of William Duesbury of Derby and its history now became part of the history of that factory. The so-called Chelsea-Derby Period has more aptly been re-named Derby-Chelsea or Duesbury-Chelsea, but the finest days were over and little further in the way of significant innovation can be said to have emanated from the London factory. The main influences of the ensuing decade came from the Court of Louis XVI, typified by swags and urns on table-wares and rather sentimental figures.

By 1784, Duesbury concentrated the manufacture of porcelain in Derby and thus, about forty years after the beginning of its brilliant history, Chelsea came to its end.

MUSEUMS AND COLLECTIONS

Collections of Chelsea porcelain may be seen at the following:

GREAT BRITAIN
Bedfordshire:	Cecil Higgins Art Gallery, Bedford
	Luton Hoo
Cambridge:	Fitzwilliam Museum
London:	British Museum
	Victoria and Albert Museum

U.S.A.
Boston, Mass.:	Boston Museum of Fine Arts
Williamsburg, Va:	Colonial Museum, Kauffmann Collection

FURTHER READING

The Gold Anchor Wares by F. Severne Mackenna, Leigh-on-Sea, Essex, rev. ed. 1969.
English Porcelain, 1745–1850, edit. by R. J. Charleston, London, 1965: 'Chelsea Porcelain' by J. V. G. Mallet.
Chelsea and other English Porcelain, Pottery and Enamel in the Irwin Untermyer Collection by Yvonne Hackenbroch, London, 1957.
The Red Anchor Wares by F. Severne Mackenna, Leigh-on-Sea, 1951.
The Triangle and Raised Anchor Wares by F. Severne Mackenna, Leigh-on-Sea, 1948.
Chelsea Porcelain by William King, London, 1922.

Worcester Porcelain

*Fig. 1 **Dessert-basket dish** marked with a script 'W' in blue, Worcester, c.1768–76. Length 11 ins. Dyson Perrins Museum, Royal Porcelain Works, Worcester.)*

The superiority of early Worcester porcelain lay in its qualities of heat resistance; it was also beautifully decorated – hence the enthusiasm of today's collectors of eighteenth-century porcelain

J. Beckerley

J. Beckerley

Our knowledge of eighteenth-century Worcester porcelain is much greater following the archaeological excavation on the site of Warmstry House where, in 1751, the Worcester Porcelain Company was founded.

The fifteen original partners headed by Dr. John Wall, a surgeon, and William Davis, an apothecary, made a fine soft-paste, or artificial, porcelain. They used soap-rock mined at the Lizard in Cornwall, clay from Barnstaple and sand from the Isle of Wight. This recipe was used by Miller and Lund's porcelain factory in Bristol which started in 1748 or 1749 and was bought lock, stock and barrel by Worcester in 1752. It is now almost certain that the Worcester factory was formed when it was known that this take-over would come about; thus, as the recipe was the same; and the Bristol workers and moulds came up the River Severn to Worcester, it is very difficult to distinguish between Bristol and early Worcester. For those wares of up to about 1752 or 1753, a descriptive title of Bristol/Worcester is used, except for the very rare pieces that have the embossed word 'Bristol' or 'Bristoll' under the base.

These early Bristol/Worcester wares are among the most charming and sought-after of English ceramics. Many of the shapes are based on silver vessels and the moulds were probably taken directly from silver sauce-boats, cream-jugs and teapots. The patterns were mainly *chinoiserie*, many of them looking very like Bristol delftware styles. The coloured wares frequently copied Chinese *famille rose* and *famille verte*, these enamels sinking much further into the glaze than on the Oriental hard-paste porcelain and presenting a much softer appearance; the under-glaze cobalt painted wares, after the early tendency of the cobalt to run and blur a little had been conquered, were of superb quality, unrivalled in this country.

Marks are few on these early pieces and comprise either some nick-like cuts or incised saltire crosses on the bases of pieces. These are called the 'Scratch Cross Family', or painters' marks. The scratch marks were probably workmen's marks, put on by the potter or foreman before the piece was fired. It should not be assumed that any piece of ceramic having a cross cut in its base is early Worcester, as it is not an uncommon mark to find scratched in many nineteenth-century factories' wares. The painters' marks are generally in under-glaze blue and are in the form of symbols or initials, usually under the base but sometimes at the bottom of the handle or inside a teapot lid.

From about 1754 or 1755, a typical Worcester style developed. The shapes became more natural to the ceramic medium, less obviously derived from silver shapes, and were of fine proportions and quality. One great advantage of the Worcester body over that of other English factories was that it did not crack or craze when in contact with boiling liquids, and no eighteenth-century Worcester is ever found that has the slightest trace of crazing. This led the factory to concentrate on the making of useful wares, principally tea and dessert wares.

Decoration could be of three types: under-glaze blue painting, over-glaze colour enamel painting and over-glaze black printing. Blue painting continued in a *chinoiserie* style, and painters' marks continued up to about 1758, when the first Worcester factory marks of a crescent and a 'W' took over. A few direct copies of Chinese originals were executed and these have a different Chinese-type mark, the greater majority of Worcester blue-and-white pieces being marked. From about this time a fretted square mark, based on a Chinese seal mark, was used for patterns which had under-glaze blue and over-glaze enamel colours combined, or the square mark could be put on pieces intended for fine over-glaze decoration. The greater majority of over-glaze decorated wares are unmarked; this also applies to over-glaze printing.

The process of printing seems to have been brought to Worcester in about 1755 by an experienced enameller, Robert Hancock. Printing

coloured prints of *Les Garçons Chinois* at the top of the vase show how effective this can be. In about 1760 under-glaze blue printing was introduced and this eventually ousted blue painting by the 1780s.

Over-glaze painting could cover a very wide range: from flowers and birds in the Meissen style (Fig. 3) of the early to mid-1750s; the Chinese and Japanese styles of the late '50s to '60s; to the sophisticated London styles of the late '60s to '70s. These are broadly the dates of the general introduction of the styles at Worcester although the periods of course tended to overlap.

The splendid ground colours that are now so keenly sought by collectors are headed by the deep cobalt blue grounds, either a solid blue (called by such names as *gros* blue, or wet blue) or a scaled blue (Fig. 1). The scales were painted in a dark cobalt over a first pale wash of cobalt which gives an attractive, fragmented appearance to the background of reserved panels which, after the glaze was fired, were decorated with Japanese-style decorations in the 1760s, fabulous birds in the early 1770s and simpler flower groups in the late 1770s and 1780s. Other ground colours quickly followed; at first yellow, then pea green (generally called apple green), turquoise (or *bleu céleste*, seen in Fig. 5) and claret. Some of these grounds, such as the yellow, were done in a scaled version and these are among the rarest of all.

Fig. 4 *Some Worcester marks.*
First row: typical painters' marks *of 1751–c.1758, in blue.*
Second row: factory marks from *c.1758–76, on painted wares.*
Third row: printed marks from *c.1760–93, on blue printed* *wares.*
Fourth row: Flight and Barr *marks from 1793, incised.*

was to revolutionize the English ceramic industry and was highly regarded when first used. The earliest Worcester printing was of curious battleships, squirrels and so forth in a rather dull smoky brown colour; these are generally called 'smoky primitives'. By 1757, the year of the first dated pieces commemorating the King of Prussia, the standard had become very fine and an example of the splendid jet black enamel transfer printing had reached a quality shown in the illustration of the vase decorated with an equestrian portrait of King George II (Fig. 6). Below the battle trophies can be seen the initials 'R H', the word 'Worcester' and an anchor; although it could be assumed that the 'R H' stood for Robert Hancock, it is likely that, in fact, they stood for Richard Holdship, one of the partners, the anchor being a rebus of his name. Holdship later went to Derby to introduce the printing process there and Hancock became a partner in his place. Some of the printed pieces were tinted or washed over in enamel colours to produce effective but easily made coloured wares, and the

Reproductions and copies abound

Care should be taken over most of these ground-colour wares as a considerable number of copies or fakes were produced in the late nineteenth and early twentieth centuries. A lot of these fakes should be obvious to anyone who has taken the trouble to learn the basic differences in sight and touch between soft-paste and hard-paste porcelain. Most are in a hard-paste body and produced in France, many by the firm of Samson of Paris.

Many copies of Worcester were produced in earthenware by the firm of Booths of Tunstall and the Worcester china factory of Grainger and Co. The Worcester Royal Porcelain Company itself produced a large number of reproductions in the last quarter of the nineteenth century; these, however, are always in bone china, a much clearer and more translucent body than porcelain and the pieces will have the later factory marks on them. There are nineteenth-century pieces, however, with an over-glaze printed mark removed by acid or an impressed mark obliterated by grinding which are now masqueraded as Dr. Wall items (that is, pieces made under his management between 1751 and 1776). One characteristic of the eighteenth-century Worcester green ground was that it would not take gold directly on top of the ground, although this was not the case with the later chrome greens.

From about 1760, transfer prints could be made under-glaze in cobalt blue. Although marks on over-glaze printed pieces are few and far between, most of the blue and white printed pieces are marked. The mark, usually a crescent, is a printed one on printed wares and the archaeological excavations have shown an interesting sequence in the form that the crescent takes. When the copper-plate was first etched and engraved it included an

Fig. 5 **Teapot** with turquoise (bleu céleste) ground, c.1775. **Coffee-pot** with reserved panels in yellow ground, c.1765. **Sugar-bowl and cover** with reserved panels in green ground (note that the gilding does not overlay the green), c.1770. **Coffee-cup and saucer** with painting by the 'Cut Fruit painter' on panels reserved in a claret ground, c.1770. (Dyson Perrins Museum.)

Fig. 6 **Vase and cover**, c.1758. Printed in black with George II above a depiction of Liberty and below a scene of Les Garçons Chinois tinted in enamel colours. (Dyson Perrins Museum.)

Fig. 7 **Teapot** marked with a cross, Worcester, c.1755. Modelled panels painted in pale blue with chinoiserie scenes. (Dyson Perrins Museum.)

6

7

J. Beckerley

78

open crescent; this crescent would be printed at the same time as the main subject, cut and attached under the base. If the pattern was a popular one the copper would become worn and would need to go back to be re-cut. To indicate this, horizontal lines were engraved across the crescent. If the copper had to be re-cut a second time, an inner line was engraved down the crescent. If a third repair was necessary a letter (E, L or R) was added to the crescent, or the crescent was turned into a man in the moon's face; the latter therefore indicates a much worn and repaired print.

After the death of Dr. Wall in 1776 the factory was managed by William Davis until his death in 1783 and was then bought by Thomas Flight for his two sons. The period from 1776–93 is known as the Davis/Flight period, a rather undistinguished period compared with the earlier one, in which great competition led the factory to cheapen their wares and to introduce a large quantity of transfer prints of a violet tone of blue in the style of Chinese Nankin wares. As well as the continuing use of a very small crescent, we find a new factory mark of the so-called Chinese Disguised Numeral Marks, for so long wrongly ascribed to the Caughley factory. Some simple, coloured wares continued to be made, generally blue-bordered, with over-glaze flowers, or merely gilt, and the shapes and decorations have a neo-classical touch about them. In 1793, Flight was joined by Martin Barr and the Flight and Barr period up to 1807 shows a steady improvement of quality and the use of a mark showing an incised 'B' with the lower half of the 'B' larger than the upper, or the continuing use of a very small crescent.

In about 1788 Robert Chamberlain started a separate factory in Worcester at first decorating white ware bought from Caughley and from Flight and Barr, and later (by the mid-1790s) making his own porcelain.

Recognising unmarked Worcester of the Dr. Wall or Davis/Flight period can be helped by visiting the main collections, but practical hints (as long as they are not taken as being completely fool-proof) are that most wares of these periods will show a green translucence when held up to an electric light, later wares can show a strawy-orange colour; most Worcester rims exhibit a rather sharply chamfered edge; most foot-rings are of a well turned, basically triangular shape; the inside flanges of covers are wiped clear of glaze.

After about 1760 there is generally to be seen a glaze-free margin (often a little ragged line of dry biscuit) just inside the foot-ring under the base. This was produced by wiping the glaze away with a pointed tool to stop the glaze running down the foot and sticking it to the kiln during firing; the process is called pegging. This should not be called glaze shrinkage or retreating glaze, as glaze does not shrink when firing, but flows. One should never attempt to test whether this is dry biscuit by running a lead pencil around the inside of the foot. No mark indicates a glazed surface, but the lead mark on biscuit would ruin the piece. Likewise one should not test whether or not a piece is soft-paste by filing it; admittedly if a cut is made the piece is likely to be soft-paste porcelain, but the value of the piece will have been ruined. Finally, glaze from the late 1760s to about 1793 shows a tendency to bubble, and patches of sanding frequently occur. 🙰

J. Beckerley

MUSEUMS AND COLLECTIONS

Worcester porcelain may be seen at the following:

GREAT BRITAIN

London: British Museum
               Victoria and Albert Museum

Worcester: Dyson Perrins Museum

U.S.A.

Chicago, Ill.: Chicago Art Institute

FURTHER READING

Royal Worcester Porcelain, 1862 to the Present Day by Henry Sandon, 1972.
Caughley and Worcester Porcelain, 1775–1800 by Geoffrey Godden, London, 1969.

Early Wedgwood

Fig. 1 **Black basalt vase** in the 'Etruscan' style, Wedgwood and Bentley, early 1770s. Wedgwood popularised vases painted with designs copied from the 'Etruscan' vases in the collection of Sir William Hamilton which were illustrated and published in a set of four volumes.
(Josiah Wedgwood and Sons Ltd., Barlaston, Staffs.)

Of all the Staffordshire potters, the name of Josiah Wedgwood clearly stands out as the most enterprising and significant

Josiah Wedgwood was the son of a potter, and belonged to a family long established in Staffordshire. His father was unsuccessful – a bequest in his will of £10 to the young Josiah was never paid – but his uncles had a flourishing pottery business and other members of the family had been potters in the past. Potting, therefore was in his blood, and it is not surprising that he adopted this profession. He was born in 1730, and came to manhood at a time when fashions in ceramics were dominated by the rococo designs of Chelsea, Bow and Worcester. Staffordshire, however, had little contact with the sophisticated tastes of London; most of what was produced there was provincial in style and crude in execution.

As a young man, Josiah Wedgwood observed that Staffordshire potters were trying to make ends meet by lowering the quality of their work; poor work fetched a poor price, which led to still lower standards and even worse returns. It was this practical lesson in economics which determined him in the belief he held throughout his life that it was not the cheaper but the better article which more easily found a buyer. The qualities which sold his work were the standard of design and finish, and the endless inventiveness which impelled him, time and time again, to produce a new type of ware or a new variant on an accepted theme before his rivals had caught up with his previous novelties.

We can see the beginnings of this inventiveness when he was still young. At the age of twelve, he caught smallpox and this left him with a form of abscess on his knee which prevented him for long periods from using a potter's wheel. A career as a thrower of pots was clearly impossible for him. Probably for this reason, he turned his mind to the

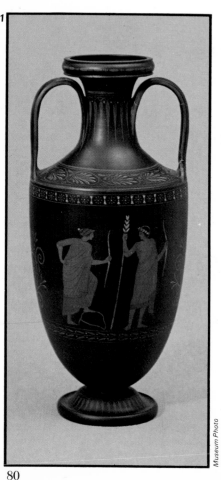

Museum Photo

80

Fig. 2 *Cauliflower teapot,*
Wedgwood, late 1750s.
This type of piece had been made
during the 1750s at the china
factories in London, but until
Wedgwood invented his deep
green glaze suitable for use on
earthenware nothing of this
kind was made in Staffordshire.
Josiah Wedgwood and Sons
Ltd.)

Fig. 3 *Coffee-pot in Queen's*
ware, Wedgwood, late
eighteenth century.
The printed decoration was
carried out by Sadler and Green
of Liverpool.
Josiah Wedgwood and Sons
Ltd.)

Fig. 4 *Black basalt ware,*
Wedgwood, late eighteenth
century.
Josiah Wedgwood and Sons
Ltd.)

chemistry of ceramic bodies and glazes, which could lead to new types of pottery different from the salt-glazed stoneware and variegated agate ware which the Staffordshire potters had been turning out for decades.

Cabbages and other vegetables were imitated in earthenware

His partnership with Thomas Whieldon from 1754 to 1759 allowed him plenty of time for such experiments, which he recorded methodically and in great detail in his *Experiment Book*. Whieldon was a very successful potter, making a good living with marbled and agate wares, but he was in sympathy with the new ideas of the younger man. Wedgwood's chemistry (which he recorded in a quaint language of his own, describing clays as 'bibulous' when he meant that they absorbed a lot of water) produced towards the latter end of the partnership a deep green glaze which was a complete novelty for use on earthenware. Such a colour suggested foliage, and it was soon possible to imitate in earthenware the amusing cabbages and other vegetables which had previously been made only by the porcelain factories. Soon cauliflower and pineapple tea-sets and leaf-patterned plates were being made in Staffordshire and finding a ready market (Fig. 2).

By 1759, the partnership with Whieldon came to an end and Wedgwood was ready to start in business on his own. Whieldon generously allowed Wedgwood to take with him the secrets of his experiments, and the ware Wedgwood made, when first his own master, carried on the same tradition as the Whieldon-Wedgwood factory. So much so, that whether a particular piece is Whieldon, Whieldon-Wedgwood, or very early Wedgwood is often open to argument.

Wedgwood leased from his uncles a small factory called the Ivy House, where he made green-glazed ware and agate ware and worked at his project for a new near-white earthenware body. His experiments led him to perfect a cream-coloured earthenware containing ground, calcined flint. In 1763 he described it as 'a species of earthenware for the table quite new in its appearance, covered with a rich and brilliant glaze bearing sudden alterations of heat and cold, manufactured with ease and expedition, and consequently cheap, having every requisite for the purpose intended' (Figs. 3, 6 and 7).

This creamware body brought Wedgwood's name before a much wider public than had previously been concerned with the remote Staffordshire potteries. He was delighted to hear that his ware was becoming the subject of conversation in London, and in 1765 he received an order for a tea-service from Queen Charlotte. His brother, then in London, was told to 'put on the best suit of clothes you ever had in your life' and hurry to the Palace for instructions. The teaset has unfortunately not survived, but the Queen was pleased with this and other pieces he made for her, and two years later Wedgwood was allowed to style himself 'Potter to the Queen'.

Though other factories, in particular the Leeds Pottery, made very fine cream-coloured earthenware, it was his own perfected variety of it, which Queen Charlotte allowed him to call 'Queen's Ware', which was the foundation of Wedgwood's fortunes.

Output of the ware soon outstripped the capacity of the painters to decorate it, but fortunately

Museum Photo

Museum Photo

Fig. 6 *Soup-tureen* in Queen's ware, Wedgwood, late eighteenth century. Based on a contemporary silver shape, this design is illustrated in the catalogue of Useful Wares, 1774 (Josiah Wedgwood and Sons Ltd.). Wedgwood adopted the name Queen's ware for his newly perfected creamwares after he had successfully executed an order for a tea service from Queen Charlotte in 1765.

Fig. 5 *Dinner-plate* from the dinner service of Catherine the Great, Wedgwood, 1773–74. Each piece in this service bears a scene of an English country house or garden. This piece with its 'antique' folly is one of the few pieces which has not remained in Russia. (Victoria and Albert Museum, London.)

transfer printing for pottery had by then been invented, and was being carried out by the firm of Sadler and Green in Liverpool (Fig. 3). For many years, Wedgwood sent all the ware which he wanted decorated in this way to Liverpool, ninety difficult miles away. At first, the crates went by pack-horse, and it is not surprising that Wedgwood was one of the prime movers in the project for a canal linking the Trent to the Mersey. When it was finished, it flowed past his new factory and reduced costs from tenpence to a penny-halfpenny per ton mile.

Wedgwood sent innumerable letters to Sadler and Green about the designs to be put on the ware, and he scorned many of the patterns which the printers thought suitable. He was particularly displeased by 'the scrawling childish sprays of flowers, which he thinks very clever, but which will not do for us'. Wedgwood had already moved away from such a rococo style. Wedgwood ware printed by Sadler and Green was often sent the half mile from their premises to the Liverpool docks, whence it was exported to the American colonies. Orders were often taken for special services ornamented with family coats of arms, but the most spectacular order for creamware came from the Empress Catherine of Russia. Already in the early 1770s she had had a large dinner-service, now in the palace at Petrodvorets, decorated with a pink husk pattern. In 1773 she ordered a huge dinner and dessert-service, including every sort of tureen, sauce-boat and dish as well as the plates: nine hundred and fifty-two pieces in all (Fig. 5). Each piece was to be decorated with a different view of an English house, garden or other particularly interesting scene. It took over a year to produce a total of 1,244 hand-painted designs. Wedgwood was on tenterhooks during this time, in case the Empress should cancel the order, or even die, before he could send the service. However, it reached the Empress late in 1774, and she paid the bill – a little over £2,700 – at once. Wedgwood's profit (the records are not clear) may have been as little as £100, but the reputation this great undertaking made for him, at home and abroad, more than compensated him for this meagre return.

By the end of the eighteenth century, Wedgwood's cream-coloured earthenware was being sent to France, Holland, Germany, Italy and America. In the early nineteenth century, the Shah of Persia bought a set of tableware; and the Emperor of China, given a present of Wedgwood ware by a diplomatic mission, had it copied by the imperial potters.

Adam's ideals translated into ceramic terms

As a young man, Wedgwood remarked that few of his contemporaries in Staffordshire 'attended to the elegance of form'. If there is one quality which characterises the work of the first Josiah Wedgwood, it is this. We have already noted that he was born in 1730, and started as an independent potter in 1759. The previous year, in 1758, another artist, Robert Adam, had settled in London, and had begun his dramatic rise to the position of the most influential architect and decorator of his time. It was Wedgwood's special talent to see that the Adam ideals could be translated into ceramic terms, and

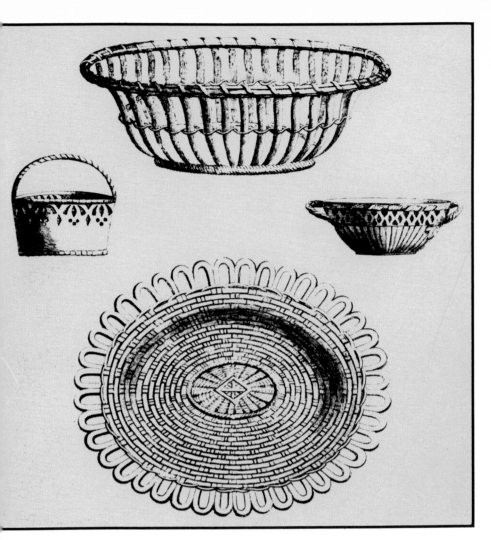

Fig. 7 *Designs for Queen's ware baskets, from the catalogue of Useful Wares, 1774.*

that pottery could be made appropriate to the Adam interior. In this he was years ahead of the other pottery firms, who mostly continued with rococo styles for another decade. By the middle of the 1760s he was producing vases and urns based on the classical designs which inspired Adam, and imitating the so-called 'Etruscan' vases then being dug up in Italy. Neo-Classicism, elegant and austere, remained the Wedgwood style until the end of his life. Even in the domestic wares where convenience was essential and there was less scope for decoration, the pieces retain the elegance of form characteristic of Adam taste.

In arriving at this particular idiom, Josiah Wedgwood was greatly helped by Thomas Bentley. Though the partnership between them was not formalised until 1769, they had known each other since 1762, and Wedgwood relied greatly on the knowledge and sensibility of his friend. Bentley had a business in Liverpool, a town which Wedgwood had to visit in connection with the printing of his wares, and they met there on an occasion when Wedgwood's knee incapacitated him and Bentley was sent by a mutual friend to entertain the invalid.

Bentley had had the classical education which Wedgwood lacked. In addition he had a wide and cultivated taste and quickly responded to the new Adam fashions. From 1767 they worked together, and Wedgwood began his series of letters in which he deferred to Bentley's superior judgement on all points of design. In 1769 the partnership was legally instituted, and Bentley took charge of the London end of the business and supervised the painting-shops at Chelsea.

The connoisseurs of the day were much interested in classical antiquities, and particularly admired the red and black pottery vases being discovered at that time in Etruscan tombs. Though it is now known that these were mostly made by Greek craftsmen, eighteenth-century collectors naturally considered them to have been made by Etruscan potters. The British Ambassador at the court of Naples, Sir William Hamilton, made a fine collection, and published volumes of plates showing his pieces in detail. Wedgwood and Bentley had copies of the books and, seeing the possibilities of copying them, soon made a name for their 'Etruscan' vases (Fig. 1).

Wedgwood had already found a suitable ceramic body. He had recently evolved a dense black stoneware, much more vitrified than earthenware, with a smooth surface which, in time, took on a faint patina. He called this ware 'basalt', thinking that it looked like basaltic rock, and boasted that 'the black is sterling and will last for ever' (Fig. 4).

The potters of antiquity had made red clay vases, which they covered, except for the areas of figure decoration, with some form of slip. This fired black, leaving the figures in the red of natural clay. Wedgwood, having perfected a body which was already black, was able to use a simpler technique; all he had to do was to paint the figures in red on his basalt pots. Copying both the shapes and the figure designs from Hamilton's books, he made remarkable approximations to the Greek originals, and they proved extremely popular (Fig. 1). Mr. Cox, his London agent at the time, was 'mad as a March hare for Etruscan vases', and more than four hundred of a single design were sold in a year.

So fascinated were both Wedgwood and Bentley by this style that when they opened their new factory for ornamental wares in 1769, they called it 'Etruria', after the district in central Italy where the ancient Etruscans had lived. To celebrate the occasion, Wedgwood and Bentley made six 'First Day's Vases' in the Etruscan style. Wedgwood did the throwing; Bentley turned the potter's wheel. The vases bear the date and the boast *Artes Etruriae renascuntur* : 'the arts of Etruria are reborn'.

MUSEUMS AND COLLECTIONS

Wedgwood pottery may be seen at the following:

GREAT BRITAIN

Barlaston:	Wedgwood Museum, Josiah Wedgwood and Sons, Ltd. (appointment necessary).
Cambridge:	Fitzwilliam Museum
London:	Victoria and Albert Museum
Nottingham:	City Art Gallery and Museum
Port Sunlight:	Lady Lever Art Gallery
Stoke-on-Trent:	Hanley Museum

U.S.A.

Birmingham, Ala.:	Birmingham Museum of Art
Merion, Pa.:	Buten Museum of Wedgwood
Shreveport, La.:	R. W. Norton Art Gallery

FURTHER READING

The Collector's Book of Wedgwood by Marian Klamkin, Devon, 1972.
Wedgwood Ware by Alison Kelly, London, 1970.
Proceedings of the Wedgwood Society edited by Geoffrey Wills, London, 1955 onwards.
Wedgwood by Wolf Mankowitz, London, 1953.

Blue and White Wares

Fig. 1 *Five pieces of porcelain,*
Lowestoft, 1760–67.
These under-glaze blue, relief-
moulded pieces are usually
associated with the name of
James Hughes, a Lowestoft
potter.
(G. Godden Collection.)

Fig. 2 *Jug, Liverpool, c.1765.*
Painted in under-glaze blue,
height 5⅞ ins.
(Victoria and Albert Museum,
London.)

Chinese porcelain was blue and white and so the English, who loved anything oriental, were delighted with the blue and white wares made in their native factories

Porcelain painted in under-glaze blue was first produced in China during the fourteenth century, but it was not until three hundred years later that it was imported into Europe by the Dutch East India Company. In the early years of the eighteenth century, European potters were starting to produce porcelain, but the early French and German factories made comparatively little attempt to imitate the Chinese blue and white wares, which had by this time become popular and fashionable.

When the first English factories started to manufacture porcelain in the late 1740s, they immediately set about trying to meet the considerable demand which had grown up for china decorated in under-glaze blue. Competition was keen, as there was not only imported Chinese porcelain to be considered, but also delftware and, later, cheaply produced types of pottery such as creamware and pearlware. However, the ideal was to resemble the Chinese as closely as possible, and in this respect no pottery could compete with the translucent, fine, delicate porcelain.

With very few exceptions, blue and white porcelain was made for everyday use, and most factories found it a very good selling line. It was comparatively cheap to produce and helped to finance their more costly and ambitious ventures in polychrome-decorated porcelain and figures. As one might expect, nearly all the under-glaze blue decoration was derived from the Chinese, but the effect achieved by the English painters was quite unintentionally entirely different. While much of the symbolism and subtlety of the Chinese designs was missing, this was replaced by a naive but most attractive assimilation, which, while truly English in style, was nevertheless completely Chinese in inspiration.

While the majority of the painted designs show a marked Chinese influence, the potters looked elsewhere for the inspiration for their shapes. Some were derived from the Continental factories, others were taken from contemporary English pottery,

especially salt-glazed earthenware. But perhaps the main inspiration was that afforded by English silver designs, an influence that can be seen on such objects as sauce-boats, cream-boats, mugs and coffee-pots.

Of the eighteen or so factories that produced blue and white porcelain in this country, fifteen made soft-paste porcelain and the other three a hard paste. Each of these factories developed its own potting and decorative mannerisms, but identification is complicated by the considerable amount of inter-factory copying which took place. In addition to this, each factory went through various stages of stylistic development, and in some cases products varied startlingly in appearance over a comparatively short space of time.

In the early stages of production, factories often progressed through trial and error. Whereas Worcester, for example, managed to produce some fairly sophisticated porcelain shapes almost immediately (Fig. 3), other factories spent their early years struggling to master the practical difficulties of producing a tractable porcelain body. Consequently, not only do the paste and the tone of under-glaze blue vary from factory to factory, but they also vary according to the stage of each factory's development.

Most of the finest blue and white porcelain was made in England in the period between the early 1750s and about 1770. During this time some beautifully potted and decorated pieces were produced, and although the emphasis was, of course, on practicality, this did not prevent the potters from creating a most charming blend of *Chinoiserie* to embellish the fine and elaborate shapes of the rococo period. After about 1770, with the increased use of transfer prints, the percentage of pieces with hand-painted decoration decreased. Most of the printed designs were somewhat uninspired and much of the painted decoration was done without the care and individuality so noticeable in the earlier period. In fact, little attempt was made to give the porcelain a more than purely functional appearance.

The renowned Chelsea factory concentrated almost exclusively on the production of polychrome-decorated wares and figures. Consequently, blue and white pieces are extremely rare, only a dozen or so examples being recorded. In contrast, the Bow factory (1749–1775) made quite a speciality of their blue and white and, from the early 1750s until the late 1760s, only the Worcester factory

Fig. 3 *Teapot*, Worcester, c.1755.
This example illustrates the facility with which Chinese-style decoration was assimilated into English rococo design.
(Private Collection.)

Fig. 4 *Coffee-pot*, Bow, c.1750.
Height 7 7/10 ins.
The handle placed at 90° to the spout is a rare feature.
(Victoria and Albert Museum.)

Fig. 5 *Teapot*, Longton Hall, c.1758. *Height 5 7/8 ins.*
The crabstock handle and the angle and shape of the spout are typical features of Longton Hall porcelain.
(Victoria and Albert Museum.)

Fig. 6 *Tankard*, Worcester, c.1754. *Height 5 3/4 ins.*
The combination of strength and simplicity in both shape and decoration is characteristic of Worcester tankards in the early 1750s.
(Private Collection.)

Fig. 7 *Hexagonal vase*, Worcester, c.1755.
Height 11 1/2 ins.
This is a rare example of a piece of blue and white ware intended for a purely decorative purpose.
(Victoria and Albert Museum.)

could equal their output. Most of the early pieces are thickly and robustly potted, and the under-glaze blue is usually remarkably bright and vivid. The magnificent coffee-pot in Figure 4 shows typical decoration of the period, although its shape is decidedly uncommon. By the late 1750s, the potting had become less clumsy and the blue tone somewhat darker. At this time, powder blue decoration became something of a speciality at Bow. This is so called because the under-glaze blue was blown or dusted on to the porcelain in a powdered form, rather than painted on with a brush in the usual way. By the early 1770s, both the quality of the porcelain and its decoration had deteriorated to such an extent that many of the late pieces resemble earthenware.

Soft-paste blue and white porcelain was made at Bristol between 1749 and 1751, but examples are now very scarce. In 1751, the factory was transferred to Worcester and for the next ten years or so some of the finest blue and white porcelain ever made in Europe was produced. No other English factory could equal the quality of the Worcester potting or the delicacy of its moulded and painted decoration. Indeed, the moulded tea-wares (Fig. 3), sauce-boats and cream-boats are amongst the greatest achievements of this celebrated factory. These wares usually have rococo panels or reserves delicately painted with Chinese fishing scenes. Other shapes made in this period include some fine, heavily-potted bowls, large jugs, rose-water-bottles and tankards (Fig. 6). The latter were produced in a wide variety of splendid shapes and sizes, the design and decoration of almost all showing an attractive blend of care and vigour. Nearly all the Worcester wares of this period show a beautiful green translucency when held up to direct light. The wares of the 1760s, while still retaining much of their previous elegance and charm, seem to lack something of the flair and individuality so characteristic of the earlier pieces. By 1775, most of the blue and white was transfer printed, and, although the high standards of potting remained unchanged, all traces of the former rococo splendour had disappeared.

Technical problems solved, many attractive pieces were made

The Longton Hall factory (c.1749–1760), in Staffordshire, was one of the first to make blue and white porcelain. However, its earliest products reflect, in their clumsiness and lack of elegance, the tremendous problems facing the mid-eighteenth-century potters. By about 1755, many of these difficulties had been overcome, and for the next five years some attractive pieces were produced, such as the delightful little teapot in Figure 5. Nowadays Longton Hall porcelain is scarce and highly prized by collectors.

Like Chelsea, the Derby factory was chiefly pre-occupied with the production of coloured wares and figures; consequently, their blue and white was regarded as a comparative sideline. For some reason, not many tea-wares were made, and the bulk of their blue and white output consisted of plates, dishes, baskets, sauce-boats and small, leaf-shaped pickle-trays.

The general description of 'Liverpool porcelain' is misleading as there were, between 1754 and 1800,

no less than seven factories within the city, all of which at one time or another manufactured porcelain. Although most of those factories show certain recognisably Liverpool characteristics each developed its own individual style of decoration, and sometimes its own particular potting mannerisms. For example, although the Chaffers factory (1754–1765) derived most of its basic shapes from Worcester, its paste and style of decoration are unmistakably those of Liverpool. In fact, the Chaffers' painting shows a most attractive fluency which is much less noticeable on the porcelain made at Christian's factory (1765–1776), which succeeded it. These latter pieces are neatly potted and pleasantly painted, but there is a lack of imagination and individuality in most of the potting shapes and designs. Seth Pennington's factory (1769–1799) made porcelain, some of which is poorly potted indifferently decorated and generally lacking in artistic merit. However, many of the earlier pieces have a rugged charm which is, to some tastes, more appealing than Christian's neat predictability.

Some of the most attractive Liverpool wares were those made at William Ball's factory (1755–1769). The shapes were, for the most part, derived from Bow, and this influence can be seen both in the vigorously potted vases and sauce-boats and in the smaller, more neatly potted articles such as tea-wares, cream-boats and the chamber candlestick in Figure 8. The under-glaze blue is attractively bright and the style of painting is reminiscent of delftware. Very different is the porcelain made at William Reid's factory (c.1755–1761). These fascinating wares show a remarkable lack of sophistication beside their contemporary Liverpool counterparts, but, for all that, they have a peculiar and distinctive charm. A small quantity of blue and white was produced at Samuel Gilbody's factory (c.1754–1761), but examples are hard to find and harder still to identify.

The porcelain made in the small Suffolk town of Lowestoft between 1757 and 1799 was primarily intended for a local market. This is reflected in the comparatively large number of pieces which were dated and inscribed with the names of East Anglian towns and villages. Most of the Lowestoft decoration is unpretentious, almost to the point of naivety, and in fact not only was much of the painting done by women, but it is believed that children also worked at the factory. However, far from being unattractive, the simple, unsophisticated designs have an altogether individual allure, particularly in the case of the pre-1770 pieces (Fig. 1). In this period the painting was done in a pleasing, delft-like style which matched splendidly the sensibly designed everyday objects made at the factory. Subsequently the wares lost some of this freedom of decoration, but they retained to the last their charming and totally characteristic simplicity.

The Caughley factory (1772–1799) in Shropshire was another which made a speciality of its blue and white ware. Most of the shapes were derived from Worcester, and some attractive and individual results were achieved. No other factory produced as many miniature tea-services, and these delightful pieces are still quite plentiful today (Fig. 10). Much of the Caughley decoration was transfer-printed, and therefore the factory's many potting shapes are of more interest than their often somewhat pedestrian designs.

The only English factories to produce a true hard-

A. C. Cooper

6

A. C. Cooper

7

K. Hoddle

K. Hoddle

K. Hoddle

K. Hoddle

Fig. 8 *Chamber candlestick,*
William Ball's factory, c.1760.
Diameter 5¼ ins.
The bright tone of under-glaze
blue is characteristic of this
factory. Chamber candlesticks
in blue and white are rare.
(Victoria and Albert Museum.)

Fig. 9 *Jug and cover, Lowestoft,*
c.1775. Height 7 ins.
This is, for Lowestoft, an
unusually elaborate and well-
painted design. The dashes on
the knop are a typical feature of
the factory.
(Victoria and Albert Museum.)

Fig. 10 *Part of a miniature*
service, Caughley, c.1780–85.
These delightful pieces were
intended either for children or as
travellers' samples.
(Victoria and Albert Museum.)

paste porcelain were those established at Plymouth (1768–1770) and Bristol (1770–1781). Neither factory made a large quantity of blue and white, and these pieces are admired today as much for their rarity as for their artistic merits.

Considerably less than half the porcelain mentioned above bears a factory mark. From about 1768 until the middle of the 1770s, most of the Worcester wares are marked with a crescent, and some pieces of Caughley, Plymouth and Bristol have their own factory mark. No other factories used marks on their blue and white porcelain, although sometimes a painter's or workman's mark can be seen. Therefore the collector must learn to distinguish pieces of blue and white by considering their style of decoration, glaze, shape, paste, design and foot-ring. This is neither as complicated nor as difficult as it might appear, and after a little experience one's instinct replaces the conscious process of attribution. However, it is wise to remember that no amount of reading or visits to museum collections can compare with the instinct, knowledge and experience which comes with the actual handling of the porcelain.

MUSEUMS AND COLLECTIONS
Blue and white porcelain may be seen at the following:

Birkenhead:	Williamson Art Gallery and Museum
Brighton:	Art Gallery and Museum
Cambridge:	Fitzwilliam Museum
London:	British Museum
	Victoria and Albert Museum
Norwich:	Castle Museum
Plymouth:	City Museum and Art Gallery
Worcester:	Dyson Perrins Museum

FURTHER READING
The Price Guide to Eighteenth Century English Porcelain by Simon Spero, Antique Collectors' Club, Woodbridge, 1970.
Caughley and Worcester Porcelains by G. A. Godden, London, 1969.
The Illustrated Guide to Lowestoft Porcelain by G. A. Godden, London, 1969.
English Blue and White Porcelain of the Eighteenth Century by B. M. Watney, London, 1963.

English Lustreware

Originally an ancient Mesopotamian technique (later used in Moorish Spain) lustre in gold, platinum and pink was a popular pottery decoration in early nineteenth-century England

Fig. 1 *Cup and saucer, probably New Hall, Stafford-shire, c.1815. Bone china with enamel colours and pink lustre, diameter 5¾ ins. (Victoria and Albert Museum.)*

Almost all the most popular styles of decorating pottery and porcelain originated in the Near and Far East. In the case of iridescent lustre, the pottery of Mesopotamia and Egypt was of a far more suitable material to receive this manner of decoration than that of China. Excavations at Samarra, Baghdad and Fostat, near Cairo, have revealed evidence of the technique on both a clear lead glaze and an opaque tin glaze, from about 850 A.D. in the case of Mesopotamia, and around 1100 A.D. in Egypt. The lustres used in these centres were always of various tones of yellow, graduating to a rich coppery brown, never silver, gold or pink as used in nineteenth-century England.

The first appearance of lustreware in Europe occurred not later than the twelfth century, when the Arab geographer Edrisi, writing of Calatayud in the year 1154, writes: 'the gold-coloured pottery is made which is exported to all countries'. Later writers speak of 'the beauty of the gold pottery so splendidly painted at Manises', near Valencia. This type of pottery was the result of the Arab invasion of the Iberian peninsula in 711, but the traditional styles of Hispano-Moresque wares were continued long after the final expulsion of the Moors from Spain at the end of the fifteenth century. Modern wares based on the earlier designs can still be purchased in the tourist markets of Spain today.

Hispano-Moresque lustrewares were exported to Italy via Majorca, resulting in the term '*maiolica*' being adopted by the Italians to refer to their own tin-glazed earthenwares, which, by the end of the fifteenth century, were being made in many centres such as Florence, Faenza and Castel Durante. Two centres specialised in lustrewares: Deruta and Gubbio.

The various techniques of preparing the materials and the special firing conditions essential for lustreware have been well recorded, and there is no evidence to suggest any deliberate attempts by potters to keep their methods secret. Many accounts of the process are available, including those of a Spanish tile-maker in 1385; the famous mid-sixteenth-century account of the potters' art by Piccolpasso; the late nineteenth-century work of the English pottery decorator William de Morgan; and the outstanding ceramic chemist William Burton, who in 1907 addressed the Society of Arts on his findings concerning lustre decoration.

The dating and attribution of the popular English lustreware is very difficult. Many dated examples are merely commemorative and very few pieces bear the mark of a potter. Experiments may well have been carried out by Josiah Wedgwood during

89

his partnership with Thomas Bentley (1769–80), but there seems little doubt that it was during the early years of the nineteenth century that potters started to use gold and platinum to achieve the decorative English and Welsh lustrewares sought after by many collectors today.

Platinum, which was first discovered in South America in about 1750, has many advantages over silver: apart from being more lustrous, it never tarnishes and so was to prove ideal for reproducing silver and silver-plated metal in the more humble, and less costly, form of pottery.

There seems little doubt that the credit for the introduction of the new lustre processes used by the early nineteenth-century English potters must go to John Hancock, who, writing in a Staffordshire paper in 1846 at the age of eighty-nine, tells of his having carried out such decoration for Mr. Spode and Messrs. Daniel and Brown.

Platinum was used to acquire a lustrous silver effect in various styles, of which the heavy pottery reproduction of silver and plate must be considered one of the less successful. Much lighter and more pleasing effects were obtained by the process referred to as 'resist lustring' (Fig. 2). In this instance, the blue flowers were painted on to the

fired body of the ware (biscuit) prior to the application and firing of the glaze, the under-glaze blue being obtained by using the metallic oxide of cobalt. The painted areas were coated with a waxy solution and the object was then dipped into a prepared platinum solution, which adhered only to the un-protected parts.

An alternative method of decoration was to apply the lustre over the glaze, to which coloured enamel was usually first added by stencilling through prepared paper patterns. The jug illustrated in Figure 3 is today probably the most sought-after type of lustreware; here the silver designs appear to have been applied by hand on to a previously fired canary-yellow enamel ground. Jugs seem to outnumber by far the other objects in this colour, although mugs, plates, vases and figures are known.

The pastille-burner in Figure 4 depicts a well-known model made at the Wedgwood factory in 1805, when the factory was under the direction of Josiah Wedgwood II, son of the founder of the pottery at Burslem in 1759. This pastille-burner, in early classical form, was made at the Etruria factory, where production continued from 1769 until about 1946, when the move to the model factory at Barlaston took place. Lustrewares are rarely

2

3

C. Cannings

4

Museum Photo

5

marked, but to find actual dated pieces, such as this, is exceptional. 2 February, 1805, a date impressed on several examples, obviously commemorated some special event in the history of the factory. The most plausible explanation (put forward by Mrs. Jean Gorely, a well-known American Wedgwood specialist and collector) is that it was on this day that Josiah Wedgwood II was successful in bringing about a sought-after improvement in the pyrometer for the recording of kiln temperatures invented by his father. The coppery lustre effect is acquired by using gold lustre over either a brown earthenware or a black stoneware (basaltes), the use of the latter resulting in a much deeper tone of copper. Wedgwood made the full range of lustre colours, which in most cases can be identified by their consistent use of the name 'WEDGWOOD' impressed into the clay. The Victoria and Albert Museum has an especially attractive silver-resist candlestick of about 1810 bearing a similar mark.

The most common lustrous colour found on wares produced by many factories, in widespread localities, is pink. Pink lustre is obtained from gold and was used in a variety of ways. Gold on a red earthenware results in a copper effect; when this same gold is applied to a white or cream-coloured ground, the result is pink. This can often be proved by looking at the inside of copper-lustre jugs which have a white clay-slip lining on a red body; where the lustre sometimes runs over the rim, it can be seen to become pink in tone. Many shades of pink, ranging from a pale rose to a deep purple, were obtained by varying the thickness of the metallic lustre. The dish in Figure 5 with the painted pink lustre border is a good example of the depth of colour possible on a white ground.

The Wedgwood factory also specialised in a pink lustre applied in an all-over mottled manner, sometimes referred to as 'moonlight lustre'. A whole variety of wares were decorated in this rather garish manner, including shell-shaped wall-pockets, shell-dishes, vases, cups and saucers, jugs and beakers. The peak of the production of these wares was about 1810 to 1815.

The fact that John Hancock claimed to have introduced the English styles of lustre decoration when working for Spode certainly suggests that this was the first Staffordshire factory to produce such pieces. Hancock also makes it clear that Henry Daniel and John Brown of Hanley, who were engaged only in decorating wares made by other

7

8

Museum Photo *Museum Photo*

Fig. 9 **Plate,** *William Rivers factory, Hanley, Staffordshire, c.1818–22. Painted in pink lustre on a white earthenware body, marked 'RIVERS', impressed, diameter $8\frac{1}{4}$ ins. (Victoria and Albert Museum.)*

Fig. 10 **Teapot,** *probably John Davenport & Co., of Longport, Staffordshire, c.1820–25. Platinum lustre, impressed anchor mark, height $5\frac{3}{4}$ ins. (Victoria and Albert Museum, London.)*

Fig. 11 **Jug,** *Staffordshire, c.1830–31. Decorated with a black transfer-print of George IV under a pink lustre wash, and inscribed 'TO THE MEMORY OF HIS LATE MAJESTY KING GEORGE IV', height $5\frac{1}{2}$ ins. (Victoria and Albert Museum.)*

Museum Photo

Museum Photo

Fig. 12 **Bowl**, 'MOORE & CO.
Southwick', Sunderland,
c.1810–20. Printed on one side
with a poem and on the other
with an oval panel containing a
scene entitled 'A East View of the
Cast Iron Bridge over the River
Wear built by R. Burdon, M.P./
Span 236 feet height 100.
Begun Sepr 1793. Open'd
9 Augt 1796', diameter 5¼ ins.
(Victoria and Albert Museum.)

potters, were through his help similarly engaged. Spode seemingly favoured the splashed type of pink lustre, some of which is impressed 'SPODE', but no examples of silver lustre are recorded with a similar mark.

Apart from these major concerns mentioned, numerous other Staffordshire potters were engaged in producing wares in the popular lustres during the first half of the nineteenth century. Marked examples are known by the following: Bailey & Batkin (1814–c.1827), Bailey & Harvey (1833–35), David Wilson (c.1802–18), Thomas Lakin (1812–c.1817), Shorthose (1807–23), Peter Warburton (1802–12), Thomas Harley (1802–8), Copeland & Garrett (1833–47), Thomas Minton (from 1793) and Ralph Stevenson (c.1810–32). In all, there were about seventy potters engaged in this work.

The cup and saucer in Figure 1 is of a type usually attributed to the New Hall factory, which finally ceased in 1835. The Staffordshire jug in Figure 11, with a black transfer-print under a pink lustre wash, commemorates the death of George IV. It is an interesting confirmation of the change in style of the jugs of the second quarter of the nineteenth century: the bold robust form of the earlier wares gave way to the fussier Revived Rococo, which did not offer the same appropriate areas of plain surfaces for decorating. Such pieces rarely bear marks, and attribution to any particular potter is usually impossible.

Perhaps one of the best-known types of lustreware is that illustrated in Figure 8. Such plates, with basket-pattern borders, are attributed on the evidence of recorded marked examples to the Cambrian Pottery, Swansea. Although a pottery existed in the area from about 1764, it was between 1802 and 1810, during the partnership of George Haynes and Lewis Weston Dillwyn, that the production of finer and more distinctive wares was introduced. The output of lustrewares from this Swansea pottery was certainly not considerable; they can usually be dated to about 1820 to 1840, when the factory was under the sole charge of Dillwyn. The pottery was taken over by Evans and Glasson in 1850. Although plates such as this are most characteristic, many lustred mugs, jugs and cream-jugs in the form of cows were produced.

Sunderland, in Tyne and Wear, is probably the best-known pottery centre associated with early nineteenth-century lustreware. Many of the wares produced by about six of the major companies in the area were marked, and attribution is often a little easier than with Staffordshire wares. One of these was the North Hylton Pottery, originally established in 1762 by William Maling. This factory remained in the hands of the Maling family until taken over in 1815 by an earlier manager of the concern, John Phillips. Phillips was already running the Sunderland, or Garrison, factory, which he had leased in 1807 from Thornhill & Co., the previous owners. Both these factories were continued by the family, under different partnerships, until final closure, the Garrison Pottery in 1864 and the North Hylton Pottery in 1867.

The North Hylton Pottery is reputed to be the first undertaking in the north of England to decorate wares with transfer-prints, of which the view of the famous iron bridge of 1796 is undoubtedly the most popular. There are in all a total of about twenty-seven versions of this historic construction, which in some cases can be dated by accompanying details. Five of the later views were engraved after the reconstruction of the bridge in 1859 (Figs. 7 and 12).

During the partnership of Dixon, Austin & Co., (1820–26), many other lustrewares, now popular with collectors, were made, including figures of Joan of Arc, Napoleon, the Duke of Wellington, Nelson and John Wesley. It is interesting to note that this factory also produced carpet-bowls, used for an indoor game of bowls and usually only associated with Scottish factories.

Collectors must be cautioned against reproductions of many of the more popular lustrewares that have been produced during more recent years by such Staffordshire factories as A. E. Gray & Co. Ltd. (1934–61), and the even better-known firm of William Kent of Burslem, who made many reproductions of early models until 1962.

MUSEUMS AND COLLECTIONS

English lustrewares of the early nineteenth century may be seen at the following:

GREAT BRITAIN

Barlaston:	Wedgwood Museum (appointment necessary)
Cambridge:	Fitzwilliam Museum
London:	British Museum
	Victoria and Albert Museum
Newcastle:	Laing Art Gallery and Museum

U.S.A.

Fairfield, Conn.:	Fairfield Historical Society
Neehan, Wisc.:	John Nelson Bergstrom Art Center and Museum
Washington D.C.:	Smithsonian Institution
Winterthur, Del.:	Henry Francis du Pont Winterthur Museum

FURTHER READING

Old English Lustre Ware by John Bedford, London, 1965.
Old English Lustre Pottery by W. D. John and Warren Baker, Newport, Mon., 1951.
Collecting Old English Lustre by Jeanette R. Hodgson, Portland, Maine, 1937.
Pink Lustre Pottery by Dr. Atwood Thorne, London, 1926.

 # Transfer-printed Ceramics

Robert Chapman

Fig. 1 **Plate**, *Wedgwood, c.1809. Cream-coloured earthenware, printed, painted and gilt with the water-lily pattern in brown, marked with 'Wedgwood' impressed, diameter 8 ins. Part of the Darwin service, this plate has a version of the water-lily pattern which was only made between 1808 and 1811. The pattern was later produced in blue, red and polychrome. (Victoria and Albert Museum, London.)*

Fig. 2 **Souvenir plate**, *Evans and Glasson, Swansea, mid-nineteenth century. Transfer-printed with a view of St. Michael's Mount, Cornwall, marked 'EVANS & GLASSON SWANSEA' in a triangle, impressed, diameter 6 ins. (Private Collection.)*

Fig. 3 **Plate**, *possibly Staffordshire, mid-nineteenth century. Transfer-printed with a puppy, unmarked, diameter 3⅜ ins. This plate may have been part of a child's tea-set of the type made in Staffordshire and elsewhere. (Private Collection.)*

Fig. 4 **Plate**, *English, mid-nineteenth century. The centre transfer-printed, the moulded flowers in the border painted by hand, diameter 5¼ ins. The moral for young and old reads: 'We cannot spend time better than learning to spend it well'. (Private Collection.)*

First practised at Worcester, the technique of transfer-printing on ceramics soon spread to the other factories, where it generated new and attractive forms and patterns for an eager market

The process of transfer-printing on chinaware originated, so far as is known at present, in or about 1751. In that year, an Irish-born engraver, John Brooks, who was then living in Birmingham, attempted to patent an invention for printing decoration on both enamel and china.

Printing on ceramics was first carried out on porcelain at Worcester. There, some jugs and other articles were produced bearing on them a portrait in black of King Frederick the Great of Prussia, with the initials of the engraver, Robert Hancock, and the date 1757 (Fig. 6). Soon afterwards the same factory and several others were busily manufacturing large quantities of blue-printed ware in close imitation of that currently being imported from China: this last was decorated by hand before application of the glaze, has an unbroken glossy surface and is known as 'under-glaze blue'. In contrast, other colours are more sensitive to heat, so were put on after the glaze was fired; they are termed 'over-glaze' colours.

Under-glaze blue decoration was possible because cobalt blue resists the change in heat needed to melt the glaze. It allowed the decoration to be applied before the glaze was fired.

The exploiters of the virtues of cobalt were the Chinese, whose blue-painted Nanking ware had been exported to Europe in increasing quantities since the late sixteenth century. Brought to the West by the various national trading companies, it was comparatively cheap and more satisfactory for daily use than any ware of European make available at the time.

The scene changed, however, when Josiah Wedgwood made substantial improvements in the composition and manufacturing processes of his local Staffordshire pottery. By 1780 he had introduced a whitened version of his celebrated creamware, and before long it was found that the new china, named by him 'Pearl ware' and quickly imitated by other potters, formed an excellent background for blue printing.

In brief, the process involved engraving on copper plates in much the same manner as was done for book-illustrations, but using special ink and paper for the printing. The paper was a strong, thin tissue which conformed to the shape of an article when it was pressed on to it for transferring the ink impression. The piece of china to be decorated was given an initial firing in the kiln, and was in this biscuit state when the transfer was applied. After this it was again fired to remove oils in the ink, and then coated with glaze and given a third, final firing.

The earliest surviving examples of the process as used on pottery date from the early 1780s, and among them is the long-popular willow pattern. It is said to have been first used by Thomas Turner at the Caughley factory in Shropshire, to which he had gone after being a pupil of Hancock at Worcester. Traditionally, the design was created by Turner and engraved by his apprentice, Thomas Minton, who later established a factory of his own.

The willow pattern, which is not copied directly from any known Chinese original, is very close in its superficial resemblance to imported Nanking work. It must have caught the imagination of the public, and was so greatly in demand that innumerable other makers copied it, with variations, at the time and subsequently (Fig. 9).

There was a very rapid increase in the spending-power of the population as the nineteenth century advanced; blue-printed pottery became immensely popular and there were few factories in Staffordshire which did not make it in quantity. New patterns were continually introduced, while the shapes of plates, dishes, tureens and other pieces varied from time to time according to prevailing fashion for classical simplicity or rococo curves.

Chinese-inspired designs lost favour and were replaced by European scenes, many of them copied from engravings in books, and it is an interesting exercise to trace examples to the particular volumes in which they first appeared. For instance a Spode plate shows a view of the bridge at Solaro, near Rome, copied from a plate in a book of views of the city and its vicinity published in 1797–98. The attractive floral border resembles many others in general appearance, although most of them differ in detail. They are a feature which was once thought to provide a definite clue to identification of the maker, but this is not true in every instance.

Fig. 5 *Commemorative mug*, *English, c.1852. Transfer-printed in blue-black with 'The Duke [of Wellington] at Waterloo' and on the reverse with a view of Walmer Castle, Kent, where the Duke died on 14 September, 1852, height 3¼ ins. (Private Collection.)*

Fig. 6 *Tankard by Robert Hancock, Worcester, 1757. Porcelain, transfer-printed in black with a portrait of Frederick, King of Prussia, initialled by Hancock and dated, height 4⅝ ins. (Private Collection.)*

Fig. 7 *Egg-cups and holder, English, mid-nineteenth century. Transfer-printed in blue with a Chinese pattern, height 5¼ ins. Although Chinese-inspired designs eventually lost favour and were replaced by European scenes, they were very popular at this period. (Private Collection.)*

Fig. 8 *Soup-plate, Wedgwood, early nineteenth century. Transfer-printed with a design of a Chinese vase standing on a table amid flowers and bamboos, marked 'WEDGWOOD', impressed, diameter 9¾ ins. (Private Collection.)*

The designers and engravers were often independent craftsmen who worked simultaneously for several factories, and it was quite common for a pleasing border or centre pattern to be copied and used by several factories.

The Wedgwood firm's first blue-printed wares came on the market in about 1805, when Spode and Minton were both engaged in supplying the demand for them. Old Josiah Wedgwood died in 1795, and had, it was later reported, stoutly refused to make any such ware because of solicitations from his painters, who feared it would result in their dismissal. It was when his son Josiah II was head of the pottery that a change took place, and it was realised that they must cater for the prevailing fashion or lose a considerable amount of worthwhile business. In late 1805 and early 1806 there are references in surviving letters to the firm's embarking on services decorated with 'the Chinese figure in the centre' and the 'New Chinese pattern with Urn', which are most probably one and the same: the pattern on the plate in Figure 8.

Very soon afterwards engraved floral patterns of distinctive types were introduced, some of which were also taken from book-illustrations. It is thought that John Wedgwood, eldest son of Josiah I, may have been responsible for their use, as he was a very keen botanist and in 1804 assisted in founding the Royal Horticultural Society.

From about 1808 the same firm occasionally used an unusual colour for their printing: a brown, varying in intensity from piece to piece (Fig. 1). The ware was sold after being embellished with hand-painting at the factory, no doubt to compensate for the uneven tints. Gilding was added to heighten the effect of the pattern, but it proved too expensive to sell in quantity.

The Staffordshire firms exported large amounts of blue-printed ware, not only to the British Colonies but also to the recently independent United States, which did its best to manufacture all its own requirements. However, the imported pottery proved unbeatable for quality and price. Some of the Staffordshire makers concentrated on that market, decorating their goods with patterns engraved for the purpose. These showed views of buildings in many cities, steamboats, ships and, not least, portraits of George Washington and succeeding presidents.

A series of pieces bearing the arms of the various States was made by Thomas Mayer, of Shelton, and, like a majority of the wares destined for the market, it is in a noticeably deep blue. In contrast, porcelain for home sale, at least after 1830, was often so pale in colour that it can be mistaken for faulty manufacture. From about the same date, printing in pink and shades of green also became popular. Towards the end of the century, dark blue was favoured in England, and was usually given a 'flown', or blurred, effect to suit the taste of the time.

A further development occurred in the 1840s when the firm of F. & R. Pratt, of Fenton, successfully introduced multi-colour printing. It was achieved by engraving each colour on a separate copper plate, with the finished work normally comprising red, blue, yellow and black or brown. Carefully arranged and engraved in stipple (small dots) the finished work could show a full range of colours; gilding was sometimes added.

The most familiar employment of Pratt's process was for decorating the curved lids of flat pots used for the packing of all kinds of products, from pomade to meat paste. In some instances the subject on the lid referred to the contents; for example,

Author's Photo

Robert Chapman

Robert Chapman

a scene of shrimpers at work denoted shrimp or prawn paste, while a man shooting a bear implied a hair-preparation compounded from bear's grease. Others reproduced popular oil-paintings by well-known artists, contemporary and otherwise, including Gainsborough, Wilkie and Landseer.

Needless to say, the firm of Pratt soon had imitators. The range of products was extended to include tea- and dessert-services, vases, pottery-framed pictures and bread-platters, many of which bore the same decoration as the pot-lids. The superiority of Pratt's productions lay in the great skill of their engraver, Jesse Austin, who sometimes signed his work with his name in full or with his initials. Many of the original copper plates engraved by Austin and others were rediscovered at the beginning of the present century and put to use again. They then appeared on a type of pottery somewhat different in composition from the original, with a tendency to show fine cracks all over the glaze, a condition known as 'crazing'.

A further use for transfer-printing came about in the second half of the nineteenth century, when patterns were executed in outline in a reddish-brown colour and then over-painted by hand. The resulting wares were very much cheaper to produce than if they had been completely painted by skilled artists. The process was often employed on porcelain, and at a glance the work can easily pass as having been executed entirely by hand.

Cheaper still was the use of transfers printed in a full range of colours by means of lithography: a printing process relying on the natural antipathy of

97

Robert Chapman

Fig. 9 **Dish,** *Bovey Tracey Pottery, Devon, mid-nineteenth century. Transfer-printed (somewhat carelessly at the edges) with the willow pattern, width 15½ ins. (Private Collection.)*

Fig. 10 **Cheese-dish and cover,** *English, second half of the nineteenth century. Transfer-printed in under-glaze blue and hand-painted over the glaze in red and gold, height 8½ ins. (Private Collection.)*

oil and water. The desired pattern is drawn with a greasy crayon on porous stone; when damped and rolled over with oil-based ink the latter will adhere only to the crayon marks. Paper in contact with the inked surface comes away bearing an imprint, and this can be repeated with any number of colours as required. Litho-printed patterns are usually recognisable by their sharp outlines and an absence of brush-strokes. It is true to say they are generally found only on articles of inferior quality.

Mention should be made of the so-called 'bat printing', a process used on porcelain in the early years of the nineteenth century. It involved the use of a plate engraved mainly in stipple, but an oil was employed in place of ink and printing took place on a thin slab, or 'bat', of glue. The bat was a little less flexible than paper, and the process was completed by dusting the oil-printed design with powdered pigment. It resulted in a very delicate picture with fine lines and dots, and it was used over the glaze in black or orange.

Queen Victoria's reign saw the increasing use of trade-marks on all types of merchandise, and a much larger proportion of pottery and porcelain was marked than had hitherto been the case. The marks, of many varieties, were mostly printed; on pottery the majority of marks consisted of the initials of the maker within a decorative framing, with or without the addition of the name of the pattern or a reference number. The presence of the royal coat of arms is not uncommon, as it was adopted by a number of makers apparently for patriotic reasons, not because they were in a privileged position. Another mark found frequently is the Staffordshire knot, which was combined with initials by a number of the county's potters. The various initials can usually be deciphered by referring to one of the available books of marks which list their names and when they were active. The word 'England' was added to marks from 1891 and the legend 'Made in England' came into use during the twentieth century. In addition to the willow pattern, quite a number of others have enjoyed a long life or have been revived from time to time. The later copies can often be recognised by their inferior quality and a study of any marks will generally settle remaining doubts.

MUSEUMS AND COLLECTIONS
Most museums in England have pieces of nineteenth-century transfer-printed pottery and porcelain on display or in their reserve collections.

FURTHER READING
Blue and White Transfer Ware, 1780–1840 by A. W. Coysh, Newton Abbot, 1970.
Staffordshire Blue by W. L. Little, London, 1969.
'Underglaze blue-printed Earthenware with particular reference to Spode' by J. K. des Fontaines in **Transactions of the English Ceramic Circle,** Vol. 7, Part 2, 1969.

Robert Chapman

 # American Porcelain

Although there were attempts at producing true porcelain in the Colonies before the Revolution, most wares were imported from England and China until 1825

The material culture of Colonial America was, quite understandably, complex. Such varied factors as geographical isolation, English colonial policy and an ever expanding frontier contributed to the composition of a society which differed in many ways from that of England. However, by the mid-eighteenth century some parts of the Colonies had developed to the point where a respectable emulation of English social patterns was possible. In such places as Boston, Philadelphia and the great plantations of tidewater Virginia, a rather high level of material culture was maintained by the well-to-do. Porcelain was included in the many possessions that enabled the prosperous Colonial American to live in a style comparable to his counterparts in England. Two broad generalisations serve to describe the situation. First, virtually all the porcelain in use was imported. Second, this porcelain was predominantly Chinese, though some English porcelain was imported at the end of the Colonial period.

In recent years, archaeological research has enabled American scholars to arrive at firm conclusions about the type of Chinese porcelain imported by Americans during the period from about 1725 to 1775. Excavations of widespread Colonial sites reveal a remarkably consistent pattern. Blue and white Chinese porcelain decorated with stylised landscape scenes or with foliate motifs was predominant. Of course these porcelains, decorated only in under-glaze blue, were cheaper than the more elaborate over-glaze enamelled pieces. Wasters from Colonial sites indicate that much of this simple blue and white porcelain was of reasonably good quality – thinly potted and well painted. In general, pieces from tea- and dinner-services have been most frequently found in archaeological sites, but punch-bowls and mugs are not uncommon. Contemporary newspaper advertisements provide further evidence of a substantial and well-established trade in Chinese porcelain by the middle of the eighteenth century. For example in 1767 a New York china vendor advertised 'India China, enamelled and blue and white Bowls, Caudle Cups, etc., . . . Nankin China Mugs, Salt Cellers, etc., etc.'

Though blue and white Chinese export wares comprised the main body of porcelain used in Colonial America, more expensive porcelains were not uncommon. Archaeology, documented pieces and literary sources all establish that some fine over-glaze, polychrome-enamelled Chinese porcelains also were present in limited quantities. More modestly decorated polychrome wares were present in greater numbers, and fine punch-bowls seem to have been in common use by the time of the Revolution. It should be remembered that during the Colonial period there was no direct American trade with China, and that imported Chinese goods came in via England.

On a considerably smaller scale, English porcelain, especially the cheaper blue and white

wares, was imported after the middle of th century. As with the Chinese porcelain, tea- an coffee-services or part-services and dinner ware were predominant. Much of the blue and whit English porcelain found during archaeologica excavations is from Worcester or from the severa Liverpool factories. This is significant, as Bristo (near Worcester) and Liverpool were the two chie English ports serving the American trade. Even o the frontier in the midst of the American wildernes some of the English seem to have maintained relatively high material culture. In the wealthie parts of the Colonies, it is quite probable that fin English porcelain was present in limited quantitie For example, the documentary sources relating t Colonial Williamsburg, Virginia, mention Chelse figures.

Though Colonial Americans imported nearly all c their fine ceramics, local potteries soon appeared i the settled areas. Supplying nearby markets, thes small potteries made coarse earthenware an stoneware for everyday use. Little was attempted i the way of better ceramics, though some creamwar and possibly some delftware was produced befor the Revolution. Ambiguous documentary source

2

Fig. 1 (Previous page) *Jug*, *Tucker factory, Philadelphia, c.1830. Height 8½ ins. As with most Tucker wares, the decoration on this jug is in the French manner. (Smithsonian Institution, Washington D.C.)*

Fig. 2 *Mug and bowl*, *Chinese export, c.1800. Decorated with the Great Seal of the United States, the borders of the Nanking pattern. Height of mug 6 ins, diameter of bowl 7⅝ ins. (Smithsonian Institution.)*

Fig. 3 *Sweetmeat-dish*, *Bonnin and Morris factory, Philadelphia, c.1771. Height 5½ ins. (Smithsonian Institution.)*

Fig. 4 *Plate*, *Sèvres, 1785. Cornflower pattern, length 10 ins. This was used as state china by John Adams, the second President. (Smithsonian Institution.)*

Fig. 5 *Bowl*, *Niderviller, c.1780–82. Diameter 10 ins. This bowl is from a dinner service presented to George Washington by the Comte de Custine of Niderviller. (Smithsonian Institution.)*

Fig. 6 *Plate*, *Chinese export, c.1775–90. Decorated in blue and white with a standard landscape. Length 14 ins. This blue and white service also belonged to George Washington. (Smithsonian Institution.)*

5

6

suggest the possibility that porcelain was made at an earlier date, but the first proved manufactory was established in Philadelphia in 1770 by Gouse Bonnin and George Morris. This pioneering commercial effort was short lived, the factory surviving only two years. The blue and white soft-paste porcelain made by Bonnin and Morris was roughly in the style of Worcester. From the fewer than twenty pieces that have been identified to date, it appears that this porcelain was of reasonably satisfactory quality and that the modelling and painting were better than might be expected. The diminutive sweetmeat-dish in Figure 3 is representative of Bonnin and Morris porcelain. Sauce-boats, baskets, covered jars and cups and saucers are also known. But, with the one minor exception of Bonnin and Morris of Philadelphia, all pre-revolutionary American porcelain appears to have been imported.

With the conclusion of the Revolution and the advent of the new republic, the situation did not change to any great extent. Possibly one might have expected the immediate, full-blown birth of an American porcelain industry. Such was not the case. The technology, the impetus and the know-how simply were not present. Rather, the pre-revolutionary situation persisted. Chinese porcelain was imported in even greater quantity, but now directly from Canton in American ships. The dominance of the English in the overall American ceramic market was interrupted only by the Revolution. After 1785 an increasing stream of creamware, pearlware, stoneware and porcelain poured across the ocean and England's profitable ceramic trade with the newly born United States has continued to the present time.

During the Revolution a fine Niderviller service was presented to George Washington

In the particular area of porcelain, the only notable change was a minor one. The French, who had assisted the Colonies during the Revolution, were able to sell some porcelain to America. This trade was limited, and it appears that a good proportion of the surviving French porcelain owned by Americans during the early republic was purchased by Americans in France or imported to special order. One of the more important French porcelain services acquired during this period is the Sèvres dinner-service purchased by John Adams, the second President of the United States. Adams acquired this service before 1800 (it has 1783, 1784 and 1785 date-letters in the mark) and used it as his state china when he became President. The rather commonplace cornflower pattern on the service shown on the plate, in Figure 4, perhaps reflects New England restraint.

In fact, as early as 1782, while the Revolution was still in progress, the Comte de Custine, proprietor of the Niderviller factory, presented a fine porcelain service to George Washington (Fig. 5). Thus, contrary to the general trend in which English and Chinese porcelains dominated, American Presidents from Washington until Lincoln frequently exercised an option for dinner-services of French porcelain. Sèvres, Niderviller, Rue d'Angoulême, Dagoty and Nast are all represented in what survives of the presidential china of the early republic. Presidential taste was not necessarily

101

Fig. 7 *Vase, Chinese export, c.1850. Decorated with polychrome painting in the 'rose medallion' style.*
Height 15½ ins.
After about 1825, the quantity and quality of Chinese export porcelain declined. A new form of decoration became popular, called 'rose medallion' which was characterised by compartmentalised foliate motifs, exotic birds and scenes with figures.
(Smithsonian Institution.)

Fig. 8 *Vase, Tucker factory, Philadelphia, c.1830. Painted and gilt decoration.*
Height 14⅛ ins.
Started in about 1825 by William Ellis Tucker, this factory produced the first true porcelain in America, and the factory continued, under various names, chiefly Tucker and Hemphill, until 1838. The style of decoration on the white, hard-paste wares was much influenced by French designs, as seen on this neo-classical urn which owes its inspiration to Sèvres products of this period. The establishment of the Tucker factory marked the beginning of a flourishing porcelain industry in the United States.
(American Museum in Britain, Claverton Manor, near Bath.)

Fig. 9 *Cup and saucer, Tucker factory, c.1830. The cup, twelve-faceted and decorated with a stylised vine motif. Height 2½ ins. The saucer sixteen-faceted and picked out in gilt. Diameter 5½ ins. Made during the Tucker-Hulme partnership, this cup and saucer are part of a service made for the Hulme family. The saucer has an incised mark on the base.*
(John Judkyn Memorial, Freshford Manor, near Bath.)

Fig. 10 *Jug, Tucker factory, 1828. Painted with polychrome flowers and gilt. Height 9 ins. The initials 'ES' painted in gilt under the spout are believed to be for the original owner, Elizabeth Slater.*
(American Museum in Britain.)

reflected in the American market. Advertisements by china sellers in late eighteenth-century American newspapers were common, but in nearly every instance only Chinese and English porcelain were mentioned. Occasionally it is possible to discover an advertisement such as one in a New York paper in 1796 offering 'a few French China table sets'. Thus, the conclusion must be that the market for French porcelain in the early republic was relatively limited.

Larger amounts of English porcelain were imported, and most of this was probably blue and white until after 1800 when polychrome porcelain became somewhat less expensive. Though specific references are unusual, some of the post-Revolutionary advertisements do provide helpful information. For example in 1791 a Baltimore china vendor reported that he had for sale 'Liverpool China, in Boxes'. The various Liverpool manufactories had a slight competitive edge in that they were located in a seaport engaged in the American trade.

As a matter of logic, it would seem likely that the early years of the nineteenth century saw some incursion into the American market by the burgeoning porcelain factories of Germany, but such was not the case. Contemporary literary sources, business records and archaeological investigations all indicate that practically no German porcelain was exported to the United States during this period. A notable exception – again pointing to the fact that the White House was atypical – was a Meissen/Berlin family service belonging to John Quincy Adams, the sixth President (1824–28). This service, decorated in under-glaze blue with the decoration known as 'onion pattern', once again indicates a certain predilection for blue and white.

William Ellis Tucker was the pioneer of the porcelain industry in the U.S.A.

All contemporary evidence indicates quite strongly that Chinese export porcelain continued to be the porcelain most commonly in use during the years after the Revolution. As with the other types previously discussed, blue and white was predominant, but the quality of paste, glaze and decoration was generally inferior to pre-revolutionary imports. Though the trade was primarily in American ships after 1785, little else differed. America's China trade was essentially the same as that conducted from Canton by various European countries or their trading companies.

Most wares were decorated in stock patterns and imported for sale by china dealers in the coastal cities or for sale at dockside auction. An example of this sort of ware can be found in a large blue and white platter decorated with an unexceptional Chinese landscape scene (Fig. 6). This plate was part of a service owned by George Washington. Of more interest were services made or decorated specially to order in Canton. Sometimes these contained patriotic scenes or symbols. A bowl and mug (Fig. 2), decorated with polychrome versions of the Great Seal of the United States, typify this genre. Other services were made with standard patterns and borders, but individually embellished with the owners' monograms.

A number of pieces of exceptional Chinese export porcelain made especially for the American market have survived. Most have more historical interest than aesthetic merit. In this category are pieces from George Washington's 'Society of the Cincinnati' service. The Society of the Cincinnati was a select fraternity made up of ex-officers who had served in the Revolution. Several services of Chinese export porcelain were decorated with versions of the Cincinnati emblem, and one was acquired by Washington. Although the iconography is pedestrian and the border common for that time, the association with Washington seems compelling, and pieces from this service command exceptional prices.

After about 1825, as the China trade declined and as the quality of Chinese export porcelain also declined, a new decorative style termed 'rose medallion' became popular. The large vase in Figure 7, dating from the middle of the nineteenth century, is typical of this class.

After 1820 English and, to a lesser degree, French porcelains maintained a substantial share of the American market. As the China trade fell off, the United States made tentative steps towards establishing its own porcelain industry. As noted earlier, an abortive venture – that of Bonnin and Morris of Philadelphia – had endured for only two years, about 1770–72. After the Revolution, a few more inconsequential attempts seem to have been made, but it was not until 1825 that a degree of commercial success in porcelain manufacturing was achieved. Again, the place was Philadelphia. There, William Ellis Tucker, the son of a successful china seller, established a factory which continued until 1838. Both in form and in decoration, Tucker porcelain was inclined to be influenced by the French (Figs. 1, 8, 9 and 10).

After the breakthrough by Tucker, American porcelain manufactories began to establish themselves, and by 1875 the United States had a true porcelain industry. But, as has been shown, this was slow in coming. The history of porcelain in America – both before and immediately after the Revolution – is essentially the history of porcelain imported from China and Europe.

MUSEUMS AND COLLECTIONS

American porcelain and imported pieces may be seen at the following:

GREAT BRITAIN

Bath:	American Museum in Britain, Claverton Manor
London:	Victoria and Albert Museum

U.S.A.

New York:	Metropolitan Museum of Art
Washington D.C.:	Smithsonian Institution
Williamsburg, Va.:	Colonial Williamsburg
Winterthur, Del.:	H. F. du Pont Winterthur Museum

FURTHER READING

Eighteenth Century Ceramics from Fort Michilimackinac by J. Jefferson Miller II and Lyle M. Stone, Washington, 1970.
Here Lies Virginia by Ivor Noel Hume, New York, 1963.
Chinese Export Porcelain for the American Trade by Jean M. Mudge, Newark, Del., 1962.
The Pottery and Porcelain of the United States by Edwin A. Barber, New York, 1909.

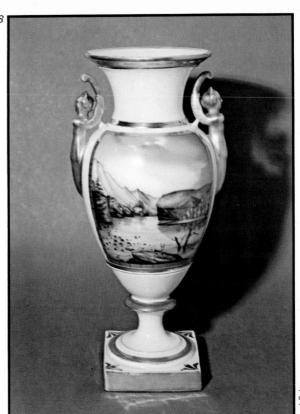

8

9

10

Staffordshire Figures

A. C. Cooper

Fig. 1 **Watch-holder**, Staffordshire, c.1850. Pottery decorated with the complete range of colours, height 10¼ ins. This watch-holder illustrates a typically maudlin legend, in which Llewelyn, Prince of North Wales, slew his faithful hound, Gelert, thinking the dog had attacked his baby son and heir. The child had, in fact, been dragged to safety by Gelert, and the blood Llewelyn had seen was that of a wolf from which he had saved the baby. (Oliver Sutton Antiques, London.)

Fig. 2 **Theatrical figure** by John Lloyd of Shelton, Staffordshire, c.1840. Porcelain, height 12 ins. It represents an early opera or melodrama, possibly Artaxerxes by Thomas Arne. (Oliver Sutton Antiques.)

A treasure-house of gaily painted, primitively moulded figures, made throughout Queen Victoria's reign, awaits the collector of Staffordshire groups

When Queen Victoria came to the throne in 1837, a new kind of pottery, unlike any which had preceded it, began to appear in that area of north Staffordshire which we call the 'Potteries'. Book after book has given the beginning of the Queen's reign as the date when this dramatic change of style took place. It is as though the girl Queen had sat up in bed one morning in Kensington Palace and said to her mother, the Duchess of Kent, 'Mama, I am quite tired of Mr. Walton's dreary little sheep and lambs, and Mr. Sherratt's horrid bull-baiting groups. I have decided to start a new style, with simple, oval bases and lots of lovely cobalt blue, and while I'm at it, I want a bedroom of my own'.

In fact, such figures had first appeared in the 1820s, and the change of style was, as always, gradual. Figures in the manner of Walton, with

the stylised leafy tree (bocage) as a background, continued to be made after 1837, and the rustic groups in the manner of Obadiah Sherratt continued until the middle of the century. By the beginning of Victoria's reign the new style was gaining in popularity and vast numbers of figures were produced of varying interest and quality.

Staffordshire figures made in the eighteenth century have attracted collectors for many years; they can be very expensive and most of the finest are in private collections or museums. It was inevitable, therefore, that collectors should turn to the nineteenth century. They little expected the treasure-house that was awaiting them.

The earliest collectors of these Victorian-style figures are recorded in the first decade of this present century, but no serious work of research was published until much later, in the 1950s. The result has been that collectors have inherited a great deal of inaccurate and misleading information passed on by word of mouth. Myths and legends die hard, and some appear to have acquired near immortality. Before sorting the wheat from the chaff, let us see how the figures differed from their predecessors and how they developed during the century. They were made from a much whiter clay

Fig. 3 **Two figures of Garibaldi** *by Thomas Parr, Staffordshire, c.1861. Heights 8¾ and 14½ ins. Both these figures of the great Italian revolutionary Garibaldi, were based on a print in a supplement to the Illustrated London News dated 26 January, 1861. Their maker, Thomas Parr, modelled fine, complex figures in the round well into the flat-back period. These groups were expensive even when they were first made. (Oliver Sutton Antiques.)*

Fig. 4 **Sailor and boy,** *Staffordshire, c.1854. Height 15½ ins. This is a rare example of a fine Staffordshire group. (Oliver Sutton Antiques.)*

Fig. 5 **Two figures of Little Red Riding Hood,** *Staffordshire, c.1848. Height 7½ ins. The group on the left is very rare; that on the right is one of a matching pair. (Oliver Sutton Antiques.)*

than the Walton and Sherratt groups; they were brightly decorated with passages of under-glaze cobalt blue and a wide variety of cheerful over-glaze enamel colours and much use was made of good quality gold decoration. It is wrong to group them together and call them 'Staffordshire pottery', for many of them were porcellaneous and a great number of other clay bodies was also used.

Made from plaster-of-Paris moulds, the primitive back-street Victorian potters showed great ingenuity in producing an apparently complicated figure from quite simple moulds. That they were forced into simplicity of line by the economics of the potting is our good fortune and does nothing to detract from their achievement. As the century progressed, figures gradually stopped being moulded in the round and developed into flat-back figures

Fig. 6 *Austria's head lie there,*
Staffordshire, c.1820. Porcelain,
height 6½ ins.
This fine pre-Victorian figure
represents the actor Mr. Holmes
as Faulconbridge in
Shakespeare's King John, *Act III,*
Scene II.
(Oliver Sutton Antiques.)

Fig. 7 *Clock piece,*
Staffordshire, c.1848.
Height 9½ ins.
This delightful group of
unknown dancers, probably
performers at a travelling
fairground theatre, is a good
example of the ingenuity of the
Staffordshire potters. It shows
their skill at producing
apparently complicated figures
from a simple two-piece mould.
Such clock pieces were often
bought by working-class people
who could not afford real clocks
on their mantels.
(Oliver Sutton Antiques.)

Author's Photo

intended to be viewed from the front only, usually on a mantelpiece above the fireplace (Fig. 1). After 1860 the colours tended to become more subdued and, although many of the figures continued to be brilliantly designed and carefully decorated, much less use was made of the intense cobalt blue. These are their main physical aspects, but their real significance lies in the subjects chosen by the potters.

The neo-classical influence of Wedgwood and the Wood family and the rustic tradition of Walton and Sherratt were the main forces at work in the first quarter of the nineteenth century. On mantelpieces all over England, sheep and lambs were protected by slightly hyperthyroid shepherds and shepherdesses. *The Four Seasons* jostled for attention with *Diana* and *Apollo*; *Faith, Hope and Charity* bore silent witness to the liberality of *Ceres* and *Pomona*, and *Andromache* mourned interminably over the ashes of *Hector*. Village boys and girls demurely displayed their proficiency in reading, not daring to raise their eyes to the sour-faced gaze of *John Wesley*. Bulls and bears were baited; sailors said *Farewell*, but *Returned* in time to take their place beside *Elijah* and the *Widow of Zarapeth*.

Around 1820 to 1840, one small but important group of figures appears. They are so completely different from their rustic and neo-classical contemporaries that some authorities have dated them to the period 1840 to 1845. They share many of the characteristics of the early Victorian figures, including the whiter body-clay, cobalt blue and gold decoration. They are fine quality, often porcellaneous, with a simple, solid base on which the figure is supported by a short column, and they are moulded in the round so that they may be viewed from any angle (Fig. 6). Slightly later examples are closer still to the Victorian style except that the base is often left open.

Just as the eighteenth-century bocage figures of Chelsea and Derby had influenced the Walton school, the nineteenth-century theatrical figures of Derby and Rockingham were reflected in these pre-Victorian Staffordshire figures which appeared in about 1820. As more and more workers were swept into the towns by the late tide of the Industrial Revolution, the demand for entertainment grew and created new gods and goddesses, and it was to the world of entertainment that the Staffordshire potters now turned for inspiration. Madame Vestris had ousted Minerva and, in doing so, had established the new age and the new style. It seems only fitting that one of her greatest successes was to be called *Olympic Revels.*

Models of the young Queen greeted Victoria's accession

Many of these early figures have been mistaken for Rockingham and even today collectors will often find them being offered for sale as such. The Rockingham factory produced porcelain for only sixteen years, from 1826 to its closure in 1842. All the figures were marked beneath the base with the Rockingham Griffin and/or 'ROCKINGHAM WORKS, BRAMELD', together with an incised mould-number from 1 to 120. If the figure is very small, it may carry only the mould-number and an unidentified code C1 1, 2, 3, 4, etc., up to 15. If the figure does not conform to these standards, it will almost certainly be Staffordshire porcelain and has every right to be judged as such, on its own merits, for some of them are very fine indeed (Fig. 2).

The accession of the young Queen, of course, gave a tremendous boost to the potters and many figures were made of her and her family, although the theatre continued to inspire the potters throughout the century. Many such figures were copied by the modellers from prints, thus making it sometimes possible to identify an untitled figure. Lithographed music-covers, prints in the *Illustrated London News*, and in books, were all used in this way. The solving of such puzzles can be an absorbing and fascinating pursuit, combining as it does the best features of a crossword puzzle and a detective story. Once identified, a figure naturally gains considerably in value, but this is nothing compared with the pleasure gained in the research.

The vast majority of these delightful Staffordshire figures was made in small, primitive factories sometimes employing only a handful of workers, many of whom were children. Attempts have been made to identify the products of particular potters, but this is a specialist pursuit and quite unnecessary to the enjoyment of the average collector. A bare

A. C. Cooper

Fig. 8 *Jules Perrot as Gringoire and Carlotta Grisi as Esmeralda from the ballet* La Esmeralda *shown at Her Majesty's Theatre, 9 March, 1844, Staffordshire, c.1845. Heights 9½ and 10 ins.* (*Oliver Sutton Antiques.*)

Fig. 9 *Two figures of Napoleon, Staffordshire, c.1845. Heights 24 and 2¾ ins. That on the left is the tallest figure and one of the rarest.* (*Oliver Sutton Antiques.*)

handful are marked, but most of them carry no factory-mark of any sort. As the figures grow in popularity, they have inevitably attracted the attention of the forgers, some of whose output is now much better than the early crude attempts at deception. The safeguard for inexperienced collectors, as always, is to find a specialist dealer who is prepared to take the time and trouble to pass on his knowledge to beginners.

Victorian Staffordshire figures reflect the age in which they were made, as much as any other primitive folk art of any period before or since. Few of the potters could read or write, so prints and music-covers assumed great importance for them. They talked; they talked at work and in the ale- and spirit-houses, and the most interesting news of the day would filter down from *The Lamb* and the hotel bar. It would reach the bar parlour of *The Foaming Quart*, or one of the hundreds of other low ale-houses where the potters were drinking, and sometimes – just sometimes – the magic worked. The great kaleidoscope of Victorian England swirled about them until an image, a tiny coloured fragment of it, froze in the mind like the frame from a modern cinema film.

When the potters' attention was caught, the image was slapped into clay, either modelled on a convenient print, or from his imagination. Royalty, Protestants, Catholics, actors, boxers, murderers and politicians – nothing escaped them. Wars, battles, generals on superb prancing horses, saints, sailors, sinners and the American lady who invented bloomers, the figures are quite literally a potted history of the nineteenth century, of absorbing interest to the enquiring collector and as cheerful as a brass band on a sunny day.

MUSEUMS AND COLLECTIONS

Staffordshire figures may be seen at the following:

GREAT BRITAIN
Brighton:	Art Gallery and Museum
Cambridge:	Fitzwilliam Museum
London:	Victoria and Albert Museum

U.S.A.
Grand Rapids, Mich.:	Grand Rapids Art Museum
High Point, N. Carolina:	High Point Historical Society

FURTHER READING

The Victorian Staffordshire Figure, a Guide for Collectors by Anthony Oliver, London, 1971.
Staffordshire Portrait Figures and Allied Subjects of the Victorian Era by P. D. Gordon Pugh, London, 1971.
A Collector's Guide to Staffordshire Pottery Figures by H. A. B. Turner, 1971.
Staffordshire Portrait Figures of the Victorian Age by Thomas Balston, London, 1958.

A. C. Cooper

The Artist Potters

Working on the principles of Ruskin and Morris and often without professional training, the artist-potters brought new decorative motifs and a refreshing lack of sophistication to Victorian ceramics

The pottery of the Arts and Crafts Movement was inspired by the same revulsion from the technical virtuosity and stylistic aridity of High Victorian production that stimulated William Morris and his colleagues in other fields. The Firm itself produced a limited amount of pottery, mostly tiles decorated with designs by D. G. Rossetti, E. Burne-Jones, Albert Moore, Simeon Solomon and other well-known painters.

In the 1860s William de Morgan (1839–1917) became closely associated with Morris and his 'Fine Art Workmen' at Red Lion Square, London. De Morgan had been a student at the Royal Academy Schools but the instruction there had weaned him of his ambition to become a painter. Under Morris' influence – but independently – he painted decorative panels on furniture designed by Philip Webb, and made stained glass. In 1869 he produced his first experimental ceramic tile and quickly became fascinated by the technical challenge involved in lustre finishes. Pottery was not an area in which Morris' enterprise was particularly active, so De Morgan set up his kiln at 40, Fitzroy Square, where, with scarcely any professional advice, he instructed himself in the ceramic arts by a laborious process of trial and error.

It was not really until his move to Cheyne Row, Chelsea, in 1872 that De Morgan began to make a viable product. Here he took on an assistant, Frank Iles, who was kiln-master throughout the later years of the pottery. The tiles which De Morgan was now producing sold well and he acquired more equipment, moved into larger premises at Orange House, Cheyne Row, and enlisted further staff. The Passenger brothers, Charles and Fred, joined as painters in 1877 and '79 respectively. They were the first, and they remained with the pottery longer than any other of the many decorators, men and women, who worked for De Morgan; Joe Juster was probably the most talented (Fig. 2).

The tiles, dishes and many of the bowls and vases were at first bought by De Morgan as blanks from potteries in Staffordshire and south-west England. Subsequently he began to fire his own wares from clay supplied by the Morgan Crucible Company of Battersea. His method of painting the tiles – the colours were applied to a ground of white slip – is significantly similar to the technique of the Pre-Raphaelites who sometimes painted on a moist white ground in an attempt to simulate the effect of fresco. Throughout his career as a designer of pottery decoration, De Morgan exploited the effects of lustre. In this respect he tried to match the achievements of the Hispano-Moresque and Italian decorators; in his masterpieces of lustre decoration which he called the 'moonlight and sunset suite', he combined gold, silver and copper lustres on single pieces, a considerable feat of technique.

Apart from lustres, De Morgan extensively used Persian colours: green, blue and red. Decorative motifs, too, were sometimes derived from Persian pottery, but also from nature and the grotesque designs with which Raphael and his assistants had decorated the Loggie of the Vatican in the sixteenth century. Unlike Morris, De Morgan's appreciation of past styles did not exclude those of the Renaissance and classical antiquity. In 1892 he wrote, from Florence, to Halsey Ricardo, the architect whom he had taken into partnership in 1888: 'I hope to find when I come back a mine of pots that might be Greek, Sicilian, Etruscan, Moorish, Italian Renaissance – anything but Staffordshire'. His antipathy to the traditional home of national production is characteristic of Arts and Crafts thinking.

From 1882–88, William de Morgan's pottery was at Merton Abbey, alongside Morris' workshops. But when the ideal factory, of which the two designer-craftsmen had dreamed, remained a 'fictionary', to use their expression, the time spent travelling grew irksome to De Morgan. He moved back to Fulham and set up his kilns at Sand's End. From 1892, due to ill health, he spent half the year in Florence where he formed and trained a band of painters whose work was sent back to England.

Towards the end of his life De Morgan wrote best-selling novels and in 1907 retired from the pottery, which continued under Halsey Ricardo until it finally closed in 1911.

A pottery sharing some points in common with De Morgan's enterprise was the Della-Robbia

Company Ltd., which was established by Harold Rathbone at Birkenhead, Merseyside, in 1894, and which continued in production until 1901. Rathbone had been a pupil of Ford Madox Brown. As the name of the pottery implies, many of the wares produced were derivative from Renaissance models in both shape and decoration, and wall-reliefs were also manufactured. Vessels of Islamic shapes are found and there is much decoration which is quite distinctive, often tending towards abstraction and geometric patterns. There is some crudity but much integrity and originality in Della-Robbia pottery. Output was divided between decorative and architectural wares; the pottery's most important work in the latter category was a fountain, since demolished, in the courtyard of the Savoy Hotel in London. This was the work of Rathbone himself.

In the nineteenth century salt-glazed stoneware was being used mainly in the manufacture of drain-pipes, roof-tiles, very large containers for liquids, and flower-pots. From about 1870, it was also used for a considerable quantity of art pottery for three significant reasons. First, because of its consistency and high firing-temperature it does not allow itself to be manipulated or coloured freely; it is impossible to create from it the kind of lavish and intricate china which the Victorians generally admired. Second, it provides the decorator with a very direct means of expression, needing only one firing; the inexperienced craftsman can soon obtain satisfactory results. Third, in contrast to china and porcelain, the extensive use of which in Europe dates from the eighteenth century, salt-glazed stoneware recalls a more romantic age.

Doulton's of Lambeth were a company producing architectural and sanitary stoneware. John Sparkes, head of the Lambeth School of Art, was imbued with principles of art education derived

R. Todd-White

R. Todd-White

Angelo Hornak

Fig. 4 **Vase** *by C. H. Brannam, Barnstaple, 1888. Earthenware with* sgraffito *decoration through slip.*
Called 'Barum ware' after the Roman name for Barnstaple, Brannam's pottery was hand-thrown. This piece is signed with the initials 'WB' for William Baron, the decorator. In 1899, Baron started his own pottery at Barnstaple.
(Author's Collection.)

Figs. 5 and 8 **Pair of figures,** *Fulham, London, C. J. C. Bailey and Co., late nineteenth century. Salt-glazed stoneware.*
From about 1870, Bailey produced artistic stoneware at the Fulham Pottery. These figures of street-sellers are decorated in the limited range of colours characteristic of salt-glazed ware.
(Fulham Public Library, London.)

Fig. 6 Left: **Carrara ware vase,** *Doulton, Lambeth, 1887–90. Enamelled stoneware decorated by Ada Dennis and Mary Denley.*
Right: **Lambeth Faience vase,** *Doulton, Lambeth, 1889–91. Under-glaze decorated earthenware, painted by Esther Lewis, Ada Dennis and Mary Denley.*
(Doulton and Company Ltd., London.)

Fig. 7 Left: **Lizards on a rock,** *Doulton, Lambeth, early twentieth century. Salt-glazed stoneware modelled by Mark V. Marshall.*
Right: **Vase,** *Doulton, Lambeth, early twentieth century. Salt-glazed stoneware decorated by Mark V. Marshall.*
(Doulton and Company Ltd.)

4

5

R. Todd-White

from William Dyce, and was also an ardent Ruskinian. He was anxious that his students should find at Doulton's pottery a useful and practical application of their artistic training. But to Henry Doulton the idea of an art-studio in his pottery did not appeal. A friend of Doulton's, however, Edward Cresy, an architect, became an enthusiastic admirer of *grès de Flandres*, the decorated stoneware made in the neighbourhood of Cologne from the sixteenth century. He encouraged Doulton to undertake the manufacture of a similar ware.

Finally, in 1866, under this dual pressure, Doulton invited Sparkes to send along one of his students to the pottery. The student was George Tinworth who became a highly accomplished modeller and whose talents won early recognition for Doulton Ware. At the 1871 International Exhibition in South Kensington, the ware impressed

critics and public; Queen Victoria ordered some examples to be sent to Windsor.

Decoration of Doulton Ware took different forms. Patterns were incised and coloured; borders and rims were carved; stiff slip was applied in spots and trails. A distinctive style of decoration was created by Hannah Barlow whose incised drawings of animals and children in landscapes quickly became popular. Arthur Barlow, her brother, and Florence Barlow, her sister, were among many other Lambeth School art-students who decorated Doulton Ware. Perhaps the most original of the Doulton artists was Mark V. Marshall, who joined the pottery in about 1876. His modelling and decoration are both of the highest quality (Fig. 7). As the success of Doulton Ware grew, new types of art-pottery were added to the range. Different bodies were used as well as different kinds of

brothers all became proficient at each other's skills. Charles became the business manager and ran a shop in Brownlow Street, London.

Martinware, to which the brothers gave their name, is rich in the variety of its shapes. Decoration is incised and coloured in a similar manner to that of Doulton stoneware but it usually has less geometrical patterning; flowers, fishes, insects, and grotesques are common motifs, the treatment being sometimes Japanese (Fig. 1) and sometimes Renaissance. R. W. Martin modelled figures and grotesque birds, known as 'Wally birds', which are usually found as tobacco-jars, the heads forming the lids.

The last firing of Martinware was in 1914. Much of the later work the brothers produced has an abstract quality which relates it to subsequent studio-pottery. Their method of working, as a sort of co-operative, bears comparison to the studio set-up of, for instance, Bernard Leach at St. Ives, Cornwall.

Many of the small family concerns in Devon turned to the production of artistic pottery in the last quarter of the nineteenth century. Some of them gained considerable reputations, and their wares were retailed by large London stores such as Howell & James and Liberty's. They manufactured slip-decorated earthenware, the ornament of which either reflected the universal vogue for the Oriental, or exploited the souvenir market with marine motifs. There were potteries at Watcombe, Aller Vale, Fremington and several at Barnstaple. Perhaps the best was C. H. Brannam's Litchdon Pottery at Barnstaple which produced Barum Ware from 1879; at first this was of a high quality (Fig. 4), but after about 1890, probably due to an insatiable demand, standards dropped.

At the Sunflower Pottery, Clevedon, near Bristol, Sir Edmund Elton made artistic pottery from 1879 until his death in 1920. It is characterised by its quaint shapes and a coloured — sometimes particoloured — slip ground on which is raised decoration of stiffer slip usually in the form of flowers. The story of Elton's early struggles to overcome technical difficulties, with scarcely any professional training or advice, is fascinating, but does not necessarily compensate for the aesthetic limitations of his rather mannered pottery.

decoration, as seen on the vases in Figure 6.

Salt-glazed stoneware was also made at the Fulham Pottery which had been acquired in 1864 by C. J. C. Bailey (Figs. 5 and 8). He encouraged the manufacture of artistic pottery and in about 1872 enlisted the services of the French landscape painter and artist-potter J. C. Cazin, who had fled to London from Tours after the fall of the Commune in 1871. His ornament was geometrical, although he used naturalistic flowers in a Japanese style.

Robert Wallace Martin also worked at the Fulham Pottery as a modeller until he set up his own kiln, first at Shepherd's Bush in 1873, moving to Southall in 1879. He worked with his brothers, Walter and Edwin, who as students at the Lambeth School of Art had been taught by Cazin, and who had also worked for a time at Doulton's. Walter was thrower and Edwin decorator, although the

MUSEUMS AND COLLECTIONS

Pottery of the Arts and Crafts Movement may be seen at the following:

GREAT BRITAIN

Leicester: Museum and Art Gallery
Liverpool: Sudley Art Gallery and Museum
London: Fulham Public Library
Victoria and Albert Museum
William Morris Gallery, Walthamstow

FURTHER READING

Doulton Stoneware and Terracotta 1870–1925: Part I, exhibition catalogue by Richard Dennis, London, 1971.
William de Morgan by William Gaunt and M. D. E. Clayton-Stamm, London, 1971.
Royal Doulton 1815–1965 by Desmond Eyles, London, 1965.
Victorian Pottery by H. Wakefield, London, 1962.
Nineteenth-Century English Ceramic Art by J. F. Blacker, London, 1911.

Rookwood Pottery

Fig. 1 *Rookwood ceramics,*
late nineteenth century. From
the left: Ewer with dragon motif.
Initialled by Albert R. Valentien.
Vase with portrait of Chief Joseph
of the Néz Percés, signed by
W. P. McDonald, height 14 ins.;
Bowl with Japanese flower motif.
(Metropolitan Museum of Art,
New York. Gifts of W. M.
Sawyer, 1945, and E. J. Kaufman
Fund, 1969.)

Founded by the socialite daughter of a wealthy Cincinnati family to further her interest in pottery decoration, the Rookwood Art pottery rose to great artistic heights and won widespread recognition

Museum Photo

The Rookwood Pottery, because it was founded by a woman in the days when there were few women *entrepreneurs*, probably received more gratuitous publicity during the first twenty years of its existence than any other American enterprise.

The magazine and newspaper writers of the period seemed to delight in telling how Mrs. Maria Longworth Nichols started the venture because she was unable to find a suitable place elsewhere in which to conduct her experiments in china painting and under-glaze pottery decoration, which had been stimulated by the widespread interest in the subject following the Centennial Celebration of the United States in 1876.

The fact that Mrs. Nichols was the socially prominent daughter of one of the wealthiest families in Cincinnati and the wife of the president of the Cincinnati College of Music made her good local copy. Newspaper-writers of the city reported in detail how she spent the summer of 1880 converting a little schoolhouse, given to her by her father, into a pottery; how she named it 'Rookwood' after the name of her father's estate, and because, she said, 'it reminded one of Wedgwood', which she felt lent a certain prestige to the new enterprise.

The newspapers also recorded that the first kiln was drawn on 25 November, 1880, and that Mrs. Nichols emphasised that her primary interest was in the production of a better art pottery rather than the achievement of a commercial success. They told how three of Mrs. Nichols' friends: Edward P. Cranch, a lawyer with artistic talents; Clara Chipman Newton, a former schoolmate; and Laura A. Fry, a skilled woodcarver and china-painter, joined with her to form the nucleus of a decorating department; they described the Rook-wood School for Pottery Decoration, which Mrs. Nichols organised in the expectation that it would provide a training-ground for future artists for her pottery.

Mr. Joseph Bailey, an experienced English potter who had migrated to the United States in 1848, gave some sound advice to Mrs. Nichols in the initial stages. In 1881, he joined the enterprise as factory superintendent.

During the first three years of its existence, expenses greatly exceeded income and Mr. Joseph Longworth, Mrs. Nichols' father, continued to make substantial contributions toward financing the venture. In spite of this and other difficulties, the little business grew steadily.

In 1883, Mr. William Watts Taylor, an old friend of Mrs. Nichols, was named manager of the pottery.

Under his direction the production of art pottery was expanded. New designs were introduced, and those that did not sell well were eliminated from the line. He also streamlined sales, appointing as national sales agent Davis Collamore & Co., a leading distributor of fine china, glass and crystal; and he instituted a policy of selective distribution, permitting only one leading retailer per city to handle the Rookwood line. In an effort to trim losses, he discontinued the pottery school. As a result of these changes the operation showed a modest profit by 1886, and by 1889 it had recouped all its earlier losses.

During its first three years, the production of the Rookwood Pottery was divided between art pottery, the primary interest of Mrs. Nichols, and commercial and utility wares, which were made solely to help defray expenses. The early output of art pottery was characterised by a variety of techniques as the organisation groped for a distinctive style. Among them were carved, incised, stamped and impressed designs, applied decoration in high relief, frequent embellishment with gilt, over-glaze painting and slip-painting under the glaze. This latter style, aided by the development of the airbrush technique for applying evenly blended backgrounds in rich, warm colours, soon became the most popular and was referred to as 'Standard Rookwood'.

From a few limited colours which would with-stand the heat of the kiln, the pottery succeeded in developing a wider range, and also employed tinted glazes and coloured clay bodies which added to the beauty and variety of its wares. In 1884 came the accidental development of an aventurine glaze having bright golden crystals appearing deep under the surface. The effect was given the name 'Tiger Eye', but this result could not be produced with certainty and what caused it to occur remained undiscovered.

Many visitors were attracted to the Rookwood pottery on the banks of the Ohio River

The widespread publicity Rookwood received attracted many visitors to the pottery. Prominent Cincinnatians as well as visitors to the city called to inspect this 'new art industry' on the banks of the Ohio River. Oscar Wilde and Seymour Hayden, an English etcher, were among the early travellers who are known to have toured the pottery.

Mrs. Nichols' husband died in 1885, and the following year she married Bellamy Storer, a well-known Cincinnati lawyer. From that time on, her interest in the pottery gradually declined until, at the end of 1889, she transferred the ownership of the business to Mr. Taylor and moved with her husband to Washington D.C. when Mr. Storer was elected a member of the United States Congress.

Under Mr. Taylor's management the production of art pottery continued to expand and new shapes were added to the line each year. The manufacture of commercial and utility items had been phased out except for infrequent orders that came in for souvenirs or for pieces commemorating special events. Floral decorations on the rich brown, orange and yellow blended backgrounds of Standard Rookwood and on the cool pink and white grounds of a style designated as 'Cameo', dominated the output of the decorating department which had

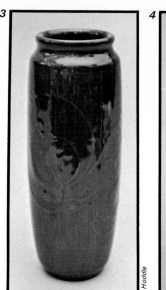

K. Hoddle

K. Hoddle

Fig. 2 *Jar, decorated by H. Wilcox with lilies on a green ground, Rookwood, shape no. 892B, 1900. (Bethnal Green Museum, London.)*

Fig. 3 *Vase, decorated by A. R. Valentien with dragons on an aventurine ground, Rookwood, shape no. S1363, 1898. (Bethnal Green Museum.)*

Fig. 4 *Vase, decorated by Constance A. Baker with poppies on a black and brown ground, Rookwood, shape no. 17C, 1900. (Bethnal Green Museum.)*

Fig. 5 *Bottle-shaped vase, decorated by K. Shirayamadani with a pattern of arrowhead flowers, Rookwood, shape no. 654C, 1900. (Victoria and Albert Museum.)*

114

grown to a staff of thirteen full-time artists.

Mr. Taylor's first moves on taking over the ownership of the pottery were to incorporate the business and to lay plans for its further expansion. As it had thoroughly outgrown the facilities available at the little schoolhouse, he designed the layout for a complete new pottery housed in an attractive English Tudor-style building. It was constructed on the top of Mount Adams, overlooking the central business district of Cincinnati, and operations were transferred to the new location in the spring of 1892. The decorating department was immediately expanded by the addition of six new artists.

The following year Rookwood was prominently displayed at the World's Columbian Exposition, more popularly known in the United States as the Chicago World's Fair. Here it attained added recognition by receiving the award for art pottery and was praised as 'an indigenous American art' Several European museums acquired examples of its production for their collections.

While most of the output continued to be Standard Rookwood, three new styles were introduced:

'Iris' was the name given to ware having light blue, grey and white blended grounds under a high glaze; 'Sea Green' designated a 'limpid opalescent sea-green effect with a favourite decoration of fish moving under water' under a high glaze; 'Aerial Blue' denoted a bluish-tinted high glaze used over decorations on light blue and grey blended grounds.

Although floral themes continued to be the most characteristic during the 1890s (Figs. 2, 4 and 5), other decorative styles appeared. Among the innovations were: under-glaze, slip-painted portraits of American Indians (Fig. 1); Negroes; cats, dogs and other animals. Figures taken from Old Masters such as Van Dyck, Rembrandt, Franz Hals, Caravaggio and others were painted on vases and plaques; and wares were embellished with silver overlays applied by the Gorham Manufacturing Company of Providence, Rhode Island, one of the country's leading silversmiths. Under the influence of the developing Art Nouveau trends, several of the artists attempted to interest the pottery in making sculptured art forms, but this style apparently proved unpopular in the salerooms and was not encouraged by the management.

During the summer of 1897, the pottery was visited by the English writer Rose G. Kingsley, who told the Rookwood story in an article which appeared in the December 1897 issue of the prestigious *Art-Journal.* The management at Cincinnati was highly pleased and ordered a supply of reprints for use in Rookwood's promotional activities.

In 1899 the building on Mount Adams was enlarged by the addition of more studio-space for the art staff, more space for the salerooms, which were attracting an increasing number of visitors, and more work-room for the potting department. The work-force was expanded and the art department increased to thirty-six members.

When Rookwood was awarded the Grand Prix at the 1900 *Exposition Universelle* in Paris, its position as America's foremost art pottery was assured. Many more European museums acquired examples of its wares, and the Pottery from that time on seldom missed an opportunity to publicise its international recognition and acceptance.

During the 1890s the Pottery had sent several of its more talented decorators to study in Europe, believing that this would be directly in the Pottery's 'artistic interests'. Rookwood had never lost sight of the original goal of its founder, the making of better art pottery, although it no longer emphasised that this interest exceeded the desire for commercial success.

One of the artists sent abroad was Artus van Briggle, who later founded the Van Briggle Art Pottery in Colorado Springs. When he returned to Cincinnati, he brought back the idea of a dull or matt glaze which he had seen in Europe. Although Rookwood began experimenting with matt glazes as early as 1896, it was not until 1901 that matt-glazed ware became a regular part of the Pottery's production. Several styles of matt-glaze decoration were developed and were described as 'Mat Glaze Painting', 'Incised Mat Glaze', 'Modeled Mat Glaze', and 'Conventional Mat Glaze'. In 1904, a transparent matt glaze known as 'Vellum' was perfected. Its use encouraged the painting of detailed landscapes and seascapes on vases and plaques. These proved popular and their production was continued for many years, although they were sold at comparatively high prices as they were costly to produce.

The development of a matt glaze also gave rise to the manufacture of decorative tiles and medallions for architectural use, a field that gave promise for further development. This led to the second expansion of the pottery's facilities on Mount Adams. A new addition was built in 1904 to house the architectural department. During the next decade Rookwood architectural products were supplied for more than seventy prominent commercial and office buildings throughout the United States, and hundreds of Rookwood mantels and facings for fireplaces and coloured-tile bathrooms were installed in private residences. But the large staff required to design and make the architectural products, coupled with the low selling-prices forced by competition, kept the profit margin down, and the operation of the architectural department proved a disappointment to the management.

Until approximately 1910, Rookwood art pottery was almost entirely confined to pieces individually decorated by the artists, who customarily signed their work with their initials or monogram. Exceptions were the ware having the 'Tiger Eye' or aventurine effect which did not require further ornamentation. Each piece was also dated, a feature which distinguishes Rookwood from most other art pottery, and given a number which identified the shape (Fig. 6). All artist-signed pieces were unique creations and never duplicated; even matched pairs differed slightly in execution.

Several years after the development of matt glaze, however, the company began to make ware in which the design, either incised or modelled in relief, could be cast directly in the mould. Such pieces could be duplicated in quantity and the method was employed with greater frequency as the demand increased for items which could be sold at lower prices.

William Watts Taylor, who had guided the Rookwood Pottery to its greatest achievements, died in 1913. Following his death, the Pottery continued to trade on the reputation and acceptance it had built up during his leadership, but it never surpassed its earlier successes. The new management lacked Mr. Taylor's perception and his business judgement, and a series of mistakes, coupled with the Great Depression of the 1930s, led to the bankruptcy of the firm in 1941 and the eventual suspension of production.

The last few years have seen a renewed interest in art pottery in general and a new appreciation of Rookwood in particular which has stimulated the demand by collectors for the products of America's foremost art pottery.

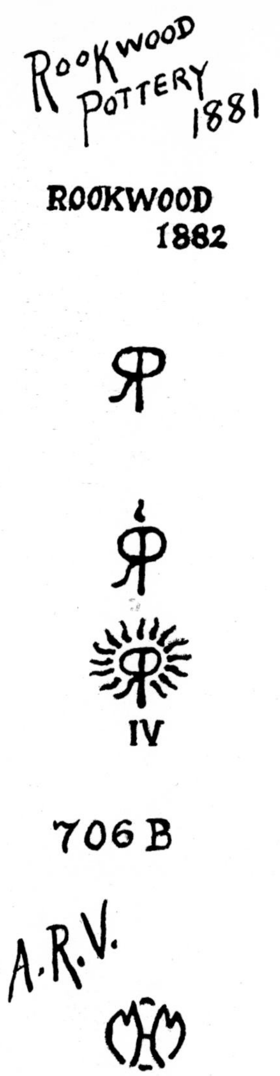

*Fig. 6 **Principal Rookwood pottery marks.** From the top: 1880–81, painted or incised. 1882–86, impressed. 1886, reversed R-P officially adopted although used by the decorator Brennan from 1883. 1887, one flame point added for that year and an additional one for each year until 1900. 1904, Roman numeral added below the R-P mark with fourteen flames to indicate the year of the new century, as here for 1904. **shape number** impressed on the bottom of each piece. When followed by a letter, it showed that shape was made in two or more sizes. **initials and monogram** of two artists. These are usually found incised, impressed or painted on individually decorated pieces.*

MUSEUMS AND COLLECTIONS

Rookwood pottery may be seen at the following:

FRANCE
Sèvres: Musée National de
                                   Céramique
GREAT BRITAIN
London: Bethnal Green Museum
                                   Victoria and Albert Museum
ITALY
Faenza: Museo Internazionale della
                                   Ceramiche
U.S.A.
Cincinnati: Cincinnati Art Museum
Washington D.C.:   Smithsonian Institution
U.S.S.R.
Leningrad: State Hermitage Museum
WEST GERMANY
Berlin: Kunstgewerbemuseum
                                   Staatliche Museen
Hamburg: Museum für Kunst und
                                   Gewerbe
Nuremberg: Gewerbemuseum der
                                   Landesgewerbeanstalt
Stuttgart: Landesgewerbeamt
                                   Baden-Württemberg

FURTHER READING

'Rookwood Pottery in Foreign Museum Collections' by Herbert Peck in **The Connoisseur,** London, September 1969.
'Some Early Collections of Rookwood Pottery' by Herbert Peck in **Auction Magazine,** New York, September 1969.
The Book of Rookwood Pottery by Herbert Peck, New York, 1968.
Pottery and Porcelain of the United States by Edwin Atlee Barber, New York, second edition 1901.

Furniture

Some of the most beautiful furniture designs have been inspired by antiquity. Graceful sabre-legged *klismos* chairs depicted on Greek vases, elegant couches and tables discovered, at Pompeii and Herculaneum, together with a wealth of classical details were all much admired during the long period of Neoclassicism that lasted from the 1760's to about 1825. Following wide-spread interest in Napoleon's Egyptian campaign at the end of the eighteenth century, Egyptian motifs were added to those of Greece and Rome in the continuing Neoclassical repertoire.

From the rare pieces surviving from the Middle Ages, it is known that styles in domestic furniture tended to reflect the prevalent Gothic church architecture of the time. Oak furniture was ornamented with pointed arches, carved linenfold panelling (to represent scrolls of parchment), tracery and medallions. Such details persisted for some time after the Renaissance had introduced new ideas.

By the 1500's, there was an increasing awareness of the applied arts. The most significant piece of furniture to be found in Italian houses at this time was the *cassone* or dower chest. Wealthy Italians acquired a great many *cassoni* and not much else, preferring to concentrate on richly painted ceilings and sculpture. The classically proportioned *cassone*, however, received the full decorative treatment of carving, gilding and painted panelling.

English furniture at the time of the Renaissance showed the influence of other Protestant countries in Europe rather than Italy. Oak furniture, built to last, was of sturdy panel-and-frame construction, with mediaeval-style carved decorations and ornate bulbous legs. Joined stools were the usual form of seating with one or two box-like chairs for important people, but luxury-loving Elizabethans favoured huge beds hung with rich fabrics, and court cupboards on which to display their silver plate.

By the early seventeenth century, the opulent baroque style had assumed an important role in Italy. Extremely elaborate carving and gilding was the hallmark of furniture in this style and it became almost sculptural in appearance. Gilded scrolls, cupids and floral motifs flowed over furniture replacing the formerly simple lines of structural elements. Elsewhere on the Continent, the baroque taste was less flamboyant than in its home-land, reaching perfection in late-seventeenth-century France with the work of André-Charles Boulle, a master cabinetmaker who produced sumptuous pieces for the palaces of Louis XIV, the Sun King.

When King Charles II was restored to the English throne in 1660, he introduced ideas in furniture design that he had admired during his exile in Holland. Dark oak and Puritanical simplicity went out of fashion and lighter woods and more elaborate styles came in. The cabinetmaker achieved new status as his skills were in demand to produce veneered furniture with popular marquetry (inlays of contrasting woods in a floral pattern) and parquetry (geometric pattern) decorations.

Legs on chairs and tables were turned in many-twisted spirals, chair backs were high, elaborately carved and inset with panels of imported cane. Later in the century, in the period known as William and Mary, refugee Huguenot craftsmen who had fled persecution in France, introduced elements of the high baroque style reflected in elaborately gilded stands, picture frames and tables in some of the great houses of the time. Other furniture was becoming more refined, designed for comfort and convenience with special-purpose items like gaming tables, and upholstered wing chairs in wide use. By this time, too, the new elegant lines of the Queen Anne style were already apparent.

The elongated S-curve was the principal feature of Queen Anne furniture, and was epitomised in the grace-ful cabriole legs to be found on chairs, tables and case furniture. Changes were immediately seen in chair backs and seats. Previously square and straight, they were now rounded and more closely resembled the human form. The carved shell, inherited from the baroque, continued to be the favourite motif and was carved on crest rails, table and chair legs and case pieces. Walnut veneer was popular as were painted or japanned finishes in simulation of imported Chinese lacquer, and mirrored furniture.

A great many cabinetmakers were working in the American Colonies by the end of the first century of settlement. The furniture they made reflected their varied English, Dutch, and German origins. They copied popular European styles, but using native woods and great imagination imbued them with an individual flavour.

The Rococo style, which became fashionable in France after 1715, began as a reaction against the ornate qualities of the preceding baroque phase; the emphasis in rococo was on lighter woods, delicate carvings of flowers and vines and asymmetrical curves. The elegant furniture of the Louis XV period is typical of French rococo at its height, both in the more elaborate Court furniture and the pretty country pieces made by craftsmen in the Provinces. In England, the famed cabinetmaker, Thomas Chippendale, interpreted Rococo with such designs as ribbon-backed mahogany chairs. At the same time, he introduced a range of pieces in the Chinese style, catering to the taste for Chinoiserie, and also revived the Gothic style. In America fashion-conscious cities like Philadelphia and Boston produced superb mahogany and cherry furniture for Colonial use in the manner of Chippendale.

Archaeological discoveries in the mid-eighteenth century sparked a keen interest in the study of classical cultures. Soon the curves and frivolities of rococo were replaced, both in England and in France, with more disciplined geometric lines and classical decorations. Mahogany became less fashionable as woods more suitable for the refined neo-classical taste were employed in cabinetmaking. Veneered finishes were revived, inlaid with delicate satinwood panels or inset with decorative lacquer or porcelain.

The tailored elegance of Louis XVI furniture in France reflected the newly refined taste, while Scottish architect Robert Adam designed houses and their interiors calling for classical columns and decorative plasterwork. Inspired by Adam, the furniture designs of George Hepplewhite and Thomas Sheraton had a lasting influence on late-eighteenth-century England and America. The Hepplewhite style is associated with shield-backed chairs, serpentine curves and slender, tapered legs while designs of Thomas Sheraton inclined toward square lines significantly in chair backs. The furniture of the New Republic in America incorporated the best of both in the Early Federal style.

Interest in Napoleon's Egyptian campaign of 1798 was largely responsible for the introduction of Egyptian details in the period known as Empire. Winged sphinxes, griffins, swans, lions' masks and animal paws were all utilised in the decoration of furniture.

The invention of machines that could mass-produce furniture cheaply signalled the end of the era of great cabinetmaking. By the 1830s, more people than ever before could buy furniture in the latest taste. A number of favourite styles were revived, notably Elizabethan, Gothic and Rococo, each fussier and more elaborate than the original. As a protest against the declining taste of machine-made furniture, a pioneer English designer, William Morris, began making hand-crafted functional furniture of mediaeval simplicity. Morris's efforts formed the foundation for the Arts and Crafts Movement in the latter part of the nineteenth century. A natural outgrowth of Arts and Crafts was Art Nouveau whose decorative details were taken from free-flowing plant forms of the popular Japanese decorative arts. By seeking inspiration in nature, Art Nouveau furniture was the only style of the nineteenth century that did not take its designs from the past.

Elizabethan Oak

Wealthy Elizabethans wanted comfort and beauty around them, and the quality of their furniture and furnishings reflects their affection for sumptuously decorated beds, tables and chairs

The England of Elizabeth I was a land of stable government based on a strong monarchy, of material prosperity and of vigorous national self-confidence. Overseas trade and domestic industry were both expanding rapidly and the first adventurous attempts were being made to found colonies. National confidence was strengthened by the successful challenge to the religious leadership of the Pope and the naval might of Philip II of Spain, whose Armada was defeated in 1588 in its attempts to transport troops to conquer England.

The vigour of national life fostered a love of ostentatious decoration

The character of an age tends to be reflected in its furniture; thus we see the rising wealth of Elizabethan England reflected in the increased quantity of furniture and furnishings produced by its craftsmen, while internal security encouraged a greater emphasis than ever before on domestic comfort and the vigour of national life fostered a love of ostentatious decoration.

The Reformation had, to a great extent, kept England from direct contact with Italy and the changes in constructional and decorative techniques in craftsmanship brought about by the classical Renaissance. Cultural contacts were closest with Protestant countries such as Germany and the Low Countries, where the Renaissance was interpreted in a complex and ornate version far removed from the chaste classicism of Italy, but full of appeal to contemporary English taste.

Printed pattern books of architectural and furniture designs from those areas were imported into England. The most celebrated furniture designs of this kind were those published in about 1580 by the Dutch artist Vredeman de Vries (1527–c.1604). It was from such foreign sources that three of the most distinctive kinds of Elizabethan ornament were derived: strap-work (intricate repeated arabesque and geometrical carving in low relief), inlay, or 'markatree' (the insertion of different coloured woods below the surface of the decorated section, to a depth of about one-eighth of an inch, to form floral or geometrical patterns), and bulbs, sometimes of grotesque proportions, on table legs, bed posts and similar supports. Elizabethan furniture remained largely medieval in form, absorbing these new types of decoration as a concession to modern taste. Flemish influence was further increased by numbers of Protestant craftsmen who fled to England to escape persecution in the Netherlands.

The growing affluence and comfort of the time were described by William Harrison in his *Description of England*, written in 1577–87: 'The furniture of our houses also exceedeth and is grown in manner even to passing delicacy; and herein I do not speak of the nobility and gentry only, but likewise of the lowest sort'. The rich, he continues, had 'great provision of tapestry, Turkey-work, pewter, brass, fine linen and thereto costly cupboards of plate', while inferior artificers and many farmers 'had learned' to garnish their cupboards with plate, their joined beds with tapestry and silk hangings and their tables with carpets and fine napery'. The ornate furniture of the rich is clearly shown in the inventories of the household contents of some of the great houses, like those made of Lord John Lumley's possessions in 1590 and 1609.

The principal constructional technique in Tudor furniture-making was that of the panel and frame. The panel, enclosed in a groove within a rigid framework of stiles (i.e. uprights) and rails, was allowed a freedom of movement which prevented the wood from splitting (this occurred when it was fixed by nails or pegs). The frame was made with the mortise and tenon joint, the mortise being the socket or slot into which the projecting tenon fitted exactly. The two pieces were then pegged. The joiner was the craftsman responsible for this technique, but the carver and turner were also important workers engaged on furniture, while the upholsterer saw to such things as the cushions, the fixed coverings of seats and bed curtains and the

Fig. 1 *Joined stool*, c.1600. Oak, height 21 ins. The stool was still the commonest form of seat in the Elizabethan home and this four legged type was developed in about 1550. (Victoria and Albert Museum, London.)

Fig. 2 *Box-shaped armchair*, first half of the sixteenth century. Oak, height 43 ins. (Victoria and Albert Museum.)

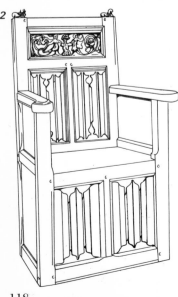

carpenter made simpler pieces. But highest in prestige was the cofferer, the first furniture craftsman to be permanently employed at Court. This man, as his title shows, at first made travelling trunks and chests for royal use, his particular skill consisting of covering them with leather and other fine materials. Later his activities included chairs, desks and screens. The Court cofferers are the only Elizabethan furniture craftsmen to escape complete oblivion, as references to their work have survived in the royal records preserved in the Public Record Office, London. The best known cofferers of the time were members of the Green family, William, John and Thomas, successively royal cofferers from about 1550 until the end of the century.

Oak was the chief wood for fashionable furniture. Before 1550 joiners had also used other native woods such as walnut, ash and elm. In Elizabeth's reign more use was made of these woods as well as of chestnut, beech, cedar and fir, and at the same time, to make the now fashionable coloured floral and chequer patterns in inlaid decoration, holly, bog oak, poplar, box, sycamore and ebony were employed.

Furniture was a valuable commodity in Tudor England and many Elizabethan houses contained pieces which had been in use from the first half of the century. Among these, special respect was accorded to the panel-back chair (which also had panels beneath the arms and seat), as social convention reserved this type for the master of the house (Fig. 5). The rest of his family sat on stools (Fig. 1) and benches. Another kind of seat was the settle, a bench with arms and back and sometimes a box beneath the seat. A light conversation chair, the caquetoire – from French, *caqueter*, to gossip – (Fig. 3) which had a tall, narrow panelled back and was open beneath its splayed arms and seat, was derived from French prototypes for ladies' use in parlours and bedrooms.

'Cupboard' – an open table for cups and plate

'Cupboard' is a word to treat with caution in its Tudor sense, for it meant originally a cup-board, that is to say, an open table for cups and plate and not, as in modern usage, a structure completely enclosed by doors. Some Tudor cupboards nevertheless were beginning to acquire enclosed sections, and examples of the different kinds – open, closed or partly closed – were being made. Some food cupboards, for instance, had pierced doors for ventilation. On the other hand, it is uncertain whether the livery cupboard, which also held stores of food – in this case the rations doled out daily to servants in large households – had doors or not.

The aumbry, originally a wall recess, then an enclosed space in a piece of furniture, was another term for a receptacle with doors, this time for keeping food for distribution by the almoner to the poor. There were also hall and parlour cupboards in two stages in which the upper stage alone, and sometimes both stages, had doors; while the press cupboard was entirely enclosed by doors. 'Cupboards' as used in Tudor inventories was thus to remain a puzzling term, although by about the end of the Elizabethan period it was beginning to acquire its present meaning.

The most costly piece of Tudor furniture was the great bed, expensive because of its rich hangings, not because of its woodwork. Four corner posts and a panelled headboard to support the tester (the canopy round which the curtains were drawn at night) formed the usual framework after 1550, replacing the canopy formerly hung from the ceiling.

All these pieces were still being made in Elizabeth's reign. The clue to their date lies mainly in their decoration. There were, however, significant changes in some instances in the framework of established types. And finally, there are some distinctly Elizabethan pieces.

The traditional panel-back chair (Fig. 5) is an excellent example of the changes which had occurred by the end of the century. In 1600 the heavy and clumsy early Tudor version had become altogether lighter by the removal of the panels from under the seat and arms. The joiner now had much greater freedom of design. The chair arms curved downwards in the centre for the sitter's elbow and scrolled outwards over the arm supports, while the latter

Fig. 3 *Caquetoire or conversation chair, late-sixteenth century. Oak, height 48 ins. This style of light chair, with its single panelled back, was supposedly made for ladies. It derives, as the name suggests, from French models. (Victoria and Albert Museum.)*

3

Fig. 4 *Draw table and bench from Broadway, Somerset, first half of the sixteenth century. Oak, height of table 34½ ins., length of bench 65 ins. (Victoria and Albert Museum.)*

Museum Photo

Museum Photo

and the front legs (i.e. the former front stiles of the seat panel) were turned in columnar and other forms. The backs of these chairs were often inlaid with floral ornament or perhaps with a coat of arms, and ornamental scrolled sections at the top and sides ('head' and 'ear' pieces) were added both for decoration and to shelter the occupant from draughts.

Towards the end of Elizabeth's reign another type of lighter chair made its appearance, to join the caquetoire. This was the back stool which in contemporary meaning was not a chair at all as it did not have arms, but was literally a stool with a back support raised clear of the seat. It was based on the recently developed joined stool which had four turned legs splayed slightly outwards. The reason for its development is not completely clear. It does, however, coincide with the growing fashion for houses to have a separate small dining parlour. When, in former times, the family dined on the raised dais at one end of the great hall, those who sat on benches or stools could rest their backs against the wall. In the dining parlour, on the other hand, the table was in the centre of the room, and it seems reasonable to suggest that the back stool was a simple expedient for providing the support formerly given by the wall.

'Chairs of clothe of gold, velvet and sylke'

Great houses also had richly upholstered chairs as proved by inventories of the time. In 1590, for instance, Lord Lumley had seventy-six 'chairs of clothe of gold, velvet and sylke' and eighty stools similarly upholstered. Such chairs and stools have all disappeared and it is impossible to say whether they were made abroad or in England. It is likely, however, that many were of the traditional X-frame form, of which one surviving example can be seen in Winchester Cathedral. This is the oak chair, originally covered with blue velvet, which was made in about 1550 and is said to have been used at Queen Mary's wedding to Philip II of Spain.

In sharp contrast to these luxury chairs were the strictly utilitarian turned (or 'thrown') chairs found in the kitchens of large houses and, more generally, in smaller manor houses and in farmhouses. These chairs had their structural members turned in a variety of ways, often in bizarre fashion. The Elizabethans also used a light folding chair which seems to have copied Italian models. This type has been given the name of a Glastonbury chair through the mistaken supposition that it was based on the design of one which belonged to the Abbot of Glastonbury who was executed in Henry VIII's reign.

The dining parlour inspired the introduction of the draw table (Fig. 4), which could be extended to about double its length by pulling out two leaves beneath the top. This saved space when the table was not in use for meals. It is a truly Elizabethan development, for the earliest contemporary reference to one is found in the inventory of the Duke of Somerset's furniture, drawn up in 1552, and it was just the kind of piece to lend itself to the ornate decoration of the time. Minute chequer inlay is sometimes found running round the whole of the frieze, but the outstanding features are the enormous bulbs on the legs. These were often of 'cup and cover' form (so

called because of its similarity to a silver covered cup), and their carved decoration consisted of gadrooning – edging of concave flutes or convex reeds – and acanthus leaves, both taken from Classical sources.

The Great Bed of Ware, with elaborate carvings, was wide enough to sleep four couples

Another Elizabethan innovation was the court cupboard. This, a cup-board in the old literal sense, was an open three-tiered side-table. It was the 'prestige-piece' of the period, for the shelves held the family plate when important guests were entertained. The upper and central friezes often contained drawers which were decorated with strap-work. The supports were of bulbous form or in the shape of heraldic beasts, while the base platform had inlaid decoration. The name 'court' remains something of a mystery – perhaps from the French *court* (short) as these pieces were rarely more than four feet high, or more probably because they may have been first used on formal occasions at Court. Some examples of these cupboards had an enclosed central compartment in the upper stage with canted sides. While, as has been seen, the earlier types of cupboards all continued to be made, food cupboards were now often hung on the wall and had turned spindles in their doors.

Beds sometimes reached enormous proportions. The wooden tester became so heavy that it no longer rested on four posts but on two large foot-posts standing clear of the bed frame, and on an elaborate carved and inlaid headboard. The most famous bed of the time is the Great Bed of Ware (Fig. 6), first mentioned in 1596 and referred to by Shakespeare in *Twelfth Night*. This bed, and others of the time, often included intarsia work – inlaid perspective views – in their headboard panels. Intarsia was based on Italian techniques, but reached England through imported Flemish pattern books.

Another decorative feature was the split baluster, made of turned pieces split down the middle, then glued to the carcase. One long-established error connected with intarsia (or inlay) work in Elizabeth's reign has arisen over the so-called 'Nonsuch chests', which are decorated with inlaid patterns of formal architectural views supposed to represent Henry VIII's Palace of Nonsuch, Cheam, Surrey, England, demolished in the seventeenth century. There is no evidence to connect these views with Nonsuch and it now seems clear that the chests were of German or Flemish origin.

Wealthy Elizabethans loved rich and gay upholstery. Cushions, wall hangings, bed curtains and imported tapestries and carpets (the latter being used to cover tables and court cupboards) all added colour and comfort to the interior. One favoured material was Turkey-work which seems to have been produced only in England and was made in the manner of a hand-knotted carpet, copying the designs of the larger carpets imported from the Middle East. In medieval times painted furniture seems to have been common. By Elizabeth's reign this custom was dying out, to be replaced by carved and inlaid decoration or, in the case of plain surfaces, by wax polishing.

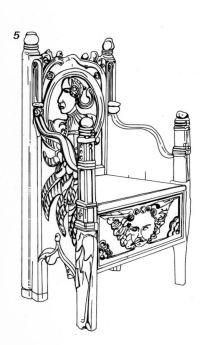

5

Fig. 5 **Armchair**, *probably Scottish, c.1550. Oak, height 42¼ ins. This chair illustrates the fusion of gothic and renaissance motifs.* (*Victoria and Albert Museum.*)

Museum Photo

Fig. 6 ***The Great Bed of Ware,***
*1580. Carved oak with inlaid
decoration, length 11 ft. 1 in.,
width 10 ft. 8½ ins.
Wide enough to sleep four
couples, it has become one of the
most famous beds in English
history, and the subject of
numerous literary allusions. Sir
Toby Belch, in* Twelfth Night
*encouraged Sir Andrew to write
'as many lies as will lie on thy
sheet of paper although thy
sheet were big enough for the
Bed of Ware in England'. It was
probably made for Sir Henry
Fanshawe of Ware Park but by
1616 it had been moved to an inn.
(Victoria and Albert Museum.)*

MUSEUMS AND COLLECTIONS

Elizabethan furniture may be seen at the following:

Derbyshire:	Hardwick Hall
London:	Victoria and Albert Museum
Norfolk:	Stranger's Hall, Norwich
Northamptonshire:	Burghley House
Nottinghamshire:	Wollaton Hall
Somerset:	Montacute House
Warwickshire:	Shakespeare's Birthplace Trust Properties, Stratford-upon-Avon
Wiltshire:	Longleat

FURTHER READING

Furniture 700–1700 by Eric Mercer, Section 4, 'The sixteenth century', London, 1969.
The Connoisseur's Complete Period Guides (ed. by Ralph Edwards and L. G. G. Ramsey), 'Furniture' by John Hunt in **The Tudor Period 1500–1603,** London, 1968.
Furniture in England: The Age of the Joiner by S. W. Wolsey and R. W. P. Luff, London, 1968.
Dictionary of English Furniture (ed. by P. Macquoid and Ralph Edwards), London, 1954. Abridged version, **Shorter Dictionary of English Furniture** (ed. by Ralph Edwards), London, 1964.
The Englishman's Chair by John Gloag, London, 1964.
A Short Dictionary of Furniture by John Gloag, London, 1964.

Early Italian Furniture

Furniture in Italy gradually conformed to the renaissance ideal and expansive public display was replaced by expensive private delight.

Wealthy Italian families in the early years of the fifteenth century took little interest in the furnishing of their palaces. It might appear surprising that those who patronised painters, sculptors, goldsmiths and architects so avidly should consider furniture a necessary but unimportant feature in a room, impermanent and apt to detract from the overall decorative scheme for which, perhaps, one of the greatest fresco painters of the day had been responsible.

In 1400 taste throughout Europe was for carved oak wall-panelling and for panelling on articles of furniture such as the chest, the medieval way of life, and thus the decorative standards, were generally haphazard. A room might contain splendidly ornate silk wall-hangings, rough linen-fold oak panelling, a central fire brazier and an enormous dining-table, all beneath a colourfully painted beamed ceiling. Gradually, however, attitudes towards furniture in Italy were changing; after about 1450 the new design and decorative elements in the Fine Arts

Fig. 1 **The Nervi Cassone,**
Florentine, late-fifteenth century.
This piece illustrates the
renaissance cassone at its best.
It is exquisitely proportioned and
the painted panels are obviously
the work of a skilled craftsman.
(Courtauld Institute Galleries,
London.)

Fig. 2 **Bed,** *Tuscan, c1550.*
This type of bed was much more
popular than the canopied four-
poster; even in their bedrooms,
the Florentines loved to be
surrounded by ornate carving
and lavish gilding.
(Palazzo Davanzati.)

Fig. 3 **Armadio, or cupboard,**
possibly from Mantua, c.1580.
The armadio *developed from the*
cassone; *this piece, with its*
elaborate grotesques, shows the
decorative exaggerations of the
mannerist style.
(Palazzo Davanzati, Florence.)

Figs. 4 and 5 **Cassone or**
marriage chest, *Venetian, c.1500.*
The ivory inlay of this cassone
has both Eastern and medieval
characteristics typical of northern
Italy.
(Rijksmuseum, Amsterdam.)

122

were regularly applied to the construction of furniture – the forms of all furniture conformed to the laws of just proportion, geometric panelling and inlay appeared on the *cassoni*, or marriage chests, and four-poster beds grew classical columns. By the 1530s, the period of mannerist decorative elegance and excesses, furniture had established its position in the decorative whole as the emphasis changed from expansive public display to expensive private delight.

Chests filled with the dowry and belongings of the bride

The principal article of furniture in the Renaissance was the *cassone*, so named because during the marriage procession these large rectangular chests, filled with the dowry and belongings of the bride, were carried through the streets to the groom's palace (Figs. 1, 4 and 5). Since they were displayed publicly, these objects were often very expensively and beautifully decorated, sometimes with painted panels executed by the best-known painters of the time; Botticelli and Perugino, for example, are recorded as having executed *cassone* panels. As the cupboard and the chest of drawers only evolved at the beginning of the sixteenth century, the *cassone* was in universal use for the storage of linen, clothes, valuables and all sorts of domestic paraphernalia; there could be as many as fifty *cassoni* in one Florentine palace, placed against the walls as well as in the traditional position at the end of the bed. At first

123

6

Museum Photo

Fig. 6 *Savonarola, or folding X-chair,* Florentine, c.1550. *Carved oak.* (Victoria and Albert Museum.)

7

Museum Photo

Fig. 7 *Sgabello, or stool,* one of a pair, Florentine, c.1500. *Walnut decorated with gilding. Despite its small size, this stool has a marvellously architectural appearance, both in its proportions and in the use of a frieze motif. The carved scroll-work displays a roundness of treatment that differs from mannerist use of the same forms.* (Victoria and Albert Museum, London.)

sight the fifteenth century *cassone* may not appear to differ radically from its immediate predecessor, the medieval chest; both objects are basically the same long-box shape, sometimes on feet, otherwise on a flat base, the interior being undivided except for one end where there was frequently a small box-drawer for holding jewels and other valuables. On closer inspection it will be seen that the new formal and decorative characteristics of the *cassone* reflect some of the many and significant stylistic changes of the Renaissance.

The first and most important difference between the medieval chest and the Renaissance *cassone* is one of proportion; the gothic style is in general characterised by spiky elongation of forms, and the medieval chest, of tall, slim proportions, often has carved gothic tracery decorating the front. In fifteenth-century Italy, however, the chest assumed the balanced proportions ordained by classical design and also became a superbly architectural object with applied pilasters, carved friezes and imposingly articulated lids and bases (Fig. 4.) Many different decorative methods were used; sometimes scenes and figures derived from the Roman running frieze were described in *pastiglia* (moulded and painted plasterwork), as a variation on the painted wooden panel already mentioned.

Naturalistic and geometric use of inlay to give illusions of space

One of the most significant innovations was in the use of illusionistic inlay of wood. The front of the *cassone* was divided evenly by heavily framed square panels in which a naturalistic or geometric pattern was inlaid to give the illusion of space. In the borders there are sometimes geometric abstract patterns derived from illusionistic Roman mosaics under excavation at the time. These devices had a long life as decorative features of European furniture; the rectangular panel in high relief became the principal motif on baroque cabinets, and it was still popular at the end of the eighteenth century. Classical running patterns in various forms have been in continuous use on furniture until the introduction of modern machine methods.

The *cassone* always remains a fascinating, fundamental object in the history of European furniture; not only does it display the first use in furniture of certain important ornamental methods, but from its basic form grew many of the pieces of furniture that were soon to be so familiar. An obvious mutation occurs from the *cassone* into the *cassapanca*, the solidly proportioned wooden-backed bench from which in turn the standard upholstered sofa was eventually to emerge in the seventeenth century. By the beginning of the sixteenth century the *cassone* itself had become more elegant, with concave curved end-sections on tallish feet. It created the basic shape of the commode, although drawers did not yet appear in the front.

The *cassone*, due to its prestige function as a marriage chest, was the only object in which any artistic interest was regularly expressed. Nevertheless, there are other pieces of furniture which have undeniable attractions to our eyes, one of these being the folding X-shaped arm-chair, called either a Savonarola or Dante chair according to certain small differences of form. (Fig. 6.) Although basically pre-renaissance in design, the Savonarola

chair has an assured elegance and a sophisticated balance of semi-circular volumes. All chairs had to be easily movable and it is admirable that a collapsible chair should possess such quality of design.

The lady of the house was surrounded by rugs and cushions from the East

Towards the end of the century a completely new type of chair emerged called the *sgabello*. (Fig. 7.) The double scroll-shaped straight back is repeated in the legs giving a severe outline to the side view. The invention of such chairs is presumably to be connected with the gradual development of the large dining-table which did not become a regular feature until the mannerist period. At the beginning of the renaissance period, the only type of table was merely a rough oak top laid on wooden trestles, but by the end of the century, tables in Tuscany are known to have had large legs sculpted to reproduce the end section of antique sarcophagi; it was for this that the *sgabello* was designed. However, one very rarely sees a true renaissance table of this type, for most are of a later date with an excess of ornament and with an exaggeration of the carved forms on their legs which places them firmly within the mannerist period. There are also in existence a certain number of smallish, solid hall-tables, supported by a central pedestal, that are stongly reminiscent of Roman stone furniture.

The renaissance bedroom is the most difficult room in a *palazzo* to reconstruct; one wonders what personal comforts the lady of the house gathered around her for the long hours when her husband retreated into his own haven, the *studiolo*. It is interesting to recall that she had no cupboard in which to keep her possessions until the introduction of the *credenza*, or side-cupboard, in the sixteenth century. Until then the *cassone* sufficed. No doubt a loom normally stood by the window; the floors were brightened with rugs and cushions brought back by travellers from the East and the walls were decorated by painted leather 'wallpaper' or by tapestries. The bed, placed on a raised dais, dominated the room; the four-poster, the most imposing type of bed, was, however, less popular than the characteristically Tuscan type with an ornately carved headpiece and four tall twisted columns at each end, surmounted by classical urns carved from wood. (Fig. 2.)

The renowned Lorenzo the Magnificent exemplifies many of the characteristics of the Renaissance and of particular interest is a letter from Lorenzo to his son Giovanni who was then studying in Rome. The letter advises against the tasteless display of wealth in contemporary decoration; a well-ordered and refined household is to be preferred to pomp and display. Much more desirable is the distinction which comes from possessing a few rare antiques (sculpture), and fine books. There is a complete disavowal of interest in contemporary furnishings and the same taste is described in Castiglione's *Il Cortegiano* (English translation, 1561), written in Rome but describing the Court of Federigo da Montefeltro at Urbino – it is a taste which denied decorative excess and demanded the type of well-proportioned, architecturally imposing furniture that has here been described.

Hamlyn group

Fig. 8 ***Table top*** *inlaid with pietre dure, or semi-precious stones, designed by Ligozzi and Poccetti, Florence, 1633–49. This fine example of pietre dure contains agates, jaspers, lapis lazuli and chalcedonies on a black marble ground. It was designed for Ferdinando II de' Medici. (Museo dell' Opificio delle Pietre Dure, Florence.)*

MUSEUMS AND COLLECTIONS

Collections of Renaissance Furniture are on view at the following:

FRANCE
Paris: Louvre
                     Musée des Arts Décoratifs

GREAT BRITAIN
London: Courtauld Institute Galleries
                     Victoria and Albert Museum

ITALY
Florence: Museo Horne
                     Museo Nazionale (Bargello)
                     Palazzo Davanzati
                     Palazzo Vecchio

U.S.A.
Muncie, Indiana: Ball State University Art Gallery
New York: Metropolitan Museum of Art

FURTHER READING

A History of Italian Furniture from the Four-teenth Century to the early Nineteenth Century by W. Odom, New York, 1966–67.
Furniture and Interior Decoration of the Italian Renaissance by F. Schottmüller, New York, 1928.

Lacquered Furniture

Fig. 1 **Miniature tansu or chest containing drawers,** *Japanese, second half of the eighteenth century. Length 9¾ ins., height 9 ins., depth 4¾ ins.*
Miniature pieces of furniture were made for the Girls' Festival in the third day of the third moon, a festival created by Tokugawa Ienari as a counterpart to the Boys' Festival. Although it is an eighteenth century piece, the shape and ornament of this chest are of earlier design.
(Phillips and Harris, London.)

Fig. 2 **Sho-dana or shelf cabinet,** *Japanese, second half of the eighteenth century.*
Like all Japanese furniture, this cabinet is designed to be used and seen from a low viewpoint in the sparsely furnished houses of Japan. It is of a type never used in China, and has an entirely Japanese delicacy. The shape is probably of seventeenth century origin, and the Karakusa ornament is probably sixteenth century.
(Phillips and Harris.)

R. Todd-White

Using a skilled and extremely time-consuming technique, Chinese and Japanese artisans produced lacquer furniture of a quality and beauty rarely seen in Europe

The art of lacquering was probably first used in China in conjunction with furniture-making at the time of the mighty Han empire, around the first century A.D. The craft was placed under the direct patronage of the emperor and imperial workshops were set up in various provinces. Even then, there were specialists in all stages of manufacture, analogous to those of seventeenth-century porcelain-making. There were the artificers of the basic wood shape, the preparers of the cloth base, the applier of the lacquer, the polisher, the gilder, the incisor and the painter.

In Japan, lacquer was probably first made for the embellishment of furniture during the Nara period in the eighth century. Throughout the later periods it was necessary to obtain special permission to possess an article of luxury. Lacquered furniture and utensils were, therefore, made only for the Court or the nobility, and, as Japan was a country of frequent natural and human turbulence, little furniture of quality survives. In China, too, little survives for the same reasons and it appears that apart from the palaces, or the grandest rooms in the houses of the gentry, it was unusual to have all the furniture, or even complete rooms, of lacquer.

Oriental lacquer became known in Europe through Portuguese and Spanish traders

Oriental lacquer was unfamiliar to the West until more recently than porcelain, which began to reach Europe sporadically by the fourteenth century, but it was not until the late sixteenth century, when the mariners of Portugal and Spain plied their commerce with the Far East, that lacquer utensils and the occasional piece of furniture found their way to Western buyers.

Marco Polo, in China for seventeen years during the late thirteenth century, had heard of the fabulous 'gold' accoutrements – saddles, boxes and tables, many of which must have been embellished with gold lacquer – that were sent from Japan to the Imperial Court of China. Both porcelain, prized for its twin virtues of translucence and resonance, and lacquer, another completely strange and magical substance, were paid the compliment of imitation in Europe and were richly mounted in precious metals or gilt-wood. The inventory of Catherine de' Medici, who died in 1589, listed lacquer objects, and Mazarin's inventory of 1653 listed lacquer of identifiably Japanese origin. European furniture certainly began to be influenced by imported lacquer in the early seventeenth century.

For a fuller appreciation of lacquer furniture, it is necessary to describe briefly how it was made. The same basic method of making lacquer is employed all over the East. It has been made in Burma, Siam (much esteemed in the seventeenth century), Korea, and principally in China and Japan, both with long imperial traditions, reaching perfection in the latter. Discounting later, and less well made imitations, the true art was one of infinite exactitude.

Resin from the *Rhus Vernicifera* (*Urushi-no-ki*) is tapped in the same way as rubber from the tree. The resin is strained, refined and sometimes blended before being put into air-tight jars. The quality differs according to the season of tapping, the soil, the age of the tree and the climatic conditions under which it is grown and also the part of the tree from which the sap is taken. The skilled lacquerer will select the type appropriate to the article on which it is to be used. After the application of one coat of lacquer – and there may be as many as three hundred on a deeply carved finished article – the piece is put to dry in an atmosphere of a particular temperature and humidity. It is then polished and the process repeated. In the case of furniture, the application is on a carcase of soft-wood, expertly dowelled together by the Chinese and Japanese joiners using wood or bamboo pins; neither nails nor screws and little glue were used until the late nineteenth century. The Chinese lacquer screens, so popular in Europe, have leaves made up of two or three planks held together merely with pegs, a tribute to the lasting tensile quality of lacquer. The Oriental craftsman seasoned his material with great care; lacquer furniture lasts extremely well since good lacquer is impervious to water and the base moves very little.

Japanese furniture was designed to be seen and used from a low viewpoint

The style of living varied in China and Japan and this accounts for some of the differences in the furniture of the two countries. The Japanese dwelling with its wooden-posted framework was simple, even austere, divided by sliding paper screens and protected by wooden shutters on the exterior walls. Rooms were very sparsely furnished and occupants sat or knelt on the mats on the floor. Furniture was limited to trunks, both large and small, for storage, writing-boxes, small tables and trays for the tea-ceremony, shelf cabinets and chests. Everything was designed to be seen and used from a low viewpoint.

The *sho-dana* (shelf cabinet) in Figure 2 makes a beautiful small table in a Western house, but was not originally designed for the viewpoint of a man standing or seated on a chair. It is a piece not used in China, and is entirely Japanese in its delicacy. This example dates from the second half of the eighteenth century. It shows a shape that originated probably in the mid-seventeenth century and the *Karakusa* design was probably first used a century earlier. The same could be said of the *tansu*, or chest, in Figure 1. It is in fact a miniature; not designed as would have been the case in England, as an apprentice piece or trade sample, but as an object for the Girls' Festival in the third day of the third Moon, created by Tokugawa Ienari. The festival was a counterpart to the Boys' Festival in the fifth Moon and there would be, among other things, an exhibition of historical dolls and miniature pieces of furniture to celebrate the next generation of motherhood.

Chinese houses would be more familiar to the

3

European visitor. They possessed stools in abundance (chairs were the prerogative of rank or age) and tables of a greater variety of heights than the Westerner commonly uses for eating, writing and the display of an object or vase of flowers. Some tables, which appear to us uncommonly low, were placed upon the *kang*, a raised, built-in, heated bed particularly popular in North China, but seldom found in lacquer. Figure 3 shows an elegant lady of the seventeenth century, posed, in much the same fashion as her European counterpart, against a cherished possession, a table with lacquered legs.

The sideboard (*lien san*), with drawers above and cupboard beneath, is rare in lacquer; bookshelves are less rare. The Chinese loved symmetry and order and the casual arrangement of our rooms would have been anathema to them. Pairs of chairs might be arranged on each side of a table, all matching; *armoires* were placed in rooms of state and, in palaces, they were often of large proportions with hat cupboards above.

One type of table peculiar to China was the household altar-table, sometimes made in pairs. Figure 5 shows a magnificent example in dark tobacco brown lacquer from the early years of the seventeenth century. The underlying form is of great beauty and strength. The decoration on the top, with dragons among clouds within a shaped surround, and on the legs and frieze, is not incised but painted gold.

The differences between Chinese and Japanese lacquer furniture are noticeable in the styles of decoration of the two countries. There is a world of

A. C. Cooper

Fig. 3 **Dish**, *Chinese, of the K'ang Hsi period (1662–1722). Porcelain.
(Christie, Manson and Woods, London.)*

Fig. 4 **Cabinet**, *Japanese, third quarter of the seventeenth century. Height 29½ ins. The highest qualities of the Japanese craftsman, brought out in cabinets of this sort, had a profound influence on European furniture.
(Phillips and Harris.)*

Fig. 5 **Household altar-table**, *Chinese, early seventeenth century. Length 6 ft. 3 ins. This magnificent dark tobacco brown and gold altar-table is of a type peculiar to China.
(Spink's.)*

Fig. 6 **Cabinet**, *Japanese, mid-seventeenth century. Height 27 ins. Of exceptional quality, this cabinet with its hardstone decoration would have cost more in 1650 than now.
(Phillips and Harris.)*

Fig. 7 **Cabinet**, *Chinese, third quarter of the seventeenth century. Height 31¾ ins. This excellent copy of Japanese lacquer emulates the raised gold (taka-makie) work of Japan.
(Phillips and Harris.)*

Fig. 8 **Cabinet**, *Japanese, early eighteenth century. Height 13 ins. This fine example shows why Oriental lacquer-work was so esteemed in Europe for its beauty and intricacy.
(Phillips and Harris.)*

difference between even a fine quality, small-size Chinese coromandel screen and the Japanese painted paper partitions of screens. Coromandel lacquer would have been coarse and overwhelming in the small-scale Japanese house. The Chinese have a great sense of the mass of an object and the balancing of masses. They often think in terms of volume, of the filling of the space, rather than the drawing of the line round it. Designs upon ceramics or lacquer furniture are appropriate to the object, and executed with great verve. The top of the remarkable table in Figure 5 has a design of three dragons within a shaped panel, with ten more cavorting round the border. To our eyes the execution of the design in painted gold is remarkable, being done with a certain artistic freedom; precise without being finicky.

Japanese decoration is achieved with great exactitude and labour

The Japanese, however, with their taste and aptitude for incredible precision of finish, do not appreciate such work to the same extent. On the whole they approach design differently; they think in terms of line and the balancing of shapes. The lacquer designs are usually more open than the Chinese, more naturalistic though at the same time more severe. They were not as fond as the Chinese of incising and inlaying different coloured lacquers in another coloured ground. Their designs were built into the lacquer surface by drawing in the materials themselves, gold or silver dust, pieces of

metal and by the carving of laboriously raised surfaces. As so often in the Japanese character, there is a contradiction: a seemingly simple design of some asymmetrically placed blades of grass, achieved, as it were, only by the swift, sure stroke of a brush, is copied with an almost unbelievable exactitude and labour in the long process of lacquer working, achieving exactly the same impression of spontaneity.

In fifteenth-century China, the imperial lacquer workshop was re-established in Peking, and the vermilion lacquers from the reign of Yung-lo and Hsuan-te have retained their contemporary fame. Figure 10 shows a rare survival of a small table from that century; furniture in this style of lacquer is most uncommon, and though the technique evolved ultimately into the carved Cinnabar lacquer of the eighteenth century, the shape of this table could well be found in other techniques in the succeeding four centuries. Very often it is embellished with mother of pearl inlays in a black ground, the shape being borrowed by the Japanese and similarly embellished.

Another very rare survival of carved red lacquer is shown in the magnificent folding chair of about 1600 in Figure 9, which would have been used in a hall or taken outside. It is in so-called *guri* lacquer, in Chinese, *Chien Hwan Hsiang Tsao*, being the description of a kind of grass that the pattern resembles. The thick lacquer is carved with a wedge-shaped tool revealing, rather like geological strata, alternate levels of light and dark red. Examples of this type of lacquer are known from the Yuan dynasty; the Japanese copied it, but as in China

129

9

R Fortt

10

A. C. Cooper

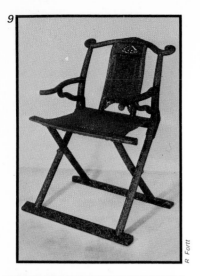

Fig. 9 **Folding chair,** *Chinese, c.1600. Carved* guri *lacquer. (Spink and Son Ltd., London.)*

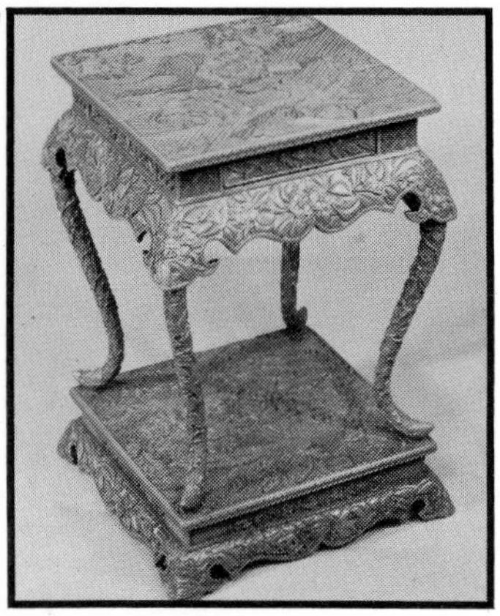

Fig. 10 ***Low table,*** *Chinese, fifteenth century. Vermilion carved lacquer. (Christie's.)*

the output largely consisted of small boxes.

Mother of pearl inlays picked out with painting in gold (*raden*) have an ancient lineage in lacquer-work and furniture. In the Shosoin at Nara are preserved Chinese T'ang and possibly a few Japanese utensils, chests, musical instruments and cabinets. At this time, the influence of T'ang China was eagerly absorbed, and indeed in the organisation of the traditional Japanese house and in the Gagaku music of the imperial household, we see and hear things essentially unchanged since the eighth century.

The highest quality work was to be seen in the cabinets, so much admired in Europe

The first *raden* lacquers of the Japanese imitated T'ang wares and, by the sixteenth century, the method was again used for the first lacquer wares made expressly for Europeans; utensils, trunks and cabinets. From these, a yet more splendid form of cabinet was developed which, although made by the Japanese to stand on the floor according to their convention, was used differently in Europe. The Japanese had now, by the beauty of their designs and the refinement and development of scores of named techniques, become superior in the art to the Chinese who, even in the sixteenth century, paid vain visits to learn a similar proficiency. It is in these marvellous cabinets that we see displayed, in a manner beautifully suited to European interiors, the highest qualities of the Japanese artist craftsman (Figs. 4 and 6).

Artists of the highest calibre painted for the lacquerer, and their designs were often borrowed by painters. Figure 6 shows a cabinet which might be assigned to the middle years of the seventeenth century. The animals, the pattern around the drawer fronts and on the dividers, the use of hardstones and the quality of the raised gold (*taka makie*), all point to a date around 1650. None of the few cabinets of similar type now in the National Museum of Denmark, formerly in the Royal Cabinet of Curiosities, the collection started around 1635, attain this quality. Few examples of this excellence reached Europe in the ship-loads that arrived in Antwerp from the East which were then much more expensive than they are now.

A great number of exotic pieces were imported into Europe

Because of the historical development of the East India trade, these cabinets would have been more familiar in Continental houses than English ones. When, in 1679, Evelyn remarked of the rich lacquer cabinets at the house of the Portuguese Ambassador, 'I think there were a dosen', he was expressing surprise at the quantity of these rare and exotic pieces.

Seventeenth and eighteenth century Europeans distinguished more readily than we do now between the various qualities of lacquer and cabinets, as of course did the Chinese and Japanese. It is noticeable that the finest French furniture of the eighteenth century used the equivalent lacquer of the 1670s or 80s. The front of the great *secrétaire en pente* which was sold in London for a large sum was veneered with lacquer that must have come from a cabinet of the type illustrated in Figure 4.

This piece also shows the refinement of the gilt copper mounts. Other sorts of Chinese and Japanese lacquer furniture might have them in brass, silver, *pai tung* (pewter) sometimes engraved, or *cloisonné* enamel. A peculiarity is that the Japanese artist worked out his designs and their location in the space without regard for the subsequent application of hinge straps or lock plates. The rich sobriety of the early examples noticed above was also taken over by the Chinese when they paid the Japanese the compliment of copying their wares. Europeans also copied both Chinese and Japanese lacquers, creating some of the most beautiful furniture of the seventeenth and eighteenth centuries.

Quality depended on sufficient time and exacting standards

A very fine cabinet from the first years of the eighteenth century is shown in Figure 8. The ground colour is dark brown, unlike the lustrous black of the previous examples, and a greater variety of colours are used. The design of the lock-plate is more elaborate; the carrying handles are of gilt-copper rather than of iron. In slightly earlier examples of a comparable quality, the flower-heads might have been in hardstone, mother of pearl, *repoussé*, or solid metal. Fine lacquer furniture could be made only when the time of a skilled artist was immaterial, and as long as an extremely exacting standard was satisfied. Unfortunately, demands and standards have changed and furniture of this quality will never be made again.

MUSEUMS AND COLLECTIONS

Oriental lacquer furniture may be seen at the following:

DENMARK
Copenhagen: National Museum

FRANCE
Paris: Musée Guimet

GREAT BRITAIN
London: Victoria and Albert Museum

NETHERLANDS
Amsterdam: Rijksmuseum

U.S.A.
Cleveland: Cleveland Museum of Art
New York: Metropolitan Museum of Art

FURTHER READING

Chinese Art by R. Soame Jenyns and William Watson, London, 1963.
Chinese Domestic Furniture by G. Ecke, reprinted London, 1963.
Japanese Art Lacquer by U. A. Casal, London, 1961.
'Guri Lacquer of the Ming Dynasty' by Sir H. Garner, **Transactions of the Oriental Ceramic Society**, Vol. 31.

The Age of Walnut

With the revived optimism of the restoration of Charles II and the extensive rebuilding in London after the Great Fire, oak furniture fell from favour. Walnut became the fashionable wood and continental veneering and marquetry gave elegance and lightness to the pieces

Fig. 1 *Detail of a marquetry box, English*, c.1670. *Various woods. Marquetry was the most fashionable form of furniture veneer of this period. Many different woods were used, dyed, stained or scorched to the right colour. Sycamore was dyed green to form 'harewood' which made up the foliage of the ever-popular floral marquetry.* (*Victoria and Albert Museum, London.*)

A. C. Cooper

Sixteen hundred and sixty, the year of Charles II's restoration to the English throne after eleven years of exile abroad, was an important landmark in the history of English furniture. For almost a quarter of a century progress in the arts and crafts in England had been seriously hampered, first by the quarrel between Charles I and Parliament, which had led to the Civil War and the King's execution in 1649, and secondly by the eleven years of Puritan rule imposed by Cromwell.

During his exile, Charles II had become fully acquainted with the high standards of furniture design and craftsmanship in France and Holland and on his return he was determined to introduce these standards into England. His example, and that of his luxury-loving Court, was eagerly followed by the aristocracy, landed gentry and merchants, encouraged both by the inevitable reaction to Puritan austerity and by the rising national prosperity brought about by trade and colonisation. The spirit of the age was aptly summed up by the famous diarist, John Evelyn, when he wrote in 1685, on the occasion of Charles II's death, that the King had 'brought in a politer way of living which passed to luxury and intolerable expense'.

The furniture industry received an unexpected stimulus when the Great Fire of London in 1666 destroyed a large number of houses and their contents. To speed the rebuilding of the capital, and with the lessons of the recent catastrophe clearly in mind, the authorities adopted a standard scheme for new houses, dividing them into four main types, and ordered them to be made of brick and stone instead of timber framing. Typical new dwellings had an entrance hall and staircase, two or three rooms on each floor and were two to four storeys high with a garret, depending on the size of the building.

131

The desire was for elegant and compact pieces

Inside, walls were covered with painted pine panelling, and ceilings with moulded plaster. Large sash windows replaced the old casements, making the interiors much brighter than before. In this new setting the traditional oak furniture was altogether too bulky and clumsy; the desire was for more elegant and compact pieces. The answer lay in veneered furniture made with all the most up-to-date processes from the Continent, and in the use of more varied and more convenient types of furniture.

Veneers were thin sheets of wood especially selected for the beauty of their pattern, or figure, which were sawn from blocks and glued to the carefully prepared flush surfaces of the carcase or frame. Saw-cut veneers varied from about one-sixteenth to one-eighth of an inch in thickness (and were therefore thicker than modern machine-produced veneers) and, as they repeated the pattern of the block from which they were sawn, they could be laid on to the carcase in a number of attractive ways to match or reverse the pattern. Among particularly interesting figures were oval 'oyster' pieces cut transversely from small branches of trees, crotches cut from the intersection of branch and trunk, and burrs – taken from the malformation of tree trunks which produced a tangled mass and not a regular figure and were difficult to use as they tended to curl.

The wood most often associated with this period is walnut, so much so that the late Stuart era is usually referred to as 'the Age of Walnut'. But although walnut, especially the continental variety which was imported because of its fine figure, was well favoured, there were other timbers which were constantly in demand, including yew, maple, elm, mulberry, ash and kingwood. For oyster pieces, the favourites were olive and laburnum.

Even more woods were required for marquetry, a form of veneering in which intricate patterns were cut in a series of veneers and then fitted on to the prepared surface very much in the manner of a jigsaw puzzle (Fig. 1). For this technique a great variety of colours was called for, and veneers were dyed, stained or scorched to get the right shade. For most of Charles II's reign floral marquetry was fashionable, and to get the green colour for leaves, sycamore was stained and given the name of hare-wood. Parquetry was a form of marquetry which employed geometrical patterns and, for these, oyster pieces were used, set in thin lines of light coloured woods such as box, holly or sycamore.

These new techniques reached England from the Continent and were taught to English craftsmen by immigrants from Holland and France. The old joiner's technique of panel-and-frame was now outmoded, for it could not provide the flush

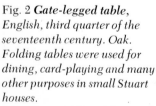

Fig. 2 **Gate-legged table**, *English, third quarter of the seventeenth century. Oak. Folding tables were used for dining, card-playing and many other purposes in small Stuart houses.*
(Victoria and Albert Museum.)

Fig. 3 **Companion figure**, *English, c.1690. Painted wood. Painted realistically in contemporary dress, these dummy figures were a charming Stuart conceit.*
(Victoria and Albert Museum.)

Fig. 4 **Sleeping-chair**, *one of a pair, English, c.1675. Gilt wood with contemporary upholstery. The winged back of this chair, designed to keep out draughts, can be adjusted by ratchets.*
(Ham House, Surrey.)

132

Museum Photo

Fig. 5 **Armchair**, *English,
c.1675.
Carved, gilt and painted wood
with dolphin motifs; original
satin brocade upholstery.
(Ham House.)*

Fig. 6 **Table**, *English, c.1675
Carved and gilt walnut and
softwood with silver mounts.
(Ham House.)*

Museum Photo

Fig. 7 **Bookcase of the Samuel
Pepys type**, *c.1665–70. Oak.
(Victoria and Albert Museum.)*

Museum Photo

surface for veneers, and the joiner had to give way to the cabinet-maker. Oak, so long the traditional woodworker's material, went out of fashion for the best furniture. Joinery, however, continued to flourish in country areas where old methods were largely untouched by the dictates of fashion.

Flowers and foliage and occasionally birds were set in oval panels

Mention of the cabinet-maker takes us naturally to the cabinet, the great prestige piece of the Restoration. Cabinets made with expensive materials such as precious woods, ivory and tortoise-shell, and enriched with metal mounts, sometimes of silver, had been made on the Continent since about 1650. Foreign cabinets of this date can be seen today in England but these have almost invariably been imported by dealers in fairly recent times. In general, the English cabinet of the post-1660 era copied contemporary Dutch and French models (Fig. 11). Its interior was enclosed by two large doors and consisted of many drawers of different sizes arranged around a central cupboard also containing drawers. The cabinet was supported on a stand – another continental innovation – with four or six legs united by waved stretchers. It was used as a receptacle for documents and the valuable collections of small curiosities, such as coins and medals, in which rich men invested a great deal of their money. In the days before banks could offer any real security it was very useful in case of an emergency to have family papers and valuables in one place for easy removal. These early English cabinets were usually decorated with parquetry of oyster pieces of olive, laburnum or walnut, or with floral marquetry. Flowers and foliage and occasionally birds were set in oval panels and surrounded by borders of oyster pieces of walnut veneer. This attractive display of colour, even though there is often some fading after three centuries, makes these cabinets the most brilliantly decorated pieces of furniture ever produced in England. One peculiarly English feature emerging from this foreign influence is the drawer with convex front which is often found in the frieze of the cabinet below the moulded cornice.

Another type was the 'Indian' cabinet imported from Japan and China by the East India Company. Decorated with lacquer on the front door and sides and on the drawer fronts, it had elaborate gilt copper hinges and lock-plates. The Chinese were fond of decorating cabinets with figures set in landscapes, while the Japanese concentrated on animals, flowers and birds. It was Chinese decoration which was mostly imitated by English craftsmen whose substitute for lacquer, varnish mixed with paint colours, became known as japanning. They preferred bright grounds of reds, greens and tortoise-shell, while genuine lacquered cabinets almost always had a black ground. English japan, however, is a poor substitute for lacquer. It cracks and fades in strong sunlight and most japanned furniture of this time has disappeared. Even when it has survived it has usually been heavily restored. Oriental cabinets required a stand for use in England and they were often given an elaborately carved and gilt (or silvered) support (Fig. 8).

The chest of drawers developed into its modern form by the end of Charles II's reign. For some time after 1660 it was usual for the upper section to have a deep drawer which, because of its weight, moved in and out on bearers attached to the inside of the carcase, the sides of the drawer being grooved to slide on them. By 1685 the present familiar arrangement was achieved in the pattern of two short, shallow drawers at the top and three long, deeper ones beneath, now moving in and out on runners. For decoration, chests of drawers often had floral marquetry or matched walnut veneers. Various decorative devices were used to mask the gap between drawer and carcase. The earliest was the half-round or double half-round moulding attached to the framework. Later the moulding or beading was attached to the edge of the drawer as an ovolo or 'quarter-round' lip moulding. All these developments meant, of course, that the chest was at last beginning to lose its long-established popularity.

Chairs typify the flamboyant spirit of Charles II's England

Chairs of Charles II's reign are a byword for their elaborate ornamentation, but in fact the first new type to appear in the decade after 1660 was a light and simple cane chair with its back and seat composed of a mesh of split rattans derived from a kind of oriental palm imported by the East India Company. This kind of chair, which was already known in France and Holland, was unusual in that it was found in ordinary houses before it became fashionable in higher society. It used the cheap method of spiral turning on all its structural members. There seems little doubt that many of these chairs were supplied in sets to the new houses built in London after the Great Fire, and that they began to replace stools, which had for so long been the common type of seat.

It was not until about the middle of Charles' reign that chairs of this kind lost their earlier simplicity when they began to be adopted in large households. Their height was increased and the framework of the cane panel in the back, set in spiral-turned uprights, was elaborately carved as also were the deep cresting and the front stretcher (which often matched each other). The arm supports and front legs were formed of elongated scrolls, and the arms themselves, of round or oval section, scrolled boldly over their supports. Made of walnut, or of beech stained to imitate walnut, these chairs perhaps typify better than any other piece of furniture the flamboyant spirit of Charles II's England (Figs. 9 and 10). Many had a patriotic motif in the cresting in the form of a crown supported by *amorini* – 'boyes and crowne'.

The simpler form of cane chairs remained popular in smaller houses. This was indeed the age of cane chairs, so much so that upholsterers petitioned Parliament for protection against the importing of canes. Their petition was unsuccessful and cane chairs continued to be made in large quantities until well into the eighteenth century. Very similar in style and decoration to the more elaborate chairs were day-beds which, after 1660, copied the *lits de repos* then fashionable in France. Now they began to resemble couches, and one end had a back which in some cases was adjustable. The

Fig. 8 *Cabinet on stand*,
English, c.1670–80. The cabinet
japanned, the stand silvered
wood; the cabinet mounts of gilt
copper.
Japanning, a process using
coloured varnishes, was widely
used in imitation of oriental
lacquer-work during the
seventeenth century.
(Victoria and Albert Museum.)

Fig. 9 *Detail of an armchair,*
English, c.1675. Walnut and
cane.
Chairs in the reign of Charles II
are known above all for the
elaborate ornamentation of their
carving, as this detail of a
chair-back amply illustrates. The
pascal lamb forming the crest, is
lost in a profusion of angels,
cherubs and swirling foliage. The
caning is typical of the period.
(Victoria and Albert Museum.)

Fig. 10 *Set of chairs, English,*
c.1685. Walnut and cane.
This set of one armchair and six
matching straight chairs is typical
of everyday furniture in the late
seventeenth century. Twisted
supports and caned seats and
backs are frequently found, while
the matching cresting and front
stretcher are more fanciful but
still commonplace features.
(Victoria and Albert Museum.)

seat and back were made of cane set in frames of walnut which were carved and turned in the prevailing mode (Fig. 13).

But in spite of the complaints of upholsterers against cane chairs, upholstered chairs employing rich materials, which were often fringed, remained a prominent feature of late Stuart furniture (Fig. 5). About 1670, the famous large upholstered winged armchair, then known as an 'easie chair' made its appearance. The wings were no doubt added to keep draughts out. Ham House, Surrey, has a pair of interesting upholstered winged armchairs with adjustable backs worked by ratchets (Fig. 4). They were made about 1675 when Ham house was being refurnished and are entered as 'sleeping chayres' in the inventory of the contents of the house which was drawn up in 1679.

New types of writing furniture also appeared at this time. The much improved postal services in London after the Great Fire, and in the country generally, led to a great increase in letter-writing. The earliest writing-cabinets, called variously scriptors, scriptoires and scrutores, were, like so many other new pieces, taken directly from continental models (French: *escritoire*). They were box-like structures, mounted at first on stands, and had a large fall-front which let down on chains or stays to provide a flat writing surface, disclosing numerous small drawers and pigeon-holes for letters. Later, in Charles' reign, a chest of drawers was used to form a steadier support for the heavy superstructure. These writing-cabinets made a fine field for decoration in parquetry, marquetry or beautifully figured walnut and other woods. The large fall-front, however, was awkward in one respect – all papers had to be cleared off the desk before it could be shut up. By 1700 the bureau was being introduced. This was more convenient

embossed silver key-plates and handle escutcheons and silver ring handles on the interior drawers. The other scriptor at Ham House, which also has silver mounts, is decorated with veneers of burr walnut. Scriptors were luxury pieces found only in rich households; elsewhere the small writing-desks of traditional form continued in use.

Another new piece of furniture was the domestic bookcase (Fig. 7). Samuel Pepys made, on 23 July, 1666, what must be the earliest reference to this type of furniture: 'Comes Simpson the joiner; and

because its sloping fall-front left space at the back on which to clear papers when the hinged front part was folded.

Two well-known and attractive scriptors at Ham House which are also in the 1679 inventory, are of smaller dimensions than the usual kinds. One, described as a 'Scriptoire of Prince Wood, garnished with silver', is veneered with oyster pieces of kingwood (a deep brown wood allied to rosewood and also known as princewood) and is supported on a kingwood stand with a drawer in the frieze and spiral-turned legs with carved volute feet joined by waved stretchers (Fig. 12). The interior has fourteen pigeon-holes and six veneered drawers. This splendid piece of Carolean furniture has

he and I with great pains contriving presses to put my books up in: they now growing numerous, and lying one upon another on my chairs'. Pepys had a number of these bookcases made and twelve are preserved in the Pepys Library, Magdalene College, Cambridge. From this time, bookcases were to be an established part of the rapidly growing libraries of large houses.

As separate eating rooms evolved, the old draw table went out of fashion and its place was taken by oval or circular gate-legged tables with two flaps, which could be conveniently set up for meals, then folded and removed (Fig. 2). Plenty of useful small tables stood about the house, often with spiral-turned legs, flat-waved stretchers, and

Fig. 11 *Cabinet on stand, English, late seventeenth century. Walnut and marquetry. Based on continental models, cabinets of this sort were the prestige pieces of the Restoration era, and were used for the storage of valuable documents and small curiosities. (Victoria and Albert Museum.)*

Fig. 12 *Scriptor on stand, English, c.1675. Kingwood oyster veneer with silver mounts. Made from deep brown king- or princewood, a wood closely allied to rosewood, this scriptor or writing-desk contains fourteen pigeon-holes and six veneered drawers. (Ham House.)*

Fig. 13 *Day-bed, English, c.1670–80. Walnut and cane. Copied from the French lits de repos, day-beds became popular after about 1660. (Victoria and Albert Museum.)*

decoration of parquetry or marquetry. They served a number of purposes, including card-playing, but tables made especially for cards did not appear until William and Mary's reign, in spite of the great passion of the time for all kinds of card games and gambling. On the other hand, tables designed for the toilet emerged quite clearly after 1660. It was fashionable to make up a set called 'table, glass and stands', composed of a dressing-table beneath a mirror flanked by a pair of candlestands. Most dressing-tables were small unless their owner was rich enough to afford one of the elaborate silver toilet sets for which a larger surface was essential. Knole, Kent, has a silver dressing-table, but walnut, ebony or olive were the woods usually employed.

Rich men still spent lavishly on beds, particularly those in the state bedrooms reserved for important visitors. New houses had higher ceilings and consequently the height of beds increased, often to exaggerated proportions when ostrich plumes were added to the four corners of the testers. The framework was no longer left exposed but was entirely covered with expensive materials. The King's Bed on display at Knole, is equipped with one of the most extravagant sets of hangings recorded. Curtains, valances, tester and bases are of gold cloth lined with faded coral taffeta, all embroidered with silver, gold and coloured silks. This bed can be dated to 1670–80 and was said to have cost some £7,000.

MUSEUMS AND COLLECTIONS

Restoration furniture can be seen in its original setting at the following:

GREAT BRITAIN
London: Victoria and Albert Museum
Sevenoaks, Kent Knole
Richmond, Surrey: Ham House

U.S.A.
Trenton, New Jersey: William Trent House

FURTHER READING

'Walnut Furniture' by Edward T. Joy in **The Connoisseur's Guide to Antique Furniture**, edit. by L. G. G. Ramsey and Helen Comstock, London, 1969.

'Furniture' by R. Fastnedge in **The Connoisseur's Complete Period Guides**, *The Stuart Period*, edit. by R. Edwards and L. G. G. Ramsey, London, 1968.

Furniture Making in Seventeenth and Eighteenth Century England by R. W. Symonds, London, 1965.

Boulle and Louis XIV

A-C Boulle, son of a carpenter, was to become one of the most influential designers in the history of furniture. Made of inlaid tortoise-shell and brass, mother-of-pearl, gold and silver, his magnificent creations indeed achieved their aim to glorify the Sun King

The name of André-Charles Boulle (1642–1732) is synonymous with furniture of a monumental style and magnificence indicative of the highest rank and largest fortune. Designed for official splendour rather than private comfort, it expresses status just as effectively as the great marble and gilded baroque palaces for which it was designed. Just as Charles Lebrun's intention at Versailles was to create a setting which would exalt the person of the 'Sun King', so Boulle's furniture was conceived in the same spirit.

The partnership between Boulle and Louis XIV began in 1672 when, on the death of the royal cabinet-maker Jean Macé, lodgings and workshops in the Louvre became vacant. Colbert nominated Boulle as the best cabinet-maker in Paris. Trained as a painter, and already in 1669 employed by the Crown in that capacity, he excelled at architecture, engraving, bronze work and monogram design as well as painting and marquetry. The son of a carpenter, he was related to Pierre Boulle, a Swiss cabinet-maker employed by Louis XIII, so his background, training and

Fig. 1 **Decorated mirror back** attributed to Boulle, 29¾ x 21¾ ins. Made for Charlotte de Saint-Simon, daughter of the author of the Mémoires. (By permission of the trustees of the Wallace Collection, London.)

Fig. 2 **Kneehole desk** in contre-partie. The dominant role of the brace veneer gives this piece a particularly opulent character; expense was never considered by Boulle's patrons. (Private Collection.)

Fig. 3 **Writing table** by Boulle, 1715. Made for Maximilian Emanuel, Elector of Bavaria. (Louvre, Paris.)

aptitude fitted him even at the early age of thirty for the royal warrant. The King did not hesitate. Boulle succeeded Macé and was thus set on the path he was to follow, with his sons, for the next half century; the production of furniture for the royal palaces at the Louvre, Versailles, the Trianon, Fontaine-bleau, Marly and St. Germain. Louis XIV wished to furnish each of these and end the medieval practice of taking his furniture with him every time he changed residence.

The scale of royal patronage meant that Boulle could accept few private commissions, though he is known to have worked occasionally for the Duc and Duchesse d'Orléans, the Prince de Rohan and the bankers Samuel Bernard and Pierre Crozat. Members of foreign ruling families such as Philip V of Spain, the Prince Bishop of Cologne and the Elector Maximilian of Bavaria obtained furniture from Boulle and in 1688 the Siamese ambassadors were given a coffer to present to their Empress

4

Giraudon

Fig. 4 *Cabinet on Stand*, c.1670. *Veneered with floral marquetry on an ebony ground using light coloured woods. The crowning feature of the gilt-wood gallery emphasises the architectural character of this cabinet. (Musée des Arts Decoratifs, Paris.)*

Fig. 5 *Wardrobe designed by Boulle. Ebony with gilt-bronze mounts.*
This cupboard combines the charming floral marquetry seen also in Fig. 4 with elegant classical detail running in a band down the centre front. The lions' heads and rosettes which decorate the base are also inspired by antiquity. (Louvre, Paris.)

as an example of the finest standards in French cabinet-making.

The genius of Boulle raised cabinet-making to an art and endowed French furniture with an unmistakably national character. Prior to this, seventeenth-century French furniture consisted of a medley of ideas inherited from Italian and Dutch sources. When Boulle, fired with Lebrun's classical spirit, and responding to the royal sense of greatness, used his superlative technical skills to match the products of the *Manufacture Royale des Meubles de la Couronne* and created furniture in the grand manner, the supremacy of Parisian cabinet-making was assured, and in this, as in the other arts, France assumed the leadership in Europe.

Bérain's delightful grotesques featuring monkeys, chinoiseries and fanciful figures heralded the Rococo

Essential to Boulle's style was his perfection of the technique of brass and tortoise-shell marquetry. These materials had been used by Italians since late in the sixteenth century and the inventories of Cardinal Mazarin and Anne of Austria (Regent and mother of Louis XIV) include

cabinets inlaid with metal, mother-of-pearl, horn and semi-precious stones. At first Boulle used this technique in the rather solemn manner of Lebrun, then, from 1690 after Lebrun's death and when the impulse towards a less formal style had come from the king himself, he collaborated with the designer, Jean Bérain (1639–1711) whose delightful grotesques featuring monkeys, chinoiseries and fanciful figures have a light-hearted character heralding the rococo movement (Fig. 2). The procedure involved the gluing together of thin sheets of brass and tortoise-shell, then the pattern – either a dignified Lebrun arabesque or a charming Bérain grotesque – was set out on a paper pasted on the surface and cut out with a saw. The cut layers were then separated and replaced together to make two types of marquetry: one with a tortoise-shell ground with the pattern of brass, called *première-partie* (Fig. 13) and the reverse, or *contre-partie*, with a shell pattern on a brass ground. Great accuracy and patience was required in the arrangement of these panels, which were then glued as veneers on to plain carcases, usually of oak. The symmetrical character of the marquetry was emphasised by its use for matching pairs of armoires, cabinets and tables, and the first and counterpart panels were also used to decorate the inside and outside of cupboard doors. Those parts of the furniture not

Fig. 6 **Commode.** *The contrast between the tortoise-shell and brass inlay and gilt-bronze mounts combines with the monumentality of design to produce an effect of great sumptuousness.*
(J. de Rothschild Collection.)

Fig. 7 **Commode in contre-partie.** *The application of Boulle marquetry to the gently curved surfaces of this piece announces the future development of the eighteenth-century commode.*
(Louvre.)

Fig. 8 **Commode.** *This historic piece, the earliest documented commode, is one of a pair delivered by Boulle in 1708 for the King's Bedroom at the Trianon. It combines features of the chest with the eight legged support of the desk.*
(Grand Trianon, Paris.)

Connaissance des Arts: J. Guillot

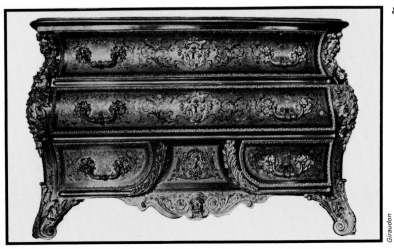

Giraudon

8

George Rainbird, Ltd.

139

Fig. 9 **Clock-vase on pedestal.**
The motif of love conquering time in gilt-bronze derives from a composition by Pordenone (1484–1539). (Versailles.)

Fig. 10 *Design for the* **Clock-case** *illustrated in Fig. 9.*
The source is known to us through a print by Ugo de Carpi which may have been in Boulle's collection.
(Musée des Arts Decoratifs, Paris.)

covered by the marquetry were veneered in ebony and occasionally coromandel wood. The brass was sometimes engraved (Figs. 1, 8 and 13), and colour was introduced in the form of a foil on which the tortoise-shell was laid, while elements like horn, silver, ivory, pewter and mother-of-pearl were sometimes incorporated into the pattern.

This expensive and elegant technique had one serious disadvantage; for the application of such different substances as metal (silver, brass and pewter) and animal products (horn, ivory, tortoise-shell and mother-of-pearl) on to wood meant that, since each of these reacted differently to varying conditions of temperature and humidity the veneers were constantly lifting from the carcase, itself subject to warping and distortion.

To counteract the fragility of his marquetry, Boulle fixed gilt-bronze mounts to the more exposed parts of his furniture, and these, like his inlay patterns, were of a classical character and combined so splendidly with the flat marquetry panels that their practical purpose was eclipsed. In achieving this alliance between cabinet-making and bronze work, Boulle established the essential features of French furniture right up to the Revolution.

He owed his freedom to combine these techniques, using both metal and wood, to his privileged position at the Louvre which exempted him from the rigid specialisation enforced by the guild system on its members. So considerable was Boulle's sculptural ability that he could model, cast, chase and gild his own bronzes, and consequently the output of his workshop was of the highest quality. Besides mounts for cabinet-making, accessories such as balustrades, grilles, light fittings and fire-dogs were made under his supervision.

Boulle was responsible for both the design and the execution of his furniture

Although Boulle collaborated with Lebrun and Bérain, he also designed independently. There are fine pen and chalk drawings for furniture attributed to him in the Louvre and the Musée des Arts Décoratifs (Fig. 11) and he published a series of engraved designs under the title *Nouveaux Desseins de Meubles et Ouvrages de Bronzes Gravés par André-Charles Boulle*. He was thus responsible for both the design and the execution of his furniture, and much of his impact stems from his superlative sense of style. In the formation of his style, his experience as a collector must have played an important part.

Like Rembrandt, Boulle never missed an auction and had to endure great financial difficulties as a result of his purchases. Among his Old Master drawings were forty-eight illustrations of Ovid's *Metamorphoses* by Raphael, Rubens' travel sketch-book and two hundred drawings by Stefano della Bella of ballet and theatrical performances; his collection of prints covered all the great Italian and Flemish masters and among forty oil paintings was a beautiful Correggio. He owned six thousand medals, wax models by Michelangelo, examples of the work of his great contemporaries, Coysevox, Coustou and Girardon, as well as plaster casts of antique sculpture. The greater part of this outstanding collection was burnt in the fire that

consumed his premises in 1720, so we have little evidence to link his collection to specific examples of his work, though it would seem that the inspiration for the *Marsyas* and *Apollo and Daphne* reliefs on the great Wallace Collection armoires must come from these Raphael drawings (Fig. 12).

An inventory of the stock which perished in this fire gives us valuable information about the range of activities carried out by Boulle and his staff of twenty assistants. Boxes containing wooden marquetry representing flowers, fruit and animals, and pictures of hunting scenes, were burnt, but the record of them proves that his skill as a marquetry worker was not restricted to his tortoise-shell and brass technique. An example of his skill in assembling wood marquetry is the Louvre armoire (Fig. 5). The severe architectural character of wardrobes such as this one, is worthy of the most grandiose conceptions of Lebrun but, since most of them are now only to be seen in the sober setting of museums, it is difficult to appreciate how well they must have harmonised with the great mirrored walls and painted ceilings of Versailles.

Various cabinets of great splendour are attributed to Boulle and he brought this favourite piece of seventeenth-century furniture to a climax before it went out of fashion. He produced versions of the bureau, a piece of furniture that was increasingly in demand as learning was once more considered an occupation for the nobleman. The *bureau Mazarin* was brought up to date with its surface, including eight legs of baluster or scroll form, decorated with Boulle marquetry. Boulle also developed a simple rectilinear table with three drawers in the frieze, of which the centre drawer was recessed and the whole veneered and enriched with gilt-bronze mounts, and this piece, the *bureau plat*, assumed great importance in the following century. Another type, with drawers resting on the top surmounted by a clock, is represented by the bureau of the Elector Maximilian Emanuel, which dates from 1715 (Fig. 3).

The strength of the contemporary literary movement is reflected in Boulle's designs for bookcases with glazed doors, and the current passion for classical antiquity was expressed in the commissions for medal cabinets. Fifteen of these were supplied for Versailles, and five of them are now in the Louvre Collection. The importance accorded to clocks and barometers is indicated by the number of cases designed by Boulle (Fig. 9) as well as pedestal supports (Fig. 13). Boulle *torchères* and *guéridons*, circular trays supported by a thin shaft resting on three legs, were designed to carry candelabra and these were placed on each side of the many elaborate marquetry tables that lined the mirror-clad walls of Louis XIV's great apartments.

The emergence of the commode came as a result of much experimentation by Boulle (Figs. 6, 7 and 8). It originated as a version of the bureau but with fewer drawers which extended the whole width. Sometimes the commode was provided with doors and the top covered in either marquetry or marble. The earliest documented examples are the Mazarine commodes formerly in the Bibliothèque Mazarine, now in Versailles, made in 1708–9 for the King's bedroom at the Trianon (Fig. 8). Here Boulle has applied his marquetry to a curved surface in an attempt to meet the fashion for furniture of a less rectilinear and severe character and, though the inspiration for this piece is the classical sarcophagus,

the experimental quality of the design is indicated by the addition of a second set of feet to bear the weight of the drawers and top.

Besides pieces of such importance, Boulle's workshop produced smaller luxurious objects; mirror- and picture-frames, ink-stands and jewel caskets, all using his characteristic marquetry which displays the same dignified spirit and uses the same motifs as his furniture.

His most ambitious achievement was the Grand Cabinet of the Dauphin, completed between 1680–83, which was considered to be one of the wonders of Versailles. Here he was responsible, not only for the furniture, but also for the marquetry frames of the Venetian glass mirrors set in the walls. His parquet floor was a masterpiece of inlay, and included highly elegant monograms of the Dauphin and his wife. Damp caused the rapid dilapidation of this room but an idea of what a Boulle style interior was like can be obtained from a study of the picture at Versailles, believed to be that of the Grand Cabinet de Monseigneur at Meudon.

A study of the history of furniture reveals that Boulle's work has always been appreciated. Even in the eighteenth century, when his tortoise-shell and brass marquetry was replaced by tropical woods and his classically inspired gilt-bronze mounts and rectilinear forms by carved surfaces and asymmetrical rococo bronzes, pieces of Boulle were regarded with the greatest respect and the day-book of Lazare Duvaux records that Madame de Pompadour collected it. With the classical revival under Louis XVI, cabinet-makers such as Levasseur and Montigny, who had been trained by Boulle's sons, found a ready market for the restoration and imitation of Boulle. Because of its inherent fragility, the majority of the pieces associated with Boulle have been extensively restored. This creates a further difficulty because Boulle did not stamp

his work and some of his followers attained such a high degree of excellence that, unless there is documentary proof, it is often difficult to determine which pieces are original. The Wallace Collection contains a knee-hole desk, veneered in *contre-partie* Bérainesque marquetry which was catalogued as seventeenth-century until cleaning revealed the maker's mark – that of Le Gaigneur, an *émigré* craftsman who worked in the Edgware Road, London, in about 1815.

Admiration for Boulle reached its zenith in Europe in the middle of the nineteenth century and this resulted in a flood of copies and drastic restoration. Because of this, much Boulle has a Victorian flavour which does not commend it to people of taste. It should be recognised, however, that Boulle's achievements were considerable: under the patronage of a king who understood the value of luxury as a means of dominating others, he was able, through his grasp of classical principles, to temper magnificence with restraint and thus give his furniture the quality of greatness. 🕮

MUSEUMS AND COLLECTIONS

Furniture by Boulle may be seen at the following:

FRANCE
Paris: Louvre
          Musée des Arts Décoratifs
GREAT BRITAIN
London: Jones Collection, Victoria and Albert
          Museum
          Wallace Collection

FURTHER READING

Furniture by F. J. B. Watson, London, 1956. (Wallace Collection Catalogue with introduction and notes).
Les Boulle by Henry Havard, Paris, 1892.

William and Mary

Despite the fact that there was a Dutch king on the throne, the predominant influence on English furniture during the last years of the seventeenth century was French. The Huguenots who fled to Protestant England brought with them the sophisticated designs of the Louis XIV style

Fig. 1 *Cabinet, c.1700. Walnut veneer with floral marquetry of various woods and ivory. This piece, made for the marriage of George Lawson and Margaret Trotter, both members of Yorkshire families, illustrates an unusual lightness and freedom in the use of marquetry. (Victoria and Albert Museum.)*

Fig. 2 *State bedstead, c.1695. The frame is of pine, covered with crimson velvet and white silk, richly trimmed with red braid. The headboard bears the cipher and earl's coronet of George Melville, created first Earl of Melville in 1690 by William III. (Victoria and Albert Museum.)*

The reign of William and Mary marks the baroque phase in the design of English furniture. Some of its manifestations can be seen towards the end of the century in the magnificent carving and gilding of such pieces as side-tables, mirrors, picture-frames and stands, the sumptuous upholstery on seat furniture and beds; the tall and elegant backs of chairs developing for the first time into curvilinear forms; the bold arches above cabinets and other case-furniture; the development of arabesque marquetry; and the vogue for flowing X-shaped stretchers on seats, stands and tables.

Political events played an important part in the development of English furniture at this time. In 1688, the Catholic James II, Charles II's brother and successor, lost his throne because of his attempts to gain toleration for his fellow Catholics and when, in 1689, the crown was settled jointly on William of Orange, the Dutch Stadtholder, and his English wife, Mary, James' daughter, a more formal atmosphere was evident at Court. John Evelyn, the celebrated diarist, described William, when he first saw him, as 'very stately, serious and reserved', words which in many ways form an apt description of the furniture which the new reign produced.

Even more decisive was the influence of the Huguenots who took refuge in England after Louis XIV's revocation in 1685 of the Edict of Nantes, by which Henry IV, in 1598, had granted toleration to Protestants in France. Even when they were tolerated, the Huguenots had still been barred by their religion from advancement in political and professional careers, and they turned their energies largely to the decorative arts. Thus, in 1685, France lost large numbers of her best crafts-men who fled to Protestant countries taking their skills with them. Those who came to England introduced the very latest French techniques and designs, the height of baroque fashion.

It was the Huguenot Daniel Marot (*c*.1663–1752),

who exercised the most powerful influence on late Stuart furniture styles. He was a true all-rounder – architect, decorator, landscape gardener and designer in a variety of crafts, including metalwork and furniture. He fled from France to Holland in 1684, anticipating the revocation, and entered William's service.

Marot's decorative flair was perhaps most vividly marked in tapestries, hangings and upholstered furniture. He also designed a Chinese cabinet room which was a pioneer attempt in the adaptation of Oriental motifs to European use. His work became widely known in England after the publication of his engraved designs, first in parts then in a collected edition in 1702, under the title of *Oeuvres du Sieur D. Marot, architecte de Guillaume III, roy de la Grande Bretagne*. He had obviously been inspired by the work of two out-standing contemporary French designers, Jean Bérain (1639–1711) and Jean Lepautre (1618–82), in whose designs can be detected the first signs of the movement from the late Baroque to the Rococo.

Another Huguenot who made a great reputation for himself in England was Jean Pelletier, carver and gilder, who appears in the royal accounts from 1690 to 1701. He supplied the royal households with carved and gilt mirror-frames, tables, screens and stands. At Hampton Court, near London, there are two sets of gilt stands which can confidently be attributed to Pelletier's workshop. Pelletier can be credited with introducing into England the magnificent baroque fine gilt furniture of the kind which distinguished Louis XIV's Court. His work undoubtedly inspired other fine gilt furniture produced by John Gumley and George Moore for George I and also on display at Hampton Court.

Another foreign craftsman, this time of Flemish or Dutch extraction, was Gerreit Jensen (whose name is found anglicised as Johnson). He was furnishing royal households from *c*.1680 to 1715, and is the only man in England at that time who is known to have made furniture inlaid with metal in the manner of André-Charles Boulle. Jensen also worked in arabesque marquetry; a writing-table (1690) and cabinet with glass doors (1693) decorated in this fashion are at Windsor Castle.

The William and Mary period is noted for some of the tallest chairs ever made in England – the backs sometimes measured two and a half times the height of the seats to the floor. Gracefulness was gained by the use of baluster forms for the uprights of the chairs instead of the earlier spiral turning of the 1670s. Front legs were still scrolled, but from about 1690 straight legs became more common, and these were either of baluster shape or square

Fratelli Fabbri

2

Museum Photo

and tapered. The tops, or cappings, of the legs acquired a variety of attractive shapes, mushroom, pear, square, etc., which are a distinctive feature of this period (Fig. 8). The height of the chairs was increased by fixing the arched cresting above the uprights instead of tenoning it between them. The filling of the backs was composed of carved scroll-work, foliage or imported cane, which was now of much finer mesh than the kind formerly used. Although the front stretcher of many chairs was frequently carved to match the bold arched scroll of the cresting, in other cases it was abandoned altogether and replaced by a curved X-shaped stretcher meeting beneath the seat in a central platform with a finial (Fig. 8). Walnut was still fashionable for these chairs, but less expensive examples were made of beech stained to resemble walnut.

The ceremonial chair under a canopy, used by William, is still at Hampton Court

Rich upholstery materials were used, however, on the finest chairs of the time. The winged armchair, now a permanent feature of English homes, had thickly padded scrolled arms and deep, padded seats, upholstered in tapestry, needlework, Genoa velvet, brocatelle, brocade, embroidered silk and braid threaded with gold and silver. Some of these materials were made in England after silk-weaving had been introduced by Huguenots who settled in Spitalfields, London.

Upholstered single chairs attained a particular elegance, with their tall, narrow, rectangular backs which were sometimes shaped at the top, probably in imitation of the arched cresting of carved and caned chairs. A well-known set of walnut seat furniture from Burley-on-the-Hill, Leicestershire,

143

A. C. Cooper

Fig. 3 **Writing-desk**, or scriptor, English, c.1690. Walnut with arabesque, or seaweed, marquetry of various woods. The sloping front opens out and is supported on the two hinged legs of the stand. (Victoria and Albert Museum.)

Fig. 4 **Winged armchair** known as an 'easie chair', c.1680. Walnut upholstered with leather. The wings were added as draught excluders. The adjustable back is worked by ratchets. (Victoria and Albert Museum.)

Fig. 5 **Circular stool** carved and gilt, c.1690. This stool still has its original brocade, embroidered in silk and silver thread. Vast sums of money were spent on fabrics at this time. (Boughton House, Northants.)

made in about 1690, has eight single chairs shaped in this manner which still retain their original brightly-coloured needlework upholstery. The Burley set includes two settees, without wings and with comparatively small padded arms; their backs are composed of two chair-backs with the same attractive shaping at the top as the single chairs.

The King's Presence Chamber at Hampton Court still contains the ceremonial chair under a canopy which William used when receiving distinguished visitors. It is flanked by a pair of stools for the use of officials. Stools were made in various shapes: rectangular, square and circular (Fig. 5). Some had six or eight feet and accommodated two persons. Daybeds or couches retained their popularity in great houses and were now usually fully upholstered instead of having cane seats and backs covered with mattress and cushions.

Japanned chairs, and indeed japanned furniture generally, imitating oriental lacquer, became increasingly popular. In 1688 Stalker and Parker's *A Treatise of Japaning and Varnishing* appeared as a manual of instruction. Illustrated with pseudo-Oriental scenes, figures, birds, etc., it made japanning a fashionable pastime for enthusiastic amateurs at home and greatly increased the demand for the work of professional japanners. The latter gained a notable success in 1701 when Parliament, in response to their outcry against foreign competition, raised the tariffs on Oriental lacquered goods and thus assured for home producers a near-monopoly of the domestic market.

One of the most remarkable advances in chair design in the whole of English furniture history occurred in the last decade of the seventeenth century. This was the appearance of the curvilinear chair (often known as the 'Queen Anne chair' though it decidedly overlapped the limits of the Queen's reign).

A new and distinctive type of walnut chair seem also to have come from Holland at this time and i described as being 'in the style of Daniel Marot' The back of this type had a curvilinear fram filled with pierced carved ornament. The front leg were of cabriole form joined by stretchers. It i possible, however, that the inspiration for the new design was a type of Chinese chair which wa imported by the East India Company and had yoke-shaped cresting and a simple central splat concave at shoulder level. Whatever the origin by about 1700 a chair of 'bended-back' type wa beginning to emerge. Such chairs had a centra splat, pierced and carved in early examples an later taking graceful vase or fiddle forms. Fo generations, chair-backs had traditionally bee square or rectangular in shape as they had bee developed by joiners from the 'panel backs' Now this quite sudden break into a curved shape opened a whole new field of design for the chair maker. In addition the cabriole leg, as it finall evolved, was the first type of leg that did no require stretchers to support it. Early cabriole legs on the Continent took the form of animals' legs ending in hooves, and at first English chairs used narrow versions of these, still preserving stretchers and adopting either hoof or club feet. As the cabrioles became sturdier and wider at the knee the stretchers were dispensed with.

The early bureaux, which stood on stands having two gate-legs which swung forward to support the top, were narrow enough to stand conveniently against the wall between windows for maximum light. At about the end of the century, this type itself was succeeded by the bureau-cabinet – a combination of chest of drawers, desk and cabinet which, in its evolutionary stage, simply consisted of these three completely separate sections. The sloping top of the central desk was supported on two slides, or lopers.

g. 6 *Day-bed*, c.1695. Gilt-
ood with Genoa velvet
holstery.
emple Newsam House, Leeds.)

g. 7 *Design for a State bed* by
aniel Marot (c.1663–1752).
ictoria and Albert Museum.)

g. 8 *Gilt chair*, covered with
t Genoa velvet, c.1690. The
ited, baluster legs have
ushroom cappings and the
rved, X-shaped stretcher
eets beneath the seat.

The cabinets for collections of 'curiosities', which had been the prestige pieces of the post-Restoration era, were still being made but were now decorated with arabesque marquetry and surmounted by arched pediments in a variety of forms. It was more usual to support them on a chest of drawers, owing to their heavy weight, than on an open stand. Cabinets, lacquered or japanned, also remained in fashion, supported on gilt or silvered stands resembling the baroque side-tables in Marot's designs. Another, newer type of cabinet had glazed doors and an interior fitted with shelves for displaying china.

As with turning, marquetry of the William and Mary period illustrated the general tendency

inspired some of the more elaborate side-tables found in fashionable households. These marked the beginning of the great period of English gesso work. Gesso was a composition of size and whiting which was laid on the wood (usually deal) in successive layers. When hard and smooth, it was treated with clay in preparation for the application of gold leaf as either water- or oil-gilding. In rarer instances it was silvered. Less luxurious side-tables were often used, though they were attractive enough with marquetry or japan decoration; their S-scrolled legs and curved stretchers were typical of the time.

At this time, the first tables specifically designed for card-playing appeared, with oval or circular

7

towards quieter forms of decoration. The former bright floral designs began to change in about 1690 into more sober shades of brown, buff and gold.

At about this time appeared the final phase of English marquetry, concentrating on arabesque patterns, the more complicated forms of which produced the version named 'seaweed' after its shape. This latter type, which no doubt owed much to Jensen's influence, used only two shades in spite of its complicated patterns – a light one (in syca-more, pear, box or holly) for the designs, and a darker one (walnut) for the background.

Grinling Gibbons (1648–1720), the greatest of all English wood-carvers, flourished at this time. He excelled in mural decoration in Wren's churches and in great houses. Only one piece of furniture by him can be positively identified on documentary grounds – a table with a walnut top set in a carved limewood frame which he presented to John Evelyn and which is now at Christ Church, Oxford.

The general tendency of mirrors to become tall and upright followed the trends of the time. They had arched headings frequently filled with mirror-glass and finished off with carved crestings. On some there were glass borders set in coloured glass banding or in gilt mouldings.

It was undoubtedly French influence which

folding tops and baluster or tapered legs, two of which swung out to support the table top.

Writing-tables were similar but had rectangular folding tops. The attractive knee-hole table, used for dressing, had a number of small drawers and baluster legs on ball or bun feet. The knee-hole was sometimes arched and had two flanking suspended finials.

MUSEUMS AND COLLECTIONS

William and Mary furniture may be seen at the following:

GREAT BRITAIN
London: Victoria and Albert Museum
Richmond, Surrey: Ham House
U.S.A.
Trenton, New Jersey: William Trent House
Warwick, New York: Warwick Historical Society

FURTHER READING

English Cabinets by J. F. Hayward, Victoria and Albert Museum, London, 1973.
Cabinet Makers and Furniture Designers by Hugh Honour, London, 1969.
World Furniture ed. by Helena Hayward, London, 1965, '**England 1660–1715**' by A. Coleridge.

Early American Furniture

Fig. 2 *Keeping-room*, American, seventeenth century. Of typical early colonial type, this living-room, or parlour, has a low ceiling and a scarcity of windows. Despite the enforced crudeness and simplicity of their furniture, it has a certain functional charm very attractive to modern eyes.
(The American Museum in Britain, Claverton Manor, Bath.)

Fig. 3 *Slat-back single chair*, New Jersey, c.1710. Maple with a rush seat.
There were many different chair designs in colonial America, but all seem old-fashioned in comparison with English examples of the same period. Most single chairs were assembled from turned members, as is this example, but the seats varied. The simplest type was plain timber, which would have been softened with a cushion, but leather, held in place with large brass-headed nails, and woven rush were also popular, and undoubtedly more comfortable.
(H. F. du Pont Winterthur Museum.)

Fig. 1 *Chest of drawers* probably by Thomas Dennis, Massachusetts, 1678. Carved and painted wood, width 44¾ ins. Made for John and Margaret Staniford, this elaborate chest has the date 1678 carved in the centre of the top drawer. It is ornamented with Elizabethan strap-work carving and applied turning, and the whole is brightly painted. It was very likely made, as was the custom of the time, when the young couple were setting up home.
Henry Francis du Pont Winterthur Museum, Winterthur, Delaware.)

Furniture in the early colonies was simple; made from local woods, it was essentially functional, although its purity of line and proportion gives it a quality pleasing to the modern eye

The first English settlers in North America attempted, between 1586 and 1603, to establish themselves in Virginia, a name given to the area in honour of Queen Elizabeth I. It was not until 1620, with the arrival of *The Mayflower* and *The Speedwell* and their cargo of one hundred and twenty dissenters, that colonisation was successfully begun.

The men and women came to a strange and hostile land with little hope of returning, and once their own small stock of supplies was expended they had to fend for themselves in every way. The settlers had the task of providing their own food, shelter, and any other requirements from the sea and the forest. Trees were felled to clear the land for cultivation and to provide timber for buildings as well as for such furniture as was essential. This latter would have been of the simplest description and has perished long ago.

Doubtless each arrival had with him a chest holding clothing and other belongings; beds would have been little more than a pile of skins on a wooden floor, while plain stools, benches and tables would have been knocked together as soon as time allowed.

The oldest surviving pieces of furniture made in the country date from the third quarter of the seventeenth century, and owe their continued preservation to the fact that they are outstanding examples in one way or another. They are complex in design involving skilful workmanship, and therefore have an artistic attraction causing them to be appreciated and cared for by successive owners.

Such pieces can be authenticated by the type of timber of which they were made. Oak was most frequently used in England for much of the century and the same applied to America, but the species found there was lighter in colour and reveals its origin to an expert. Pine, maple and other local woods were also employed by the colonists, but being relatively soft these woods are less durable and articles made from them are not plentiful.

The appearance of pieces was dictated by the skill of the makers, by the available materials, and by the taste and wealth of buyers. The latter not only led an enforced, unsophisticated existence in the new colony, but had in many instances come from provincial homes and were unaware of urban modishness; the younger people born in New England knew little, if anything, of smart London styles.

In the seventeenth century the time-lag between town and country was a matter of several years – a city style did not influence outlying towns and villages for a decade or more. An even longer interval elapsed between the adoption of an innovation in the capital and its appearance in, for instance, far away Virginia. Thus it is frequently found that what was currently appealing to the colonists had been popular in England as much as thirty years or half a century earlier.

Boxes held Bibles and other precious possessions

The variety of articles was limited by the comparatively elementary requirements of users. Chairs which were reserved for the head of the household were outnumbered by stools and benches; tables were of various sizes according to needs; boxes held Bibles and other precious possessions. The list is completed with beds, chests and cupboards. The two last-named were the pieces to which much attention was paid. At first, as in Europe, the chest was no more than a large box with a hinged lid; then a drawer was added in the base (Fig. 6). Finally the rising lid was dispensed with and it became the chest of drawers (Fig. 1). Of all New England furniture, it was given the most distinctive appearance and is unlikely to be confused with a similar piece made elsewhere in the world.

Cupboards followed English lines, with the two-tiered Elizabethan and Jacobean court type and the enclosed buffet being made as late as 1680. Although sometimes ornamented with carving similar to that found on their prototypes, the use of American timber is a pointer to their origin. At about the same date others were ornamented with applied turned sections, split in half and painted black to provide a contrast with the background.

A further feature of chests and of some other pieces was the use of paint to emphasise or replace carving (Fig. 12). Red and yellow were popular, and their use must have helped to brighten house interiors relying for their daytime illumination on small panes of glass, or more often on sheets of semi-opaque oiled paper.

Of the men who actually made the surviving furniture little is known, and many of the attributions are to an area rather than to a person. A notable exception is a chest, on the back of which is inscribed: 'Mary Allines Chistt Cutte and Joyned by Nich. Disbrowe'. Disbrowe would appear to have been born in Essex, England, in about 1612, and by 1639 was living in Hartford, Connecticut. The chest has been dated to about 1680 when Mary Allyn was twenty-three years of age. It would have been her 'hope' chest, for holding the trousseau she was to need in 1686, on her marriage to John Whiting.

Many of the chests were made as 'hope' or 'dower' chests

No other pieces made by Disbrowe have come to light, but similar examples to the single survivor are known as 'Hadley' chests. They gained their name from the town of Hadley, Massachusetts, and are distinguished by their carved decoration of entwined flowers and leaves covering the entire front surface, often centring on the initials of their first owner. A study of the initials has shown that most of the original possessors lived in or about Hadley, where the chests were made between the years 1675 and 1740.

Comparable chests, with hinged tops and one or more drawers in the base, came from elsewhere in the Valley. They are known variously as 'Tulip', 'Sunflower', 'Connecticut' or 'Hartford' chests. Each has the upper portion of the front divided into three panels which are carved with formal representations of sunflowers or tulips and have additional ornament in the shape of split turnings, painted black and applied to relieve the otherwise plain uprights (Fig. 6).

The foregoing piece may be compared with the chest illustrated in Fig. 1. It was probably made by Thomas Dennis of Ipswich, Massachusetts, for John and Margaret Staniford; in the centre of the bottom drawer is carved the date 1678. The chest is not only carved with strap-work of Elizabethan pattern, but bears applied turning and is brightly painted. The carving and other details are accented with colour, and the overall effect may be thought to reflect the aspirations of a couple setting up house.

The fact that many of the chests were made specifically as 'hope' or 'dower' chests, and were embellished with the initials of their owners and sometimes with the date of their making, has undoubtedly led to their preservation; articles

with less intimate associations have been discarded long ago. Most of these chests are now in museums where, even if they no longer have a practical function, they are kept safely for all to see.

Chairs of the time varied in their design, but again are old-fashioned in comparison with contemporary English examples. In most cases they are assembled from turned members supporting a seat of plain timber, which was made more comfortable with a cushion. Alternatively, there were seats of woven rushes (Fig. 3) or of leather, the latter held in place by large brass-headed nails.

The first Governor of Plymouth Plantation, John Carver, who came over with the Pilgrim Fathers,

Fig. 4 *Table or candle-stand*, Connecticut, late seventeenth century. Maple and pine, painted red, height 23 ins.
This sturdy little stand once belonged to Peregrine White, who was born on The Mayflower in Cape Cod Harbour in the year 1620.
(American Museum in Britain.)

Fig. 5 *Cabinet*, perhaps by James Symonds, Salem, Massachusetts, for Thomas and Sarah Buffington, 1676. Oak, cedar and maple, with the initials TSB. Height 17¼ ins.
(H. F. du Pont Winterthur Museum.)

Fig. 6 *Chest*, Connecticut, 1670–90. Oak and pine, the front three panels carved with a tulip pattern. Width 4 ft.
(American Museum in Britain.)

gave his name to one type of armchair. It has stout turned uprights and plain round stretchers joining the legs, and the back contains three horizontal turnings of which the lower two are linked by three turned uprights (Fig. 10). The seat is of rush, and the chair has a heavy throne-like appearance to be expected in the seat of someone who was in authority.

Another historic armchair is the one which once belonged to an Elder of the Plantation, William Brewster, and is preserved in Pilgrim Hall, Plymouth, Massachusetts. Like the carver it is made from lengths of turning and has a rush seat. It differs from it, however, by having the back inset with two rows of short uprights, while the same arrangement appears between the front legs.

and at each side. The carver and brewster armchairs were copied, usually with some variations in design, from about 1650 onwards. The principal difference lies in the number of turned uprights in the back and elsewhere, which are frequently fewer in number than in the prototypes. While both of these chairs had their back turnings running vertically, a third type featured horizontal flat strips of wood. The descriptive term 'slat-back' is usually applied to them in the United States, although comparable English versions are generally known as 'ladder-backs'. The example shown in Fig. 8 was made in New England in the last quarter of the seventeenth century, and is constructed of

8

9

D. Balmer

Museum Photo

Museum Photo

maple, ash and oak, and has a rush seat.

Confusingly, present-day writers in the United States describe a normal armchair as a 'carver', and refer to eighteenth-century and later sets of chairs as comprising, say, 'six singles and a pair of carvers'. Thus the original chair belonging to John Carver has given rise to a generic term, and has kept alive the name of one of the founding-fathers of the country.

The stool was made from various woods, and does not differ greatly in appearance from those that must have been recollected by the older settlers existing in their youth (Fig. 13). No doubt they were once plentiful, but hard use over the years has resulted in scarcity today. The same remarks apply to long benches or forms, which were con-

structed in a similar manner to the stools. Both were made with mortise and tenon joints held together with wooden pegs or dowels, and both were subject to equally heavy wear and tear.

Then, as now, tables were an important feature of a room. Large ones were given sturdy bases of oak and a removable top, so that if the space was required the whole article stacked easily out of the way. The top was not always of the same timber as the base, but as it was usually covered with a cloth or carpet this disparity was of little importance.

Smaller tables followed European patterns, with turned legs united by plain stretchers and sometimes having carving on the front of the frieze drawer. Some of them were based more on Dutch

149

than on English prototypes, with shaped and pierced brackets providing stability and decoration where the legs joined the horizontal members below the top. Another type, the gate-legged table, with additional legs at each side to swing outwards and support the hinged top, began to appear at the end of the century. It was made either with open swing-legs to match the remainder of the underframe, or with the gate of solid triangular form which earned it the name of 'butterfly-table'.

The foregoing does not exhaust the list of what was in daily use among the colonists. Not least was the Bible-box, mentioned earlier, which was used for holding documents and other personal property. Other minor pieces of furniture must have come and gone without leaving a trace of their existence, but a few have withstood the passage of time. An example is the simple table in Fig. 4, which once belonged to Peregrine White, who made his entry into the world in 1620 aboard *The Mayflower* in Cape Cod harbour.

Although the earliest of the arrivals in the country must have had austere homes, a greater degree of comfort became possible once a stable community was established. This largely took the form of colourful curtains, cushions and table-covers, which have now vanished. Records of them remain in inventories, and one made following the death of Major-General Edward Gibbons, of Boston, noted: 'thirty-one cushions, of which eleven were window cushions, four damask, four velvet, two leather, and two Turkey-work'. The latter was a variety of coarse work made in imitation of Turkey carpeting.

The men who laboured to furnish the homes of New England had no illusions about their skill or the unsophisticated nature of their output. The great majority of them described themselves as 'joiners', and the first record of a cabinet-maker does not occur until 1681. He was named John Clark, of whom nothing else is known except that he worked in Boston, and is the sole representative of those superior craftsmen to be so described in documents prior to 1700. By that date the population of the country was expanding very rapidly, villages and hamlets were becoming sizeable towns and the standard of living was fast catching up with that of Europe.

Fig. 10 *Armchair of carver type, New England, late seventeenth century. Named after the first governor of Plymouth Plantation, John Carver. (American Museum in Britain.)*

Fig. 11 *Chest of drawers, New England, late seventeenth century. Mahogany and pine. Width 41 ins. (American Museum in Britain.)*

Fig. 12 *Toilet Table, Boston, c.1700. Painted wood. Width 31⅛ ins. (H. F. du Pont Winterthur Museum.)*

Fig. 13 *Joint stool, Boston area, c.1700. Walnut, height 23 ins. In the early colonies, the great simplicity of household furnishings meant that chairs were, in general, reserved for the head of a household. Stools and benches were used by the rest of the family, and few have survived the hard daily use given them over the years. (H. F. du Pont Winterthur Museum.)*

MUSEUMS AND COLLECTIONS

Early American furniture may be seen at the following:

GREAT BRITAIN

Bath:	The American Museum in Britain, Claverton Manor

U.S.A.

Boston:	Boston Museum of Fine Arts
New York:	Metropolitan Museum of Art
Sturbridge, Mass:	Old Sturbridge Village
Winterthur, Delaware:	Henry Francis du Pont Winterthur Museum

FURTHER READING

American Furniture 1660–1725, by G. A. Gilborn, 1970.
American Furniture by Helen Comstock, New York, 1962.
Colonial Furniture in America by L. V. Lockwood, New York, 1926.

Queen Anne Furniture

Fig. 1 **Bureau-cabinet**, 1710–20.
Burr-elm veneer.
One of the most subtle and
beautiful figures chosen for fine
pieces, burr veneer was cut from
a root or crotch of the tree.
(Victoria and Albert Museum,
London.)

Fig. 2 **Day-bed** by Giles
Grendey, c.1730. Japanned
beechwood.
The shape of the back and legs,
and the caned seat, preserve the
earlier fashion of c.1710.
(Victoria and Albert Museum.)

Fig. 3 **Dressing-mirror and
desk on matching stand**, c.1710.
Amboyna veneer with kingwood
and rosewood banding.
This charming piece, with its
pivoting mirror, is typically
English in style and convenience.
(Victoria and Albert Museum.)

Designed by the craftsmen of the period rather than by professional designers, Queen Anne furniture is distinctive for its functional, comfortable and highly decorative elegance that holds great appeal for modern eyes

Queen Anne furniture is generally the most popular of all English styles. Its pleasant walnut veneer, usefulness and air of comfort and affluence typify the very best in the English vernacular tradition. The style began as a simplification of its seventeenth-century inheritance, but after about 1712 ornamentation again became fashionable. As a whole, the style is characterised by refinement and artistry of design that shows a considerable advance over that of William and Mary.

Queen Anne was not distinguished for her lively personality, and her Court was probably the dullest that had been in England up to that time. The Queen herself did nothing to direct the progress of fashion, and about the time of her accession, if not before, one can detect a kind of pause in furniture design. The pause represents a moment when patrons and craftsmen alike wished to discard the foreign and generally useless elaboration of late seventeenth-century furniture and, by reducing it to practical forms, to retain only the essentials of the design. The campaigns that Dutch William

had successfully conducted against Louis XIV had the curious effect of weakening the economy of Holland while strengthening that of England. With growing confidence, therefore, the craftsmen in London, whether they were native or immigrant, could shake off their previous dependence on Dutch fashions.

The contours and carving on furniture became smoother. Fragile caned chairs and stools, and the hard, high settees that were made for posture rather than for comfort, were replaced by pieces more suited to the shape of the human body. Fall-front writing-desks survived for a little, but before long gave way entirely to the more convenient bureau. Cabinets and cupboards became less elaborate and fussy. All these pieces were economically designed with a view to their function rather than to the display of an abundance of material and crafts-manship. At the same time, cabinet-makers perfected the technical improvements that had started a few years previously, stronger case con-struction and better dovetailing helped to establish the superiority of English furniture over its Dutch counterparts.

It is curious that, in an age which saw the building of such houses as Castle Howard and Blenheim Palace, drawings of furniture by archi-tects are almost unknown. Essentially the Queen Anne style seems to have been dictated by the craftsmen themselves. To them we may attribute the domestic character and gentle contours. There was a general lack of classical detail. In the reign of William III most furniture, whether chairs, bureau-bookcases or beds, had the height emphasised

151

Fig. 5 'Bended-back' chair,
c.1710. The arms are of the over-
scrolled type called 'shepherd
crook' arms. (Mallett's.)

Fig. 6 **Dining-chair**, c.1710.
Walnut veneer with scrolled
back and relief scallop shells
and husks. (Mallett's.)

by very elaborate crestings or pediments topped by finials. From 1700 there was a tendency to bring down the height and to make a piece appear more stable by directing the eye to an apparently low centre of gravity. This difference is parallel to that between the high gabled terrace-houses of Amsterdam and those built in London at the same time.

Their new sense of proportion allowed the London makers to dispense with much elaboration. The splendid marquetry tradition dwindled almost overnight to the occasional use of small panels of inlaid arabesques. After 1700 such panels were only incidental to the decoration and contributed nothing to the form of furniture (Fig. 7). Parquetry, too, was restricted. The overpowering and often startling contrasts of late seventeenth-century styles were unacceptable in the new century.

In general, the decoration of case furniture was limited to the choice of a single fine walnut veneer, or to two or more sheets of veneer cleverly matched with their reflecting patterns laid side by side. The wood was carefully chosen for its marking, the best having a burr figure, cut from the root or a crotch of the tree (Fig. 1). Normally, the veneer was bordered by cross-bandings and a narrow line of herring-bone pattern, all of the same material and identical colour. English walnut was the best variety, and its colour might be described as a warm grey-brown; but as the home supply became less, French and Italian walnut was imported. The continental variety has a darker colour tending towards olive, and a darker figure. Virginian walnut, imported from the American colonies, is a hard, dark wood without much figure. It was generally used for solid work, rather than for veneering.

Good quality elm furniture tended towards woodworm and is uncommon today

Yew, which today we find most attractive, never became really popular at this period. On the whole, elm had much better possibilities; it tends to be coarse in grain, but when cut at the root for a burr figure it can be so fine as to be almost indistinguishable from walnut. Elm was considerably cheaper, but soft, light and very appetising to woodworm. Consequently good quality elm furniture tends to be uncommon today. The burr elm veneer could be curiously stained in such a way as to produce a mottled figure like mulberry wood. The firm of Coxed and Woster in St. Paul's Churchyard, used this technique on bureau-bookcases (Fig. 8).

Olive and laburnum might still be used occasionally, both having a beautiful and delicate grain. Rosewood and kingwood, imported from Brazil, at one time used chiefly for cross-banding, soon became unfashionable. Generally, then, the choice of woods appears to be more restricted than during the seventeenth century. The former richness of surface and colour was replaced by a uniform but subtle texture.

Some new types of furniture were invented, all of them pieces that were typically English in their style and convenience. The dressing-mirror was now not merely a framed looking-glass, but was pivoted between two uprights; the stand included fitted drawers, and often a small writing flap (Fig. 3). These dressing-glasses appeared around

1700 and were made for over a hundred and twenty years. A knee-hole dressing-table about three feet wide, with nine drawers and a back cupboard for slippers, was also intended for use as a writing-table. The bachelor's chest appeared rather later. It was essentially a light, movable piece for a person of small personal needs; it would hold clothes and the folding top opened to make a table. When inns and lodgings offered little but discomfort, such an object was most useful. Although bachelors' chests are obsolete today, they have become valuable and interesting collectors' pieces.

Two other developments of about 1710–20 are by no means obsolete. The card-table grew around 1710 from the rather small seventeenth-century piece that was designed for piquet, into the Queen Anne card-table, about three feet wide, which was intended for four-handed games such as ombre and quadrille. Today it remains of ideal size for our whist and bridge.

The tallboy, or chest-upon-chest, was also developed at this time as it was more capacious than the already existing chest-on-stand. By the eighteenth century the chest of drawers had been accepted in all fashionable circles as a more convenient clothes store than the coffer, though it is surprising that as late as 1726 Daniel Defoe wrote that the manufacture of these objects was centralised in London; but it is evident that most fine furniture must have been made there. Not only was it the metropolis of fashion, but only there could be found the concentration of skills needed to produce furniture at reasonable cost. The cabinet-maker, carver, gilder, chair-maker, upholsterer, glass-maker and metal-worker all enjoyed separate trades, and the quality achieved in furniture depended very largely on the degree of specialisation and co-operation between craftsmen.

Whereas in the seventeenth century chairs might still be made by the joiner and carver, soon after 1700 a new type of chair developed that made a specialist chair-maker absolutely necessary. The Queen Anne chair is one of the finest products of the period. Its curves give comfort to the sitter besides forming a pleasing and strong design. At the time, these were known as 'bended-back' chairs (Fig. 5). The back, rising from firmly splayed back legs, and the cabriole front legs, were best when carved out of solid walnut, elm or beech, despite the extravagant use of wood. The tenon and mortice joints which held the frame together achieved a much firmer chair than the William III type. Stretchers between the legs were soon dispensed with.

Not all chairs of the period had cabriole legs; but the cabriole leg is rightly regarded as a distinctive innovation of this period. On chairs and stools it was sturdy, but when supporting tables or stands for bureaux and cabinets it might be elongated and refined. Its origin is mysterious. It is said variously to be Dutch, Chinese, or derived from an animal's leg. In its early form, around 1700, it was of square section; this shape persisted and was often used with grandiose effect well into the 1720s. It lent itself to variations such as 'broken' knees or feet. When the leg is rounded, it has gentle curves that seem almost sculptural. The earliest examples retaining the 'Braganza', or flattened scroll, foot are rare. The deer foot, or *pied de biche*, is generally early, but similar pony-hooves can be found up to

153

7

8

9

Fig. 7 *Settee*, c.1710: Walnut veneer with marquetry panels. Contemporary needlework, showing the Fall of Phaeton. (Christie's, London.)

Fig. 8 *Bureau*, possibly by Coxed and Woster, c.1700–10. Stained figured elm inlaid with pewter banding. (Christie's.)

Fig. 9 *Side-table*, c.1715. Gilt gesso with the crest of Lord Cobham. Originally from Stowe House. (Victoria and Albert Museum.)

Fig. 10 *Table top*, probably 1723. Gilt gesso with the arms of Cholmondeley impaling Walpole. This elaborate table top shows the influence of the

about 1730. The knees were carved with side mouldings, sometimes scrolled, or ornamented by turned bosses. Within certain limits the makers showed considerable invention in the decoration of the cabriole leg (Fig. 7).

Queen Anne's reign passed through war to peace, and in 1714 the Stuarts lost the crown to the Hanoverians. It is around 1713, the date of the Peace of Utrecht, that one detects a revival of ornament. While simple shells, carved in relief, and mouldings were in use quite early, more elaborate decoration is apparent during the second decade of the century. On the cresting of a chair a new kind of scroll-work appeared, suggesting that the frame was made not of wood but of curling-up leather or strap-work. Foliage sprouted at salient points. The carved shell became stylised, sometimes so much as to be confused with a stiff form of honeysuckle, and might be set on the elegantly scrolled hip of a chair leg, with husks trailing below it (Fig. 6).

These artificial motifs were of French origin,

Such furniture implied pomp and circumstance, and it is not surprising that these pieces were often inspired by French patterns. In fact, a revival of Louis XIV influence in both form and decoration is obvious in the years following the Peace Treaty of 1713. The designs of Daniel Marot and Jean Bérain were once more taken as models, as they had been before 1700 (Fig. 9). The adaptable nature of this universal style can be appreciated by comparing, for instance, a table top with a design for a formal knot garden (Figs. 10 and 11). Both show the same vigour in an underlying strap-work pattern, which is softened by touches of scrolled leaves and other stiff foliate decoration.

Tall mirrors leafed with gold or silver had carved and pierced crestings which revived, but with a greater confidence of design, the fashions of William III in which the Marot influence had been paramount. Towards 1720, however, a distinct type of mirror appeared with a spreading flat frame, shaped and carved in relief. Here again the French style in the carved ornament was repeated with subtle variations; but at the same time it became mixed with the same naturalistic innovations that we have already noticed on the chair. Beside the interlaced strap-work, demon faces and shells, there appeared eagle heads, luxurious acanthus and other foliage. When set beside such animated details, the French patterns can look old-fashioned, artificial and 'precious'.

Japanned furniture continued in the tradition already set in the seventeenth century. The vogue for *chinoiserie* was steadily increasing up to 1730, and the patterns, with figures in pleasure gardens or mountain landscapes, tended to become rather stereotyped. Perhaps more attention was paid to the genuine lacquer imported from China, and rather less to Stalker and Parker's quaint adaptations from it in 1688. Japanning on black and dark green grounds was the most common, but the large and expensive bureau-cabinets decorated in gold on a brilliant scarlet ground somehow seem to us more typical of the period (Fig. 2). These pieces show a love of colour that one would not have suspected from a knowledge of sober walnut furniture alone.

A. C. Cooper

universal French style and the same vigorous strap-work pattern as the formal knot garden (Fig. 11). (Christie's.)

Fig. 11 *Design for a garden* by Daniel Marot. Engraving c.1700. (Victoria and Albert Museum.)

K. Hoddle

and can be found on furniture up to about 1730; but during the 1720s another type of carved decoration appeared that was more naturalistic, even animated. The carved acanthus leaf found a vigorous freedom, and eagles' heads appeared on the arms of chairs. The eagle head might seem the logical extension of the claw-and-ball foot (Fig. 6), which had appeared earlier; some writers say it was used as early as 1710.

Two kinds of furniture show special richness of surface treatment: those in gesso and 'japan'. Gesso furniture had a magnificent revival up to about 1730 when the fashion for it lapsed. Between ten and twenty layers of chalk and parchment size were laid on a shaped or partly carved piece of furniture and, when it had hardened, the decoration was carved into it. Then the whole was gilt or, more rarely, silvered. Thus, the high relief carving had a wooden basis while the low relief existed only in gesso. Differences in texture could be obtained by pouncing the ground, or by applying sand to produce a rough surface, and burnishing the raised ornament. The resulting furniture was fragile, intended for display rather than for use. It generally consisted of sets of mirrors, side-tables and torchères for state-rooms; sets of gesso chairs, too, were opulent luxuries, and were made with increasing elaboration up to 1730 (Fig. 4).

MUSEUMS AND COLLECTIONS

Queen Anne furniture may be seen at the following:

Cornwall:	Antony House
Gloucestershire:	Dyrham Park
Hampshire:	The Vyne
London:	Hampton Court Palace
	Victoria and Albert Museum
Oxfordshire:	Blenheim Palace

FURTHER READING

The English Country Chair: an Illustrated History of Chairs and Chairmaking by Ivan G. Sparkes, Bucks., 1973.
English Furniture, 1550–1760 by Geoffrey Wills, Enfield, 1971.
English Furniture Styles 1500–1830 by Ralph Fastnedge, London, 1955.
Furniture Making in Seventeenth and Eighteenth Century England by R. W. Symonds, London, 1955.
Georgian Cabinet Makers by Ralph Edwards and Margaret Jourdain, London, third edition, 1955.
English Furniture from Charles II to George II by R. W. Symonds, London, 1929.

American Colonial Furniture

Fig. 1 **Fall-front desk** by
*Edward Evans, Philadelphia,
1707. Walnut, red pine and white
cedar.*
*This magnificent desk is the
earliest known piece of signed
and dated Philadelphia furniture.
(Colonial Williamsburg,
Virginia.)*

The increased demand for elegance and comfort in the Colonies during the eighteenth century led to the production of handsome, well-proportioned furniture based on English designs

In England, the eighteenth century witnessed a brilliant flowering of all the arts aided by the expansion of commerce and trade in addition to political and social stability. While England moved into this period of graciousness, the Colonies followed, but at a slower pace. New wealth on both sides of the Atlantic assumed a material form in stately houses furnished in an elaborate and refined manner.

At the beginning of the century, a third generation of Americans was already living in the Colonies, still retaining many of the basic traditions of their ancestors in matters of taste. However, the rural arts and crafts of the seventeenth century were transformed into a culture which was now urban in character. In Philadelphia, Quaker traditions were in evidence and in New York could be seen a strong Dutch influence. In New England, the Puritan standards which had been established soon yielded as trade and ship-building industries flourished. Cities such as Boston, Newport, New York and Philadelphia grew and developed rapidly as commercial shipping centres. Trading with England, especially in tobacco, brought many goods, including furniture, directly to the southern states. It seems apparent, therefore, that styles were not at first transmitted from within the Colonies, but reached separate regions through various commercial means.

Eighteenth-century houses were based on the spacious architectural plans of the Renaissance. Although the frontier vigour of earlier houses was no longer evident, the resulting benefits in spaciousness and comfort more than offset this loss. These symmetrically planned houses now contained several rooms, including a central hall, a dining-room and two parlours. One of the parlours was usually formal, containing chairs, sofa, mirror, several small tables and perhaps a desk (Figs. 6 and 9). The second parlour was for the family and would often contain a day-bed, chairs, pine tables, a cradle and general family furniture (Fig. 4).

The settlers of the previous century had, of necessity, to be adept at a variety of crafts. This versatility was responsible for a type of furniture which involved no special skills. In contrast, the eighteenth century was an age of specialisation. Along with the builder and the silversmith, the cabinet-maker was now able to devote all his time to his particular trade. However, unlike the silver of this period, which was stamped with the maker's mark, attributions of furniture to a single maker cannot be readily made as the labelling of furniture was not yet in practice. A single exception to this is a fall-front desk by Edward Evans of Philadelphia. His name, and the date 1707 branded on one of the drawers, establishes it as the earliest signed piece of Philadelphia furniture (Fig. 1).

The eighteenth century was an age of specialisation

The William and Mary style, based on the application of veneers, required professional skill far beyond that of a mere joiner. Fortunately, by the early eighteenth century sufficient numbers of skilled cabinet-makers were already working in the Colonies. Without these trained cabinet-makers to interpret the new styles from England it would have taken a much longer time for earlier Jacobean styles to be replaced.

As oak was the wood best suited to seventeenth-century furniture, so walnut was best suited to the baroque forms of the William and Mary and Queen Anne styles. Walnut is close-grained and lends itself to carving while veneers can be cut from it to give splendid surfaces to desks, tables and chests. Since walnut is not attacked by worm, does not splinter easily, and takes a fine finish, especially when burled, much of this wood was brought to England from the Colonies. By 1730, the South Sea Company had established trade with England for black walnut from the forests of Pennsylvania. Other native woods used were pine, maple and a variety of fruit-woods – pear, apple and cherry. Mahogany was introduced into America in the 1700s; however, it was only used occasionally for

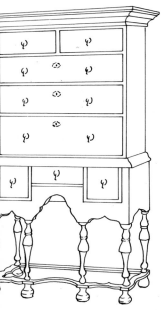

Fig. 2 **Highboy,** American,
1700–20.
This piece has trumpet legs.

Fig. 3 **Bonnet-top highboy** by
John Pimm, Boston, c.1740–50.
Maple and pine with japanned
decoration.
This masterpiece of American
furniture was made by Pimm for
Commodore Joshua Loring of
Boston. The decoration is in
imitation of Oriental lacquer-
work, and was probably painted
by Thomas Johnson.
(Henry Francis du Pont
Winterthur Museum,
Winterthur, Delaware.)

3

4

Fig. 4 **Room from the Samuel Wentworth House**, *Portsmouth, New Hampshire, built 1671, panelled c.1710. (Metropolitan Museum of Art, New York.)*

Fig. 5 **Gaming-table**, *American, c.1740–50. The oval hollows are for gaming counters.*

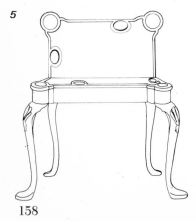

case furniture in the American Queen Anne period and did not become of major importance until the second half of the century.

The introduction of a new style meant additional changes in the construction of furniture. Interiors of case pieces were more accurately joined and particular care was taken in the dovetailing of the drawers. Usually the grain of the wood provided sufficient ornament, but this did not preclude embellishments of scrolls and foliage. Metal hinges, handles and back-plates were mainly imported. In addition, a few pieces of furniture were decorated to simulate Chinese lacquer.

The use of veneer was only one of the innovations employed with William and Mary furniture; carving also became bolder. The vigorous carving of baroque details was incorporated into the existing rectilinear furniture shapes producing visual contrasts of light and shade. The Spanish foot, resembling a semi-flexed fist resting on knuckles, was a move away from the unsophisticated feet common to the period (Fig. 8).

For America, the William and Mary style was significant in that it introduced many new furniture forms: the highboy, the lowboy, the slope-top or slant-top desk, the upholstered easy chair and a

great many types of utilitarian tables. It should b remembered that pattern books were scarce an that, from the beginning, the American craftsme took fundamental furniture forms and proceede from there to develop an indigenous style.

One of the most notable innovations of the perio was the upholstered arm-chair. The entire fram except for the legs and feet was covered wit perpetuana (a durable wool and silk materia much favoured in eighteenth-century America Upholstery improved the appearance of thes chairs as well as their comfort. Some dining-room contained sets of side-chairs and matched arm chairs which were either caned or upholstered, an carving on the back, arms and feet gave added grac to these pieces. Sofas and settees were als introduced.

The storage chests of the earlier period under went a considerable change. There were still th simple chest of drawers, but now the drawers wer veneered, the divisions of the front were accente by mouldings and the whole piece rested on ball turnip feet. A further practical innovation was th raising of the chest upon a framework of legs an stretchers from which resulted the earliest form high chest. In America, it is more commonly calle

8

Fig. 6 **The Readbourne Interior.** *The Philadelphia scroll-armed easy chair dates from the 1730s. Note also the shell-carved Philadelphia chairs and the New York tea-table with ball and claw feet. The Boston highboy is seen in Fig. 3.* *(H. F. du Pont Winterthur Museum.)*

Fig. 7 **Armchair**, *Philadelphia, c.1740–50. Walnut.* *(H. F. du Pont Winterthur Museum.)*

Fig. 8 **Lowboy** *with Spanish feet and deeply scrolled and arched skirt, New Jersey area, 1730–50. Maple.* *(Parke-Bernet Galleries, New York.)*

(Fig. 1). This desk was essentially a chest of drawers, topped with an additional section containing small drawers, pigeon-holes and a writing surface. Occasionally, a cupboard with panelled doors was added on top of the desk, creating another form called the 'secretary'. The increased space allowed for storage of books as well as papers.

The import of ceramics, with their utilitarian and decorative appeal, increased the demand for other new forms of furniture for storage and display. Corner-cupboards, as well as several varieties of table, were used to fulfil this need.

By 1725, the fundamentally baroque character of the William and Mary style had merged with the more sophisticated Queen Anne style. For the most part, there was little change in the basic types of furniture although, as might be expected with the increasing wealth and complexity of Colonial life, more specialised types of furniture were also made. In addition to the greater skills exhibited in furniture construction and finish, there was a new concern for the co-ordination of all the elements of interior design.

A respect for the natural qualities of the wood

Queen Anne furniture at last lost the stiffness of the furniture of earlier periods and a clear and distinct elegance emerged. Although American models were based on English styles, they were simpler than their counterparts. Whereas English furniture relied on carving and gilding for decoration, American furniture craftsmen always had a respect for the natural qualities of the wood, and sought to achieve delicate and graceful forms through simplicity.

The most important element of Queen Anne design was the cyma curve – the elongated S-shape called by Hogarth 'the line of beauty'. The use of this curve went beyond decoration; it was part of the structure itself. The cyma curve is ubiquitous throughout the furniture of this period and is most noticeable in the serpentine cabriole leg. Complementing the cyma curve legs were the curved seats, chair-backs, table aprons and scroll tops of the highboys.

The Queen Anne style is epitomised in the chair, in that it required a variety of skills – those of the upholsterer, the joiner, the carver and the turner – and is capable of reflecting Colonial tastes of this period on its own. It is the side-chair which best serves to illustrate regional differences. In general, American Queen Anne chairs are smaller than those of England. They possess an organic unity which makes use of both a bold outline and a subtle interplay of curves (Fig. 6). New England chairs were tall, square-seated, and usually had stretchers connecting the legs; the pad foot was commonly used. New York chairs were broad and heavy, also with a square seat; in addition, there was an early adoption of the ball-and-claw foot, in the Queen Anne style. This feature was not adopted fully by other regions until around the middle of the century. The stiles (back posts) had reversed curves which matched the vase splats. Carving on the back cresting of New York chairs had strong Dutch characteristics.

The most important centre at this time was Philadelphia, and it was here that the Queen Anne

the 'highboy'. This form lost favour in England after the Queen Anne period, but remained popular in the Colonies throughout the period 1700–80. From the beginning, the highboy was built in two pieces for convenience of moving, with both upper and lower portions containing drawers (Fig. 2). The finest William and Mary highboys exhibit a beautiful use of burled walnut, whereas others were painted black and decorated with colour imitating Chinese motifs. Many variations occured in the turning of the legs and the scrolling of the stretchers. Some earlier pieces had turned legs, usually six, with bell, cup, or trumpet turnings (Fig. 2). The façade of the highboy also underwent several modifications involving the moulding around the drawers, the curving of the apron and the elaboration of the cornice. Crossed stretchers between the legs were sometimes used instead of the customary connecting stretchers. Tear-drop handles first, and later, bail, or half-loop, handles were used on the highboy drawers of the William and Mary period. The lowboy, which was at first a support for the high chest, was also used as a separate piece.

Another piece of furniture which developed in this period was the slant-top, or slope-top, desk

159

Fig. 9 *The Perley Parlour,*
Boxford, Massachusetts, 1763.
Built for the leader of the
Boxford Minute Men, Captain
Perley. The panelling is painted
in imitation of grained cedar, and
the pilasters are marbled. The
furniture is all of the period.
(American Museum in Britain,
Claverton Manor, Bath.)

Fig. 10 *Corner, or roundabout,*
chair, Philadelphia, c.1740–50.
Walnut.
(H. F. du Pont Winterthur
Museum.)

chair achieved its greatest refinement. The straight line was completely eliminated: the square seat was replaced by the horse-shoe or compass seat, which was in further harmony with the curving splat and stiles; and the elimination of stretchers gave the chair a continuous undulating line. Another Philadelphia characteristic was the chamfered stump leg and the trifid or drake's foot. The Philadelphia arm-chair shows an integrated blending of the arms with the back and the seat (Fig. 7). The carving of shells on the back cresting and knees of Philadelphia chairs was naturalistic, emphasising the alternation of concave and convex shell radials. An innovation in chairs of the period was the corner, or roundabout, chair with the back curving around two sides and a corner pointing to the front (Fig. 10).

The cabriole leg adapted well to the popular highboy. Regional differences included long slender legs on pieces from New England (Fig. 3), as compared with the shorter legs of the Phila-

The lasting popularity of the Queen Anne style in America cannot wholly be attributed to a provincial time-lag. It is evident that the Colonial cabinet-maker as well as his client preferred the style. In fact, American Queen Anne furniture rivalled those styles which followed as late as the third quarter of the century.

No discussion of American furniture of this period would be complete without mention of the familiar Windsor chair. Brought from England in the early 1700s and established by the 1730s, the Windsor chair remained popular with all classes throughout the Colonies. Simple, utilitarian, and made of the most readily available woods, the Windsor achieved a lean elegance, combining lightness with strength. The chairs were frequently painted green, with coloured lines added as decoration. Like other styles brought to America from outside the Windsor chair was developed and modified, with new forms emerging which were totally unknown in the land of its origin.

Museum Photo

delphia highboys. The flat tops of highboys of the William and Mary period gave way in the Queen Anne period to scroll-top and bonnet-top pediments above the cornice.

In tables, other significant changes were made. The drop-leaf table with cabriole legs replaced the gate-leg. Tea-drinking, fashionable in America as in England, gave rise to a variety of tea-tables, some with marble tops and others with a protective moulding round the edges. This use of a heat-resistant surface on a table can be considered as a forerunner of the popular sideboard. Another notable form was the gaming-table which could be folded in half and moved about easily (Fig. 5). Smaller pieces of furniture, such as candle-stands and fire-screens, were now placed on cabriole tripod stands, but retained their characteristic columnar form.

MUSEUMS AND COLLECTIONS
American furniture may be seen at the following:
GREAT BRITAIN
Bath: The American Museum in Britain, Claverton Manor

U.S.A.
Boston: Boston Museum of Fine Arts
New York: The Metropolitan Museum of Art
Philadelphia: Philadelphia Museum of Art
Winterthur, The Henry Francis du Pont
Delaware: Winterthur Museum

FURTHER READING
American Furniture by Helen Comstock, New York, 1962.
American Furniture of the Queen Anne and Chippendale Periods by Joseph Downes, New York, 1952.

The Ebénistes of Louis XV

Fig. 1 **Commode** by Bernard van Riesenburgh, mid-eighteenth century. Set with Japanese lacquer panels. (By gracious permission of H.M. the Queen.)

Fig. 2 *Commode by Pierre II Migeon, mid-eighteenth century. French lacquer in imitation of Chinese lacquer, with marble top. Note the richness of the colours on this fine, simple piece. (Musée des Arts Décoratifs, Paris.)*

Fig. 3 *Commode by Antoine Gaudreau after a design by the Slodtz brothers, the gilt-bronze mounts by Caffiéri, delivered to Louis XV, for whom it was made, in 1739. This magnificent piece remained in the King's bedroom until his death in 1774, proof of the long-standing royal predilection for the Rococo. (Wallace Collection.)*

Fig. 4 *Commode by Bernard van Riesenburgh, mid-eighteenth century. Lacquered in the Chinese style with vernis Martin. The division between the drawers has been ignored so that the front may be treated as a single pictorial unit. (Metropolitan Museum of Art, New York. Collection of Mr. and Mrs. Charles B. Wrightsman.)*

Fig. 5 *Drop-front secrétaire by Jean-François Dubut (died 1778), mid-eighteenth century. A curved rococo silhouette has been applied to the secrétaire design, creating a form which was popular for two centuries. (Wrightsman Collection.)*

Fig. 6 *Table by Bernard van Riesenburgh, mid-eighteenth century. Inlaid with tulipwood, ebony, mother of pearl and horn stained green, blue and red. The highly polychromatic effect shows the brilliance of French ébénisterie in its original condition. (Wrightsman Collection.)*

Fig. 7 *Corner cupboard, one of a pair by Jacques Dubois (1693–1763), mid-eighteenth century. This restrained rococo piece bears a mask of Diana in ormolu above another mount symbolising husbandry. This is an unusual combination of stock mounts. (Wallace Collection.)*

Cabinet-making under Louis XV was carried out by a team of highly skilled and original craftsmen, who produced magnificent pieces of furniture for the Courts of Europe

During the reign of Louis XV, the French cabinet-maker, or *ébéniste* (the name refers to the use of ebony for the earliest veneered furniture), was the most accomplished in Europe. Foreign Courts ordered their finest furniture from Paris or had French models copied at home, and the aesthetic and technical stimuli of working in France combined with a prodigious scale of patronage to attract the most talented craftsmen from southern Germany, Flanders and other traditional wood-working centres of Europe.

Thus, the *ébéniste*, unlike the *menuisier* or chair-maker, was not of exclusively French origin. Nor was he able to work anonymously, for the Guild Statutes of 1743 required members to stamp their work; it is this practice which allows us to identify the style of certain craftsmen. Their role was to take a carcase of inexpensive wood, usually oak, and on it to build a complicated system of veneers from foreign woods of contrasting grains and colours, and then to bind the whole together with splendidly cast mounts of gilt bronze. This operation, a synthesis of various technical processes, was perfected by André-Charles Boulle (1642–1732) and Charles Cressent (1685–1768), who effected the alliance between marquetry and bronze which is the essential feature of French *ébénisterie*.

In 1739 Antoine Gaudreau (1680–1740) delivered the commode illustrated in Figure 3 to the King's bedroom at Versailles; the double bowed profile of this piece, the *bombé* front and tall curved legs affirmed the victory of rounded forms, used here with such virtuosity that the surfaces seem almost to move. Just as this piece was designed to harmonise with the decorative scheme of the room and the rococo mounts echoed the motifs on the wall panelling, so pieces of a less grand character, smaller, lighter and easier to move, were made to suit the smaller proportions of the private apartments into which fashionable French society had withdrawn; the interdependence of furniture and interior decoration was complete.

Designs for furniture came from a few gifted craftsmen but were generally provided by the ornamentalists, specialists in design like Meissonnier, Pineau and the Slodtz brothers, these last being responsible for the design of the great commode in Figure 3. Also influential in guiding the taste of cabinet-makers and helping to bring veneering, marquetry and gilt-bronze techniques into line with current fashion, were the *marchands-merciers*. These dealers in expensive objects and fashionable furniture were most effective in devising new combinations of materials and techniques; one of these, Poiriet, is believed to be responsible for the introduction of Sèvres plaques to furniture, while Lazare Duvaux, who supplied Madame de Pompadour, may have developed the use of lacquer. Thoroughly understanding the taste of their clients, the *marchands-merciers* knew how to tempt them and how to stimulate craftsmen so that each piece became a delight to the eye.

This meant that furniture had to be colourful and because of the discoloration of age it is difficult for us to appreciate how brilliant the marquetry must have appeared in its original condition. The favourite tulipwood was prized for its red and white stripes, whereas now it has assumed a uniform honey-colour, and there were at least fifty other such exotic woods available to the cabinet-maker. His range was also increased by the practice of staining and tinting pale woods, each master having his own jealously guarded methods. These woods were applied in the form of veneers or marquetry patterns: geometric subjects such as squares, lozenges, triangles and chequered patterns were popular as well as stars, herring-bone and basket work patterns. Pictorial subjects featured teapots, teacups, vases, ewers, intertwined garden implements and musical trophies, but the most exacting work was involved in the assembly of floral motifs. The simpler designs show sprays of flowers trailing elegantly across entire surfaces, sometimes with birds perched on the stems; otherwise the floral motif is confined to a centre panel with stems and bouquets emerging from baskets or vases, and framed by several fillets of different varieties of wood.

Decorated lacquer was prized for its asymmetrical composition and glittering gold motifs

The taste for the colourful and the exotic was also met by the use of imported Chinese and Japanese lacquer panels (Figs. 1 and 8). These were prized for their asymmetrical composition and glittering gold decoration; although there was some red lacquer, black grounds were the most common. The fashion for Oriental lacquer stimulated the French to produce a substitute called *Vernis Martin*, named after the perfectors of this process, the Martin brothers (Guillaume, died 1749; Etienne Simon, died 1770; Julien, died 1782; and Robert died 1765). In 1730 and again in 1740, they were granted the exclusive monopoly to make lacquer of the Oriental kind and their own version, called *chipolin*, which had garlic as a vital ingredient of the formula. *Vernis Martin* (Fig. 4) was available in a wide colour range and was sometimes combined with figures and patterns inspired by Boucher or Greuze, giving a thoroughly French stamp to a technique originating in the East.

All veneer, marquetry and lacquer furniture was combined with gilt-bronze mounts. Only in very rare cases could the *ébéniste* follow the example of Boulle and Cressent, and have these made in his own workshop. In the Louis XV period, an *ébéniste* such as Marchand, who had infringed Guild regulations without the exemption of a royal warrant, found his workshop ransacked and his living jeopardised, as well as having to face expensive legal proceedings. The gilt-bronze mounts, the products of a group of specialists—modeller, caster, chaser and gilder—originally intended to protect the most vulnerable parts of the furniture, became increasingly decorative and tended to eclipse the cabinet work; they invaded the marquetry panel

5

6

7

Fig. 8 *Corner cupboard* by *Bernard van Riesenburgh, mid-eighteenth century. Set with a lacquer panel.*
(*H. M. the Queen.*)

Fig. 9 *Cartonnier in the style of Bernard van Riesenburgh, mid-eighteenth century. Marquetry veneer.*
The cartonnier was made to stand near a writing-table, and was used for filing papers.
(*By permission of the Trustees of the Wallace Collection, London.*)

instead of restricting themselves to framing, or t defining the architectural outlines of the piece. I spite of the great richness of this ormolu decoratio using vegetable, floral and plant forms, the inna French sense of elegance and proportion save these exuberantly modelled and opulent moun from exaggeration; however daring the asymmetr however languid the curves, the final result always balanced and poised.

It seems rather paradoxical, as each piece furniture resulted from the combined efforts several specialists, each striving to excel in h particular field, that the Guilds should hav stressed the importance of the stamp of the *ébénist* who was, after all, only one of a team. This ma have been due to a recognition that the art of th *ébéniste* lay in a skilful combination of the elemen provided by different craftsmen as well as the actu construction of the furniture. It is also interestin that many of these *ébénistes*, whose work s perfectly expresses the triumphant French rococ spirit, should have come from abroad.

Among these, Bernard Van Riesenburgh, Flemish origin (died 1767), second of a line three bearing the name, settled in Paris around 172 Received Master in 1730 and succeeded by his so Bernard III, he produced work so reflecting curre sophisticated taste that his name is constantl recurring in the accounts of Lazare Duvaux. Th mystery of his stamp – the initials B.V.R.B. – w solved only in 1957 but, since then, scholarship h identified much of his work. He made luxur furniture executed in various techniques, usin marquetry, both Oriental and European lacque and Sèvres porcelain plaques. He was, incidentall the first to apply Sèvres in this way. His ve distinctive marquetry consists of trailing sprays flowers in purple-wood, sometimes enlivened wit stained shell or horn (Fig. 6). His mounts ar equally individual and may have been modelled b his son, Bernard III. They often take the form scrolled ribs or flat bands, around which flor motifs are entwined, framing his marquetry panel He tended to emphasise the silhouettes of his piec with a narrow moulding of gilt bronze or bras running right down to the feet (Figs. 4 and 6).

His name is associated with many exquisit creations designed for the bedroom or boudo where the lady of fashion, seated at her dressin table, would receive her closest friends, listen to th latest gossip, discuss what was going on at th theatre, and scribble her messages and note Bernard Van Riesenburgh created a series luxurious pieces for this utterly feminine enviror ment; thus, for the first time in history, pieces furniture were made which were of the highe quality but small in scale. Typical of these is th *table en chiffonière* intended to keep oddments materials, or *chiffons*, and sometimes fitted wit writing equipment (Fig. 10). Other boudoir piec associated with this *ébéniste* are bedside tabl on which objects intended for use in the night we placed, including the *medianoche*, or midnig snack. The artist François Boucher owne another specialised piece called a *vide poche* mac by B.V.R.B.; this was a small table with a dee rim round the top on which objects taken from th pockets could be placed at night. B.V.R.B.'s wor outstanding in its superlative quality and stylis poise, was so prized by his contemporaries that i sale catalogues he was referred to by his Christia

Fig. 10 *Table en chiffonière by Bernard van Riesenburgh, mid-eighteenth century. This work-table exemplifies the superlative cabinet-making lavished on the smallest items of boudoir furniture, made popular by Madame de Pompadour. (Wrightsman Collection.)*

Museum Photo

name, an honour he shared with his predecessor A-C. Boulle and his great contemporary, Oeben.

Jean-François Oeben (*c.*1720–63) was born in Franconia in South Germany, the son of a postmaster. Soon after his arrival in Paris, his aptitude was recognised by the youngest son of A-C. Boulle, and he shared the Boulle family workshops in the Louvre. He held the royal warrant from 1754 until he died, and enjoyed a great reputation for immaculate craftsmanship and originality. He excelled at highly elaborate pieces containing secret compartments and mechanical devices; such are his *tables à transformation* combining several functions in one piece, and his *table à la Bourgogne*, a small chest of six drawers concealing a bookcase. As *ébéniste du Roi*, he was exempt from the Guild regulations and was thus able to work as both *ébéniste* and *mécanicien*. As he was also exempt from the rule about stamping, much of his finest work is not signed. His pictorial marquetry was celebrated for its realistic character – a favourite form is baskets of flowers naturalistically rendered and framed with interlaced ribbon. The outer edge of his panels usually have two or more very slender strips of contrasting ebony and boxwood. His pieces, usually of simple form, combine solidity with great elegance, and he was the first *ébéniste* who attempted to conceal the heads of the screws fastening the bronze mounts to the carcase, hiding them behind foliated motifs.

His supreme achievement, the great roll-top desk of Versailles, made for Louis XV from 1760 to 1769, was posthumously completed by his successor, J. H. Riesener (1734–1806) who was to become the greatest *ébéniste* of the Louis XVI period. This masterpiece of ingenuity, with its marquetry by Wynant Stylen and bronzes modelled by Duplessis, cast and chased by Hervieu, was the subject of the most exhaustive experiments before the mechanical locking systems by Oeben were perfected.

New pieces appeared – smaller, with elaborate and unusual fittings

Gilles Joubert (1689–1775) succeeded Oeben as *ébéniste du Roi*. Among his prolific output was the famous *table volante* for royal use at Choisy, which could be removed from the diner by an elaborate mechanism. Similarly representative of this desire for privacy was the dumb waiter or oval table with shelves on which bottles of wine, plates and table accessories were placed. One of these was put beside each diner, again dispensing with waiters. Another specialised piece of furniture had a built-in wine-cooler; this was called a *rafraichissoir*. It was similar in form to a *jardinière*, a stand with a deep, lead-lined top to hold cut flowers.

A dynasty of *ébénistes* shared the name Pierre Migeon. Pierre II Migeon, the most successful member of the family, was both *ébéniste* and dealer, employing forty craftsmen. He was particularly favoured by Madame de Pompadour and also worked for the King. Small pieces, especially those with unusual or elaborate fittings, were his particular line; he made a speciality of water-closets which he supplied to the royal ladies.

Another Fleming, R.V.L.C. (Roger Vandercruse, also known as Lacroix or Delacroix), is associated with the rise in popularity of desk furniture. Both the *secrétaire à abattant* (drop-front secretaire, Fig. 5), and the roll-top bureau were developed by him; he was one of the first to combine porcelain plaques with cabinet-making and to use satin-wood inlaid with ebony. The interest in all types of locking furniture shows the importance attached to privacy at this time.

As every activity of polite society had a specialised piece of furniture, many varieties of gaming and work tables were made, and light-weight occasional tables, *en cas*, just for convenience. Among many delightful versions of the lady's dressing table, there is Germain Loudin's beautiful heart-shaped piece with its drawer springing out on each side in butterfly form. In the years 1750 to 1760, this enchanting style was the height of fashion.

The achievement of the long list of *ébénistes* working in the Faubourg St. Antoine, during the Louis XV period was that they used their great talents in the service of a *clientèle* prepared to lavish large sums of money on fine furniture; the results are masterpieces of craftsmanship as redolent of the rococo spirit as a painting by Boucher or Fragonard.

MUSEUMS AND COLLECTIONS

Louis XV furniture may be seen at the following:

FRANCE
Paris: Musée des Arts Décoratifs

GREAT BRITAIN
Aylesbury: Waddesdon Manor
London: Victoria and Albert Museum
                           Wallace Collection

U.S.A.
Los Angeles: J. Paul Getty Museum
New York: Frick Collection
                           Metropolitan Museum of Art
Washington, D.C.:   National Gallery of Art

FURTHER READING

The Louis Styles (Furniture): Louis XIV, Louis XV, Louis XVI by Nietta Apra, London, 1972.
Guide to Furniture Styles: English and French, 1450–1850 by John Gloag, London, 1972.
The Wrightsman Collection, 2 vols. by F. J. B. Watson, New York, 1965.

Riesener and Louis XVI

Riesener was one of the most renowned cabinet-makers to contribute to the spread of French taste across Europe, and he holds an important place in the history of furniture

Like many cabinet-makers at the Court of Louis XVI, Riesener was a German. He was the son of a court usher and was born at Gladbeck, near Essen, on 4 July, 1734, moving at an early age to Paris where he entered the workshop of Jean-François Oeben, cabinet-maker to Louis XV.

Jean-Henri Riesener was twenty-nine when Oeben's death left him in charge of the workshops. In 1767, following a custom which was fairly common when it was to the advantage of both parties concerned, he married Oeben's widow, Françoise-Marguerite, and on 23 January, 1768, he received his *Maîtrise* (Mastership).

When Riesener took over Oeben's workshop, Louis XV's great desk called the '*Bureau du Roi*', ordered in 1760 for Versailles, had not yet been finished. It was to be completed under his supervision; he put his signature on it and had it delivered to Versailles in 1769. He did the same for other commissions which were in hand at Oeben's death.

Riesener was made Cabinet-Maker to the Crown and received orders for costly, intricate furniture

In July 1774 he was granted the title of Cabinet-Maker to the Crown, replacing Gilles Joubert. The great period of his career had begun. Almost immediately he received an order for a marquetry commode decorated with ormolu for the King's room at Versailles, which he replaced the following year with another yet more magnificent one, now at Chantilly (Fig. 7).

It was during this time that he received many orders for writing-desks, and also for multi-functional tables. For instance, in 1778 he made a charming table (now in the Metropolitan Museum, New York) for Marie Antoinette, which, at the push of a button, could be converted into a dressing-table with numerous compartments, or into a writing-desk. At the time it cost 4,000 *livres*.

These costly orders for valuable furniture went to furnish the chief royal palaces – Versailles, Fontainebleau, Trianon, Marly. From 1774 to 1784, the total amount Riesener made was 938,000 *livres* – in those days a very considerable sum – making him both famous and prosperous. His portrait, painted by Antoine Vestier in 1786 (now at Versailles), shows the great cabinet-maker as a man elegantly dressed in a velvet morning coat, silk waistcoat and lace cuffs, his right elbow on a very attractive table which he must surely have made (Fig. 2). He holds a pencil in his right hand which seems to suggest that he was eager and proud to be portrayed practising his craft as a furniture designer.

He was forced to submit to drastic financial restrictions

But early in 1784, the sorry financial plight of the *Garde Meuble* administration forced it to restrict its spending. Most of the orders went to the cheaper cabinet-makers such as Beneman and Stöckel. Riesener had to submit to a drastic reduction of his prices for furniture already supplied; orders for new work were cut to about one-sixth of their former value. He took badly to these restrictions, and preferred to give up his official duties to Beneman, who had a more flexible and less exacting nature.

Riesener kept, nonetheless, a large personal clientele and, in particular, the patronage of Marie Antoinette. In the 1780s he furnished her own apartments at Fontainebleau, and made a writing-desk and a commode, both decorated with lacquered panels, for her apartments at St. Cloud (Fig. 6). It is interesting to note that these pieces of furniture are decorated with lacquered panels rather than marquetry panels of precious woods which would have been more costly. His clients also included several members of the royal family, great nobles and rich *fermiers généraux* (tax administrators).

The Head Steward of the *Garde Meuble de la Couronne*, the famous Thierry de la Ville d'Avray also sent for Riesener. When Thierry moved into an apartment in the *hôtel* of the *Garde Meuble*, he ordered Riesener in 1784 to alter a low bookcase made by Gaudreau for Versailles forty years previously. Several months later, Thierry de la Ville d'Avray wanted a pendant to this piece so he

commissioned Riesener to make him a copy.

In 1776 Riesener's wife died leaving him with an only son, Henri François, who was to become a highly talented portrait painter. He was re-married in 1783, when he was nearly fifty, to a very young girl, Marie-Anne Grezel; but his second marriage does not appear to have been happy as he was divorced a few years later.

Like many others, Riesener was ruined by the Revolution. He did not try to build up a new clientele, although his competence was such that he might have been appointed arbitrator by the Tribunal of Commerce. With his clients now mainly political exiles, his life ended sadly. When the *Convention* sold the royal furniture, he bought back certain pieces he had made and tried on two occasions, first during the Terror and afterwards during the *Directoire*, to sell them privately, both times without success.

Magnificent marquetry and elegant curved panels

In 1795 he was told by the *Directoire* to remove from his furniture the royal emblems, called the 'trade marks of the feudal system'. He was even asked to obliterate the royal emblems on the desk which, together with Oeben, he had made for Louis XV. Society's taste had changed; the painter David had made fashionable the quite different neo-classical style. Riesener was forced to close his workshop. He died in poverty on 8 January, 1806, in his house in the rue Saint Honoré.

Riesener's work displays a very great variety. The contours of his first pieces of furniture are curved and his marquetry tables follow Oeben's tradition. He excelled in the craft of marquetry – combining the different woods in arabesques, flowers, birds and various emblems. The famous *Bureau du Roi* begun by Oeben displays the excellence of his skill as a cabinet-maker. The whole desk is veneered with precious woods, even inside the drawers. The back part, hidden by the cylinder when closed, is decorated with mosaics in chequer-work patterns and rose shapes. The magnificent marquetry on the outside is matched by the elegant curved panels depicting the royal symbols of the arts and the sciences (Fig. 1), those of war and commerce, and fruits and shells symbolising earth and sea.

Furniture made for the apartments of the royal family incorporated the products of highly skilled craftsmen

Made in 1775, the commode which is today housed at Chantilly is truly royal in its richness and strength (Fig. 7). The fullness of its shape, the outstanding quality of the four ormolu statues which support it, the exuberance of its decoration, the thickness of the marble – all this profusion is understandable only when one realises that it was ordered for the King's room in the *petits appartements* at Versailles. The shape of the central trapezoidal projection, decorated with superb marquetry, is characteristic of Riesener and is found in many pieces of his furniture.

Adorned with fleurs-de-lis and the coats of arms of the daughters of France, the desk which is now

Fig. 3 **Drop-front secretaire** with the mark of the Château de Trianon by Riesener, 1783. Thuya wood panels with purplewood borders, the mounts in the style of Gouthière and the giltbronze plaque chased with a scene of a sacrifice to Love in the manner of Clodion, height 54½ ins.
Made for the use of the Queen at the Petit Trianon, this secretaire bears a plaque chased with one of the scenes most frequently used by Riesener.
(Wallace Collection, London.)

Fig. 4 **Roll-top desk** by Riesener, 1774. Marquetry of precious woods, gilt-bronze mounts, height 44 ins.
Made for the Comte de Provence, later Louis XVIII, this piece remained at Versailles until the Revolution. It is in the pure rectilinear style of Louis XVI.
(Waddesdon Manor, Buckinghamshire.)

Fig. 5 **Corner cupboard,** one of a set of two cupboards and three commodes by Riesener, 1786. In 1786, Marie Antoinette redecorated the Salon des Nobles at Versailles, ordering these five pieces with blue marble tops to match the fireplace. They were moved to the Tuileries in 1789, and have only recently been returned to their original home. (Versailles.)

Fig. 6 **Secretaire** with the marks of the Queen's Garde Meuble and of the Château de Saint Cloud by Riesener, c.1787. Ebony with black and gold lacquer panels, unusually rich ormolu mounts with the cipher of Marie Antoinette by Gouthière, and a black marble top.
(Metropolitan Museum of Art, New York, bequest of W. K. Vanderbilt, 1920.)

Fig. 7 **Commode** by Riesener, 1775.
This truly royal commode, with its full shape, exuberant decoration, thick marble top and outstanding ormolu figures, was ordered for Louis XVI's own room in the petits appartements at Versailles.
(Musée Condé, Chantilly.)

preserved at Waddesdon Manor in Buckinghamshire was perhaps made for Madame Adélaïde in 1776. Although less magnificent, its general lines are very similar to those of the *Bureau du Roi*. Another roll-top desk, which is today in the same collection, is quite different in that the legs are straight and truly in the Louis XVI style. This desk was delivered in 1774 to the Comte de Provence, the future Louis XVIII, and it embellished the *appartements* at Versailles until the Revolution (Fig. 4).

A more refined style was adopted by Riesener to humour Marie Antoinette

The jewel cabinet belonging to the Comtesse de Provence must date from 1780; it was made in the traditional style of this type of furniture and set on tall legs (Fig. 9). Less magnificent than that made by Schwerdfeger for Marie Antoinette, it is nevertheless very richly decorated with ormolu. It is recounted that in 1811 the Comte Daru proposed to

Connaissance des Arts: R. Bonnefoy

buy it for the Empress Marie Louise. This offer was rejected because, as Daru observed: 'Her Majesty wants to have everything brand new; and not to buy back old stuff'. George IV of England showed better judgment when, at a sale in 1825, he acquired this magnificent piece of furniture. Ever since then, it has been part of the English royal collection.

Riesener's style became more refined and elegant under the influence of Marie Antoinette, whose whims he wanted to humour. For her boudoir at Fontainebleau, which was decorated with Pompeian arabesques by the Rousseau brothers, Riesener produced two extremely fine pieces of furniture – a roll-top desk and a work-table which combine marquetry of mother of pearl with ormolu and polished steel (Fig. 8).

It was probably in 1787 that he made a commode and a writing-desk (Fig. 6) for the Queen's apartments at St. Cloud, the castle which Louis XVI had

just bought from the Duc d'Orléans and which the Queen furnished at great expense. These two pieces of furniture are decorated with lacquered panels, which are rarely found in his work. These pieces also have the central trapezoidal projection which is typical of much of Riesener's work. One cannot fail to admire the floral motifs in ormolu, which is chased so beautifully that it could be the work of a goldsmith, and which never displays any such defect as the head of a nail fixing the ormolu in position; Riesener always employed excellent craftsmen for his work in this medium.

As well as these marvellous pieces of furniture which he made for royal residences, Riesener also made rather less ornate pieces of furniture which were equally beautiful. The beauty of the satin-like mahogany and the purity of line chased with only light ormolu to set off the reflections in the wood make every piece a masterpiece.

A meticulous care in his work was characteristic of Riesener. His furniture consistently displays a sense of harmony and proportion, is always well-balanced and shows a kind of logic in the use of the most ostentatious decoration.

MUSEUMS AND COLLECTIONS

Riesener's work may be seen at the following:

FRANCE
Paris: Musée du Louvre
Versailles: Château de Versailles

GREAT BRITAIN
Aylesbury: Waddesdon Manor
London: Wallace Collection
U.S.A.
New York: Metropolitan Museum of Art

FURTHER READING

Cabinet Makers and Furniture Designers by Hugh Honour, London and New York, 1969.
French Furniture and Interior Decoration of the 18th Century by Pierre Verlet, London, 1967.

French Provincial Furniture

Fig. 1 **Console table**, Liège, c.1760. Carved and gilt, marble top.
(Musée de Lièges.)

Fig. 2 **Sideboard**, Liège, mid-eighteenth century. Walnut, elaborately carved with rococo motifs.
(Musée de Lièges.)

Fig. 3 **Cabinet**, Liège, mid-eighteenth century. Carved walnut with glazed doors and sides to the upper section.
(Musée de Lièges.)

3

Pierre Jahan

Pierre Jahan

Pierre Jahan

Fig. 4 **Armoire**, *Normandy, eighteenth century. Plainly worked oak with brass fittings. (David Allan Collection, London.)*

Fig. 5 **Drop-front secretaire** *by Hache, Grenoble, c.1765. Polychrome floral marquetry on a ground of knotted walnut panels. (Musée Lyonnais des Arts Décoratifs.)*

The increased use of engravings and craftsmen's manuals brought a high standard to the furniture of the French provinces, while local traditions in design and decoration were still upheld

Now that Parisian furniture of the eighteenth century is the preserve only of the very rich, the attention of collectors has been focused increasingly on the work of French provincial *menuisiers* of the reigns of Louis XV and XVI, particularly in England, where its simple elegance has always appealed as much as the ormolu extravagances of a Cressent commode or the lush marquetry of a Riesener bureau. This interest in provincial furniture is also reflected in a deeper study of the subject; recent research has unearthed for the first time the names of many important provincial craftsmen and the stylistic idiosyncrasies of many regions.

At first sight rococo and neo-classical designs seem to have spread over France with an apparent uniformity, and the influence of Paris, and more particularly of Versailles, certainly cannot be over-estimated. The Château de Montgeoffroy, for instance, in the depths of Anjou, has retained its original furniture ordered by the Maréchal de Contades between 1775 and 1780, all of it from the best-known Parisian makers – chairs and sofas by Gourdin and Boucault, commodes and *encoignures* (corner-cupboards) by Heurtaut. Often such craftsmen were imported for quite a length of time to carry out a commission in the provinces, and in many such cases they had a lasting effect on native styles and techniques. Thus, Bordeaux was never far behind Paris furniture fashions, largely due to the patronage of its *intendant*, the Marquis de Tournay, who employed a team of carvers and designers, including Victor Louis and Barthélémy Cabirol, directly controlled from Versailles by Jacques Gabriel. Dijon, too, benefited from the power of the Condés who first lured the *ébéniste* Demoulin from his workshop in the Faubourg Saint-Antoine.

A second important factor in the uniformity of French furniture design was the increase in engravings and craftsmen's manuals. No provincial *menuisier*'s bench was complete without its copies of Delafosse, Watin or Delalonde designs. By the middle of the century these tended to be not just simple engravings of furniture but detailed diagrams of the necessary construction. The plates for Diderot's *Encyclopédie* of 1751–72 (Fig. 9) are an illustration of how explicit such pictorial direction could be.

Little is known on the whole about the lives of provincial *menuisiers* but, if the rules of their Guild are anything to go by, their apprenticeship must also have encouraged a certain uniformity of style. Apprenticed at the age of eleven, the potential member of the Guild became a *compagnon* at fifteen, and was then expected to work in other towns and for different masters. How seriously this so-called '*tour de France*' was taken cannot now be gauged, but judging by the persistence of clearly regional designs and techniques throughout the eighteenth century it is likely that most craftsmen were too poor to go far beyond their own provinces.

An important role played by the Guild was to ensure a high standard of workmanship among furniture-makers all over France. On the whole less corrupt than other guilds, it often did not hesitate to punish its own highest officials; thus René Renault of Tours had a number of oak and walnut *buffets* seized for using defective wood, even though he had twice been Warden of his company.

It is clear, then, that the Guilds had strict control over the technical proficiency of their members, but at the same time little influence as regards ability to design. For, despite the standardisation encouraged by them and helped by the spread of engravings, and despite the leadership of Paris in every field of the arts, there were striking differences not only between court furniture and country furniture, but between one village and another. The reasons for this are mainly geographical. The weaker a province's communications with the capital, the stronger were its local traditions and forms. Thus, remote and mountainous areas like Lorraine or the Pays Basque continued to produce simple furniture of purely medieval construction and decoration right through the eighteenth century. A bed-end with balusters and panels now in the Musée des Beaux-Arts, Rennes (Fig. 11), seems at first sight, at least to English eyes, to date from the early seventeenth century. Yet it is firmly inscribed '1759' just below the top rail. Beds of almost exactly this pattern were still being made in Finistère in the mid-nineteenth century.

Rococo and neo-classical ornament were often mixed

A differentiation must be made here between the furniture of the gradually emerging middle class under Louis XV and XVI, the *noblesse de la robe* and the lesser nobility, and the constant under-current of peasant furniture, to which these beds in fact belong. It is obvious that the latter was more resistant to novelty and fashion than the former, not least because of the different functions it was designed to fulfil. A satinwood *bonheur-du-jour* would have been as out of place in a farmhouse of the Auvergne as a solid, oak-panelled coffer in the drawing-room of Madame de Sévigné. Different life-styles demanded utterly different kinds of furniture.

The *armoire* (Fig. 4) was the most important piece of furniture in every peasant household. It was a large, rectangular, standing wardrobe, which significantly had become almost extinct in court circles after the death of Louis XIV. Its design and construction – usually of two large doors with four or six fielded panels – retained on the whole its original, late medieval shape. This was disguised, as the century progressed, with the odd rococo motif, the panels becoming asymmetrical cartouches, the aprons and cornices curved, and the handles and escutcheons moulded ormolu especially in metal-producing areas, for example Poitou. Since *armoires* were very often made to celebrate marriages or to contain bridal dowries, they frequently bear initials and dates. Sometimes such a date can be misleading, however, since it was the custom in various regions to plant a tree at the birth of a child; it was then cut down to make an *armoire* for the grandchild at his birth.

Fig. 6 **Sofa** belonging to a large [se]t of seat-furniture, Montpellier, [c.] 1780. Painted beechwood with [th]e original embroidered covers. [(P]rivate Collection.)

Fig. 7 **Detail of a chair-front** in [th]e Lyonnais style, Rhône valley, [m]id-eighteenth century. [T]he sophisticated influence of [L]yon spread down the valley of [th]e Rhône as far as Nîmes and [M]ontpellier. [(M]usée Lyonnais des Arts [D]écoratifs.)

Fig. 8 **Armchair** signed by [N]anot, in the Lyonnais style, [R]hône valley, mid-eighteenth [ce]ntury. [T]he furniture of the Nogaret [sc]hool in Lyon and the pieces it [in]fluenced have a simple, [fl]owing grace. [(M]usée Gadagne, Lyon.)

Pierre Jahan

Loïc – Jahan

Loïc – Jahan

173

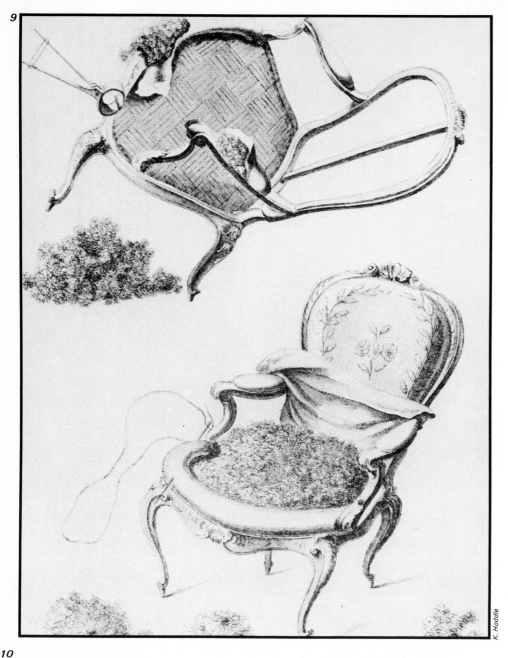

9

10

The *buffet*, or dresser, was likewise an obje
unknown to the Paris *marchand-mercier* and agai
therefore, liable only to have surface decoratio
with a smattering of rococo or neo-classical orna
ment, more often than not a mixture of both. Almo
always this decoration, like the geometrical pattern
of the Middle Ages which still survived in backwar
districts, was liberally applied with no regar
to the structure of the piece of furniture, a
example of that horror of bare surfaces which
a hallmark of the primitive artist.

It must be admitted that many of these peasan
pieces, beautiful though they are, come near
to being folk art than fine art. The slightly mor
ambitious works of craftsmen in provincial town
such as Lyon, Toulouse, Rouen or Liège are perhap
worth studying in more detail, partly because o
their intrinsic quality and partly because it
occasionally possible to pierce the veil of anonymit
which surrounds their creators. It is extreme
unfortunate for furniture historians that the law
of 1743 which forced Parisian cabinet-makers t
stamp their goods were never systematicall
extended to the rest of France. Only a very sma
minority of leading provincial *menuisiers* use
stamps, among them the famous Pierre Nogaret o
Lyon and his successors Parmantier and Lapierre
Froydeveau of Strasburg, and the Hache famil
of Grenoble. A few towns seem to have had thei
own guild and date marks, like the fleur-de-li
poinçon found on many Lille pieces of the mid
century, but these are extremely rare. Liège, whicl
went through a golden age of furniture-makin
during the 1750s and '60s, has hardly any names o
craftsmen to its credit.

Before looking at these towns separately, it i
useful to note the difference between the material
each used. The woods usually employed for th
finest French furniture in the eighteenth centur
were walnut and beech, but whereas Parisia
pieces and those supplied to the royal palaces wer
almost invariably painted or gilt, provincial crafts
men were often happier to leave them plain
Nogaret's chairs, usually of waxed walnut, but witl
rococo carving even more luxuriant than many o
his Parisian contemporaries, show this practice t
its best advantage. Fruitwoods, too, were employe
throughout the provinces, particularly hornbeam
pear and cherry, their rich colours and grain pat
terns used to great decorative effect. Oak was als
popular for the larger pieces of carcase furniture
especially in the west, Normandy, Brittany, Picardy
Artois and the Pays Basque, although its intract
ability for the carver made it more suitable fo
simpler utilitarian pieces made by the village joiner
Walnut was of course the staple wood for highe
quality furniture all over France, but at the sam
time every district had its speciality: olivewood
in Provence, pine in the Auvergne, knotted eln
and ash in Burgundy and Bresse. Far more tha
in England with her colonial supplies, mahogan
was a great luxury in France and was in genera
use only around the great ports, Bordeaux, Nante
and Saint-Malo, particularly in the late eighteent
century. Sometimes confused with it is the deep re
patina of chestnut (Fig. 12) particularly favoured ir
Brittany, Périgord and the Auvergne.

Stylistic differences between the regions wer
to some extent conditioned by the differen
materials used. In areas with very hard woods
again the west, but also Alsace and Lorraine

Fig. 9 *Plate from Diderot's Encyclopédie*, edition of 1771. Explicit instructions for upholstery and cabinet-making were an essential part of the provincial menuisier's equipment, and helped to spread the latest Parisian styles. *(Victoria and Albert Museum, London.)*

Fig. 10 *Commode, Provence, mid-eighteenth century. Olivewood. Mouldings, rather than carving, form the decorative detail on this piece. (Musée Contadin, Carpentras.)*

Fig. 11 *Panelling from a lit seigneurial, Brittany, 1759. Carved and turned oak. This imposing bed is an example of the time-lag between Paris and the provinces; the design and technique are of the sixteenth century, yet such beds were made well into the nineteenth. (Musée des Beaux Arts, Rennes.)*

Fig. 12 *Commode and armchair, Toulouse, c.1800. Chestnut. Pier-glass, Toulouse, c.1800. Carved and gilt. This ensemble shows not only the limitations of provincial work – the flat carving on the mirror and ungainly proportions of the commode – but also its charm and naive vigour. (Private Collection.)*

mouldings are more important than carving in the decorative scheme (Fig. 10). Panels are given boldly chiselled surrounds of convex and concave borders; bases and cornices are emphasised by countless strips of beading; richness is achieved not by swags of flowers or elaborate cartouches but by the shaped outlines of every space, the recession of layer upon layer. Elsewhere, notably in Normandy and the north-east (especially in what is now Belgium), the softer woods encouraged a tradition of incredibly rich carving. In the Pays Basque the decoration is also rich but peculiarly hollowed out, more like engraving than carving in relief. Very often the motifs on all these pieces are a strange mixture of Louis XV and Louis XVI styles: twisted cartouches and shells jostle with classical urns and *paterae*. Yet the synthesis is more endearing than jarring. In fact, provincial pieces frequently give more of an appearance of unity than their Paris counterparts; the strict demarcation there

11

12

between *menuisier*, *ébéniste* and *sculpteur*, preserved by the various guilds, does not seem to have been so strong outside the capital.

Carving, marquetry and plain carpentry were all in a day's work for the average small-town furniture-maker, and it is not therefore surprising if his results were rather different from those of the teams of specialists who produced furniture for the King and Court. The quality of the carving is on the whole flatter (Fig. 12), the marquetry less ambitious, in geometrical rather than naturalistic and *trompe l'œil* designs, and the shapes less subtle, particularly the *bombé* fronts and sides of commodes. Nevertheless certain areas, through either their wealth or their strong contacts with Paris, attained a far greater sophistication. Lyon, famous for its silks and damasks, predictably excelled in seat-furniture where the coverings were as important as the frames. The chairs and sofas of the Nogaret School (by makers such as Carpentier, Geny and Lapierre) capture the elegance of Paris makers such as the Foliots but show an even more accentuated movement and supple line.

The influence of Lyon spread in turn down the valley of the Rhône to centres like Nîmes and Montpellier, where a simple and elegant rococo style was succeeded by a chaste neo-classical style soon after Lalive de Jully's innovations and the Pavillon de Louveciennes (Fig. 6). Pillot's work in Nîmes is particularly beautiful and has strong relations with Nogaret's in Lyon. Very sophisticated furniture, too, was made at Liège in the southern Netherlands; the Musée de Liège has preserved splendid, locally made *boiseries*, commodes and console tables (Fig. 1) very closely based on Paris models though with an added robustness in the carving which is not unattractive. It is rare to find elsewhere in French provincial furniture the luxuries of gilding, of lacquer and of marble on such a scale. Even the secondary pieces of furniture from this school at Liège, walnut sideboards and cabinets (Figs. 2 and 3), adapt advanced rococo motifs to traditional shapes with far more confidence than the usual provincial designs.

But the appeal and the charm of French provincial furniture lies not so much in its sophistication or its documentary interest as in its naive inspiration. 'En art comme en amour', as Anatole France wrote, 'l'instinct suffit'.

MUSEUMS AND COLLECTIONS

French provincial furniture of the eighteenth century may be seen at the following:

FRANCE

Paris: Musée des Arts Décoratifs
Musée des Arts et Traditions Populaires

The best collections are still to be found in the provinces themselves, especially in the museums at Quimper, Nantes, Fontenay-le-Comte, Bordeaux, Lyon, Arles, Bayonne, Clermont-Ferrand and Nancy.

FURTHER READING

Les meubles régionaux en France by Claude Salvy, Paris, 1967.
Le mobilier des vieilles provinces françaises by J. S. Gauthier, Paris, 1960.
Styles Régionaux, a series featuring each province in turn, published by *Plaisir de France*, Paris, from 1959.

English Chippendale

Fig. 1 **Standing shelves** with a pagoda cornice, based on a design in Chippendale's Director, 1762. Japanned and lacquered. (Kedleston Hall, Derbyshire.)

Fig. 2 **'Pagoda' cabinet** in the manner of Chippendale, made for Uppark, Sussex, mid-eighteenth century. Lacquered and japanned, inlaid with ivory and pietre dure.
The inconsistencies of chinoiserie decoration can be seen to perfection in this cabinet. The pagoda which surmounts the piece is decorated with japanned oriental ornament whilst some of the panels below are in Italian pietre dure. The upper drawers are mounted with carved ivory medallions of Homer and Brutus in the classical mode. (Uppark, Sussex.)

The name of Thomas Chippendale is equated with quality and elegance in furniture design as the Rococo yielded to the simpler lines of neo-Classicism

J. Bethell

Transglobe

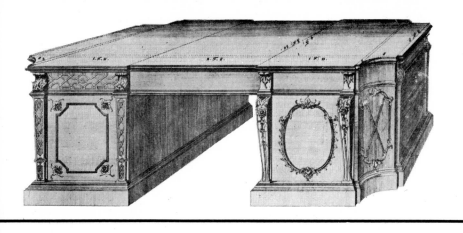

R. B. Fleming

Fig. 3 **State Bedroom,** Nostell Priory, West Yorkshire, designed by James Paine, 1750s, furnished by Thomas Chippendale. Work at Nostell Priory was begun in 1733 under the auspices of the owner, Sir Rowland Winn. When he died in 1765, his son took the commission from Paine and gave it to Robert Adam. Chippendale worked as cabinet-maker under both architects.

Fig. 4 **Design for a library table** from the first edition of The Gentleman and Cabinet-Maker's Director by Thomas Chippendale, 1754. Further editions were published in 1755 and 1762.

Whether or not he was employed in these two famous Yorkshire houses in his youth cannot be proved but these gentlemen were certainly among his most important clients at the height of his career.

In fact, the answer to the enigma may well be that Chippendale was introduced to his clients, and consequently to the London scene, by some of the leading architects of the period. Mr. Desmond FitzGerald (of the Victoria and Albert Museum) has suggested, for example, that James Paine, the architect, may have introduced him to Sir Rowland Winn of Nostell Priory in about 1730, as Paine was working for Sir Rowland at that date. Mr. FitzGerald further suggests that Paine may have persuaded Chippendale to go to London with him in about 1745 in order to study drawing and design, get in touch with craftsmen, designers and engravers, and possibly set up in business together. There, Chippendale could have attended either Hogarth's or Gravelot's schools of design in St. Martin's Lane and, if he did, he would have made useful trade contacts in Old Slaughter's Coffee House, their favourite meeting-place.

There is, furthermore, another link between Chippendale and Paine – the Earl of Northumberland. Paine was employed at various of his houses; Stanwick in North Yorkshire, Syon House in London and Alnwick Castle in Northumberland; Chippendale dedicated the first edition of his *Director* to the Earl. Paine also designed the Middlesex Hospital in 1765 when the Earl, by then Duke, was Chairman of the Board and significantly 'it was that celebrated artist, Mr. Chippendale', who designed and executed 'a rich and elegant frame' for the now lost portrait of the Duke for the Courtroom. Finally, amongst the Paine drawings in the Victoria and Albert Museum, there are three projects for 'octagon' glazed shop fronts, one of these labelled 'Cabinet Ware House'. Mr. FitzGerald suggests that one of these may have been for Chippendale's premises, known in 1758 as 'The Cabinet and Upholstery Warehouse, at the Chair in St. Martin's Lane.'

'... he went with me to Cobbs, Chippendale's and several others of the most eminent cabinet makers to consider of proper Furniture for my Drawing Room'

There may well have been a connection between John Carr, another Yorkshire architect, and many of Chippendale's clients in Yorkshire. Carr, for example, had been employed at Harewood House until he was superseded by Robert Adam. A further link is found in John Spencer's diary, in which we read of a London visit in April, 1768, when Spencer was introduced by Carr, his architect for Cannon Hall, to various members of the trade: 'Mr. Carr went with me to Mr. Tyler the Statuary . . . from thence he went with me to Cobbs, Chippendales and several others of the most eminent Cabinet Makers to consider of proper Furniture for my Drawing Room'.

However, Chippendale, whose business acumen can teach us all a great deal, hunted with the fox and rode with the hounds, and he certainly retained the highly important Harewood account (Fig. 11) after Robert Adam replaced John Carr, the neo-

Chippendale's career, which, judged on results alone, must be regarded as a great success story, is also something of an enigma. How did a completely unknown young man, born in 1718 at Otley in West Yorkshire, son of John Chippendale, a 'joyner', find the funds or backing necessary to set himself up in business in St. Martin's Lane, London, by the age of thirty-five?

Nothing, to date, is known of Chippendale's career between his birth and his marriage in 1748 to Catherine Redshaw at St. George's Chapel, Hyde Park. It has been suggested that, during his formative years, he may have worked at Farnley Hall, near Otley. He doubtless served his apprenticeship in Yorkshire and it is traditionally held that, during this period, he may have made the dolls' house at Nostell Priory (Fig. 5) to a design by James Paine, and may have been employed at Harewood House, near Leeds, by Mr. Henry Lascelles, who had purchased the estate in 1739.

Transglobe

5
6

Fig. 5 **Doll's House** at Nostell
Priory, said to be the early
work of Chippendale under the
supervision of James Paine, 1740
Sir Rowland Winn was one of
Chippendale's earliest and
greatest patrons. It has been
suggested – and there appears
to be a certain amount of
evidence – that Chippendale
served his apprenticeship at
Nostell Priory.

Fig. 6 **Secrétaire**, attributed to
Chippendale, c. 1770–75.
Satinwood inlaid with various
woods.
The recumbent figure and the
vase are of ivory on an ebony
ground.
(Harewood House, West
Yorkshire.)

Fig. 7 **Open armchair** designed
by Robert Adam and made by
Thomas Chippendale, 1764. Gilt-
wood, upholstered in damask.
This chair originally formed
part of a suite comprising ten
chairs and three sofas, made for
Sir Lawrence Dundas.
Chippendale charged prices
which were high for that date –
£20 for each chair and £54 for
each sofa. On top of this, Sir
Lawrence had to supply the
damask for the upholstery.
(Victoria and Albert Museum,
London.)

Fig. 8 **'Ribband-back' chair** of
Director design, c. 1760.
Mahogany.
(Victoria and Albert Museum.)

178

classical marquetry and decorated furniture at
Harewood House bearing witness to his genius.
However, it has only recently come to light that,
in the case of Sir Lawrence Dundas' suite of neo-
classical seat-furniture (Fig. 7), both Chippendale
and Adam were involved in its production and
that they therefore collaborated on a furniture
commission. It is not clear which of the two introduced the commission to the other, although, as
Adam's design for the sofas is dated 1763 and
Chippendale's account is dated 1765, these dates
suggest that it was, in fact, Adam who introduced
Chippendale to Sir Lawrence. Indeed, one would
expect the architect to introduce the cabinet-
maker to the client, Chippendale doubtless paying
an introductory commission to Adam.

'. . . a very pretty Connoisseur in furniture.'

Finally, Chippendale may well have had a similar
relationship with the fashionable and celebrated
Scottish architect, Sir William Chambers, a noted
rival of his fellow countrymen, the Adam brothers.
This connection was, at times, far from placid,
as is shown by a letter from Chambers to Lord
Melbourne in 1773 concerning the furnishings of
the house, which Chambers was building for his
client on the site in London where Albany now
stands: 'Chippendale called me up yesterday
with some designs for furnishing the rooms which
upon the whole seem very well but I wish to be a
little consulted about these matters as I am really a
very pretty Connoisseur in furniture. Be pleased
therefore if it is agreable to Your Lordship & My
Lady to order him to show me the Drawings at
large for tables, Glasses etc., before they are put in
Hand as I think from his Small Drawings that some
part may be improved a little'. Chambers and
Chippendale had obviously just had an acrimonious
quarrel, and it is again probable that it was the
architect who had called in the cabinet-maker,
since Chambers' appeal to his clients was aimed

at keeping Chippendale in his place.

These four architects, Paine, Carr, Adam and
Chambers, may well have been responsible for
introducing Chippendale to many of his clients,
Paine and Carr, in particular, to his considerable
Yorkshire patronage. As in the case of Chambers
and Chippendale's dealings with Lord Melbourne,
it appears that a cabinet-maker, albeit a leading
one, was often on a rather different social footing in
relationship to the client, than was an architect:
there were, after all, many amateur gentleman
architects. This may help to explain why we know
so little about the personality of Chippendale.
The glimpses that we have of him are, with few
exceptions, from somewhat oblique sources such a
business letters, advertisements and similar
material. It is strange that no portrait of him i
extant and that there are no known references of a
descriptive nature to him in any contemporar
diaries or letters.

This lack of material relating to Chippendal
may, in fact, be a most revealing piece of negativ
evidence. We have descriptions and portraits o
some of his rivals. John Cobb, for example, i
described in *Nollekens and his Times* by J. T. Smith
as that 'singularly haughty character . . . one of th
proudest men in England . . . he always appeared i
full dress of the most superb and costly kind, i
which state he would strut through his worksho
giving orders to his men'. William Hallett, anothe
of Chippendale's rivals, appears to have bee
determined to become accepted as a gentlema
and, with this end in view, he built himself
mansion on the site of Canons, the Duke of Chandos
house in Middlesex. He is shown, in a family grou
portrait by Francis Hayman, holding the plans o
Canons in his right hand. His name is also couple
with that of Thomas Bromwich, a highly successfu
specialist in wall-papers, by the poet Richar
Cambridge in his *Elegy written in an Empt
Assembly Room* (1756) in which Cambridg
speaks '. . . of scenes where Hallett's genius ha
combined, With Bromwich to amuse and chee
the mind . . .'. There is even in existence a miniatur

portrait of a provincial Scottish cabinet-maker, George Sandeman of Perth.

'Household Furniture in the Gothic, Chinese and Modern taste'

We do know that Chippendale had social aspirations and that he was a self-publicist, for he joined the Society of Arts at the age of forty-two, in 1760, and his publication of *The Director* is a prime example of his consciousness of the importance of public relations and advertising media. Had he become 'accepted' in the social sense of the word there must surely have been more references to him in contemporary literature. In spite of his membership of the Society of Arts and his fashionable wedding at St. George's Chapel, he was never accepted, except in his trade and professional capacity, by the 'Gentlemen' to whom, with the 'Cabinet-makers', he addressed his *Director*, 'as being calculated to assist the one in the choice, and the other in the execution of the Designs . . .', as he explains in the preface.

Chippendale must have quickly realised his limitations and decided to concentrate on building

often incorrectly interpreted, version of the forms of the French *rocaille*, or *genre pittoresque*. Lock probably taught Chippendale how to handle the 'Modern' or 'French' style, with its birds, shells, foliage, water, rocks, C-scrolls and *rocaille* work.

Chippendale, in addition to being a cabinet-maker in the very widest sense, was also a businessman. His business morals, in fact, do not appear to have been very high, as, in 1769, he was in trouble with the customs for importing French chairs in an unfinished state, which he was declaring at a very low value and then intending to finish in his own warehouse. But, in all fairness, his principles seem to have been no worse than those of many of his contemporaries. His eye for the main chance must have dictated his move to London, for we find him there, at the age of thirty, living in Conduit Court, Long Acre. Four years later, in 1752, he moved to Northumberland Court, where he stayed for two years before moving again, this time to 60, St. Martin's Lane, where he remained for the rest of his life.

The move from Yorkshire, the cost of these various premises, his stock and his wage bill, must have come from some outside source. It has already been suggested that Paine may have been involved in

up a cabinet-making business in which he employed every kind of specialist craftsman. He also had on call professional designers such as Matthias Lock and H. Copland who were not only there in a consultant capacity to his clients, but also helped him to compile his famous publication, *The Director* – 'Being a large collection of the Most Elegant and Useful Designs of Household Furniture in the Gothic, Chinese and Modern Taste'.

The third of the stylistic trends on which he based his designs in the first edition was the 'Modern' taste. This refers to the anglicised, and

Chippendale's move to London, and Chippendale's two most influential Yorkshire clients, Sir Rowland Winn of Nostell Priory and the Lascelles family of Harewood House, are both possible early patrons. Dr. Lindsay Boynton, in the journal of the Furniture History Society 1968, writes: 'The tone of some of the letters [between them] suggests that Sir Rowland Winn held a special place among Chippendale's patrons'. On one occasion, Sir Rowland mentioned his 'custom and protection', and on another describes his patronage as a 'friend's protection'. Chippendale refers to Sir Rowland as 'my patron'

179

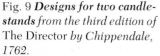

Fig. 9 *Designs for two candle-stands from the third edition of* The Director *by Chippendale, 1762.*

Fig. 10 **Dressing-table,** *c.1760. Rosewood and gilt, height 6 ft. 9½ ins., length 4 ft. 2 ins. (Lady Lever Art Gallery, Port Sunlight, Merseyside.)*

These references imply, as local tradition records, that there was a special relationship between the two men and it is possible that Sir Rowland was not only Chippendale's patron, but also his elusive backer.

In 1754, the year of his move to St. Martin's Lane, he took as his partner James Rannie, who appears to have invested a considerable sum in the business. Rannie, who is described in contemporary documents as 'Upholder and Cabinet-Maker', probably specialised in the 'upholding' (or interior decorating) and upholstery side of the business, Chippendale presumably devoting his energies to the cabinet-making side.

We thus find Chippendale in 1755, set up in the heart of the trade in St. Martin's Lane with a partner and several possible backers. In the same year he insured his premises with the Sun Insurance Company for £3,700, which was a considerable sum. This interesting document tells us a great deal about the details of his business. Later in the same year, a disastrous fire broke out in his premises in which the 'chests of twenty-two workmen were consumed'.

This was the year, 1755, in which the second edition of *The Director* was published; in 1766, four years after the third edition was published, James Rannie died. In 1771, his clerk-accountant, Thomas

Fig. 11 *A drawing from a page entitled 'French chairs' from the third edition of* The Director *by Chippendale, 1762.*

Haig, was taken into partnership and in the same year, the sale of part of the stock was announced in *The Public Advertiser* '. . . to be sold by Auction by Mr. Pervil . . . All genuine Stock in Trade of Mr. Chippendale and his late Partner, Mr. Rennie . . .'. This advertisement is also of great interest as it gives a detailed list of the various categories of pieces which were to be sold. The sale really brings to an end the first phase of Chippendale's career when he was a champion of the rococo taste in this country. As far as he was concerned, it had served him well and, through *The Director*, he had attracted to his premises a large and influential coterie of clients.

Chippendale rapidly followed Adam as an exponent of the Chinese taste

However, Thomas Chippendale was primarily a business-man, and he must have quickly realised that the Rococo was doomed to fall before the neo-classical style, which was by that time being so ardently canvassed by Robert Adam, 'Athenian' Stuart and some of their clients, not to speak of the echoes of a similar movement which were reaching England from Paris. Chippendale, presumably having decided that neo-Classicism was the coming thing, rapidly followed Adam in becoming a leading exponent of the 'Antique' taste. Thus, he devoted the latter years of his career to producing the very finest furniture in the neo-classical tradition whether it was painted, japanned, gilded or of marquetry

obtain commissions from the Crown – William Vile having been appointed Cabinet-Maker to the Royal Household in 1761. In 1762 he therefore dedicated, without prior sanction, several copies of the third edition of his *Director* to Prince William Henry. The Prince, or his advisers, probably indicated that his behaviour over the matter was dubious, reprehensible and impertinent, to say the least, and he was ordered to withdraw the page. In 1768, however, we find Chippendale once again writing to Sir Rowland Winn, as usual apologising for his tardy delivery dates and adding: 'I hope to perform better for the future but it was all owing to the great quantity of unexpected business which I did not know of nor could I refuse doing it as it was mostly for the Royal Family'. It is tantalising that the royal accounts have not, to date, yielded any corroborating evidence.

Why was Chippendale's name so readily accepted by his own and successive generations? His extant *œuvre* speaks for itself and presumably has always done so, but the principal reason why his name has always been synonymous with the finest canons of English mid-eighteenth century cabinet-making is undoubtedly due to his innate understanding of the importance of public relations as exemplified by the publication of his *Director*. ✶

Fig. 12 *Library table probably designed by Adam and made by Chippendale for the library of Harewood House, West Yorkshire, c.1770. When Chippendale saw that Adam and his neo-classical followers were gaining popularity, he abandoned the Rococo and took to decoration based on 'Antique' motifs. (Temple Newsam House, Leeds.)*

(Fig. 12). Some of his most successful essays in this genre, and indeed in the transitional taste linking the Rococo with the neo-Classical, can be seen at Harewood House and Nostell Priory, often in the rooms for which Chippendale's firm originally supplied them (Fig. 3).

Chippendale also seems to have cast a keen eye at the French and Continental markets. Some copies of the third edition of *The Director* were published in French, and in an advertisement in *The British Chronicle*, March 1763, it is stated that 'the descriptions of the said Plates are printed also in French, for the Convenience of Foreigners'.

It appears that Chippendale was very keen to

MUSEUMS AND COLLECTIONS

Chippendale furniture may be seen at the following:

GREAT BRITAIN
Gloucestershire:	Badminton House
Sussex:	Uppark
Tayside:	Blair Castle
West Yorkshire:	Harewood House Nostell Priory
Wiltshire:	Corsham Court Wilton House

Examples may also be viewed in the following museums:

London:	Victoria and Albert Museum
Merseyside:	Lady Lever Art Gallery, Port Sunlight
West Yorkshire:	Temple Newsam House, Leeds
U.S.A. **Holyoke, Mass.:**	Holyoke Museum, Wistonehurst

FURTHER READING

Chippendale and his Contemporaries by John Kenworthy-Browne, London, 1973.
Chippendale by Edward T. Joy, Feltham, 1971.
Chippendale Furniture, the Work of Thomas Chippendale and his Contemporaries in the Rococo style by Anthony Coleridge, London, 1968.
'Thomas Chippendale and Nostell Priory' by Lindsay Boynton and Nicholas Goodison in **Furniture History**, vol. IV, London, 1968.
Adam, Hepplewhite and other Neo-classical Furniture by Clifford Musgrave, London, 1966.
Thomas Chippendale by Oliver Brackett, London, 1930.

American Chippendale

As influential in the Colonies as in England and Ireland, the Chippendale style was supremely dominant in American furniture until the coming of the Revolution

Of all the names associated with furniture and its design, that of Chippendale is the most familiar.

Thomas Chippendale was born in 1718 and died in 1779, and his son Thomas was born in 1749 and died in 1822, having run his father's firm since his death. Essentially Thomas Chippendale the elder was a publicist. The extent to which

Fig. 1 **The Deming Parlour** built for Jonathan Deming, an officer in the Continental Army and a prosperous merchant, Colchester, Connecticut, c.1778. This interior is smaller in scale than a comparable room of the later eighteenth century in England. Because the house from which it was taken was basically of timber frame construction, the original builder found it necessary to conceal one of the structural timbers in the corner behind a two-sided pilaster. A richly coloured Caucasian dragon carpet covers the floor, and the red damask curtains are hung in the contemporary manner. The contents, proceeding clockwise from the left, are as follows:

Wing chair, Newport, Rhode Island, c.1770–75. Mahogany and other woods, the front legs stop-fluted. Height 46 ins.

Looking-glass in the 'Chinese Chippendale' manner using a favourite Chippendale device as finial, the ho-ho bird, American, c.1770–80. Cross-banded mahogany with water-gilding. Height 45 ins.

Pembroke table, American, c.1775–80. Mahogany with pierced C-scroll cross stretchers. Height 28 ins., top when open 0 x 31½ ins.

Tassel-back chair made for the Van Rensselaer family, New York, c.1760–70. Mahogany. Height 38½ ins.

Secretary-bookcase with swan-neck broken pediment, characteristic flame finials and fan decoration, and short cabriole legs, attributed to Joseph Hastings or John Leavitt of Suffield, Connecticut, c.1755–65. Cherry. Height 8 ft. 2½ ins.

Small looking-glass labelled on the back 'John Elliott [1713–91] No. 60 South Front Street between Chestnut and Walnut Streets, Philadelphia, sells wholesale and retail looking glasses in neat mahogany frames etc.'. Walnut. Height 18 ins., width 8½ ins.

Tripod table, American, c.1780–85. Cherrywood, height 26¾ ins.

(American Museum in Britain, Claverton Manor, Bath.)

Fig. 2 **Highboy**, Philadelphia, c.1765–75. Mahogany with carved shell and fan motifs and quarter-round fluted columns. Height 7½ ft.

(American Museum in Britain.)

Derek Balmer

183

Fig. 3 *Chair, Massachusetts,*
c.1765–75. Mahogany in the
Chippendale manner but with a
Queen Anne style kidney-shaped
seat. Height 37½ ins.
(American Museum in Britain.)

Fig. 4 *Chair, one of a pair*
labelled on the back with metal
plates bearing the name Hopkins
for the original owner, John
Estaugh Hopkins of Haddenfield,
New Jersey, possibly made by
Samuel Nickle (who returned to
his birthplace, Haddenfield, in
1776 for three years), c.1776–79.
Mahogany in the Chippendale
manner but with a Queen Anne
style spla:. Height 40 ins.
(American Museum in Britain.)

Chippendale himself was responsible for the designs shown in his famous pattern-book, *The Gentleman and Cabinet-Maker's Director* (first edition 1754) is not certain, and he probably employed designers such as Matthias Lock to assist him.

Without doubt, however, the book was immensely significant, for it represented the fashions set by all the leading London cabinet-makers and it was to influence the design of furniture in various British colonies, not least in North America. Just as public buildings in the American colonies were influenced by James Gibbs' *The Rules for Drawing the Several Parts of Architecture* (1732) and domestic buildings by Batty Langley's *Builder's Jewel* (1754), so Chippendale's *Director* influenced colonial American furniture design in the second half of the eighteenth century.

The term 'American Chippendale' is usually applied to furniture forms derived from England in the mid-eighteenth-century post-walnut, pre-satinwood epoch. Though this style was derived from England in the middle of the eighteenth century, its adoption in America occurred in the latter half of that century.

Large quantities of mahogany were imported from the West Indies

Three basic types of mahogany were in use in both England and America in the second half of the eighteenth century. These were the varieties from Cuba, San Domingo and Honduras. The finest of them was the Cuban, a wood that is characterised by great weight, hardness and closeness of grain. When it is worked, minute white flecks of a chalky character appear in the wood. Honduras is lighter in weight and colour. The mahoganies from San Domingo and Jamaica fall somewhere between Cuban and Honduras in quality. Flame mahogany refers to the character of the grain, and it is taken from the 'pair of trousers', the name given to the first branch or crotch of the tree. Another much sought-after 'figure' (meaning the character of the grain) was mottled, and often referred to as 'plum pudding' mahogany.

Nevertheless, in the Chippendale period in America, cherry was more often used than mahogany by Connecticut cabinet-makers. Throughout the U.S.A. the main structure of carcase furniture was of softwood, whereas in England hardwood such as oak was favoured.

Virginian walnut, known in the timber trade as 'black' walnut or 'bastard' walnut, sometimes has a reddish colour akin to mahogany. This variety of walnut was used in England in the last phase of the walnut period when English walnut was scarce and the walnut famine in France resulted in an embargo on the export of this variety to England in 1730.

Once Britain had gained mastery of the New Netherlands in 1674, British political power and subsequent socio-political influence extended from Massachusetts almost to Florida. This was a vast area whose population, whether of British descent or not, tended to adopt not only the British language but also the British way of life, and this was reflected in the furnishing and decoration of their homes. It is thus not surprising to discover that

American furniture in the manner of Chippendale was created by men who were not exclusively of British descent. George Gostelowe who worked in Philadelphia was of Swedish extraction, and Andrew Gautier was a Huguenot.

Some of the most remarkable makers of this sumptuous furniture were Quakers, for example the Goddards and the Townsends of Newport, Rhode Island, and William Savery of Philadelphia. In the whole history of American colonial furniture the Townsends and the Goddards (the two families intermarried) are truly remarkable for the quality of their work and for the number of them of different generations who made furniture, altogether some twenty individuals from three generations. Of the Townsends, Christopher and his sons John and Job and his grandsons Job Junior and Edmund were well known, while of the Goddards the best known was John.

Block-front carcase furniture (where the centre front recedes in a shallow concave curve between slightly convex ends) seems to have been unique to North America. Certainly Chippendale illustrated no furniture of this type in the first edition of *The Director*. It is thought that the style originated in the area of Boston, Massachusetts, in the second quarter of the eighteenth century and, it later assumed a Chippendale character. The first known documented piece is a fine bureau-bookcase signed 'Job Colt 1738' now in the Henry Francis du Pont Museum at Winterthur, Delaware. A fine block front bureau in the American Museum in Britain at Bath is interesting in that the outward projection are carved out of the solid and not made of separate pieces of wood. The fall-front of this bureau and the drawer fronts are thus made from pieces of wood of considerable size (Fig. 5).

Another characteristically American furniture form was the highboy, a type that is also occasionally block-fronted. In England the chest-on-stand of the late seventeenth and early eighteenth centuries was abandoned in favour of the tallboy or chest-on-chest where the lower section is supported on low bracket feet. In contrast the highboy is supported on high cabriole legs, the top being surmounted by a swan-neck broken pediment sometimes known in America as a 'bonnet top' (Fig. 2). The centre of the pediment is usually embellished with a cartouche, of the type illustrated in the first edition of *The Director* except that in America the belly (the area originally designed for a heraldic device) of the cartouche has shrunk to insignificance. Chippendale illustrated a few examples of the chest-on-stand which he called the 'chest on frame'. The stand or frame is of a very simple kind and encloses no drawers within its frieze. In the eighteenth century the highboy was known as a 'high chest of drawers'. These are usually elaborately carved as it was customary for such pieces to be exhibited in the drawing room despite the fact that they were designed to contain belongings of a personal nature.

The lowboy, as its name implies, was composed in effect of the lower part of the highboy, and was often elaborately embellished with carving. Most of the brass hardware that occurs on highboys and other American furniture of this period was imported from England, but it is known that there were American makers. English provincial 'Chippendale' chairs often exhibit features of Queen Anne or early Georgian character and a

Derek Balmer

Fig. 5 *Block-front bureau, possibly Boston, Massachusetts, c.1770. San Domingo mahogany. Height 44½ ins. (American Museum in Britain.)*

Fig. 6 *Dowel and tenon construction, which continued in use in the Colonies as late as the end of the eighteenth century. Though very strong, this primitive method was abandoned in sophisticated English furniture early in the century.*

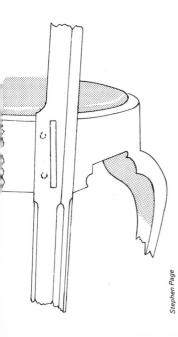

Stephen Page

strong, though very much earlier type of construction. That which was true of the English provinces was also true of the English colonies in North America. It is by no means unusual to see American chairs of 'Chippendale' form with Queen Anne back-splats or kidney-shaped seats (Figs. 3 and 4) while dowelled-through tenons continued to be employed in America, even in sophisticated furniture, up to the late eighteenth century (Fig. 6). In England this feature had died out in all but country furniture by the early eighteenth century. Of course there are exceptions which avoid these anomalies so that identification is dependent upon more subtle points such as the less extreme line of the 'back-foot' (a chair-makers' term for the back leg) as compared with the English examples which are less vertical. However, in America, cabriole legs tended to be somewhat curlier than in England.

In America, as in England, chair-making was a distinct department of furniture manufacture, its specialist requirements demanding specialist craftsmen. The reason for this division of labour is simple: a chair contains few right-angles, a fact which complicates the joints and renders cramping up (holding the parts rigid while the glue dries) difficult. In particular, on curvilinear examples, especially in France, it was customary to leave projections on the component parts of a chair in order to facilitate the application of cramps when gluing up. These projections were subsequently carved off. Another method frequently employed involved the use of a long strip of flexible metal on each end of which was bolted a block of wood; the strip of metal could then be wound round in form and built up with G-cramps or sash cramps on the blocks. For this reason it is often difficult to repair chairs though in the eighteenth century tourniquets were sometimes employed in addition to the methods already mentioned. There were, on both sides of the Atlantic, craftsmen who made

both chairs and case furniture but they were the exception, and it was usual for them to emphasise this fact in their trade cards as did Jonathan Gostelowe of Philadelphia whose card declared him to be a 'Cabinet and Chairmaker in Church Alley'.

Another form of furnishing that is much associated with the name of Chippendale is the so-called 'Chinese Chippendale' mirror-frame. As a rule, American furniture did not achieve a full flowering of 'Chinese', 'Gothick' or 'French' Chippendale though a much modified *bombé* form for chests of drawers was adopted. Generally speaking, American examples are infinitely simpler than those made in the mother country and are comparable with English provincial specimens, being of cross-banded mahogany and parcel-gilt.

Large numbers of English mirror-frames were imported into the U.S.A., the extreme elaboration of the carving coupled with that most difficult method of gilding on a gesso ground, water-gilding. John Elliott of Philadelphia, whose trade label was printed in both English and German, imported large numbers of English mirrors.

Records exist of 'handicraft slaves' and their relative values

Records dating from before the American War of Independence prove that there were many skilled craftsmen in the country. In Boston, for example, there were one hundred and fifty known cabinet-makers, chair-makers and carvers prior to the American War of Independence, while in Newport there were over fifty. In the South, craftsmen-slaves were able to produce good work. Thomas Elfe of Charleston, whose records for the year 1768 to 1775 have survived, wrote of many 'handicraft slaves'; for instance, 'four sawyers valued at £1,400 and five cabinet-makers at £2,250'.

In America the influence of Chippendale drew to a close with the founding of the new republic. Thomas Jefferson's house, Monticello, was designed in a Palladian manner. The new republic demanded new furniture forms and if Palladian architecture was scarcely new, the furniture forms that emerged were certainly of a different order. ◾

MUSEUMS AND COLLECTIONS

'American Chippendale' furniture may be seen at the following:

GREAT BRITAIN
Bath: American Museum in Britain, Claverton Manor

U.S.A.
Boston: Boston Museum of Fine Arts
New York: Metropolitan Museum of Art
Philadelphia: Philadelphia Museum of Art
Williamsburg, Va: Colonial Williamsburg
Winterthur, Del: Henry Francis du Pont Winterthur Museum

FURTHER READING
Centuries and Styles of the American Chair by Robert Bishop, New York, 1972.
The Cabinetmakers of America by Ethel Hall Bjerkoe, assisted by John Arthur Bjerkoe, New York, 1957.
American Furniture of the Queen Anne and Chippendale Periods by Joseph Downs, New York, 1952.

Hepplewhite Furniture

Fig. 1 **Pembroke table top**, *late eighteenth century. Marquetry decoration representing floral wreaths.*
According to Sheraton, this type of table, with its hinged flaps, derived its name from 'the lady who first gave orders for one of them', possibly the Countess of Pembroke (1737–1831). In this example by an unknown cabinet-maker, the decoration has a freedom and charm which is still rococo in spirit.
(Victoria and Albert Museum, London.)

186

Hepplewhite, like Chippendale and Sheraton, owes his posthumous fame to his book of designs which had a wide circulation towards the end of the eighteenth century

George Hepplewhite, having been apprenticed to the firm of Gillow, in Lancaster, came to London and by 1760 was making furniture in Redcross Street, Cripplegate. He died in 1786. This is virtually all we know of the man whose name is used for a style of furniture covering roughly the years 1775 to 1790.

In 1788, two years after his death, there appeared *The Cabinet-maker and Upholsterer's Guide*. It is this book which has made Hepplewhite famous; in fact it was produced by A. Hepplewhite and Co., that is, by his widow, Alice, who had continued the business. A folio volume, with an introduction and notes to one hundred and twenty-three engraved plates, it contained some two hundred and sixty illustrations for many types of household furniture, details of cornices and mouldings and a plan for a typical room or 'parlour'.

Alice, widow Hepplewhite, was clearly an efficient and enterprising businesswoman. There had been few published books on furniture since

Figs. 2, 3 and 4 **Designs for chairs** *from* The Cabinet-maker and Upholsterer's Guide *by A. Hepplewhite and Co., 1788. These designs have the combined elegance and utility which made Hepplewhite's furniture so popular.* (*Victoria and Albert Museum.*)

Fig. 5 **Design for a pier-table** *from Hepplewhite's Guide, 1788. This design is closely related to the card-tables, which folded in half to give a shape similar to that of a pier-table, made by Hepplewhite and other designers of the day.* (*Victoria and Albert Museum.*)

Museum Photo

the mid-1760s, when the vogue for the Rococo had started to decline. She published a work on a scale comparable to Chippendale's *Director*, the 1762 edition of which had two hundred plates. A second edition of *The Guide* with an additional plate was published in 1789. The 'improved' third edition of 1794 had two further plates, and fourteen of the old ones were altered to include fresh designs.

In studying the plates of *The Guide* one concludes that Hepplewhite had neither antiquarian nor architectural training. From the 1760s, Robert Adam and others had directed fashion away from the Rococo and *Chinoiserie* towards Neo-classicism. In the hands of an architect, or of a top furniture designer, the ornaments were arranged together with clarity, vigour and vitality. The *rinceau*, or acanthus scroll, for example, would have a tense outline like a wound spring, recalling the Ionic volute. Other ornaments would flow or cluster round the main construction lines in logical sequence. It is this ordered logic and discipline which is lacking in the designs of *The Guide*. With Hepplewhite the *rinceau* tends towards the ovoid and terminates awkwardly. The leaves and husks wander limply over the surface; festoons hang badly and, although the design may be decorative and charming, it shows no proper knowledge of ancient Rome, whence it was derived. Moreover, the neo-classical repertory of ornament is sometimes mixed with a flower-head or a ribboned bunch

of leaves, bringing with it a lingering flavour of the rococo period.

Neo-classicism was much softened in the designs for, instead of Adam's severe geometrical outlines, there are gently undulating serpentine fronts, or the serpentine apron curving to shaped feet. The furniture in *The Guide* is useful and decorative, but it gives no sense of any underlying architectural proportions.

'To combine the elegance and utility, and blend the useful with the agreeable'; to 'convey a just idea of English taste in furniture for houses'; to adhere to 'such articles only as are of general use and service': these intentions are expressed in the introduction to *The Guide*. Any attempt at originality is disclaimed – 'we designedly followed the latest or most prevailing fashion only, purposely omitting such articles whose recommendation was mere novelty' – and many of Hepplewhite's designs published between 1788 and 1794 reflected the taste of at least ten years before. Some designs for chairs would not seem out of place in Robert Manwaring's book on chair-making of 1765, and Hepplewhite actually illustrates a 'Chinese Chippendale' fret to support hanging shelves.

Considering the enormous quantity of high-quality furniture that survives from Georgian times, it seems extraordinary that we know so little of its makers. Sir Ambrose Heal has listed the names of well over two hundred cabinet- and chair-makers operating between 1774 and 1794. Among them

Fig. 6 *Secretaire bookcase*, c.1790. Figured satinwood decorated with marquetry and painting. The straight cornice, ornamented with semicircular motifs, is an unusual feature in this design. (*Victoria and Albert Museum*.)

Fig. 7 *Armchair*, c.1780. This armchair, in the Hepplewhite style, shows French influence and is known as 'French Hepplewhite'. (*Norman Adams Ltd., London*.)

Mark Gerson

are upholders, carvers, gilders, turners, founders, glass-grinders and other craftsmen related to the furniture trade. Some of these are known to us through trade directories, trade-cards, rate-books, bills or even through the presence of labels which sometimes remain pasted in the drawers or on the underside of furniture. But of their individual achievements we know little.

In the late eighteenth century George Seddon owned one of the largest manufacturing firms in London, about which we have some detailed information.

The show-room was described by Sophie von la Roche, a visitor from Germany, who went to Seddon's in 1786 and wrote in her journal at some length. She noted all manner of finished and unfinished articles, 'from the simplest and cheapest to the most elegant and expensive . . . Charming dressing-tables are also to be seen, with vase-shaped mirrors, occupying very little space and yet containing all that is necessary to the toilet of any reasonable person. Close stools, too, made like a tiny chest of drawers, decorative enough for any room. Numerous articles made of straw-coloured service wood . . . ; their own saw-house too, where as many blocks of fine foreign wood lie piled, as firs and oaks are seen at our saw-mills. The entire story of the wood, as used for both inexpensive and costly furniture and the method of treating it can be traced in this establishment'.

Seddon, unlike his contemporaries, dealt in upholstery, glass-cutting for looking-glasses, the casting and gilding of mounts and lock-making, the related trades to cabinet-making. If fabrics were not actually made by Seddon, carpets were at least cut to order, and 'a great many seamstresses' were busy making curtains and bed-covers. Seddon's factory was burnt down three times, in 1768, 1783 and 1790. In 1768 the loss was £7,300 (he had omitted to pay his insurance premium and was refunded only £3,000). In 1789, the stock-taking totalled £118,926 of which the carpets were worth over £20,000. Sophie von la Roche tells us that he was 'foster-father to four hundred employees'.

Notwithstanding his vast output, a large part of which must remain with us today, only a handful can actually be traced to Seddon's firm. A set of painted satinwood shield-back chairs of about 1790 is known from a bill and, because of this, similar fine painted chairs are often associated with his name (Fig. 8).

On the evidence of *The Guide*, we may assess the position of Hepplewhite among his rivals. The numerous designs for chair-backs (Figs. 2, 3 and 4) and settees, though somewhat outmoded for their date (1788–94), are in fact of considerable merit, and Hepplewhite may well have specialised in chair-making, possibly for the wholesale trade. The same may be said of the many canopy beds which, since he did not cater for very rich patrons, are remarkably elaborate. Case-furniture such as bureaux, secretaires, chests of drawers and

Owner's Photo

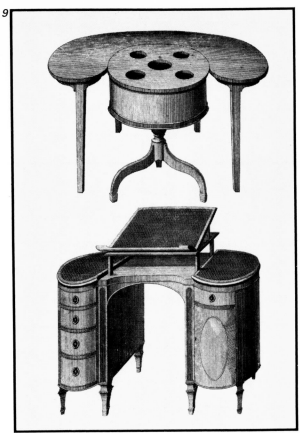

9

Museum Photo

Fig. 8 **Pair of painted armchairs**, c.1785–90. This decorative style of floral details, garlands and ribbons is popularly associated with George Seddon (1727–1801), a cabinet-maker of considerable output in the eighteenth century. (Mallet and Son Ltd., London.)

Fig. 9 **Designs for a wine-table and a reading-table** from the third edition of Hepplewhite's Guide, London, 1794. The cylindrical top of the wine-table revolves so that the guests, seated along the oval table, may reach any of the bottles resting in the cavities. (Victoria and Albert Museum.)

Fig. 10 **'Rudd's' dressing-table**, probably made before 1775. A similar table appears in the Guide of 1788 and is described as 'possessing every convenience which can be wanted or mechanism or ingenuity supply'. (Christie, Manson and Woods, London.)

Fig. 11 **Dressing-table** with shield-shaped mirror. Mahogany. (Christie's.)

numerous kinds of tables are well represented in *The Guide*, but their style is not exciting. For all these mahogany is usually specified; but very many surviving examples from the period are in fact of satinwood, more or less inlaid, according to the pocket of the purchaser, and intended for the drawing-room or other rooms used by the ladies.

The patterns for dressing-chests and shaving-tables are perfectly competent, though less elaborately fitted than Thomas Shearer's designs. (Together Shearer and the firm of Hepplewhite published a book of designs and prices in 1788.) The 'Rudd's' table (a type of table the original of which was made for a Captain Rudd) in Figure 10, which is thought to have been made before 1775, bears the trade-labels of Thomas Scott, whom Ambrose Heal mentions as a specialist in such pieces.

An improvement in the third edition of *The Guide* included changing the designs of fourteen chairs and three sofas, including some archaic chairs and all those with oval backs. New chair designs included five more shield-backs and seven

with the square backs fashionable in about 1790. A few of these show quite definite Sheraton influence. In addition, there were twelve designs for chair backs 'proper to be executed in mahogany or japan'. Japan would seem the more likely, considering their style. These quite pleasing designs show some French influence and might be called 'poor man's Sheraton'.

The final plate is a design for a Dining Parlour. (Sophie von la Roche remarks at Seddon's showrooms: 'the scheme for a dining-room, designed both for practical use and for ornament, took my fancy most . . .'). It shows the fully developed sideboard flanked by pedestals. Parlour or dining-chairs (without arms) and a sofa are arranged round the walls, and above them are square looking-glasses and girandoles, or branched candle-brackets. The four windows each contain a window-seat and are separated by pier-tables and pier-glasses. *The Guide* informs its readers: 'For a Dining Room, instead of the pier tables should be a set of dining tables' Presumably these were to be brought out

10

A. C. Cooper

11

A. C. Cooper

and assembled only at meals, when the parlour became a dining-room. There is no design for a dining-table in *The Guide*. Formal meals were becoming the fashion, but a dining-table as we know it, permanently set up, seems not yet to have appealed to Hepplewhite's patrons. On the other hand, those who were rich enough to have a drawing-room besides a dining-parlour, should have in it two sofas, and a confidante opposite; 'the sideboard also should be removed, and an elegant commode substituted in the place. The remaining space may be filled up with chairs'.

These were the basic furnishings of the main rooms. Matters did not stop here, for in a society increasingly dominated by women, and profoundly conscious of social class, numerous smaller pieces were necessary. Pole screens to set by the fire, urn-stands for tea, recently invented Pembroke tables (Fig. 1) for breakfast or needlework, and elaborate dressing- and writing-tables, were increasingly in fashion to be used when sitting in elegant conversation, at one's toilet, or writing letters and diaries. The ladies' rooms (the drawing-room, boudoir, dressing-room and bedroom) were furnished preferably in satinwood, cross-banded with exotic woods and inlaid with marquetry; or, less expensively but equally fashionably, with japanned furniture. The parlour and the library, being more masculine and functional, were normally furnished in mahogany.

From *The Cabinet Makers London Book of Prices*, and *Designs of Cabinet Work*, the combined work of Shearer and Hepplewhite's company, we see that Shearer was the better draughtsman. His crisp etching, detailed shading and exaggerated perspective account for the superior quality of his engravings. He shows sharp mouldings and gives scales in feet and inches, whereas Hepplewhite's scales often make no coherent sense. Shearer's firm outlines, particularly to serpentine fronts, and the feet and legs narrowed to fragility, provide an elegance which is lacking in *The Guide*.

In some cases Shearer was definitely mor advanced than *The Guide* in his experiments. Th patterns for glazing-bars for bookcase doors is a example. Shearer shows very elegant designs c spindle-thin, interlaced arches, whereas Hepple white, in 1788, favoured simpler curves. Shearer writing- and dressing-tables are closer to th intricate needs of ladies of the time than an shown by Hepplewhite.

Thomas Sheraton in his introduction to Th *Cabinet-maker and Upholsterer's Drawing Boo* (1791–94) was extremely critical of *The Guide*. Th illustrations to his book are impressive from th point of view of their draughtsmanship and perspec tive; on both these scores Hepplewhite was criti cised. Besides designs for chairs and dressing-table (some of which are not really so far removed from Hepplewhite's designs) and bookcase doors obviously deriving from Shearer, the *Drawing Boo* contains an abundance of newer patterns, full o mechanical contrivances and French sophistication Of *The Guide* he writes: 'if we compare some o the designs . . . with the newest taste, we shall find that this work has already caught the decline, and perhaps, in a little time, will suddenly die i disorder'. He praises Shearer's *Book of Prices* a Hepplewhite's expense.

In support of Hepplewhite, it can justly be said that *The Guide* has never wholly passed out of use Whereas Sheraton's style, though it 'dates' well inevitably recalls the 1790s, Hepplewhite's pattern have been used consistently right up to the presen century for universal, uninspired, domestic fur niture. Examples are the ever popular shield-back chair (Figs. 3 and 4) and the cellaret sideboard, which was designed to hold winebottles. Both these pieces and others characteristic of English furniture, have been made well by generations of craftsmen, with o without direct reference to *The Guide*, where first they were illustrated.

Fig. 12 ***Design for a pier-glass*** from Hepplewhite's Guide, London, 1788.
In this design, the decoration is mainly used without discipline and the neo-classical repertory of ornament is mixed with flower-heads and ribbons.
(Victoria and Albert Museum.)

Fig. 13 ***Pembroke table*** in the style of Hepplewhite, late eighteenth century.
The top of this table is cross-banded in satinwood and inlaid with a delicate, classical design.
(Mallet's.)

Museum Photo

Owner's Photo

MUSEUMS AND COLLECTIONS

Hepplewhite furniture may be seen at the following:

GREAT BRITAIN

Barnsley:	Cannon Hall Art Gallery and Museum
Colchester:	The Minories Art Gallery
Hove:	Hove Museum of Art
Leeds:	Temple Newsam House
London:	Geffrye Museum
	Victoria and Albert Museum

FURTHER READING

Adam and Hepplewhite and Other Neo-Classical Furniture by Clifford Musgrave, London, 1966.
Shearer Furniture Designs with an introduction by Ralph Fastnedge, London, 1962.
English Furniture Styles from 1500 to 1830 by Ralph Fastnedge, Harmondsworth, 1955.
The London Furniture Makers (1660–1840) by Sir Ambrose Heal, London, 1953.
The Cabinet Maker and Upholsterer's Guide by A. Hepplewhite and Co., London, 1788, reprinted by the Thames Facsimile Company, 1953.

Sheraton

T. SHERATON
N. 106, Wardour Street, Soho.

Teaches Perspective, Architecture and Ornaments,
makes Designs for Cabinet-makers, &c.
and sells all kinds of Drawing-Books &c.

R. B. Fleming

Fig. 1 Trade-card of Thomas Sheraton, engraved by Barlow, c.1795. Sheraton's relationship with the furniture trade in London was two-sided; on the title-page of his Drawing-Book of 1793, he described himself as a 'Cabinet-Maker', whereas on this card, the emphasis is on his role as a teacher, designer and seller of drawing books. (British Museum, London.)

Thomas Sheraton — teacher of perspective, architecture and ornament; author, publisher and preacher; and the talented creator of a new furniture style

Thomas Sheraton (1751–1806) appears never to have owned a business, but there is good evidence that he was trained as a cabinet-maker and worked at this trade in someone else's business for part, perhaps for much, of his life. A good deal of technical knowledge is evident in his writings, and contemporary comment in his obituary stated that he had been a journeyman cabinet-maker for many years whereas after 1793 he made his living chiefly by writing. His own testimony bears this out; on the title-page of *The Cabinet-Maker and Upholsterer's*

Drawing-Book, of 1793, he described himself as a cabinet-maker, whereas his trade-card (Fig. 1), bearing his Wardour Street (London) address of 1793–95, announced that he taught perspective, architecture and ornament, made designs for cabinet-makers and sold all kinds of drawing-books. His statement about making designs is interesting evidence of a two-way relationship between Sheraton and the trade, for he often acknowledged in the *Drawing-Book* that he obtained ideas from cabinet-makers.

The only recorded instance of his designing for a commission, however, is for Broadwoods when they made a grand piano in 1796 for Godoy, favourite of Queen Maria Louisa of Spain. Since there is no evidence that Sheraton ever set up on his own as a cabinet-maker we should not expect too much of attempts to identify furniture made by him. There are reports of workmen employed by him; of furniture for which his bill is said to exist

191

Fig. 2 **Design for a cabinet**,
*Plate 14, dated 1793, in the
appendix of the* Drawing-Book
*by Thomas Sheraton, London,
1793. Engraving by G. Terry.
This design is of the type by
Sheraton often considered
feminine or effeminate – slender
and fragile with delicately
painted decoration.
(Victoria and Albert Museum,
London.)*

Fig. 3 **The 'Weekes' cabinet**
*in the manner of T. Sheraton,
late eighteenth century.
This elegant cabinet is inset with
a clock and has neo-classical urns
round the top.
(Temple Newsam House, Leeds.)*

2

A. C. Cooper

Fig. 4 **Design for a sideboard**,
*Plate 29, dated 1791, of
T. Sheraton's Drawing-Book.
Engraving by G. Terry.
(Victoria and Albert Museum.)*

Fig. 5 **Bookcase** *after a design
dated 1806 in Sheraton's*
Encyclopaedia, *early
nineteenth century.
The severe lines of this fine bookcase are softened by the richness
of the veneering.
(Victoria and Albert Museum.)*

Fig. 6 **Lady's writing cabinet**
*in the manner of Sheraton, late
eighteenth century.
Delicately painted with flowers,
this piece is also inset with two
Wedgwood plaques.
(Lady Lever Art Gallery,
Port Sunlight, Merseyside.)*

Fig. 7 **Commode** *in the manner
of T. Sheraton, c.1790.
Satinwood.
(Victoria and Albert Museum.)*

192

3

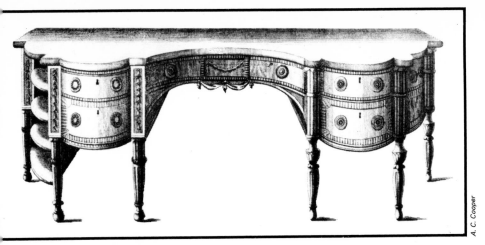

6

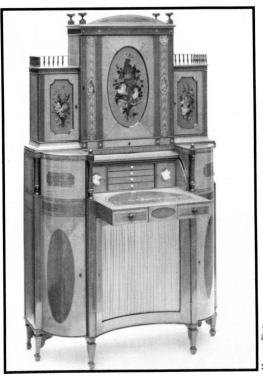

(but which cannot be found); and recently of a long-case clock labelled 'Thomas Sheraton' which was found in County Durham. However, the last item cannot be authenticated without further evidence.

The breadth of Sheraton's interests led him into many different activities. A notable example was Baptist theology and preaching; he spent a good deal of time travelling and writing in this cause and eventually joined the ministry. Adam Black, later a publisher, worked for Sheraton at one time and gave a succinct pen-portrait of his employer: 'He lived in an obscure street [Broad Street, near Golden Square], his house half shop, half dwelling-house, and looked himself like a worn-out Methodist minister, with threadbare black coat. I took tea with them one afternoon. There were a cup and saucer for the host, and another for his wife, and a little porringer for their daughter. The wife's cup and saucer were given to me, and she had to put up with another little porringer. My host seemed a good man, with some talent. He had been a cabinet-maker, was now author and publisher, teacher of drawing, and, I believe, occasional preacher. I was with him for about a week, engaged in most wretched work, writing a few articles, and trying to put his shop in order, working among dirt and bugs, for which I was remunerated with half a guinea. Miserable as the pay was, I was half ashamed to take it from the poor man.' Elsewhere, Black noted of Sheraton, 'He is a man of talents . . . a scholar, writes well; draws, in my opinion, masterly; is an author, bookseller, stationer, and teacher. We may be ready to ask how comes it to pass that a man with such abilities and resources is in such a state? I believe his abilities and resources are his ruin, in this respect, for, by attempting to do everything, he does nothing.'

Sheraton's books betray something of what we should call 'a chip on the shoulder', particularly about the education he lacked but strove, in the best nonconformist tradition, to acquire. Indeed, his ambitions went further: not only did he personally teach drawing, but he was also anxious that his *Drawing-Book* should persuade cabinet-makers to learn about drawing, especially in relation to architecture and perspective. His predecessors in the field of furniture design had tended to pay lip-service rather than anything else to these subjects which, perhaps through Sheraton's advocacy, came to form part of the curriculum for aspiring cabinet-makers and others in the next generation: the age of self-help and of Mechanics' Institutes.

Adam Black thought Sheraton himself drew 'masterly'. Yet only one drawing is at present attributed to him, which is now in the Victoria and Albert Museum (Fig. 10). Being unique, there is no possibility of establishing its credentials by comparison; nor can we simply accept the signature on it for the same reason, since none of his correspondence has been found. Here again, there is an obvious contrast with Chippendale, a number of whose drawings exist, even if they are not particularly distinguished. Nevertheless, Sheraton's talent for drawing is apparent through his published designs and notably in his *Drawing-Book*. Sheraton's deservedly high reputation rests on this book rather than on his *Cabinet Dictionary* of 1803 (interesting as much of its information is) and still less on his *Cabinet-Maker, Upholsterer, and General Artist's Encyclopaedia* of 1804–1807, some plates of which were published posthumously. This

193

Fig. 8 *Frontispiece of the Drawing-Book by T. Sheraton, London, 1793. Engraving by Hawkins.*
Over the page Sheraton has written in the 'Frontispiece Explained':
'...I have, by the figure on the right hand, represented Geometry standing on a rock, with a scroll of diagrams in his hand, conversing with Perspective, the next figure to him, who is attentive to the Principles of Geometry as the ground of his art; which art is represented by the frame on which he rests his hand. On the left, seated near the window, is an artist busy in designing; at whose right is the Genius of Drawing, presenting the artist with various patterns. The back figure is Architecture, measuring the shaft of a Tuscan column; and on the back ground is the Temple of Fame, to which a knowledge of these arts directly leads'.
(Victoria and Albert Museum.)

last was over-ambitious and, by Sheraton's death in 1806, covered only 'Astronomy' to 'Canada'; its inconsistency and even incoherence were such that it has been suggested that its author's mind had given way. However, Sheraton's theological tract *A Discourse on the Character of God as Love*, written in 1805, is perfectly clear and rational.

At all events, Sheraton never repeated the success of his *Drawing-Book*, which attained three English editions and a German translation by 1802, and at least eight more printings thereafter. Unlike earlier books of its kind (notably Chippendale's *Director*) which, although influential in the trade, also sought aristocratic patronage, the *Drawing-Book* was aimed at cabinet-makers themselves. Eighty per cent of its subscribers were connected with one or another of the cabinet trades, and many of them were from the provincial towns. This was to be expected, for England's marked growth in population meant that London's predominance, though still important, was not as overwhelming as it had been. Consequently, it is from the late eighteenth century that we find provincial cabinet-makers emerging from their former obscurity.

Sheraton must have realised that the time was right to give these craftsmen a lead in order to attract the custom of the large middle class in England. He was, after all, a teacher, and there is much of the teacher in the *Drawing-Book*. He did not claim that the designs in it were wholly original; rather, as he made quite clear, he found that no one workshop was first class in all branches of design and so he visited one after another, collecting ideas, giving credit where credit was due, and adding his own improvements where he could. He thus presented a summary of what he thought was best in London design, both to his numerous fellow cabinet-makers in England and to those in her colonies, in Europe, and in the United States. This in itself was a notable achievement. But Sheraton probably aimed still higher. The *Drawing-Book* includes a great deal about geometry and perspective which has generally been dismissed as tedious and irrelevant. Taken by itself, no doubt it is; but Sheraton's comments on the 'unalterable principles' of the 'sublime science of geometry' indicate that he was trying to link furniture design to permanent principles which would raise it above mere fashion and give it a lasting quality (Fig. 9). At the same time, however, Sheraton knew very well that the applied ornament on furniture, as opposed to its basic lines, was dictated by rapidly changing fashions. To reconcile the impermanent with the permanent appears to attempt the impossible. Yet Sheraton felt the need to try, and the reason is not difficult to discover. He wrote at a time when the old idea of a permanent standard of taste had been abandoned to such an extent that architecture was being bombarded by style after style – Gothic, Chinese, and so forth, grafted on to the prevailing classical taste. Where architecture led, furniture was sure to follow.

Sheraton seems to have been torn between the need to conform with current trends (his *Cabinet Dictionary* is important as the first publication with a Regency flavour), and to reform them, hence the duality of his designs. Some are of the rather pretty kind often considered feminine or effeminate: slender and fragile pieces, sometimes with delicate, painted decoration (Fig. 2). Others are not only more austere but in their predominantly square or rectangular elevations and round or elliptical plans show the influence of the contemporary neo-classical architects (Figs. 9 and 11). In clean-lined furniture such as this, it is possible to see a link with modern designers, even though their materials may be different; if so, then Sheraton may be held to have succeeded both in educating his contemporaries and in influencing his successors. 🥀

8

194

A. C. Cooper

MUSEUMS AND COLLECTIONS

Sheraton furniture may be seen at the following:

GREAT BRITAIN
Leeds: Temple Newsam House
London: Victoria and Albert Museum
Port Sunlight: Lady Lever Art Gallery

FURTHER READING

The Cabinet Dictionary by Thomas Sheraton, London, 1803. Reprinted New York, 1970.
The Cabinet-Maker and Upholsterer's Drawing-Book by Thomas Sheraton, London, 1793. Reprinted with an introduction by L. Boynton, New York, 1970.
Sheraton Furniture by Ralph Fastnedge, London, 1962.
English Furniture Designs of the Eighteenth Century by Peter Ward-Jackson, London, 1958.

Fig. 9 *'Houses & Chairs in Perspective'*, Plate 24, dated 1792, of T. Sheraton's Drawing-Book. Engraving by G. Terry. Drawings such as this, with their search for permanent principles which would rise above the fashions of furniture, illustrate Sheraton's motto from his frontispiece (Fig. 8): *'Time alters fashions and frequently obliterates the works of art and ingenuity; but that which is founded on Geometry & real Science, will remain unalterable.'* (Victoria and Albert Museum.)

Fig. 10 **Design for a mirror**, signed *'Thos. Sheraton'*, c.1790. Water-colour. (Victoria and Albert Museum.)

Fig. 11 **Designs for 'A Bidet Dressing Table' and 'A Night-Table Bason Stand'**, Plate 7, dated 1793, of Sheraton's Drawing-Book (Appendix). (Victoria and Albert Museum.)

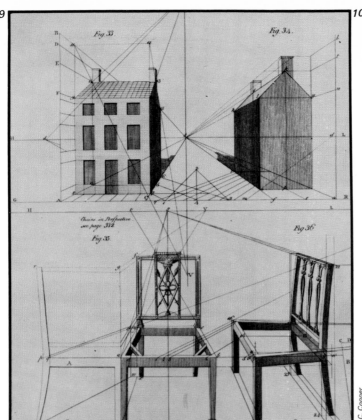

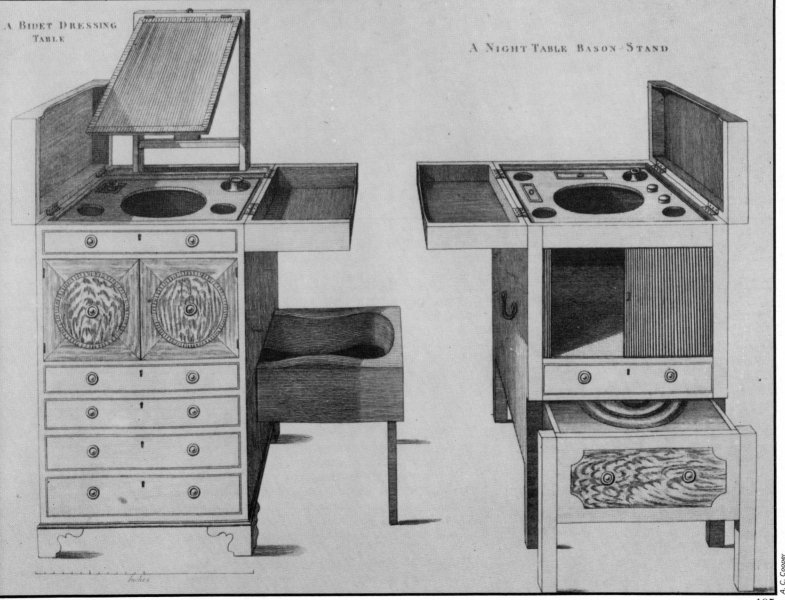

Early Federal Furniture

Museum Photo

Association Photo

196

> In the late eighteenth century it was observed that, as regards furniture, Americans 'will habitually prefer the useful to the beautiful, and they will require that the beautiful should be useful'

Fig. 1 **Side-chair**, one of twenty-four made in Philadelphia, c.1796. Maple, painted black and with colours, height 38½ ins. These superb chairs in the Hepplewhite style were ordered in 1796 by Elias Hasket Derby, a wealthy merchant of Salem, Massachusetts. (Metropolitan Museum of Art, New York. Gift of Mrs. J. Insley Blair, 1947.)

Fig. 2 **Sideboard**, one of a pair by John Aitken, Philadelphia, c.1797. Mahogany, width 5 ft. 11 ins. Acquired by George Washington for his Banqueting Hall at Mount Vernon in 1797, this handsome piece relies on perfection of proportion and line rather than on detail for its effect. (Mount Vernon, Virginia. Courtesy of the Mount Vernon Ladies' Association of the Union.)

Fig. 3 **Case of drawers** by William Lemon, carved by Samuel McIntire of Salem, Massachusetts, 1796. Mahogany, height 8 ft. 6½ ins. One of the masterpieces of American craftsmanship, this chest in a style derived from Chippendale was also ordered by Elias Hasket Derby of Salem. (Boston Museum of Fine Arts, Boston. M. and M. Karolik Collection.)

As the storm of what Americans call 'The Revolution' (1775–83) subsided, the Thirteen Colonies, diverse in their economic interests and in their political cleavages, found themselves joined together in a loose Confederation of States. The English 'oppressors' had been expelled with the decisive American victory at Yorktown in 1781. Americans were no longer under the domination of the King and 'the lust of dominion or lawless ambition' of the Parliament.

But rarely does a new political freedom immediately emancipate the arts of a nation. Only after a decade of recuperation did America again begin to urge herself toward the economic and political stability necessary for a resurgence of creative energies. It was the ratification of the new American Constitution by a majority of the States by 1788 that drew the diverse American people together and brought new vitality and direction to their arts.

Since the new form of government embodied many of the democratic principles of ancient Greece and Rome, the tangible accoutrements which the new American 'senators' associated with the classical period became fashionable. From Maine to Georgia, many embraced neo-classical form, proportion, and ornamentation, either by transforming their 'plain farmer's houses' into modest domestic temples or by building entirely new ones. George Washington redesigned Mount Vernon, his plantation overlooking the Potomac River in Virginia, into what we see today; Thomas Jefferson designed Monticello freely choosing from classical precedent. To furnish these houses Americans continued, as before the Revolution, to look primarily to England for inspiration in furniture design.

In the designs illustrated in Hepplewhite's *The Cabinet-Maker and Upholsterer's Guide* (1788), *The Cabinet-Maker's London Book of Prices* (1788 and 1793), and Sheraton's *The Cabinet-Maker and Upholsterer's Drawing Book* (1793–94), Americans found a new style consistent with the ideals embodied in their new government. The style was simple, straightforward and unpretentious, without the heavy forms or elaborate ornamentation of the previous periods. The American cabinet-maker borrowed from these English sources (and from actual imported examples) and reworked their designs into what is now known as the 'Federal Period' in American furniture history as codified by Mr. Charles F. Montgomery in his authoritative pioneer study, *American Furniture: The Federal Period*. For the first time, Montgomery has revealed the conditions which surrounded the fabrication of Federal furniture, and regionalised the use of construction techniques and the preference for certain woods by American cabinet-makers between 1790 and 1825.

But it was the interpretation by each American cabinet-maker that made his own creation individual. Some craftsmen tried to be as correct as possible in classical details, following English designs. Others blended neo-classical ornamentation with traditional forms. More often, the American cabinet-maker chose freely from among the sources available, combining, for example, elements from several designs by Hepplewhite with ornamentation from Sheraton. Most often he adapted the designs to meet his own requirements or those of his patron, although there are pieces which are direct copies. He innovated and developed as he chose, limited only by his vision, his proficiency in the control of his materials, and his customer's taste and ability to pay. Thus, while there is no unified American interpretation of the English designs clearly recognisable as being American, there often seems to be a different emphasis in an American piece from that of its English counterpart.

Careful study of construction details and ornamentation used in labelled or documented examples, combined with positive identification of secondary woods which are indigenous to America, yields a distinct pattern of regional techniques which enables the identification of a larger group of furniture forms from each of the American urban design centres. Boston, Newport, New York, Philadelphia, Williamsburg and Charleston were augmented in the early years of the Republic by small, though no less important towns. Salem, Baltimore, Annapolis and Richmond rose to increased importance with the wave of new wealth mostly derived from invigorated sea trade with the Orient (for the seas were now free for American ship captains to trade wherever they pleased) and the American South and West. The new 'senators' required fashionable, or what they thought to be fashionable, furnishings for their houses. Likewise, their 'venture cargoes' sent abroad were in the latest styles. Thus, pieces of American furniture can often be found many miles, even a continent, away from their place of fabrication.

One such piece is the secretaire shown in Figure 4. On the basis of two paper labels of the Salem cabinet-maker Nehemiah Adams, a member of the co-operative enterprise which made furniture for export around 1800, the piece was sold in Capetown, South Africa, as 'a unique and charming piece made in the United States'. It remained far from home until about 1940, when it was purchased and returned to America. Though not unique as advertised (over a dozen related examples have survived), it is a distinctive interpretation seemingly inspired by Plate 52 in Sheraton's *Drawing Book*. The Massachusetts cabinet-maker has changed the design, substituting a secretary drawer in the lower section for the fall-front lid and drawers of Sheraton's upper section, and replacing the lid with glazed doors. He has simplified and extended the top into balanced sweeping S-curves similar to the design shown in Plate 3 of *The London Book of Prices* (1793), while eliminating the Adam-like ornamentation of the frieze and top and exchanging the diamond motif ornamentation for oval veneers and tracery.

The quality of, and the preference for, carved motifs on the flat surface of mahogany furniture that can be documented as the work of Samuel McIntire help to identify a larger group of objects made in Salem. McIntire was an important architect as well as a designer and maker of fashionable furniture. His hand is best identified in the carved details of baskets of fruit, swags, urns, *putti*, and

4

Museum Photo

cornucopias, all masterfully executed on the 'case of
drawers' made by William Lemon for Elias Hasket
Derby, a wealthy Salem merchant, in 1796 (Fig. 3).
It is considered one of the masterpieces of American
eighteenth-century cabinet-making. The form is a
survival from the Chippendale style, reiterated by
Hepplewhite in Plate 54 of his *Guide*, modified by
Lemon, and updated by McIntire's vigorous carved
detail.

Elias Hasket Derby also imported elegant furniture from nearby Boston and distant Philadelphia.
In 1809 Thomas Seymour charged Derby's
daughter for the 'Large Mahogany Comode'
(Fig. 7) and for 'Mr Penniman['s] Bill for Painting
Shels on Top'. It is one of the most successful and
sophisticated American combinations of inlaid and
carved satinwood and mahogany, further ornamented with painted decoration. The elegance
achieved by the carefully selected curly-maple
veneered drawer-fronts contrasted with the cross-
grained rosewood skirt and the carved mahogany
posts of the front, is further enhanced by the
contrasting segments and painted shell of the top.
It is a marvellous combination of exuberance and
restraint.

From Philadelphia, Derby ordered twenty-four
oval-back chairs from his agent in 1796 (Fig. 1), also
without doubt patterned after the *Guide* of 1788.
Their success lies in the boldness of design, in the
effectiveness and dexterity of the hand which
painted the back and in the unexpected strength
of construction which has enabled them to survive
in spite of their delicacy of line.

As Philadelphia remained the new nation's
political and fashion capital until 1800, it was only
natural for America's first President to buy much of
his furniture for Mount Vernon there. In 1797,
George Washington acquired a tambour desk with
bookcase, based on Plate 69 of Hepplewhite's
Guide, from John Aitken, a prominent Philadelphia
cabinet-maker. Aitken infused his own sense of
proportion by raising the height of the bookcase,
adding a simple top, and altering the drawer-
arrangement to develop a continuous semicircle in
the apron of the base. The designs for both the top

and the tracery on the doors are again adaptations
from *The London Book of Prices*, Plate 3.

For his new banqueting hall Washington's
accounts record his payment for 'two side-boards'
(Fig. 2). The sideboards are pure Hepplewhite
(without the ornamentation). They appear to reflect
the same concern that Washington expressed
regarding his imported chimneypiece for the same
room – that it would be 'too elegant and costly . . .
for [his] own room and republican style of living'.
Thus, rather than an extensive use of ornate inlays
with swags and bell-flowers, Washington chose a
plainer style, which he considered to be more fitting
to his new way of life.

With the sideboard, Aitken has taken Hepplewhite's basic design and added a pair of doors,
concealing a shelf, under the central drawer. He
changed the design and the proportion; he transformed the piece into a seemingly more useful
form, one which found great popularity in many
American houses by the end of the eighteenth
century, while retaining the movement and grace
called for in the original design.

This same change occurred in other American
cabinet-making centres along the Atlantic seaboard. However, it was in New York City that the
American version of the sideboard was developed
and refined to the highest degree with the 'diver-
sified contour[s]' and the 'light and shade' called
for by Robert Adam's aesthetic theory.

At the same time that Aitken was working on
Washington's furniture in Philadelphia, John
Shaw, a Scottish-born cabinet-maker of Annapolis,
created the elegant secretaire (Fig. 6) now in The
White House in Washington, D.C. It is generous in
size, refined in proportion and distinctive in execution, though rather behind the times for 1796, the
year in which it was made. The delicacy of the
pierced scrolls and plinth at the top is a successfully individual refinement found on several pieces
of the period. The inlaid shells and *paterae* and the
carved cornice further enhance this distinguished
piece. It demonstrates Shaw's ability as a cabinet-
maker and the refined taste of its original owner,
John Randall.

But it was in Baltimore that some of the most
glorious pieces of high-style Federal furniture were
created. The lady's cabinet- and writing-table
(Fig. 5) is one such piece. Closely related to several
plates in Sheraton's *Drawing Book*, it is one of the
most sophisticated of the small group of tables to
have survived; so close is it in feeling and detail that
it could be mistaken for one of its English counterparts. The inclusion of the banded oval looking-
glass, the mitred satinwood door-fronts with inset
painted and gilt oval glass panels of biblical and
mythological figures, and the overall proportions
and composition are the American cabinet-maker's
contribution. His choice of contrasting woods and
his technical skill place this anonymous craftsman
among the most proficient in America.

Thus, during the eighteenth century, the design
of American furniture remained under English
influence. Following the Revolution, as we have
seen, the design-books of England's cabinet-makers
found immediate acceptance in the new Republic.
But it was the individual interpretation of these
designs infused with the inherent creative energy of
the American cabinet-maker, modified by the taste
of his patron, which formed America's furniture of
the Federal Period.

Museum Photo

6

White House Photo

7

Museum Photo

MUSEUMS AND COLLECTIONS
Early Federal furniture may be seen at the following:
GREAT BRITAIN
Bath: American Museum in Britain
U.S.A.
Boston: Boston Museum of Fine Arts
New York: Metropolitan Museum of Art
Washington D.C.: Smithsonian Institution
Winterthur: Henry Francis du Pont
                              Winterthur Museum

FURTHER READING

The American Heritage History of American Antiques from the Revolution to the Civil War by Marshall B. Davidson, New York, 1968.

American Furniture: The Federal Period by Charles F. Montgomery, New York, 1966.

John and Thomas Seymour by Vernon C. Stoneman, Boston, 1959.

Later Federal Furniture

Fig. 1 *Tambour desk,* label of
John Seymour and Son, Boston,
1794–1804.
Mahogany, height 41⅝ ins.
(*The Henry Francis du Pont
Winterthur Museum.*)

Fig. 2 *Grecian couch,* Salem,
Mass., 1805–15. *Mahogany and
cane, height 38 ins.*
(*The Henry Francis du Pont
Winterthur Museum.*)

**In the first quarter of the
nineteenth century, the cabinet-
makers of the United States,
combining various European
styles, produced furniture of
quiet distinction**

When building recommenced after the Revolution
the old styles continued for a few years, but after
1800 the treatment of interiors tended toward the
classical. The influence of Robert Adam is seen in
details of doors, windows, mantels and entablatures;
plain walls were favoured instead of panelling, and
classical details were used in cornices, chair-rails
and mouldings. They were also included in the composition ornaments that decorated Adam-style fireplaces, with their chimneypiece mirrors of gilt and
tinted glass surmounted by eagles or leafy urns.
Such was the setting for Federal furniture.

In the furniture itself, widespread changes in
style and cabinet-making followed in the years
after the establishment of the United States. During
the forty years of the Federal era, American
cabinet-makers took advantage of the expanding
prosperity and the emergence of new markets for
furniture. Thus, the neo-classical style became
current almost immediately after the adoption of
the Federal Constitution in 1788.

American Federal furniture includes Hepplewhite, Sheraton, American Directoire and Empire
styles. The early Federal style is sometimes named
after the two English furniture-designers George
Hepplewhite and Thomas Sheraton. The use of
antique sources was characteristic of Robert Adam,
and both Hepplewhite and Sheraton were adapters
of the Adam style in which the ornament was
antique but the basic style was not. Hepplewhite's
designs were published in 1788, and Sheraton published a series of designs between 1791 and 1794.
The name of Hepplewhite is given to the delicate
inlaid and carved furniture of the late 1780s and
early '90s, and that of Sheraton is used to designate
furniture employing turned or reeded supports and
bowed or hollowed facades, first made in America
in the early 1790s. However, these names are confusing because there is an overlapping of styles. The
term 'Federal' seems more appropriate since many
of the pieces were carved or inlaid with the
American eagle, the symbol of the Federal Union.

Early Federal design, between 1795 and 1815,
emphasised colour and surface-decoration as
opposed to form, which had been the dominant
note in the furniture of the early eighteenth century.
The proportions of furniture became light and
delicate. The straight line was the basis of design
and the structural lines of the furniture were
rectangular, with uncomplicated semicircular or
elliptical curves. The legs are straight, tapering to a
narrow foot. The square-back chair with turned
legs, reeded motifs and certain carved elements was
introduced in the late 1790s. These forms and
motifs continued to be popular until about 1815.

The Federal style brought changes in the forms
of furniture. The dining-room as a separate room
required furniture for storing silver and china and

200

Fig. 3 **Bed**, *Massachusetts,
1800–10. Mahogany, birch and
pine, height 8 ft. 4 ins.
This bed is exhibited in the
Benjamin Franklin Room at the
Museum with other pieces
probably made in or near Boston,
Franklin's birthplace.
(The Henry Francis du Pont
Winterthur Museum, Delaware.)*

on which the table was mounted was designed in the form of two parallel lyres and rested on carved legs. Pembroke tables became the fashionable form for tea-tables. Other innovations included the dressing-table and the lady's sewing-table. A new type of desk, the tambour, had sliding doors made up of vertical strips that moved horizontally to uncover pigeon-holes and small drawers (Fig. 1). Other desks are topped with bookcases (Fig. 4).

The earliest type of Federal chairs are the ladder-back or slat-back with Marlborough legs (straight tapered legs of square section), stretchers, three or four pierced slats and upholstered seats. From about 1790 vase- or urn-backed chairs were popular, but five or ten years later square-backed Sheraton-type chairs with plain, upright, 'X' or gothic splats and sturdy, straight stretchers were the most popular. Settees followed similar styles and the uphol-stered sofa was also based on straight lines. After 1800, chair-design was based on what was known of antique classical chairs. The chair-back had a solid, thick, curving top-rail supported by thin stiles, with either a horizontal splat or a lyre, harp, or 'X'-shape to serve as a back support. An innovation of the Federal period was a type of chair that is distinctly American – the Martha Washington or 'Lolling' chair (Fig. 8). It is a tall, upholstered chair with scrolled, open arms and legs of cylindrical or quad-rangular form joined with plain stretchers.

Early in the nineteenth century a more faithfully classical style developed, based on contemporary scholarship. A design-book by Thomas Hope, *Household Furniture and Interior Decoration*, published in 1807, spread this second phase of the Federal style. London price-books also included engraved designs of furniture, which contributed to the widespread knowledge of English furniture. The late Federal style (1815–25) was also influenced by some of Thomas Sheraton's later designs, which were characterised by Greco-Roman forms – *klismos* and curule chairs – and animal supports. The presence of French craftsmen working in America in the opening years of the nineteenth century was another factor in the development of this phase of the Federal style. Furniture became increas-ingly heavy and bold. It absorbed the Greco-Roman and Egyptian influences of French Directoire and Empire furniture, and is referred to as 'Regency' or 'Empire', depending upon the predominance of English or French characteristics.

From the beginning of the nineteenth century, New York City was the centre of fine cabinet-making. Although New York had many accom-plished cabinet-makers, the most famous was Duncan Phyfe (1768–1854), whose workmanship and interpretation of English Regency forms became a model for other cabinet-makers. Duncan Phyfe worked in New York from 1795 until his retirement in 1847. His early work reflects Sheraton's influence. The most characteristic Phyfe chair is the scroll-back chair with carved top-rail and one or more crosses in the back; reeded stiles and outflaring, reeded feet. Other Phyfe chairs have lattice-backs, ogee-scroll-, lyre- or harp-backs combined with Grecian legs. Some scroll-back chairs have carved front legs ending in paw-feet. Chairs of this type became the standard type made in New York in the mid-Federal period (1800–15).

In Salem, Massachusetts, the combination of Samuel McIntire (1757–1811), carver, and Jacob Sanderson (1757–1810), cabinet-maker, produced

for serving. The sideboard, which began as a table, was supplied with drawers. The typical dining-table of the era could be dismantled into several smaller tables. Shapes vary and the legs are square or round, and sometimes fluted; late examples have a series of balusters with heavy carving. The sofa-table was long and narrow with drop leaves and legs joined by simple stretchers at each end. The lyre card-table in Sheraton style was a favourite design at the beginning of the nineteenth century; the standard

Fig. 4 *Secretaire, known as the 'Sister's Cylinder Bookcase' modelled on Sheraton's* The Cabinet Dictionary *of 1803, Baltimore or Philadelphia, c.1811, Mahogany with satinwood veneers and inlays, height 7 ft. 7 ins.*
A straight, drop-front desk is substituted for the cylinder roll-top of Sheraton's design and a graceful pediment echoes the pyramid of the base.
(Metropolitan Museum of Art. Gift of Mrs. Russell Sage and other donors, 1969.)

Hepplewhite-type chairs and Sheraton-influenced square sofas carved with festoons of drapery, fruit, flowers, *paterae*, ribbons, stalks of wheat, cornucopias, fluting and occasionally a carved eagle.

The furniture of the Boston cabinet-makers John (*c*.1738–1818) and Thomas (1771–1848) Seymour presented the richest interpretations of Sheraton design in the Federal period. The pieces included superb desks with tambour shutters and light wood inlays of husks, inlaid discs and string-inlaid panels.

By 1815 the French phase of the Federal style was in vogue. The French Empire bed, or sleigh-bed, made to be placed against the wall, marble-topped tables with caryatid or columnar supports and massive pier-tables were characteristic articles of furniture. The requirements for fine furniture of the later Federal era were different. The lines are usually more vigorous, the masses heavier, the scale larger and the wood darker, giving a more sober, but richer appearance. The general effect is also more dignified.

The foremost exponent of the French phase of the late Federal style was the New York cabinet-maker Charles-Honoré Lannuier (1779–1819). Lannuier made some of the most elaborate furniture

Fig. 5 **Card-table** *by Charles-Honoré Lannuier (1779–1819), c.1813. Rosewood, bird's-eye maple and satinwood with gilt-brass and gesso ornament, height 31 ins.*
Lannuier, a New York cabinet-maker, made some of the most elaborate furniture produced in America at this period.
(Metropolitan Museum of Art, New York.)

Fig. 6 **Armchair,** *attributed to John and Hugh Findlay of Baltimore, 1805.*
(Baltimore Museum of Art.)

Fig. 7 **Federal room,** *1800s; the mantelpiece from the house of Moses Rogers, New York, 1806; the chimney-glass, New York or Albany, c.1805; the chairs made in the shop of Duncan Phyfe (1768–1854), 1807,*
(The Henry Francis du Pont Winterthur Museum.)

produced in America (Fig. 5). His furniture is often a skilful combination of Directoire, Consulate and Empire styles. The furniture was ornamented with gilt carvings of acanthus leaves, caryatids, dolphins and animal feet. Ormolu mounts depict classical scenes of gods and goddesses, and hand-sawn brass inlay borders in the Greek key pattern were often used. Furniture of a simpler type was made by Lannuier for the New Jersey home of Napoleon's brother Joseph Bonaparte. A pair of pedestal card-tables were made with water-leaf carving, reeding and brass paw-feet. The brass inlay included a lyre, six-pointed stars and classical urns.

In Philadelphia, Joseph B. Barry made similar furniture based on Sheraton and French designs. He designed French-style pier-tables with columns resting on massive mahogany platforms and decorated with ormolu mounts.

There was a revival of interest in painted furniture towards the end of the eighteenth century. Much painted furniture was designed in England around 1790 and American furniture-makers quickly followed the style.

The finest workmanship and most elaborate in design is the painted furniture produced in Baltimore. While many Baltimore cabinet-makers may have produced this furniture, the numerous advertisements for the work of John and Hugh Findlay suggest that the Findlays were the most prolific producers of this type of furniture.

The following extract from the *Federal Gazette and Commercial Daily Advertiser*, 8 November, 1805, describes this furniture: 'Elegant, Fancy Japanned Furniture . . . all colours, gilt ornamented and varnished in a style only equalled on the continent . . . with real views, Fancy landscapes, Flowers, Trophies of Music, War, Husbandry, Love, etc. . . . Window and recess seats, painted and gilt in the most fanciful manner, with and without views adjacent to this city'.

Such painted scenes were also popular on fancy chairs made in New York and New England. A set of six chairs with views of the Hudson River (New York, 1815–25) are in the Henry Francis du Pont

Winterthur Museum. Settees, card-tables and work-tables were often decorated in similar manner. In fact, the popularity of painted furniture grew rapidly and so much of it was made that after 1820 it became known as 'country furniture' and the fashion declined rapidly.

Although American Federal furniture was for the most part modelled on English furniture and followed English ideas, it was not an imitation. Many components are similar, but they are combined in different ways. One difference between American and European furniture was the wood used. Although mahogany was the primary wood used by American cabinet-makers of the Federal period, the secondary woods used were those that grew in the region where the furniture was made. A careful examination of these secondary woods not

203

Fig. 8 *Federal Parlour,
Massachusetts, 1790s;
secretaire, Connecticut or
Rhode Island, 1790–1810;
Martha Washington chair,
c.1800. (The Henry Francis
du Pont Winterthur Museum.)*

rical patterns of squares, lozenges, triangles and zig-zags. To provide points of interest, inlays of *paterae*, flowers, leaves, shells, fans, bell-flowers or eagles were used. The woods employed in stringing and inlay included holly, satinwood, boxwood, ebony and the cheaper maple and birch. Brass inlays were occasionally found on furniture made in New York and Philadelphia, and inlays were sometimes imported from England. There were also craftsmen in American cities who specialised in making inlays. Although the records of suppliers and makers of inlays are sparse, there seems little doubt that, while some cabinet-makers produced their own inlays, a large proportion of inlays used in city shops were bought ready made. This accounts for the similarity of inlays used on furniture. Patterned stringing was favoured in Boston, Salem and other centres in New England, whereas plain stringing, cross-banding and inlaid shells, eagles and flower motifs are often found on the work of cabinet-makers working in the New York area. Many three-part husks or bell-flowers, inlaid shells, eagles and flower motifs are found on Baltimore furniture and Philadelphia furniture.

Owing to the limited supply of valuable wood, the practice of veneering was used after 1790. The principal woods used in veneering American Federal furniture included bird's-eye maple, mahogany, rosewood, satinwood, sycamore, amboynawood, tulipwood and zebrawood. Figured birch was often used on the fronts of chests of drawers and on card-tables in the New England area.

Carving was another method of ornamenting Federal furniture. The finest carving is that of Samuel McIntire on Salem furniture. The carving on Duncan Phyfe furniture is also of high quality. Philadelphia carving is often scratchy and flat, and Baltimore carving varies in quality, some of it being extremely coarse. The motifs most often used were wheatsheaves, drapery, vines and baskets of fruit.

In the most famous pieces of Federal furniture, such as the Seymour tambour desks or the Massachusetts secretaire, there is an interplay of form, inlay and colour and subtle harmonies of line. The materials, workmanship and design are also so inter-related as to produce unity. These are the qualities which distinguish fine furniture, and the cabinet-makers of the Federal era produced many such pieces.

only gives a clue to the regional origin of American furniture, but also aids in distinguishing to some extent between American and English furniture of the same style. The presence of tulip or poplar is a sign of American manufacture, and white pine is also generally regarded as proof of American origin. For less expensive furniture, birch and maple were used and often stained to resemble mahogany. Native softwoods such as pine were stained or painted; some furniture was made of bird's-eye maple and a few pieces of satinwood.

In the Federal period after 1790, veneers and ornamental inlays became one of the principal methods of ornamenting furniture. Light and dark inlaid lines and patterned stringing or banding composed of different coloured woods became a common feature. This decoration tended to be in geomet-

MUSEUMS AND COLLECTIONS

American furniture may be seen at the following:

GREAT BRITAIN
Bath: American Museum in Britain
U.S.A.
Baltimore, Md: Baltimore Museum of Art
Boston, Mass: Boston Museum of Fine Arts
Dearborn, Mich: Henry Ford Museum
New York, N.Y.:   Metropolitan Museum of Art
Winterthur, Del: Henry Francis du Pont
                             Winterthur Museum

FURTHER READING

American Painted Furniture, 1668–1880 by Dean A. Fales, New York, 1972.
Nineteenth-century America: Furniture and other Decorative Arts, Metropolitan Museum of Art, New York, exhibition catalogue, 1970.
American Furniture: The Federal Period by Charles F. Montgomery, Winterthur, 1966.

Consulate and Empire

Fig. 1 *The Bedroom of the Empress Josephine*, *Château de Malmaison. Carved and gilt wood with gilt-bronze mounts in the form of cornucopias, swans and an eagle.*

Although Empire furniture was a natural development from the style of Louis XVI, the prevailing taste for classical antiquity and the new interest in Egypt provided its characteristic decorative motifs

The excavations at Pompeii and Herculaneum in the mid-eighteenth century and the foundation of the *Académie d'Herculanum* in 1755 inspired a revival of interest in the architecture of classical times. The publication of many scholarly books continued this development towards the neo-classical style and by 1770 decorators had abandoned their struggle to maintain the old style.

In the opinion of philosophers, historians and artists, classical Greece set an ideal for which modern civilisation yearned. Orators and pamphleteers of the French Revolution pointed out the moral values and material spirit of Antiquity, and designers endorsed this notion with a style which evoked the ancient and glorious past.

The Revolution hastened the acceptance of the *style à l'antique*. Much fine furniture was consigned to a bonfire beneath a Tree of Liberty in the forecourt of the Gobelins factory and the national treasures were dispersed. After the excesses of the Revolution, the agile French mind could hardly endure for long such a void in the decoration of daily life. The government set about forming a Jury of Art Manufacturers in order to promote a national art form unencumbered by obsolescent monarchical embellishment.

The fashion which succeeded the end of the Terror is referred to as *le style Directoire*. The Directory continued only four years, from October 1795 until November 1799, not sufficiently long to develop an individual style. But Directoire design may be said to encompass the final years of the reign of Louis XVI, the period of the Convention (1792–1795), and the term occupied by the

205

Connaissance des Arts: J. Guillot

Fig. 2 *The bedroom of the Emperor Napoleon, Château de Malmaison, recently redecorated using objects associated with Napoleon. The bed was Napoleon's at the Tuileries.*

Fig. 3 *Commode by Jacob-Desmalter, early nineteenth century. Gilt-bronze mounts and marble top. (Château de Compiègne.)*

Fig. 4 *Guéridon, French, early nineteenth century. Mahogany, and gilt bronze. (Sotheby and Co., London.)*

Figs. 5 and 6 *Throne chair probably by Georges Jacob, c.1805. Painted and gilt wood, velvet upholstery. This chair à gondole has arms in the form of winged lions. (Victoria and Albert Museum, London.)*

Directory itself, followed by part of the Consulate. After 1799 Napoleon put a stop to further depredations upon the French nation's artistic heritage, although this came too late to preserve the splendid royal collections from being broken up.

Despite the overthrow of the *ancien régime*, there was a strong continuity between the previous *style Louis XVI* and the formulae adopted during the Directory. Several elements associated with the Empire had made their appearance at the end of the reign of Louis XVI. The most notable and frequently employed of these was the *buste de femme* surmounting a tapering term with the narrowing lower end resting on bare or sandalled feet. Other innovations were classical, allegorical relief figures, sometimes in white on a blue ground in imitation of Wedgwood Jasper ware, and metal furniture. Bronze patinated green, wrought iron and steel, were employed to construct small elegant pieces of furniture, such as *guéridons* (Fig. 4), tripods, work-baskets and little tables *pour le lunch à l'anglaise*. Leading *ébénistes* such as Etienne Avril (1748–91), Guillaume Beneman (*Maître-ébéniste* 1785), and Gaspard Schneider (*Maître* 1786) were already continuing the luxury of the *ancien régime* with the precise, dry, restrained, classical ornament

associated with the oncoming Empire style.

Cabinet-makers were encouraged to return to their former high standards of craftsmanship

With the advent of Napoleon came a new chance for the decorator. The stripped apartments required refurnishing. But the political and intellectual scene now necessitated a *décor sobre*. The abolition of the professional corporations which had maintained strict surveillance over standards of craftsmanship proved to be a grave misfortune. After 1793, contemporary cabinet-makers became more inclined to skimp their work and use poor materials. Napoleon, however, personally supervised the setting up of modern manufactories and actively encouraged a return to higher standards. To enhance the prestige of the new order, Napoleon applied himself to refurnishing the royal residences. In 1799 Napoleon acquired the Château de Malmaison. In 1802 St. Cloud was taken over, in 1804 the Palais de Fontainebleau was refurbished for Pope Pius VII, and a year or two later Compiègne, the Elysée, Rambouillet,

A. C. Cooper

Museum Photo

206

Fig. 7 **Pedestal table**, French, early nineteenth century. Mahogany with gilt-bronze mounts.

Occasional tables with round, revolving tops were used for serving wine or tea and could also be moved about the room and used as pedestals for lights. (H. Blairman and Sons, London.)

Fig. 8 **Pedestal cabinet**, one of a pair in the manner of Georges Jacob, French, early nineteenth century. Burr-chestnut with gilt-bronze mounts and white marble top.

These desirable pieces were often called athéniennes after a painting by J. B. Vien, La Vertueuse Athénienne, in which one first appeared. In addition to their function as cabinets, these rare examples might have held heavy candelabra, perfume-burners, flower-vases or wash-basins. (Sotheby's.)

Versailles, St. Germain and Meudon received the same treatment. In Italy and the Netherlands further royal residences were refitted. In 1799, the First Consul commissioned Charles Percier (1764–1838) and Pierre François Léonard Fontaine (1762–1853), shortly to become the chief architects and arbiters of taste in the Empire, to initiate plans for the restoration of the interiors and remodelling of the Château de Malmaison (Fig. 2). The designs of these two decorators were soon to transform cabinet-making throughout Europe, Russia and America. Their drawings were published in a notable volume: Recueil de Décoration Intérieur de Percier et Fontaine (1812). Both designers, never-theless, owed much to an exceptional artist named Jean-Demosthène Dugourc (1749–c.1810). Dugourc displayed a marvellous facility for composition and was the precursor of the Empire style in furniture and decoration. Under Louis XVI he had executed many designs for both royal and private residences. Obliged to leave France for Spain in 1799, Dugourc's genius remained unacknowledged by his contemporaries.

Shining gilt-bronze mounts, drawn from Greek or Roman sculpture

With the disappearance of carved ornament and absence of marquetry, the craftsmen of the Consulate and Empire period substituted sculp-tured bronze and gilding, either matt or burnished to throw up subtle highlights, in order to sharpen up the rigid shapes and symmetry of the furniture. Whereas menuisiers of the eighteenth century had taken pains to soften angles and create curves, strict technicians of the latest antique style requested only sophisticated and severe architec-tural forms; and figures such as caryatids became more academic in conception. Pierre-Philippe Thomire (1751–1843), whose workshop included eight hundred artisans by 1806, and the artist Olivier were the master craftsmen in gilt bronze of this era and all their work is distinguished by fine casting and chiselling of furniture mounts.

The gilt-bronze mounts used to embellish furniture of the period were cast in many different shapes. There were wreaths of ivy or vine-leaves, formalised laurel branches, chaplets of oak-leaves interlaced with fluttering ribbons, palmettes, pine-cones and bouquets. Most of these applied bronzes were drawn directly from Greek or Roman sculpture.

Eagles were popular, symbolising Imperial Majesty, and swans were used in deference to the Empress Josephine; so were bees and hives, the emblems of Napoleon's family. Human figures played a considerable role, either draped as Victories proffering garlands or blowing trumpets, or else diaphanous as goddesses in floating draperies. There were Bacchic masks, Hermes, Isis, helmeted heads of warriors, and figures emblematic of Liberty. Plain surfaces could be further offset by circlets of stars, winged flambeaux, thunderbolts, trophies of lances and bundles of fasces. Music, too, was represented by the lyre, cymbals and pipes.

The wood to which the bronze mounts were attached was mainly a hard, rich Cuban or Nicaraguan mahogany, sometimes plum-pudding, flame or speckled. In 1810, however, its importa-tion and employment in the Mobilier Impérial was

forbidden by Imperial Decree. The English block-ade of France made the selection of quality woods from abroad more difficult. But other woods came into fashion: ebony, rosewood, yew, walnut, oak, beech, satinwood, olive, maple, burr-elm, burr-ash and fruitwood. Surfaces were wax-polished and varnished. The carcase was generally of oak and covered with selected veneers. Inferior materials could thus be disguised by unscrupulous cabinet-makers, a malpractice all too frequent, following the collapse of the Guilds at the time of the Revolution.

Napoleon himself was averse to over-elaboration – 'les meubles de trop de richesse' – and the adroit Percier had often to simplify a luxuriant design. On many an occasion the Garde Meuble was admon-ished to modify the programme. One of Percier's aquarelles submitted to Napoleon bears the note: 'simplifier les ornements, c'est pour l'Empéreur'.

A prodigious promoter of the style à l'antique, Baron Dominique Vivant Denon, must be the most expert, industrious and suave character in the annals of art plunder. He had received an excellent education, had made an early appearance at the Court of Louis XV and had been appointed Keeper of the Royal Cameos; he was also Madame de Pompadour's professeur. He was engaged in diplo-matic activity in St. Petersburg and Naples, drew and etched after the Old Masters for seven years in Italy before returning to France in 1788, and on being saved from the guillotine the following year through the influence of the painter David, was com-missioned to design uniforms for the Republican army. Denon was one of the official artists who accompanied Napoleon to Egypt in 1798 for the purpose of examining and recording the antiquities. It was Denon who emphasised the vogue for Egyptiana in furniture. A keen collector himself, he was responsible for selecting the finest pieces of plunder for packing up and dispatching to France. Denon never missed anything of quality, and from 1804 was Inspector-General of French Museums. He became the foremost exponent of the classical ideal, turning Paris into a repository of the art of Europe, immense archives which could be readily available to practising designers.

The Jacob family made furniture for the painter David and for the Emperor himself

The most celebrated name among the many menuisiers and ébénistes of the age is that of Jacob. The industry of this family extended over a lengthy period and produced pieces of outstanding quality. Georges Jacob (1739–1814) was an expert innovator who dominated French furniture design until the end of the eighteenth century. It was he who favoured mahogany for chairs in the English fashion. To him is attributed the introduction of accotoirs rampants (sloping arm-rests), le dossier ajouré en lyre (lyre-shaped backed chairs) and gerbes en carquois (wheat-sheaves in the form of quivers). He adapted his furniture design from Greek and Roman prototypes, and made furniture for the painter David which was derived from specimens depicted on Etruscan and Greek vases, all carved out of a sombre mahogany resembling the deep patina of bronze. In 1796 Georges con-ceded the management of his workshop in the

207

Giraudon

Fig. 9 *Secrétaire à abattant*,
French, early nineteenth century.
Burr-wood with gilt-bronze
mounts.
This exceptionally severe
example of a popular Empire
style is virtually undecorated.
Except for the restrained mounts
in the classical style – heads,
palmettes and other characteristic
Empire motifs – the wood alone
is the major decorative feature.
The fall-front, which forms a
writing surface, and the doors
below conceal a variety of
drawers, compartments and
mirrors.
(Musée des Arts Décoratifs, Paris.)

Fig. 10 *Dressing-table*, Jacob-
Desmalter, early nineteenth
century. Yew with delicately
chased gilt-bronze mounts.
Originally the property of the
Empress Josephine, this splendid
dressing-table is supported on
four lyre-shaped legs. The
supports to the mirror also serve
as candelabra.
(Musée des Arts Décoratifs.)

rue Meslée to his sons, Georges (1768–1803) and François Honoré Georges (1770–1841), the younger becoming the eminent designer who maintained the fame of his father until the demise of the elder brother on 21 October, 1803, under their mark 'Jacob Frères, rue Meslée'. Public demand became so great that the expanded *atelier* completed commissions for the leading personalities of the day, such as the Emperor himself, Mademoiselle Mars and Madame Récamier at whose residence, according to the brothers Goncourt, 'mahogany raged throughout the room'.

Under the Empire was evolved a variety of novel furniture forms

By 1803, François Honoré Georges Jacob, known as 'Desmalter', was sole proprietor of the *atelier*, *La Maison de Jacob-Desmalter et Cie*. He used native woods, often adding a patination in *vert antique* encrusted with mother of pearl, ebony, porcelain or faience plaques and steel. He was the main supplier to the *Mobilier Impérial*.

Among the most distinguished *ébénistes* of the Napoleonic period were Bernard Molitor (born 1730); Félix Rémond, a pupil of Riesener; the brothers Mansion. Jean-Baptiste-Bernard Demay (1759–1848) and Jean-Antoine Bruns (*Maître* 1787) were also well-known craftsmen. Denières and Matelin were famous for bronze mounts.

Under the Empire, a variety of novel forms in furniture design were evolved. Commodes were

fitted with a pair of doors to conceal the drawers. This type was designated as a *bas d'armoire* (Fig. 3). The *chiffonier*, a development of the commode, often contained seven drawers and was then termed a *semainier*. Drawer-handles were cast in the form of lion's masks with rings or gilt-bronze knobs. Flanking columns and a marble top created an architectural effect.

Most popular was the *secrétaire à abattant*, a development of the renaissance cabinet with various miniature interior compartments, drawers and mirrors (Fig. 9). The front, beneath which were larger drawers, could be dropped to form a writing-flap. Another variety of the fall-front desk, but without lower drawers, was the *secrétaire de Compiègne*: four balusters or columns set on a plinth supported the cabinet with the back either open or faced with mirror-glass. The *bonheur du jour* grew squarer and loftier in elevation whilst the *bureau plat* assumed palatial proportions. The top rested upon a console of winged animals' legs terminating in claw feet, or was supported by refined X-pattern stretchers after the fashion of Greco-Roman tables. Tables, usually circular, were more or less accurate reproductions from antique representations, the tops, sometimes of variegated marble or inlaid woods, resting on lion monopodia, Doric, Ionic or Persic columns or triple monopodia formed of gryphons, lions or sphinxes.

Work-tables, *tables à fleurs* or *jardinières* were a feature of the salon. The top consisted of sheet metal painted and varnished to contain the blooms, the circular form being preferred to the rectangular variety. *Guéridons* and small round or octagonal occasional tables were much in demand (Fig. 7). Elegant tripods inspired by antiquity in round or hexagonal shapes were also used as stands for heavy candelabra, perfume-burners, flower-vases or wash-basins. These *athéniennes* were constructed of mahogany, gilt-wood, bronze patinated green and heightened with gold, iron or oxidised steel. They often came in pairs (Fig. 8).

The *serre-papiers* (filing cabinet), resembling a funerary urn set on arched claw-legs and adorned with bronze mounts, found a place in the library beside the *écritoire*, and a work-table could be combined with a *poudreuse* of which the top could be raised to display a looking-glass and a small drawer. It was the lesser partner of the *grand toilette* (dressing-table), a recent arrival in the French boudoir. A splendid example has survived from the Tuileries Palace finished in yew-wood and decorated with delicately chased ormolu mounts. It is supported by four lyre-shaped legs. The supports to the octagonal mirror also serve as candelabra (Fig. 10).

A magnificent style of decor, highly acceptable throughout Europe and beyond

Consoles and side-tables were designed to stand on single monopod supports topped with a marble slab and were either semi-circular *(à la lunette)* or rectangular in shape. Under the Directory, chairs retained the delicate structure employed in the reign of Louis XV but were modified to simulate the Greek *klismos* with sabre legs *(pieds étrusques)*. The X-framed stool in imitation of the Roman folding curule chair found favour as did a *causeuse* to seat two persons and a *chauffeuse* for drawing up to the fire. Particularly attractive was the form *à gondole* with the arms reclining on winged griffins, sphinxes, swans or lions (Figs. 5 and 6).

The *méridienne* was simply an elongated extension of the chair. Sometimes one end was made higher than the other with a lofty back to provide a sense of enclosure.

Bedroom furnishings were dominated by the bed, the most magnificent object of all. The bed stood on a dais, one long side being placed parallel to the wall with the headboards and facing side sprinkled with a profusion of gilt-bronze mounts (Fig. 1). Often the bed was devised like an elegant barque *(en bâteau)*. A dome or tent-shaped canopy was frequently suspended above, from which sweeping draperies descended to be captured by projecting bosses, lances or arrows in military style. The fashionable *chaise-longue* (day bed) (Fig. 11) was inspired by the ancient *triclinium* (the couch running round three sides of a table on which the Romans reclined). Since the famous painting by David depicting Madame Récamier reclining on one, this modified version of the bed was referred to as a *récamier*.

The boudoir ensemble was not complete without a *grand miroir à la Psyché*, an original invention of the First Empire resembling an oval or rectangular cheval-glass slung between twin columns or terms fitted with candle-sconces and decorated with gilt-bronze mounts.

Finally the bookcase assumed an increasing importance in the early part of the nineteenth century. Such pieces were intended to rest on a stout plinth without feet and came in varying dimensions. The books were protected by doors with glass panes, pleated silk or grilles furnished with beautifully manufactured locks and long bolts as on French windows.

The Emperor Napoleon's puppet monarchs were not slow in extending the new Empire style throughout their subservient states, and it quickly became popular. France had produced a magnificent style of decor which proved highly acceptable throughout the western hemisphere and beyond. 🕸

Fig. 11 **Day-bed,** design No. 130 from the Collection de Meubles et Objets de Goût by La Mésangère, Paris, 1818–35. Colour engraving. (Bibliothèque Nationale, Paris.)

Connaissance des Arts: J. Guillot

MUSEUMS AND COLLECTIONS
Consulate and Empire furniture may be seen at the following:
FRANCE
Compiègne:	Musée National du Palais de Compiègne
Fontainebleau:	Musée National du Château de Fontainebleau
Paris:	Hôtel Beauvais
	Musée des Arts Décoratifs
	Musée Marmottan
Rueil-Malmaison:	Musée National du Château de Malmaison
Versailles:	Musée National du Château de Versailles

FURTHER READING
Empire Style (Furniture), 1804–1815 by Nietta Apra, London, 1972.
The French Empire Style by Alvar Gonzalez-Palacios, translated from the Italian, London, 1970.
Empire Furniture 1800–1825 by Serge Grandjean, London, 1966.
Les Ebénistes Parisiens (1795–1830) by D. Ledoux-Lebard, Paris, 1951.
Mobilier National de France: Les Sièges de Georges Jacob by Ernest Dumonthier, Paris, 1921.
L'art décoratif et le mobilier sous la République et l'Empire by Paul Lafond, Paris, 1900.

Regency

Fig. 1 *Armchair in the Egyptian manner, English, early nineteenth century. Carved and gilt wood.*
(Mallett and Son Ltd., London.)

Fig. 2 *Upright chamber pianoforte, sometimes known as a 'giraffe', by 'M. & W. Stodart Makers to their Majesties . . . Golden Square, London 1806'. Satinwood and faded mahogany with ebony stringing, height 8½ ft.*
(Bowes Museum, Barnard Castle, Durham.)

Fig. 3 *Pair of torchères or pedestals in the manner of George Smith's Designs, published in 1808. Painted and gilt wood.*
(Normanby Hall, Scunthorpe, Humberside.)

Fig. 4 *Chimney-piece mirror in Normanby Hall, Scunthorpe, c.1810. Gilt wood with a type of classical frieze found on mirrors throughout England.*

Fig. 5 *Circular drawing-room table, English, 1812–15. Kingwood, gilt. Seen in the drawing-room, Southill Park, Bedfordshire, by Henry Holland, built 1796–1800.*

210

Crocodiles, sphinxes and dolphins – such was the extravagant decoration of Regency furniture

Though less so than that of our own day, Regency taste was eclectic and synthetic, and not until the Egyptian ingredient has been added does the synthesis become complete enough for the style to be unmistakably different from all preceding ones.

Isolated examples of Egyptian taste have occurred in every epoch of post-renaissance Europe. In the second half of the eighteenth century they became more common, following publication by several authors of Egyptian designs. By 1784 there was at least one Paris drawing-room decorated in the Egyptian fashion, and what may be architecturally the earliest Egyptian room in Britain, at Cairness, Grampian, bears the inscription, 'Compleated MDCCXCVII'.

Once again the name of Thomas Hope occurs as a pioneer of taste. As a young man he had paid visits to Egypt, and by 1800 his London mansion contained a furnished Egyptian room, whose massive couches and chairs incorporated a wealth of Egyptian motifs and applied scholarship. But, though initiators of taste, Hope's productions in this, as in other fields, were too scholarly, too expensively made and 'too bulky . . . to be commodious for general use'.

The peace of 1802–3 between England and France gave a chance to the much more light-hearted version of Egyptian taste developed in France following the return from Egypt of Napoleon and his staff in 1799. This *retour de l'Egypte* style of the Consulate period was both scholarly and fanciful; in both countries from about 1804 onwards, the swing was away from the former towards the latter. Hieroglyphics (their meaning not yet elucidated) were used ornamentally: the sphinx, correctly male and wingless, grew wings and changed his sex, and the whole vocabulary of sun-discs, draped heads, papyri, crocodiles and lotus buds were used in delightful, but often indiscriminate, profusion.

French and English painters, whose work was so vital to the evolution of Regency taste, used the new 'outline' technique which lent itself so readily to the art of engraving and it was by this art that the spirit of the Regency was – literally – delineated, and disseminated to the wider public.

Artists, illustrators and engravers worked in harmony: Percier and Fontaine's *Interior Decoration* of 1801 inspired Thomas Hope's *Household Furniture and Interior Decoration* of 1807. Hope was followed by George Smith's derivative publica-

tion – with the same title – in 1808; Rudolph Ackermann's *Repository of Arts, Literature, Fashions, Manufactures, etc.* appeared in monthly numbers from 1809 to 1828 – the Regency equivalent of our twentieth-century glossy magazines – besides a number of short-lived publications.

On furniture the greatest single influence was probably George Smith's collection of designs of 1808, catering as it did for Greek, Roman, Egyptian, Chinese and gothic taste alike. If he had a trade mark it is the lion or other animal monopodium. Figures 3 and 9 both illustrate interpretations into actual pieces of furniture of the designs prevalent at this phase. Such pieces were repeated – with minor variations – many times over, but the period also gave birth to a number of extraordinary productions such as crocodile-legged couches and the unique set of dolphin furniture shown in Figure 8.

Historically-minded readers may like to recall that the Prince (after a brief spell in 1806) finally became Regent in February 1811. It was during the decade of the constitutional Regency that the style, the evolution of which we have observed, became fully absorbed into the everyday life of the middle class, a middle class enormously enlarged, enriched by war and concerned as never before to be 'in the fashion'. For them were built those distinctive, well proportioned terraces and villas which still grace Britain's towns and countryside, and the original furnishings of which form the bulk of the elegant, unpretentious Regency pieces in circulation today.

One of the sure signs of the full acceptance and assimilation of a style is its application to objects with a purely specialised function. The wine-cooler and the 'giraffe' piano (Fig. 2), are examples of these. Indeed, pianoforte cases of various shapes and sizes gave rise to some of the finest displays of Regency ingenuity and showmanship, from the modest, but often finely veneered, 'square' pianofortes of the 1780s, to the magnificent brass-inlaid grands made by Motts, Broadwoods and other firms from 1810 onwards.

Brass decoration became increasingly popular on Regency furniture up to about 1805 in the form of thin string-lines and beading and afterwards with broad sheet-brass scrolling and floral forms; sometimes, on important pieces, these developed into full panels of brass marquetry. By the end of the constitutional Regency (1820) brass had almost entirely replaced boxwood, ebony, etc., for inlay purposes on furniture of all types and sizes, from bookcases to clock-cases.

Like all living things, styles and movements carry within themselves the seeds of their own alteration and decline. The changes in taste which eventually transmuted Regency into Early Victorian are discernible at least as early as 1815. Foremost among

3

5

6

7

8

Museum Photo

Museum Photo

Fig. 6 *Lamp-standard, one of a pair by William Collins, 1823, to George Smith's design of 1808. Gilt bronze, height 10 ft. 6 ins. These magnificent five-branched lamp standards were made for Bath House, Piccadilly. (Bowes Museum.)*

Fig. 7 *Dolphin centre-table, English, c.1820. Carved and gilt wood, with circular inlaid marble top, height 2 ft. 4 ins.*
Pair of griffin armchairs, English or French, early nineteenth century. Parcel-gilt carved wood, covered in velvet, height 3 ft. 3 ins. (Mallett and Son Ltd.)

Fig. 8 *The Dolphin suite of furniture by William Collins, c.1813. Carved and gilt wood. This famous suite was presented to Greenwich Hospital in 1813. (Royal Pavilion, Brighton.)*

Fig. 9 *Commode, probably English, c.1820. Figured mahogany with marble top and ormolu cornucopia lock-plates; the free-standing Doric columns have ormolu bases, capitals and abaci, length 4 ft. 3 ins. (Bowes Museum.)*

Fig. 10 *Three-shelf bookcase, English, c.1824. Mahogany. A silver plate on the top of this handsome piece states that it was 'formed to receive 41 volumes of the Regent's Edition of Latin Classics'. It was presented by George IV on March 19, 1824. (Bowes Museum.)*

these changes were the Regent's own leanings: if, during the Revolutionary and Napoleonic era he had shied at things French, after the Bourbon restoration he returned to them with new enthusiasm. From 1815 he led a full-scale revival of Louis XIV and Louis XV styles with a special penchant for boulle, and factories specialising in this decoration sprang up in London. From now on, furniture for the royal palaces and the seats of the nobility increasingly deserted the Regency style in favour of Louis XIV and even rococo designs.

The drawing-table was an early and simple example of this royal nostalgia for the *ancien régime*, and its solid oak construction typifies another fashionable departure – the use by cabinet-makers for the first time since the seventeenth century of home-grown timbers in preference to exotic veneers. This movement is taken further in an important publication of 1820, Richard Brown's *Rudiments of Drawing Cabinet and Upholstery Furniture*, where naturalistic British flowers and foliage tend to replace the classical anthemion and acanthus, while delicate, reeded edges give way to plain D-ends. Not only in Brown's *Rudiments* but in P. & M. A. Nicholsons' *Practical Cabinet Maker* of 1826–27 this growing clumsiness and heaviness of proportion is discernible, which, though it retains classical forms, leads us straight into the Victorian era. The turned leg replaces that Regency trade mark, the scimitar. These are not the lightly turned and fluted legs of 1800 but an altogether stumpier and thick-set version, deeper and more profuse turning being made possible by the improvement in lathes.

The real pioneers of taste are sometimes able to anticipate subsequent trends by up to twenty years. Before 1820, for instance, certain rooms at Thomas Hope's Surrey mansion, Deepdene, Dorking, had the appearance of almost perfect specimens of Early Victorian – say 1845 – interiors. Lansdowne Tower at Bath was completed by William Beckford well before 1830, but contemporary illustrations of its furniture and of its Crimson Drawing Room make us think of 1850 at the earliest.

Pieces of furniture bearing an actual date – all

too rare at this period – frequently compel us to modify doctrinaire opinions. The massive gilt candelabra of 1823, one of which is shown in Figure 6, look back in style to around 1810; indeed, the only other known furniture by their maker, William Collins, is the 1813 Dolphin suite (Fig. 8). The bookcase illustrated in Figure 10, with its assured proportions and rich neo-classical carving, typifies the best in Hope's *Household Furniture*, yet its inscription tells us that it was made in 1824.

The mahogany commode in Figure 9 is perhaps one of the most difficult pieces to date of all those illustrated here. Its ormolu mounts, pillars and marble top have obvious affinities with the French Consulate and Early Empire, but the number of specimens in this country would seem to indicate an English origin for it. It is a significant piece because it typifies (and probably antedates) the great output of Regency-flavoured post-Napoleonic furniture that we know as Biedermeier, which covered the countries of Northern Europe throughout the 1820s and 1830s.

MUSEUMS AND COLLECTIONS

Regency furniture may be seen at the following:

GREAT BRITAIN
Brighton: Royal Pavilion
Faringdon: Buscot Park
Grantham: Belvoir Castle
Liverpool: Town Hall
London: Victoria and Albert
                Museum
Scunthorpe: Normanby Hall

FURTHER READING

Late Georgian and Regency Furniture by Christopher Gilbert, Feltham, 1972.
Regency Furniture 1800–1830 by Clifford Musgrave, London, 1970.
Regency Furniture 1795–1820 by Margaret Jourdain, London, 1934. Revised and enlarged by R. Fastnedge, London, 1965.

Biedermeier Furniture

Fig. 1 **Bed,** *designed by the architect Karl Friedrich Schinkel (1781–1841) for Queen Louise of Prussia. Pearwood veneer. (Charlottenburg, Berlin.)*

Fig. 2 **Sofa,** *German, c.1835. Typical of much south German furniture, this sofa is severe in ornament and imposing in its scale. (Münchner Stadtmuseum, Munich.)*

Fig. 3 **Sofa,** *Austrian, c.1820. Fruitwood with ebony and gilt decoration. The use of light-coloured wood was a characteristic of Biedermeier, but here the inspiration came from France. (Bethnal Green Museum, London.)*

214

The Biedermeier period saw a return to a simpler style of furniture, more in tune with current conditions and epitomising the relaxed, easy atmosphere following the Napoleonic Wars

Biedermeier furniture faithfully reflects the needs and tastes of the generation that came after the Napoleonic Wars. Self-consciously modest, it acts as a conductor between the severe classicism of the Empire style and the tasteless exuberance and technical virtuosity of the later nineteenth century. The name itself is an amalgam of the names of Biedermann and Bummelmeier, two comic characters who epitomised the cheerful philistinism of middle-class Germans in the 1830s. Biedermeier has become linked with the word *bourgeois* for more than alliterative reasons. The patriotic fervour which accompanied the War of Liberation gave rise to the hope that the German states, fusing their political differences in a common sense of nationhood, would come together to form a united Germany. It is not too far fetched to link the collapse of this ideal, with its heroic and classical overtones, with the emergence of an almost anti-heroic style. This style reflected the self-confidence and sentimentality of a class protected politically by Metternich and the Holy Alliance, and economically by stringent controls after 1815.

In the Austrian Empire the financial reforms of Count Stadion were especially important for the development of a new style. His deflationary policy resulted in an acute shortage of money at a time when private credit hardly existed in Austria. In the German lands merchants had to contend with renewed competition from English manufactured goods, and in Hungary and Galicia landowners faced the threat of imported Russian wheat. There simply was not enough money for new building projects or lavish schemes of decoration.

The Emperor himself gave the lead in cultivating a simpler style in tune with the changed conditions. Franz der Gute was scarcely a heroic character.

A. C. Cooper

Museum Photo

Angelo Hornak

Fig. 4 **Work-table.**
*Although the lyre-shape is
strongly neo-classical, the round
form is a prominent feature of
the Biedermeier style.
(Schleswig-Holsteinisches
Landesmuseum, Schleswig.)*

Fig. 5 **A pair of chairs,** *German
or Austrian, c.1830. Oak.
The shape of the chairs is based
on a style popular throughout
Europe during the first three or
four decades of the nineteenth
century. Many such chairs
survive in mahogany or light-
coloured wood, often
decorated with metal mounts.
These are of oak and are very
solidly made, which may suggest
that they were made by a
provincial chair-maker.
(Private Collection.)*

The virtuous, narrow figure hurrying along the
corridors of Schönbrunn was hardly the man
to inspire a return to the baroque splendours and
financial extravagances of the eighteenth century.
Practical, inexpensive furniture was all that was
needed and all that the bad state of Austrian
finances allowed. Derived from classical example,
Biedermeier furniture 'suited the modest size and
unostentatious needs of comfortable bourgeois
houses'. Workshops such as Danhauser, which
flourished between 1804 and 1838, produced
furniture in which the severity and tension of
Empire design was softened into a more relaxed
style, where comfort took precedence over appearance. One of the most popular innovations was
the sofa (Fig. 2). Rectangular, with high back and
sides, sofas looked deceptively hard: in fact their
depth and solidity made them very comfortable.
Armchairs, too, became more comfortable as
changing fashions permitted men to sit back and
take their ease; upholstery was brightly coloured.

The neo-classical *torchère* was transformed into
a massive pedestal, surmounted either by a

piece of statuary or by a flambeau whose proportions presaged the monstrous light-fittings of the
1860s and '70s. One new and omnipresent feature
was the piano, the polished surface of which
became a resting place for clocks, pieces of porcelain and the inevitable basket of flowers. There
was also a vogue for cabinets (Fig. 10), to house
collections of any objects which might proclaim
the artistic sensibility of the household.

The less severe appearance of furniture led to a
less formal arrangement of the rooms as a whole.
Flowers, screens, work-tables and knick-knacks
of all sorts helped to give a sense of humdrum
family life. Paintings by Georg Kersting (1783–
1847) and Franz Heinrich (1802–90) amply
demonstrate what is often called 'the quiet
happiness of Biedermeier'.

Although Biedermeier was essentially a product
of south Germany, its greatest exponent was the
Prussian architect and designer Karl Friedrich
Schinkel (1781–1841) (Fig. 1). Despite the prover-
bial dreariness and meanness of the Prussian Court,
Schinkel was encouraged to produce furniture and

Fig. 6 Cupboard, *north German,*
c.1820. Mahogany with gilt
plaster decoration.
The use of gilt plaster and
mahogany together derives
from late Empire forms.
(Bethnal Green Museum.)

Fig. 7 Writing-desk, *German,*
c.1835.
This is an unusual piece, the
nationality of which was in doubt
for some time. The rich use of
veneers as surface decoration
gives it a much less severe
appearance than many German
pieces of this date.
(Bethnal Green Museum.)

Fig. 8 Work-table, *German or*
Austrian, c.1835. Veneered with
very light-coloured wood and
retaining its interior fittings.
(Victoria and Albert Museum,
London.)

Fig. 9 A living-room, *Lübeck.*
Though this room, as arranged,
looks typical of the decade
1860–70, much of the furniture is
earlier. The sofa is in the style of
the 1850s, but pieces in this style
were being made into the 1860s.
Note that the cupboard is very
similar to that in Figure 6. The
mirror over the cupboard dates
from the '30s and is hung at the
correct angle. The chairs date
from the '40s, and the
arrangement of the curtains and
the pattern of the wallpaper from
the same decade.

even jewellery for the Prussian Royal Family. His style combines the aesthetic delicacy of neo-Classicism with the functional and restrained qualities of Biedermeier. Schinkel's reward for being the most original of all German designers was a commission to design the new school of artillery.

Despite Schinkel, the Biedermeier style in south Germany was certainly more attractive than its northern counterpart. In Austria, light-coloured fruitwoods were popular (Figs. 3 and 8) and there was less use of heavy veneering or inlay. The Viennese sat on cherrywood sofas to read the comedies of the Austrian playwright and poet Grillparzer while, in the vast barrack of Berlin, Prussians sat forward on mahogany chairs upholstered in black horsehair to listen to the dynamic logic of Hegel.

In the 1840s Biedermeier gradually gave way to the curves and flourishes of the neo-rococo revival in Vienna. In the north, the romantic movement led to the dramatic rediscovery of medieval Germany and the long night of the Gothic Revival.

Fig. 10 *Collector's cabinet on stand,* German, c.1835.
*The cabinet is veneered in bird's-eye maple and
decorated with transfers in the form of mezzotints
of German scenes. Inside is a number of shallow drawers.
The stand is very much in the rococo revival style and has
pronounced cabriole legs. Cabinets of this sort were often
made as master works by craftsmen who had completed
their apprenticeship, for they readily lent themselves to
elaborate veneering and delicate carving and were
therefore ideal tests of a craftsman's skills.*
(Bethnal Green Museum.)

10

MUSEUMS AND COLLECTIONS

Biedermeier furniture may be seen at the
following:

AUSTRIA
Vienna: Schloss Schönbrunn
GERMANY
Munich: Munchner Stadtmuseum
Schleswig: Schleswig-Holsteinisches
                     Landesmuseum
GREAT BRITAIN
London: Bethnal Green Museum
                     Victoria and Albert Museum

FURTHER READING

Biedermeier Furniture by Georg Himmelheber,
London, 1974.
World Furniture ed. by Helena Hayward,
London, 1965.
Biedermeier: Deutschland von 1815–1847 by
Max von Boehn, Berlin, 1923.

Shaker Furniture

Shaker furniture, with its ingenuity, simple design and excellent workmanship, is admired throughout the world as a fine example of functional art

Shaker furniture is a physical manifestation of the discipline and moral values of a religious group which created the austere style that is so admired today. It is as if the precepts of modern designers were conceived and executed in the early nineteenth century long before the modern concept of functionalism was mentioned.

The Shakers were a religious sect founded by Mother Ann Lee in England during the eighteenth century. In 1758, when Ann was twenty-two years old, she became a Quaker; she later married and had four children. It was religion that gave her the power to become a leader during a period when women did not normally have such rights. In prison, where she was sent in 1770 for profaning the Sabbath, she meditated and began to believe that she was the daughter of Christ.

Mother Ann, her husband and a few of her sect left England for the Colonies in 1774. The group, with the exception of Ann's husband who left her for another woman, founded a settlement in Watervliet, New York, where they could farm, garden, prosper and practise the many rules of their religion.

The history of the growth of the Shaker families is remarkable, for Mother Ann decreed celibacy and it was only through conversion that new Shakers could join. The rules of each settlement were strict. Hard work was required, and frivolity was unknown; only the 'dancing' at their religious services offered any respite. The Shaker religion was at its height in 1860 when eighteen settlements with 6,000 members were located in the United States – in New England, New York, Ohio and Kentucky. What is also remarkable is that such a small group should have been so original in their thinking and arts while remaining so rigid in their social behaviour. Their inventions were many and included the flat broom, the automatic spring, the

Fig. 1 **Room** *in the style of the early nineteenth century. (American Museum in Britain, Claverton Manor, near Bath.)*

clothes-peg, metal pen-point, a chair-leg that tilted, the threshing machine, pea-sheller, apple-corer, static electricity machine and the circular saw.

Mother Ann said: 'Do all your work as though you had a thousand years to live, and as you would know you must die tomorrow'. If a Shaker baked a pie or made a chair, the result was to be as close to perfection as possible. Perhaps it was this philosophy, together with the prohibition on unnecessary decoration, that led to the Shaker style.

Shaker furniture is an extension of the religious beliefs of the group and, in order to appreciate the design and ingenuity of the Shaker craftsman, the ideology must be considered. Some Shakers believed that the furniture designs were originated in heaven and transmitted to the craftsman through angels. The quality of workmanship was always high and the wood carefully selected for suitability and well seasoned. Old-growth pine, maple, cherry, pear, apple and walnut were all favoured.

Designs had to conform to religious principles

Many of the Shakers came from rural areas and were familiar with the work of the country craftsman; provincial styles influenced all the work done in the Shaker villages. When a convert joined a Shaker community, he brought with him his family, his money and his humble possessions.

It was the country furniture of the times that furnished the Shaker homes – Windsor chairs, banister-back, slat-back and Dutch-style chairs, stretcher-tables, chests of drawers, cottage beds and candlestands. The need was so great that all furniture was accepted and used even though the pieces might have been ornate.

The communal groups began to build their own houses and meeting-places by 1788. Converts were often very poor and could not afford to buy furniture. The first chair-factory, blacksmith's shop and tannery were in use in New Lebannon (Mount Lebannon), New York, by 1789. In a few years, the Shakers were also making bricks, whips, felt hats, silk, nails, medicine, shoes and woollens. They made almost everything that was needed for the community except satin and glass.

The furniture-makers were, however, faced with a problem of design. They had to follow the teachings of Mother Ann, who said: 'Whatever is fashioned, [let] it be plain and simple . . . unembellished by any superfluities which add nothing to its goodness or durability'. Some designs, such as the highboy, the canopy-bed and elaborate chairs, were not only difficult to make, but also too ornate for the religious teaching. Some plain forms such as candlestands, trestle-tables, slat-back chairs and low-post beds were acceptable, but the cabinet-makers adapted the designs to conform with their materials, needs and religious views. No carving, inlays or veneers were used. Turnings were used only in a functional way, with no excess permitted. The designs became more and more restrained until even the bu'k of wood was diminished to the absolute minimum. Chair-posts were sometimes as small as half an inch in thickness and were rarely over an inch in diameter. 'Sinful' mishandling of the furniture was never permitted in Shaker dwellings and many of the lighter pieces have survived.

There are a few design characteristics that can be noted in all Shaker pieces which are a result of the drive toward simplicity and usefulness. Rod-shaped and slightly tapered turnings on the furniture legs can be found; they often have almost no foot. Metal mounts are omitted, only simple, turned pegs being used for drawer-handles. Exposed dovetailing has a decorative value, but was only included for structural reasons. Large chests and counters had sharply angled bracket feet designed to hold great weights. Beds had large wooden castors for ease of movement. Extra drawers or drop-leaves added to the usefulness of many tables and stands. Many chairs, tables and stands were designed very low by today's standards. The finish used on all pieces was similar: red, yellow and green stain and a light varnish or oil were used on the furniture made in all the settlements.

The backs of pieces of furniture were as perfectly finished as the fronts. No Shaker pieces are found with poor finishing, sloppy paint-work or uneven measurements.

That some new forms were developed seems consistent with the inventive nature of the Shaker. The sewing-desk was a form which differed from society to society. Combination pieces were made for dual purpose. One type of chair had an extra top-rail to hold the folded bedspread. Pegboards for the walls, swivel stools and wall clocks seem to be unique to the Shakers.

The earliest cabinet-makers among the Shakers started with chairs. The craftsman kept refining the ladder-back chair until the characteristic design appeared. The first factory-made chairs appeared in 1789 and they were evidently sold to surrounding areas the following year. From this time until about 1860, the three-slat side-chair was made. This chair had turned front and back uprights, the rear uprights ending in acorn-shaped finials. The slats were slightly concave, to adjust to the shape of the user's back, and were about twelve inches long and two and a half inches wide. The arms were shaped, slightly flared and held to the front upright by sockets. Two box-stretchers on the legs helped to give the chair structural soundness. The legs were made of plain turnings.

The rocking-chair was popular among the Shakers

The seat was of rush, splint or a colourful and popular woven tape that was made by Shaker women and sold to surrounding communities (Fig. 2). Most chairs were made of maple. Some were made of birch, cherry or butternut, with pine, ash or hickory for specialised parts.

The dining-chair was a special Shaker form. It was made so low that it could be pushed under the table when not in use. The chair usually had one slat across the back and was twenty-five inches high, with the seat set only sixteen inches from the floor. The seat was wider in the front than in the back, for added comfort. There was a two-slat version of the low dining-chair, but the design seemed to be a regional one. A one-slat chair appears in Massachusetts, and in later years, the two-slat variety appeared in New York and New Hampshire.

The rocking-chair was one of the most important Shaker designs and was popular with the many elderly people who lived in Shaker communities.

Fig. 2 *Ladder-back chair from Pleasant Hill, Kentucky, first quarter of the nineteenth century. Cherry or walnut painted red, with the original seat-tapes. These seat-tapes were a popular Shaker product and were sold to surrounding communities. (Shakertown, Pleasant Hill, Kentucky.)*

Fig. 3 *Tailoress' counter from Watervliet, New York, 1820–30. Pine and curly maple.*
The first Shaker settlement was founded in 1774 by Mother Ann at Watervliet, the origin of this beautiful piece. Note the fine grain of the wood, discreet moulding along the drawers, simple turned knobs and delicate but sturdy tapered legs.
(American Museum in Britain.)

Fig. 4 *Round stand from New Lebannon, c.1820. Cherry, height 27 ins.*
Evolved from the early candlestand, these round stands were made for the retiring-room. They were very important to the Shakers, whose rules stated that 'one or two stands should be provided for the occupants of every retiring-room'.
(American Museum in Britain.)

220

The rocking chair was similar to the side-chair, but had four slats and arms in several different styles. Five types of rocker were made; the scroll-arm, rolled-arm, front upright with mushroom end (Fig. 1), cross-rail and armless sewing-rocker are the types now recognised. Each one was named for its most obvious design feature. Some rockers were made with drawers which held sewing-equipment, with special tray-like arms and with other refinements. The male Shakers, like most men, could not resist tipping back their side-chairs, so an inventive member of the sect developed a tilting-chair. A ball-and-socket device was made to fit the back legs so that they remained vertical when the chair was tipped.

Shaker chairs were so well made and so cheap that thousands were sold outside the Shaker settlements. In 1807 the chairs were sold for seventy-five cents each. By 1828 a rocker cost two dollars and fifty cents. The chairs were advertised in newspapers, and sales brochures were distributed. Marked examples are occasionally found with a 'No. 3', or another number ranging from one to eight, according to size, on the label. The chair was larger, wider and higher, and made to suit the physique of the buyer.

The Shakers ate in communal dining-rooms; the brothers at one sitting and the sisters at another. The dining-table was of a trestle type with a shoe foot, and had two or three boards in the top. The rectangular top was up to twenty-eight inches wide and up to eight feet long. One very large communal dining-table that still exists is twenty feet long. A characteristic underbracing is seen on most of the tables and benches. The parts were joined with mortice and tenon joints. Early tables and benches were stained dark red, but later a light stain and varnish were used that allowed the grain of the wood to show.

Shaker beds were cots only three feet wide

Shaker chests were made with simple, moulded edges and turned wooden knobs (Fig. 3), and were often built into the room as a permanent part of its design (Fig. 6). Mushroom-shaped turnings as knobs were preferred at some settlements. The cupboard doors were narrow, held closed with wrought-iron catches. Each member of the society had a limited number of drawers and cupboards

Fig. 5 *Press*, 1850s, reflecting 'worldly' turnings on the legs. (*Shaker Museum, Auburn, Kentucky.*)

allotted to them for their own personal use.

The free-standing chests were of two types: a high chest slightly over five feet tall, made of maple, birch or butternut, and a small chest that was under three feet high. The high chest had four full-width drawers topped by four half-width drawers in two tiers. The low chest had one row of half-width drawers and three full-width drawers.

Shaker beds were simple cots, about three feet wide (Fig. 7). The bed had a short headboard and a shorter footboard. Almost all of the beds were painted green. Each bed had rollers or castors so that it could be moved for easier cleaning. The bed was made with lightweight slats that could 'give' with the body – a great improvement over the ropes that were used on 'worldly' beds.

The Shaker stands were numerous. The rules of the Shakers stated: 'One or two stands should be provided for the occupants of every retiring-room'. The sewing-shops had stands for one or two workers. The washstand, of course, was important for cleanliness; it often had a tapered shaft sup-

turning or curve of the leg is seen on a press or stand (Fig. 5); even a shaped apron on a chest might be rarely found in Ohio. The character of the design, the simplicity of the approach and the obvious attention to excellence that marks all Shaker furniture remained in even the less pure examples dating from the 1860s.

Today, there are only twelve living Shakers who reside in Shaker communities in Maine and New Hampshire. Mother Ann predicted that one day there would be too few Shakers remaining to bury the dead, but she also had another vision; that when the Shakers numbered less than seven, there would be a great revival. Although the religious views of celibacy and perfect order seem to have little appeal to the masses today, it is interesting that the culture of the Shakers, their architecture and furniture has been of increasing interest to the United States. The old Shaker villages are being preserved and restored and the furnishings of the Shakers are known throughout the world as fine examples of functional design.

Fig. 6 *Shaker storeroom.* Cupboards were often built into a room as a permanent part of the architecture in Shaker houses. Here, a typical Shaker chair hangs from a pegboard, as was the custom when the floors were being cleaned. (*Henry Francis du Pont Winterthur Museum, Winterthur, Delaware.*)

Fig. 7 *Shaker bedroom, with a Pleasant Hill walnut bed and a cherry washstand, both made in the first quarter of the nineteenth century. Shaker beds were simple cots with lightweight slats instead of the rope bases, common then. Almost all were painted green.* (*Center Family House, Shakertown, Pleasant Hill.*)

ported by three rod-like feet. Round-topped stands that were evolved from the early candlestand were made for the retiring-room (Fig. 4); square-topped sewing-stands with small, underslung drawers were used for sisters in the workrooms.

The Shakers made almost every type of furniture needed for the settlements. Clocks, boxes, box desks, baskets, work-tables, stoves, standing-racks to hold bedding, racks of shelves to hold dishes, bookcases, wood-boxes, blanket-chests and small hanging-cupboards are still to be seen.

Although Shaker furniture was supposedly made by closely following the designs passed on to the craftsmen by angels and the rules of Mother Ann, by the 1850s the influence of the 'worldly' people could also be seen in some pieces. The change was particularly apparent in the furniture of the Kentucky Shakers. Slat-back chairs, with flattened back stiles, and bentwood chairs were made. Tables, stands, and desks were often heavier in construction and lost some of the characteristic Shaker delicacy.

Furniture produced in the East was often made of maple, cherry, butternut and other similar woods, but in Ohio and Kentucky, poplar (whitewood) and black walnut were favoured. Sometimes, an extra

MUSEUMS AND COLLECTIONS

Shaker furniture may be seen at the following:

GREAT BRITAIN
Bath: American Museum in Britain, Claverton Manor

U.S.A.
Boston, Mass: Boston Museum of Fine Arts
Philadelphia, Pa.:   Philadelphia Museum of Art
Shaker Heights, Ohio: Shaker Historical Society
Winterthur, Del.:   Henry Francis Du Pont Winterthur Museum

FURTHER READING

A Reappraisal of Shaker Furniture and Society by Mary Lyn Ray, in Henry Francis du Pont Winterthur Museum, 1973.
The American Shakers and Their Furniture by John G. Shea, New York, 1971.
Religion in Wood, a Book of Shaker Furniture by E. D. and F. Andrews, Indiana, 1966.
American Country Furniture 1780–1875 by Ralph and Terry Kovel, New York, 1965.
The Shakers: Their Arts and Crafts, Philadelphia Museum of Art, Philadelphia, 1962.

Victorian Gothic

English gothic furniture, so called because it incorporated details of English gothic architecture, was a style unique in its vigorous invention and humorous inconsequence

Furniture in the gothic style, which has come to be so closely associated with the first half of the nineteenth century, was being made in certain forms as early as the mid-eighteenth century. Most of the firms which produced furniture for the fashionable market at this time, and in particular that of Thomas Chippendale, had made a gesture towards supplying the gradually increasing demand for a style which would be more appropriate for use in pre-classical houses than the current rococo or neo-classical modes.

Nevertheless, before 1800, most of the gothic pieces were simply standard productions of the time with a little gothic architectural detail grafted on to them. The Chippendale-style chair of about 1760 shown in Figure 1 is a typical example of that firm's output, except that some gothic arch shapes have been introduced into the carving of the back instead of the more usual rococo or ribbon ornament.

Even such an enthusiastic connoisseur as Horace Walpole (1717–97), who began creating his fantastic 'medieval' house at Strawberry Hill in 1749, did not insist on gothic furniture. Contemporary illustrations show him seated in his library on the typical English mid-eighteenth-century chair, which had close affinities with French rococo. As the eighteenth century drew to a close, however, the fashion for building romantic houses in what was imagined to be a medieval manner greatly increased, and a new sort of knowledgeable clientele began to require furniture in an appropriate style.

It is perhaps desirable at this stage to define a little more precisely the exact use of the term 'gothic' as applied to nineteenth-century furniture, especially as the vast diversity of fashionable styles at this period tends to make the picture rather confusing.

The word is here used to describe only that furniture which incorporates details of gothic architecture. Pointed arch shapes, crockets, column clusters, leaf mouldings, ball flowers, even wheel-window forms; all were pressed into service to

Fig. 1 **Chair**, *in the manner of Thomas Chippendale (1718–99), c.1760. Mahogany. This is an eighteenth century gothic piece, the architectural detail grafted on to a standard design.* (*Victoria and Albert Museum.*)

Fig. 2 **Armchair**, *English, c.1830. Gilt beech.* (*Victoria and Albert Museum, London.*)

Fig. 3 **Bed**, *from* A Collection of Designs for Household Furniture and Interior Decoration *by George Smith, published 1808.* (*Weinreb and Douwma, Ltd.*)

Museum Photo

A. C. Cooper

Angelo Hornak

ornament and add distinction to the style. Since hardly any genuine medieval furniture existed, designers embarked on a programme of fanciful creativity with the happy inventiveness which so distinguishes the early 1800s.

Although the results do not in the least resemble the few pieces of rude furniture which have survived from the Middle Ages, they left us a style which is unique and delightful in its vigorous invention, humorous inconsequence and skilful adaptation.

As the nineteenth century advanced, the spirit of historicism and quasi-scholarship which is noticeable in the architecture of the period began to influence furniture-design. Suites of furniture in the Jacobean, Elizabethan or François I styles began to make their appearance, following with more or less accuracy the appearance of their models. None of these should be confused with

gothic, and they constitute a completely separate area of study.

The general expansion of the furniture industry at the beginning of the nineteenth century was directly related to the expanding market of the growing middle classes, many of whom turned to novelty in their search for identity. The gothic, and other types of 'fancy' furniture helped to satisfy this need. Another factor which undoubtedly influenced taste away from neo-classicism and Continental styles during the first twenty years of the century was the continuing war with France. In the characteristic thinking of the time, a gothic or 'English' style was felt by many people to be more patriotic. It is even said that the Prince Regent's taste for Orientalism was consciously acquired in place of his true preference for fine French furniture in the Louis XIV or Empire styles.

Already, during the second half of the eighteenth century, pattern-books of furniture had begun to include a few gothic examples. Chippendale's *The Gentleman and Cabinet-Maker's Director* (1754) contains several, and soon it was considered essential for any new work to show at least some pieces in this style, together with some suggestions for gothic decoration.

Pattern-books and Ackermann's Repository encouraged the gothic trend

Pattern-books in the late eighteenth and early nineteenth centuries fulfilled very much the same role as the present-day home-decorating magazines, and so many were produced that it is not possible to list them all. Perhaps the most influential of any English publication was Ackermann's *Repository of the Arts*, which appeared monthly from January 1809 to December 1828. Although it was not a pattern-book in the true sense, out of the two hundred and forty parts, one hundred and eighty-nine contained a coloured plate devoted to some aspect of furniture or interior decoration, and many gothic pieces were included (Fig. 10).

While the *Repository* reached a wide public, its contents were of course not as concentrated as those of the contemporary pattern-books, and all of these followed the new enthusiasm in some measure. *A Collection of Designs for Household Furniture and Interior Decoration* by George Smith, which first appeared in 1808, had many gothic examples, even an incredible state bed (Fig. 3), together with chairs, sofas, a dressing-table, canterburies, library tables and bookcases. *The Encyclopaedia of Cottage, Farm and Villa Architecture and Furniture* by J. C. Loudon, the first edition of which is dated 1833, contained designs for gothic pieces in, appropriately, a rather simple style. It is interesting to observe, however, that the quality of the designs is not nearly as assured as that of the neo-classical, in which vocabulary Loudon obviously felt himself much more at ease. It is also interesting to note the generally 'improving' tone of the whole work, symbolised in its title of encyclopedia, and very indicative of the trend towards the more correct styles of the middle of the century.

Gothic furniture came to be considered appropriate for the more solemn and masculine apart-

Fig. 4 *Housekeeper's cupboard, Cheshire, c.1830. Oak with ebony detail and mahogany crossbanding, height 7 ft. 6 ins. The gothic elements give lightness and interest to an otherwise cumbersome piece. (Private Collection.)*

A.C. Cooper

Fig. 5 **Carver Chair,** one of a set of two carvers and six side-chairs, designed by A. W. N. Pugin (1812–52) for Scarisbrick Hall, Lancashire, 1837.
(Victoria and Albert Museum.)

Fig. 6 **Two dining-chairs,** from a set of twelve from Attingham Hall, Shropshire, English, c.1840. Mahogany with brass reliefs of vine leaves and grapes. These are similar to the chairs in the dining-room at Eaton Hall shown in Figure 7.
(Mallett and Son, Ltd.)

Fig. 7 **Dining-room,** a print from the series Views of Eaton Hall by J. C. Buckler, 1826.
Eaton Hall, near Chester, was built by William Porden and extended by William Burn. The interior was decorated in the strictest gothic manner.
(Royal Institute of British Architects, London.)

ments – the hall, the library, sometimes the dining-room, occasionally a bedroom, although the boudoir and the drawing-room usually retained the frivolity and lightness of the current French styles. Notwithstanding, the gothic style did enjoy a brief vogue in France during the wave of enthusiasm for English fashion which marked the restoration of the monarchy. French *faux gothique,* or *style cathédrale,* is nevertheless fairly easily distinguishable by a certain shallowness of ornament, and by the wood used, which was nearly always mahogany or maple. Also, the base wood of carcase furniture was usually oak, while in England the veneer was sometimes applied to softwood, and the show-wood was more likely to be oak. Sometimes it was painted, or even gilt.

In America also the gothic style found favour, and some beautiful furniture was designed by the

house was cased up in town-hall gothic by Alfred Waterhouse (1830–1905) in the late 1860s, largely obliterating the Porden interiors, and it has now been completely demolished and the furniture and fittings dispersed.

Of course many other well-known architects of the early nineteenth century built gothic houses, and a few examples must suffice: James Wyatt (1746–1813) designed a huge gothic house at Ashridge in Hertfordshire (1808–17) for the Earl of Bridgewater, John Nash (1752–1835) designed some fine gothic interiors at Ravensworth Castle, Co. Durham (1808) and Shanbally Castle, Co. Tipperary (1812), and for all such houses it is likely that at least some gothic furniture would have been required.

A large number of houses were also fitted up with gothic interiors, the most typical and most famous

architect Alexander Jackson Davis for Lyndhurst, the house that he was building for William Paulding in 1841. A section on furniture in the gothic style is included in *The Architecture of Country Houses* by Andrew Jackson Downing, published in 1850 and obviously based on Loudon's *Encyclopaedia.*

Few houses were completely furnished in the gothic style, and undoubtedly the most remarkable was Eaton Hall, in Cheshire, built for the 2nd Earl Grosvenor by William Porden (1755–1822) between 1803 and 1812, and subsequently extended between 1820 and 1825. The whole interior of this extraordinary house was fitted up in the strictest gothic manner (Fig. 7), all the furniture and light-fittings were specially designed and even carpets with gothic borders were specially woven. The firm of Gillow of Lancaster seems to have produced most of the furniture, as was the case in many great houses of this period, but it is probable that it was designed by Porden. Chairs from Attingham Hall in Shropshire similar to those to be seen in the view of the dining-room have been sold in London (Fig. 6). Unfortunately the whole

of which is Windsor Castle. Sir Jeffry Wyatville (1766–1840) decorated many of the rooms in this style during the alterations that he supervised for George IV and the furniture that he designed was in fine characteristic style (Fig. 9).

Many houses also had a gothic room or two, even though the general style did not accord. For example, Thomas Hopper (1776–1856) designed a magnificent gothic conservatory for the Prince Regent at Carlton House in 1811 and Sir John Soane (1753–1837) transformed one of the rooms at Stowe, Buckinghamshire, into a gothic library in 1806. When the middle of the century approached, however, as has been previously remarked, the taste for gothic was superseded by the fashion for more historicist styles, which were believed to be closer to their antecedents. The catalogue of the Great Exhibition of 1851 contains hardly any examples of gothic furniture other than those in the Medieval Court, designed by A. W. N. Pugin (1812–52). This reflects the trend in architectural taste, as attention shifted from the early romantic gothic of Nash, Porden, Wyatville or

225

8

9

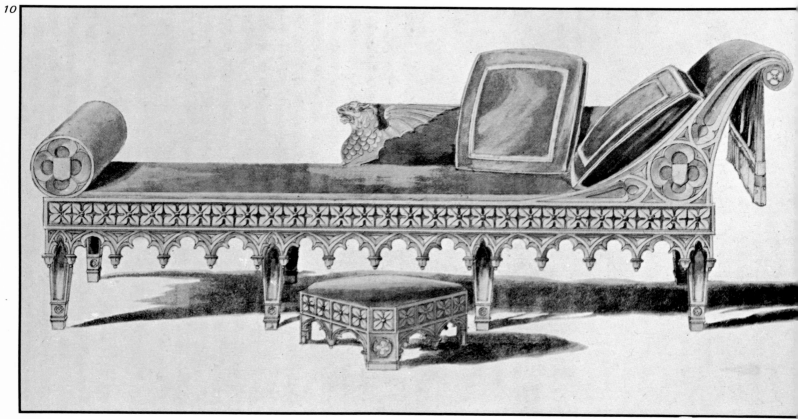

10

11

Fig. 8 **Table-top**, *probably designed by A. W. N. Pugin c.1847. Walnut inlaid with a gothic design. (Victoria and Albert Museum.)*

Fig. 9 **Design for the south wall of a dining-room at Windsor Castle**, *attributed to Sir Jeffry Wyatville (1766–1840). Water-colour over black chalk. (Sotheby and Co. Ltd.)*

Fig. 10 **Gothic sofa**, *from* Repository of the Arts, *a monthly published from 1809 to 1828. It contained designs for many gothic pieces. (Private Collection.)*

Fig. 11 **Dining-chair**, *one of a set of six, English, c.1835. (Private Collection.)*

226

Pugin himself, to that of the solemn, correct, churchy revivalists like Waterhouse, Scott, Teulon or Burgess.

The only exception to this trend in furniture was in the field of ecclesiastical and church furnishing, and for this the gothic style was employed right up to the end of the nineteenth century, and indeed well into the twentieth.

The most important and, as it happens, the last figure to be associated with the design of gothic furniture in the period under review is Augustus Welby Northmore Pugin, whose name is now so closely associated with the early gothic revival. He produced furniture and decoration of outstanding competence, although he is primarily known as an architect and publicist of moral theories on build-ing. It should not be forgotten that he designed not only the furniture for his various commissions, but the whole range of interior fittings as well. He worked with J. G. Crace & Sons, the famous firm of decorators and manufacturers, and collaborated with them in the design of wallpapers, textiles, schemes of decoration and furnishings.

K. Hoddle

Museum Photo

Fig. 12 *Design for a conversational sofa* by L. N. A. Cottingham, 1842. Water-colour. This piece was for Snelston Hall, Derbyshire. (*Victoria and Albert Museum.*)

Fig. 13 *Cabinet, designed by A. W. N. Pugin and made by J. G. Crace, c.1850. Carved oak with brass panels and mounts. This piece, in fifteenth-century style, was exhibited at the Great Exhibition of 1851. (Victoria and Albert Museum.*)

vocabulary as other practitioners of this style, his furniture has a very individual character. His whole approach was fundamentally different in that he did not see the decorative details of gothic architecture as a means of ornamenting already accepted furniture forms, but rather did he try to reconsider the whole design programme, which he then tried to express in gothic terms. His stature is evident when his productions are compared to those of his contemporaries.

In the normal commercial field, the style of gothic furniture changed remarkably little during the years from 1820 to 1850. From the beginning, designers showed a considerable knowledge of gothic ornament and a considerable skill in applying it but, for the opposite reasons to those which make Pugin's furniture so convincing, a lot of the less thought-out designs look papery and frivolous by comparison.

It has to be admitted that a certain awkwardness and naivety is often evident, brought about by the insoluble problems of grafting purely architectural forms on to objects of domestic utility. In this way it is not unusual to find cupboards suggesting choir-screens, chests looking like tombs and chairs which evoke flying buttresses.

Some of the most engaging productions in the gothic style are perhaps those which are least excessive. Provincial furniture-makers turned out simple utilitarian pieces in large quantities, on which expressions of gothic are used very sparingly, merely to heighten or give liveliness to furniture which would otherwise be rather dull, or to add fantasy where it would not normally be expected. On the cupboard made in Cheshire about 1830, known as a housekeeper's cupboard (Fig. 4), the ebony stringing lines in gothic arch shapes completely transform a large and cumbersome object by the introduction of unusual decoration. The rest of the piece is mostly of oak. Similarly the chair (Fig. 11), although it has a very standard seat-frame and legs, typical of the 1840s, is lifted right out of the commonplace by the gothic back.

Gothic furniture seems so often to be illuminated by the glow of unexpected and arbitrary fantasy that one must concede that it is in this that its special charm must lie.

Pugin's most famous work is that which he did on the interiors of the new Houses of Parliament, London, built between 1840 and 1865, where he worked in conjunction with the architect Sir Charles Barry (1795–1860) from 1844 until his death. In this one building the full range of his talent can be seen in a gorgeous panoply. Characteristic of his very personal style are the chair, now in the Victoria and Albert Museum, London (Fig. 5), that he designed in about 1840 for Scarisbrick Hall, Lancashire; the beautiful octagonal table made around 1847 for Abney Hall, Cheshire (Fig. 8), also in the Museum, and the great cabinet made by Crace to Pugin's design and exhibited at the Great Exhibition of 1851 (Fig. 13).

Although Pugin used basically the same design

MUSEUMS AND COLLECTIONS

Nineteenth-century gothic furniture may be seen at the following:

FRANCE
Paris: Musée des Arts Décoratifs
GREAT BRITAIN
London: Victoria and Albert Museum
Windsor: Windsor Castle
U.S.A.
Tarrytown, N.Y. Lyndhurst

FURTHER READING

The World of Victoriana by James Norbury, Feltham, 1972.
Nineteenth Century English Furniture by Elizabeth Aslin, London, 1962.
Regency Furniture Designs, 1803–1826 by John Harris, London, 1961.
Regency Antiques by Brian Reade, London, 1953.

Arts and Crafts Furniture

Although the Arts and Crafts Movement in furniture encompassed a multitude of styles, it was rooted in the desire for good, simple design and solid construction

In 1867 Bruce Talbert's *Gothic Forms Applied to Furniture* was published and C. L. Eastlake's *Hints on Household Taste* came out the following year. These two books heralded the production of what is termed 'Art Furniture', in reality a mainly gothic style suited to the needs of the general public.

Eastlake's book found favour and obviously influenced many people, and Talbert – originally a woodcarver – designed furniture for several large commercial firms, the sideboard in Figure 6 illustrating a style much copied at the time. But, even allowing for the public's growing interest in furniture and interior decoration, it is now generally accepted that it was William Morris (1834–96) who kindled the flame which grew into the Arts and Crafts Movement.

Morris moved into his newly built Red House in 1860 to find that 'only in a few isolated cases – such as Persian carpets, and blue china or delft for vessels of household use – was there anything then to be bought ready-made that he could be content with in his own house'. To remedy this state of affairs Morris and his friends set themselves to designing and making, and from this somewhat unusual beginning the firm of Morris, Marshall, Faulkner and Company was born, and the beginnings of the Movement.

Following Morris' lead, many architects, craftsmen and designers became interested in the revival of good design and honest craftsmanship; from this interest various guilds and societies emerged, the first being the Century Guild, founded around 1882 by the architect A. H. Mackmurdo (1851–1942). The aim of the Guild was to 'render all branches of art, the sphere no longer of the tradesman but of the artist'. The furniture designs were carried out by professional firms of cabinet-makers and range from small oak writing-desks (Fig. 2), to beautifully

A. C. Cooper

Owner's Photo

Fig. 1 **Chair**, designed by E. W. Godwin (1836–86) and made by Watt, c.1877. Ebonised wood with split-cane back and seat.
Inspired by Japanese design, Godwin produced furniture far ahead of its time with many features sought for by present-day designers.
(Miss Elizabeth Aslin Collection.)

Fig. 2 **Writing-desk** by A. H. Mackmurdo (1851–1942) for the Century Guild, c.1886. Oak.
Only an architect such as Mackmurdo could have designed so unified a piece. As with all the furniture made for the Century Guild, the work was carried out by a firm of professional cabinet-makers.
(William Morris Gallery, Walthamstow, London.)

Fig. 3 **Dresser**, designed by W. R. Lethaby (1857–1931), c.1900. Oak inlaid with various woods.
The floral patterns on this famous piece show clearly the influence of Morris.
(Victoria and Albert Museum, London.)

Fig. 4 **Dresser**, designed by Ernest Gimson (1864–1919), c.1900. Oak with simple gouged decoration and chamfers.
Unlike the work of Morris, which offers flat surfaces as a field for painters, Gimson's pieces allow the proportions, timber and workmanship to speak for themselves.
(Mrs. F. L. Griggs Collection.)

made large and elaborate satinwood pieces. Due to the co-operative nature of the Guild it is impossible to attribute designs to any one person with certainty. There is little doubt, though, that Mackmurdo was the first to design furniture with Art Nouveau features; if only because of this the work of his Guild must be noted.

In 1884 a group of architects formed the Art Workers' Guild and from this, to enable selective exhibitions to be held, came the Arts and Crafts Exhibition Society. The phrase 'Arts and Crafts', coined by the bookbinder Cobden-Sanderson, was here adopted. Four years later, in 1888, C. R. Ashbee opened his Guild and School of Handicraft in the East End of London, and later wrote: 'The Arts & Crafts Movement began with the object of making useful things, of making them well and making them beautiful . . . this movement, which began with the prophetic enthusiasm of Ruskin and the titanic energy of Morris'.

In the climate of the time (one architect wrote that they were living in an intellectual ferment), exhibitions were numerous and much of the furniture displayed was 'strikingly original'. Prominent among the furniture-designers were three architects, Sidney Barnsley (1865–1926), Ernest Barnsley (1863–1926) and Ernest Gimson (1864–1919). The work of these three men, who had been in constant contact with William Morris and greatly influenced by him, was to exert an enormous influence on other craftsmen and designers.

Towards the end of 1890, Gimson and Sidney Barnsley formed, with a few friends, the firm of Kenton and Company, and engaged professional cabinet-makers to execute their original designs. Pieces were also exhibited by the Arts and Crafts Exhibition Society and were shown at an exhibition at Barnard's Inn.

The firm lasted until 1893, when Gimson and the Barnsley brothers moved to the peace and quiet of the Cotswolds, there to follow the gospel of Morris. For a few years these three 'gentle men' worked together, pooling their ideas and making furniture with their own hands. In time, Sidney Barnsley, acquired the skill and expertise of a professional cabinet-maker. In 1901, skilled craftsmen were employed in a small workshop in Cirencester (Gloucestershire), but in 1903 a move was made to Sapperton, where Daneway, a magnificent manorhouse, was rented. The ground-floor rooms were used as showrooms, and the out-buildings converted into workshops.

From this time, Sidney Barnsley designed and made furniture entirely with his own hands (Fig. 5); Ernest Barnsley designed some furniture while working mainly as an architect (his great work, Rodmarton Manor, for which he made every drawing, is a storehouse of most interesting furniture designed by him, his brother Sidney and Ernest Gimson); Gimson concentrated on furniture-design, employing up to twelve cabinet-makers at the Daneway workshops.

The early pieces, especially those made by Sidney Barnsley, were experimental both in design and in construction; mostly they were of oak with large, flat surfaces, unadorned by carving, painting or any other form of ornament. These pieces are a natural follow-on from the early pieces of William Morris, but, whereas his furniture offered flat surfaces as a field for painters, the Cotswold pieces allow the proportions, the quality of the timber and

the workmanship to speak for themselves (Fig. 4).

Gimson, although he received instruction in chair-making and did, in fact, make a few chairs himself, was not a skilled worker in wood and, until his untimely death, worked mainly at the drawing-board. The large number of drawings he left testifies to his industry and, contrary to much that has been written about him in the past, he produced furniture of a wide variety, using many woods other than oak. Originally it was his intention to produce plain pieces at moderate cost but, with growing interest and demand, expensive pieces of increasing sophistication were made (Fig. 7).

Gimson's Dutch foreman, Peter Waals, was a cabinet-maker of great skill and experience who set a standard which became the accepted norm for the work produced. In 1916, a critic wrote: 'To a cabinet-maker it is a sheer delight to open and shut the door in a sideboard made by Ernest Gimson; it swings back into its place with the mathematical accuracy of the breech-block of a gun'.

Each piece of work was made under constant supervision. Gimson visited the workshops two or three times every week and often designs were modified to suit the timber or construction. Every handle, whether of wood, steel, brass or silver, was made with meticulous care, blacksmiths being employed who also made fire-irons, candle-sconces, hinges and other items. Much church work was undertaken, and Gimson developed a remarkable flair for knowing just what could be achieved in different materials. The shaping seen on the horse-drawn wagons in general use at the time influenced many of the designs, and Ernest Barnsley in particular developed the use of chamfers to a considerable degree. The effect on some of the large oak pieces is most pleasing, making full use of the play of light and shade.

In 1902 C. R. Ashbee moved his Guild and School of Handicraft to Chipping Campden, where a wide variety of work was produced. Ashbee, too, had been influenced by William Morris, especially politically, and also by the writings of Ruskin, and it is necessary to remember this when studying

Fig. 5 **Cabinet on stand**, *designed and hand made by Sidney Barnsley (1865–1926), c.1910. Quarter-cut English oak with black and white inlay, simple gouged decoration and hand-made iron handles.*
In 1903, Barnsley moved to Sapperton, and from then on designed and made all his furniture with his own hands.
(Mrs. F. L. Griggs Collection.)

Fig. 6 **The Pet Sideboard**, *designed by B. J. Talbert (1838–81) for Gillow's and shown at the London International Exhibition of 1871. Carved boxwood panels, long strap hinges.*
Originally a woodcarver, Talbert designed Art Furniture in a gothic style suited to the needs of the public, for several large commercial firms.
(Victoria and Albert Museum.)

Fig. 7 **Cabinet**, *designed by Ernest Gimson and hand made in his Cotswolds workshops, c.1900. Walnut with fielded panels emphasising the quality of the wood, black and white inlay, hand-made handles and simple chamfers.*
Despite his intention to produce plain, cheap pieces, Gimson achieved great sophistication on occasion. (Private Collection.)

1867. His furniture is light, graceful and far ahead of its time (Fig. 1), and in direct contrast to many of the heavy, gothic pieces and ebonised cabinets, consisting mainly of small shelves, bevelled mirrors and turned spindly supports, intended to display the knick-knacks so beloved of the Victorians.

Another active member of the Arts and Crafts Exhibition Society was W. R. Lethaby (1857–1931), whose work and ideas exerted great influence by virtue of the fact that he was the first Inspector of Art Schools for the London County Council; two years after, he was appointed Principal of the Central School of Arts and Crafts. Later he became the first Professor of Design at the Royal College of Art and was finally appointed Surveyor to the Fabric of Westminster Abbey.

A dedicated follower of William Morris and his principles, Lethaby was a member, with Gimson and Sidney Barnsley, of Kenton and Company. He designed furniture using a wide range of materials from unstained oak to polished inlaid mahogany pieces made by Morris & Company and large commercial firms. The range of his work is typical of the time and illustrates only too well the difficulties facing the historian. His best-known piece (Fig. 3) shows many of the best features of Arts and Crafts furniture, while the floral inlay, similarly used by Gimson and the Barnsleys in their earlier work, shows clearly the influence of Morris' designs.

Sir Ambrose Heal (1872–1959) was reared in the Arts and Crafts Movement. He was much influenced by the work produced at Sapperton and, while making some impressive exhibition pieces, his firm also manufactured extremely well-made, simple pieces, mostly in oak, for the ordinary market. In his autobiography, Sir Gordon Russell has paid tribute to the influence exerted on him by the work of Ernest Gimson and C. R. Ashbee. In recent years, these two firms of Heal's and Gordon Russell have set a standard envied throughout the world.

It is only comparatively recently that the furniture of the Arts and Crafts Movement has been appreciated for the influence it exerted on furniture-design in this century. Gimson's and the Barnsleys' well-designed furniture kept alive the best traditions of English craftsmanship, handing down Morris' ideas to the present.

some of the furniture produced by the Guild. Employing some fifty craftsmen, Ashbee encouraged co-operation between the crafts and, wherever possible, exploited the possibility of the piece to 'carry a message'.

The aims and ideals of the Guild and School exerted a great influence on the Continent (at one Vienna exhibition some fifty-two pieces were shown) but the furniture lacked the refinement of Gimson's pieces. Indeed, one Continental critic wrote: '. . . even in his decorative objects, which might be taken for domestic folk art . . . The furniture displayed here leaves the Viennese (with a few exceptions) fairly cool. The workmanship when compared with that of our own present-day craftsmen . . . is rather primitive'.

Ashbee complained bitterly of his designs being plagiarised by some of the big London firms, and there is little doubt that this contributed in no small measure to the demise of the Guild in 1909.

Perhaps the most astonishing furniture of this period was that designed by E. W. Godwin (1836–86). An architect, stage-designer and friend of Whistler, he was inspired by the displays of Japanese craftsmanship at the International Exhibitions in London and Paris, of 1862 and

MUSEUMS AND COLLECTIONS
Furniture of the Arts and Crafts Movement may be seen at the following:
GREAT BRITAIN

Bilbury, Glos.:	Arlington Mill
Cheltenham:	Art Gallery and Museum
Leicester:	The Newarke Houses Museum
London:	Victoria and Albert Museum
	William Morris Gallery, Walthamstow

FURTHER READING
The Anti-Rationalists by Sir James M. Richards London, 1973.
The Arts and Crafts Movement: A Study of its Sources, Ideals and Influence on Design Theory by Gillian Naylor, London, 1971.
Furniture Design Set Free by David Joel, London, 1969.
Nineteenth Century English Furniture by Elizabeth Aslin, London, 1962.

Art Nouveau Furniture

Fig. 1 **Furniture** by Victor Horta (1861–1947), c.1898.
In 1898, Horta built for himself the Maison Horta at 25 rue Américaine (now the Musée Horta), in which he indulged to the full his personal style. His deep belief that all the elements of a house should harmonise to form a unified whole led him to design every piece of furniture; and although most of the furniture has been removed from the house it has been to some extent replaced by similar pieces to retain the original atmosphere. The terra-cotta colour of the walls has been restored, and the petal-like forms of the canapé and chair blend perfectly with the striped marble table-top and its sinuous silver ornament.
(Musée Horta, Brussels.)

Fig. 2 **Chair** by V. Horta, c.1898. Oak re-covered with brown velvet. Made by Horta for his own house, this chair has now been restored to its original place.
(Musée Horta.)

Fig. 3 **Furniture** by Henry van de Velde (1863–1947), 1898. Mahogany. Unlike Horta, van de Velde relied entirely on line in his furniture, using no mouldings or other ornament. In this suite, the use of parallels and dynamic, structural curves is of the utmost importance.
(Galerie L'Ecuyer, Brussels.)

Fig. 4 **Double table** by Gustave Serrurier-Bovy (1858–1910), c.1900. Mahogany.
Serrurier never used any surface ornament on his furniture, not even paint. He felt that all ornamentation and fantasy belonged to the walls and window-panes of a room, leaving the controlled line of his furniture to speak for itself.
(Claude Simon Galerie d'Art, Namur.)

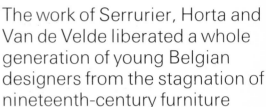

The work of Serrurier, Horta and Van de Velde liberated a whole generation of young Belgian designers from the stagnation of nineteenth-century furniture

At some point in the 1880s, Belgium became the centre of contemporary art, and in the field of the decorative arts supplanted England in the lead. After the revolution brought about in the concept and practice of the arts by Ruskin and William Morris, and later in the Aesthetic Movement, England turned away from Art Nouveau: 'The strange fact is that, having in effect created Art Nouveau in the 1870s, England abandoned and even shunned the style once it became a fashion' (E. Aslin in *The Aesthetic Movement*).

Owing to the increasing material potential of a country which was the most industrially advanced on the Continent, and to the new demands brought about by the rapid growth in population, the rising industrial bourgeoisie of Belgium was able to indulge in houses and furniture in the contemporary idiom.

Furniture designers wished to create a total effect based on a unity of style which would be distinct from the confusion and eclecticism which had preceded it. Like Morris and Viollet-le-Duc, they felt that art should be extended to the smallest detail of the environment. It was in this mood that *Les Vingt* (The Twenty), whose exhibitions had until then been devoted to the fine arts only, introduced the applied arts to their Salon of 1891. In 1893 two whole rooms were needed to contain them. That year the group was dissolved, but at the same time Octave Maus laid the foundations of *La Libre Esthétique*, which united every aspect of the arts – painting, sculpture, graphic art and the applied arts. Their first Salon opened on 17 February, 1894.

A social duty to introduce art into everyone's daily life

Artists now felt it a social duty to involve themselves in everyday problems and to introduce art into everyone's daily life. The return to unpretentious materials and true craftsmanship had been retained from the teachings of Morris and Viollet-le-Duc. If some designers accepted that, with machinery, their furniture would become more

233

widely distributed, the problem of mass production had not yet seriously arisen. Machinery helped the artisan without in any way influencing the process of manufacture; although furniture was produced in quantity, pieces were often individually finished and were not truly identical.

Gustave Serrurier-Bovy (1858–1910) and Henry van de Velde (1863–1947) used initially native woods such as beech and oak, and these were also used, although sparingly, by Victor Horta (1861–1947). Their furniture was also influenced by the import of woods from the Congo, the use of which was encouraged by Leopold II; fine-grained woods were favoured such as citrus and mahogany which allowed a clean line, as well as fluidity and precision of form.

The main characteristic of Belgian furniture of this period is its architectural quality, which shows itself in two different ways. First of all,

first salon of *La Libre Esthétique* in Brussels showed in its severity a marked divergence from the ideas of his predecessors. His encounter with the Paris *milieu* of 1900, where he decorated one of the restaurants of the Exhibition, the Pavillon Bleu, modified his style and signalled a new feeling for movement and the controlled curve. He was perhaps the first to break away from the era of workshop technology and he designed a suite of completely collapsible 'Silex' furniture in birchwood. Serrurier-Bovy never used artificial aids or paint, and kept all decorative fantasy and ornament for the walls or window-panes. A true follower of Viollet-le-Duc, whom he liked to invoke, he maintained rigorous standards of logic and solidity in every piece that left his workshops (Figs. 4 and 7).

Horta's furniture was based on the same principles as his architecture. He held that the form of the building should determine the form of the

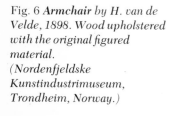

Fig. 5 *Magasin Habana* decorated by H. van de Velde, 1898. This tobacco-shop in Berlin is a superb example of the harmony imposed by Van de Velde on any interior he designed. The door-frames, wall-painting, shelves and even the incidental chairs blend to make a rhythmically patterned unit.

Fig. 6 *Armchair* by H. van de Velde, 1898. Wood upholstered with the original figured material. (Nordenfjeldske Kunstindustrimuseum, Trondheim, Norway.)

most of the furniture was designed to fit in with a particular architectural scheme and it does not often stand on its own merits. This is particularly true of the work of Horta, but applies also to that of Van de Velde and to a certain degree to pieces made by Serrurier. Second, furniture of this period can be called architectural because it is mainly the work of architects. Serrurier and Horta sought to achieve unity of spirit between architecture and furniture, and Van de Velde, a self-taught man, concentrated on the home and its decor; at the same time each of these designers showed a marked individualism. The curve of the furniture represents not so much the flower but the stem (Horta), or the smooth sinuosity of waves (Van de Velde).

A new feeling for movement and the controlled curve

Serrurier-Bovy was at first inspired by English design. He visited London and imported Liberty furniture and accessories for his shop in Liège. But, as early as 1895, the study that was exhibited in the

furniture, logic being the supreme consideration. For him, logic in this respect did not only concern matters of construction or function, although these were not forgotten; it also implied that each part should fit properly and harmoniously into the whole. His architect's office was sometimes transformed into a sculptor's studio for, when he was involved with a detail concerning architecture or furniture-design, he would first make a plaster maquette so as to provide a precise model for the craftsman. His careful handling of space is evident in even the smallest detail. The rhythm of curve and counter-curve which is typical of his work, and which often occurs in the rounded angles of his furniture, is underlined by a restrained and subtle use of moulding. Also, the tones of the woods he used are clearly designed as features in the general style of the house, and there is a harmony of mass and colour in the door-frames, panelling and painted decoration (Figs. 1 and 9). He was the uncompromising creator of a homogeneous and forceful style (Figs. 2 and 9).

Van de Velde approached the problem of furniture in an experimental manner. At his own home,

Bloemenwerf, the furniture has an almost medieval logic, although there are already signs of the flowing line which he was later to develop more strongly. He is the most linear of the designers, and did not use moulding. For him, the curve as an element of design was '*dynamographique et structural*'; he used it first as a series of parallels, and then to encircle larger areas which are edged with subtle carvings (Figs. 3, 6 and 8). The furniture he built in Germany was even lacquered in pure white. He thought deeply both about the form and construction of furniture and also about its emotive effects. He remained influenced at all times by the two-dimensional work that he had done as a painter.

A whole generation of young designers was now set free of the old prejudices and showed evidence of their talent and originality. Some are still comparatively unknown, among them Paul Hankar, Georges Antoine Peereboom and Georges Hobe. �

Fig. 7 **Wardrobe** by G. Serrurier-Bovy, c.1900. Light mahogany. This complex and supremely functional piece was exhibited at the Salon de la Societé des Beaux Arts in Bordeaux. (Mme. Soyeur Collection, Brussels.)

Fig. 8 **Furniture** by H. van de Velde, 1898. Mahogany. The chair, stand and picture-frame are part of the suite seen in Figure 3. In the frame is a Japanese print, highly fashionable around the year 1900. (Galerie L'Ecuyer.)

Fig. 9 **Chair** by V. Horta, c.1900. Carved light and dark woods, covered in leather. Note also the wall and floor designed by Horta. (Musée Horta.)

MUSEUMS AND COLLECTIONS

There is very little Belgian Art Nouveau Furniture in public collections, but examples may be seen at the following:

BELGIUM
Brussels: Galerie L'Ecuyer
              Galerie d'Art
              Musée Horta

SWITZERLAND
Zurich: Kunstgewerkemuseum

FURTHER READING

Art Nouveau: Revolution in Interior Design by Rossana Bossoglia, London, 1973.
Le Monde de Henry van de Veldé by A. M. Hammacher, Paris, 1967.
Art Nouveau by R. Schmützler, London, 1964.

235

Glass

The beauty and luxury of glass was appreciated by both the Mesopotamians and the Egyptians at least 3,500 years ago, but exactly who uncovered the secrets of making it is lost in legend. The Egyptians first had shiny glazes on their beads and by 1500 B.C. were producing containers by winding threads of molten glass around a central core. Centuries afterwards, probably in the more sophisticated Roman period, the technique of glass blowing was developed.

Glass is made of silica (sand) mixed with a variety of fluxes such as potash, soda or lime and heated at a high temperature until the mixture (the batch) melts, producing a thick, plastic liquid. The molten glass (the metal) can be poured into a mould, blown, pressed and manipulated into any number of forms. Each type of flux produces a different characteristic in the finished glass. The purer the raw materials, the finer and clearer the end product. The addition of minerals to the batch produces coloured glass.

One of the oldest ways to shape glass is by pouring it into a mould, but after the blow pipe was invented, perhaps 2,000 years ago, glass could be blown in moulds, a time-saving method of producing utilitarian objects.

The tools needed to make free blown glass have changed little over the centuries. A blob of molten glass (a gather) is withdrawn from the furnace on the end of a long, hollow pipe. The glassmaker blows into the pipe, expanding the gather into a hollow, spherical form. A cylindrical shape can be made at this stage by swinging the gather at the end of the pipe. The vessel in the process of being made is then transferred to a long rod called a pontil rod (or punty) for further work and frequently reheated at the furnace to retain its plasticity. The glassmaker constantly rolls the pontil rod back and forth along the extended arms of his special seat (the chair) as he continues to fashion the piece or smoothes it on a special slab, (the marver). Glass in the process of formation can be cut with shears, twisted, pulled, bent and tooled into the desired shape. As work progresses, tiny gathers of metal are withdrawn from the furnace and applied to the piece as stems, handles, feet and other decorative devices.

The finished piece is cracked off the pontil rod – a rough spot can often be detected underneath old glass – and placed in an annealing oven where it is allowed to cool and harden very slowly. At the end of the process, the glass is ready to be engraved, decorated and polished.

Crude window glass and bottles were commonly produced at glasshouses throughout Europe in the mediaeval period, but artistic glassmaking stemmed from the industry on the Venetian island of Murano, which was firmly established by the thirteenth century. For the next three hundred years, the finest glass of the time was made here in a tightly controlled monopoly. The Venetians used opaque *lattimo* glass for their splen-

did goblets and ornaments which reflected the decorative trends of the Renaissance in elaborate enamelling. By the sixteenth century, when Venetian glassmaking was at its peak, exquisite *crystallo* was created, a glass so fragile and delicate that its beauty lay in its transparency and form alone. Magnificent winged goblets with slender trailed decorations were among the most cherished objects in Europe. Another Venetian innovation was *lattacinio*, a sheer glass with the appearance of lace made by enclosing opaque white glass threads in the clear metal.

Eventually, the secrets of Venetian glasshouses spread as some of the craftsmen were able to leave Murano and settle elsewhere. In the seventeenth century, forest glasshouses in Bohemia were making distinctive goblets and beakers decorated with engravings or colourful enamelled peasant motifs. Coloured glass was also made in Bohemia and in 1674, the famous ruby glass appeared.

The English glass industry received a boost at this time from George Ravenscroft, a seventeenth-century glassmaker who was attempting to improve the quality of his Venetian-inspired wares. Ravenscroft applied a Roman technique of adding lead oxide to the batch to produce a glass that was extremely hard, clear and brilliant making it suitable for deep cutting and wheel engraving.

Ravenscroft's 'glass of lead' was in wide use by the eighteenth century for the finest English glass including elegant wine glasses with their handsome assortment of baluster, knopped and air twisted stems.

One of the first American industries was undoubtedly glassmaking, but none of the early glasshouses survived for long mainly because of the lack of skilled craftsmen in the Colonies. It was some one hundred and thirty years after the first settlement that glassmaking became a successful venture. Caspar Wistar, a Pennsylvania German buttonmaker, began producing his bluish green 'South Jersey tradition' glass in 1739 and he was followed by Henry William Stiegel who made flint glass to rival imported English tablewares and coloured perfume bottles blown in patterned moulds.

The nineteenth century was an era of great innovation and expansion in the glass industry everywhere. Glasshouses in France, Germany, England and elsewhere produced opaque coloured glass that resembled porcelain in appearance. French factories such as St. Louis and Baccarat developed *millefiori* ('a thousand flowers') glass for vases and paperweights and the unique opaline wares.

A major technological advance was made in the 1820's when a machine for pressing glass in decorative moulds was patented in America. For the first time, mass-produced patterned glass closely resembling hand-cut crystal was available to a wide market. Catering to the new demands for elaborate glass, Bohemian factories developed a more sophisticated style. Colour was its hallmark and pieces that were in the ornate fashionable taste of the day were made in quantity.

The demand of the nineteenth-century public for elaborate glass led to the production of art glass, created when chemical processes were applied to produce exotic and unusual finishes. American factories, whose artistic endeavours in this field rivalled those in France, made a wide variety of art glass with names like Peach Blow, Wild Rose, Amberina and Burmese. In Britain there was a revival of the sophisticated Roman technique of cameo cutting, demanding the combined skills of glassmaker and carver. Everywhere, imagination and ingenuity were applied to glassmaking.

Glass was a perfect medium for the fluid movements of Art Nouveau. Emile Gallé produced outstanding ornamental glass in this style and inspired others like the great American designer and glassmaker, Louis Comfort Tiffany. Long-fascinated with the qualities of ancient glass, Tiffany created iridescent glass of extraordinary beauty in his Favrile pieces whose patterns of peacock feathers, tulips, lilies and dragonflies so perfectly reflect the asymmetrical yet natural lines of Art Nouveau.

Venetian Glass

At a moment when superb skill was turned for the first time to the production of secular objects, glass became one of the most important luxuries.

Museum Photo

The glass industry in Europe – for the production of glass other than window glass – began in Venice. The Venetians established a highly developed industry with a vast export trade which virtually dominated the rest of Europe until the middle of the seventeenth century and all subsequent development in European glass stems from the Venetian tradition.

Venice, a great trading nation geographically situated between Western Europe and Asia, with trading stations all over the Near East, had a flourishing glass industry with a considerable trade by the thirteenth century; but Venetian glass is not datable before the fifteenth century. The finest period is from 1500 to 1550.

Venetian, like Roman, glass is a light and thin-walled soda glass, made from raw materials obtained by the Venetians through their trade. It consists of soda ash, imported either from Spain or Egypt, and white pebbles from the Po or the Ticino, together with lime in the form of powdered marble or crushed sea shells to give this very delicate substance added stability. By the end of the tenth century there were probably glass-workers in Venice making simple glass objects such as bottles and flasks, possibly with the help of craftsmen from Byzantium or Syria where there were well-established glass industries at this period.

In the thirteenth century the glass industry became a monopoly of the Venetian Republic and in 1292 the glasshouses were established on the island of Murano, where they still exist today. This move was made not only to avoid the risk of fire in Venice itself, where all glasshouses had to be not less than fifteen paces from any dwelling-place, but also to

Fig. 1 *Illumination from **The Travels of Sir John Mandeville** (published between 1357 and 1371) illustrating early glass-making, Flemish or German, fifteenth century. (British Museum, London.)*

Fig. 2 **Green glass enamelled goblet with portrait head in cartouche and gilded foot,** *Venetian, c.1480. Height 6¾ ins. Early Venetian glass illustrates forcibly the splendours of renaissance Italy. Magnificent gilding and enamelling to resemble gems was common on such goblets which were often made to commemorate a betrothal or marriage. Great artists of the day were sometimes commissioned to decorate these glasses. (Victoria and Albert Museum London.)*

Fig. 3 **Enamelled beaker decorated with two Mermen,** *Venetian, c.1490. Height 5 ins. Renaissance motifs were commonly painted on drinking-glasses, whose basic shapes were often influenced by designs for silver. It was not until the sixteenth century that specific glass shapes were developed. (Victoria and Albert Museum.)*

the Venetian glass-workers could produce blue, green, purple and opaque white glass, and the latter was probably used in the first recorded experiment in the making of European porcelain, by Maestro Antonio di San Simone, in 1470. Some of the glass was made in imitation of semi-precious stones, such as onyx, agate and chalcedony (Fig. 4), but the great feature of fifteenth-century Venetian glass is the use of enamelled decoration (Figs. 2 and 5).

Enamelling on glass first appeared in Venice in the mid-fifteenth century. Great use was made of dark backgrounds of coloured glass to display the beauty of the enamel decoration, which was painted in fusible enamel and fired by baking in a small oven. This is an Islamic technique of the thirteenth and fourteenth centuries, but it probably developed independently in Venice from the use of enamel on metalwork. The decoration on enamelled glass had similarities with contemporary renaissance decorative motifs and was used not only in a pictorial fashion but also in coloured spots of enamel, giving a gem-like effect comparable with the decoration on contemporary goldsmiths' work (Fig. 5). It was mainly used, in its pictorial form, for the decoration of goblets and chalices, often commissioned to commemorate a betrothal or a marriage, and there is a very strong influence between this form of decoration and contemporary painting (Fig. 3). Vivarini, the early Venetian painter, probably did some pictorial decoration on glass, but this type of elaborate decoration was comparatively short-lived and in the sixteenth century it rarely appears.

The Venetian glass industry reached its height in the sixteenth century. There was enormous prosperity and the huge export from Venice dominated the rest of Europe. In this period of increased trade and, consequently, of increased wealth, when the ideas of the Renaissance were spreading from Italy to the rest of Europe, glass became not only a highly desirable luxury, but also a great status symbol; the finest pieces were sent from Venice to the princely Courts and rich merchants' houses. A great number of the pieces were not made for practical use, but were collected by connoisseurs and used as display objects by those who wished to emphasise their fashionable taste – and their wealth – in the eyes of society. In the sixteenth century, the increased development in the technical skill of the Venetian glass-workers led to the vast expansion in trade. Shapes specifically suitable for glass were evolved, and there was less dependence on shapes of metalwork and ceramics, as previously.

Venetian glass of the sixteenth century is fanciful and fantastic, much lighter in design and far less massive in shape and size than glass of the fifteenth century. A glass similar in appearance to rock crystal, called *cristallo*, one of the most prized objects of the century, was created and became immediately fashionable. There was very little surface decoration and use of coloured glass at this period. What enamelled decoration there was, was carried out on a clear ground and was mostly made for the export market. Glass objects appear in Venetian paintings, showing the luxury and splendour of Venetian life. Mirror glasses were also made from the beginning of the century and a French traveller in 1584 writes of glass musical instruments.

The *cristallo* developed in Venice in the sixteenth century was probably discovered about 1450 and was often tinged with a pale grey colour. This was

establish a state industry so rigidly controlled that the establishment of glasshouses elsewhere could be prevented. The Venetian glass-workers were organised in an elaborate guild system and were virtually prisoners of the state, with very restricted freedom of movement. They were forbidden to emigrate from Venice on pain of death. The export of glass-making materials and of cullet, the broken and waste glass, was also forbidden so as to keep the secret of glass-making in Venice. Glasshouses were nonetheless established in Bologna and Ferrara in the thirteenth century, and in the sixteenth and seventeenth centuries there was a widespread establishment of glasshouses on the Venetian pattern elsewhere in Europe.

Early Venetian glass was simple – jugs, carafes and bottles – but in the fifteenth century, with the great impetus of the Renaissance, glass became one of the most splendid and elaborate art forms of the period. Fifteenth-century Venetian glass was heavy and massive in shape, closely influenced by contemporary silver, and it was not only brilliant in colour but also a vehicle for magnificent and grandiose decoration. The splendour of renaissance Italy is illustrated very forcibly in these early pieces of Venetian glass. By the end of the fifteenth century

Fig. 4 *Ewer in imitation chalcedony*, Venetian, c.1500. Height 12 ins.
By the late fifteenth century, Venetian glass-makers had reached a high degree of technical proficiency. They were able to produce many different effects, one of which was the imitation of semi-precious stones such as onyx, agate and chalcedony.
(*Victoria and Albert Museum.*)

Fig. 5 *Cup and cover* with enamelled decoration, Venetian, late-fifteenth century. Height 18 in.
Although most fifteenth-century enamelling was done on dark-coloured glass backgrounds, this is a fine example of the use of cristallo.
(*Victoria and Albert Museum.*)

Fig. 6 *Nef, or boat-shaped ewer*, attributed to Armenia Vivarini, Venetian, mid-sixteenth century.
Armenia Vivarini was a descendant of the painter Antonio Vivarini. This piece is typical of the fantastic and elaborate articles which were made in glass in the sixteenth century to grace the tables of the rich throughout Europe.
(*Museo Vetrario.*)

Fig. 7 *Reliquary of cristallo with a high foot sprayed with gold and enamelled decoration*, Venetian, late-fifteenth or early-sixteenth century.
Glass used for religious purposes during the Renaissance followed quite closely the forms of table-glass.
(*Museo Vetrario, Murano.*)

Fig. 8 *Casket with lid of white net glass*, Venetian, mid-sixteenth century.
Glass-making was at its height in the sixteenth century.
Magnificent pieces of vetro de trina or lace-glass such as this casket were made not just for practical purposes, but for collectors who desired them for their beauty and intricacy.
Shapes were devised to show off the material to perfection, as in the knops on the top of this piece.
(*Museo Vetrario.*)

Fig. 9 *Hexagonal bottle with threads of milk glass on exterior*, Italian, late sixteenth or early seventeenth century.
(*Museo Vetrario.*)

Angelo Hornak

dissipated in the sixteenth century by blowing the glass more thinly. Refined by the use of manganese, *cristallo* was the most famous glass made in Venice and was not allowed to be sold by pedlars or by stall-holders. It is mentioned as being displayed by the glass-workers at the Ascension Day Fair in Saint Mark's Square.

An air of fantasy in keeping with contemporary design

Venetian *cristallo* was so fragile that it could not be refired for decorative purposes because of the risk of distortion and so, in the sixteenth century, a great emphasis was placed upon elaborate shapes and upon decorative borders, stems and handles, applied to the glass itself. The only other form of decoration to be used was diamond-point engraving – never very popular in Venice and rarely figurative, as in English glass of the period – and some fine applied gilding. *Cristallo* was used to great effect to create fantastic and elaborate articles, such as the magnificent *nefs*, or boat-shaped ewers, which graced the tables of renaissance Europe (Fig. 6). Objects such as these were highly desirable, not only for their beauty, but also for their originality and for their air of fantasy which is very much in keeping with contemporary design.

The Venetians also produced *latticinio* (reticulated, filigree or lace-glass), first mentioned in its most elaborate form in 1540. This is glass with the incorporation of an opaque or coloured glass thread used in the metal and it involves a highly complicated and difficult process. In its most complex form, as *vetro de trina*, or lace-glass (Venice had a world-famous lace industry), it was evolved to produce fantastic and elaborate objects for the purpose of display (Fig. 8), but it was also used, in its simpler form as a common type of decoration in glass in the late sixteenth and early seventeenth centuries (Fig. 9).

Another elaborate form of glass which appears in sixteenth century Venice is ice-glass, or crackle-glass, which first appeared in the middle of the century and which was a very short-lived fashion.

The discovery of the trade route to the East by Vasco da Gama in 1497–98 had a long term effect on Venetian trade generally. With the rise of other glass industries in Europe, Venice was beginning to decline as the paramount influence upon European glass by the end of the sixteenth century. As early as the mid-fifteenth century a serious rival industry had appeared at L'Altare, near Genoa. Glass-workers from Normandy had established a glass-workers' guild there to spread the secret of the craft and to establish new glasshouses. Their wares were similar in type and style to Venetian glass. Throughout the sixteenth century Venetian domination was constantly being eroded by the proliferation of glasshouses making Venetian-inspired glass, the most important being that of Antwerp, founded by Venetian workmen in 1541.

It is in the development of drinking-glasses that Venice had her greatest and most long-lasting influence. The shapes, developed from the early beakers and goblets, had a profound effect upon the glass that was made outside Murano until the middle of the seventeenth century, when individual national styles began to appear. The exaggerated shapes of the stems of Venetian glasses, the moulded baluster stems of the sixteenth century and the seventeenth-century winged stems with their elaborate trailed decoration, in particular, had enormous influence. 🕸

MUSEUMS AND COLLECTIONS

Collections of Italian glass are on view at the following:

AUSTRIA
Vienna: Österreichisches Museum für Angewandte Kunst
CZECHOSLOVAKIA
Prague: Museum of Decorative Art
FRANCE
Paris: Musée du Petit Palais
GREAT BRITAIN
Birmingham: Art Gallery
London: British Museum
Victoria and Albert Museum
St. Helen's: Pilkington Glass Museum
U.S.A.
New York: Corning Museum of Glass
Metropolitan Museum of Art
Washington, D.C.: Smithsonian Institution
WEST GERMANY
Cologne: Kunstgewerbemuseum
Munich: Bayerisches National-museum
West Berlin: Kunstgewerbemuseum

It is also possible to visit the factories in Murano, to watch the manufacture of modern Venetian glass. The factories are open every day except Sunday.

FURTHER READING

Masterpieces of Glass, British Museum, London, 1968. The catalogue for the 8th International Congress of Glass held at the British Museum.
Italian Blown Glass from Ancient Rome to Venice, by G. Mariacher, London, 1961.
Glass, by W. B. Honey, Victoria and Albert Museum Handbook I, London, 1946.

Early German and Bohemian Glass

Fig. 1 *Goblet and cover engraved by Gottfried Spiller (died 1721), Potsdam, c.1700.*
The Potsdam factory was founded in 1674 by the Elector Frederick William of Brandenburg. The engraved decoration is of bacchanalia.
(Victoria and Albert Museum, London.)

Museum Photo

Throughout the seventeenth century, a distinctive national style was emerging in German and Bohemian glass. New techniques of cutting, enamelling and colouring placed these exquisite wares among the most prized of all Europe

The swelling curves and irregular protuberances of the baroque movement found expression in the interiors of secular and, in particular, ecclesiastical buildings enriched by painted ceilings, intricate metalwork and gilt statues in voluminous, flowing robes. To set off this new splendour, colourful stained glass was ousted and supplanted by a plain, colourless window-pane permitting maximum penetration of undiluted light.

In the early years of the seventeenth century sweeping changes were made in Italian-inspired glass-making in Germany and Bohemia. Venetian and medieval Frankish-Rhenish influences which flourished side by side were gradually allotted their proper niche in the glass-maker's craft, thus encouraging the emergence of a distinctive national style.

Due to the crippling drain on natural and economic resources, and the devastation brought about by the unrestrained violence and plunder committed by armies and foreign mercenaries during the Thirty Years' War, the transition was slow, and remnants of medieval beliefs, superstitions and artistic concepts lingered on.

A significant period in Bohemian glass-making came during the later sixteenth century, when the nobility sought to augment feudal revenues by establishing glass-works on their vast and amply forested estates. This enterprise benefited from an influx of German glass-makers who could no longer tolerate the astronomical price of essential wood fuel brought about by the rapid expansion of the native mining industry. Privileges were granted to these immigrants who grew prosperous, inter-married and soon formed the nucleus of industry.

It was usual practice, if not indeed obligatory, for the continental craftsman to fill in the immediate years after serving his apprenticeship – the *Lehrjahre* – with a period of travel – the *Wanderjahre* – a perfect insurance against stagnation. A somewhat different aspect of the glass trade was represented by the glass-pedlar, who wandered from town to town selling his wares. One such glass-hawker, setting out with his heavy walking-stick, is shown in a woodcut from Georgius Agricola's famous book, *De Re Metallica* (Fig. 10). A huge contraption on the pedlar's back holds glasses of all sorts packed in straw. Glass-maker's tools are lying about untidily, but the focal point in the illustration is the beehive-shaped glass furnace subdivided into the firing chamber, founding chamber and annealing chamber. An open door allows a glimpse of a tavern-like service counter where the glass-worker would quench his thirst – most likely free of charge – a provision still observed in some glasshouses in the nineteenth century.

The glass-hawker was often trained as an engraver and glass-painter

The glass-hawker was often trained as an engraver and glass-painter, well able to decorate a customer's purchase to order. The Bohemian glass-seller Georg Francis Kreybich made about thirty journeys between 1683 and 1721, which took him all over Europe, including Murano and Moscow. The diaries he kept are extremely informative and entertaining.

The mountains and forests of Bohemia, Silesia, Moravia and, on the German side, Bavaria, Thuringia, Saxony and Franconia, were ideal locations for the establishment of glasshouses. Silica, soda (or potash) and lime are the main components of glass. In the forest areas there was an abundance of beechwood supplying fuel and potash, and most other essential raw materials were present in rocks and soil. Apart from window-glass, forest glasshouses produced hollow glass in a thick metal of greenish colour and bubbly consistency.

Fig. 9 *Humpen presented to Caspar Steiner of Volpersdorf by Christian Preussler, Bohemian, 1680. Decorated with enamelling. The decoration depicts the glassworks at Zeilberg. The Preusslers were a large family of glass-makers and this Humpen would have been made in the Zeilberg works which they owned. (Museum of Arts and Crafts, Prague.)*

Gabriel Urbanek

Venise', comparable to specimens made at Verzelini's London glasshouse. However, it is in seventeenth-century Prague that the art of glass engraving and cutting by the wheel received a new and unparalleled significance. The abundance of rock-crystal and other minerals caused the art of the lapidary to flourish, and the art-loving monarchs, Rudolf II at Prague, Wilhelm V of Bavaria and Christian II of Saxony, vied with each other in engaging the finest artisans from far and near. At the Bavarian Court, the work of famous Milanese lapidaries had a significant influence on the Strasbourg cutter Valentin Drausch, who may well have been the master of that great artist innovator, Caspar Lehman (1570–1622).

By way of Munich and Saxony, Lehman arrived in Prague in 1588, already an experienced cutter of gems, rock-crystal and glass. Lehman's astonishing achievements in transferring lapidary techniques to the thin, hard brittleness of Venetian *cristallo* represents one of the marvels of artistic glass-making and when a robust glass metal was at last developed successfully, Lehman had been dead for over half a century. Early cutting techniques were shallow and broad, but Lehman's work has a vigorous quality far advanced of his time, and his designs were frequently based on contemporary Flemish and Italian engravings. After a quarrel with the Emperor's adjutant, Lehman left Prague in 1606 to work at the Court in Dresden, but returned in 1608. He was knighted by the appreciative Rudolf, and in 1609 was granted a monopoly for the application of glass engraving. After his death, the monopoly was inherited by a gifted pupil, Georg Schwanhardt.

The effects of the Thirty Years' War and the Counter-Reformation prompted Schwanhardt to settle in Nuremberg, a free city, and lay the foundation for a flourishing centre of glass decorators and engravers. A number of Lehman's pupils established workshops elsewhere, as for instance Caspar Schindler in Dresden and Jan Hess in Frankfurt. The technique of polishing parts of the matt-cut was one of Schwanhardt's innovations which greatly enhanced the reflective property of the glass surface.

Nuremberg goblets often show fine engraving, and it is during this period that the glass artist begins to add his signature to his work. Of Lehman, we have only one signed specimen, a conical beaker dated 1605 (Fig. 8), with shallow engraving and deeper undercutting, representing allegorical figures and coats of arms, although several engraved panels and glass vessels attributed to him have survived.

By about 1660–70, a robust colourless potash-lime glass had been perfected, and cutting and engraving became bolder with heavy wheel engraving in high relief and intaglio (*Hoch und Tiefschnitt*). Enamelling was still popular, but became increasingly confined to domestic or household utility ware and of suitably less refined workmanship and character. Engraved and cut glass, however, joined the ranks of the aristocracy, and was favoured by the nobility and the wealthy *élite*. The finest work was produced in Silesia during the late seventeenth and early eighteenth centuries in the manner of rock-crystal engraving, which is also echoed in the form of the vessel, as for instance in the boat- or shell-shaped specimens reminiscent of the Italian Renaissance. The decorative treatment and form of Silesian glass expresses a horizontal movement as opposed to the strictly vertical design concept in Bohemian cut glass of the period.

During the second half of the seventeenth century, the glass decorators emerge as a group of professional artists, removed from the influence and conditions of the glasshouse. Guilds were formed for glass-painters, engravers and a number of allied sections, with the earliest guild established in 1661 by Count Johann Oktavian Kinsky, in Chřibská (Kreibitz).

Several German glasshouses such as Kassel, Potsdam and the Lauensteiner Hütte, were greatly influenced by the development of Ravenscroft's lead crystal. However, early attempts at applying the English formula were frequently affected by the glass disease of crizzling.

The Potsdam factory was founded in 1674 by the Elector Frederick William of Brandenburg. Here, Johann Kunckel, a man of great scientific and artistic talent, developed his famous *Gold-rubin* (gold-ruby) glass, obtained by the addition of gold and a complicated firing technique. Green and blue glass was also produced at Potsdam, and though plain facet cutting was preferred for coloured vessels, some of the finest glass engravers such as Gottfried Spiller and Martin Winter (d.1702) were employed by this factory (Fig. 1). Kunckel's book, *Ars Vitraria Experimentalis* (1678), forecasts a revival of the early Christian *fondi d'oro* glass, and Kunckel himself made use of gold-leaf in glass decoration.

The transition from a pure blown-glass style to a cut-crystal style swept aside the two hundred year old Venetian monopoly within a few decades. This was to a large extent due to the ability and inspiration of the seventeenth-century Bohemian and German glass-worker who emerges as an individual glass artist, quick to appreciate and interpret the infinite possibilities of his chosen material.

Fig. 12 *Reichsadler* (*Imperial eagle*) *by Hans Burgkmair (1473–1531), 1510. Woodcut.*

Fig. 13 *Reichsadler* glass showing the use of the Imperial Eagle motif. Enamelled. (Victoria and Albert Museum.)

Fig. 10 **Glass-blowing,** *woodcut from* De Re Metallica *by Georgius Agricola, Basle, 1556.*

Mansell Collection

Fig. 11 **Goblet** *cut in facets and engraved with a portrait of Leopold I, Bohemia, c.1700. (Museum of Applied Art, Prague.)*

Museum Photo

MUSEUMS AND COLLECTIONS

German and Bohemian glass of the sixteenth and seventeenth centuries may be seen at the following:

GREAT BRITAIN
Cambridge:	Fitzwilliam Museum
Edinburgh:	Royal Scottish Museum
Lincoln:	Usher Art Gallery
London:	British Museum
	Victoria and Albert Museum

CZECHOSLOVAKIA
Jablonc:	Museum of Glass
Prague:	Museum of Applied Art
	Museum of Decorative Art

GERMANY
Berlin:	Kunstgewerbemuseum
Cologne:	Kunstgewerbemuseum
Munich:	Bayerisches Nationalmuseum
Nuremberg:	Germanisches Nationalmuseum

U.S.A.
New York:	Corning Museum
Ohio:	Toledo Museum of Art

FURTHER READING

Bohemian Engraved Glass by Zuzana Pesatová, Prague, 1968.
German Enamelled Glass by A. von Saldern, New York, 1963.
Glass in Czechoslovakia by Karel Hettes, Prague, 1958.
Das Glass by Robert Schmidt, Vienna, 1922.

Early Looking Glasses

*Fig. 1 **Looking-glass**, 1730–40. This piece suggests the manner of Benjamin Goodison, carver to George II. Carved and gilt wood. (Sotheby's, London.)*

*Fig. 2 **Looking-glass in silver frame**, engraved with the cipher of William III, c.1697. (Windsor Castle. By kind permission of H.M. the Queen.)*

Of rather crude construction when production began, English looking-glasses progressed to become works of art in their own right, with frames of great complexity and beauty

Mirrors of the early Middle Ages were usually polished gold, silver or bronze plates; in the fifteenth and early sixteenth centuries steel was added to the range of reflecting metal surfaces. Although there had been earlier experiments with metal-backed glass, the results were so dark, spotted and distorted that looking-glasses were not serious rivals to polished metal plates until after the establishment of the specialized Italian glass-houses at Murano, early in the sixteenth century. Not until the nineteenth century did the term 'mirror' oust 'looking-glass' or 'glass' in common parlance.

Early glasses were usually small toilet mirrors

Inventories of Henry VIII's possessions show that he owned several small, imported 'glasses to look in', but in some instances there is a contradiction, because the 'glasses' are specifically described as being made of steel. Until the manufacture of English looking-glasses commenced in the seventeenth century, the majority of those who could afford mirrors of any kind still used small plates of polished metal.

Early in the reign of James I, one of the King's favourites, Sir Robert Mansell, obtained a patent for making looking-glasses, and brought over 'many expert strangers from foreign parts beyond the seas to instruct the natives of this Kingdom in the making of looking-glass plates'. In 1620, the importation of foreign glass was prohibited. When Mansell's patent was renewed in 1623, he was able to state that at his manufactory in Southwark he provided employment for five hundred people in the 'making, grinding and foyling of looking-glasses'. Although the ban on imported mirrors was lifted in 1624 it did not prevent Mansell from

expanding his manufacture to other glasshouses in provincial towns in England, Wales and Scotland.

None of these early glasses appears to have survived, but as they were of blown glass and of poor reflective quality, due to lack of skill in grinding and polishing, they would have distorted the image. Moreover, as they were mostly small toilet mirrors, they were doubtless scrapped when plate glass became available. This was after 1663, when Charles II granted a patent to George Villiers, second Duke of Buckingham (1628–1687), to set up his glasshouse at Vauxhall, London.

In 1664, imported mirrors were once more banned and the Worshipful Company of Glass-Sellers and Looking-Glass Makers was incorporated. Thence mirrors, although remaining valuable, expanded their usage from the realm of toilet requisites into that of luxury furnishing and interior decoration. On 19 September, 1676, John Evelyn, visiting Vauxhall, wrote in his diary that they made 'looking-glasses far larger and better than any that come from Venice'. Although this was doubtless true Vauxhall plates seldom exceeded three feet in length, and examples sometimes less than two feet long were described in inventories as 'great glasses'.

Variety in colour and rich elaboration were much to the fore

To make these expensive luxuries more important, it was usual to enhance them by wide and elaborate frames, further increased in height by crestings. Two rarities (Figs. 4 and 6), both dating from the 1670s, would probably have ranked as great glasses, although the frames enclose glasses less than three feet in height. The example in Fig. 6 has the frame covered with fabric embroidered with Stuart stump-work (relief needlework), which displays the usual naïve lack of proportion between human figures, birds, beasts, insects, fruit and flowers common to textile work of the period. What makes it possibly unique is the pristine freshness of its colouring, due to its still being in the original oak outer case and enclosed by a pair of doors with pierced brass hinges and mounts. Some wide frames of this

Fig. 3 **Mirrored cabinet,**
probably by John Channon,
London, c.1735. Mahogany
with gilt-brass mounts.
This is a fine example of the
mirrored furniture which
reflected day or candlelight.
(Victoria and Albert Museum.)

Fig. 4 **Looking-glass,** *1670–80.*
Carved and silvered wood.
This rare and elaborately carved
frame displays to perfection
the late seventeenth-century
love of ornate furniture.
(Victoria and Albert Museum.)

Museum Photo

Museum Photo

Fig. 5 **Looking-glass,** *1670–80.*
The frame of straw-work.
Although many people think that
straw-work was done only by
French prisoners of war in the
Napoleonic period, it was in fact
a craft hobby of amateurs much
earlier. The pieces of straw were
cut out and attached to the
wooden base like elaborate
marquetry.
(Victoria and Albert Museum.)
248

period, covered in flat needlework or stump-work,
were additionally ornamented with scalloped outlines (Fig. 5). This example is even rarer than
stitchery, being an early example of straw-work
decoration, on a grey silk ground.

The range of wooden mirror-frames available in
the last quarter of the seventeenth century was
vast, both in covering materials and in finishing
techniques; in accordance with the fashion,
naturalism in the depiction of motifs, variety in
colour and rich elaboration were much to the fore,
irrespective of the medium chosen.

In a period of great liking for high-relief,
naturalistic carving, the presiding genius was
Grinling Gibbons, who executed beautiful work
within the orderly framework of Sir Christopher
Wren's decorative architectural schemes. In
domestic furniture, such as mirror-frames,
Gibbons' technically brilliant compositions are

often too large in scale, and they tend to overpower
the small plates enclosed within the complex of
delicately carved fruit and flowers, or shells and
seaweed, accompanied by chubby *amorini*.
A frame which incorporates many of the usual
motifs employed by Gibbons, but treated in a more
formal manner, is shown in Fig. 4. This frame,
the wood finished with burnished silvering,
incorporates in the cresting the arms of Gough of
Perry Hall, Staffordshire, granted in 1664. It
exemplifies how a plate only about thirty-four
inches high was doubled in height by framing and
cresting.

Charles I collected Old Masters; his son's
predilection for young mistresses with extravagant
tastes engendered a demand not only for silvered
furniture but also for furniture covered in repoussé
and engraved silver plate. Nell Gwynn possessed not
only silver framed 'great looking-glasses' but also

Fig. 6 Looking-glass, 1670–80. The frame of stump-work. Being still in the original oak outer case, the coloured silks of this charming piece have retained their original freshness. Private Collection, formerly in the Fred Scull Collection.)

Author's Photo

Fig. 7 Looking-glass, second quarter of the eighteenth century. Walnut veneer with parcel-gilt carved ornament. Becoming gradually heavier in their detailing, and using mahogany veneer, architectural mirrors of this sort were made until the middle of the century. Sotheby's.)

Sotheby's Photo

an ornamentally embossed silver bedstead. Furthermore, she vied with the Duchess of Portsmouth in the ostentatious extravagance of a mirror-panelled room. John Evelyn was most indignant: in September 1675 he recorded: 'I was casually shewed the Dutchesse of Portsmouth's splendid appartment at White-hall, luxuriously furnished, and with ten times the richnesse and glory beyond the Queene's; such massy pieces of plate, whole tables, & stands of incredible value'. The description probably refers to a type of dressing-suite consisting of a wall mirror above a table flanked by a pair of *guéridons* or *torchères* – tall, floor-standing candlestands; such suites were made in all the fashionable finishes, but in the course of time the four matching pieces have usually become separated.

A somewhat larger table was also used, on which could be arranged the silver toilet set, which included among its many pieces a pair of candlesticks and a strutted mirror. The majority of these sets were repoussé with or without chasing, but a few were quieter in taste, being chased only with *chinoiserie* decoration.

At Windsor Castle there is a silver-framed mirror of the architecturally controlled style of the William and Mary period (Fig. 2). Dating from about 1697, the frame, with its pediment bearing the royal arms and cipher of William III, brings the total height to seven feet, six inches. It was presented to the King by the Corporation of London.

Other frames in vogue towards the end of the seventeenth and in the early eighteenth centuries were of japanned wood, of framing overlaid with strips of bevelled silver plate and, probably most popular of all, the convex or 'cushion' types, which were frequently veneered with walnut, olivewood, ebony or laburnum; they were usually surmounted by a fretted cresting. Additionally, many frames were decorated with floral marquetry, following the general fashion in furniture. First came formal isolated marquetry panels. These were followed by continuous and more naturalistic floral marquetry, sometimes including ivory jasmine flowers and stained green foliage. Finally, at the end of the century, came the much quieter arabesque marquetry.

With the opening of Queen Anne's reign, several comparatively fresh trends were apparent. Mirrors were now considered necessary decorative features in all important rooms and their valuable contribution to reflecting both daylight and candlelight was given due consideration in positioning. The regularity of eighteenth-century domestic architecture and the usual proportions of windows and width of pier walls between them brought about considerable standardisation in the placing of furniture, particularly in rooms used for formal entertainment. In a room with two windows there were three pier walls, and in a room with three windows there were four.

Pier walls were dark, not only because of their position, but also because of heavy window draperies. It became customary, therefore, to hang long and decoratively framed mirrors on pier walls, frequently with matching console-tables below. To reflect more light, matching mirrors might be provided on the wall opposite. If the chimney-piece came opposite the window, it would probably have a mirrored overmantel; if at the end of the room, it might be matched by a large console-mirror opposite. In a sitting-room with two or four windows, the central pier was often occupied by one of the fashionable bureau-bookcases with mirrored doors and candle slides below, so that the candles were reflected in the mirrors.

As large glasses were now the vogue, but mirror sizes were still limited, it became normal practice to joint them. This might be accomplished by butt-jointing the shallow bevelled plates, or by covering joints with an ornamented, gilt or carved metal or wood strip, or by means of a strip of bevelled, silvered glass.

Another variant of the frame itself was *verre eglomisé*, a decorative technique fashionable about 1690 and popular for some twenty-five years. Intricate arabesque and other designs in gold or silver were worked on the backs of glass border strips, on grounds of black or coloured enamel. In 1691, soon after the introduction of the fashion from France, a Mr. Winches of Bread Street was advertising his mastery of the craft.

Reference has been made earlier to eighteenth-century mirror-faced furniture; Fig. 3 must be as fine an English example as exists. It dates from about 1735, is of mahogany, inlaid with engraved brass with gilt brass mounts. It is attributed by the Victoria and Albert Museum to John Channon of St. Martin's Lane. As yet little is known of the Channon family, but such work of theirs as has come to light in recent years suggests that they were in the first rank of their trade.

In the first half of the eighteenth century, instead of jointing up silvered plates to make overmantels more important, landscape, seascape or architectural paintings were placed above plates, in the same frame. Sometimes the two are not contemporary, the looking glass being cut and framed to suit an existing picture. 🙰

MUSEUMS AND COLLECTIONS
English looking-glasses may be seen at the following:
GREAT BRITAIN
Birmingham: Aston Hall
Leeds: Temple Newsam House
London: Ham House
Hampton Court Palace
Victoria and Albert Museum
Sevenoaks: Knole
Stamford: Burghley House
Near Tonbridge: Penshurst Place
Windsor: Windsor Castle
U.S.A.
Miami, Florida: Vizcaya-Dade Country Art Museum
Boston, Mass.: Women's City Club of Boston

FURTHER READING
A Family of Looking-glass Merchants by D. J. V. Fitzgerald, London, 1971.
English Looking Glasses by Geoffrey Wills, London, 1965.
Shorter Dictionary of English Furniture by Ralph Edwards, Vol. II, London 2nd edit. 1969.
Furniture Making in Seventeenth and Eighteenth Century England by R. W. Symonds, London, 1955.

Eighteenth-Century English Wineglasses

Late eighteenth-century English glass is complex, varied and unsurpassed in its delicacy. Decoration of stems and bowls was of infinite variety and of the highest craftsmanship

Fig. 1 *Incised-twist wineglasses (left to right):* **Moulded funnel bowl,** *1760. 5¾ ins.* **Green with veined and lined cup bowl and twisted incised stem,** *1750. 5¼ ins.* **Trumpet bowl,** *1760. 5¼ ins.* **Hammered bowl,** *1760. 5¾ ins.* *(Author's Collection.)*

Fig. 2 *Mixed-twist wineglasses, (left to right):* **Multi-spiral air gauze and opaque twist,** *1760. 6¾ ins.* **Alternating opaque and air twists,** *1760. 6 ins.* **'Nipt diamon wais',** *1760. 7½ ins.* **Air column and opaque thread,** *1770. 5¾ ins.* **Ale-glass with multi-ply opaque spiral,** *1770. 7½ ins.* **Festoon engraved bowl,** *1770. 6 ins.* **Hop and barley engraved bowl,** *1765. 7¾ ins.* *(Author's Collection.)*

Fig. 3 *Wineglasses with twisted stems (left to right):* **Goblet with latticinio twist,** *1775. 7¾ ins.* **Ladder moulded bowl,** *1770. 5⅞ ins.* **Ratafia-flute,** *1770. 7¼ ins.* **Knopped stem,** *1760. 6⅝ ins.* **Firing-glass,** *1770. 4 ins.* **'Honeycomb' hammered bowl,** *1760. 6 ins.* **Straight sixteen-ply gauze,** *1760. 6¼ ins.* **Knopped with latticinio twist,** *1760. 6 ins.* **Two-piece glass,** *1760. 6¾ ins.* *(Author's Collection.)*

Fig. 4 *Wineglasses with opaque twist stems (left to right):* **Four knopped,** *1775. 6¾ ins.* **Triple knop,** *1770. 6½ ins.* **Double knop,** *1770. 6¼ ins.* **Swelling knop,** *1775. 6¼ ins.* **'Captain' wineglass,** *1760. 6¾ ins.* **Pan-topped bowl,** *1770. 6⅛ ins.* **Double ogee bowl,** *1760. 6⅞ ins.* **Ale-glass with flared bowl,** *1770. 7¾ ins.* *(Author's Collection.)*

The third quarter of the eighteenth century is a particularly interesting time in the evolution of the English glass industry. With the demise of the air-twist stem and the development of the highly decorative mixed colour and opaque-twist stems of this period, there is a definite and marked decline in decoration by wheel engraving on the bowls of these later glasses.

This does not mean that the bowls ceased to be decorated at all, rather that engraving tended to be of formal swags and drapery instead of individual designs. There also came into vogue probably the two most decorative and attractive forms of decoration on glass ever to be devised: gilding and enamelling.

A small and not very attractive group of glasses appeared right at the beginning of this period displaying the incised-twist stem (Fig. 1). The incised twist as a form of decoration had been known for many centuries, and there are several Venetian and *façon de Venise* glasses decorated in this style; for some reason, this particular stem again came into vogue from 1750 to 1765. Some authorities believe that glass-makers were losing business to the porcelain trade and that by employing a form of porcelain decoration they could keep pace with their competitors.

These incised-twist stems tended to be sturdy and strong and were not at all attractive to the eye, at a time when style and beauty far outweighed practicality. Their popularity was short lived and they are now, in consequence, very difficult to find. The majority had tall, round-funnel bowls, which were decorated with hammering or moulding on the lower half and usually set on plain, straight columnar stems; very few were knopped or had folded feet, and fewer still were coloured.

It is easy to understand why the incised twist was unpopular, but in view of the fact that the opaque twist was an outstanding commercial success, it i difficult to comprehend how neither mixed- no colour-twist stems really caught the public fancy They are highly decorative and some of the colour are most attractive. Although colour twists com mand a very high price on today's market, there ar probably more colour than mixed twists to be found There is some uncertainty as to when these glasse first appeared but without a doubt there were mixed twists being made from approximately 1750 to about 1775; colour twists were made throughout the same period and probably even later.

Most mixed twists are made by the combination of air threads forming a column down the centre of the stem and various forms of opaque twist surrounding it. There are so many variations on this theme, however, that it is impossible to be definite about the designs (Fig. 2). In some cases an opaque core is surrounded by a ribbon of air, and in other the whole of the centre of the opaque twist is blown as a hollow 'worm' of air. The majority of both mixed- and colour-twist stems are found on simple wineglasses, and it is exceptionally rare to find either goblets, ale- or cordial-glasses with these types of stem.

Rare and beautiful glasses with stems of intriguing complexity

The rarest of all these glasses are the mixed-twist composite stems, air- and colour-twist stems and a combination of air, opaque- and colour-twist stems. Because of the existence of air and colour together, one must assume that colour twists were first made at a slightly earlier date, but the majority were produced in the third quarter of the eighteenth century. Most of the colours themselves were not opaque, but translucent, and were formed by canes of coloured glass inserted into the make-up of the stem. Each colour has a definite rarity value; the most sought-after is canary or yellow, and in decreasing rarity come green, black, lavender, chocolate, russet-red, rubber-red, grey-blue, mauve, orange, turquoise, dark and light blues, reds of many hues, and almost any colour combinations. The most common of these combinations is red and green, or red and blue.

It seems extraordinary that these most attractive

glasses commanded so little respect and popularity at the time of their manufacture, representing only three per cent of all glasses manufactured at this date. We have very little factual knowledge of their cost and therefore do not know whether it was their high price or the fact that Englishmen did not care for such garish decoration that condemned them to such a short life.

The dating of the white opaque-twist stem is very difficult, but it is doubtful whether there are in fact any specimens made earlier than about 1750; they were certainly being made as late as 1800. The twist itself was made by placing rods of opaque-white enamel glass upright in a circular mould. The clear glass was then poured into the mould and the resulting block was re-heated, drawn out and twisted with exact regularity. If some of the more complex of these stems are studied in detail, it can be seen that as many as thirty-six white canes were used to form this complicated process of decoration and single, double and triple series twists are in themselves a miracle of craftsmanship.

The definition of these three terms is quite simple: a single twist is merely one design of ribbon twisted throughout the stem; a double twist, two designs; and a triple – the most complicated – would have three different designs of twist interwoven to form one stem. The variation and number of these opaque-twist stems is quite enormous and must extend into several hundreds. It is quite obvious that because the focal point of the drinking-glass was now the stem, rather than the bowl, engraved decoration fell from favour.

Variations and decorations on the bowls became highly elaborate

Almost every type of bowl can be found on opaque-twist glasses, although some of the older types, such as the drawn trumpet and the mead bowls are very rare indeed. The most common of all bowls was the ogee and round-funnel bowl. Variations and decorations on the bowl became highly elaborate with hammering, moulding and fluting; the rarer types of bowl such as the double ogee, pan-topped, octagonal and bucket, were all in evidence. In the closing years of the eighteenth century and the beginning of the nineteenth century, the unattractive cup bowl also made its appearance.

The decoration within the stem itself was usually enough, but there are quite a few knop-stemmed glasses. The most common of all was the central swollen knop, but as many as four knops have been recorded (Fig. 4). In the earlier air-twist period, knopping became a fine art, but it seemed to die away in the latter half of the century as the internal decoration of the stem rather than the bowl became the focal point.

Commemorative glasses of this period are rarer than those of the earlier air-twist period, another example of the important effect of the stem as the principal area of interest. The most common engraved pieces are the simple ale-glasses and wineglasses decorated with hops and barley or fruiting vines (Fig. 6).

The rarest opaque twists are those with folded feet. After the Excise Act of 1746, the folded foot went out of common use except by special order

251

Fig. 5 *Colour-twist wineglasses* (*left to right*): **Opaque twist edged with bright blue**, 1780. 5½ ins. **Opaque spiral edged with emerald green**, 1770. 5¾ ins. **Air gauze and royal blue thread twist**, 1750. 7 ins. **Green core surrounded by white with an outer red thread**, 1755. 6½ ins. **Opaque white ribbon edged with translucent emerald green, intertwined with a mauve thread**, 1780. 6½ ins. **Canary-yellow twist on white core**, 1770. 5¾ ins. **Cordial-glass with mauve core**, 1770. 7 ins. **Opaque twist with red spiral**, 1770. 5 ins. **Opaque twist edged with red and green**, 1765. 6¾ ins. (*Author's Collection.*)

Fig. 6 *Engraved opaque-twist glasses* (*left to right*): **Ale-flute with hops and barley**, 1770. 7¼ ins. **Cordial-glass with band of flowers**, 1765. 6½ ins. **Ale-glass with symbolic fruit and flowers**, 1765. 7⅛ ins. **Ale-glass with hops and barley**, 1780. 7¾ ins. **Ale-glass with crossed hops and barley**, 1765. 7½ ins. **Cordial-glass with flowers and leaves**, 1780. 6½ ins. **Ale-glass with hops and barley**, 1770. 7¼ ins. **Ale-glass with hops on a pole and barley on the reverse**, 1760. 8 ins. (*Author's Collection.*)

Fig. 7 *Gilt and enamelled glasses* (*left to right*): **Gilt cider-glass** from the atelier of **Giles of London**, 1775. 7½ ins. **White enamelled wineglass by Beilby**, 1775. 6 ins. **Gilt wineglass by Giles**, 1780. 5¾ ins. **White enamelled wineglass by Beilby**, 1775. 6 ins. **Armorial masonic firing-glass with the arms of the Grand Lodge of England by Beilby**, 1765. 3⅛ ins. **White enamelled wineglass by Beilby**, 1770. 6⅞ ins. **Gilt wineglass by Giles**, 1780. 6 ins. (*Author's Collection.*)

Fig. 8 *Opaque twists with folded feet* (*left to right*): **Sweetmeat with double ogee bowl**, 1760. 6½ ins. **Wine-goblet**, 1760. 7¼ ins. **Ratafia-flute with vertically moulded bowl**, 1770. 7¼ ins. **Sweetmeat with dentil rim**, 1770. 6½ ins. **Wineglass**, 1770. 6¼ ins. **Wineglass with multi-ply latticinio gauze stem**, 1770. 6¼ ins. **Sweetmeat**, 1765. 6¾ ins. (*Author's Collection.*)
All measurements given refer to the height of the glasses.

and for luxury glasses. It is for this reason that the majority of opaque-twist sweetmeats, a great rarity in their own right, have folded feet. These specially ordered pieces would be of greater weight and therefore far more expensive than normal glass. Only four per cent of all opaque-twists have folded feet and usually these are examples of extremely high quality (Fig. 8).

Many gilt and enamelled glasses are highly decorative and of fine craftsmanship

Probably the most intriguing decoration on opaque-twist glass is gilding and enamelling. We know very little about the men and women who carried out this extraordinary craft as few of them are named in records and even fewer signed their works. In the field of gilding we know of only three or four. Absolom of Yarmouth signed simple holiday trinkets and, although his glasses were quite decorative, they were not of the finest craftsmanship. What is known of Giles of London is on record due to the fact that he went bankrupt and his entire stock was catalogued and sold by Christie's. Michael Edkins, a really talented enameller and gilder of glass who lived in Bristol, worked for Isaac and Lazarus Jacobs who were gilders to George III. There are several pieces signed 'Jacobs' but none of them are drinking-glasses, as the Jacobs gilding was mainly confined to water-bowls, decanters and plates in Bristol blue.

The art of gilding on glass is highly skilled and requires a great deal of artistry and patience. Gilding and enamelling are allied crafts; the decoration in either case is painted on to the bowl and then the glass is fired in a small kiln until the gilding or enamelling is quite firm. These glasses are exceptionally rare and very valuable.

We know of no enamellers by name other than Michael Edkins and the highly talented Beilby family of Newcastle. We know quite a lot about the Beilby family because Thomas Bewick, an apprentice taken into their house, recorded details of life with them in his autobiography. Practically the whole family contributed to the fine arts of this country during the eighteenth century and for that reason alone they are remarkable. The father of the family was William Beilby. By trade, he was a jeweller and silversmith living in Durham, but his business failed and he moved to Newcastle upon Tyne around 1760.

Of William's seven children, five survived. Elizabeth married and left the home; William the son became a glass enameller, having first learned the trade of enamelling at Bilston, and Ralph became an engraver and carver on silver and other metalwork and later engraved Thomas Bewick's book illustrations. Another son, Thomas, had also learned enamelling, but he became a drawing-master and lived in Leeds. There remains Mary, who also learned the family trade of glass-enamelling and was 'in constant employment of enamel painting on glass'.

Through Mary Beilby, the feminine influence became apparent in the decoration of their glasses

It is fairly certain that all Beilby enamelled glasses were made between the years 1762 and 1778 (Fig. 7) and that Mary had no hand in the enamelling in the early years. By 1768, when Mary was nineteen years old, enamelled glasses by members of the Beilby family suddenly took on a definitely feminine touch. No longer were they confined to armorials; rustic subjects, as well as conventional scenes, suddenly appeared, while landscapes with classical ruins, obelisks and the like also made themselves apparent. Regrettably, in 1774, Mary Beilby suffered a stroke and as she and her brother had always worked as a pair, the enamelling of glasses was not carried on for much longer. In 1778, with the death of their mother, William and Mary retired to Scotland and it can be safely assumed that their work of painting on glass

ceased at that time. There are no known glasses dating from the last twenty years of the eighteenth century enamelled in the style of the Beilbys.

The eighteenth century was the golden age of English glass, as of many other forms of decorative art. It is the combination of delicacy and practicality in the glass of this period that makes it unique, and it was also probably one of the greatest commercial successes that England has ever known. 🙢

MUSEUMS AND COLLECTIONS

English glasses of the late eighteenth century may be seen at the following:

GREAT BRITAIN

Belfast:	Ulster Museum
Bristol:	City Art Gallery
	Harvey's Wine Museum
Cambridge:	Fitzwilliam Museum
London:	Victoria and Albert Museum
Manchester:	City Art Gallery
Oxford:	Ashmolean Museum
St. Helens, Lancashire:	Pilkington Glass Museum
U.S.A. New York:	Corning Museum of Glass

FURTHER READING

The Ingenious Beilbys by James Rush, London, 1973.

An Illustrated Guide to 18th Century English Drinking Glasses by L. M. Bickerton, London, 1971.

Irish Glass in the Age of Exuberance by Phelps Warren, London, 1970.

The Collectors' Dictionary of Glass by E. M. Elville, London, 2nd impression, 1969.

English and Irish Antique Glass by Derek Davis, London, 1964.

English, Scottish and Irish Tableglass by Bernard Hughes, London, 1956.

American Colonial Glass

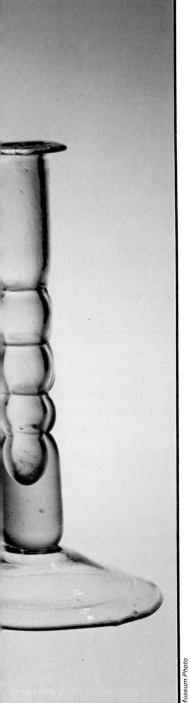

It was not until the middle of the eighteenth century, with the factories of Wistar and Stiegel, that the Colonies began to develop a true glass industry of their own

In 1608 and again in 1621 attempts were made to establish a glass factory in Jamestown, Virginia, giving rise to the claim that glass-making was the first industry in English-speaking America. But both failed. Several other attempts were made in the seventeenth century to establish glass-works elsewhere in the Colonies, but these, too, were abortive. It was not until the eighteenth century, when about a dozen more attempts were made, that some degree of success was achieved. The most noteworthy and best-known glasshouses of that century were those established by Casper Wistar, Henry William Stiegel and, later, John Frederick Amelung.

Casper Wistar was not a practical glass-maker, but a successful brass button manufacturer in Philadelphia who had come there from the Palatinate in 1717. In 1739 he employed his capital to purchase a large tract of land and build a glass-house in what came to be called Allowaystown, or Wistarberg, about thirty miles to the south east of Philadelphia (Fig. 6). Wistar imported his glass-makers, the first four coming from Rotterdam, as shown by an agreement dated 7 December, 1738. As their names suggest – John William Wentzell, Casper Halter, John Martin Halton and Simon Kreismeier – these men were Germans or Dutch.

Later he imported other skilled workers from Germany.

Wistar's glasshouse produced primarily window-glass and bottles but, while these necessities were the basic products of his factory, his workers also made limited quantities of tableware from the same material from which the window-glass and bottles were made. These 'off-hand' pieces, made primarily for the workers' own families and for the local market, are characterised by individuality and were influenced by the Germanic tradition with which the workers were familiar. They were utilitarian and bold in form, sometimes almost crude, and were often decorated with applications of the same glass in the form of threading, gadrooning, prunts, trailing patterns and sometimes even bird-shaped finials (Fig. 1).

These pieces from Wistar's factory and later South Jersey glasshouses are referred to today as 'South Jersey Type' glass and the general style, which gradually spread to window- and bottle-glasshouses in New England and New York State, is called the 'South Jersey Tradition'. The Germanic influence on these glasses can be readily noted by comparing the two sugar-bowls shown in Figure 7. The origins of the South Jersey Tradition, however, may be traced well beyond the eighteenth century to the *Waldglas* produced in the small glasshouses of central Europe in the fifteenth, sixteenth and seventeenth centuries.

After Casper Wistar's death in 1752, his glass-house was carried on by his son, Richard. The following advertisement from the *Pennsylvania Gazette*, of 28 September, 1769, suggests the nature of the products of this fairly successful glasshouse. The difficulty of competing with imported wares is also suggested by Richard Wistar's plea for support of American manufacture:

Fig. 1 *Left:* **Covered sugar-bowl with chicken finial,** *German, last third of eighteenth century. Colourless glass. Wistar imported many of his glass-blowers from Holland and Germany. With them they brought their old traditions, and many pieces with animal finials were made after prototypes such as this.*
Centre and right: **Covered sugar-bowl** *and* **candlestick,** *attributed to a South Jersey glass-works, possibly Wistar's, c.1760–80. Olive green and aquamarine glass. Height of candlestick 6½ ins.*
(Corning Museum of Glass, Corning, New York.)

Fig. 2 **Pattern-moulded glass** *attributed to Stiegel's glass-works, Manheim, c.1769–74. From the left:* **Salt-cellar.** *Cobalt blue glass.* **Covered sugar-bowl.** *Cobalt blue glass, height 6⅛ ins.* **Creamer.** *Amethyst glass.* **Creamer,** *English, third quarter of the eighteenth century. Pattern-moulded glass.*
A comparison of the Stiegel creamer with the one of English origin on the right indicates the difficulty of distinguishing Stiegel's work from contemporary English or European glass.
(Corning Museum of Glass.)

Fig. 3 *Two enamelled tumblers
with inscriptions, probably made
in Europe and enamelled
at Stiegel's glass-works,
Manheim, 1772–74. Height 4 ins.
(Corning Museum of Glass.)*

Fig. 4 *Bottle of the type
produced in Wistar's glasshouse,
probably of English origin,
dated 1767. Height 9 ins.
(Corning Museum of Glass.)*

'Made at subscriber's Glass Works between 300 and 400 boxes of Window glass consisting of common sizes 10 x 12, 9 x 11, 8 x 10, 7 x 9, 6 x 8. Lamp glasses or any uncommon sizes under 16 x 18 are cut on short notice. Most sort of bottles, gallon, 1/2 gallon, and quart, full measure 1/2 gallon case bottles, snuff and mustard bottles also electrofying globes and tubes &c. All glass American Manufacture and America ought also encourage her own manufacture. N.B. He also continues to make the Philadelphia brass buttons noted for their strength and such as were made by his deceased father and warranted for 7 years.

RICHARD WISTAR.'

It has always been assumed, on the basis of his 1769 advertisements, that Wistar produced all of the glass he offered for sale, but manuscripts in the possession of a descendant include letters from Richard Wistar in which he ordered crown window glass from Bristol in 1759 and later, and enquired about the pieces of 'hollow ware' in 1767. Thus, a degree of caution must be used in interpreting his advertisements.

Richard Wistar continued to operate the glasshouse in Allowaystown until 1780, when he offered the business for sale. There were apparently no takers, and glass-making operations ceased. Despite its importance in the history of American glass-making, no products are known which can definitely be attributed to it. An English bottle of a type which was probably made there between 1740 and 1780 is illustrated in Figure 4. The South Jersey Tradition continued until about 1860, and found its fullest expression and development in New York State glasshouses during the period 1835–50 (Fig. 7).

Henry William Stiegel, born in Cologne in 1729,

came to America in 1750 and settled in Shaefferstown, near Lancaster, Pennsylvania, where many of his fellow countrymen were living. He was an iron-worker by trade, married to the daughter of iron-master Jacob Huber, the successful owner of a local forge. In 1758, after the death of his father-in-law, Stiegel took over the iron works, rebuilt it and named it Elizabeth Furnace, after his wife. He later built another iron furnace at Charming Forge, and apparently both prospered. With profits from his iron furnaces, Stiegel established a small glass-works at Elizabeth Furnace which began producing bottles and window-glass in September 1763. In November 1765, together with Philadelphia partners, he established a glasshouse in Manheim, a small town near Lancaster which he founded. Here, tableware as well as bottles and window-glass were produced. A third glasshouse, also located in Manheim, was begun in 1768 and completed in 1769, to which additions were made in each of the next three years.

Stiegel specialised in the production of fine tableware

Stiegel's advertisements referred to the firm as the American Flint Glass Works. Here he produced colourless and coloured flint glass and fine tableware of many varieties, including engraved and enamelled glasses. This was the first glasshouse in America to specialise in the production of fine tableware, which emulated both English and Continental glasses. He employed, at the peak of his production, about one hundred and thirty men who had come primarily from England and Germany. Stiegel advertised fairly widely and his products

256

were marketed as far away as Boston. At the time of his failure on 5 May, 1774, Stiegel listed unsold glass with dealers or agents in York, Hanover and Carlisle, as well as Manheim (Pennsylvania), Hagerstown, Fredericktown and Baltimore (Maryland), and New York City. He probably also sent some glass to the West Indies. The bankrupt Stiegel was thrown into a debtors' prison in the autumn of 1774 but was released by Christmas. He died at Charming Forge on 10 January, 1785.

The 'Stiegel Tradition' flourished in the Midwest

Although Stiegel was not a practical glass-maker, he was very successful in emulating the various types of English glass in demand in the Colonies at the time, as well as the common engraved and enamelled Germanic wares with which his fellow Pennsylvania Germans had been familiar in their homeland. With a few exceptions, it is impossible to distinguish between products which may have been made in one of his glasshouses and those produced in England or on the Continent during this period. Stiegel imported glass-blowers and enamellers from Germany and glass-blowers from the Bristol area of England. Because the output of his workmen was closely controlled, the products from Stiegel's factories were far less individual in character than those produced in the South Jersey Tradition. Pattern-moulding as a decorative technique was widely used in his glasshouses. The use of

this technique was continued in many of the glass-houses established in the early nineteenth century west of the Allegheny Mountains, an area termed, in American glass-making parlance, the 'Midwest', of which Pittsburgh was the centre (Fig. 6). This presumed Stiegel influence resulted in what is called today the 'Stiegel Tradition'.

Though many of his pattern-moulded glasses cannot be distinguished from their counterparts in England or Europe, pocket-bottles, which were once found largely in Pennsylvania bearing a diamond daisy or a daisy in hexagonal pattern, appear to have no European counterparts or prototypes and may be attributed with a degree of certainty to Stiegel. They were probably made in his second Manheim factory between 1769 and 1774. With these exceptions, it is impossible to distinguish Stiegel's products, but we know from his advertisements and his account books, which are still extant in the Historical Society of Pennsylvania, Philadelphia, that his factories produced a wide range of tableware and other glass. A partial listing in one of his account books '. . . for glass sold and sent out' to various stores and agents for the months of November and December 1769 included 'Quart Moulded Decanters, Pint Decanters of all sizes, half pint ditto, Quart, Pint, half pint and gill and half gill tumblers, Wine and Water glasses, Wine and Beer Glasses, quart, Pint and half pint Mugs, Bowls, Specie Bottles, half pint Cans, Cream Jugs, Smelling Bottles, Vinegar Cruets, Sugar boxes with covers, Chain Salts, Mustard Pots, Pocket Bottles, Jelly, sillabub and Free mason glasses, Phials of all

Fig. 8 **Decanter**, *possibly made at Stiegel's glass-works, Manheim, c.1770. Free-blown of colourless non-lead glass and engraved, height $9\frac{7}{8}$ ins. (Corning Museum of Glass.)*

Sorts, Candlesticks, Fine Wine glasses, common tail wine glasses, and Toys of all Sorts'. One can speculate that the entries for 'Chain Salts', 'Sugar boxes with covers', and 'Cream Jugs' are of the types illustrated in Figure 2, which are indistinguishable from English glass of these types.

Stiegel produced enamelled glasses for the local German inhabitants

Presumably some of the tumblers and mugs produced were sketchily engraved with floral and geometric designs in what we term today a 'peasant' or 'folk' manner, like the mug in Figure 5 and the decanter in Figure 8. Such glasses were widely produced on the Continent and those thought to have been made by Stiegel must be referred to today as 'Stiegel-type' glasses, rather than 'Stiegel glasses', because of the uncertainty of their origin. The same terminology must be applied to enamelled glasses like those in Figure 3, which Stiegel began producing in 1772, undoubtedly to supply the local Pennsylvania German market. They closely imitated the same type of enamelled peasant glass with which these people had been familiar in their native land. About a dozen enamelled tumblers are known bearing English inscriptions with a Germanic flavour expressing the following sentiments: 'We Two will be True', and 'My Love you like me do' (Fig. 3). While these glasses, too, may have been made in Europe for the American market, they are likely to have been enamelled in Stiegel's factory.

MUSEUMS AND COLLECTIONS
Early American blown glass and English prototypes may be seen at the following:

GREAT BRITAIN

Bristol:	Bristol City Art Gallery
London:	Victoria and Albert Museum
Newcastle-upon-Tyne:	Laing Art Gallery and Museum
Sheffield:	City Museum
York:	Yorkshire Museum

U.S.A.

Boston:	Boston Museum of Fine Arts
Corning, N.Y.:	Corning Museum of Glass
Dearborn, Mich.:	Henry Ford Museum and Greenfield Village
New York:	Metropolitan Museum of Art
Philadelphia:	Philadelphia Museum of Art

FURTHER READING
Chats on Old Glass by R. A. Robertson, revised with a new chapter on American glass by Kenneth M. Wilson, New York, 1969.
Two Hundred Years of American Blown Glass by George S. and Helen A. McKearin, New York, 1950.
Stiegel Glass by Frederick William Hunter, New York, 1950.
American Glass by George S. and Helen A. McKearin, New York, 1941.

Irish Glass

For the last quarter of the eighteenth century, and several decades more, glassmaking in Ireland enjoyed a golden age. Glasshouses in Cork, Dublin, Belfast and particularly Waterford produced the elaborately hand-cut pieces that are synonomous with the best in Irish glass

The successful manufacture of glass in Ireland in the last quarter of the eighteenth century and the first half of the nineteenth was due entirely to political causes. The more important of these stimulated the expansion of industries in the country, many of which had remained in a state of stagnation struggling to endure against great odds.

Irish manufacturers in general had received little or no encouragement during the eighteenth century, when they were prohibited from exporting their goods and sales were limited to the home market. This condition was imposed by the English government in deference to the wishes of their own manufacturers, who were content to have a steady, if small, number of buyers conveniently close at hand. However, the outbreak of the American War of Independence in 1775 led to a threat that the French might invade Ireland in order to launch an attack on England. The possibility of such an event gave the Irish an opportunity that they did not hesitate to exploit. Under the able leadership of the statesman and orator Henry Grattan, they were able to procure constitutional freedom from Westminster, and no longer did the Dublin parliament have meekly to await London approval before their decisions became law. Grattan also obtained for the Irish the right to trade wherever they wished, and thenceforward they were permitted to make what they pleased and sell to whomsoever would buy.

The English glass-makers had to pay a duty on their products which lessened their sales by making the wares expensive; its imposition also caused inconvenience. Customs agents were stationed in every glasshouse, where they checked all the processes and ensured that the full and exact amount of duty was paid. With a corps of tax-collectors conveniently stationed wherever they were required, it was not a difficult matter merely to increase the duty whenever more money was required. This was done in 1777; four years later the process was repeated and the makers began to look about them for ways of circumventing the hardship.

Ireland now offered an opportunity to glass-makers, for in that country glass was free of tax and there were no restrictions on trade. Soon after 1780 Englishmen began to cross the Irish Sea to escape the extortions of their government and endeavour to increase their profits. At the same time, the Irish themselves were not slow to take advantage of the chance for which they had waited so long.

One firm of glass-makers had managed to prosper in Dublin with the aid of financial assistance from the Royal Dublin Society, which had been founded to encourage local arts and manufactures. Richard Williams and Company was founded in about 1764 by a group of Welshmen and nine years later was able to announce that they 'had brought the manufacture to as great perfection as carried on abroad'. In 1777 they built a new glass house in Marlborough Street, Dublin, and continued in business until 1829.

The Waterford Glass-House was established in 1783

It is, however, the glasshouses that were established from 1783 onwards, by or in conjunction with English craftsmen, that resulted in the production of the distinctive Irish glass. The best-known and longest lasting of these was the one which advertised in the *Dublin Evening Post* on 4 October 1783 'Waterford Glass-House. George and William Penrose having established an extensive Glass Manufactory in this city, their Friends and the Public may be supplied with all kinds of plain and cut Flint Glass, useful and ornamental; they hope when the Public know the low Terms they will be supplied at, and consider the vast expence attending this weighty undertaking, they will not take offence at their selling for Ready Money only. They are now ready to receive orders, and intend opening their Warehouse the 1st of next month. Wholesale Dealers and Exporters will meet with proper Encouragement. Sept. 22, 1783'.

The two Penroses were brothers, moneyed merchants with no knowledge of the processes of glass-making but sufficient business acumen to seize the opportunity of the moment. The essential

Fig. 2 **Water-jug** marked 'Waterloo Co Cork', 1815–35. Moulded base and engraved ornament, height 6 ins. The Waterloo Glass House Company was founded in the year of the battle of Waterloo, 1815, and went bankrupt after twenty years. (Delomosne and Son, Ltd., London.)

Fig. 3 **Covered vase on a square foot**, c.1800. Height 11 ins. This fine vase relies on good proportions with simple mouldings and fluting for effect. (Cecil Davis, Ltd.)

Fig. 4 **Condiment set**, c.1825. The holder silver plate, the bottles cut with diamonds in the Irish style, overall height 9¼ ins. The diamond patterns were cut by hand on an iron wheel and polished on a wooden wheel. (City Museum and Art Gallery, Plymouth.)

2

Raymond Fortt

3

Wallace Heaton Ltd.

4
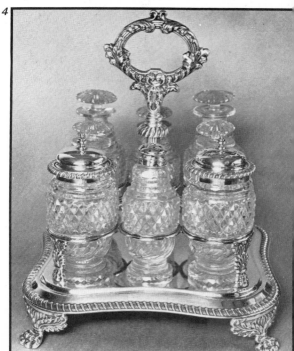

R. Todd-White

Fig. 5 *Pair of covered sugar-bowls*, Irish, c.1790. Cut with a Van Dyck border, height 7 ins.
One of the charms of Irish glass is that, being cut by hand, it is not always perfectly regular.
(Delomosne and Son, Ltd.)

Fig. 6 *Decanter*, one of a pair marked 'Cork Glass Co', c.1800. The bodies part-moulded with flutes and cut with shallow patterns, height 9¾ ins.
(Delomosne and Son, Ltd.)

Raymond Fortt

expertise was provided by an Englishman, John Hill, who had been working at Stourbridge and left there for Waterford in company with what was described as 'the best set of workmen that he could get in the county of Worcester'. Hill stayed only three years and left suddenly for an unknown reason, but not before he had passed on all his secrets to a fellow-Englishman, Jonathan Gatchell. As a result, Gatchell was elevated from clerk to manager and in time succeeded to ownership of the firm. Relatives carried on after him until 1851, when the business was closed, leaving behind it a reputation that remains undiminished today.

Less than one hundred miles to the south-west of Waterford is the city of Cork, where no fewer than three glasshouses were opened and closed in a period of sixty years. The first of these was the Cork Glass Company which was established in 1783, the same year as that at Waterford. It remained in business until 1818, but three years before that, in the year of the battle of Waterloo, a competitor appeared on the scene, appropriately named the Waterloo Glass House Company. Finally, in 1818 came the Terrace Glass Works, which was closed in 1841, six years after the Waterloo Company had gone bankrupt.

Many small makers came and went

Other manufactories in the country were at Dublin and Belfast. In the capital, Dublin, in addition to the Williams glassworks mentioned above, was that of Charles Mulvaney which started in about 1785, but although he called himself a maker it is possible that he dealt in goods made by others. Soon afterwards Thomas and John Chebsey were operating a glasshouse near Ballyborough Bridge, but it closed after only ten or eleven years in 1797 or 1798. Belfast, in the north of the country, was the site of a works established by a Bristol man, Benjamin Edwards. He was succeeded by his son of the same name who ran the concern from 1812 until

about 1829, and successive members of the family kept it running until about 1870.

The foregoing were the makers who came and went, but while they can be identified by name their products are mostly indistinguishable and cannot always be differentiated from contemporary English productions. Being free of tax, the Irish could be more lavish with their material but, in spite of the level of duty payable in England, equally heavy pieces were made there. It was the imposition of a tax in Ireland in 1825 that slowly but surely killed off what had been a short-lived industrial and artistic venture with considerable potential for the future.

In the pioneer English book on glass, *Old English Glasses*, published in 1897, the author Albert Hartshorne wrote 'There is no information that the glass made at Dublin and Cork had any special characteristics of metal or form, beyond those common to the generality of glasses in England at the end of the eighteenth century; but Waterford glass is usually to be distinguished by its pale blue tinge'. The possibility of Waterford products being easily recognisable in comparison with other varieties was seized on by the uninformed and only in recent years has the view been modified. A dealer who specialised in Irish glass wrote in the twenties that it differed from English because it is 'tougher and stronger than any other', 'gives a sense of warmth to the touch', and while 'British glass has a clear, definite, bright ring' much of Irish make has what was termed a 'peculiar throb'. Doubtless it was good sales-talk, but it does not withstand examination. The blue and grey tinge found in a proportion of surviving old glass, which may or may not be Irish, is due only to faults in manufacture such as inaccurate weighing and careless mixing of ingredients.

Waterford is stated to have made a point of attempting to produce a perfectly colourless glass, and as long ago as 1920 Dudley Westropp, then Curator of the Irish National Mus m, Dublin, wrote quite firmly: 'As far as I can judge from examining many authentic pieces, the metal of

8

Fig. 7 *Pair of boat-shaped salts,*
c.*1800. Diamond cut,*
height 3⅜ ins.
Elaborately cut table wares are
generally considered to be
characteristic of Irish glass.
(Delomosne and Son, Ltd.)

Fig. 8 *Square-based turnover*
bowl, c.*1800. Height 8 ins.*
Most esteemed of all Irish glass
wares are the massive serving
bowls, such as this 'turnover'
bowl named for its curled rim;
they glisten with reflected light
from their cut surfaces.
(Delomosne and Son, Ltd.)
262

Waterford glass is much whiter than that of other of
the old Irish glasshouses'.

Marked by slightly raised wording under the base

A few of the Irish manufacturers marked their
products, and provided future collectors with
indisputable evidence of some portion of their output. In each instance the marking takes the form
of slightly raised wording under the base of the
article, which was executed during its making by
blowing the object in a mould prepared with the
necessary lettering. Carelessness in the glassworks
and subsequent wear and tear often result in the
marks being difficult to decipher and sometimes

they are so faint as to be overlooked altogether. The
makers concerned and their marks are: B. EDWARDS
BELFAST; CORK GLASS CO.; PENROSE WATERFORD;
WATERLOO CO., CORK.

In addition there were a number of retailers who
had goods marked in a similar manner with their
names: ARMSTRONG ORMOND QUAY; J. D. AYCKBOWN
DUBLIN or J D A; MARY CARTER & SON 80 GRAFTON
ST., DUBLIN; FRANCIS COLLINS DUBLIN; C M & CO.
(Charles Mulvaney).

Inscriptions, crests and Masonic symbols are now rarely found

The majority of marked pieces are wine-
decanters and finger-bowls, while water-jugs and

Raymond Fortt

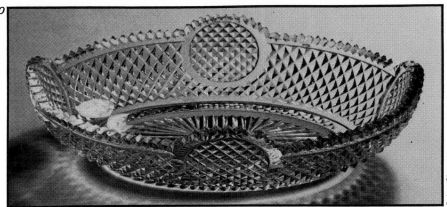

Robert Chapman

Fig. 9 *Boat-shaped bowl,*
c.1790. *Flat-cut with a shaped
rim, on a moulded foot,
height 8 ins.*
*Until about 1800, Irish glass
often featured shallow 'slices',
cut away from the surface or
giving a bevel to the rim.*
(Delomosne and Son, Ltd.)

Fig. 10 *Oval bowl,* c.1820. *Cut
with small diamonds on the sides
and with radiating flutes beneath
the base, width 9 ins.*
*At around this date, the 'Age of
Exuberance' set into Irish glass-
making, and the cutters gave full
play to their fancy, using every
combination of strokes possible.*
(Private Collection.)

dishes have been recorded in small numbers. The decanters, bowls and jugs share the feature of a row of short, upright shallow flutes round the lower part of the body. These were moulded and show none of the sharp precision of cutting. The decanters of the various makers exhibit variations, but they are less pronounced than was once thought and it is unsafe to rely on them for identification in the case of an unmarked example.

Some of the decanters and other articles were devoid of ornament except for the fluting, but many were given cut or engraved decoration. Cork noticeably favoured use of the vesica, a pointed oval, which frequently appears on pieces from the city, but occasionally more ambitious patterns were attempted there and elsewhere. Inscriptions, crests and Masonic symbols are recorded, and while probably plentiful at one time they are now rare.

Although the decanters and other marked pieces are unquestionably Irish in origin, they are not in the public mind characteristic of that country's glass. Truly representative are the elaborately cut pieces for use at the dining-table; pieces that recall the name 'Waterford' throughout the world. The standards of glassmaking at Waterford were extremely high and only the purest materials were used in the manufacture of the brilliant, silvery lead crystal. The wide range of tablewares produced primarily for export included three-ringed decanters with mushroom stoppers, candlesticks, drinking glasses, compotes, cream-jugs and all kinds of covered dishes. Of them all, the most esteemed are the massive serving-bowls, some with curled rims ('turnover' bowls), which glisten with hundreds of points of light reflecting from their cut surfaces. The cutting was performed by holding the blank article against revolving wheels of various materials, deep cuts being made with a wheel of iron fed with a trickle of water and sand which did the work. When the incisions had been made they were polished on wooden wheels using a soft powder. Before starting, the pattern was marked out to guide the craftsman, but the completed decoration relied greatly on the experience of his eyes and hands and its charm lies in the human touch, the slight inaccuracies revealed on close inspection.

The patterns which were in use up to about 1800 were often composed of shallow 'slices' cut away from the surface or giving a bevel to the rim. After that date, the 'Age of Exuberance' set in, and the cutter gave full play to his fancy by using a wide combination of strokes to increase the brilliant effect of his work. Complexity extended to construction, with some of the largest bowls being made with a separate foot, and flat dishes given a base on

which to revolve as a 'lazy Susan'. At the 1851 Great Exhibition the Waterford company exhibited a table centrepiece composed of no less than forty pieces, 'so fitted to each other as to require no connecting sockets of any other material'. The Exhibition closed on 11 October, but, alas, the glass-makers had found themselves unable to surmount their business difficulties and had advertised a sale of their entire stock in the September. It was the end of an enterprise that had endured for almost seventy years, but one that remains internationally known today.

In spite of words to the contrary about the alleged colour of Waterford glass, the blue-grey legend persisted for many years. Foreign manufacturers busy supplying the antiques market in the decade 1920 to 1930, carefully tinted their 'genuine Waterford', but took less trouble to make it in correct shapes and with proper cut ornament. A new company was started at Waterford in 1948 and makes copies of some of the products of its forerunner. Thirty different pieces chosen from antique collections have been painstakingly reproduced to preserve the characteristics of the old glass. The range includes such well-known items as the three-ring decanter, turnover bowl and boat-shaped bowl. Marked decanters have been reproduced, and any with particularly clear wording on them should be examined with care.

MUSEUMS AND COLLECTIONS

Irish glass may be seen at the following:
GREAT BRITAIN:
London: Victoria and Albert Museum
Bedford: Cecil Higgins Museum
Cambridge: Fitzwilliam Museum
IRELAND:
Belfast: Ulster Museum
Dublin: National Museum of Ireland
U.S.A.:
New York: Corning Museum of Glass

FURTHER READING

Irish Glass: the Age of Exuberance by Phelps Warren, London, 1970.
English and Irish Glass by Geoffrey Wills, London, 1968.
A History of English and Irish Glass (2 vols.) by W. A. Thorpe, London, 1929.
English and Irish Glass by W. A. Thorpe, London, 1927.
Irish Glass by M. S. Dudley Westropp, London, 1920.

263

Later Bohemian Glass

Museum Photo

Fig. 1 **Decanter**, *Bohemian,
c.1840. Ruby glass, cut on the
wheel, height 12¾ ins.
Much Bohemian coloured glass
had engraved portraits or
topographical views in the
panels. This, however, is an
undecorated piece, impressive on
account of its heavy, flawless
texture and bold shape.
(Victoria and Albert Museum,
London.)*

Fig. 4 **Vase**, *Bohemian,
c.1830–40. Glass, cut and
engraved on the wheel, with
yellow and pink stains and
silvering, height 8 ins.
The Biedermeier period in glass
manufacture was characterised
by elaborate surface decoration
in various forms, either in a
repeating pattern or applied
irregularly, and a chunkiness of
the glass itself.
(Victoria and Albert Museum.)*
264

Bohemian glass-workers resumed
their former supremacy by
adopting vivid colours and bold,
often faceted, forms

The Napoleonic Wars brought disaster to the glass-houses of Bohemia. For the better part of twenty years, the markets in Spain and the Americas were closed and trade with Britain, the Low Countries and Holland disrupted. But the eighteenth-century supremacy of Bohemian cut and engraved glass had been threatened even before the French Revolution, as the fashion for English and Irish lead glass – simple, facet-cut, lustrous and relatively cheap – became popular throughout Europe.

When Napoleon was exiled to St. Helena in 1815 (a scene frequently depicted on glass by Bohemian artists), and the Congress of Vienna restored the old royal families, the glasshouses faced an uncertain future. The British had undercut their traditional markets and the decorative coloured and opaque glass of Clichy, St. Louis and Vonêche (later Baccarat) had established the fashionable French Empire style.

Just as Bohemia had met the challenge of porcelain by the introduction of opaque white glass in the eighteenth century, so her glassworkers in the nineteenth developed an entirely new style and composition of glass and recaptured, during the Biedermeier period, their former supremacy.

The romantic revolution was under way, the most fruitful and original era of change in European cultural history since the Renaissance. At the same time a profound economic transformation took place: the Industrial Revolution spread outwards across the Continent, creating new wealth in different hands and bringing railways, even to remote Bohemia, by the 1860s. Speed of movement as much as the new liberalism freed art from its predominantly aristocratic patronage. The triumph of the middle classes was reflected, through their demands for luxury, in all the domestic arts, and glass followed suit. While the nobility still ordered imposing tableware and ornate chandeliers, there grew up a far more diverse requirement for decorative objects in glass for both display and use. Above all, in the first enthusiasm of the rediscovery of landscape, the German public bought souvenirs – delicate and expensive, perhaps, but essentially no different from the 'trifle from

Brighton' and the glass toys of Stourbridge.

Surprisingly, considering their enormous production in the nineteenth century, Bohemian and Silesian glasshouses remained backward in adopting modern technology: as late as 1870, only twelve of the hundred and sixty-nine largest furnaces were burning coal. In the early part of the century, most glassworks were still strictly controlled by the families who owned them, and their sons were apprenticed to the business as agents in foreign markets.

During the period which may be called Empire (1795–1815), a reversion took place from formal magnificence; glass-blowers concentrated on simple, plain shapes, producing cylindrical tumblers or decanters, bowls and vases very similar to contemporary English patterns. Even the English style of facet and diamond cutting was followed closely. Later, in' the Biedermeier period, the classic design was a trumpet-shaped beaker with a heavy foot, often facet-cut, called the *Ranft-becher*. The diversity of forms became so great as to defy classification, and almost every object of domestic use, from snuff-boxes to candlesticks, was made in decorative glass. It is this exuberance that marks the second great age of Bohemian glass.

Portraits in the form of medallions, silhouettes or painted parchment were used as decoration

Older traditions survived, of course. The first great artist in the neo-classical mode belongs almost wholly to the eighteenth century. Johann Josef Mildner (1763–1808), of Gutenbrunn in Lower Austria, used the *zwischengoldglas* technique to decorate glasses with portrait medallions. This involved setting a sheet of gold leaf, often on a red ground, into circular recesses in the side and base of the glass and etching the portrait or design, then laying another disc of glass over it, so that the surfaces fitted exactly. Silhouettes or portraits painted on parchment served equally well, and Mildner's work on clear and opaque white tumblers was usually given fire-gilt borders of a very high standard.

Another artist in the eighteenth-century mode whose signed pieces are extremely valuable is the engraver Dominik Biemann (1800–57), whose workshop engraved ornamental glass. Biemann was one of the first artists to follow the tourist trade; he spent

Fig. 2 **Beaker**, *Bohemian, c.1830–40.* Lithyalin *glass, height 4¼ ins.*
Lithyalin *is a marbled glass invented in 1823 by Friedrich Egermann (1777–1864), who had a glasshouse at Blottendorf in Bohemia. This beaker illustrates the wide variety of marbled colours that could be produced by this method.*
(Victoria and Albert Museum.)

Fig. 3 **Mug**, *Egermann factory, c.1830.* Hyalith *glass, height 4½ ins.*
Hyalith *was invented in 1822 by Count George Buquoy in imitation of Wedgwood's black basalt. To compete with the porcelain so popular at the time, eighteenth-century Bohemian glass-workers introduced an opaque, white glass; hyalith glass was a later experiment towards the same end.*
(Richard Dennis Antiques, London.)

4

Fig. 5 **Tumbler**, Bohemian, 1830. *Clear glass with engraving cut through a ruby flash, height 4⅝ ins.*
This highly decorated glass illustrates the combined use of several of the techniques practised by Bohemian glassworkers at this period. The flash is a layer of surface colour applied to clear glass.
(Victoria and Albert Museum.)

Fig. 6 **Footed beaker**, Bohemian, c.1830–40. *Faceted on the wheel, the foot stained yellow, the bowl painted in transparent enamel colours, height 5 ins.*
A vivid yellow was one of the most popular colours in Bohemian stained-surface glass.
(Victoria and Albert Museum.)

Fig. 7 Left: **Covered goblet**, *Bohemian, c.1850. Engraved clear glass with coloured coating, height 11 ins.*
The engraving, in the manner of Karl Pfohl, is of a startled horse. Pfohl was one of the finest nineteenth-century Bohemian glass-engravers. Seven panels on the opposite surface of the goblet reflect the horse in miniature. These reflecting panels are found only on the highest quality engraved glass.
(Richard Dennis Antiques.)

Right: **Beaker**, *Bohemian, c.1825. Engraved clear glass, height 6½ ins.*
The beaker has five panels, four with views of Baden and the fifth bearing the name of its original owner. Souvenir glass was very popular in the spas of Europe, supplying the tourist trade with engraved portraits and landscapes.
(Richard Dennis Antiques.)

Fig. 8 **Cup and cover**, Bohemian, c.1840. *Opaque white glass, height 8 ins.*
(Bethnal Green Museum, London.)

Fig. 9 **Tankard**, Bohemian, early nineteenth century. *Glass, cut and engraved on the wheel, height 7 ins.*
(Victoria and Albert Museum.)

5

Museum Photo

6

each season at the fashionable spa of Franzensbad, undertaking commissions and working on special orders – exquisite portraits and landscapes.

The names of the finest engravers include Karl Pfohl, Mattoni of Carlsbad and the families of Moser, Pelikan of Meistersdorf and Simms of Gablonz. They often signed their work, but a host of unknown craftsmen depicted small masterpieces – horses, mountaineers with ropes, children at play, or public buildings, palaces and views of towns.

The great wealth of the souvenir market was opened up with the invention of painting in transparent enamel colours. Immediately it became possible to paint in far greater detail and with more sensitivity than earlier artists using opaque colours. From about 1810 a series of major artists gave vent to their feeling for landscape in its wild and romantic aspects. Mountain scenes, ruined castles and gothic fantasies appealed to the sense of awe, while genre scenes of children and animals satisfied the sentimental. Expensive mementos recalled picnic suppers by the banks of the Rhine or vistas of Prague or Charlottenburg. The highest standards of painting were achieved by the Mohn family: Samuel Mohn (1762–1815), who settled in Dresden in 1809, and his son Gottlöb (1789–1825), who worked chiefly in Vienna. Signed pieces by either are rare and expensive. The father painted simple naturalistic landscapes, views of cities and churches, and the son indulged in romantic pastorals and sentimental allegories.

Followers of the Mohns worked in Berlin and Bohemia as well as Vienna, and in all the spas and watering-places – such as Carlsbad, Marienbad, Teplitz and Baden (Fig. 7, r.) views of which appear on tumblers and goblets with increasing regularity after 1815. Anton Kothgasser (1769–1851) of Vienna carried the fashion to its peak; his portraits, genre scenes, moonlit views and illustrations of proverbs, usually set in elegant gilt borders, are technically superb, if rather stylised, works of art. There was no lack of imitators, given an eager public, and the

fashion remained vital until the 1850s although the standard, especially on glasses designed for export, had begun to decline.

Engraved and cut clear glass was produced in great quantity throughout the nineteenth century mostly for the export market. Designed for a mass market, it reflected commoner tastes and is generally heavy and repetitive. In Germany and the Austro-Hungarian Empire, the tables of less wealthy city-dwellers and country farmers would have been decorated with cheap machine-made pressed glass or clear and coloured glass with crude enamel designs. These, with sprays of flowers, birds, or more modern emblems, such as railway trains, hark back to the seventeenth century and may be compared with English souvenir glass from Stourbridge and Nailsea with which they are often confused.

Innovation was for the wealthy new patrons, whose taste dictated the use of new colours and materials. Bohemia's response to this demand in the 1830s and '40s was the most colourful in the long history of glassmaking – colour in the glass metal itself or superimposed by painting, staining and overlay.

Just as white opaque glass (*milchglas*) had been made in imitation of porcelain, nineteenth-century inventors strove to match the black basalts of Wedgwood. In 1822 Count George Buquoy succeeded in creating a dense black glass which he called *hyalith* (Fig. 3), and also a red glass, curiously like sealing-wax. Enhanced with formal designs of *chinoiserie* scenes in fire-gilding, the effect of his tall vases and tea- or coffee-sets is monumental. A year later, in 1823, Friedrich Egermann (1777–1864) introduced similar wares at his glassworks at Blottendorf in northern Bohemia. Later he developed what he called *lithyalin*, a marbled glass of astonishing variety, like jasper or agate, whose colours ranged from brick red streaked with green, to deep blues and purples (Figs. 2 and 10). These, too, were gilded and

painted, sometimes with simple mottoes like *'Erinnerung'* (Remembrance). *Hyalith* and *lithyalin* were used prolifically for vases, beakers, table-sets, scent-bottles, inkwells and candlesticks, and a wide range of designs can be found in trade catalogues of the 1840s.

Egermann was a notable inventor; he discovered the gold stain, made with silver, which Kothgasser often used as a background colour, and he made possible the cheap manufacture of ruby glass, by replacing the gold with copper. A wave of striking colours characterised the 1830s, as new substances like antimony and uranium were added to the metal. Turquoise, topaz, chrysoprase, and the shades of uranium green called *Annagrün* and *Annagelb* came from the factory of Joseph Riedel. But new colour in glass was only one of many innovations bringing the finest glassware within range of the middle-class market. Stained glass (clear glass given a surface colour) was widely popular and to the eighteenth-century purple stains were added vivid reds, greens, yellows and sometimes a layer of gold or silver arabesques in high relief (Figs. 4 and 6).

Cased glass was a much prized and highly secret process

The most noted technique, however, was that of overlay, or cased, glass, in which the glass vessel was encased in opaque glass or glass of another colour; these surfaces were then cut away in broad facets to reveal the contrasting layers beneath. The panels would be shaped and then finely gilded, painted or engraved as the designer's fancy chose. Until the 1850s, the process remained a secret in Bohemia. Decanters and sets of glasses, lustres and tall vases were for sale for high prices in London, Paris and New York until imitators caught up and repeated the technique.

The variety of decoration, even on the basic

tumbler, beggars description, and a collector could spend a lifetime without exhausting the richness of Biedermeier glass. One should mention the *Perlbecher*, a beaker with a closely woven net of multi-coloured glass beads round the base of the bowl, and the many goblets bearing portraits of monarchs or notables in sulphide cameos, similar to those produced by Desprez in France and Apsley Pellatt in England. At both ends of the market, Bohemian supremacy lasted until the 1848 Revolution shook the whole of Europe. The uneasy amalgam of placid prosperity and liberal intellectual aspirations dissolved, to be succeeded in central Europe by a decade and more of reaction and repression.

Even without that check to artistic confidence, Bohemian glassworks could hardly have fought off, for the whole nineteenth century, the competition from Britain and America. Cutting costs was the answer; and for every fine example of an engraved goblet or a painted overlay tumbler, a dozen factory-made lifeless copies were sent out in the 1850s and '60s. Modern methods of production helped to emphasise the trend. Design deteriorated; form became heavy. The restless search for novelty produced pearl satin glass and imitations of Venetian *latticinio*, *millefiori* and aventurine glass – yet the results were not inspiring. Vast quantities crossed the Atlantic, and the firm of Lazarus and Rosenfeld of New York distributed what they called 'Bohemian art glass ware' – lamps and vases in 'Rose de Bohème' and 'Green de Bohème' – cheap things from Altrohlau and Steinschönau which had an equally depressing effect on better English and American equivalents.

The originality of Bohemian glassware was saved by a few enterprising industrialists and the deliberate policy of the Austro-Hungarian authorities of stimulating trade schools of design and decoration – the first at Kamenicky Senov in 1839 and another at Novy Bor in 1870. The intense mood of pan-Germanism prevalent at the time of German

10

R. Todd-White

Fig. 10 *Jug, Egermann factory,*
c.1820. Lithyalin *glass,*
height 8¾ ins.
(Victoria and Albert Museum.)

Fig. 11 **Goblet,** *Bohemian,*
c.1840. Glass, cut and engraved
through a layer of yellow stain,
height 7 ins.
(Victoria and Albert Museum.)

unification encouraged revivals of the Teutonic tradition of glass decoration. The Viennese glass designer Louis Lobmeyr strove to coordinate these factors in a single centre and, with the help of Viennese and Bohemian craftsmen, he produced on the one hand excellent glassware in the seventeenth- and eighteenth-century tradition (including enamelled and *schwarzlot* drinking-glasses and engraved and gilded goblets) and on the other hand a series of modern designs in clear, thin-walled glass, not unlike those of his contemporary, James Powell, of the Whitefriars glasshouse in London.

Others followed: the Moser glassworks at Carlsbad, and Meyers Neffe at Adolfov. While it was true that in 1890 the factory of W. Hirschmann at Munich could issue a trade catalogue of standard replicas of antique glass, and many Bohemian factories were flooding the world market with cheap imitations of Stourbridge cameo carving made rapidly, in very low relief, with the use of hydrofluoric acid, the last quarter of the century was a period of experimentation, rather than archaism, and it led, as happened with French Art Nouveau, towards the blossoming of its German equivalent, Jugendstil.

The iridescent glass which Lobmeyr first exhibited in 1873 became a speciality of the Neuwelt factory, and in 1879 Henrichs and Company, distributors of Bohemian glass in New York, announced the arrival of 'the finest selection of iridescent glass and bronze glass ever assembled under one roof'. J. Lötz of Klostersmühle in Austria produced a new method of obtaining iridescence in 1898 and achieved a *succès d'estime* at the famous Paris Exhibition of 1900.

MUSEUMS AND COLLECTIONS

Nineteenth-century German and Bohemian glass may be seen at the following:

AUSTRIA
Vienna: Kunsthistorisches Museum
CZECHOSLOVAKIA
Prague: Museum of Applied Art
                           Museum of Decorative Art

GERMANY
Berlin: Kunstgewerbemuseum
Cologne: Kunstgewerbemuseum
Munich: Bayerisches Nationalmuseum
Nuremberg: Germanisches
                           Nationalmuseum

GREAT BRITAIN
Cambridge: Fitzwilliam Museum
Edinburgh: Royal Scottish Museum
Lincoln: Usher Gallery
London: British Museum
                           Victoria and Albert Museum

U.S.A.
Corning, N.Y.:   Corning Museum of Glass
Toledo, Ohio: Toledo Museum of Art
Flint, Michigan: Flint Institute of Art

FURTHER READING

Continental Coloured Glass by Keith Middlemas, London, 1971.
Bohemian Glass, a Victoria and Albert Museum handbook, HMSO, 1965.
Glass in Czechoslovakia by K. Hettes, Prague, 1958.
Europaische Glas by R. Schmidt, Berlin, 1927.
Gläser der Biedermeier Zeit by G. Pazaurek, Leipzig, 1923.

Victorian Glass

During the first part of the nineteenth century fashionable society demanded cut-glass, engraved and painted tablewares of greater and greater ostentation

It is difficult to form a worthwhile judgement about the quality of 19th century English glass because the overall picture is still incomplete. The glasshouses produced an enormous quantity of tablewares to satisfy the demands of an ever-expanding market. Allowing for the inevitable casualties, surviving glasses are still like sands from the sea and it will be some time before it is possible to have a balanced estimate of the glass-makers' contribution to the country's useful manu-factures. To judge by the clumsy appearance of so much of the furniture and pottery of the day, it may well turn out that the flexible age-old craft of glassmaking suffered less from the shoddy ideals of the Victorian new rich – so neatly portrayed by Charles Dickens when he described the Veneerings in 'Our Mutual Friend' – than did other crafts which were more easily exploited by mass production.

Fig. 1 **Goblet,** *probably Stourbridge, c.1845–50. Opaque white glass with painted decoration, height 6¾ ins. (Victoria and Albert Museum, London.)*

Fig. 2 **Carafe,** *designed by Richard Redgrave for Henry Cole's Summerly's Art Manufactures, made by J. F. Christy, Lambeth, design registered 1847. Enamelled and gilt glass, height 9¼ ins. (Victoria and Albert Museum.)*

Fig. 3 **Water-jug,** *made by W. H. and B. Richardson of Wordsley, marked 'Richardson's vitrified', design registered 1848. Clear crystal glass, painted in enamel colours, height 9¼ ins. (Victoria and Albert Museum.)*

2

3

Museum Photo

R. Todd-White

R. Todd-White

R. Todd-White

Fig. 4 **Wine-cooler,** *English or Irish, c.1815–25. Clear cut glass, height 14¾ ins. (Victoria and Albert Museum.)*

Fig. 5 **Covered vase,** *possibly by Thomas Hawkes of Dudley, late 1830s. Double-walled glass, the outer wall cut, the inner wall painted and gilt, height 14¾ ins. (Victoria and Albert Museum.)*

Fig. 6 **Claret-jug,** *with silver mount made by Benjamin Smith, Jun., Duke Street, Lincoln's Inn Fields, London, and hallmarked London 1841–42. Cut glass, height approx. 11 ins. (Victoria and Albert Museum.)*

Fig. 7 **Standing bowl,** *probably made by James Powell and Sons, London, c.1851. Silvered glass, ruby layered with cut decoration, height approx. 7 ins. (Victoria and Albert Museum.)*

The other difficulty in dealing with the subject is that, even now, we are still too close to that late Georgian and Victorian world to be certain about dates. An example of this difficulty, among many, is to be found in the typical decanter of the second half of the century – bulbous, long-necked, often with three lips and retaining its popularity, with only slight variations of detail, for a good fifty years. There are, too, the various levels at which manufacturers would try out new notions. Obviously the better-off and socially ambitious would be more likely to buy fresh designs, not necessarily because they were attractive but because they were new. There are always people willing to purchase something just because it is expensive and there was always a mass market, as there is today, for the bizarre as long as it was cheap.

To trace these various strands is not easy in so vast a production. One can, however, indicate certain trends and, thanks to numerous documented pieces and the pattern-books of many famous firms, not go too far astray as to dates. But a vast amount of patient research still awaits the dedicated student. As to pattern-books, Hugh Wakefield has noted that one firm alone, Thomas Webb and Sons of Stourbridge, have some twenty-five thousand items in their main series of patterns between 1837 and 1900. Multiply this mass of material several times to cover the records of other famous glassmakers and one can see that future researchers will not lack evidence; their difficulty will be to deal with it.

During the first twenty or thirty years of the nineteenth century fashion demanded cut glass, not the elegant shallow-cut decanters and glasses which were the ideals of the 1770s and '80s, but a far heavier shape which could take deep cutting. It is curious how speedily a method designed to provide an added brilliance to so beautiful a material, without in any way obscuring the fluid forms derived from the skill of the glass-blower, became decadent. Pomposity began to replace a natural, easy growth; deeper and deeper cutting required thicker and thicker glass and that in its

turn demanded greater weight, so that some of the bowls and other table wares of the time, with their deep mitre cutting and ponderous shapes, seem to have taken the well-upholstered figure of the Prince Regent himself as their model.

The English flint-glass, with its comparatively high lead content, lent itself particularly well to both engraving and cutting, and there are few things more satisfying, or which require more skill in the making, than the best cut glass of the years immediately preceding and after the turn of the century. But a lamentable amount of inferior work was also put on the market, so that Ruskin's harsh words in his *Stones of Venice,* exaggerated though they are, must at the time have echoed the opinions of many worthy people: 'The peculiar qualities of glass are ductility when heated, and transparency when cold. . . . All work in glass is bad which does not, with loud voice, proclaim one or other of these qualities. Consequently all cut glass is barbarous, for the cutting conceals its ductility and confuses it with crystal'. All such pronouncements, uttered as it were *ex cathedra,* make their author look ridiculous (Ruskin was fond of this kind of statement) but his words have at least some merit, that they do sound a warning, and had they only been taken with a few grains of salt, might well have restrained many a glassmaker of the mid-nineteenth century from perpetrating some of his worst excesses.

A reaction against heavy cutting led to a fashion for engraving of varying degrees of delicacy

The early years of the century can perhaps be represented by the cut-glass wine-cooler of Figure 4, its date about 1815–25, an aldermanic, weighty object lavishly mitre cut from stopper to foot, an admirable example of a taste which is hardly ours of a hundred and fifty years later but which was greatly admired all over

271

Europe. Decanters, also at first decorated with this rather graceless type of cutting, showed considerable variations within a period of twenty years: a bulbous body with horizontal pattern cutting, with ball or mushroom stoppers and concentric rings round the neck, then a shape with vertical sides and pillar cutting, and about 1850 cut with pointed arches – a strange side-line of the fad for gothic architecture, the greatest monument of which is the Houses of Parliament.

At the same time there were signs of a reaction against heavy cutting on strongly rounded shapes. Globular decanters, bowls and similar vessels were often cut with rows of shallow hollows, with or without wheel engraving; by the 1860s and '70s engraving of varying degrees of delicacy was the fashion, and cutting did not come back into favour until late in the century, when it was once more regarded as highly respectable – as one phrase had it, 'the old legitimate trade'.

Some of the most interesting vessels made during the mid-century were of clear glass and painted – jugs and goblets, for instance, from the firm of W. H. B. and J. Richardson of Stourbridge, were painted with flowers and leaves. A great many of the glass designs commissioned by Henry Cole (the presiding genius of what was destined to become the Victoria and Albert Museum) for his Summerly's Art Manufactures in about 1847 were for clear glass vessels with painted decoration. Some were made by Richardson's, but the best known of them, and the most imitated by others, was a series decorated with water-plants, carried out by J. F. Christy of Lambeth after a design by the painter Richard Redgrave R.A.

'Suggestive ornament' was used as decorative indications of the purpose of the vessel

The carafe shown in Figure 2, intended for water, the green plants growing from the base and curling inwards in a natural manner as they reach the shoulder, is an exceptionally harmonious example of what used to be called 'suggestive ornament', that is, ornament used to indicate the purpose of the vessel.

Another no less charming example of painted glass, its date 1848, is seen in Figure 3, the flower-painted jug, its shape a commonplace in contemporary pottery. But this treatment was more frequently used not on clear glass but on white opaline glass; much of this was in the form of decorative vases rather than tableware, but there were many such items as the flower-painted goblet shown in Figure 1. It was a mid-century taste which was not, like the deep cutting of the earlier part of the century, in favour abroad.

These are far closer to the inherent possibilities of glass than most of the tortured, extravagant designs produced with such misguided ingenuity during the twenty-five years from about 1835 to 1860. While it is correct to assert that the glass-manufacturers never quite achieved the elaborate vulgarity of their brethren the potters, they did at times come very close. There is no accounting for tastes, but the two pieces shown in Figures 5 and 7, the covered vase and the standing bowl, are surely likely candidates for a chamber of horrors. The former, possibly by Thomas Hawkes of Dudley in the late 1830s, is of double-walled glass, the outer layer cut, and painted and gilt within, vaguely reminiscent of some Germanic baroque silver ancestor. The latter is of ruby layered, silvered glass, emulating Bohemian coloured glass of its day – about 1851. It is thought to be by James Powell and Sons.

Here a word must be said in favour of the so-called Nailsea glass, really an offshoot of the bottle-making industry. It is mostly brownish or greenish, speckled or striped, and, though wholly unpretentious and cheap, was aesthetically far more satisfying than the laborious and ambitious confections mentioned above. However, by about 1840, it seems to have gone out of fashion for use as tableware because by then pressed glass had become a popular and inexpensive substitute for elaborately cut clear glass, so that the lower orders were able to keep up with the opulent Joneses.

A confection which would have surely delighted the Veneerings is the claret-jug in Figure 6 – a cut-glass decanter mounted lavishly and skilfully with silver vine leaves, the handle added as a vine stem to turn the vessel into a jug. It was made by Benjamin Smith, Jun., of Duke Street, Lincoln's Inn Fields in 1841.

As for goblets and wineglasses the solid, sturdy traditions dating from the early years of the century died hard whether cutting or engraving or both methods were employed. The goblet shown on the left in Figure 10 is of clear cut glass, decorated in the upper part with a grey enamel wash and an etched landscape design, and might be dated to about 1815. The goblet on the right is wheel-engraved with the initials C.A., festoons and the date 1840. A less ponderous style of about the same date is seen in the group of green-tinted wineglasses in Figure 8, the shallow fluting and stems of which hark back to eighteenth-century fashion, while the two champagne-glasses in Figure 9, made of thin glass delicately engraved and with elegant looped stems, presumably dating from a few years earlier, pay tribute to a not yet wholly forgotten Venetian tradition.

Later still the architect Philip Webb designed a notable group of highly sophisticated and simple glasses for Powell's. It was not obvious at the time, but his pioneer work, soon followed by other designers, did a great deal to remove some of the complicated clutter which makes it so difficult to form a balanced judgement of the achievements of an industry with so many ramifications.

MUSEUMS AND COLLECTIONS

Early nineteenth-century glass may be seen at the following:

GREAT BRITAIN

London: Victoria and Albert Museum
             The Bethnal Green Museum

FURTHER READING

Glass through the Ages by E. Barrington Haynes, London, reprinted 1964.
How to Identify English Drinking Glasses and Decanters, 1630–1830 by D. Ash, London, 1962.
Nineteenth Century British Glass by H. Wakefield, London, 1961.
Glass-making in England by H. J. Powell, London and New York, 1923.

Fig. 8 *Group of wineglasses,*
English, c.1840. Engraved green
glass.
(Delomosne Antiques.)

Fig. 9 *Champagne-glasses,*
made by George Bacchus and
Sons, Birmingham, c.1830. Clear
glass with twisted threads of blue,
white and pink, the glass on the
left having an engraved bowl,
height 5¼ ins.
(Victoria and Albert Museum.)

Fig. 10 Left: *Goblet, Davenport*
factory, Longport, c.1815.
Clear glass, cut on wheel,
decorated with an etched wash
of grey enamel, height 7⅞ ins.
Right: *Goblet, English, 1840.*
Wheel-engraved glass with the
initials 'CA', height 6½ ins.
(Victoria and Albert Museum.)

A. C. Cooper

Museum Photo

R. Todd-White

273

Nineteenth-Century American Glass

Museum Photo

Fig. 1 **Apple paperweight,** *New England Glass Company, 1853–80. Blown glass, height approximately 4 ins. The apple rests on a cushion of clear crystal glass. (Corning Museum of Glass, Corning, New York.)*

Important technical developments and the skill of nineteenth-century glassmakers in America resulted in pressed, cut, patterned and coloured glass of astonishing variety and stylishness

The *Boston Daily Journal* of 26 February, 1850, carried an advertisement by the glass-merchants W. R. and A. H. Somner, promising to supply not only the latest patterns in Waterford and English glass, but also 'American glassware made to order from metal of uncommon brilliancy to match any pattern desired whether of foreign or domestic manufacture'.

Some researchers believe glassmaking to have been the earliest American industry, and we know that the first Colonists established a glasshouse at Jamestown, Virginia, in 1608. From that date, glassmaking pursued a somewhat sporadic course with a fair number of factories emerging and closing down again after brief activity or amalgamating with a more prosperous establishment. Glassworks were frequently forced to move due to circumstances either of the economics or of the natural resources of the chosen area, and often the glassworkers themselves decided upon a change and joined a new glasshouse. During the later eighteenth century such enterprising glassmakers as Henry William Stiegel and John Frederick Amelung arrived from Europe, and their work left an indelible imprint on the history of American glassmaking.

A traditional American glass design is the so-called 'South [New] Jersey' style produced in glasshouses of this region during the later eighteenth and early nineteenth centuries. It is represented by free-blown, clear glass, adapted to pleasing and well-balanced forms of cream-jugs, bowls and dishes in attractive colours – amber, aquamarine, purple, blue and green – which could be produced by varying the quantity of the natural mineral content in the raw material. The most distinctive form of applied decoration is the lily-pad motif, resembling the stem and pad of a water-lily, and apparently an entirely original conception (Fig. 2).

Applied bands and loops in glass of contrasting colours, as may be found on some specimens of the Pittsburgh Flint Glass Manufactory of Bakewell and Co., show the influence of Bristol and Nailsea. Thomas Caines, son of a Bristol glass-maker, arrived in Boston in 1812 and was instrumental in setting up the South Boston Flint Glass Works, a subsidiary of the Boston Crown Glass Manufactory. A further factory, the Phoenix Glass Works, was established by the Caines family in 1820.

By 1815, some forty glasshouses were in operation in various parts of America, but these concentrated mainly on the manufacture of bottles and window-glass by the crown technique. Prior to the Treaty of Ghent in 1814, the war of 1812 and the blockade of American ports by the British made the Americans realise that home manufacture of fine table-glass was desirable. By 1840, about thirty American glasshouses were engaged in the production of tableware.

American cutting styles were predominantly influenced by English and Irish glass, which was

Fig. 2 **Pitcher**, *South Jersey type, possibly Lancaster or Lockport glassworks, New York, c.1840–50. Free-blown glass, with applied lily-pad decoration, height 7⅛ ins. (Corning Museum of Glass)*

Fig. 3 **Pitcher**, *Dorflinger Glass Works, New York, 1852–63. Cut glass, height 12⅛ ins. (Corning Museum of Glass.)*

Fig. 4 **Candlestick**, *probably Pittsburgh area, c.1815–40. Purple-blue pattern-moulded glass, height 10¼ ins. (Corning Museum of Glass.)*

Fig. 5 **Celery-vase**, *Bakewell, Page and Bakewell, Pittsburgh, c.1825. Cut glass, height 7½ ins. This was given by the Bakewells to Henry Clay Fry when he opened his glass factory in Pittsburgh in about 1867. (Corning Museum of Glass.)*

Fig. 6 **Oil-lamp**, *possibly Midwest, Pittsburgh area, c.1835–40. Blown, pressed and cut glass, height 17 ins. (Corning Museum of Glass.)*

imported in large quantities throughout the nineteenth century. By the middle of the century, Bohemian glass techniques had also made their mark upon the industry.

Bakewell's glass was highly praised for its quality, variety, beauty and brilliance

The first American glasshouse to produce cut and engraved tableware was very probably the Pittsburgh Flint Glass Manufactory, established by Benjamin Bakewell and Edward Ensell, an English glass-blower. Beginning operations in 1808, the partnership was dissolved in 1809, and the firm traded subsequently under various trade names (Fig. 5). Quality was extremely fine, with regard to both the white metal of their lead glass and the workmanship of the cutters and engravers.

It was fashionable for the stranger to Pittsburgh to pay a visit to the Bakewell glasshouse. Anne Royall in *Mrs. Royall's Pennsylvania* (Washington, 1829) writes rapturously of the quality, variety, beauty and brilliance of Bakewell's glass and assures us that it is equal, if not superior, to the Boston glass.

In his *Personal Narrative of Travel* (1817), Elias Pym Fordham wrote 'Mr. Bakewell's works are admirable. He has excellent artists, both French and English. His cut glass equals the best I have seen in England'. Henry Bradshaw Fearon in *A Narrative of a Journey* (London, 1818) expresses astonishment at finding such elegant and excellent perfection in glass on the other side of the Atlantic, although he adds that a number of specimens had been cut from a London pattern. In the absence of

a factory-mark, it is frequently impossible to be certain whether a specimen was an Anglo-Irish import or a home product.

Bakewell's produced a superb service of table-glass, made to order in 1817 for President Monroe. This is described as having been of brilliant double flint metal, engraved and cut by Mr. Jardelle, 'in which this able artist has displayed his best manner' with the arms of the United States decorating each piece. Another engraver and cutter of European extraction, William Peter Eichbaum, was employed by Bakewell's in 1810 and 'in that year cut the first crystal chandelier to have been produced in America'.

Until about 1820, the position of Bakewell's as manufacturers of fine, cut and engraved flint glass had few rivals. The factory made glass over a period of seventy-four years and finally closed down in 1882.

By 1816, the general depression had reached its height. The country was hard hit by commercial disasters, due partly to loss of foreign trade, and partly to the fact that, following the Treaty of Ghent, England swamped the American market with British wares which were heavily subsidised and prevented competitive home manufacture. For the more enterprising glass-makers transport facilities by road were poor and fraught with danger. On the other hand, the early years of the nineteenth century witnessed tremendous advances in another field of communication – water. Due to the development and expansion of the steamboat industry, hitherto unnegotiable routes began to open up, and river traffic proved a boon for the internal market.

In 1817, a group of Boston businessmen

7

8

Fig. 7 *Comport, covered bowl and plate*, Boston and Sandwich Glass Co., c.1830–40. Lacy pressed glass. *(Corning Museum of Glass.)*

Fig. 8 Left: *Sugar-bowl with cover*, probably Providence Flint Glass Works, 1831–33, or possibly Boston and Sandwich Glass Co., c.1830–40. Lacy pressed glass.
Centre: *Lamp*, New England Glass Co., c.1830. Lacy pressed glass.
Right: *Inkstand*, Boston and Sandwich, c.1830. Lacy pressed glass.
(Corning Museum of Glass.)

Museum Photo

Museum Photo

purchased the defunct Boston Porcelain and Glass Company, and in February 1818 the factory commenced production as the New England Glass Company. By the act of corporation, the associates, 'their successors and assigns' were privileged to manufacture 'flint and crown glass of all kinds in the towns of Boston and Cambridge'. The company became so successful that by 1865 five hundred men and boys were employed in various parts of the large plant. In time, the company expanded and a number of branches and subsidiaries were established, generally in neighbouring areas.

The youngest and possibly most dynamic of the original partners was Deming Jarves (1790–1869), who left the New England Glass Company to establish his own glassworks at Sandwich which was incorporated in 1826 as the Boston and Sandwich Glass Company. The tireless Jarves founded a number of branch firms, for instance the Cape Cod Glass Company and the Mount Washington Glassworks (famous for its 'Burmese Glass') for members of his family, and the New England Glass Bottle Company for the exclusive manufacture of bottles. It was at Jarves' instigation that the New England Glass Company began to manufacture its own red lead (litharge) from Missouri lead, an essential ingredient of flint glass. The supply of red lead to other glasshouses proved a profitable business for the company. For the manufacture of the high-grade clay pots needed in glassmaking, Stourbridge clay was imported from England. It is therefore not surprising that the lead glass produced by the New England Glass Company was of excellent quality. Particular emphasis was given to form and outline, and

grapes and other fruit, intaglio-cut landscapes and figures, faceted stems and star-cut bases were decorative devices applied to the early products of the company.

By the middle of the century, Bohemian-style cutting had become fashionable and European craftsmen, such as the German Louis Vaupel (Lewis Vaupal) at the New England Glass Company, were engaged to work for the larger American glasshouses. The resultant Bohemian-style glass could easily hold its own with the European models which had been obtained expressly for the purpose of study and copying. Cutting was frequently applied to good ruby-stained or cased glass, and, according to the recipe-book of John H. Leighton of the Boston and Sandwich Glass Company, this colour was obtained by the addition of oxide of gold to the batch. Specialists were engaged in every facet of the trade and workmen moved freely from one factory to another.

Production of cut glass was always costly and some of the executives, particularly men like Deming Jarves, encouraged production of mould-blown glass which would allow a variety of patterns, still in fine lead glass, to be manufactured more cheaply. Utilisation of the three-part mould was particularly suitable since it facilitated the lifting out of wares with complicated patterns.

A most significant development was achieved with the perfection of a practical glass-pressing machine, and once again the commercial application of this revolutionary technique is attributed to the ability and zeal of Deming Jarves, though he would not admit that this was a purely American invention. What he did maintain however was that 'America can claim the credit of great improvements in the needful machinery which has advanced the art to its present perfection'. Bakewell and Company obtained a patent for their pressed-glass furniture knobs in 1825; Enoch Robinson and Whitney of the New England Glass Company followed suit with their patent for pressed-glass knobs in 1826. A number of other glasshouses were granted patents for pressed wares, and most of these were situated along the eastern seaboard, particularly in the New England region. G. E. Pazaurek, in his unsurpassed *Gläser der Empire und Biedermeierzeit*, writes that apparently the first pressed drinking-glass with scale-cut pattern (*Schuppenschliff*) was made by Deming Jarves at Sandwich, Massachussetts, but most likely the first pressed objects were flat, such as the American so-called 'cup-plates'. These are small plates, three or four inches in diameter, in which the cup was set when the tea was poured into the saucer for cooling prior to drinking, so as to protect the table or linen from tea-stains.

When glass is blown into a mould, the inner surface of the specimen will correspond to the outside contours. In pressing, the glass mass is pressed into the mould by means of a plunger with a long handle, and consequently the interior glass surface will not follow the pattern but remain relatively smooth. It is the designer of the metal mould who must be considered as the real artist, and one of the finest craftsmen chosen by Jarves was probably Hiram Dillway, who remained with the Boston and Sandwich Glass Company all his life (d.1887).

Early American pressed ware was normally of

Fig. 9 *Dolphin candlesticks*, *probably Boston and Sandwich, mid-nineteenth century. Pressed glass.* (*Corning Museum of Glass.*)

fine quality lead glass, and once the piece was pressed into shape it was usually considered complete – edges and joins remained rough and unfinished. By the mid-nineteenth century three quarters of the American glass production consisted of pressed ware. The influence of this technique was enormous and revolutionised the glass industry in all parts of the world; in England, Apsley Pellat patented his process for glass-pressing techniques in 1831 and 1845.

The new 'lacy' glass had the delicate appearance of textiles or embroidery

During the early period of pressed-pattern glass (*c.*1825–50), a new phenomenon occurred in American pressed-glass design. This was the so-called 'lacy', now highly valued by collectors. Lacy glass patterns show a stippled background having the delicate appearance of textiles or embroidery; quite possibly the inspiration for the style came from Europe, perhaps from France, for it has decorative motifs similar in character to French designs. The actual source of the stippled background has never been fully explored; if there is a French influence, the fact that stippling represents one very specialised facet of the silversmith's craft, and that it was applied particularly to certain French and Russian work of this and earlier periods, is perhaps relevant. Early lacy glass is usually of fine quality, and patterns are so varied and numerous that to determine provenance in the absence of a factory-mark requires a great deal of study (Fig. 8).

The momentous changes and advances in the fields of politics and industry found a suitable response in a prolific output of commemorative glass objects, particularly in the cup-plates which were produced to more than six hundred different designs. Pictorial and historical pocket-flasks which were free-blown or pattern moulded appeared in large quantities and represent a study in themselves. First produced in about 1780, they continued throughout the ensuing century in numerous colour variations, and are much sought after by collectors. Among the most popular pressed objects are the delightful salt-cellars of trough-like shape and French-inspired rococo or Empire designs in both plain and coloured clear glass. Apart from the usual tableware (Fig. 7), pressed-glass whale-oil lamps came into fashion after 1820. These often consist of a pressed base and free-blown font and may incorporate cut and engraved decoration.

The earliest lacy glass has coarse stippling which becomes finer and more intricate in later ware. To exploit to the full every nuance of the delicate patterning, the glass metal had to be not only ductile, but also fluid, and this was achieved with the very high temperatures obtained by coal-fired furnaces. For these reasons, the moulds too were heated prior to being filled. The variety and richness of pattern could not conceivably have been accomplished by hand-cutting. Very much like French paperweights, American lacy glass is valued by the rarity of its design and colour.

About the middle of the century, America produced paperweights in many techniques. Floral bouquets were enclosed in the glass or miniature fruit rested on a *latticinio* bed, as produced by Nicholas Lutz who had come to the Sandwich Glass Company from the St. Louis glassworks in French Lorraine. *Millefiori* weights made of multi-coloured glass canes enclosed in a clear glass matrix were a speciality of John L. Gilliland, who apparently worked not only for his own factory at Brooklyn, New York, but also for a number of other glasshouses. The portrait weights with sulphide enclosures in the manner of Apsley Pellat's *Cristallo-ceramie* technique were based on existing designs of coins and medals. More original are the fruit paperweights produced mainly by the New England Glass Company (Fig. 1), which were attractively coloured single fruit, nearly life-size and blown, resting on a clear glass cushion. These were mostly produced by a Frenchman, François Pierre, who had been apprenticed at the Baccarat factory. During the later half of the century, there appeared paperweights pressed into the shape of some interesting landmarks such as the Plymouth Rock, and other weights in pressed glass are found which represent books or animals, and in addition are cut or engraved.

The development in 1864 of a cheaper substitute for lead glass – the lime soda glass developed by William Leighton of the Wheeling Glass Factory in West Virginia – proved disastrous for some of the manufacturers of high quality lead glass. There followed an increase in pressed-glass production, but a lowering of quality, and a number of the New England glass factories were slow to adapt themselves to this cheaper method. Many of the glassworkers were loath to utilise an inferior substitute for their high quality metal, but, 'there was no fun in carrying on at a loss, interesting though it may be to see workmen producing beautiful glass specimens', was the comment of the stockholders.

At the close of the century, many of the finest early glasshouses had ceased operations. The New England Glass Company closed down in 1888 and the manager at that time, Edward D. Libbey, took over the charter and moved the firm to Toledo, Ohio. There it successfully recommenced glassmaking as the Libbey Glass Company.

One of the finest modern glass factories, the Corning Glassworks, grew from the amalgamation and reorganisation of a number of unsuccessful glasshouses, and was established at Corning, New York, in 1875. A new generation of enterprising glassmakers began to explore new art forms in order to revive the industry.

MUSEUMS AND COLLECTIONS
American nineteenth-century glass may be seen at the following:
GREAT BRITAIN
Bath: American Museum in Britain
London: Victoria and Albert Museum
U.S.A.
Corning, N.Y.:   Corning Museum of Glass
Dearborn, Mich.:   Henry Ford Museum
New York: Metropolitan Museum of Art
Toledo, Ohio: Toledo Museum of Art

FURTHER READING
New England Glass and Glassmaking by K. M. Wilson, New York, 1972.
Early American Pressed Glass by Ruth Webb Lee, Massachusetts, 1946.
American Glass by George S. and Helen A. McKearin, New York, 1941.

French Paperweights

Invented by an Italian and made chiefly in the three French factories of St. Louis, Baccarat and Clichy, glass paperweights have captured the imagination of collectors since the first was exhibited in 1845

A paperweight must be handled to be appreciated. Because of the problems of reflection, photography, which has achieved such remarkable results in other fields, can provide only a suggestion of the beauty of a good paperweight.

Legend has it that glass was discovered accidentally by a group of Phoenician sailors who built a bonfire on a beach. Having no stones upon which they could rest their cooking-utensils, they used cakes of soda which they happened to have with them. On completion of their meal, they were amazed to find that the soda had disappeared. In its place was a hard, shiny substance which proved to be the first glass made by man.

Early glass paperweights were inspired by the mosaic glass beads of the ancient Egyptians

Study of the old mosaic glass beads of the Egyptians will reveal the designs which served, hundreds of years later, to give workmen their ideas for the so-called 'cane', or 'florette', patterns used in some early glass paperweights.

The process of making the cane seen in these *millefiori* weights takes time but appears fairly simple to the observer. It is composed of several rods of glass of different colours, welded together to form a large block of glass ranging from six to

Fig. 1 *Bouquet paperweight, Clichy, nineteenth century. Diameter 2¾ ins.*
(Spink and Sons Ltd., London.)
Fig. 2 *Bouquet paperweight, Baccarat, nineteenth century. Diameter 3¼ ins.*
(Spink's.)
Fig. 3 *Bouquet paperweight, St. Louis, nineteenth century. Diameter 2½ ins.*
(Spink's.)

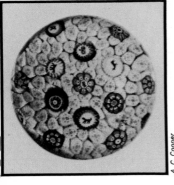

Fig. 4 *Paperweight, St. Louis,
nineteenth century.
Diameter 3 ins.
(Spink's.)*

Fig. 5 *Paperweight, Baccarat,
nineteenth century.
Diameter 3 ins.
Set with animal silhouette and
other canes, this white and red
weight is marked 'B.1848' for its
date and place of manufacture.
(Spink's.)*

Fig. 6 *Crown Imperial
paperweight, Baccarat,
nineteenth century.
Diameter 3 ins.
The spray of flowers in this
excessively rare weight is set in
clear glass, as is usually the case
with single flowers.
(Spink's.)*

twenty-five inches in length and four to five inches in diameter. This block is then reheated and drawn to the required thickness by two men pulling in opposite directions, ending up as a very long, thin stick which, when cooled, is cut into very short lengths of which various types, colours and sizes form the design. These, having been placed in a mould, are then picked up by a ball of molten glass taken from the furnace on a pontil rod and fused together, thus forming the dome which magnifies the canes. The glass-maker then takes a large wooden spatula and, while he rolls the pontil rod back and forth on a bar of wood or metal, uses this spatula to trim the weight down to its correct shape and size. It is then removed from the pontil rod, and the finished weight is allowed to cool slowly in an annealing oven at a reducing temperature, and subsequently given to the polisher to smooth away the rough pontil mark on the base, leaving it with or without star cutting as a finishing touch.

'Numerous small canes of all colours and forms, assembled to look like a posy of flowers'

Pietro Bigaglia, a member of an old family of Venetian glass artisans, is credited with the manufacture of the first glass weight. In May 1845 Bigaglia displayed his paperweights at the Exhibition of Austrian Industry in Vienna. Attending the Exhibition as an observer for the Paris Chamber of Commerce was Eugène Peligot, a professor at the Conservatoire National des Arts et Métiers and a renowned authority on glass. Impressed by Bigaglia's entry, and, more important perhaps, quick to see a potential new product for the French glass industry, which was not flourishing at the time, Peligot reported the Italian's paperweights to friends in Paris and undoubtedly carried back with him to France examples of Bigaglia's work. His report stated: 'One of the principal exhibits is that of M. Pierre Bigaglia of Venice – round-shaped millefior paperweights of highly transparent glass in which are embedded numerous small canes of all colours and forms, assembled to look like a posy of flowers.' The French glass industry at that time comprised a number of companies of which only three figure prominently in the history of paperweights: St. Louis; La Compagnie des Cristalleries Baccarat, at Baccarat in Lorraine, about sixty miles from St. Louis and not far from Lunéville; and the Cristalleries de Clichy, located in what was then a village outside Paris.

Baccarat was the largest of the French glassworks. Prior to 1845 fine crystal glassware such as table-services, chandeliers and vases, as well as cameos,

279

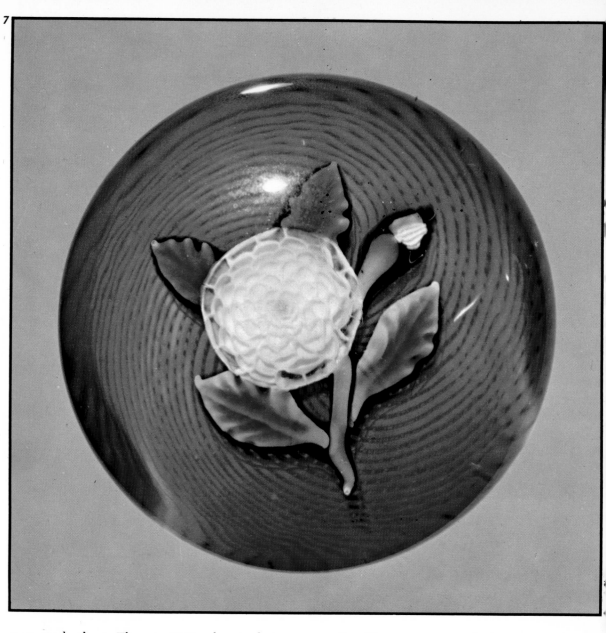

were made there. Then, in 1845, when trade was poor, it was suggested that paperweights might be a profitable new line. Baccarat did not go along with this idea, however, and the St. Louis glassworks was the first to make paperweights of the type which collectors now prize. These were far more beautiful in colour and design than those made by Bigaglia, and soon Baccarat and Clichy started to produce them. The work of each of these factories shows distinct characteristics in colouring, formation and the variety of canes and design. Baccarat weights can be divided into two groups: *millefiori*, which form roughly two-thirds of all Baccarat weights, and flowers, which comprise little less than a third. The remainder comprise such subjects as butterflies and reptiles and, more rarely, incrustations – porcelain-like cameos encased in the body of the paperweight.

Many St. Louis paperweights featured flowers, fruits, vegetables and reptiles

St. Louis had a somewhat wider range of subjects than Baccarat, employing *millefiori* less extensively, (for only about twenty-five per cent of its output) and also devoting a considerable proportion of its production to flower weights, fruit, vegetables and

reptiles. The canes are much the same as those of Baccarat, consisting of the usual hollow forms in various colours, usually four, while the tone of the colours is delicate and, in some cases, pale by comparison with Baccarat and Clichy.

Millefiori, bouquets, swirls and miniatures were specialities of the Clichy factory

Few records of the Clichy factory survive and consequently less is known of its history than of either Baccarat or St. Louis, although there are fortunately a few signed specimens which make its style recognisable.

The factory, which is known to have produced paperweights from about 1849, specialised in *millefiori* – no less than eight out of every ten being of this type – and conformed to a more standard pattern than any other factory. Other types include the sought-after Clichy overlays, which comprise less than two per cent of all types, and bouquet weights, (weights with a central motif of a bunch of flowers, in some cases tied at the base with ribbon). Swirls and miniature Clichy weights also appear fairly frequently.

In the illustrations, differences in types of bouquets of flowers are noticeable: those of Clichy

Fig. 8 Butterfly paperweight, Baccarat, nineteenth century. Diameter 3⅜ ins. Four per cent of all paperweights made at the Baccarat factory during the nineteenth century feature a butterfly. Most hover over a white flower, although a few coloured flowers are also seen, as well as the delicate white lace in this example. (Spink's.)

Fig. 9 Blue colour-ground paperweight, Clichy, nineteenth century. Diameter 3 ins. These striking weights appear in brilliant red, green, pink of various shades, yellow, mauve and many shades of blue. Occasionally they have a cane containing the letter 'C' for Clichy. (Spink's.)

Owner's Photo

Owner's Photo

Fig. 10 *Crown paperweight,*
St. Louis, nineteenth century.
Diameter 2½ ins.
A type peculiar to this factory,
St. Louis crowns are hollow,
with white filigree threads and
coloured twists rising to end
under a central cane above.
(Spink's.)

10

(Fig. 1) include two pink so-called 'Clichy roses', and the bouquet is tied with ribbon. Others display flowers, usually in pastel colours, resting on a cushion of white swirling rods – dahlias, thistles, pansies, convolvuluses, auriculas, etc. The Baccarat bouquet in Figure 2 is in a larger weight and has a pink rose in the centre, surrounded by a red primrose, a plum-mauve and yellow pansy, a yellow wheatflower with black spots, and buds. The variety of flowers differs in almost every bouquet; some contain pom-pom and other dahlias, clematis, buttercups and forget-me-nots. The spray manufactured at St. Louis illustrated in Figure 3 has a charm of its own, with snowdrops and a striped tulip, seen very rarely; in place of these a fuchsia is occasionally included among the tiny flowers.

The term 'carpet', which describes the patterned ground of a paperweight, was first used in 1855 in

A. C. Cooper

the *Catalogue des Collections du Conservatoire des Arts et Métiers, Paris.* The carpet weights differ, as seen in Figures 4 and 5, the white and red Baccarat one set with silhouettes and other canes and marked 'B.1848'. Other St. Louis carpets are composed of green or pink hollow canes set with animal silhouettes, some marked 'S.L.1848', this being the only year for dated St. Louis weights. All Baccarat carpets of this type are dated and appear in royal blue, rust red or green.

Single flowers are mostly in clear glass (Fig. 6), sometimes set on a white or coloured spiral cushion (Fig. 7). Baccarat weights have a pansy, wheatflower, primrose, buttercup, dahlia, white bellflower, bluebell, daisy, periwinkle or a red or pink cabbage rose. Baccarat butterflies were made in clear glass, hovering over a flower, or over white lace within a wreath of canes, as in Figure 8.

More are found over a white dahlia than over coloured flowers.

Occasionally the letter 'C' for Clichy was incorporated in weights from that factory

Clichy colour-ground weights are usually very striking, in colour and design, as in Figure 9; they occur in brilliant red, green, pink of various shades, yellow, mauve and many shades of blue, very occasionally with a cane containing the letter 'C' for Clichy. There are also some with translucent cushions in green, dark blue or wine red. St. Louis crowns (Fig. 10) are hollow, with coloured twists between white filigree threads rising from the base and ending under a central cane above, a type peculiar to this factory.

COLLECTING HINTS

Nineteenth-century French paperweights are considerably heavier than modern reproductions. This is the simplest test to apply. It is also easy to tell a certain amount about the age – and consequently the authenticity – of the object by the condition of the surface of the glass. Where weights are severely scratched or damaged, restoration can be done to remove the blemishes and increase the brilliance of the glass, but this must be done professionally. The lapidary has to remove the minimum amount of glass and retain the original shape. Unskilled polishing may result in loss in value of the weight, and those with deep chips should be avoided by the collector.

Paperweights vary greatly in worth. To value one requires knowledge of the different types, some of which vary in only the slightest degree. A well-illustrated book on the subject is essential to the collector.

MUSEUMS AND COLLECTIONS

French glass paperweights of the nineteenth century may be seen at the following:

FRANCE
Paris: Baccarat Showrooms
                  Musée des Arts Décoratifs

GREAT BRITAIN
Bristol: City Art Gallery
Swansea: Glynn Vivian Art Gallery

U.S.A.
Chicago: Art Institute of Chicago
Los Angeles: Francis Fowler Museum
Neenah, Wisc.: John Nelson Bergstrom Art
                  Centre
New York: New York Historical Society
Flint, Michigan: Flint Institute of Art

FURTHER READING

Glass Paperweights: an Old Craft Revived by Paul Hollister, 1975.
Glass Paperweights of the New York Historical Society by Paul Hollister, 1975.
The Encyclopedia of Glass Paperweights by Paul Hollister, New York, 1969.
Antique Glass Paperweights from France by Patricia K. McCawley, London, 1968.

French Coloured Glass

Fig. 1 **Pair of vases,** *probably St. Louis, c.1850. Blue and white spiral glass, height 6⅛ ins. Like the striped glass in Figure 2, these attractive pieces show the Murano influence in the strong, clear colours and patterns. (Kunstindustrimuseet, Oslo.)*

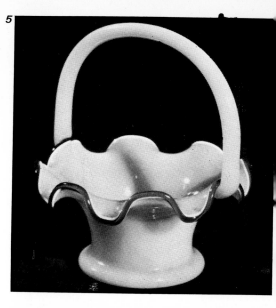

Fig. 2 **Vase**, *St. Louis, 1855.*
Blue glass with yellow internal stripes.
The Venetian heritage in French glass may be seen in the imaginative use of bright colours, often as here composed into stripes.
(Conservatoire National des Arts et Métiers, Paris.)

Fig. 3 **Two-handled vase,**
St. Louis, 1853. Green glass with marbled surface.
Textural effects were very popular on glass vessels.
(Conservatoire National des Arts et Métiers.)

Fig. 4 **Tall goblet on twisted stem** *by Georges Bontemps, Choisy-le-Roi, 1842. The cup is encased in red glass with a pattern of vine leaves cut through to the crystal base.*
The great period of the factory at Choisy-le-Roi began in 1825 when Bontemps became its technical and artistic leader. He was one of the greatest glassmakers and experimenters of his time, and the factory closed down shortly after his departure to England in 1848.
(Conservatoire National des Arts et Métiers.)

Fig. 5 **Basket**, *St. Louis, 1853. Milky-white glass with blue edges.*
(Conservatoire National des Arts et Métiers.)

From the 1820s and throughout the rest of the nineteenth century, the French were the finest makers of luxury glass in Europe

In the course of the nineteenth century French glassmakers forged ahead of the traditional producers of decorative glass – the Venetians, Bohemians and the English – and established themselves as the makers of the finest and most imaginative luxury glass of the age. This development began during the 1820s and '30s, and was the more surprising since the French until then had made no very interesting contribution in this field. Royal patronage, the government protection which under *l'ancien régime* had been so vital to the success of any French industry, had been given generously to makers of flat glass, and it was as producers of the finest mirrors and windows in the world that French glassmakers had gained their great fame. But such support for the makers of glass vessels had been only sporadic; their products had been mainly utilitarian, and when they did decorative work it was without striking originality.

But the Revolution changed the pattern of French glassmaking. The old privileges and protective measures were abolished, and from the early years of the nineteenth century no authorisation was needed to set up a glasshouse, and no protection was given to one establishment and withheld from another. At the same time, the new authorities gave vigorous encouragement to crafts and industries by the arrangement of regular exhibitions (from 1797) where the products shown were submitted to intelligent criticism and awards were given for the best goods. It was in this stimulating atmosphere of free enterprise, free competition and public interest that the French makers of glass vessels were to give their very best.

Most of the decorative glass in nineteenth-century France was produced in the factories of Baccarat (founded in 1764) and St. Louis (founded in 1767). They were both situated in Lorraine, and both were large, modern establishments with good technical resources and production capacity. That this was so was to a large extent due to the efforts of Gabriel d'Artigues (died 1848), owner-director of St. Louis from 1791 to 1797 and of Baccarat from 1816 to 1822, one of the great administrators and

glass technicians of his time. From about 1835 onwards the two Lorraine factories were run as one unit, with a joint policy of production and sales.

In the France of Louis Philippe's monarchy (1830–48), the Second Republic (1848–52) and the Second Empire (1852–70), Paris was the great centre of fashion and arbiter of taste, as it had been before the Revolution, and the Lorraine factories kept closely in touch with Paris. Between 1832 and 1855 they had a depot in Paris run by the firm of Launay, Hautin & Cie., who constantly advised the makers of what the public of Paris wanted and how fashions were changing, and Baccarat and St. Louis adapted their production accordingly. Most decorating work was done in Paris, as neither of the factories seems to have had decorating shops of any importance. In the fashionable quarters of Paris were numerous dealers in luxury goods of many kinds, including glass, who took their goods from Launay, Hautin & Cie., and who had very close and regular connections with cutters and engravers, gilders and enamellers; many of these worked with as much skill in the ornamentation and refining of porcelain and faience as with glass.

In 1843, Launay, Hautin & Cie. took in as a business associate Joseph-François Robert, an enameller at the porcelain factory at Sèvres. In 1838 he had invented a method of applying coloured enamels to lead crystal. His secrets were soon understood by other craftsmen, but Robert remained a partner in the Launay firm until 1855, and some surviving pieces carry his signature.

L'Escalier de Cristal, a firm founded in 1802 at Palais Royal, was active until 1835, specialising in the cutting, engraving and mounting in bronze of fine crystal goods – vases and boxes, clocks and mirrors, even tables and chairs. During the 1830s and '40s Jaquel, in the rue de Richelieu, sold luxury glass and executed cutting and bronze mounting of glass to specification, while in the rue du Faubourg St. Denis the firm of Cattaert carried on a similar kind of business.

Paris soon became a centre, not only for the decoration, but for the actual making of fine glass. The factory of Choisy-le-Roi was founded in 1820 in an industrial suburb to the north-west of Paris, and its great period began in 1825 when Georges Bontemps became technical and artistic leader. Bontemps was one of the great glassmakers of his time. He experimented assiduously and was the author of the most important glassmaker's manual

Fig. 6 **Designs for cut glass decanters** from a St. Louis catalogue of 1842. Decanters with this Biedermeier flavour remained popular for many years, and appear in a Baccarat catalogue as late as 1865.

Fig. 7 **Ewer and bowl**, French, c.1830. Opaline with brass mounts, height of ewer 11½ ins. (Kunstindustrimuseet, Oslo.)

Fig. 8 **Beaker**, French, c.1810. Turquoise opaline with gilt decoration, height 3½ ins., diameter 3 ins. Opaline was made in a wide variety of qualities and, after the initial milky-white period, of colours. (Richard Dennis Antiques, London.)

Fig. 9 **Tazza**, Baccarat, dated 'B1846' in centre of bowl. Millefiori glass bowl and foot, the stem with opaque white twisted threads, height 3⅝ ins. (Corning Museum of Glass, New York.)

of the period, *Guide du Verrier* (1868). At Choisy-le-Roi, flat glass and optical glass were produced as well as fine lead-crystal vessels, tinted in subtle shades of colour and decorated with cutting and engraving (Fig. 4). But in 1848 Bontemps left France for political reasons. He joined the firm of Chance Brothers in England and soon afterwards the factory at Choisy-le-Roi ceased production.

In 1848, after an introductory period of seven years at nearby Pont de Sèvres, M. Maës set up a glass factory at Clichy-la-Garenne on the south-eastern fringes of Paris. It was active until 1889, when it was absorbed into the glasshouse at Sèvres. M. Maës seems to have been the moving spirit in the firm's activities until about 1870. By mid-century, Clichy had become one of the main producers of fine glass in France, with an output amounting to one third of that of Baccarat. Apart from its signed

paperweights, few products from Clichy can be identified today, but contemporary critics spoke with enthusiasm about the factory's coloured opaline glass with gilt and enamelled decoration.

The third of the important Paris glasshouses of the period was founded in 1851 at La Villette, an industrial suburb to the north-east of the city; soon afterwards it moved to Pantin, a little further out. Under the leadership of M. Monot, the factory launched on an ambitious career of luxury glass-making; by 1867 it had achieved an importance equal to that of Clichy. Pantin continued to make fine and truly luxurious pieces, mostly of coloured glass, to the end of the nineteenth century.

The earliest efforts of post-Revolution French glassmakers were aimed at the production of cut lead crystal, after the English fashion. Some results had been achieved at St. Louis as early as 1782, but-

Museum Photo

Author's Photo

Fig. 10 **Vase**, *one of a pair, Baccarat, c.1865. Mould-blown opaline.*
Although a cheaply made piece from the design in Figure 11, the shape, colour and design of this late example of opaline are very good, and the result attractive.
(Kunstindustrimuseet, Oslo.)

Fig. 11 **'Vase moulé à guirlande en spirale'** *from the Baccarat catalogue of 1865.*
(From L'Opaline Française au XIXe siècle by Yolande Amic, Paris, 1952.)

the great achievements in this direction were attained under the leadership of D'Artigues. From the 1820s cut crystal glass was being produced in important quantities and in a rich and original style at both the Lorraine factories; it continued to be a large part of their output throughout this period and later. The magnificently dignified shapes had a distinctly neo-classical character, which was further accentuated by the insertion of sulphides, or silver-white cameo portraits of famous men and women, into the massive walls of the vessels. These portraits were made, frequently from coins, by various specialised producers in Paris, many of whom signed their works.

Eventually the grandeurs of the Napoleonic style began to give way to softer and gentler contours and cut patterns with less fierce a glitter; the models from St. Louis dating from 1842 have a comfortable, Biedermeier look about them (Fig. 6).

A distinctively French contribution of the time is opaline glass – glass with an opalescent sheen made into smooth, simple forms, mostly of classical derivation, such as urns and ewers. The best pieces were mounted in bronze and had the solidity and dignity of true Empire products (Fig. 7). During the early stages, up to about 1830, opaline was chiefly made in pure milky-white glass, but soon taste turned in favour of pretty colouring and opaline was increasingly tinted a soft rose pink, a fine apple green or a clear turquoise blue (Fig. 8). Opaline was made in a wide range of qualities, from the heaviest and most costly lead glass to the cheapest *verre commun*. As this popularity spread, the genre became somewhat vulgarised; the fine opalescent glass was replaced by a cheaper and less attractive *pâte-de-riz*, produced from 1843, and the ornaments were sometimes applied by mechanical methods. What had begun as true luxury glass had become *verre de fantaisie*, with a much less exclusive character.

The greatest finesse and originality was displayed by French glassmakers in the production of coloured glass in furnace-worked combinations. The key pieces from this group are those presented to the Conservatoire Nationale des Arts et Métiers by the glassmakers themselves and obviously considered by them particularly fine and characteristic examples of their skill. By comparison of styles and techniques, other glasses can be grouped around the dated and identifiable pieces at the Conservatoire Nationale.

The glasses are made of a fairly heavy crystal which has been tinted in colours of great purity and brilliance; by clever furnace-work, they were combined to make rich harmonies. The glasses adhere to no particular style; they are not neo-classical, Biedermeier nor historicist in taste; they are pure experiments in fine glassmaking. Their initial inspiration clearly came from Venice.

The ancient centre of colour glassmaking at Murano had been declining fast in the course of the eighteenth century, and when Napoleon entered Venice it received the *coup de grâce*; in 1806 the ancient organisation of the Murano glassmakers was dissolved by Imperial decree. It was in a spirit of nostalgia that the descendants of the old Murano masters began, about 1830, a tentative revival of the old colour techniques of the island: lace glass, aventurine, chalcedony and others.

These developments were followed with the keenest interest by glassmakers abroad, not least by

the French. In his *Guide du Verrier*, Bontemps describes how in 1839 he was able to produce lace glass, in 1844 *millefiori* – one year before Pietro Bigaglia showed his famous *millefiori* paperweight at the exhibition in Vienna.

But the glassmakers in France did not copy the admired Venetian models. In fact, had they wanted to, they would probably not have found it possible. For their own heavy, lead crystal, initially of English derivation, was very different from the brittle and lightweight metal which the Venetians had used, and it was quite unsuited to the making of those pretty, miniature glassblown details for which the Venetians were so justly famous. The Franco-Venetian glasses of the mid-nineteenth century are bold and simple in form, without any of those dexterous glassblowers' details which are so typical of the fully developed Venetian style. The Venetian heritage in the French glasses can be traced in the imaginative use of brilliant colours, composed into stripes and spirals or combined into fascinating textural effects: *millefiori* was used, not only for paperweights, but also for vessels (Fig. 9). In the application of Venetian ideas to their heavy crystal glass, the French produced some of the most captivating luxury glasses of the age.

The coloured glasses in Venetian style constituted only a small section of the whole output of French luxury glassmaking of the middle years of the nineteenth century, but the group is very important – not only because of the intrinsic beauty and charm of the pieces themselves but because they provided the starting-point from which the famous French Art Nouveau glass at the end of the century could develop. It is glasses like these which form the true background to the art glass of Eugène Rousseau, Emile Gallé and the other great French glassmakers of the last decades of the century. When their glasses in the fashionable forms of *japonisme* and Art Nouveau appeared at exhibitions which were sponsored by new organisations such as L'Union Centrale des Arts Décoratifs and which were widely publicised in the new design magazines, they were greeted as truly sensational and they became famous and influential far beyond the boundaries of France. But these achievements would not have been possible without the anonymous, experimental work with furnace-worked coloured glass in Lorraine and in Paris.

MUSEUMS AND COLLECTIONS
French glass of the nineteenth century may be seen at the following:
FRANCE
Paris: Conservatoire Nationale des Arts et Métiers
     Musée des Arts Décoratifs
GREAT BRITAIN
London: Bethnal Green Museum
NORWAY
Oslo: Kunstindustrimuseet

FURTHER READING
Continental Coloured Glass by R. K. Middlemas, London, 1971.
French Cameo Glass by Berniece and Henry Blount, 1968.
Sulphides by Paul Jokelson, New York, 1968.
'French Nineteenth-Century Glass' by Ada Polak in **The Concise Encyclopedia of Antiques**, edited by The Connoisseur, London, 1962.

English Cameo Glass

Fig. 1 **Vase**, *Thomas Webb, c.1880. White on orange cameo glass. (Alan Tillman.)*

Fig. 2 **Vase** *designed by Thomas Woodall (1849–1926) and cut by J. T. Fereday for Thomas Webb and Sons, made for the International Health Exhibition of 1884. White on amber glass. Thomas Woodall gained a bronze medal at this exhibition for his vases and bowls. (Victoria and Albert Museum, London.)*

Inspired by classical precedent the later nineteenth-century English glassmakers produced cameo glass for exhibition and commercial purposes of the best artistic and technical quality

Cameo glass, a revival of a technique known to the Romans, became one of the most important features of the English glass industry in the latter part of the nineteenth century, superb examples being produced for exhibitions and for the luxury trade. This particular form of decorative glass has always been a product demanding great skill, and pieces of cameo glass have long been regarded as collectors' items of great importance.

English cameo work of the late nineteenth century was not really related to contemporary cameo work produced elsewhere. It was almost entirely classical in inspiration, with figurative decoration, unlike the oriental inspiration of the French glassmaker Emile Gallé. What naturalistic decoration there was, tended to be overshadowed by Classicism, except in the case of mass-produced articles for a wider and cheaper market.

Cameo glass first appeared in England after the Great Exhibition of 1851 and was usually the work of local craftsmen in the Stourbridge area, which was the centre of nineteenth-century English glass-making. It is a form of cased or flashed glass, using several layers of glass in the manufacture of the vessel, usually an opaline glass on a coloured

287

R. Fortt

Fig. 3 *Vase, Thomas Webb, late nineteenth century. White on pink on yellow cameo glass. (Private Collection.)*

Fig. 4 *Vase, George Woodall, made in 1910 for the Brussels exhibition of 1911. White on sepia cameo glass depicting The Origin of Painting. (Stourbridge Town Council Collection.)*

Fig. 5 *Four scent-bottles, Thomas Webb, c.1880. White on yellow, red and green cameo glass, the tops of silver. (Alan Tillman, London.)*

Fig. 6 *Vase by John Northwood, late nineteenth century. White on amber cameo glass. This fine vase is seen with an assortment of tools used by John Northwood for the cutting and engraving of cameo glass. (Science Museum, London.)*

ground with a matt finish, the opaline shape being filled with coloured glass and then marvered. The blank was sent to a decorator's workshop, where the outer layer was partially removed and small steel rods were used to carve the relief. Shadows were obtained by controlling the density of the decoration.

This method of production, requiring such a high degree of craftsmanship and technical competence, was never a viable commercial proposition. Eventually, with the rise in demand for cameo glass, some methods of industrial production were introduced. The glass blank was treated with acid and an engraving-wheel was used, so as to produce cheaper cameo work for a mass market. The relief work was done by glass-engravers on a considerably thinner base, so that there was less ground to remove for shadowing and commercial pieces could be produced on a large scale.

Cameo work represented a comparatively short-lived fashion which was virtually over by the beginning of the twentieth century. Cheaper Continental wares had appeared on the market and the idea of a white relief on a coloured ground had been copied in the so-called 'Mary Gregory' glass, using painted decoration, and in figurative designs on ceramics.

The cameo glass of the nineteenth century is directly influenced by ancient precedent and coincided with the museum-inspired revivalism of the nineteenth century. The Portland Vase, a classical glass vase of the first century A.D., once the property of Sir William Hamilton and copied by Wedgwood, was exhibited in the British Museum in 1810. It provided an example for English pioneers in cameo work and an impetus for the development of English cameo glass.

Production of decorated glass in England, particularly after the repeal, in 1845, of the crippling glass tax, increased, and was strongly influenced by Continental imports and by the contemporary desire for elaborate ornament. Apsley Pellatt (1791–1863), the son of the founder of the Falcon Glasshouse in Southwark, produced glass towards the end of his life decorated with classical motifs in ceramic paste, known as 'crystallo-ceramie' or 'cameo incrustations', and this was displayed at the Great Exhibition of 1851; the Apsley Pellatt cameo decoration was virtually an imitation of cameo cutting. Engraved, cut and coloured glass was popular in the late nineteenth century, when cameo glass began to be of paramount importance.

The firm of Richardson of Stourbridge, which had won the gold medal of the Society of Arts in 1847 and a prize medal at the 1851 Exhibition, under the influence of Benjamin Richardson (d.1887), produced highly decorative and experimental forms of glass and was particularly skilled in the use of the acid etching process. They also employed John Northwood, the first glass-maker in England to produce cameo glass on the classical pattern.

John Northwood (1836–1902), a great admirer of Greek art, came from Wordsley and joined the Richardson firm at about the age of twelve, painting on glass in Richardson's decorating shop. He had been a prize student at Stourbridge School of Art and was greatly influenced by the trend towards museum-inspired revivalism and by the work of the neo-classical artist Flaxman. He made a serious study of classical design and by 1861 he and his brother, Joseph, had set up a decorating workshop in Stourbridge, using acid etching to produce highly elaborate ornament on glass.

John Northwood produced a famous series of cameo vases, the first being a blue vase with white overlay, inspired by a design by Professor Kiss of Berlin, c.1855. This purely experimental piece was smashed several years later and was a forerunner of the famous Elgin vase, commissioned by J. B. Stone (later of the Birmingham firm of Stone, Fawdry and Stone) in 1864 and finished in 1873. The Elgin vase, Grecian in style and inspired by the equestrian figures on the Elgin marbles, was not true cameo work, as it was executed in clear glass, probably made in Stone's glassworks. A similar subject was worked by the engraver Frederick Kny.

The Elgin vase was the direct antecedent for the cameo work produced for Northwood's cousin, Philip Pargeter of the Red House Glassworks in Stourbridge; he made a series of superb pieces – the Portland vase, the Milton vase and the Shakespeare, Newton and Flaxman tazzas, the latter pieces being awarded a Silver Medal at the Plymouth Art and Industries Exhibition of 1881.

The Portland vase, 1873–1876, for which Northwood made endless experiments in technique and in the use of various graving tools, was an exact replica of the original and it was displayed at the Paris Exhibition of 1878, on the stand of the dealer R. P. Daniell. At the same exhibition, Northwood's unfinished Pegasus or Dennis vase won a Gold Medal. This vase, commissioned by Thomas Wilks Webb, c.1875, of the Dennis Glass Works, was displayed on the Webb stand; it was finished in 1880 and sold to Tiffany of New York. Northwood also showed another piece of cameo glass at the Paris Exhibition, the Milton vase, illustrating the expulsion from the Garden of Eden as described in *Paradise Lost*, and designed in close conjunction with Philip Pargeter. This was displayed on the stand of James Green and Nephew.

One of the features of the Paris Exhibition of 1878 was the fashion for very deep cutting of glass, and the Exhibition was important for its display of cameo glass as such. The Stourbridge firm of Richardson showed work by the French medallist Alphonse Eugène Lecheverell (born in 1850) who came to Wordsley in 1877 to train Richardson's workmen in the art of elaborate ornament; Lecheverell cameo work – *Venus Arising, The Birth of Venus, Raising an Altar to Bacchus* and *Hercules and Alcestis* – was displayed on the Richardson stand, as also was the work of Joseph Locke (1846–1938), including an unfinished version of the Portland vase (Fig. 7).

The glass produced at this period was strongly classical in derivation and showed the overriding influence of the Portland vase, but in the 1880s, when the taste for cameo glass became more widespread and it was produced on a more commercial scale, some use was also made of floral decoration. The firms of Stevens and Williams and of Thomas Webb produced commercial cameo work and John Northwood was made art director of Stevens and Williams in about 1880, the decorating firm of J. and J. Northwood becoming virtually a cameo workshop for Stevens and Williams, one of the most successful and influential firms of the day.

In 1886, Stevens and Williams exhibited 'a choice collection of Table and Decorative glass in cut, engraved, rock crystal, cameo etc.', at the International Exhibition of Industry, Science and Art at Edinburgh and won the Gold Medal Diploma for art cameo glass. Northwood was followed by his son,

Derek Balmer

K. Hoddle

A. C. Cooper

John Northwood II (1870–1960), who first worked on cameos for brooches and later became director and technical manager for Stevens and Williams. His nephew, William Northwood (1858–1937), like John Northwood II, produced very little, but won a bronze medal in a national competition in 1889.

The most important follower of John Northwood was Joshua Hodgetts (1857–1933) who was employed by Stevens and Williams and who worked in the Northwood decorating shop at Wordsley. Hodgetts, who had also been to the Stourbridge School of Art, was a knowledgeable amateur botanist and made great use of floral decoration on the wheel-cut commercial work he produced for the firm (Fig. 8), some of which was exhibited at Wolverhampton in 1902. By 1906, however, Stevens and Williams were producing crystal cameo work, which was cheaper and which used crystal glass with relief work in the style of a cameo.

Apart from the Northwood and Stevens and Williams work, superb cameo work was carried out in the cameo workshop of Thomas Webb by Thomas (1849–1926) and George Woodall (1850–1925) who had originally worked in the Northwood firm and were nephews of Thomas Bott (1829–1870) an employee of Richardson, who had moved to the Worcester porcelain factory. They were well-trained artists and went to work for Thomas Webb in about 1874. The influence of Northwood's Dennis vase at the Paris Exhibition of 1878 and the interest in museum-inspired pieces, encouraged Thomas Wilkes Webb to send George Woodall to the Continent and to the art school at South Kensington to study, and Woodall did engraving on both flint glass and rock crystal.

In 1884, Webb started to produce commercial cameo glass, using the wheel, instead of relying entirely upon carved decoration, with great emphasis upon shadow, caused by deep cutting of the overlay. Acid was used to aid the engravers and the pattern was painted in acid resistant, so as to enable a larger and cheaper production. Engraving, as such, was out of fashion in the 1880s, so labour was plentiful and, despite the competition from imported German glass painted in enamels, in imitation of cameo work, Webb had considerable success. In the International Health Exhibition of 1884, Thomas Woodall gained a bronze medal for vases and bowls (Fig. 2). Webb also patented glass

289

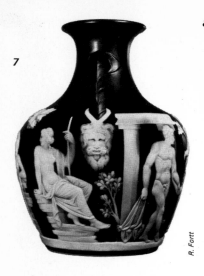

7

8

R. Fortt

Fig. 7 **Copy of the Portland Vase** *by Joseph Locke (1846–1938), made for the Richardson display at the Paris Exhibition of 1878. White on black cameo glass, unfinished.*
The Portland vase, a classical piece of the first century, was perhaps the strongest inspiration to the development of nineteenth-century cameo glass. Copies of it were made by several glassworkers, including Northwood and Locke. This version took twelve months to complete.
(Private Collection.)

Fig. 8 **Vase** *by Joshua Hodgetts (1857–1933) for Stevens and Williams, 1880–1900. White on yellow cameo glass.*
Designed in an Indian shape, this vase is decorated with naturalistic flower patterns; Hodgetts was an enthusiastic amateur botanist.
(Stourbridge Town Council Collection.)

Fig. 9 **Bowl** *designed and cut by Jacob Face for Thomas Webb and Sons, made for the 1884 International Health Exhibition. White on amber cameo glass. (Victoria and Albert Museum.)*

Fig. 10 **Vase and scent-bottle** *probably by Thomas Webb and Sons, c.1890. White on turquoise and red cameo glass. (Richard Dennis Antiques, London W.8.)*

in imitation of carved ivory in 1887, the first twenty pieces of which were purchased by Queen Victoria, and in 1888 the firm won a gold medal at Melbourne. Webb exhibited at the Paris Exhibition of 1889 and cameo work of all kinds was produced at this period.

The work done by the Woodalls themselves was mainly figurative and more personal in approach than the work produced by Northwood, although the Woodalls also relied heavily upon classical inspiration. This classical decoration was a feature of the Webb stand at the Chicago World's Fair of 1893, and was more in tune with the work of Leighton and Alma Tadema than with the decoration of the Portland vase. George Woodall was influenced by the sculpture of Canova, a book of whose work he possessed, and the firm owned Tatham's *Etchings of Grecian and Roman Architectural Ornament*, Owen Jones' *Examples of Chinese Ornament*, and *Le Style Empire XIX Siècle*, published in Paris, as well as the *Art-Journal* and the *Pottery Gazette*, all of which were used to inspire new designs of one kind or another. George Woodall was assisted by J. T. Fereday (1854–1942) (Fig. 2), by the gilder and enameller Jules Barbe and by the engraver William Fritsche (1853–1924). Work by the Woodalls was exhibited at the Franco-British Exhibition of 1908, and in 1911 George Woodall retired.

The commercial cameos produced by Webb were marked 'Webb's Gem Cameo' on the important pieces, and in the late '80s were sometimes dated. The Woodall work was usually marked 'T. and G. Woodall', 'T. Woodall' being very rare, although 'G. Woodall' before about 1895 and 'Geo Woodall' were used alone. The Woodall signature, if used, was normally placed on the opal overlay.

English cameo glass of the nineteenth century, representing as it does superb technical skill and artistic ability, is of great importance in the history of the development of the English glass industry and, although a revival of a technique known to the ancient world, it was by no means a dead or a static creation. Despite the proliferation of pieces for the sole purpose of exhibition, the commercially produced pieces, even if of inferior quality, do represent an important phase in the history of English glass design, reflecting as they do the eclecticism of the late nineteenth century. The classical inspiration of the important exhibition pieces in no way overshadows the more personal and decorative pieces with their floral decoration inspired by oriental design, and both are worthy of attention and study.

MUSEUMS AND COLLECTIONS
The preponderance of nineteenth-century English cameo glass is in private collections in both Great Britain and the United States. Very little is to be seen in museums as yet, although the Stourbridge Town Council has a good collection, and the Victoria and Albert Museum in London has a few pieces on display. The Science Museum in London is helpful for the technical aspects.

FURTHER READING
Nineteenth Century British Glass by Hugh Wakefield, London, 1961.
John Northwood by John Northwood Jr., Stourbridge, 1958.
Nineteenth Century Cameo Glass by Geoffrey W. Beard, Newport, 1956.

French Art Nouveau Glass

Fig. 1 **Vase** by Emile Gallé
(1846–1904), c.1900. Marqueterie
de verre, height 13½ins.
Gallé launched the new
technique of marqueterie de
verre in 1897. It involved
pressing pieces of semi-molten
glass into the surface of the piece
before it was cooled, and was so
difficult that many pieces were
cracked in the making.
(Alain Lesieutre Collection.)

Fig. 2 **Dragonfly vase** by Emile
Gallé, c.1900. Carved glass with
applied body and eyes.
A keen botanist, Gallé had
engraved over his door the motto
'Ma racine est au fond des bois.'
(Musée des Arts Décoratifs, Paris.)

Fig. 3 **Vase**, Daum, Nancy,
c.1900.
Milky-blue glass overlaid with
blue-grey glass and carved with
a thorn pattern, held in a gilt-
bronze mount set with glass
drops, overall height 11ins.
(Sotheby and Co., London.)

Fig. 4 **Vase in the Japanese taste**,
attributed to Eugène Rousseau
(1827–91), 1878–84. Pale yellow-
grey crackled glass overlaid with
wheel-cut coral glass, height
6½ins.
(Sotheby and Co., London.)

Fig. 5 **Trial vase** by René
Lalique (1860–1945), 1900–10.
Clear glass probably modelled by
the lost-wax process, height 8¼ins.
Lalique's early glass often has
pitted, unpolished surfaces.
(John Jesse Collection, London.)

Fig. 6 **Bowl**, Daum, Nancy,
1900–6. Enamel-painted and
acid-etched glass, width 5ins.
(John Jesse Collection.)

292

Sotheby Photo

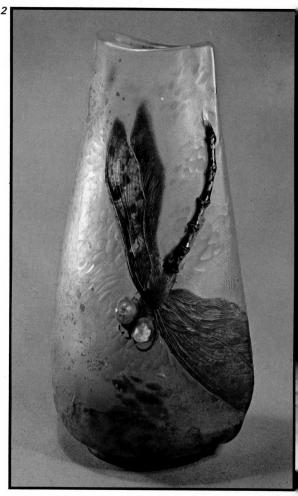

After the anonymous factory-made
glass of nineteenth-century
France, the superbly hand-made
pieces of the Art Nouveau style
formed a much needed and
popular change

French cut-crystal tableware and opaline vases of
the mid-nineteenth century were made by anonymous craftsmen working in large factories, and it
was due to the success of the individualistic
signed work of Eugène Rousseau that the idea of
glass as an art-form was accepted. The vases by

Rousseau have smoke-coloured or brownish
crackled bodies, sometimes with inclusions of
red, rust and green. His work, which is rare, was
exhibited in 1878 and 1884 and was immediately
appreciated by knowledgeable collectors. His
pupil, Leveillé, who later directed the firm,
continued to make the same type of crackled glass.
Few of his pieces are signed, and care should be
taken not to confuse them with later, unsigned,
stereotyped jugs and vases.

Like so many artists of the period, Rousseau and
Leveillé were interested in Japanese art. They were
attracted by its more obviously decorative aspects,
which led to a vase in the form of a bamboo stem
or cut with blossoming cherry trees and kimonoed
figures (Fig. 4); they did not try to reach a deeper

4

5

6

understanding of the spirit of the Far East as did the later ceramists and glassmakers. Joseph Brocard exhibited his pastiches of enamelled Islamic glass in 1867, a time when many books were published by archeologists and travellers in the Middle East, and he made very fine copies of fourteenth-century Syro-Egyptian mosque-lamps which were being acquired by museums around 1870. Although some of the pieces were signed, it is often difficult to tell them from the originals, or at least from the sixteenth-century Italian copies. Gallé also made these lamps, but his are much lighter in weight and the engraving and enamelling are not so bold. Brocard's later work, with its great freedom of drawing and delicacy of colouring, is rarely seen on the market (Fig. 9).

Emile Gallé – an outstanding and original glassmaker, both artist and technician

Emile Gallé (1846–1904) of Nancy was the most outstanding artist and technician among the French glassmakers of the late nineteenth century. Gallé's early pieces were based on historical themes with enamelling and gilding on transparent green, white or amber glass. Around 1884, these gave way to realistically drawn flowers and insects, still on transparent glass, following the aim of the official programme of the Nancy School of craftsmen to abandon 'the imitation of old styles in favour of a new principle, that of the scientific observation of live models'. During the following years, Gallé created some of his most original work in opaque coloured glass in a wide variety of techniques (Figs. 1, 2 and 7). All the pieces are signed and many are of superb quality. During the 1890s, Gallé changed his views about mass production, and the designs were cut by acid, instead of on the wheel, into the superimposed different coloured layers of glass, a technique found in eighteenth-century Chinese scent-bottles. This is called 'cameo glass' and is mistakenly referred to as 'pâte-de-verre' in French auction-room catalogues. A vast quantity of this type of glass was produced and it was very popular for wedding presents in the Middle East as well as in Europe. Gallé died in 1904, but the

Fig. 7 *Bottle and stopper by Emile Gallé*, c.1900. *Marbled glass with engraved decoration and gilding, height 6¾ ins. Gallé often used different techniques – some of them experimental – on each glass piece so that it can be difficult to sort out the various effects. (Christie, Manson and Woods, London.)*

7

8

9

A. C. Cooper.

294

Fig. 8 *Figure of Loïe Fuller* by
Amalric Walter, after 1906.
Pâte-de-verre, height 8 ins.
In 1906, Walter signed a contract
with Daum to use their kilns for
firing these figures of the
American dancer Loïe Fuller, as
well as ashtrays modelled with
birds, frogs, lizards, fish and
insects. In 1919 Walter opened
his own business, and the
production of them continued.
(Alain Lesieutre Collection.)

Fig. 9 *Bowl by Joseph Brocard,*
c.1900. Enamelled glass,
height 5⅞ ins.
Although Brocard began his
career in 1867 with pastiches of
Islamic and other Eastern glass,
his later, rarer work has a great
freedom of drawing and delicacy
of colouring.
(N. Manoukian Collection.)

Fig. 10 *Signatures and marks on*
Gallé glass.

firm continued until 1914. After the Great War, it was re-established at Epinay and lasted until 1935. Pieces produced after Gallé's death are signed with a star beside 'Gallé'. Unfortunately, many people judge the whole of Gallé's output from this poor quality glass, particularly as there is so much of it.

The Nancy firm of August and Jean Daum (1853–1909 and 1825–85) has been rather over-shadowed by Gallé's reputation. Besides vases and table-services painted with landscapes or vignettes *en camaïeu* in the eighteenth-century style, the firm adopted in 1893 the technique of acid-cut cameo glass, decorated with sprays of flowers, fruit, wild grasses or landscapes (Figs. 3 and 6). Although some pieces do closely resemble the work of Gallé, the range of colours is different; they used a large amount of orange and yellow.

René Lalique incorporated glass in his exquisite gold and enamelled jewellery

Gallé naturally had many imitators and Delatte, Arsall, Le Verre Français, D. Christian & Sohn, Muller Frères and Michel are only a few. Auguste Legras, working in the Paris suburb of St. Denis, also came under his influence, but his work can be distinguished by its pastel shades, often on an attractive creamy base. The glass of the Cristallerie de Pantin has rather flatly drawn flowers enamelled and gilt on a frosted ground, or cameo land-scapes, and is variously signed 'De Vez', 'Pantin' or 'Mont Joye'.

Besides this great following of the School of Nancy, there were a number of individualists such as Corillet who collaborated with the painter, musician, ceramist and glass-decorator Duc A. de Caranza at his Noyon workshops. The vases are painted with flowers and leaves in green, red and gold lustre, giving an appearance so similar to the pottery of the Massier family at Golfe Juan that it seems likely that De Caranza worked with them at one time. The workshops were destroyed during the Great War and consequently this glass is rare. Schneider made mottled red, grey or orange vases and jugs in rather tight forms. René Lalique, the leading designer of Art Nouveau jewellery, was already experimenting with glassmaking during this period. He had included coloured glass in his exquisite gold and enamelled jewellery in the 1890s and made a number of experimental statuettes and vases by the lost-wax technique. They often have unpolished and pitted surfaces since they were never perfected after the firing (Fig. 5).

In 1908 he was commissioned by the *parfumeurs* Coty to design a range of scent-bottles, the first time attention had been paid to the presentation and packaging of scent. It is of course through his work of the 1920s and '30s that Lalique is best known, and unfortunately very little documentation remains relating to his early pieces of glass, except for some reviews in contemporary periodicals.

There were a number of artists experimenting in *pâte-de-verre* rather than blown glass, the earliest being Henri Cros, who took the themes for his plaques from classical mythology. This is a process in which crushed glass fragments are mixed with coloured oxides, placed in a mould and slowly fired. After being allowed to cool slowly, the paste is taken from the mould and modelled with a spatula. Each artist had his own technical secret and it was a material which became very popular during the 1920s, with the work of François Décorchemont and G. Argy-Rousseau. Albert Dammouse, formerly a ceramist at Sèvres, worked in very fine *pâte-d'émail*, which is more like porcelain than glass. The fragile walls of his vases were modelled with trails of seaweed or flowers in grey, brown and blue.

Décorchemont, painter and ceramist, who died in 1971 aged ninety-one, made vases modelled with masks and flowers similar to those by Dammouse. In 1910, his material became thicker and at the same time more transparent. By 1925, his bowls, of classical simplicity, were heavy and chunky, with polished surfaces. Nearly all his pieces have a number scratched on the base, which is the date code. Works by Dammouse and Décorchemont belonging to the Art Nouveau period are rare and they are very often cracked or broken. Other artists working in *pâte-de-verre* were Ringel d'Illsach who made grotesque masks, and Georges Despret who started making figures, masks and fish during the 1890s in rather sugary colours. In 1906, Amalric Walter signed a contract with the Daum company which allowed him to use their kilns and materials for firing the pieces he made, in collaboration with Henry Bergé, the sculptor, Joseph Chéret and Victor Prouvé, of the American dancer Loie Fuller (Fig. 8), and ashtrays modelled with birds, frogs, lizards, fish and insects. Apparently these did not sell very well, and after the Great War Walter started a business on his own. Contrary to what is generally believed, Bergé did not provide him with any more models but remained in charge of Daum's workshops.

There is a series of vases signed 'George de Feure', decorated with friezes of classical figures which are often confused with *pâte-de-verre*. They are in moulded glass and were designed for the firm of Fauchon of Paris.

MUSEUMS AND COLLECTIONS

French Art Nouveau glass may be seen at the following:

FRANCE
Nancy: Musée de l'Ecole de Nancy
Paris: Musée des Arts Décoratifs
            Musée d'Arts et Métiers

GREAT BRITAIN
London: Bethnal Green Museum

U.S.A.
Corning,
N.Y.:   Corning Museum of Glass

WEST GERMANY
Darmstadt: Hessisches Landesmuseum
Karlsruhe: Badisches Landesmuseum
Kassel: Staatliche Kunstsammlungen

FURTHER READING

Carved and Decorated European Art Glass by R. L. Grover, Vermont, 1970.
French Cameo Glass by B. and H. Blount, Iowa, 1968.
'Emile Gallé' by Richard Dennis in **Antiques International**, London, 1966.
La verrerie française depuis cinquante ans by Leon Rosenthal, Paris, 1927.

American Art Glass

In the last thirty years of the nineteenth century American manufacturers produced several new types of decorative — sometimes frivolous — glass, using sophisticated chemical processes

Fig. 1 **The Morgan Vase,** *Hobbs-Brockunier & Company, Wheeling, West Virginia, c.1890. Coral, or Wheeling Peach Blow, glass, height 9⅞ ins. The form, and to a large extent the colour, of this piece emulates a Chinese ceramic vase purchased by Mrs. Pierpont Morgan for $18,000. The event created a great stir of public interest. (Corning Museum of Glass, Corning, New York.)*

Fig. 2 **Berry-bowl and stand,** *Mount Washington Glass Company, New Bedford, Massachusetts, 1880–90. Etched cameo glass, the stand of silver plate, width 8 ins. (Corning Museum of Glass. Lola Kincaid Ford Collection.)*

Fig. 3 **Covered goblet and pitcher,** *attributed to the Boston and Sandwich Glass Company, Sandwich, Massachusetts, 1870–88. Clear glass with mechanically threaded decoration, height of goblet 9 ins. (Sandwich Glass Museum, Sandwich, Massachusetts.)*

The making of 'art glass', as it was called in its heyday – about 1875 to 1900 – and as it is still called by collectors today, was due to the combination of social and technological factors: the fondness of late Victorians for highly ornate and colourful decoration and developments in the chemistry of colouring glass. These factors led to the production of many types of glass which often looked like other substances and which were sometimes novel, frivolous and by today's standards in bad taste. Nevertheless, art glass epitomises, probably more than any one other product, the late Victorian era.

Art glass was, at least in the Western world, an international style, with centres in England, Bohemia and other central European areas. It is difficult to ascertain whether it was developed first in Bohemia or in England. Both areas, but in particular England, had a strong influence on its development in America.

Silvered, or mercury, glass, along with opal-decorated glasses, may be considered the first type of art glass. A patent for the first commercially practical method for producing silvered glass was granted to Hale Thomson in London in about 1851. In America, William Leighton, an Englishman who became superintendent of the New England Glass Works, was granted a patent on 16 January, 1855, for silvered-glass door-knobs, which he claimed were superior to silver articles.

It is interesting to note, in view of this patent date, that listed among the wide variety of glass exhibited by the New England Glass Company at the New York Crystal Palace Exposition in 1853 were 'Two-hundred glass door-knobs, silvered' and 'One large silvered-glass bowl on foot, very richly engraved'.

'Opal-decorated' wares, as opaque-white or 'milk' glass was called by glassmakers, were produced in large quantities by numerous American glasshouses from the middle of the 1850s. English firms such as W. H. B. & J. Richardson, with their opal-decorated products, undoubtedly had a marked influence on American production of these wares. For example, William L. Smith and his two sons, Alfred and Harry, decorators, emigrated to America and began working for the Boston and Sandwich Glass Company in about 1855. In 1871 the Smith brothers were employed by William Libbey to operate the large decorating shop he established at the Mount Washington Glass Works. Three years later they leased this shop and apparently before 1876 moved their business to 28 and 30 William Street, New Bedford.

Vases called by the generic terms 'ring' or 'Smith

Museum Photo

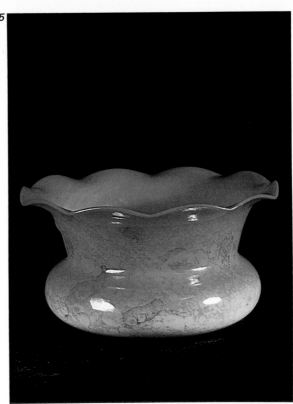

Museum Photo

Fig. 4 **Wild Rose vase,** *New England Glass Company, 1885–88. Height 8¼ ins. (Corning Museum of Glass.)*

Fig. 5 **Agata bowl,** *New England Glass Company, 1887–88. Diameter 5¼ ins. (Corning Museum of Glass. L. K. Ford Collection.)*

Fig. 6 **Plated Amberina vase,** *New England Glass Company. Height 8¼ ins. (Corning Museum of Glass. Mr. and Mrs. Richard Greger Collection.)*

Corning Museum Photo

Fig. 7 *Vase, Hobbs-
Brockunier & Company,
1886–91.
Ruby-opalescent glass pressed in
a mould with hobnails, height
6½ ins.
A paper label on the base reads
'Patented June 1, 1886.'
(Corning Museum of Glass.)*

Fig. 8 *Burmese candleholder,
Mount Washington Glass
Company, 1885–95. 'Burmese'
glass, height 7½ ins.
A contemporary price-list shows
that these candleholders were
sold for $15 a dozen.
(Corning Museum of Glass.)*

Fig. 9 *Royal Flemish bottle,
Mount Washington Glass
Company, c.1890. Colourless
glass decorated with light stains
and raised gilding, height 13 ins.
This firm was called the
'Headquarters in America for
Art Glass'.
(Corning Museum of Glass.
L. K. Ford Collection.)*

Fig. 10 *Amberina glass bottle,
New England Glass Company,
1883–88. Pattern-moulded
bi-partite glass, height 9⅞ ins.
This was the earliest sort of
shaded art glass to achieve
success, and it attracted many
imitators.
(Corning Museum of Glass.)*

Brothers', became popular and continued to be decorated by them after they left the Sandwich firm, but they were also made and decorated by other firms. Many of the blanks decorated by the Smith brothers were made in Europe, probably in Germany or Bohemia, although some were obtained from the Mount Washington Glass Company. A photograph of the Smith Brothers' display at an unidentified trade show illustrates the wide variety of opal lamp-shades decorated by them. It probably dates from about 1880. A stereoscopic view of the New England Glass Company's showroom, taken in about 1875, indicates that that firm was also a major producer of this type of ware, as was the Mount Washington Glass Company, which constantly advertised 'opal decorated wares' among its products. Frederick S. Shirley, an Englishman with consummate glassmaking knowledge and considerable business acumen, became the agent of the latter company in 1874, and under his direction it developed into the 'Headquarters in America for Art Glass Wares'.

The first bi-partite, or shaded, art glass to achieve success was Amberina (Fig. 10); it was patented on 24 July, 1883, by Joseph Locke, another Englishman, who had emigrated to work for the New England Glass Company located in East Cambridge, near Boston, Massachusetts. This glass shaded gradually from an amber colour near the base to a deep ruby or fuchsia red at the top.

Pages from Locke's sketch-book, and the relatively large number of pieces still extant, indicate the wide variety of forms and the extensive production of Amberina. Its success was so great that it was copied by the Mount Washington Glass Company, which, after being threatened with a lawsuit by the New England Glass Company, agreed to call its product 'Rose Amber', although their advertisements frequently used the terms 'Rose Amberina' and 'Amberina'.

The development of other shaded art glasswares followed rapidly. On 15 December, 1885, Shirley, of the Mount Washington Glass Company, was granted a patent for Burmese glass (Fig. 8), an opaque glass containing gold and uranium oxides which produced a glass gradually shading from a delicate pale yellow to a plushy pink colour. This glass, too, caught the public's fancy and was a great commercial success. A price-list indicates that it was made in about two hundred and fifty different forms which were available in their natural glossy, or plush, finish, called 'satin glass' by today's collectors. A number of the forms were decorated.

Shirley's business acumen and salesmanship undoubtedly helped to make Burmese the success it was. He sent as a gift to his former queen, Victoria, a tea-set decorated with what he termed the 'Queen's Burmese' pattern (Fig. 12). He subsequently received an order from the Queen for more Burmese, and Thomas Webb & Sons of Stourbridge, England, were licensed by the Mount Washington Glass Company in 1886 to produce this glass; each piece was marked on the base: 'Thos. Webb & Sons, Queen's Burmese Ware, Patented'.

Peach Blow was another parti-coloured glassware produced by the Mount Washington Glass Company. It shaded from a slightly bluish white to a pink colour, and although very attractive, appears not to have been so commercially successful as Burmese. Nevertheless, it was emulated by the New England Glass Company, whose Wild Rose

shaded from white to a deep pink colour. Both firms produced these wares in natural and plush finishes, and both decorated some of them (Fig. 4).

The most popular of the Peach Blow glasses was that made by Hobbs-Brockunier & Company, of Wheeling, West Virginia, which they termed 'Coral'. It was a cased, or plated, glass, consisting of an opaque-white interior covered with a thin layer of transparent glass shading from a pale yellowish colour at the base to a deep orange-red at the top (Fig. 1).

Very much like Coral, or Wheeling Peach Blow, except in colour is the New England Glass Company's Plated Amberina, for which a patent was issued to Edward D. Libbey on 15 June, 1886. It is apparently Amberina encasing an opaque-white glass, and is almost always pattern-moulded (Fig. 6). It was seemingly produced in limited quantities, and is much sought after by collectors.

Joseph Locke, of the New England Glass Company, was granted a patent on 18 January, 1887, for Agata glassware (Fig. 5), which was simply Wild Rose glass which had been decorated by brownish and purplish stains, usually applied in a random splotched pattern. This was achieved by partially or wholly covering an article with a metallic stain or mineral colour and then spattering it with a volatile liquid such as alcohol, benzene or naphtha. This produced a mottled effect which became permanent when fired. Agata, which is usually found in the same forms as Wild Rose, was not commercially successful, and it is rare today.

Popular satin glass was widely produced

Probably, Pearl Satin Ware, or 'satin glass', as it is most frequently called today, was one of the most popular types of art glass, and it was widely produced. Frederick Shirley was granted a trademark for Pearl Satin Ware on 29 June, 1886. Undoubtedly his glasshouse produced quantities of the ware, the satin-like finish of which was achieved by either exposing the glass to the fumes of hydrofluoric acid, or dipping it in a bath of this acid, for a few minutes. Thomas Webb & Sons was licensed in 1886 by the Mount Washington Glass Company to produce Pearl Satin Ware.

Hobbs-Brockunier & Company is one of the best-known to collectors for its art glass. A pink and white satin-ware vase decorated with an invitation to President Cleveland to visit Wheeling and the Hobbs-Brockunier factory, now in the Oglebay Museum, Wheeling, is an example of this firm's production of this type of ware. This company also produced a wide variety of art glasses bearing applied decoration, as well as a variety of novelty forms – some mould-blown, others pressed – and many coloured glasses.

In 1883 William Leighton Jr. originated a spangled glass, which was made by picking up flakes of mica on an initial gather of glass, then covering them over with a glass of another colour. Figure 7 illustrates a ruby-opalescent vase bearing a label reading: 'Patented June 1, 1886'. In February 1886, the New England Glass Company licensed this firm to manufacture pressed Amberina.

Two other types of art glass utilising applied glass for decorative effects were mechanically threaded glass (Fig. 3) and 'overshot', or 'ice', glass. The

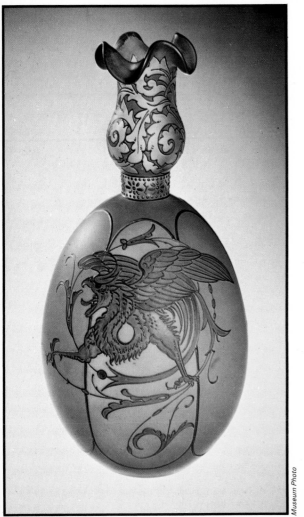

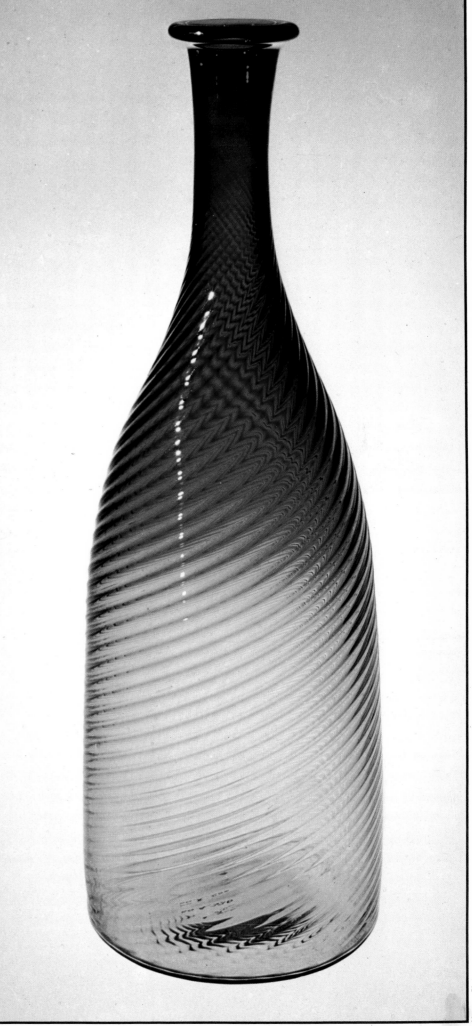

Fig. 11 *Page from a catalogue of the Pairpoint Manufacturing Company, New Bedford, Massachusetts, c.1894.*
One of the best customers of the Mount Washington Glass Company was the Pairpoint Manufacturing Company which made silver-plated mounts for art glass. It was established next door to the glassworks in 1880, and later took over the glassmaking operation.
(Corning Museum of Glass.)

Boston & Sandwich Glass Company, established in Sandwich, Cape Cod, Massachusetts, in 1825 and noted for its production of 'lacy' pressed glass in its earlier years, made both types of glasses. Often these mechanically threaded pieces were engraved above the threading with marshland scenes or foliate forms.

Numerous companies produced art glass, but obviously the Mount Washington Glass Company was justified in describing itself as 'Headquarters in America for Art Glass'. In addition to the art glasses noted above, this firm produced a wide variety of 'rich decorated' ware. This included opal-decorated glass, Albertine, Crown Milano, Napoli and Royal Flemish (Fig. 9). Except for the last, which was a colourless glass decorated with thin stains and raised gilding, all these glasses were

cameo glassmaking enjoyed a revival after John Northwood successfully copied the Portland vase in 1876, little true cameo glass was made in America. But acid-etched cameo glass was another product of the Mount Washington Glass Company. Although produced largely in the form of bowls, often intended for use in silver-plated holders, this type of glass was also used in lamps. These 'cameos' are found in translucent pink, light blue and yellow glasses cased over opal or opaque-white glass. The designs usually consist of classical or pseudo-classical motifs (Fig. 2).

The production of art glass declined as the century drew to a close and ceased by 1900. Its place was largely taken by glass in the Art Nouveau style, an entirely different artistic expression and another chapter in the history of glass.

Fig. 12 *Burmese lamp, Mount Washington Glass Company, 1885–95. Decorated with the Queen's Burmese pattern, height about 20 ins.*
A shrewd businessman, Shirley of the Mount Washington Glass Company assured the success of his Burmese glass by sending to Queen Victoria a tea-set decorated with this pattern. He subsequently received an order for more Burmese, and Thomas Webb and Sons of Stourbridge, England, were licensed to produce the glass in large quantities.
(Mr. and Mrs. Samuel Feld Collection.)

opaque white, richly enamelled and gilded. Many examples of Crown Milano and Royal Flemish glass are exotic in form and decoration.

A number of these art glasses were used in silver-plated stands or holders, and silver-plating companies purchased a considerable portion of the output of art glass. One of the best customers of the Mount Washington Glass Company was the Pairpoint Manufacturing Company. This firm was established in 1880 in New Bedford, Massachusetts, next door to the glassworks. Some of its officers were also associated with the glassworks and in 1894 the latter became part of the Pairpoint Manufacturing Company, but it retained its own name for many years afterwards. Many types of glass made by this glassworks are illustrated in catalogues of the Pairpoint Manufacturing Company (Fig. 11). It is evident from these catalogues that the same type of glass was called by more than one name.

Novelty wares of decorated opal glass were also part of this company's production. They included decorated eggs and tomato-forms to be used as salt- and pepper-shakers, sugar-sifters and containers for marmalade, sugar, sweetmeats or rose-leaves. The Smith Brothers' firm also decorated some eggs which were made to stand at an angle, to circumvent the Mount Washington Glass Company's patent for the upright egg.

In contrast to England, where the ancient art of

MUSEUMS AND COLLECTIONS

American art glass may be seen at the following:
GREAT BRITAIN
Brierley, Wilts.: Brierley Hill Library
Stevens and Williams Ltd.,
Royal Brierley Crystal Glass
Works, Brierley Hill
Edinburgh: Royal Scottish Museum
London: Victoria and Albert Museum
Newcastle: Laing Art Gallery and
Museum
Stourbridge: The Council House,
Stourbridge Town Hall
U.S.A.
Corning, N.Y.: Corning Museum of Glass
Milan, Ohio: Milan Historical Museum
New York: Metropolitan Museum of Art
Norfolk, Va.: Walter Chrysler Museum
Toledo, Ohio: Toledo Museum of Art

FURTHER READING

The Pairpoint Glass Story by George C. Avila, New Bedford, Massachusetts, 1968.
Art Glass Nouveau by Ray and Lee Grover, Rutland, Vermont, 1967.
Nineteenth Century Glass, its Genesis and Development by Albert C. Revi, New York, 1959.
Nineteenth Century Art Glass by Ruth Webb Lee, New York, 1952.

Tiffany Glass

Fig. 1 **Flower-form vase**, *Tiffany, c.1900. Green striated glass with an iridescent sheen on the inside, the base engraved 'L.C.T. T290', height 11¼ ins. (Sotheby's Belgravia, London.)*

Fig. 2 **Wisteria lamp**, *Tiffany Studios, c.1900. Leaded marble glass outlined in a verdigris with verdigris bronze base and four light-fittings marked 'Tiffany Studios New York 26854', overall height 27 ins. (Sotheby's Belgravia.)*

Fig. 3 **Vase**, *Tiffany, c.1900. Pale green lustre glass decorated with a trailing band of lily-pads in high blue-gold iridescence over black inlaid glass, height 3¾ ins. (Sotheby's Belgravia.)*

In producing his beautifully designed and executed art glass, Louis C. Tiffany was largely instrumental in giving an identity to American craftsmanship

2

3

Fig. 4 *Tulip lamp*, *Tiffany Studios*, c.1900. Leaded marble glass, the leading given a gilt-bronze patination, marked 'Tiffany Studios New York 1596', with three light-fittings and gilt-bronze base marked and numbered '587', overall height 23½ ins.
(Sotheby's Belgravia.)

Fig. 5 **Vase**, *Tiffany and Fabergé*, c.1900. Favrile glass with peacock-feather decoration in high gold, mauve and green lustre, the 'eyes' of inlaid green glass with darker centres, marked 'Louis C. Tiffany 07233'; the silver-gilt Fabergé mount by Johan Viktor Aarne. Overall height 7¾ ins.
The prefix 'O' to the number of the glass body indicates a special order. The vase was given by Louis C. Tiffany at the wedding from the White House of Miss Julia Grant to Prince Michael Cantacuzene. It was taken with other Tiffany pieces to their home in Russia, where Fabergé was commissioned to make the mount. Tiffany's peacock vases of this type represent the ultimate achievement in his technique of glass-blowing and decoration.
(Sotheby's.)

Sotheby Photo

Louis Comfort Tiffany was born in 1848. His father, Charles Louis Tiffany, had by then established himself as a jeweller and silversmith, having founded the firm of Tiffany & Young in 1837. By the year 1870, when L. C. Tiffany had reached the age of twenty-two, his father's was the smartest shop in the country and was able to present for sale what was possibly the largest collection of gems in the world. The firm's own silverware was of a very high standard and had won prizes in European exhibitions, including the Paris Exhibition of 1867.

This was a booming period for the United States. New families appeared with what seemed like limitless fortunes. The Vanderbilts, the Astors, the Goulds and the Havemeyers were in competition to dispose of vast sums, often, sadly, with more money than taste.

The young Louis Comfort, to his father's chagrin, took little interest in the business and seemed to have no enthusiasm for the commercial side of it. In 1866, he declared his desire to study art rather than go to college. His first leaning was towards landscape painting and he developed a very romantic view of nature as the pupil of one of America's leading landscape-artists, George Inness. The winter of 1868–69 was spent in Paris with Léon Bailly, who was to take Tiffany on a visit to Spain and North Africa, instilling in him a fascination for Islamic, North African and Moorish art, all of which styles he was later to adapt in his eclectic decorative schemes. An important influence on the young Tiffany was one of his father's chief designers, Edward C. Moore. Moore was a great admirer of oriental art and was, in turn, admired by Samuel Bing, the Parisian dealer and critic, whom Tiffany met on a visit to Paris and who was to become the French agent for Tiffany's work. Bing supplied Tiffany and Moore with examples of oriental art and started them off as collectors.

Tiffany had devoted most of the 1870s to painting. However, he was the first to admit his shortcomings in this field and it was Edward C. Moore who encouraged Tiffany to devote himself to the applied arts and interior decoration. In 1879, Tiffany finally determined to go into decorative work professionally and formed a partnership with

Fig. 6 **Paperweight vase**, *Tiffany*, c.1900. Two layers of tinted glass decorated between the layers with swirling green leaves and red poppies with millefiore stamens, the inside with a green-gold lustre, the base engraved '8520 N. L.C.Tiffany Inc. Favrile', height 6 ins.
The finest paperweight vases were those of this type, with sliced and embedded millefiore canes.
(Sotheby's Belgravia.)

Samuel Colman and Candace Wheeler, which he called 'Louis C. Tiffany and Associated Artists'.

He very quickly won a high reputation, and his pre-eminence as America's leading decorator was acknowledged in the winter of 1882–83, when he was invited to redecorate parts of the White House. The highlight of his decorative scheme was a vast opalescent glass screen regrettably destroyed in 1904, when Theodore Roosevelt, redecorating the White House, gave the order to 'break in small pieces that Tiffany screen'.

From surviving photographs and accounts, one can piece together the style of the Associated Artists. Their decorative work was still essentially high Victorian in feeling; their sources were many, although they were successful in achieving a sense of harmony, blending Islamic art with their own embroidered hangings and painted friezes and with tiling and panelling in the coloured glass in which Tiffany was becoming interested.

These domestic applications of glass were Tiffany's introduction to the medium – he became tremendously involved and broke up his old partnership to devote his energies to glassmaking. His former associate Candace Wheeler recalled: 'I think Mr. Tiffany was rather glad to get rid of us all . . . for his wonderful experiments in glass iridescence . . .'.

During his travels, Tiffany had formed a collection of glass – his particular fascination was with ancient glass with its marvellous nacreous iridescence, caused by decomposition while buried, and by the effects of metallic oxides. Tiffany also loved the pitted and corroded effects caused by decomposition. He saw the beauty of what were essentially imperfections in the glass. It became his ambition to learn so much about glass and its reactions to different types of chemical that he would

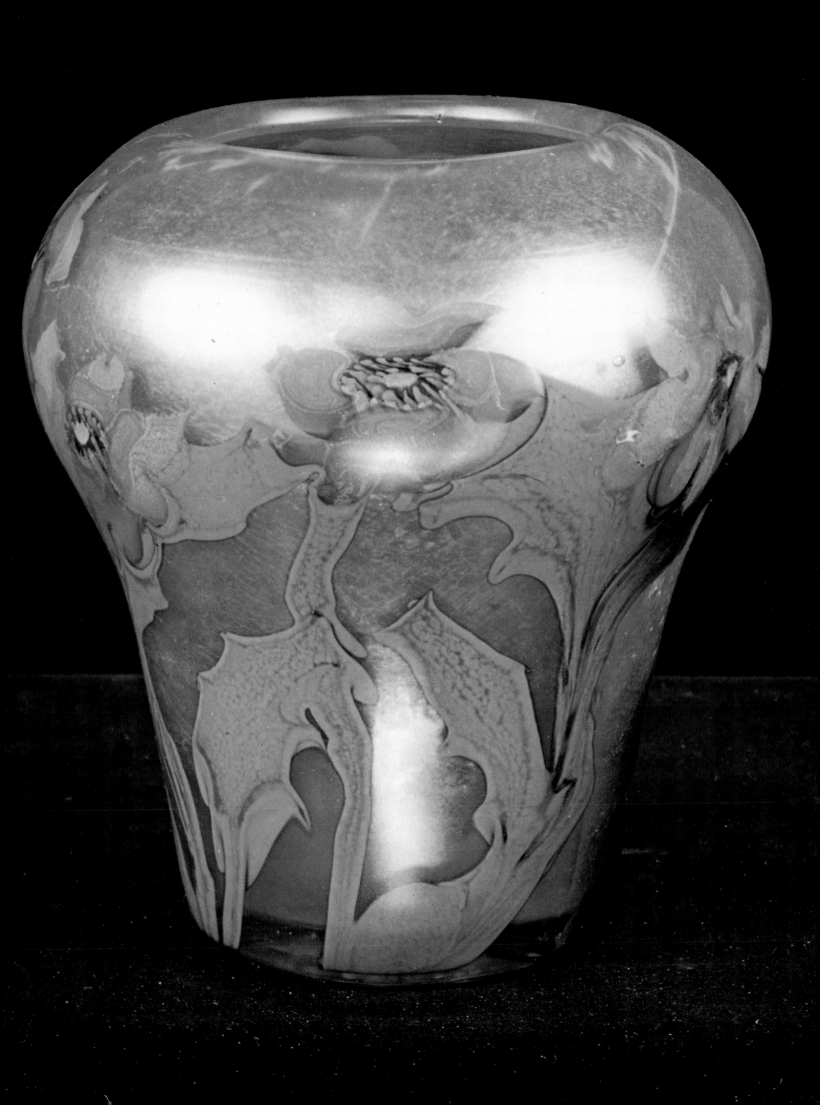

Fig. 7 *Lava vase, Tiffany, c.1900. Dark purple-blue iridescent glass with gold lustre decoration, height 5 ins. Pieces of this particularly interesting range of Tiffany glass have abstract decoration in trailed gold or silver lustre.*
(Sotheby's.)

8

Fig. 8 *Gooseneck vase, Tiffany, c.1900. Gold iridescent glass enriched with green feather lines, the base engraved '803T. L.C. Tiffany-Favrile', height 14½ ins. The form of this vase is organic, and, like much of Tiffany's work, it is of Persian inspiration. The word 'Favrile', derived from the Old English word 'fabrile', meaning 'hand-made', appears on many of Tiffany's glass pieces.*
(Sotheby's.)

Sotheby Photo

304

be able to control these accidental imperfections.

Coloured glass fascinated him; the art of stained-glass windows was a challenge he could not resist, but he was horrified by those craftsmen who were content to apply painted decoration to the glass. On this point, Tiffany felt most strongly – that any decoration in his glasswork should be integral to the glass body. If, for instance, he wanted a glass vase to be decorated with flowers, he felt it would be abhorrent to paint flowers on the vase; their presence should be represented by the texture and the colour of the glass itself.

Tiffany was further inspired by the simplicity of the forms of ancient glass, just as he was horrified by nineteenth-century efforts to mould or cut glass into shapes more appropriate for bronze or porcelain. Tiffany was pleased by the irregularity of form of a good deal of ancient glass and, as a result, one finds that much of his own glassware has a certain, probably intentional, asymmetry (Fig. 8).

One should bear in mind that not all the glass that bears his name was made by Tiffany himself, although he kept a close supervision on everything that left his workshops. Certain pieces are the result of serious experiment and their technical invention is of significance in the history of art glass. A good deal of Tiffany output, however, tends to be of more commercial quality, for he had a very large and enthusiastic clientele.

This market was kept happy with the plain gold lustre pieces which form the largest single category, designed mostly as decorative tableware – one finds vases, sets of beakers, glasses, *tazze*, bowls, finger-bowls and stands. In a patent-claim filed in 1880, Tiffany described the essential method of producing iridescent glass: 'The metallic luster is produced by forming a film of a metal or its oxide or a compound of the metal on or in the glass, either by exposing it to vapors or gasses or by direct application. It may also be produced by corroding the surface of the glass, such processes being well known to glass manufacturers'.

Tiffany found how cobalt or copper oxides could colour glass blue; how iron oxide resulted in green; how manganese oxide produced shades of violet; how gold or copper produced red; how coke, coal or other carbon oxides gave an amber colour; and how manganese cobalt and iron could combine to give a black glass. The distinctive gold lustre was achieved with gold chloride either suspended in the glass or sprayed on while the glass was still hot from the furnace. Twenty-five dollar gold pieces were used as the base. After the plain gold glass, one finds in order of frequency blue, green, white, yellow, brown, amethyst, black and red. Samuel Bing's purple prose on the subject of Tiffany's lustre glass is almost too enthusiastic to be true: 'They captivated the eye by reason of both their wonderful matt softness and, at the same time, a nacreous richness over which played, according to the breaking of the light, an infinite variety of tones in which were opalised radiations so subtle, delicate and mysterious that the water of an exquisite pearl can alone be compared to them'.

The second most numerous category is the decorated iridescent ware, although this is a fairly broad heading as it includes all types from the superb 'peacock feather' vases (Fig. 5) and the flower forms (Fig. 1) to the simpler vases decorated with a few trailing ivy-leaves or lily-pads (Fig. 3). Samuel Bing, although full of the same sense of rapture, is more

helpful in the following passage where he describes the craftsman at work on the decorated glass. 'Look at the incandescent ball of glass as it comes out of the furnace; it is slightly dilated by an initial inspiration of air. The workman charges it at certain pre-arranged points with small quantities of glass, of different textures and different colours, and in this operation is hidden the germ of the intended ornamentation. The little ball is then returned to the fire to be heated. Again it is subjected to a similar treatment (the process being sometimes repeated as many as twenty times), and, when all the different glasses have been combined and manipulated in different ways, and the article has been brought to its definite state as to form and dimension, it presents the following appearance: the motifs introduced into the ball when it was small have grown with the vase itself, but in differing proportions; they have lengthened or broadened out, while each tiny ornament fills the place assigned to it in

7

advance in the mind of the artist'. Tiffany's 'Peacock-feather' vases are the ultimate achievement in this technique and they are often further enhanced by inlaid 'evil eyes' of dark coloured glass (Fig. 10). Similarly, one finds inlaid glass in lily-pad vases such as the one illustrated (Fig. 3).

Another group that presented comparable technical problems were the 'paperweight' vases in which the floral decoration was trapped between two layers of glass. An initial form would have been blown and into its warm, soft surface would be pressed coloured glass to form flower-patterns; these would be rolled until smooth and the whole would be cased in a further layer of glass, thus giving to the surface of the object an illusion of great depth which was sometimes enhanced by a light internal iridescence. Perhaps the finest quality paperweight vases are those which incorporate *millefiore* glass – glass canes are sliced and then embedded in groups in the inner layer of glass and rolled into the surface. These are *millefiore* canes of a type used in traditional French paperweights, but Tiffany's application is all the more remarkable in that he was able to create so successfully

Fig. 9 *Favrile Cypriote vase*, Tiffany, c.1900. Opaque green glass with a partly pitted surface, numbered 'K 1379' and with a Tiffany Glass and Decorating Co. trade-label and the original verdigris bronze base, height 13½ ins. (Sotheby's.)

Fig. 10 *Peacock vase*, Tiffany, c.1900. Glass body decorated with a combed peacock-feather design of pale green and gold iridescence, the three 'evil eyes' of dark green iridescence, the base engraved '06580', height 13¼ ins. (Sotheby's.)

9

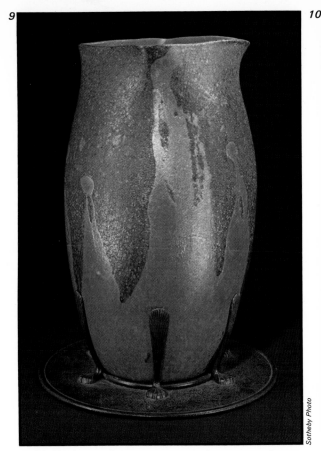

Sotheby Photo

10

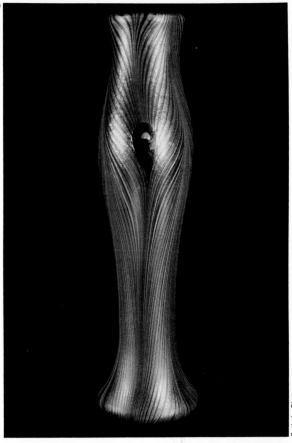

Sotheby Photo

Fig. 11 *Marks* used by Louis C. Tiffany at the Tiffany Studios.

a three-dimensional effect with so thin a body.

'Cypriote' was the name given to a type of glass most closely inspired by the corroded textures of excavated ancient glass. Nearly always found in brown or blue opaque glass, Cypriote ware is characterised by its crusty surface. This effect was achieved by rolling the body over a marver covered with pulverised crumbs of glass. Cypriote pieces are often haphazard in form and are often larger than other types of vase (Fig. 9).

Lava glass is the self-explanatory name of a particularly interesting range of Tiffany glass (Fig. 7). These pieces are generally of a dark blue lustre body with voluptuous, abstract-organic, trailed or poured, gold lustre decoration. In their very free conception of form, they are among the most revolutionary of Tiffany's works.

There are other categories such as Agate ware (coloured glasses are run together and then polished down to resemble agate) and Marblized ware (colours are blended to resemble the texture of marble), and the various glasses used in the series of leaded shades for table-lamps which helped more than anything else to make Tiffany's name a household word. From the quantity produced, and from contemporary reports, one must assume that no well-decorated (or at least fashionably decorated) home in America was complete without one.

In this series of lamps, Tiffany found a means of adapting the principles of stained-glass windows to electricity in an unobtrusive as well as a very decorative way. The lamps vary a good deal in quality; some are far more elaborate and far more subtle in the tones of glass used. The large Wisteria lamp illustrated in Figure 2 is a very good example, conceived in a fully naturalistic way. Here we have, not a lamp decorated with wisteria blossom and trees, but a lamp which is in the form of a wisteria tree. Other types have the shades decorated with dragon-flies or their bases beautifully

modelled in full relief as clusters of lily-pads.

Louis Comfort Tiffany was no great social theorist; his influence, however, was very great in giving an identity to American craftmanship. At the back of his mind was always an ambition to become a kind of American William Morris, but he found it all too easy to indulge his taste for the luxurious and the exotic. There was no return to simplicity, although there was a return to nature and inspiration from organic form. In this sense he can be called an Art Nouveau designer, but he was never attached by any dogma to the Art Nouveau movement as such. His range was far wider.

Samuel Bing concludes significantly: 'If we are called upon to declare the supreme characteristic of this glassware, we would say it resides in the fact that the means employed for the purpose of ornamentation are sought and found in the vitreous substance itself, without the use of either brush, wheel, or acid. When cool, the article is finished'. ✦

MUSEUMS AND COLLECTIONS
Tiffany glass may be seen at the following:
FRANCE
Paris: Musée des Arts Décoratifs
GREAT BRITAIN
London: Bethnal Green Museum
U.S.A.
New York: Metropolitan Museum of Art
Norfolk, Va.:   Chrysler Museum
Provincetown,
  Mass.:   Chrysler Art Museum

FURTHER READING
Louis C. Tiffany's Glass, Bronzes, Lamps: A Complete Collector's Guide by Robert Koch, New York, 1971.
Artistic America, Tiffany Glass and Art Nouveau by Samuel Bing, reprinted with an introduction by Robert Koch, Cambridge, Mass.; London, 1970.

Silver and Gold

Possession of gold and silver has always been a measure of wealth and position. The treasures of Egyptian pharaohs and other ancient kings were overflowing with gold and silver jewellery, drinking vessels and ceremonial objects, while throughout history the search for the precious ore has obsessed kings, princes and explorers alike.

Craftsmen who worked in both gold and silver called themselves goldsmiths and were part of the mediaeval guild system which imposed strict standards of quality and workmanship on its members. Gold, being a more sumptuous and expensive material, was used for magnificent jewellery and prized objects such as the exquisite snuff boxes fashioned in France during the eighteenth century. Silver was the more usual material for both church silver and valuable domestic plate and was sometimes washed with gold to produce additional richness in the form of silver gilt.

Prior to the eighteenth century, when it was customary to amass personal wealth in the form of gold and silver plate, goldsmiths were as important to a community as bankers are today. Plate could be melted down at a moments notice and turned into money when necessary. As a result, much beautiful silver of the Mediaeval, Renaissance and Mannerist periods has been lost. It was also common to melt down plates when more fashionable styles came along – not much sentiment was attached to old things, despite the skill that had gone into their creation.

Objects that survived the widespread meltings throughout Europe were generally the silver-mounted wares made in Germany, Holland and England. The amount of silver used in making the supportive ornaments for drinking cups, bowls and ceremonial salts, created from horn, shells and rock crystal, was not considered worth the trouble of breaking up the pieces.

Very little early French silver survived the royal extravagances of the seventeenth and eighteenth centuries and the destruction of the Revolution. Since French silver was widely admired outside France at the time, however, enough has been preserved to give some indication of the silversmith's artistry. Fortunately, these skills were not entirely lost. Following the revocation of the Edict of Nantes in 1685, in which it was attempted to make the Catholic faith compulsory in France, many goldsmiths who were Protestant Huguenots fled to Holland and England. The Huguenots introduced elements of the baroque taste, which was at its height in France, into the traditions of their new homelands. The techniques at which they excelled included ornamental piercing, casting (molten silver poured into moulds for handles, feet and knobs), and cut-card work (the application of silver cut-outs to smooth silver surfaces).

At the end of the seventeenth century, in an effort to prevent silversmiths melting down coins for their silver content, the Britannia Standard was imposed in England. For more than twenty years, until the law was repealed, plate had to contain more silver and less alloy than previously while the standard for coins remained unchanged. Britannia Standard silver (marked by the engraved figure from which it takes its name instead of the traditional Sterling Standard lion passant) was softer and more difficult to work although the immigrant Huguenots had no trouble. The sophisticated, unadorned and angular shapes common to the Queen Anne period silver are generally of this standard.

Among the silversmiths of Huguenot stock working in early eighteenth-century London was Paul de Lamerie who became the leading exponent of the swirling, curving Rococo taste in silver design. De Lamerie could fashion elaborate or plain ornament silver with equal skill.

The arrival of porcelain, lacquer ware and silks from China during the seventeenth century inspired a vogue for Chinoiserie that was found in all branches of the decorative arts, including silver. Spice boxes, cups, salters and cannisters for holding precious tea leaves were ornamented with motifs that suggested a Chinese origin but were in fact wholly European in concept.

Tea and coffee drinking were very popular by the end of the century, and special pots were made in silver for the purpose of serving the fashionable brews. Teapots, copied from those of Chinese porcelain, were small (because tea was expensive) and pear-shaped to enable the tea leaves to steep better when they settled in the narrow bottom. Coffeepots were tall and tapered with handles frequently placed at right angles to the spout. Contemporary paintings of family groups often included the prestigious silver and porcelain tea things. Although individual pieces of tea equipage – pots, cream jugs, sugar bowls and kettles – were made continuously, they were bought separately as funds permitted. Complete matching sets were not common until later in the eighteenth century.

Silversmiths working in the American Colonies largely followed fashions in England, although their work revealed an individualistic flavour. One of the most important craftsmen of the eighteenth century was Paul Revere, distinguished as a patriot as well as a goldsmith. The son of an immigrant Huguenot, Revere produced a wide range of silver during his varied career. He made church silver, spoons, picture frames and tankards as well as teapots richly decorated with repoussé work and gadrooning in the Rococo taste of mid-century. As fashion dictated, Revere adapted his skills to the graceful lines of the Neoclassical era. Some of Revere's silver is reproduced today such as the simple, unadorned pitcher copied from a Liverpool pottery jug.

The long romance with Neoclassicism that prevailed in Europe and America from the 1760's to the 1820's was the inspiration of many superb designs in silver. The smooth, gleaming metal was the perfect medium for the helmets, urns and columns of the period, ornamented with restrained elegance in bright cutting and engraving. By the early nineteenth century, lion's heads, dolphins and palmettes of Egyptian origin were included as the style progressed to French Empire and English Regency.

The discovery of a way of plating copper with a layer of silver in Sheffield during the 1740's gave rise to a whole range of inexpensive pieces that looked like sterling silver but brought luxurious taste within a reasonable price range. Various improvements were developed in the techniques and by the mid-nineteenth century electro-plating used German silver instead of copper as a base, thus eliminating the reddish gleam of copper that appeared when the silver plate wore thin.

Silver and silver plate fulfilled the nineteenth-century need for ostentatious display. Domestic silver wares were overburdened with applied ornaments and decorations in the general mêlée of popular styles which included Mediaeval, Gothic, Rococo as well as Chinese and Japanese. The decline in taste of the mass-produced furniture which had driven William Morris to start the Arts and Crafts Movement was also prevalent in silver. A return to the softly rounded, hand-fashioned forms to which silver lent itself so beautifully was begun and by the end of the century, the dragonflies, lilies, leaves and other plant forms of the Art Nouveau movement were reflected in silver teapots, picture frames and jewellery.

Silver Mounted Wares

The fashion for mounted wares in Tudor and early Stuart England revealed a passionate desire for the exotic both in the style of the mounts and choice of wares, ranging from ostrich eggs to gourds, horns and coconuts

1

M. R. Dudley

2

K. Hoddle

3

Museum Photo

Fig. 1 **Standing Salt** (left),
maker's mark a swan's head
erased, London, 1549. Silver-
gilt and crystal, height 8 ins.
(Trinity College, Oxford.)

Fig. 2 **Wan-Li Ewer** with
English silver-gilt mounts.
Sixteenth or early seventeenth
century. Height 10 ins.
After the 1520s, a great deal of
Ming porcelain was brought to
England, where it was regarded
as a magnificent luxury, and was
often mounted in silver,
gold or silver-gilt.
(Victoria and Albert Museum,
London.)

Fig. 3 **Katharine Parr's Jug**,
the latticinio, or milk glass
body Venetian, sixteenth
century, the silver-gilt mounts
with maker's mark, a fleur-de-lis,
London 1546. Height 6 ins.
On the cover are enamelled the
arms of Sir William Parr,
Elizabeth's uncle and
chamberlain, to whom perhaps
she presented the jug.
(London Museum.)

Fig. 4 **The Gibbon Salt**, maker's
mark three trefoils in a trefoil,
London, 1576. Silver-gilt with
an irregular five-sided pillar of
rock crystal enclosing a silver-
gilt figure of Neptune, height
12 ins; weight 57 oz. gross.
This extrordinary salt, which
was worth about £12 in 1632, is
believed to have been given as
a bribe to the Goldsmiths.
(The Worshipful Company of
Goldsmiths, London.)

J. Freeman

Fig. 5 *Ostrich Egg Cup and Cover, unmarked, c.1610. Silver-gilt mounts with ostrich motifs, height 20¾ ins. Arms of Exeter College and of Cleve. (Exeter College, Oxford.)*

P. Parkinson

Since Anglo-Saxon times at least, the rare, the curious and the valuable have been made more precious and beautiful by the addition of gold or silver mounts. During the medieval and Tudor periods, as the world was shrinking in the path of European mariners and merchants, so the treasure-houses of kings and princes and the cupboards of the wealthy were being filled with new and strange objects from India and China, Africa and the West Indies. There were ostrich eggs and fragile porcelain, mother-of-pearl and nautilus shells, gourds and coconuts. From nearer home came Venetian glass, Baltic amber, stoneware from the Rhineland, the fabulous unicorn's horn (in reality, the tusk or tooth of the narwhal), Turkish coloured pottery and varieties of rock crystal, agate and other hardstones, many of them carved in the workshops of southern Germany and northern Italy. And in England itself there was already a long tradition of working in horn, ivory and the spotted maplewood.

'Pots of earth of sundry colours garnished with silver'

Mounted wares are of two basic types: the decorative and the useful. The latter includes horn cups and beakers, wooden mazers or drinking-bowls and the leather jugs and bottles known as blackjacks, all of them favourite subjects, from medieval times onwards, for mounting with silver or silver-gilt. In addition, the middle of the sixteenth century saw the introduction of mounted stonewares, those 'pots of earth of sundry colours, and moulds, whereof many are garnished with silver' which William Harrison reported in 1587 as being used by all sorts and conditions of people all over the country.

Decorative mounted wares, for the display cupboards of the nobility and for ceremonial use, appeared in a host of lavish and imaginative guises under the inspiration of the renaissance designs which reached England by the second quarter of the sixteenth century. Some, despite their fragility, have survived to form the nuclei of rich royal and national collections. Inevitably, many have been lost, mostly those with fine and heavy mounts. In England, large numbers, especially with gold mounts, were sent to the Mint for disposal by Queen Elizabeth I in 1600 when she needed money. However, some of the less exotic pieces did have a fair chance of survival, for the iconoclasts and the tax-gatherers did not always trouble themselves over mounted wares when there were ample hoards of gold and silver vessels to satisfy them.

Several medieval mazers, the name given to bowls of spotted maplewood, appear to have been converted into all-silver bowls and standing cups during the sixteenth century, while the few that bear Elizabethan hallmarks on their mounts were possibly restored, rather than new pieces. The mazer in the Armourers' and Brasiers' Company Collection is in fact inscribed: 'Everard Frere gave this Mazer garnisht wt. silver 13 ounces wc. was new garnished ano. 1579 for y. Poor...' and it has a boss, apparently from an older mazer, presented to the Company by its first Master in 1453. Other mazers perhaps acquired new silver mounts when presented to colleges or companies, but there is no doubt that, while few new ones

were made, old mazers were still in use well into the seventeenth century. The so-called Pepys Mazer of 1510 got its name simply from the fact that Pepys recorded drinking from it when he visited the almshouses at Saffron Walden, Essex, in 1659.

It is, however, among the richer and rarer materials that one can glimpse something of the lost treasures of Tudor times. Ivory, the tusk of the Indian elephant and other tusks of whale or mammoth, were among the most popular exotic materials used in medieval times for carving and mounting (Fig. 6). However, they were gradually going out of favour and only 'oone Salte of Iuerie garnishhid with siluver guilt' appears in the royal inventory of 1574.

The fragility of materials does not seem to have deterred the Elizabethan goldsmith from lavishing rich gold and silver work on them. Among the most prized of medieval imports were ostrich eggs, often called gripe or griffin eggs in early inventories. Strange though the ostrich itself might be, the fabulous griffin, with its eagle's head and lion's body, apparently had greater appeal as creator of these large eggs with their relatively thick, pitted and yellowish shells. Their size was, of course, ideal for standing cups, but obviously most of the rich silver and silver-gilt frames made for them have acquired replacement eggs during the past four centuries.

Of highly sophisticated workmanship is the cup and cover of 1584, now in the Toledo Museum of Art, Ohio. The vase-shaped stem is flanked by four dolphin brackets, while the shell is enclosed by four alternating male and female caryatid straps in the best renaissance manner. Both the domed foot and the deep lip mount are engraved with fruit motifs between four coats of arms of contemporary date.

The origin of the shells is particularly stressed on one or two surviving cups, notably that of about 1610 at Exeter College, Oxford (Fig. 5). The domed base is chased with ostriches, the stem is formed as four ostrich legs clustered together, while three bold plumes on the tall cover support a finial in the form of an ostrich.

Another fragile and less easily replaceable material much favoured in the sixteenth century was pearl shell, the nacreous substance taken from many kinds of mollusc and known as mother-of-pearl. Ewers of mother-of-pearl feature regularly in the inventories of Queen Elizabeth, none of which appears to have survived. Most mother-of-pearl and other mounted wares bear neither hallmark nor often even maker's mark, so that the decoration and style of the mounts are frequently the only clue to date and country of origin. The pearl is usually arranged like staving and the mounts often have crenellated edges that have been worked to contain the pearl, a practical method used for small bowls and other wares until the middle of the seventeenth century.

A shell of a very different kind that had tremendous popularity throughout the period was the coconut shell which, when shorn of its rough outer covering and painstakingly polished, and often carved, provided a lustrous dark nut. The pieces merited a place in the royal collections or served as royal gifts, to judge from the coconut cups bearing the Tudor arms. Many of the most splendid coconut cups date from the fifteenth century, and have been treasured over the centuries in the

Fig. 6 *The Howard Grace Cup*, maker's mark, crossed implements, London 1525. Ivory mounted in silver-gilt, set with pearls and garnets, height 12 ins.
The mounts of this superb piece mark a transition in English style from the Gothic to the Renaissance; the former is reflected in the rope-work borders and the band of gothic lettering, while the latter is seen in the rich elaboration of renaissance motifs on the foot and cover.
(Victoria and Albert Museum.)

Fig. 7 *The Rogers Salt*, London, 1601. Silver-gilt, rock crystal and painted parchment, height 22 ins.
This is one of the last great Tudor mounted salts to be made. The cylinder of crystal contains a parchment roll painted with flowers, the arms of the Goldsmiths' Company, and an escutcheon inscribed: 'Ric. Rogers, Comptroller of the Mint'.
(The Worshipful Company of Goldsmiths.)

collections of Oxford and Cambridge colleges and the City Livery Companies.

Even in the mid-sixteenth century, rather traditional gothic styles persisted for coconut cups, perhaps to complement the simple form of the shell and its sombre colouring. With few exceptions, even those cups enriched with carving on the shell have a certain simplicity of form. From 1586 dates a beautiful standing cup, the nut carved with strap-work and armorials, including the cipher of Elizabeth I and the crest of the Sidney family, designed either for the Earl of Leicester or his nephew Sir Philip Sidney. But, rather like stoneware and pottery, coconut cups tended with time to become less extravagant and less precious examples of the mounter's art, and, indeed, became almost a provincial speciality. Most seventeenth-century cups show York or other provincial marks.

Equally widely made throughout the country were tigerware jugs. To modern eyes, this German mottled stoneware seems unremarkable, but English pottery at the time was very coarse and usually porous. A variety of German stoneware was imported into Elizabethan England: greyish wares from Cologne and the Westerwald, brownish ones from Raeren, and an interesting white ware came from Siegburg. The greater number of wares were, however, the brownish ones known as tigerware (Fig. 8). It has been suggested by Sir Charles Jackson, the authority on English silver, that the name was derived from the German *tiegel*, meaning kiln, but it seems equally possible that it meant speckled, or tabby, like a cat.

'My painted Drinking Glass, with the Silver and Guilte foote'

The import of tigerware pots and jugs into England appears to have dated from about 1540, and large numbers were garnished with silver, especially in the 1570s. It is known that they featured as prizes in the various state lotteries of the period, and this probably accounts for their ubiquity – there are surviving tigerware pots bearing provincial marks. Perhaps because they were popular rather than courtly pieces, the standard of the silver and silver-gilt mounts is not always very high, and the quality of embossing and engraving varies considerably.

One of the most fascinating aspects of sixteenth-century mounted wares is the esteem in which they were held by their owners. In the Armourers' and Brasiers' Company is a stoneware pot with silver mounts in the form of an owl, valued at 28s 6d when it was presented by Julyan, late the wife of William Vineard, in 1537. The rarity of glass in England in the first half of the sixteenth century gave it an importance equal to that of Chinese porcelain, both of which were well-represented in the royal collections of the period. Glasses mounted in gold, ewers of red or morrey glass and of 'purslaine' glass have, understandably, vanished, but one rarity with royal connections is the mounted glass pot known as Katharine Parr's jug (Fig. 3). Made of the milky white striped glass known as *latticinio* (milk) probably imported from Venice, the jug is beautifully mounted with silver-gilt, fully marked in London in 1546. On the cover are enamelled the arms of Sir William Parr, the Queen's uncle and her Chamberlain, to whom per-

Fig. 8 (above) *Tigerware Jug,*
maker's mark, a cross between
four pellets, English c.1570.
Silver-gilt mounts,
height 9¼ ins.
Note the neat bands of
engraving around the neck.
(Christie's, London.)

Fig. 9 (below) *Rock Crystal*
Ewer, the crystal Milanese,
c.1580, the silver-gilt mounts
English, maker's mark E.I.,
c.1620. Height 6⅛ ins.
(Christie's, London.)

haps she presented it. Painted glass was also much esteemed, but few pieces have survived.

Intrepid adventurers who made their way to the Orient returned with such rarities as celadon and, by the 1520s, Ming porcelain. Despite their oriental origin, there was no effort on the part of the English silversmiths to produce mounts in anything but the current European style. Even such popular inscriptions as 'Live to die and live', were used. Monstrous-looking griffin and eagle-head terminals to the spouts of ewers were by renaissance times part of the standard European ornamental repertoire (Fig. 2). Similarly, the mounts on Turkish and other coloured pottery were unmistakeably English in character.

The dark green mottled marking of the serpentine

While potters and artists strove to create hard and brilliant new materials, the gem-carvers and jewellers of renaissance Europe continued to lavish their craftsmanship on both transparent and opaque gem materials such as alabaster, marble, jasper, agate, serpentine and rock crystal. Just as the speckled surface of tigerware appealed to the Elizabethan man-in-the-street, so the dark green mottled marking of the serpentine appealed to the wealthy patron. The mounted 'serpentine pott' bequeathed by Dr. William Butler to Clare College, Cambridge is an excellent example. Queen Elizabeth owned dozens of such mounted pieces, including a serpentine collock or barrel, just one of more than a dozen serpentine wares.

Of all the precious mounted materials, however, the most splendid survivors are those of rock crystal. Royal collections no doubt had more than their share of them, for it was thought that the crystal would shatter if poison were placed in it. Queen Elizabeth had more than fifty cups, bowls and ewers of crystal, some set in gold, others in silver-gilt, and more than a dozen salts, including state salts. By tradition, the Bowes Cup of 1554 in the Goldsmiths' Company Collection is always known as Queen Elizabeth's Coronation Cup, although the owner, Sir Martin Bowes, was not then Lord Mayor, but Prime Warden of the Goldsmiths, to whom he gave the cup in 1561. Here is Elizabethan gold-smithing at its most delightful. The crystal cylinder is supported by four Atlas figures around a globe of crystal and is enclosed by four caryatid straps. Another piece of hemispherical crystal is held within the domed cover which is topped by a grace-ful female figure bearing a shield with the donor's arms enamelled on it, while the remaining surfaces of the cup from foot to finial are rich with repoussé chasing.

Yet another crystal cup in the same collection, dated 1545, though less exceptional in its quality, has a faceted bowl of rock crystal with three very slender straps holding it between the foot and the cup-shaped engraved lip. Other types of recorded cups have faceted bowls and stems, and one, of about 1600 in Yateley Church even has a steeple cover.

The rock crystal cylinder was also used for a number of fine ceremonial salts, many of them enclosing standing figures within the crystal column. Such is the silver-gilt salt of 1549 now at

Trinity College, Oxford (Fig. 1) with scrolling caryatids supporting the stone.

Many of the great state salts of the period were of architectural form and none more majestically so than the pillared Gibbon Salt of 1576 (Fig. 4), presented to the Goldsmiths in 1632 after a search had been made through the City for substandard wares. Within the columns, a cylinder of rock crystal contains a figure of Neptune, holding above his head the tiny well for the salt.

Not only rock crystal and silver-gilt, but jewels as well, decorate some salts. The Elizabethans were at times ready to accept grandeur for its own sake, as can be gauged from the records of clock salts and the rare sixteenth-century rock crystal candelabrum which appeared in Christie's, London in 1956.

By 1600, much of the glory that formed the royal and other collections had been dissipated by the needs of war, and hundreds of pieces were sent to the Mint for melting. Here and there, elaborate standing cups and salts were still mounted; the Duke of Bedford's salt at Woburn is dated to about 1610, and a few years later a Milan-carved crystal ewer was mounted in silver-gilt by an English goldsmith (Fig. 9). But the age of grand silver was virtually over with the old century, and it is with a salt of 1601 (Fig. 7), that the story of Tudor mounted wares ends: a cylinder of rock crystal in a restrained and simple setting chased in low relief with formal foliage, its cover topped with a miniature crystal and silver steeple, its cylinder of rock crystal holding a splash of colour in the parchment roll painted with flowers, the arms of the Goldsmiths' Company and an escutcheon inscribed 'Ric. Rogers, Comptroller of the Mint'.

MUSEUMS AND COLLECTIONS

Examples of silver-mounted wares may be seen at the following:

GREAT BRITAIN
Edinburgh: Royal Scottish Museum
London: British Museum
London Museum
Victoria and Albert Museum
U.S.A.
California: Henry Huntington Art Gallery, San Marino
New York: Metropolitan Museum
Ohio: Toledo Museum of Art

FURTHER READING

Tudor Domestic Silver, Victoria and Albert Museum booklet, 1970.
Illustrated History of English Plate (2 vols.) by Sir Charles Jackson, London, reprinted 1967.
Investing in Silver by Eric Delieb, London, 1967.
English Silversmiths' Work, Civil & Domestic by Charles Oman, London, 1965.
English Domestic Silver by Charles Oman, 5th Edition, London, 1962.
The Plate of the Worshipful Company of Goldsmiths by J. B. Carrington and G. R. Hughes, London, 1962.

Early American Silver

The pilgrims newly arrived in America brought with them many skills, not the least of which was silversmithing. The pieces they created are some of the most interesting in the history of American craftsmanship

There was no silversmith listed among the hundred and two 'Saints and Strangers' who landed at Plymouth, Massachusetts, in the little ship, *The Mayflower* three hundred and fifty years ago, but the men and women who made that voyage to a new life in America were soon followed by many others, chiefly from England and Holland. They included farmers and labourers, artisans and merchants, who helped to create new settlements that shortly grew into towns and cities very like those that they had left behind in Europe.

Early American silver is understandably rare, confined mainly to essential pieces such as spoons, porringers and drinking-vessels, and to church plate. Unfortunately for the historian and the silver collector, American silversmiths were entrusted with making their wares to the sterling standard without the supervision of an assay office or other authority, although in some respects, such as that of apprenticeship, the colonists had hardly more freedom than they had had in Europe. In recent years there has been extensive and rewarding research into the lives and works of a notable number of silversmiths in Boston, New York and Philadelphia, and many have now been identified.

Fig. 1 *Porringers* by John Coney (1656–1722) and Peter van Inburgh (1689–1740). (Yale University Art Gallery, New Haven, Connecticut. Mabel Brady Garvan Collection.)

Fig. 2 *Beaker and Porringer* by Robert Sanderson (1608–93) and John Hull (1624–83), Boston, 1659 and c.1655. (Loaned by the First Church, Boston Museum of Fine Arts.)

Fig. 3 *Two-handled cup* by John Coney, Boston, 1679. Height 6⅞ ins. Arms of Addington. This superb caudle cup is an excellent example of Coney's mastery of silver. (Yale University Art Gallery. Garvan Collection.)

Fig. 4 *Two-handled cup and cover* by John Coney, Boston, 1701. Height 10¼ ins. Arms of Stoughton. This magnificent cup was given to Harvard University by the Hon. William Stoughton. (William Hayes Fogg Art Museum, Cambridge, Mass.)

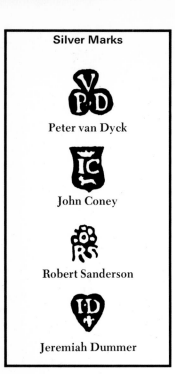
Fig. 5 *Detail of Fig. 6, showing Edward Winslow's mark.*

Fig. 6 *Footed salver by Edward Winslow, Boston, c.1695. Diameter 9¾ ins. This handsome salver has a raised gadrooned rim and stylised foliage border. (Christie's.)*

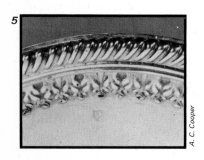

In some cases, no more than a name is known, such as that of Thomas Howard, recorded as a goldsmith in Jamestown in 1620, the year of *The Mayflower's* historic voyage. Others left not only their marks and their works, but notes and diaries that invest them with as much humanity as the rarer surviving portraits.

Nothing is yet known of the work of an English goldsmith, John Mansfield, who emigrated to Boston in 1634, perhaps to escape religious intolerance, perhaps because he feared the onset of the Civil War. It was probably in that same year that the father of a certain John Hull emigrated with his family from Market Harborough to Boston, where John and his brother are known to have worked as silversmiths. John Hull later wrote how he 'fell to learning (by the help of my brother) and to practising the trade of a goldsmith' – at which he prospered. By 1652 he was so greatly esteemed that he was appointed Mint-master for the Court of Massachusetts, electing his friend, the silversmith Robert Sanderson, to act in partnership with him.

Robert Sanderson was a London silversmith who was born in 1608 and served his apprenticeship to William Rawlins. He worked for some years in London, and it is certain that the mark RS shown below a sun in splendour was his, for he continued to use it after his arrival in America. It has been found on at least three pieces of English silver – a salver of 1635 found, in fact, in the United States and recorded by Jackson (*English Goldsmiths and their Marks, 1921*), and a chalice and paten of the same year bearing the arms of Sir Thomas Myddelton and his wife.

The setting up of the Mint indicated the growing importance of Boston

In America, Sanderson first lived in Hampshire, Massachusetts, but, by 1642, was in Watertown where the first of his three sons, all later to become silversmiths, was born. By the middle of the century he had moved to Boston, which continued to grow rapidly in importance and distinction throughout the ensuing decades. Some indication of this is shown not only by the setting up of the Mint, but by the fact that by 1680 there were enough well-established goldsmiths and bankers in the colonial capital to train several apprentices each, among them 'four ministers' sons.

In 1659, John Hull records that he 'received into my house Jeremie [usually called Jeremiah] Dummer and Samuel Paddy . . . as apprentices'. Paddy was, unhappily, a failure, but the fourteen-year-old Dummer was to become one of the most notable of the early American craftsmen. Others trained by Hull and Sanderson included William Rouse (or Ros), apparently of Dutch origin, and Timothy Dwight, born in 1654, as well as the notable John Coney who had been born in 1656.

Dummer himself, who, according to Hull in 1681, lived 'in good fashion, hath . . . a good estate', probably trained Thomas Savage, born in 1664, and Edward Winslow, born five years later. Besides the young men who were truly American by birth, a number still came from the Old World, among them Edward Webb, who lived in Boston and died there in 1718, and John Edwards, brought to Boston as a young man and probably apprenticed

to Dummer. Edwards worked in partnership with John Allen, and later alone, his two sons carrying on their father's business into the mid-eighteenth century.

Naturally, the first generation silversmiths from England continued to make silver in much the same styles as those used at home. A small dram cup by Hull and Sanderson, now at Yale, is one of the oldest recorded pieces of American silver, dated 1651. Its central flower motif and twisted wire handles makes it similar to many Commonwealth wine-tasters, but it should be noted that in colonial inventories, these small bowls are almost always termed 'dram cups' for drinking spirits. Another plain example by the same makers can be dated to 1673, while a beaker of about the same date, engraved with pendent drops below strap-work and with a stamped border at the foot, might almost have been made in East Anglia, where many of the immigrants once lived. A winecup, also at Yale, is typically English in style, while several bellied porringers, both plain in the East Anglian manner and with simple panelled decoration in the style of the 1650s, have been noted.

Apparently originals and patterns continued to arrive from England throughout the second half of the seventeenth century, but in many instances the American craftsmen were developing their own distinctive styles, especially in the pierced flat ears of porringers (Figs. 1 and 2) and in the scalloped bands around the bases, and even on each side of the moulded rib on otherwise conventional tankards. One of about 1690 by John Edwards features an unusual serrated square on the base of the handle echoed by similar cut-card work at the junction, a beaded spine, lion thumb-piece and two rows of gadrooning on the cap cover.

Gadrooning was perhaps the most favoured of all styles of decoration in late seventeenth century Boston. Jeremiah Dummer is credited with having introduced it in about 1680, and it was much used by John Coney and by Edward Winslow for the borders of salvers, cups, mugs, salts, castors and sugar caskets. John Coney's grace cup for Harvard, dated 1701, shows a late survival of Stuart caryatid handles with more up-to-date fluted and gadrooned formality, while in his footed salver of about 1695 Edward Winslow has captured the new English Baroque with a border of stylised foliage below the heavily gadrooned rim (Figs. 5 and 6). These craftsmen, in fact, developed Boston silver along very similar lines, making fine gadrooned salvers,

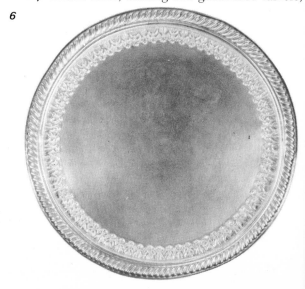

Fig. 7 *Sugar-box* by John Coney, Boston, c.1700. Length 7¼ ins. Only three of these very rare caskets made by Coney survive. (Christie's, London.)

Fig. 8 *Punch-bowl* by Jeremiah Dummer (1645–1718), Boston, c.1692. Height 3¼ ins., diameter 6¾ ins. (Yale University Art Gallery.)

Fig. 9 *Standing salt, candlestick, sugar castor and tankard* by John Coney, Edward Winslow (1669–1753) and Henry Hurst (c.1665–1717), Boston, c.1700–10. (Boston Museum of Fine Arts.)

Fig. 10 *Caudle cup* by Robert Sanderson, Boston, c.1680. (Henry Francis du Pont Winterthur Museum, Winterthur, Delaware.)

Fig. 11 *Monteith* by John Coney, Boston, early eighteenth century. (Yale University Art Gallery. Garvan Collection.)

Fig. 12 *Spout cup* by William Cowell (1682–1736), Boston, c.1700. Probably used by invalids. (Private Collection.)

Fig. 13 *Two-handled cup and cover*, maker's mark IB, probably for Jurian Blanck, New York, c.1695.
The shape of this cup is typically English, but the richness of ornament is very Dutch, as is the coat of arms.
(H. F. du Pont Winterthur Museum.)

Fig. 14 *Beaker* by Cornelius van der Burgh, New York, c.1685. Height 5⅞ ins. (Christie's.)

Fig. 15 *Tankard* by Peter van Dyck (1684–1750), New York, early eighteenth century. Height 6¾ ins.
(Yale University Art Gallery. Lent by F. P. Garvan '97 and Mrs. Garvan.)

the rare sugar-caskets (Fig. 7) based on Charles II styles (of which only eight have been recorded in American silver), and lace-back and other decorated spoons in the English manner.

Edward Winslow was also responsible for one of the three known standing salts from Boston (Fig. 9), the others being by Dummer, Edwards and Allen.

Tea, coffee and chocolate made their impact on New England as in Europe, chocolate apparently being the most popular in Boston, where Coney made a baluster-shaped pot about 1701, its spout curved and slender like those made in England some fifteen years earlier. It is, however, to New York that the student must look for the earliest teapots, two of them dated to about 1697, and another, by Peter van Dyck, c.1710, of pear shape with an almost straight spout. In 1960 a teapot of about the same date came to light, made by the

London-trained silversmith Simeon Soumain.

The silversmiths of New York have almost as long a history as those of Boston, but it was the Low Countries rather than England that proved the chief influence and source of craftsmen. New York silver is rich with Dutch names such as Bartholomew Schaats, Benjamin Wynkoop, Konraet ten Eyck, Jesse Kip and the noted elder craftsman, Cornelius van der Burgh. Others show their Huguenot descent – René Grignon and the Le Roux family as well as Soumain, and their silver is markedly European in flavour. This is especially true of their beakers and tankards, dram cups and two-handled bowls, often decorated in the Dutch manner.

One of New York's earliest and best-known pieces is Van der Burgh's beaker, now at Yale, with strap-work panels engraved with designs taken from Van der Venne's engravings for the poems of

13

12

14

15

Fig. 16 *Sugar Castor, probably from a set of three, by Peter van Dyck, New York, early eighteenth century. Height 7¾ ins. Arms of Schuyler. (Yale University Art Gallery. Garvan Collection.)*

Jacob Cats. The beaker is engraved 'Robert Sanders, 1685', and dates from about the same time as another beaker by the same silversmith, also in Dutch style, charmingly and delicately engraved with three birds, strap-work and pendant flowers and foliage.

Some of the Dutch flower motifs embossed and chased on the bowls of two-handled cups, often with scroll panels and caryatid handles (Fig. 13), are reminiscent of the styles brought back from abroad by the English Court at the Restoration, and it is perhaps some indication of the provincial outlook of the town that they were still being made in New York some forty years later. As in Europe, however, it was the Huguenot-born silversmiths who helped to lift silver styles out of the seventeenth and into the eighteenth century. A two-handled cup by Charles Le Roux, for example, has formal, although very simple, strap-work and fine harp-shaped handles in sharp contrast with the little Commonwealth and Charles II style spirit cups and porringers of the period.

The New York Dutch styles were not, however, without charm, and some very pleasant effects were achieved in minor details. Cupid masks and elaborately cast flowers were both popular terminals used at the base of tankard handles (Fig. 15), while a cut-card cast lion in relief climbing the scroll handle was a conceit affected by several makers between about 1690 and 1710.

The swift colonisation of America during the second half of the seventeenth century brought silversmiths in the train of the settlers to many East Coast towns. In Philadelphia, Cesar Ghiselin and Johannis Nys were able to forge a living making spoons and tankards, cups and porringers. Francis Richardson's father took him from New York to Philadelphia as a boy, where the Irish family Syng, from Cork, also settled about 1714. Interchange of ideas and designs as well as increased travel among craftsmen seeking fame and fortune meant a gradual development of what one might call the American silver style. Boston became less 'English' and New York less 'Dutch', as the silversmiths of the second and third generations developed an affinity of thought and design to cater for a young, vigorous and increasingly wealthy nation. 🕸

MUSEUMS AND COLLECTIONS
Early American silver may be seen at the following:

U.S.A.
Boston: Boston Museum of Fine Arts
Cambridge: William Hayes Fogg Art Museum
Chicago: Art Institute of Chicago, Illinois
New Haven: Yale University Art Gallery
New York: Metropolitan Museum of Art

FURTHER READING

Early Connecticut Silver, 1700–1840 by Peter Bohan, Conn., 1970.
The Colonial Silversmith: His Techniques and his Products by Henry J. Kaufmann, New Jersey, 1969.
American Silver by Kathryn Buhler, Cleveland, 1950.
American Silversmiths and Their Marks by Stephen C. G. Ensko, New York, 1948.
American Silver by John Marshall Phillips, London, 1949.

German Silver

German
Silver

Fig. 1 *Salt-cellar in the form of a monster, Augsburg, late seventeenth century. Height 7½ins. (Victoria and Albert Museum, London.)*

Distinctive in both conception and design, German silver in the seventeenth and eighteenth centuries was among the most lavish and magnificent in Europe

A period of intense hardship from which even the nobility were not immune followed the end of the Thirty Years' War in 1648. Not only were industry and commerce in a state of grave disrepair, but, in addition, intellectual life suffered. The old confidence in national strength had disappeared. The internal organisation of the country was chaotic; there were approximately eighteen hundred different states, some with populations of less than three hundred, all governed by an Emperor with limited powers who made laws only with the consent of the Reichstag, established at Regensburg. The picture of Germany in the middle of the century is certainly gloomy, with its crushing levies, nepotism and inefficient government. On the last score, Leopold I (1640–1705) saw his position solely as a means to promote the interests of the Catholic Church which, though arguably admirable in principle, did little to strengthen the internal structure of Germany or revive the earlier sense of optimism.

Fortunately there are always those who seek self-aggrandisement and one of the most obvious manifestations of this was in the spectacular rivalry of the lesser princes. Nothing was more suitable for ostentatious display than silver. Although the indigenous silver-mines were partly exhausted, a new source of supply was realised in America. Because obvious splendour was what mattered, the majority of the plate produced was partly or totally gilded. It was not a period that produced any startling new designs or techniques within the country; rather the designers stuck to what they knew, to the old traditions. Towards the end of the century, French influence became paramount, aided by the immigration of Huguenots who gave new life to the production of silver.

Exuberant ornamental detail was lavished on drinking-vessels

The standard of execution remained high throughout the seventeenth century and, while a preference was shown for repoussé and/or chased surfaces, the quality of engraving on occasion equalled the products of Friesland. As in contemporary architecture, there was an undoubted tendency to exuberance of ornamental detail, and this attention was lavished in particular on drinking-vessels, which form the majority of seventeenth-century German silver.

It was the custom to give a cup on any important occasion and the variety is legion. The *Riesenpokal* was unique to the German smiths; a large cup, sometimes forty inches high, it was intended solely for display. More familiar is the *Ananaspokal* (pineapple cup), the stem of which was often shaped as a tree trunk or a figure. Those with bowls decorated with large bosses (*bückeln*) continued to be produced until the end of the century, an example of the tenacity of tradition. The top cup of the *dop-*

K. Hoddle

pelpokal (double cup) was reputed to be reserved for the exclusive use of the mistress of the house. A few terrestrial globe cups survive, the globe invariably supported by a figure of Atlas. Two fine examples are in the Staatliche Akademie für Werkkunst at Berlin; one is the work of a Magdeburg smith and was engraved by Wilhelm Jansson Blaeu in 1667. It was a gift from the Mayor to the Elector of Brandenburg. The other is probably by the Augsburg smith Lorenz Biller II, and was engraved by Christoph Schmidt in 1696. Another form of surface decoration was the imitation of faceted diamonds (*diamant-bückeln*) which owes its inspiration to the Venetian glassworks.

There was a long-standing popularity for cups modelled in the form of animals

A type of drinking-vessel indigenous to the country was that of cups modelled as animals. They may well have originated as three-dimensional representations of the owner's crest or part of his coat of arms. Each has a detachable head, and their forms included those of the chamois, griffin, panther, swan and pelican in her piety. They continued in popular use until the end of the seventeenth century. They were occasionally adapted to serve another purpose; the example in Figure 1 is a magnificent salt-cellar modelled as a monster holding in its claws a scallop shell.

Fig. 2 *Beaker* by Christian Metz, Ohlau, late seventeenth century. Engraved with flowers and parcel-gilt, height 4½ ins. (Victoria and Albert Museum.)

K. Hodtle

The surfaces of tankards provided great opportunity for imaginative German goldsmiths. In the main, they chose to decorate them with chasing, the scenes represented often being of a mythological or biblical nature, and sometimes a combination of the two. Even in the last years of the century there were examples of typical high renaissance ornament, swags of fruit and flowers, garlands and strap-work. Nevertheless, these pieces remained expressions of distinct German individuality in conception and design.

In some cases a Netherlandish influence is apparent, which is hardly surprising in view of the predominance of Dutch merchants travelling in Europe. Pattern books were widely circulated and had some influence on design. The essence of the style created in Holland by the Van Vianens, and pursued to its logical conclusion by Johannes Lutma, was discretion. The style never engulfed a piece but on occasion became apparent, as for instance, on the scroll handle of a tankard or round the base of a standing cup. However, in the succeeding century the inspiration became increasingly eclectic.

There had long existed in Germany an interest in natural history; indeed, by the seventeenth century museums had been established devoted to this subject. A satisfactory manner of displaying natural objects to good advantage was mounting them in silver or silver-gilt. Cornelian, chalcedony, agate, mother of pearl, ivory, stoneware and faience were also used for this purpose. The silver-gilt cup in Figure 3 shows the unusual combination of horn and mother of pearl; the latter panels are finely engraved with hunting scenes. Equally, crystal, with its supposed property of divining the presence of poison, was popular.

Johann Melchior Dinglinger – a craftsman of extraordinary technical ability

The zenith of this art-form was reached by Johann Melchior Dinglinger; by 1708, with the assistance of his brothers Georg Friedrich as enameller and Georg Christoph as jeweller, he had completed his greatest work, a baroque creation called 'The Court at Delhi on the Birthday of the Great Mogul Aureng-Zeb'. Made for Augustus the Strong, it was housed in the Green Vaults at Dresden. Dinglinger, through his use of material and extraordinary technical ability, transcended the limitations of his craft. It is interesting but not surprising to note the influence on Dinglinger of some of the designs of the Frenchman Lepautre; the French influence was in the ascendant at this time. When in 1698 Augustus wished to have the Brandenburg rooms of his Dresden palace decorated, he summoned the French architect Raymond Leplat. The result was the latest Parisian style of restrained elegance, as exemplified by Jean Bérain.

The development of the Louis XIV style in Germany owed much to the publications of Abraham Drentwett (1647–1727) of Augsburg and Johann Jakob Priester, who worked in collaboration with Elias Adam. The latter specialised in mounts, as did Melchior Beyer. Several practising goldsmiths published designs, among them Johann Leonhard Eysler, Johann Erhard Henglin II and Johann

319

K. Hoddle

Ludwig Biller, who belonged to a well-known family of Augsburg smiths. Another from the same town was J. J. Baumgartner whose designs, published in 1727, included some *Chinoiseries*. The main centre for dissemination of the style was Augsburg, a city that remained pre-eminent in quality as well as in quantity of production throughout the eighteenth century.

It would, however, be wrong to assume that France was the only outside influence on taste. England admittedly was of far less consequence, but a ewer and basin now in the Lee of Fareham Collection, made by Daniel Schaeffler of Augsburg around 1710 and decorated simply with gadrooning, shows a strong stylistic similarity to some produced in England. In addition, when the Hanoverian Elector came to the English throne, this connection resulted in the direct copying of English designs by Hanoverian goldsmiths.

Frederick the Great was an enthusiastic patron of the arts

But by the middle of the eighteenth century, Voltaire wrote from Potsdam: 'I am in France here. Only my own tongue is spoken. German is reserved for soldiers and horses'. Outposts of resistance against French domination were apparent, as in the behaviour of King Frederick William I of Prussia (1713–40), who loathed everything French. However, his successor, Frederick the Great (1740–86) showed antipathy to his father's views and became a great patron of the arts. He was a collector on a lavish scale and had a passion for snuff-boxes, mounted in gold or silver. An edict by Frederick in 1740 forbade the importation of any

K. Hoddle

K. Hoddle

Fig. 3 *Standing cup and cover,*
German, eighteenth century.
Mother of pearl and horn with
silver-gilt mounts, height 15 ins.
(Victoria and Albert Museum.)

Fig. 4 *Beaker and cover by*
Johann Erhard Henglin,
Augsburg, c.1720. Silver-gilt,
height 6 ins.
(Victoria and Albert Museum.)

Fig. 5 *Andiron by Philip Jacob.*
Drentwett, Augsburg, 1747–49.
Height 17 ins.
This is one of the rare fire-dogs
made after the late seventeenth
century.
(Victoria and Albert Museum.)

Fig. 6 *Beaker and cover, maker's*
mark $^{SB}_{P}$, *Augsburg, late*
seventeenth century. Chased
with flower-heads and gilt,
height 6½ ins.
(Victoria and Albert Museum.)

French boxes and contributed to the eminence of Berlin silversmiths in this field. Two of the most outstanding exponents of this art were Johann Christian Neuber (1736–1808) and Heinrich Taddel, (active 1739–69), both at different times directors of the Green Vaults Museum. However, the leading exponent was the Parisian-trained goldsmith Jean Guillaume Georges Krüger, who also published designs.

Until the establishment of Augustus the Strong's factory at Meissen in 1710, the goldsmiths were unrivalled in their ability to produce an enormous range of luxury goods. If a gift was required, it invariably took the form of a piece of silver. This monopoly was terminated by the invention of true porcelain in Europe and accounts for the gradual decline in prestige of German silver during the eighteenth century. At times, the two crafts were advantageously combined in mounted wares, but the artistic emphasis in Germany was towards producing ever more magnificent examples of porcelain. The forms of decoration in the early eighteenth century, which included *Laub und Bandelwerk* (foliage and scroll-work), and stylised portrait busts, were well suited to both media (Fig. 4). Accordingly, the variety of silver produced was narrowed down; certainly it included drinking-vessels, such as goblets, beakers (often covered and

sometimes inset with coins) and tankards, as well as candlesticks, *écuelles* and boxes, but the wine-cisterns, fountains, andirons (Fig. 5) and large dishes common in the late seventeenth century became increasingly rare. It was a time of consolidation for the goldsmith; the glory of the past two centuries allowed him to take stock of his position and to adapt to the new influences.

Another reason for a decline in the output of silver was the number of wars that beset the century, in particular the Seven Years' War (1756–63), in which Frederick the Great took on the combined forces of Austria, France, Russia, Saxony and Sweden, his sole help a small financial interest from England. Although victorious, this war was yet another indication that it was the time not for expansive display but for the retrenchment of artistic endeavour.

In technique the French designs laid emphasis on chasing and flat chasing. Engraving was usually restricted to an inscription or coat of arms.

The emergence of the rococo style (*Muschelwerk*) was hardly apparent before 1730, and it was during the following decade that it reached its peak. The German version of the Rococo is distinctive. It was frequently somewhat crude in conception and marred by over-elaboration of detail. There was a tendency for whimsical designs like those of

321

Meissonnier and Claude Ballin to be lost in the ungainly shapes used. A baptismal ewer and dish, now in the Bayerisches Nationalmuseum, Munich, made in Augsburg in about 1756, is, with its welter of florid extravagance, an example of this lack of restraint. This exuberance, however, is not always apparent. On occasion the chased detail is set off by plain surfaces; the *écuelle* in Figure 7 is a rare but happy example of a less riotous and more subdued interpretation of the Rococo.

The Rococo died slowly, continuing until about 1780; but the products of the later years are somewhat stiffly executed. They lacked the earlier exuberance, which was much assisted along its course by the designers Martin Engelbrecht and Caspar Gottlieb Eissler, both of Nuremberg.

By this date, England and France were under the artistic influence of neo-Classicism; Germany, however, remained almost untouched by it. Certainly, individual examples exist incorporating loosely draped figures, wreaths, urns and Arcadian landscapes, but they are few and far between; they remain examples of an international style as opposed to one fundamentally understood and transmuted into a means of nationalistic expression. This feeling lasted out the eighteenth century and explains the decline in quality and quantity associated with its last decades. 🙰

7

Fig. 7 *Ecuelle, cover and stand by Emmanuel Drentwett, Augsburg, 1747–49. Silver-gilt, diameter of stand 9¼ ins. The German Rococo was far removed from the tasteful delicacy of the French. In Germany, shapes were often ungainly, and marred by over-elaboration of detail. This* écuelle *is a rare example of a more subdued interpretation. (Christie, Manson and Woods, Ltd., London.)*

WHERE TO SEE

German silver of the seventeenth and eighteenth centuries may be seen at the following:

GERMANY
Berlin: Kunstgewerbemuseum
Munich: Bayerisches Nationalmuseum
GREAT BRITAIN
London: British Museum
                    Victoria and Albert Museum
Oxford: Ashmolean Museum
U.S.A.
New York: Metropolitan Museum of Art

FURTHER READING

At the Court of the Great Mogul by Joachim Menzhausen (trans.), Leipzig, 1966.
Goldschmiedekunst in Dresden by Walter Holzhausen, Tübingen, 1966.
Augsburger Silbergeräte des Spätbarock by Sylvia Rathke-Koehl, Hamburg, 1965.
Deutsches Goldschmiedekunst by Heinz Leitermann, Stuttgart, 1954.
Johann Melchior Dinglinger by Walter Holzhausen, Berlin, 1946.

Chinoiserie Silver

**Although very little silver
came to Europe from the East,
the West set to decorating
silver with *Chinoiserie*, using
Eastern lacquer and porcelain
designs as inspiration**

The most fascinating aspect of Chinese influence on the decoration of European silver is the fact that *Chinoiserie* was a purely European style and never a serious attempt to copy Chinese art. It involved the use of oriental motifs during the seventeenth and eighteenth centuries in a highly romantic way (Fig. 7).

In seventeenth century Europe, there was a growing fashion for oriental objects and the Manchu or Ch'ing dynasty, founded in 1644, expanded trading possibilities with the West. By the middle of the century there was a considerable vogue for oriental design and the Manchu period, although far from being the golden age of Chinese art, was an era of great technical skill. Goods began to be made solely for export to many European countries where, being greatly in demand, they were very expensive and highly prized.

Europe at this period did not really distinguish between China, Japan and India from the artistic point of view, and European art was not seriously influenced by the Orient until the late seventeenth century, when the magnificence and exoticism of western decoration was further enhanced by equally magnificent and exotic *Chinoiseries*. Lacquer, porcelain and textiles began to influence contemporary Europe, and European craftsmen began to imitate oriental wares.

One of the earliest uses of *chinoiserie* decoration in England was for the embellishment of silver. True Chinese ornament was always symbolic – this usually escaped the European eye – and, except for filigree work, there was little silver imported into Europe from the Far East at this time. Nothing, therefore, was known about the work of Chinese silversmiths.

In 1616 a Dutch engraver, Mathias Beitler, produced a series of engravings of oriental designs, but the earliest known London pattern-book showing the use of *chinoiserie* decoration on silver is that of De Moedler of 1694.

In the seventeenth century, *chinoiserie* decoration used by silversmiths was based on lacquer-work designs from the Far East which were greatly

admired and much copied in Europe. Other
designs were taken from porcelain, which had been
imported in large quantities for some time by the
Dutch East India Company, and from contemporary travel books (Fig. 6), the most famous of
which was Nieuhoff's *Embassy*, published in
England in 1669.

All these sources created an almost totally
European and artificial concept of China; most
contemporary silver shapes continued to be used
by European silversmiths who then enlivened them
with *chinoiserie* decoration (Fig. 4), usually
engraved and of a fairly crude standard of execution
and design. Very little care, if any, was taken to

copy oriental art correctly. The fantastic birds, a
great feature of *chinoiserie* silver, the trees, the
little theatrical figures, often more Indian than
Chinese, and usually with decidedly Mongolian
features, all combined to create a new and
completely fantastic form of decoration on English
silver of the late seventeenth century. They
appeared first of all in the 1660s and became a
considerable feature of decorative ornament by the
1680s. Punch-bowls, monteiths, porringers,
tankards, caskets, vases and toilet-services were
all given elaborate *chinoiserie* decoration. Pieces
connected with tea, which was sold in London for
the first time around 1658, showed Chinese

influence, early teapots being based upon the shape of Chinese wine-pots.

Chinoiserie rooms and painted ornament were very popular during the reign of Louis XV, but eighteenth-century *Chinoiserie*, like that of the seventeenth century, bore only slight relation to genuine oriental art and anything coming from the Far East was usually further embellished in one way or another. Most of the great porcelain factories produced figures in the Chinese style. Voltaire wrote a Chinese play, *L'Orphelin de la Chine*, in 1755, and his study was embellished with Chinese decoration. *Chinoiserie* spread throughout Europe and became fashionable in the 1740s and 50s.

One of the strongest influences on eighteenth-century *Chinoiserie* was that of Boucher (1703–70), who was widely imitated and whose imaginary view of China spread across Europe through his engravings. His designs for a series of tapestries of Chinese life, woven at Beauvais in the 1740s, were

supposedly based upon Jesuit drawings illustrating scenes of oriental pastoral life, and were, once again, an almost wholly imaginary European view of China. Louis XV sent a set of these tapestries to the Chinese Emperor in Peking.

Jean Baptiste Pillement (1727–1808) had, next to Boucher, the greatest influence on eighteenth-century *Chinoiserie*. Pillement, an outstanding designer and engraver whose *chinoiserie* designs were even more fantastic than those of Boucher, had designs published in both London and Paris and was far more popular in the rest of Europe than in Paris itself. His exotic ideas had enormous influence, particularly in England.

Despite this interest, however, *chinoiserie* decoration on English silver did not seriously begin to affect traditional styles until the mid-eighteenth century. It virtually disappeared from use between the late seventeenth century and the 1740s. English *chinoiserie* silver of the eighteenth

Fig. 8 ***Teapot***, *Chinese, 1680s.*
Silver-gilt.
This rare piece of Chinese silver was made specifically for the European market.
(Victoria and Albert Museum.)

A. C. Cooper

century is unparalleled on the Continent and is almost peculiar to this country. It was usually of very high quality, displaying superb technical skill in the creation of a far more elaborate, exotic and fantastic form of *Chinoiserie* than that in use in the seventeenth century (Fig. 2).

The opening in 1715 of the East India Company's trading factory in Canton, the principal port in China, which exported goods made solely for the European trade, added to the influence of Pillement and French *Chinoiserie* spreading through engravings, gave rise to a general craze for anything from China. A highly satirised *Chinoiserie* appeared in England, reaching its height in the 1750s. *Chinoiserie* decoration was applied to everything and export goods from China were especially elaborate in order to satisfy English taste.

Eighteenth-century *chinoiserie* silver is usually away by the predominating influence of neo-Classicism in the late 1760s and early 1770s, and in the nineteenth century had almost completely disappeared. Paul Storr, Digby Scott and Benjamin Smith did not use *chinoiserie* decoration, although a sauce-tureen by John Edward in the Deccan service, made in 1806 for presentation to the future Duke of Wellington, is surmounted by a *chinoiserie* figure. There is also a salver dated 1823 by John Angell with a *chinoiserie* border in the revived rococo style. *Chinoiserie* was hardly ever used again, but Harrisons of Sheffield, exhibiting electro-plated goods at the Great Exhibition of 1851, did advertise some *chinoiserie* designs.

In the nineteenth century, China entered the modern world. As she did so, *Chinoiserie*, this romantic, fantastic and exotic European vision of her, faded away.

Fig. 9 *Inkstand*, *indecipherable maker's mark, 1759–60. The fretwork on this piece is similar to that used on Chinese wallpaper and in the gardens of the period.* (Victoria and Albert Museum.)

Fig. 10 *Pair of tea-caddies by Samuel Courtauld, 1760s. Tea-caddies were popular and appropriate objects for* chinoiserie *decoration.* (Victoria and Albert Museum.)

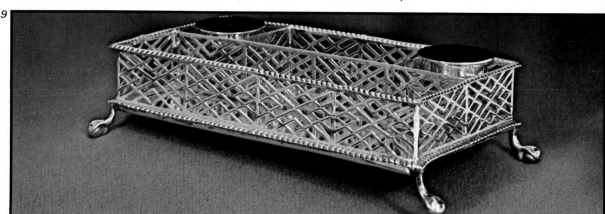

embossed or repoussé and appears first in the 1740s. An example is the De Lamerie tea-caddy of 1742, made a year before Horace Walpole remarked upon tea-drinking as being a universal habit. *Chinoiserie*, naturally enough, was widely used for objects connected with tea-drinking, and tea-caddies, called canisters until the late eighteenth century (caddy being a corruption of the Malay word *kati*, a weight used in the tea trade and equivalent to just over a pound), appeared in considerable numbers from the mid-eighteenth century (Fig. 10). The Chinese themselves had enamelled tea-caddies in the shape of European silver in the early eighteenth century.

The highly elaborate pictorial decoration, often emphasising the exotic birds so greatly loved in the seventeenth century, was eventually swept

MUSEUMS AND COLLECTIONS

There are very few good collections of *chinoiserie* silver open to the public. A fine representative collection may, however, be seen at the Victoria and Albert Museum, London.

FURTHER READING

Chinoiserie by Hugh Honour, London, 1961.
A Cycle of Cathay: The Chinese Vogue in England during the Seventeenth and Eighteenth Centuries by W. W. Appleton, New York, 1951.
Chinese Export Art in the Eighteenth Century by Margaret Jourdain and R. Soame Jenyns, London, 1950.

Queen Anne Silver

Fig. 1 **Teapot, kettle and chocolate pot** all on matching stands by Joseph Ward, London, 1719.
Octagonal shapes were very popular in the early 18th century. This superb matching set uses them with a characteristic pear-shape on the teapot and kettle. (Worshipful Company of Goldsmiths, London.)

With the introduction of the Britannia standard in 1697 and the arrival of many Huguenot craftsmen from France, English silver design entered a period of unrivalled simplicity, dignity and beauty

Fig. 2 **Tea-kettle stand** *in solid silver, unmarked, English, c.1725.*
(Victoria and Albert Museum, London.)

Fig. 3 **Teapot** *by James Smith, London, 1719–20. Height 4 ins. Bullet-shaped teapots, as pots of this sort were called, were very popular later in the reign of Queen Anne, and well into that of George I. They were made very small in recognition of the high price of tea.*
(Victoria and Albert Museum.)

Fig. 4 **Tea-canister** *by Nathaniel Roe, London, 1713.*
These attractive containers for a very expensive commodity, tea, were not called caddies until late in the eighteenth century.
(Worshipful Company of Goldsmiths.)

The Queen Anne style is considered as having begun in the last decade of the seventeenth century, and a number of important factors affecting the craft of silversmithing were at work in the Queen's reign and that of her successor, George I. One was the quality of the silver itself. From 27 March, 1697, until 1 June, 1720, English silversmiths were compelled by statute to work metal of a higher standard than sterling. This is generally known as the Britannia standard, because the lion-passant mark was replaced by a figure of Britannia, which denoted the presence, in 12 oz. (Troy) of metal, of $11\frac{1}{2}$ oz. of pure silver as against the $11\frac{1}{10}$ oz. of the sterling standard. For much of this period, therefore, English domestic silver was of the Britannia standard and bore the appropriate marks.

Another important factor was the arrival in England and Ireland of large numbers of Huguenot craftsmen, among them plate-workers. These immigrants were refugees from the persecutions instituted by Louis XIV against their co-religionists after the Revocation of the Edict of Nantes in 1685. The great trouble they took with their work forced the native silversmiths to emulate both their industry and their mannerisms in order to compete with them. This brought about a general raising of standards.

Of small size, in recognition of the price of tea

One form of decorative technique which was popular in the early eighteenth century on hollowware of all kinds is known as cut-card work. The Huguenots were much addicted to it, but they had neither invented nor introduced it to England, where it had been used to a limited extent since quite early in the reign of Charles II. It consisted of thin sheet silver, cut into patterns such as leaf-forms and soldered on to various parts of a vessel.

It is now necessary to consider some of the more important items of domestic plate of the period. From early in the reign of Queen Anne, silver teapots began to be made in comparatively large numbers, after appearing sparsely in the time of Charles II. They were of two main kinds. The

more characteristic was shaped like a pear with a high, domed lid, and was of either circular or polygonal section (Fig. 1). The handle, which was of wood, or occasionally of ivory, was at right-angles to the swan-necked spout, or on the opposite side, the latter arrangement being more usual in the reign of George I. In wealthy households, they were sometimes accompanied by large silver kettles of much the same shape but with swing-handles, mounted on stands, with spirit-lamps to heat the water. These massive, expensive objects were beyond the resources of many people, whose teapots were furnished with their own small stands and lamps, possibly so that the water could be boiled in the pot itself.

The other type, which increased in incidence later, was of more or less spherical form and is consequently known as bullet-shaped (Fig. 3). These pots were nearly always plain and of small size in recognition of the high price of tea. Late in the reign of George I, kettles began to be made in the same form and remained popular long after the pear-shape had fallen into disuse.

A large baroque cartouche for the owner's arms

In considering the rest of the tea equipage, it must be remembered that the later conception of a matching tea-set was less popular in the first half of the eighteenth century (Fig. 9). Many people bought the various components separately as finances permitted, and they were not necessarily in precisely the same style. The teapot and covered sugar-bowl might be of circular section, the slop-basin might be vertically ribbed, and the milk or water jug and the tea-canister of long octagonal shape (Fig. 4). The last, incidentally, were not called caddies until the late eighteenth century. Some people owned no more than one; others had sets of two or three which were locked away in cases to prevent the pilfering of the contents by servants.

Coffee-pots and chocolate-pots were similar to each other, the only essential difference being that the latter had removable finials on the lids which enabled a rod to be inserted immediately before pouring, to stir the contents. For many years the lids were mostly domed like those of pear-

K. Hoddle

K. Hoddle

Fig. 5 **Candlestick** by David
Tanqueray, London, 1720.
Height 7 ins.
This design was current before
1700.
(Victoria and Albert Museum.)

Fig. 6 **Chocolate-pot**, maker
unknown, London 1722–23.
Height 9¼ ins.
The finial is removable to allow
a stirring rod to be inserted.
(Victoria and Albert Museum.)

Fig. 7 **Tankard** by Robert
Timbrell and Benjamin Bentley,
London, 1714–15.
The hinged lid with a low dome
was a standard feature.
(Victoria and Albert Museum.)

Fig. 8 **Two-handled cup** by John
Sutton, London, 1705. Height
4½ ins.
This common household variant
of the two-handled cup was
probably used at breakfast and on
other informal occasions. The
choice of this humble domestic
vessel by the Company of Porters
suggests that they were one of the
poorer guilds.
(Victoria and Albert Museum.)

Museum Photo

shaped teapots (Fig. 6), but a lower form became prevalent in the second quarter of the century. There was great variation in the shape of the bodies; some consisted of upward-tapering cylinders, some curved inward at the base just above the foot-ring, while others were of a fully-developed baluster shape. This became increasingly popular with the passage of time and persisted throughout the eighteenth century despite the introduction of other types.

Drinking-vessels had suffered a grievous loss with the almost total disappearance of the silver winecup, supported on a stem and foot, in the middle of the seventeenth century, but this had been chiefly replaced by two-handled cups of various kinds. The remote ancestor of them all was the ancient Greek *kantharos*. In the early eighteenth century some were purely functional and of simple shape, while others were of such important and monumental aspect that, although they were capable of being used, and almost certainly were on special occasions, one cannot but think of their purpose as being chiefly ostentatious. This is especially true of covered two-handled cups in which Huguenot influence is discernible.

The commonest household variant, used at breakfast and on other informal occasions, had an expanding U-shaped body which rested not on a foot-ring but on a slight downward extension of the base, and a pair of scroll handles which might be cast, or consist of narrow ribbons of sheet silver (Fig. 8). Very few were plain. Most were ornamented with a circuit of embossed spiral gadroons alternating with hollow flutes, rising from the base of the bowl and terminating in the lower half. This decoration was usually, though not invariably, answered by an embossed cable-moulding a short distance below the rim, and there might also be a large baroque cartouche for the owner's arms, crest or monogram. The same kind of decoration appeared on many other vessels.

Like their seventeenth-century predecessors, cups of this kind are often miscalled porringers, but it has been proved beyond doubt that this designation is incorrect and that they were, in fact, drinking-vessels. They were typical not only of the reign of Queen Anne, but of that of her successor also. After George I's death, however, although they continued to be made to a decreasing extent and embellished with ornament which had long been obsolete, their proportions were gradually spoilt by their becoming too narrow in relation to their height.

Most tankards of the early eighteenth century held about two pints and involved the use of a great deal of silver but, despite the increased cost resulting from the imposition of the Britannia standard, there was no apparent diminution in the demand for them. They had already begun to be slightly narrower in the last decade of the seventeenth century than those of the Charles II period, when these pots reached their maximum width; but a further modification became almost universal after 1700. The hinged lid, which formerly had a flat or nearly flat top, now developed a low dome which became a more or less standard feature (Fig. 7), while a few of them were surmounted by

Fig. 9 *A family at tea,* attributed
to Richard Collins (d.1732),
c.1730.
The principal objects of silver
represented are a teapot, stand
and canister of 1705–20, sugar
bowl and tongs of about 1730,
and a bowl and dish which could
be either English or Scottish of
about 1730.
(Victoria and Albert Museum.)

finials, which had scarcely been seen since the reign of James I.

Various kinds of thumb-piece – also known as the billet or purchase – persisted from the late seventeenth century, including a type with voluted ends which continued after 1750. One of the more striking was in the form of a couchant lion cast in the solid, but this barely outlasted the reign of Queen Anne.

Handsome proportions and the sheen of silver in candlelight

The majority of tankards were cylindrical, sometimes with a narrow, applied moulding running around or beneath the centre of the body; but a new variety appeared in the form of a squat baluster, and this, with a more curvaceous outline, was destined to be especially popular in the second half of the century.

Not everyone could afford a silver tankard, and the production of cans or mugs burgeoned in a remarkable fashion after 1700. These miniature tankards without lids had first come on the scene

just after the Restoration in 1660, the earliest type looking something like a common form of pottery vessel, with a globular body and a short cylindrical neck. The scrolled handle was cut out of sheet silver. A few of these were made in the reign of Queen Anne, but as they were uncomfortable to hold and inconvenient to drink from, they enjoyed no great popularity and quickly disappeared.

More numerous than these were mugs of cylindrical shape, with hollow wrought handles of D-section like those of tankards, but provided with a thumb-rest at the point where the top of the handle joined the body. All these handles had a notch at the bottom, to permit the escape of hot air when they were being soldered to the body, and thus to prevent their bursting open (Fig. 12, right). The myth that this notch was intended for use as a whistle is still widely believed; in fact, no such thing as a whistling tankard or mug has ever existed.

Some of these cylindrical mugs were quite plain; a few were spoilt by closely-spaced fluting in the Huguenot fashion, but a great many had a narrow moulding applied around the body a short distance below the rim (Fig. 12, left). This feature continued only for a year or so after 1714, and may be

Fig. 10 **Monteith** by John Smith, London, 1702.
These bowls were originally intended for cooling wine glasses, suspended from the notches. But this example has a detachable rim so that the bowl may be used for punch as well. (Worshipful Company of Coachmakers, London.)

Fig. 11 **Punch-bowl and ladle** by William Darker, London, 1729. In about 1720, the elaborate Monteith with its detachable rim, as in Fig. 10, fell out of favour. Silver bowls about a foot in diameter replaced them, which relied on handsome proportions and smooth gleaming surfaces for their effect. (Christie's.)

Fig. 12 **Two mugs**, that on the left by Timbrell and Bentley, London, 1713; that on the right by Nathaniel Locke, London, 1716.
Cylindrical mugs of this sort, either with or without a narrow moulding applied just below the rim, were quite common in the early years of the eighteenth century. At the base of the handle of the right-hand mug can be seen the notch which allowed hot air to escape while the handle was being soldered to the body, thus preventing it from exploding. (Private Collection.)

considered highly typical of the actual years of Queen Anne's reign. A baluster shape was also used but became more frequent later, as in the case of tankards.

Connected with more ceremonious forms of drinking were silver punch-bowls and monteiths. According to the diarist Anthony à Wood, the latter first appeared in 1683. Their original purpose was purely to cool wineglasses, which were suspended, bowl-downward, in cold water from notches in the rim of the monteith. Bowls intended solely for the brewing of punch had level rims, but in the last decade of the seventeenth century, a dual-purpose vessel was devised, with a detachable monteith rim looking somewhat like a crown (Fig. 10). The production of these increased enormously in the early eighteenth century, but the monteith fell out of favour in about 1720, and thereafter large silver bowls were devoted entirely to the brewing of punch and had normal fixed rims without indentations. Surface decoration of any kind became rare, and punch-bowls relied for their effect on handsome proportions and the sheen of silver in candlelight (Fig. 11).

The candlesticks of the Queen Anne and early Georgian period are among the most satisfying ever made. The columnar variety of the Charles II period, with a shaft of thin, pressed silver filled with amalgam to resist denting, was made for a short while after 1700, overlapping a greatly superior design which had first occurred in the reign of William III, at the opening of the stylistic phase designated by the name of Queen Anne. This type, which was of heavy, cast metal and had a shaft which comprised bold, simple mouldings of great artistic assurance, had a self-confident dignity characteristic of the period. Some were polygonal like much other contemporary plate, the angles running over the pyramidal base up to the socket. Most were of circular section, the bases, of a modified square shape, generally having a shallow, saucer-like depression in the centre (Fig. 5). Even when divorced from their function, these candlesticks are superb objects in their own right.

MUSEUMS AND COLLECTIONS
Queen Anne silver may be seen at the following:

GREAT BRITAIN
Leeds: Temple Newsam House
London: Victoria and Albert Museum
Norwich: The Castle Museum

FURTHER READING
British Pewter and Britannia Metal, for Pleasure and Investment by Christopher A. Peal, London, 1971.
English Silver Drinking Vessels, 600–1830 by Douglas Ash, London, 1964.
English Domestic Silver by Charles Oman, London, 1947.

American Colonial Silver

Silversmiths' shops sprang up and flourished in the Colonies, producing valuable wares of great beauty which applied the American ideal of simplicity to the influential designs of English imported wares

One hundred years after America was settled, every major centre of population had a number of silversmiths' shops to supply the needs of the wealthier colonists who wished to turn their accumulated coins into objects which were useful, and identifiable in case of loss or theft. The New World silversmith generally patterned his work after English styles, following the designs that were current in the late renaissance style of the seventeenth century and, at the turn of the eighteenth century, indulging in the extravagances of elaborate baroque designs.

The richness and heaviness of the baroque style were bound to give way to greater simplicity, lightness of line, and restrained ornamentation. By 1720, the modifications of baroque elements had been introduced into American silver and were beginning to form themselves into a style distinctly their own. With an emphasis on contour, plain

1

surfaces and rhythmic curves, objects became basically circular with little decoration other than engraving.

The octagonal shape shows graphically the transition from rectilinear to circular forms. The candlestick in Figure 1, one of a pair made by Nathaniel Morse of Boston, is devoid of surface decoration, relying upon the contours of the shaped shaft and the facets of the octagonal base for success. Variety was achieved by dividing the shaft into many sections of unequal lengths, ranging from a wafer-thin disc to an elongated ogival curved section. The faceting of the base is repeated lightly in the slight faceting of the central section of the shaft, creating a pleasing repetition to unite the variations.

The octagonal shape was one of the most popular features of early eighteenth century silver. An 'Eight square Tea-Pot' was spoken of as 'the newest Fashion' in 1727, when it was offered in the *New York Gazette* as part of a prize made by Simeon Soumain. Such a teapot, with an S-shaped spout and a C-scrolled handle, was also fashioned, in about 1725, by the silversmith Peter van Dyck (Fig. 7).

A contemporary of Van Dyck, William Hogarth (1697–1764) of London, summarized the fundamental principles of the current style in his *Analysis of Beauty*. Published in 1753, this study of aesthetics is of particular interest because Hogarth was himself trained as a silversmith as well as being an excellent engraver and a painter. One of

Funk & Wagnalls

his chief theories was that there was a fundamental 'line of beauty' which was S-shaped, with just the proper amount of curvature; a line which was not too straight and not too exaggerated a curve. This line appears repeatedly in silver made in the second quarter of the eighteenth century.

It was important that the material should be suited to both purpose and design

Another aspect of beauty which Hogarth discussed was the quality of fitness. There must be a fitness of the material for the purpose of the object. This is particularly true of the minor arts, where usefulness is a primary factor. There must also be a fitness of the material for the design; that is, the properties of silver should be considered and not violated, a principle voiced earlier by Shakespeare: 'o'erstep not the modesty of nature'.

Silver was well suited to the brewing of tea.

Sometimes teapots were made in a pear shape. This was done to ensure that the tea would steep better because a maximum amount of water would be in contact with the tea leaves when they settled at the bottom of the pot. Tea was precious and the early teapots were necessarily small so that small quantities could be brewed. However, the handle of the teapot had to be of a certain size in order to be gripped by the normal hand and a curved handle fits the grip better than a square handle. Since silver is a great conductor of heat, it was not suitable for handles, and wood was usually substituted. All these factors of fitness to function and beauty of line had to be taken into consideration by the silversmith (Fig. 7).

To achieve variety in design, several different curving lines were often joined together to form a continuous, smoothly flowing line. Engraved borders and embellishments of infinite variety were added. A salver made by Jacob Hurd (Fig. 2) has a border composed of many different motifs and textures, 'to lead the eye a wanton chase', as

*Fig. 1 **One of a pair of candlesticks** by Nathaniel Morse (1685–1748), Boston, c.1720. Height 6⅛ ins. Engraved with the arms of Faneuil. (Henry Francis Du Pont Winterthur Museum, Winterthur, Delaware.)*

*Fig. 2 **Salver** by Jacob Hurd (1702–1758), Boston, c.1730. Diameter 12½ ins. Engraved with the arms of Clarke. (Yale University Art Gallery, New Haven, Connecticut.)*

Hogarth put it. Chief among these motifs were the delicate C-scroll, diapering (engraved lozenge-shaped patterns, enclosing dots or flower-heads), lightly curved leafage and flowers, and the scallop shell, which, with its many lobes, epitomised the desired roundness and united curved lines.

Engraved ciphers were well suited to the dictates of freely curving design with their circular and foliated script shapes of initials. Simeon Soumain made the cipher the chief form of embellishment on a sugar dish . . . a sugar dish now in the Mabel Brady Garvan Collection, Yale University Art Gallery. The engraving of the initials EC, for the original owner, Elizabeth Cruger, contained within a circle on the side and just above on the lid, accentuates the roundness of the form itself and the circular form of the foot and reel top. The shape of the dish was taken from that of Chinese porcelain tea bowls, and Chinese design and decoration played an increasingly important part in the mid-eighteenth century.

One of the most impressive and lasting forms of this period is the covered cup made on several special occasions by Jacob Hurd for presentation to outstanding men (Fig. 5). Although a large piece of silver, it has grace because of the simplicity of its curvilinear form. The expanse of the body is broken up by an elaborately engraved cartouche in the upper section, and by the proper placement of a mid-band, dividing the sections into pleasing proportions.

Jacob Hurd (1702–58), who was a prominent second-generation American silversmith, was a master of proper details and cohesive design. In the coffee-pot in Figure 6, he accentuated the roundness of the body with a domed lid and a round finial. Beneath the spout he added a drop, which is the same shape as the finial but only half-round. The same silhouette, cut from a flat piece of silver, was soldered just under the top of the handle. It is this thoughtful repetition of the same shape in different dimensions which gives the design originality, interest and unity in American silver of the age of Hogarth.

Fig. 3 **Teapot** by Jacob Hurd, Boston, c.1738. Silver and wood. Spherical teapots of this type became common early in the eighteenth century and changed very little through the years except for minor features such as the higher foot, broken spout and elaborate finial on this pot. (Yale University Art Gallery.)

Fig. 4 **Milk jug** by Adrian Bancker, New York, c.1740. Height 4⅛ ins. Pear shapes of this sort were popular for many purposes in eighteenth-century silver, both English and American. It was frequently used for teapots, as it allowed the maximum amount of hot water to come into contact with the rare and expensive tea-leaves when they settled to the bottom of the pot. For jugs, the pear shape was less obviously sensible, but it created a practical, steady form which was hard to tip over, and easy to pour from. Although this jug is almost plain, it has the moulded rim, elaborately curved handle, and hoof feet with shell tops which are frequently seen as details on rococo pieces. (H. F. Du Pont Winterthur Museum.)

Fig. 5 **Covered cup** by Jacob Hurd, Boston, 1744. Height 13⅞ ins. Inscribed to Richard Spry, Commander of the Comet Bomb which captured a privateer, and presented to him by several Boston merchants. (Private Collection.)

Funk & Wagnalls

Museum Photo

Museum Photo

Museum Photo

Fig. 6 **Coffee-pot** *by Jacob Hurd, Boston, c.1750. Wood and silver engraved with the arms of Clarke, height 10¼ ins.*
Note the unity of design seen in the accentuation of the roundness of the body by the dome, and the repetition of the finial shape under the spout.
(H. F. Du Pont Winterthur Museum.)

Fig. 7 **Teapot** *by Peter van Dyck, (1694–1750) New York, c.1725. (Yale University Art Gallery, Mabel Brady Garvan Collection.)*

Fig. 8 **Salver** *by Joseph Richardson, Snr., made for Mary Grafton, 1746. (Yale University Art Gallery, Mabel Brady Garvan Collection.)*

Fig. 9 **Sauce boat** *by Jacob Hurd, Boston, mid-eighteenth century. (H. F. Du Pont, Winterthur Museum. Gift of C. K. Davis.)*

MUSEUMS AND COLLECTIONS
American Silver may be seen at the following:

GREAT BRITAIN
Bath: The American Museum in Britain, Claverton Manor

U.S.A.
Boston: Boston Museum of Fine Arts
New Haven: Yale University Art Gallery
New York: Metropolitan Museum of Art
Philadelphia: Museum of Art
Winterthur: Henry Francis Du Pont Winterthur Museum.

FURTHER READING
The Genius of William Hogarth by Stuart Barton, Worthing, 1972.
American Silver, 1655–1825 in the Museum of Fine Arts, Boston by Kathryn C. Buhler, 1972.
American Silver: A History of Style, 1650–1900 by Graham Hood, New York, 1971.
Early American Silver for the Cautious Collector by Martha Gandy Fales, New York, 1970.
Early American Silver by C. Louise Avery, New York, 1968.
American Silver by John Marshall Phillips, New York, 1949.

Paul de Lamerie

Fig. 1 *Newdigate centre-piece by De Lamerie, London, 1743. Height 9⅞ ins.*
An example of rococo work of the very finest quality, this imposing centre-piece was made as a wedding present for Sir Roger Newdigate. It is highly decorative, but De Lamerie has not forgotten the practical aspects of such a large piece; the four branches are detachable. (Victoria and Albert Museum, London.)

The work of Paul de Lamerie, sometimes simple, sometimes highly decorative, exemplifies the highest achievements in English rococo silver

Paul de Lamerie (1688–1751), who 'was particularly famous in making fine ornamental Plate, and has been very instrumental in bringing that Branch of Trade to the Perfection it is now in', as was stated is one of his obituaries, is among the most celebrated of the great English goldsmiths, certainly the greatest in the eighteenth century, and is known today as the prime exponent of the rococo style in English silver.

Although a great craftsman, highly esteemed in his own day, and a prominent member of the Gold-smiths' Company, Paul de Lamerie never became a crown goldsmith, Samuel Smithin and Thomas Minors holding this position during De Lamerie's long working life. Very little is known about his life, despite the presence of a number of remarkably well-documented facts. An eighteenth-century goldsmith, however talented and successful – and

Museum Photo

K. Hoddle

Museum Photo

Fig. 2 *Sugar-castor by De Lamerie, London, 1734–35. From his Huguenot master, Pierre Platel, De Lamerie learned the techniques of French decoration which became so popular in England. On this castor are seen the characteristic details of Huguenot silver, but the piece is far less flamboyant than would have been demanded by a wealthy French patron. (Victoria and Albert Museum.)*

Fig. 3 *Pair of tea-caddies, unmarked, probably by De Lamerie, with engraving by William Hogarth, London, c.1720. Silver-gilt. Dating from De Lamerie's years at the sign of the Golden Ball in Windmill Street, London, these superb caddies are examples of his work in a simple style. (Victoria and Albert Museum.)*

Fig. 4 *Cup and cover by De Lamerie, London, 1723. Fairly restrained in its decoration, this cup follows the fashion for elaborate silver which continued throughout the eighteenth century. The proportions are faultless, and the decoration is typical of De Lamerie's superb technical skill. (Ashmolean Museum, Oxford.)*

Fig. 5 *Candlestick, one of a pair by Paul de Lamerie (1688–1751), London, 1748. De Lamerie was strongly influenced by the work of the French designer, J-A. Meissonnier, and was one of the first English silversmiths to use his exuberant rococo forms. (Ashmolean Museum.)*

Paul de Lamerie has seldom been surpassed in ingenuity of shape and richness of ornament – was regarded merely as a superior tradesman and of no social importance whatsoever. As far as is known, there are no surviving engraved or printed bill-heads of his, there is no portrait, and about the only personal relics to survive from his long and active life, apart from his will and various signatures in a very beautiful and distinctive hand, are a group of handwritten invoices dating from the 1720s.

De Lamerie lived in Soho, a Huguenot refugee district

Paul de Lamerie was born on 9 April, 1688, and was a second generation Huguenot refugee. Despite his name, he was only French in so far as his parents were both of French origin. It is not known where his parents came from in France, but most of the Huguenot refugees came from the French provinces. He himself was almost certainly born in the Netherlands and never lived in France. His father, also Paul de Lamerie, a member of a minor aristocratic family, was an army officer in the service of William of Orange in 1686.

In 1689 the De Lamerie family left for England and by 1691 they were living in Soho, London, a district filled with French Huguenot refugees at this period. The father De Lamerie probably lived on what money he had brought with him, and on the minute pension he may have received from the Crown. As a member of an aristocratic French family, however minor, he would have regarded earning his own living as being below his personal dignity, and was possibly too poor to obtain naturalisation, even if he had wanted it. He died, a pauper, in 1735.

One of the few professions a French aristocrat could follow without losing social caste altogether was that of a goldsmith, and in the records of the Goldsmiths' Company for 6 August, 1703, there occurs the following: 'I, Paul De Lamerie, son of Paul De Lamerie, of ye Parish of Saint Anne's, Westminster, Gent., do put myself apprentice to Peter Plattell, Citizen and Goldsmith of London, for the term of seven years from this day'.

By this time the family was, obviously, very poor, as Pierre Platel, a Huguenot from an aristocratic French family in Lorraine, and a leading goldsmith of the day, was never paid for De Lamerie's apprenticeship, as was customary.

Pierre Platel was probably himself apprenticed in London, registering his mark in 1699. He made some of the most splendid pieces of early eighteenth-century silver, including a service of plate for George, Prince of Wales, who became George II. Paul de Lamerie would have lived with Platel during his apprenticeship, in Pall Mall, one

Paul De Lamerie

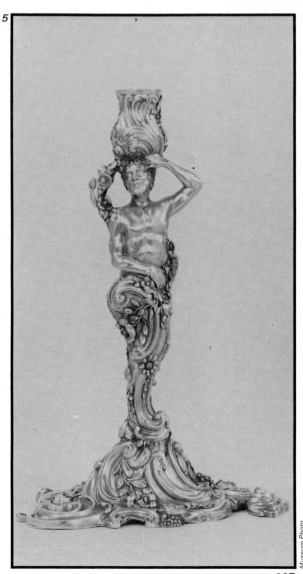

Museum Photo

6

Fig. 6 *Hallmark of Paul de Lamerie, registered in 1732 for use on silver of the Old Standard.*

Fig. 7 *Blade of a fish-slice (detail) by Paul de Lamerie, London, 1741. Pierced and engraved, width 4 ins. It was common practice in the eighteenth century for the decoration of a piece to reflect its purpose, as in the captured fish on this fish-slice. (Ashmolean Museum.)*

Museum Photo

of the most exclusive streets in London. Pierre Platel died in 1719 and it is to him that De Lamerie owed his technical skill for which the Huguenot goldsmiths were renowned, particularly in their use of cast decoration which was not customary in England at this time.

French Huguenot goldsmiths were familiar with the complicated technique required to make the fashionable silver of the day (silver with sculptural decoration in what was basically the Louis XIV style) and, because of their desire to emulate Continental fashion, made most of the important pieces of silver in England at this period, although the styles in which they worked were often far less flamboyant than those which would have been demanded by a wealthy French patron (Fig. 2). It must be remembered that eighteenth-century goldsmiths did not think in terms of individuality, but in terms of producing, to order, the finest fashionable work made by the workshop, using the mark of the master goldsmith.

At the same time as they produced flamboyant and highly decorative silver, the Huguenots made some simpler and plainer pieces as a concession to English taste and poorer patrons (Fig. 10). Paul de Lamerie himself did precisely this throughout his working life, and his earliest recorded piece of work is plain. In 1712 he became a Freeman of the City of London and registered his first mark with Goldsmiths' Hall, a mark very like that of Platel, his master, and similar to that of a French goldsmith of the period – LA, the first two letters of his surname, as was obligatory under the Act of 1697, incorporating a crown, as in Paris.

The Act of 1697 established the New, or Britannia, Standard for silver, a silver of greater purity than that used prior to 1697; this was very expensive and difficult to work. De Lamerie worked in the Britannia Standard for twenty years, although under the Wrought Plate Act of 1719 goldsmiths were allowed to revert to the so-called Old Standard if they so wished. Most goldsmiths after 1719 preferred to do so, as the Old Standard was probably easier to work.

He set up his own business and had a considerable stock-in-trade

By 1716 Paul de Lamerie was well enough established in his own right to set up his business at the sign of the Golden Ball in Windmill Street. The premises would have included a shop, and he is known to have dealt in jewellery. In 1717 he married Louise Juliott, a member of an old Huguenot family from Poitou. They had two sons and four daughters. In a fire insurance policy of 1728 his stock-in-trade, probably weighing about 3,000 oz, is mentioned as being worth about £800, a considerable sum at that time. It is from the Windmill Street period that the Hogarth tea-caddies, the Treby Toilet Service and the Walpole Salver date.

The Hogarth tea-caddies are an example of De Lamerie working in a simple style, but with superb attention to detail on a small scale (Fig. 3). Hogarth, who, like most English engravers working on silver, never signed his work, was apprenticed in 1712 to the goldsmith Elias Gamble, to learn to engrave plate. He set up on his own in about 1717. He did very little work on silver, as he had great success as an engraver and probably found engraving on silver too limited.

The famous Treby Toilet Service of 1724 was commissioned by one of De Lamerie's most important clients at this time on the occasion of his marriage, and is the most complete service of its kind (Fig. 9). There are over twenty pieces and an existing invoice states that it cost £370 13s 10d, a vast sum of money in 1724. Some of the pieces probably came from existing stock, as the ornament varies, but it is typical Huguenot work showing a superb use of flat chasing.

The Walpole Salver, named after Sir Robert Walpole for whom it was made in 1728, is another fine example of the quality of De Lamerie's work (Fig. 11). The piece was made from the discarded matrix of the Exchequer Seal of George I, which Walpole, as First Lord of the Treasury, would have received as a perquisite of office on the accession of George II.

In 1731 Paul de Lamerie became a member of the governing body of the Goldsmiths' Company, which was a high honour. By this time he was very successful indeed, was investing in property and was lending money on mortgage. It is from this period in his life that his most elaborate and magnificent pieces date.

In 1732 he registered a new mark, specifically stating on registration that it was for use on silver of the so-called Old Standard. All goldsmiths reverting to the previous standard were obliged to alter their marks after the Wrought Plate Act and his second mark (P.L., incorporating a crown) coincides with the use of altogether heavier and more decorative silver in the rococo style, for which the Old Standard was probably more suitable.

The exuberant, flamboyant and highly decorative forms of the rococo, coming from France and greatly influenced by the work of the architect Juste-Aurèle Meissonnier (who was made a master of the Paris Goldsmiths' Guild in 1725 on the personal order of the Crown), were superbly exploited by De Lamerie (Fig. 5). He was one of the first to use this exaggerated and heavily ornamental

Fig. 8 *Sideboard dish* by De Lamerie, London, 1736. Diameter 27¼ ins.
The balance between plain and ornate surfaces on this dish is one of the marks of De Lamerie's genius. The armorial decoration in the centre is unusual in that it is raised rather than engraved. (Sotheby and Co., London.)

Fig. 9 *Box, waiter and casket* from the Treby Toilet Service by De Lamerie, London, 1724. The most complete set of its kind, the famous Treby service has over twenty pieces. It was made for the marriage of one of De Lamerie's most important clients, and cost £370 13s 10d, a vast sum of money in 1724. The superb use of flat chasing is a Huguenot speciality. (Ashmolean Museum.)

Fig. 10 *Set of four trencher salts and spoons* by De Lamerie, London, 1727. The interiors gilt. As a concession to English taste, and for poorer patrons, Huguenot goldsmiths, including De Lamerie, often made absolutely plain pieces. The charm of these salts lies not in De Lamerie's usual flamboyant decoration, but in their perfect line and proportions. (Ashmolean Museum.)

Fig. 11 *The Walpole Salver* by De Lamerie, London, 1728. Diameter 19⅛ ins. Made for Sir Robert Walpole, First Lord of the Treasury, upon the accession of George II in 1727, this famous salver is one of the finest examples of De Lamerie's work. (Victoria and Albert Museum.)

8

9

10

11

A. C. Cooper

Peter Parkinson

Museum Photo

Fig. 12 *Ewer and basin by
De Lamerie, London, 1741.
Height of ewer 14¾ ins., diameter
of basin 31 ins.
(Worshipful Company of
Goldsmiths, London.)*

Fig. 13 *Rubbing of the central
engraving on the Walpole Salver
in Figure 11; it was
made from the discarded
matrix of the Exchequer Seal
of George I.
(Victoria and Albert Museum.)*

shop. Some of his most notable works were produced in Gerrard Street and he took as an apprentice Peter Archambo, who was the son of another Huguenot goldsmith, and who himself became well known. Meanwhile his daughter Susannah married Joseph Debaufre, a member of a well-known family of Huguenot watchmakers.

De Lamerie's later work in the full rococo style, with its wonderful detail and elaborate and overall decoration, is superbly illustrated in the great ewer and basin of 1741 (Fig. 12). These pieces were made for the Goldsmiths' Company to perpetuate the memory of benefactors to the Company, whose presentation plate had been melted down in 1667 and in 1711. In the Court Minutes for 9 December, 1741, it is stated that 'All the new plate lately made for the Company having been now viewed by the several Members present at this Court it was the General Opinion that the same is performed in a very curious and beautiful manner'. After the viewing, the accounts were dealt with.

In 1743 De Lamerie became Fourth Warden of the Goldsmiths' Company, the same year that he made the famous *épergne*, or centre-piece, as a wedding present for Sir Roger Newdigate (Fig. 1). It is not only highly decorative, but also very practical, as the four branches and waiters (small trays for holding sweetmeats, etc.) are detachable. This centre-piece is characteristic rococo work of the very finest quality.

After his death his 'entire stock of curious patterns and tools' was sold

In 1747 De Lamerie became Second Warden of the Goldsmiths' Company and on 2 August, 1751, he died after an illness which had lasted for some months. In his will he asked that his business should be closed down, as his two sons, Paul and Daniel, had died in infancy and there was nobody to carry it on. The stock, including jewellery and watches, was to be sold by auction and on 4 February, 1752, 'All the genuine and entire stock of curious patterns and tools' were also sold.

The work of Paul de Lamerie, illustrating as it does, with supreme technical skill and superb quality of design, the current and fashionable styles in silver of nearly forty years of the early eighteenth century, is amongst the finest silver ever produced by a goldsmith and is worthy to rank with any other great work of art of the period.

form of decoration in England, which did not become widespread until after his death.

As a leading member of the Goldsmiths' Company, Paul de Lamerie was on the committee instrumental in drawing up the Plate Offences Act of 1738, whereby all goldsmiths had to change their marks. His third and last mark, registered according to the Act, is the only one that did not resemble that of a Paris goldsmith (P.L. in script, incorporating a crown).

In the same year he had moved to Gerrard Street, where he lived until he died and where he dealt in jewellery and watches as well as running his work-

MUSEUMS AND COLLECTIONS
The silver of Paul de Lamerie may be seen at the following:

London: Victoria and Albert Museum
Oxford: Ashmolean Museum

FURTHER READING
Rococo Silver by Arthur Grimwade, London, 1974.
Paul de Lamerie by P. A. S. Phillips, London, 1968.
English Domestic Silver by Charles Oman, London, 1965.
Huguenot Silver in England 1688–1727 by J. F. Hayward, London, 1959.

Irish Silver

Good workmanship, greater rarity and subtle differences in design from its English counterpart make Irish silver both interesting and valuable to the collector

Brilliant metalwork of three very different kinds has been made in Ireland at three different times in its history. The first was during the early Christian period, when such masterpieces as the eighth-century Ardagh Chalice were created. The craftsmen of this period generally made use of a variety of base and precious metals, an abundance of jewelling and enamelling and an unlimited amount of interlacing of the kind which is seen at its most elaborate in the Book of Kells.

The arrival of the Normans in Ireland in 1170 brought a rapid change of style, and during the following centuries it seems that silver was inspired by the western European gothic tradition. Surviving examples include the De Burgo O'Malley Chalice of 1494 and the 1418 mitre and crosier of Bishop Cornelius O'Dea of Limerick. These are the finest pontificals in the country; they carry the signature of an Irish craftsman, Thomas O'Carryd.

The third and most important period began in 1637, when domestic silver was first made. In so far as it has survived, earlier work seems to have been almost entirely ecclesiastical; now came the beginnings of Irish-made spoons, tankards, drinking-cups, porringers and other such objects. Dublin, the centre of this new activity, was very much a capital city, and had close links with Bristol. It was therefore a city where English as well as Irish craftsmen were working, and who were later to be joined by exiled French Huguenot silversmiths of enormous skill – for example men such as Francis

Fig. 1 *Spoon by R. Goble, Cork, 1700. Length 7½ ins. (Victoria and Albert Museum, London.)*

Fig. 2 *Spoon by Jonathan Buck, Limerick, c1740. Length 9¼ ins. (Victoria and Albert Museum.)*

Fig. 3 *Spoon by David Pete, Dublin, 1765. Length 8¼ ins. (Victoria and Albert Museum.)*

Museum Photo

2   3

Museum Photo

Fig. 4 *Three dish-rings* by John Lloyd, Dublin, c.1770–80.
More common in Ireland than elsewhere, the dish-ring was one of the best examples of the mid-eighteenth century rococo style. They have been called 'potato-rings' mistakenly since Victorian times, when they were believed to have been used for serving boiled potatoes. In fact, they were intended to keep bowls of steaming 'bishop' (hot punch) from marking the polished mahogany of a dining-table. They are always pierced, frequently with elaborate patterns, as on these examples.
(National Museum of Ireland, Dublin.)

Fig. 5 *Sauce-boat* by Thomas Walker, Dublin, c.1738.
This superb piece, though Irish in character, would stand comparison with rococo work from anywhere in Europe.
(National Museum of Ireland.)

Fig. 6 *Monteith* or punch-bowl by Thomas Bolton, Dublin, 1704. Silver-gilt.
Many Irish designs are virtually indistinguishable from English pieces of the same date. This fine monteith is of a standard design of the late seventeenth and early eighteenth centuries.
(National Museum of Ireland.)

Fig. 7 *Cake-basket* by John Lloyd, Dublin, 1772.
Irish silver was often more sound, simple and workmanlike than its English counterparts at this date, since the shops made only a fraction of what came from large English metal-working centres such as Birmingham and Sheffield.
(National Museum of Ireland.)

Fig. 8 *Tankard* by Robert Goble, Cork, c.1695.
The greatest silversmith of Cork, Robert Goble, made the remarkable mace of the Cork Guilds as well as many fine pieces of domestic silver.
(National Museum of Ireland.)

Girard, John Letablère and Isaac D'Olier.

In December 1637, a royal charter was granted to the Dublin Goldsmiths' Company. This organisation still flourishes and by law it still assays all silver made in Ireland. The Assay Office, Goldsmiths' Hall, which contains original records and some early historical relics, is situated in the precincts of Dublin Castle and is directed by Captain Le Bas, a member of a Huguenot family recorded as working in Dublin in Georgian times.

It is common knowledge that hallmarks were introduced in order to guarantee a standard of purity in gold and silver pieces, and to prevent fraud. (The Dublin Assay Office has a curious collection of fakes, which were seized by law.) London introduced a mark as long ago as the fourteenth century; in Dublin the first marks were used in 1637–38. The marks were put on with individual punches, the number of which increased as the years went by. They began with a mark of origin, a date-letter, and a maker's mark. The mark of origin has always been a crowned harp. The date-letter is an alphabetical code which enables the year of manufacture to be discovered. The maker's mark is a private sign, generally the initials of the individual silversmith.

'This day ye duty came on'

Following the introduction of hallmarks, as a work-book in the archives of the Dublin company puts it under 21 April, 1730, 'This day ye duty came on'. The duty was sixpence an ounce, certified by a stamp of Hibernia, a figure very like Britannia, but holding a harp and a palm-leaf. Very often, when Hibernia was added, the date-letter was left out. This creates difficulties in dating Dublin silver. Some years later, in 1805, the exchequer charged the buyers of silver a further sixpence, and a mark of the Sovereign's head was added. George III looks to the right, George IV to the left, William IV to the right, and Queen Victoria to the left. After 1890, the duty disappeared, as did the Sovereign's head; but Hibernia remained. Ireland never had an equivalent of the English 1697–1720 Britannia Standard of higher silver content.

It may well be asked in what way, apart from markings, Irish silver differs from its English equivalent during the Georgian period. It is known that old Waterford glass was based on English designs, and it is interesting to see whether the same applies to Irish silver and workmanship.

At first sight the similarities are greater than the differences, yet practice enables one to detect the latter. For example, the bright-cutting on Limerick-made spoons is unlike that practised elsewhere. Late eighteenth-century Cork silver is highly distinctive. Dublin silver of the era is sound, simple and workmanlike, which is to be expected from shops which made only a fraction of what came from Birmingham or Sheffield.

Moreover, it is arguable that Ireland produced some eighteenth-century items of silver which can be claimed as more Irish than English. One is a mid-eighteenth-century pierced butter-dish, often made in the Chinese style, and probably originating from Huguenot influence on Irish workshops. The Dublin National Museum has an example which shows a shepherd leering at a

maiden from behind an unmistakably Irish Round Tower. This mid-eighteenth-century rococo spirit is seen at its best in the dish-ring, a piece of table-ware far commoner in Ireland than elsewhere (Fig. 4). The word 'dish', in this context, means 'bowl', and in fact this circular stand was intended to keep bowls of steaming 'bishop' (hot punch) from marking the polished mahogany of a dining-table. It is certainly a misnomer to call them 'potato-rings', and the Victorians were incorrect to serve boiled jacket-potatoes in them, wrapped up in a linen table-napkin; it would be proper to balance a bowl of cooked potatoes on one.

A wide variety of small, collectable items

Again, there was a considerable vogue throughout the second half of the eighteenth century for cups with two harp-shaped handles. It would be unwise to say that these were exclusively Irish, but the harp design was much in vogue in the Dublin shops. Further, the helmet-shaped cream-jugs of the first half of the eighteenth century are distinctively Irish.

The variety of small silver pieces was enormous, and there are plenty of collectable items. It is interesting to find an advertisement of 1765 which lists the most popular items stocked by a provincial silversmith and jeweller. This was issued by Collins Brehon, a freeman of Limerick city, who had his establishment opposite the Exchange under the sign of 'The Two Blue Posts'. The advertisement says that 'he makes all kinds of repeating watches and mends them in the best and safest manner . . . the said Brehon has a large assortment of touched plate, Butterboats, large and small ditto, large and small cups, Variety of touched Shoe and Knee Buckles and a large assortment of Jewellery work from the maker in Dublin, such as paste and stone, shoe and knee buckles, Garnet Hoops, Gold set lockets, Rings of different kinds, Pebble rings set around with garnets, watches, &c., he will engage; also plain and chased Coffee pots, and plate-handled knives and forks, with Cases, with several other articles too tedious to mention. N.B. He will give the highest price for old Gold and Silver and for Silver and Gold lace'.

A charm which comes from the personal and the intimate

Brehon's advertisement is a reminder that no account of old Irish silver can be complete without a note about the provincial makers of the Georgian period. Their work has a charm which comes from the personal and the intimate; it was sound and competent hand-made work, and it was up to the standard of English work in the lesser towns. A case in point is that of a mid-seventeenth-century Bandon silversmith called John Moore, who was asked to make a chalice for Cloyne Cathedral. Cloyne was a remote, tiny village, and Bandon a small market town, but John Moore's work was in no way inferior to that of more sophisticated silversmiths. It appears that he borrowed the finely made contemporary London chalice from his parish church as a model. The copy is admirable and completely competent. It has no hallmark, not

6

8

having been sent to Dublin. As an alternative, some makers used their full names, for example the seventeenth-century Fennell of Ennis, who signed the Franciscan chalices there.

It is to be expected, Irish conditions being what they were, that few provincial silversmiths sent their wares to Dublin. In small towns no guarantee of quality would be needed; each maker was known far too well to make fraud worth while.

Very little silver was made north of a line drawn between Dublin and Galway. The 'red hand' mark found on a few ancient pieces, once believed to have been made in Belfast, is now said to indicate Maltese silver. South of the line, however, a good many towns had their silversmiths. During the late seventeenth and early eighteenth centuries, a number of town marks existed. Youghal had a yawl; Galway a boat with furled sails on the yard-arm, or an anchor; Cork a tower and a three-masted ship, sometimes combined, sometimes separate. A very few examples exist of a tower indicating Kilkenny; Limerick had a two-towered castle-gate and a five-pointed star, sometimes with wavy beams. As the eighteenth century wore on these local marks died out, and only Cork and Limerick continued to produce identifiable marks. These are confusing, however, since both used the word 'sterling' or its abbreviations. This means that a Limerick piece can only be told from a Cork piece when the initials, or the style, of the maker are known or occasionally by a little fleur-de-lis mark.

Cork silver is still collectable, though rare, and tends to be found in its native county. In the middle of the Cromwellian period, on 21 May, 1656, the goldsmiths of Cork were incorporated as a Guild together with the braziers, pewterers, founders, plumbers, white-plate-workers, glaziers, saddlers and upholsterers of the city. The Guild was known as 'The Society of Goldsmiths of Cork'. The multiplicity of trades gave Robert Goble, Cork's greatest silversmith, his opportunity in the making of the mace of the Cork Guilds. It is a most remarkable piece of work, and is now in the Victoria and Albert Museum, London.

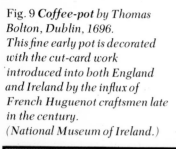

Fig. 9 *Coffee-pot* by Thomas Bolton, Dublin, 1696. *This fine early pot is decorated with the cut-card work introduced into both England and Ireland by the influx of French Huguenot craftsmen late in the century.* (National Museum of Ireland.)

Fig. 12 *Eighteenth-century Irish silver marks.* Top row: Hibernia, the date-letter for 1747 and the crowned harp of Dublin; the yawl of Youghal, c.1712; the anchor of Galway, c.1730. Bottom row: the two-towered castle-gate of Limerick, c.1710; the sterling mark of Limerick and Cork 1700–1800; the tower of Cork, c.1730.

Fig. 10 *Pair of sauce-boats* by *Robert Calderwood, Dublin, c.1737.*
Less elaborately worked than the sauce-boat of a year later illustrated in Figure 5.
(National Museum of Ireland.)

Fig. 11 *Jug, Dublin, c.1760.*
Height 6½ ins.
Much Irish silver has charm and a personal quality due to its lack of sophistication.
(Victoria and Albert Museum.)

Fig. 13 *Three casters* by *David King, Dublin, 1699.*
Vertical fluting was popular in Ireland as well as England.
(National Museum of Ireland.)

Cork 'sterling' marked silver from the mid-eighteenth century is still to be found. One notable partnership was that of Terry and Williams. Carden Terry's work is recorded as early as 1776. In 1795 he went into partnership with his son-in-law, Williams, who died soon afterwards. He continued the partnership with his daughter Jane, and many fine pieces up to 1821 bear the joint initials 'C.T. and J.W.'.

A very satisfactory form of silver collecting in Ireland is provided by spoons. Local pieces are still to be found, very often with local peculiarities such as the pointed handles, the Limerick bright-cutting in the form of the fleur-de-lis, or the Prince of Wales feathers.

Since the output of the Georgian silversmiths in Dublin was minute, and that from Cork and Limerick even less, compared with that from Birmingham, Sheffield or London, it is obvious that Irish pieces have better rarity prospects for the collector. They also show less evidence, on the whole, of mass production.

The peak of Irish output was reached at about the end of the eighteenth century, characterised by the era of bright-cut designs which reflect the light so charmingly. The demand lessened considerably from the time of the potato famine of 1847, since so many formerly well-to-do landlords were beggared and this greatly reduced the number of silversmiths. In Cork the last silversmith of the era seems to have been Kean Mahony who was working around 1840. A modern firm, Egan of Cork, produced some interesting, unassayed locally marked pieces during the Civil War of 1922.

Early Victorian silver, relatively rarer than Georgian, and also cheaper, is well worth collecting. The quality is good, though caution is needed over pieces imported from England and hallmarked in Ireland.

A little later, at the turn of the nineteenth century, came the Celtic revival under Yeats, Synge and Lady Gregory. In Ireland this produced a certain amount of silver with Celtic interlacing, which may well be worth finding.

Museum Photo

MUSEUMS AND COLLECTIONS

Irish silver may be seen at the following:

GREAT BRITAIN
London: Victoria and Albert Museum
EIRE
Dublin: National Gallery of Ireland
National Museum of Ireland

FURTHER READING

Irish Silver in the Rococo Period by Kurt Ticher, Shannon, 1972.
Irish Georgian Silver by Douglas Bennett, London, 1972.
Hall Marks on Dublin Silver 1730–1772 by Ticher, Delamer and O'Sullivan, Dublin, 1968.
An Introduction to Irish Silver by the Right Reverend Robert Wyse Jackson, Dublin, 1963.

Paul Revere

One of the most popular figures
from the American Revolution,
Paul Revere was a respected
Boston citizen, competent
engraver and prolific silversmith

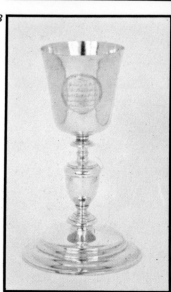

Paul Revere II (1734–1818) (Fig. 5) was, for almost a century, better known as a patriot than as a silversmith, and his first claim to fame is still remembered even as his craftsmanship receives renewed appreciation. Engraving, dentistry and operating a hardware store were also activities that Revere pursued from time to time, but for the greater part of his life his chief dependence was 'on my goldsmith's business for the expenses of my family'. The late E. Alfred Jones' *The Old Silver of American Churches* shows him to have fashioned more church pieces than any of his contemporaries in New England, and his daybooks reveal important public and private patrons.

Like many of Boston's best-known goldsmiths, he was of Huguenot descent. His father, Apollos Rivoire, was born in Riaucaud, France, in November 1702, and before his thirteenth birthday he left home, arriving in Boston probably late in 1715. He was apprenticed to John Coney, whom many consider to be the outstanding goldsmith of early New England if not the colonies.

He was still known as Paul Rivoire in 1728 when he was one of the subscribers to a life of the Reverend Cotton Mather, pastor of the Second Church; that he was buying a biography suggests careful schooling. He was Paul Revere in the record of his marriage in 1729 to Deborah Hichborn. Their second child, Paul, was born on 31 December, 1734.

The North End, where Paul grew up, was, in the words of Miss Esther Forbes (*Paul Revere and the World he Lived In*): 'a mixture of an almost London elegance of living, rubbing shoulders with poverty and vice . . . The tides of poverty washed about such islands of wealth as the Hutchinsons and their next-door neighbors the Clarks'.

In 1754 Paul Revere I died, leaving tea-sets and tankards, porringers, cans and a chafing dish, but nothing to compare with the variety or ability of John Coney's work; his son's versatility is a better reflection of his master's skill. Paul II was not yet of age to practise the craft, but in the manner of the day was permitted to carry on for his master's widow.

Revere I left another son, Thomas, of an age to begin his apprenticeship, and another, John, who became a tailor. One wonders who looked after the shop when, early in 1756, Revere II went off to fight the French at Lake George. The group came home at the end of the year and in August 1757 he was married to Sarah Orne.

In 1758 Paul was called upon to carry out the wishes of the Reverend Thomas Prince, beloved pastor of the Old South Church to which he had bequeathed 'a Piece of Plate in the Form and Height of that last presented to ye sd Church. I would have it plain and to hold a full pint' Revere's adaptation of the recently given French chalice is seen in Figure 3.

Revere was received into St. Andrew's Lodge in 1760 when 'work was commenced under it [the charter] by receiving Paul Revere, a Goldsmith and engraver as Entered Apprentice'. It is possible that he taught himself engraving. Coney had been an excellent engraver, but there is very little embellishment on Revere I's known work and of his independent engraving nothing is known, although an unsigned book-plate is attributed to him.

On 3 January, 1761, Revere II began the first of his two preserved daybooks. From its pages, one learns of many distinguished patrons. The first debit was for a 'Freemason Medal 13/4d', and he continued to charge for Masonic jewels, medals and cross-keys in silver, and for engraving plates for summonses, certificates and notifications, both to individuals and to Masonic Lodges. The second entry was to his brother Thomas, then of age and perhaps leaving the shop. The third client was Joshua Brackett, who was to succeed in 1768 to his widowed mother's inn, and who was debited for two pairs of buckles and 'one od dito'. Not debited in the daybooks is the billhead Revere engraved for him, an example of which bears a date of 1771. The entry for his buckles is slashed with a covering 'X', as most entries are; it is assumed to mean payment. Yet the next two entries are for a credit 'by Silver received', which was more than swallowed up in its ensuing debit. Less than a page was used for 1761 accounts, which do not include the baptismal basin made for Zachariah Johonnot and dated in that year when its presentation was noted and thanks enthusiastically voted by the Hollis Street church. Equal appreciation was expressed by the same church in 1773 for the 'large and costly Silver Flaggon for the Communion Table', which the daybook records: 'Zachariah Johonnot Esq./Dr.

	oz	
To a Silver Flaggon	wt 55-15 at 7/	£19 – 10 – 3
To the Making		6 – 13 – 4
To Engraving		1 – 4 – 0

The engraving included Johonnot's coat of arms in a scrolled and foliate cartouche and an inscription. Across the foot of the entry is written: 'Recd the above'.

A debit to one Williams for a 'gold necklace, gold

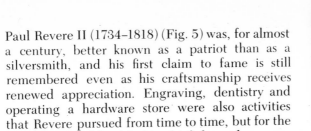

Fig. 1 *The Bloody Massacre perpetrated in King Street Boston on March 5th 1770 by Paul Revere II (1734–1818) after a design by Henry Pelham. Coloured engraving,* 9⅝ x 8⅝ *ins. (British Museum, London.)*

Fig. 2 *Covered cream-jug by Paul Revere II, Boston, 1784. Silver engraved with the crest of Colonel Swan, height* 6¹³⁄₁₆ *ins. (The Paul Revere Life Insurance Company, Worcester, Massachusetts.)*

Fig. 3 *Cup by Paul Revere II, Boston, 1758. Silver, height* 9½ *ins. (Old South Church, Boston, Massachusetts.)*

Fig. 4 *Urn-shaped Sugar-dish and cover by Paul Revere II, Boston, c.1790. Silver engraved with the initials of Hephzibah Hall, height* 9⅝ *ins. (The Paul Revere Life Insurance Co.)*

Fig. 5 *Paul Revere II by J. S. Copley, 1768–70. Oil on canvas,* 35 x 28½ *ins. (Boston Museum of Fine Arts, Boston. Gift of J. W., W. B. and E. H. R. Revere.)*

Author's Photo

Museum Photo

Museum Photo

Fig. 6 *Coffee-urn* by Paul
Revere II, Boston, 1793. Silver,
height 17⅞ ins.
*This fine urn and its matching
sugar-dish, teapot and stand are
engraved with the initials of
Burrell and Ann (Zeagers) Carnes.
(Boston Museum of Fine Arts,
Henry Davis Sleeper Collection.)*

Fig. 7 *Two goblets* from a set of
six by Paul Revere II, Boston,
1782. Silver, the interiors gilt,
heights 5 5⁄16 ins.
*The total cost of these beautiful
cups was only £37 10s. The
initials are of Nathaniel and
Mary Tracy.
(Boston Museum of Fine Arts,
Pauline Revere Thayer
Collection.)*

lockett, odd gold button, turtle shell ring lin'd with
gold, Pr of Spectical Bows and Glasses', and
mending a 'Pockett Book', represent many such
commissions unknown today but executed over his
full career. Enamelled rings, Death's head rings,
gold mourning rings, 'berring' (burying) rings and
plain gold rings were recorded. His greatest
number of items was probably spoons and buckles.
Of the latter, few are known, although he made
them for stock, neck, knees and shoes. His early
entries show more imagination or time for frivolities
than the later ones. They include: 'two Silver
Handles to two Shells for Spoons'; 'riming a China
Bowl wt Silver'; 'Turtle shell handle to a Knife';
'a Sugar Dish out of an Ostrich egg'; and 'silver
foot & rim to a shell'.

Among his clients were other silversmiths:
Nathaniel Hurd (1729–77) was debited for 'a Silver
frame for a Picture' and 'a Silver Indian Pipe wt.
9:6:0'. Samuel Minott (1732–1803) had 'two Silver
Waiters Chased wt. 22:18 To the Making £6', and 'a
large silver Salver 28 oz. Making £4'. For John
Coburn (1725–1803) he did considerable engraving.
The only candlesticks in the daybooks were for
Zachariah Johonnot Esq., who also had a unique
'Pr of Snuffers & Snuf Dish'; he was credited with
'Silver Receiᵈ at times' to cover the bill which
included a debit for 'a Counterfeit Cobb'.

Revere's earliest engraving known today is the
view of the North Battery, c.1762, one of many such
certificates charged throughout his daybooks. His
first political cartoon, taken from an English print,
was a protest against the unpopular Stamp Act of
1765, with Revere's inscription: 'The odious Stamp
Act represented by the Dragon . . . from the Liberty
Tree hangs the officer of the Crown'. His *View of
the Colledges in Cambridge* was a joint undertaking, for half its cost was debited to Joseph
Chadwick. Most of his pictorial engravings can be
traced to another source: his *View of Boston and
Landing of the Troops in 1768* (cut two years later)
was probably the design of Christian Remick.

In 1763 Revere began making numerous charges
to the artist John S. Copley (or Copely) for frames,
which led early readers of the daybooks to believe

that Revere had carved the wooden frames for
Copley's portraits on canvas despite the fact that all
the entries, which only continue until 1767, are
substantiated by the weight of gold or silver used.
Other early clients bought frames, and he served
doctors who had spatulas and probes in silver and 'a
Sett of Surgin's instruments'. His own venture in
the dental field was advertised in 1768 and his
daybook reveals 'fastning teeth 2/', and 'To cleaning you teeth & one pot dentfrice 4/6d'.

His best-known silver, the Rescinders' or Sons
of Liberty Bowl (Fig. 9), was fashioned in 1768,
yet was one of the many pieces not recorded in his
daybooks. *The Boston Gazette* of 8 August, 1768,
noted: 'We hear that the Week before last was
finished, by Order and for the Use of the Gentlemen
belonging to the Insurance Office kept by Mr.
Nathaniel Barber, at the North-End, an elegant
Silver BOWL, weighing forty-five Ounces, and
holding forty-five Jills. One Side is engraved
within a handsome Border – To the Memory of the
glorious NINETY-TWO Members of the Honourable House of Representatives of the Massachusetts-
Bay, who, undaunted by the insolent Menaces of
Villians in Power, and out of a strict Regard to
Conscience, and the LIBERTIES of their Con-
stituents, on the 30th of June 1768, Voted NOT TO
RESCIND. – Over which is the Cap of Liberty in an
Oaken Crown. On the other Side, in a Circle
adorned with Flowers, &c. is No 45, WILKES AND
LIBERTY, under which is General Warrants torn
to Pieces. On the Top of the Cap of Liberty, and
out of each Side, is a Standard, on one is MAGNA
CHARTA, the other BILL OF RIGHTS – On Mon-
day Evening last, the Gentlemen belonging to the
Office made a genteel Entertainment and invited a
Number of Gentlemen of Distinction in the Town,
when 45 Loyal Toasts were drank, and the whole
concluded with a new Song, the Chorus of which is,
In Freedom we're born, and in Freedom we'll live,
&c.'.

Although Revere is not mentioned as the maker,
his pellet mark is on the bottom of the bowl. To
meet the required capacity (45 gills) and weight
(45 ounces), which were based on John Wilkes'

Museum Photo

Museum Photo

Author's Photo

Fig. 8 **Pitcher** *by Paul Revere II, Boston, 1806. Silver, height 6 ins. This pitcher was 'Presented by The Government of the Mechanic Association TO Mʳ SAMUEL GILBERT. As compensation for his faithful and extra services while their SECRETARY'. (The Paul Revere Life Insurance Co.)*

Fig. 9 **The Sons of Liberty or Rescinders' Bowl** *by Paul Revere II, Boston, 1768. Silver, diameter 11 ins. The capacity (45 gills) and weight (45 oz.) of this bowl were determined by No. 45 of Wilkes' North Briton. (Boston Museum of Fine Arts. By subscription and the Francis Bartlett Fund.)*

Fig. 10 **Teapot** *by Paul Revere II, Boston, c.1785. Silver, height 5⅝ ins. A similar pot of 1785 is the first known by Revere to be of seamed rather than raised construction. (Sterling and Francine Clark Art Institute, Williamstown, Mass.)*

sympathetic paper (the No. 45 referred to in the quotation), he had to make a wrought rather than the customary cast foot.

Stirring events underlie his charges to Edes & Gill on 9 March, 1770:

To Engraving 5 Coffins for Massacre 6/
To Printing 200 Impressions of Massacre 5 – 0

The coffins were line-cuts for their newspaper, *The Boston Gazette*, for which he also cut mastheads. The impressions were of *A Print, containing a Representation of- the late horrid Massacre in King Street* (Fig. 1). Henry Pelham, half-brother of J. S. Copley, wrote protesting that Revere had pirated his design: 'If you are insensible to the Dishonour you have brought on yourself by this Act, the World will not be so'. But Pelham seems not to have been a good prophet.

On 15 February, 1770, Revere bought the house on North Square, then almost a century old, which is now maintained as a memorial to him. From its windows, on the first anniversary of the Massacre, he showed illuminations to keep its memory aflame and 'The whole was so well executed that the Spectators, which amounted to many Thousands, were struck with Solem Silence & their Countenances covered with a meloncholy Gloom.' (*The Boston Gazette.*)

In 1773 Sarah died, and in September of that year Revere married Rachel Walker to mother his six surviving children and give him another eight, of whom three died in infancy or early childhood. Also in September 1773, he charged to Dr. William Paine, for his bride Lois Orne whose arms the pieces bear, the most complete service known, which lacks, strangely, a sugar-bowl. The pair of porringers, some spoons, the cream-pot and the wooden box which cost 3s. 8d., are all that are missing from this service in the Worcester Art Museum (Fig. 11). In November 1773, 'That worst of Plagues, the detested tea shipped for this port by the East India Company', sent Revere 'riding express' to warn of the impending Tea Party and he was soon carrying letters to other Sons of Liberty in New York and Philadelphia.

On 1 April, 1775, the silver entries cease and no

further silver is recorded until 1781. Rent, food, and the 'use of my chaise' are intervening entries partially covering two pages. Revere was empowered to engrave and print paper currency in the five ensuing years and was sent to Philadelphia to learn how to erect a powder mill. He established one in Canton where eventually he was to have his bell and cannon foundry and copper manufactory. In April 1777 his son Joseph Warren was born, and in May his mother died; his daughter Deborah, almost twenty, was at home to help.

Revere wrote to them from Castle Island and from Rhode Island, before embarking on the disastrous Penobscot Expedition, of which he kept a careful diary, in 1779. In a post-war letter to a cousin in France, he summed up his activities: 'the year 1775 when the American Revolution began; from that time till May 1780, I have been in Government service as Lieutenant Colonel of an Artillery regiment, the time for which that was raised then expired and I thought it best to go to my business again, which I now carry on and under which I trade some to Holland. I did intend to have gone wholly into trade, but the principal part of my interest I lent to Government, which I have not been able to draw out; so must content myself till I can do better'.

His earliest coffee-pots had been single bellied; what was presumably the last of these was charged in 1772 and given three shell feet with shell attachments; the style of the coffee-pot from the Lois Paine (née Orne) service continued until the mid-1790s. One bulbous tankard by Revere is known, and a heavy one without a finial. His known pre-Revolutionary pieces are in the form of the Paine ones, but usually lack their enriched bases.

Beads, bodkins and jewellery are among many items charged in the daybooks which are not now known. 'Butter cupps' were listed at the same weights as his butter-boats which were usually tripod; three are known on a collet foot reminiscent of Bow porcelain examples. Buttons of gold, silver, stone and tortoise-shell for coat, sleeve or jacket are recorded in quantity but unidentified. Cans came usually in pairs and in sizes from half-pint to wine-quart; in the 1790s, he charged a 'hoop'd cann' which we know to be straight-sided with applied reeded bands. Casters in pairs, or single ones specifically for pepper, he produced throughout his working years. He made chains for buttons, scissors and pin-balls; a squirrel-chain made in 1772 brings to mind the portrait of Henry Pelham, *Boy with a squirrel*, which his friend Copley had exhibited in the London Society of Artists exhibition of 1765. Clasps were made for shoes, usually children's, and for cloaks; he recorded considerable 'cleaning and mending' of silver. He accepted a barrel of rum for a tankard, and a bookcase for a cream-pot. A silver chalice and an old salt went into the making of spoons in 1784, and 'Freight on some goods from France' helped pay for cans and marking spoons. He carried on a thriving harness business, much of it plated, and some silver. He riveted china dishes, put new lids to tankards and cloth bottoms to bottle stands. His porringers were often in pairs, sometimes in child's size; his handle designs varied, mainly in size. 'Large' and 'tea' were his usual designations for spoons; 'dessert-spoons' began *c.*1790, and he did not succumb to the familiar word 'tablespoon' until that decade.

Paul Dudley Sargent's coffee-pot, in the double-bellied form of Mrs. Paine's, is the only known surviving item from his 1781 charges. Thomas Hichborn's teapot (in drum form with a gadrooned border) and Nathaniel Tracy's goblets (Fig. 7) were debited in 1782. The names of many of his pre-Revolutionary clients recur subsequently, and some of his Loyalist ones, as soon as the Treaty of September 1783 permitted them to be so, acted as his agents in England. They sent him the hardware, fine materials, writing- and wall-paper with which he stocked the shop which, according to Miss Forbes, he opened 'opposite the Liberty Pole' in 1783. His silver accounts in the first daybook end in August that year, but he noted in the book, in 1784/5, the renting of his house on North Square to the miniaturist Joseph Dunkerly, whose credit 'By sundrys & p[e]r his Bill' may well have been for a charming portrait of Rachel Revere in what is traditionally regarded as a Revere gold

for Mrs. Hannah Rowe; this had a cylinder for a heating rod similar to that with which he equipped the fluted 'coffee urn' for Burrell Carnes (Fig. 6), but Mrs. Rowe's urn was twice the weight. His tankards were given higher domed covers; the new lids he sometimes charged for could have been repairs or a means of updating an old-fashioned piece.

In 1786 he advertised his removal to Dock Square, or 50, Cornhill, where he was when the first *Boston Directory* was published three years later. In 1788 he had started his 'furnass' and in 1792 cast his first church bell; of a later one, the Reverend William Bentley was to write that they 'venture to prefer it to any imported bell & so did we but from patriotism'. His only known trade-cards are for the 'Bell & Cannon Foundrey', although he engraved many for fellow tradesmen. The second *Boston Directory* of 1796 gives: 'Revere & Son goldsmiths Ann Street'. Two years later this was 'Paul & J. W. Revere' for his son Joseph Warren, who had just come of age. The early directories give Paul Jr., who predeceased his father, on Fleet Street. 'Paul Revere, bell & cannon foundrey Lynn street, house North Square' was amended in 1800 to 'house Charter Street'. In 1797, the last year of the day-books, he fashioned his now unique 'waiter' for the great Salem merchant, Elias Hasket Derby.

The bell and cannon foundry was in the area of the shipyards, and Revere began working in copper. His seaworthy fittings were much appreciated by the shipbuilders. Late in December 1800, when he had mastered the technique of rolled copper, he established his rolling-mill in the town of Canton, using water power from the Neponset River. When the hurricane of 1804 had damaged Lynn Street, he moved his foundry there. He sheathed the dome of Bulfinch's State House, the cornerstone of which he had assisted in laying in 1795; and in 1809 provided copper for boilers for Robert Fulton's steamship. He was one of the founders and first president of the Association of Mechanics for which in 1806 he fashioned one of his famous adaptations (Fig. 8) of the Liverpool pottery pitchers, apparently his last.

In 1813, Mrs. Revere died. Revere divided his time between Canton and Charter Street until his death in 1818, when it was said of him that he was 'Cool in thought, ardent in action, he was well adapted to form plans and to carry them to execution — both for the benefit of himself and the service of others'.

Fig. 11 *Silver service by Paul Revere II, Boston, 1773. Silver, the pot-handles of wood, height of tankard 9½ ins., of coffee-pot 13½ ins.*
The most complete silver service known, this one is missing only a pair of porringers, some spoons, the cream-pot and the fitted wooden box. Oddly, it never had a sugar-bowl. It was made for Dr. William Paine of Worcester, Mass. for his bride, Lois Orne, whose arms and initials the pieces bear.
(*Worcester Art Museum, Worcester, Mass. Donated from four lines of descent in the Paine family.*)

frame. A drawing of flattened bow sugar-tongs, eleven inches long, with a note of '1 oz. 2' is on the last page of this book.

On the first page of the second book, in the careful handwriting of his signature, there is a recipe 'to make Gold Sawder', with other less careful notations and a drawing of a finial. Three pages mostly record family debts, including those of Paul Jr. Fellow silversmiths who are recorded as clients were John Andrew, Nathaniel Austin, who put his own mark on Revere's spoons, Caleb Beal and Stephen Emery. In 1789 a page was devoted to 'Shop Dr. to Paul Revere Senior for Stock Ready made in the Cases'. Its total of forty-two pairs of silver buckles for stock, neck, hat, knee and shoes; shoe-clasps, buttons, brooches, spoons, ladles, spurs, sugar-tongs, hairpins, one gold necklace and seven gold rings contrasts with the hollow ware which comprised only three cream-pots and a pair of casters. One is reminded of his many credits 'by silver to make' a piece.

His teapots changed rapidly in form, and more of the 'engraved and fluted' ones of the 1790s are known than any others. With the exception of one set charged in 1764, no three-piece tea-set was charged until the 1790s; and then a fourth piece, a stand for the teapot, was usual. Cream-pots in the early 1780s were pyriform on a splayed foot; his covered one of 1784 (Fig. 2) he called a 'cream jug'. The so-called 'helmet-shapes' he made in a variety of styles; he recorded sugar-dishes, urns, vases and baskets; one of the last he referred to as a 'sugar-bowl'. His goblets for Tracy appear to be unique today; those made for Moses Hayes (in 1796) and Andrew Cunningham are in the form of his unmarked 'church cupps', which also date from 1796. In 1791 he made a plain 'tea urn'

French Gold Boxes

Fig. 1 **Crab box** *of Paris 1738–39, bearing the marks of an unidentified maker. Polished stone mounted in enamelled gold. This charming box is of the type described in a London paper in 1731 as a 'Crab-Box . . . with a Pebble-Stone Top and Bottom'. (By permission of the Trustees of the Wallace Collection, London.)*

The small gold boxes made in Paris epitomise the elegance and extravagance of French taste better than any other single group of objects

J. Freeman

These gold boxes illustrate perfectly the changes of taste in the most moneyed circles in France, and therefore in Europe, since Paris was the centre of the fashionable world. Generally called snuff-boxes today they were, of course, intended for any purpose that the owner wished, and might contain *dragées* to sweeten the breath; patches, powder or rouge for the face; wafers for fastening letters, or souvenirs of love-affairs. When they did contain snuff their use was governed by a precise etiquette dictating the exact mode of proffering and accepting a pinch, a ritual not missed by contemporary satirists.

Although during the greater part of the seventeenth century snuff was probably kept in containers akin to gunpowder flasks, references to boxes for snuff become common in the second half of the century. Their appearance is known from engraved designs (Fig. 8) but, unfortunately, no gold box bearing a French mark is known earlier than the year 1723/4 – the very brink of the appearance of the rococo style. It is quite impossible in the space available to do more than sketch the changes of form and decoration, affected as they were by the most frivolous and fickle of fashions. It is clear from

advertisements like those of Granchez in *L'Avant Coureur* that fashions in boxes changed with the greatest rapidity.

Designs for early eighteenth-century boxes were usually rectangular or oval, but these were soon superseded by those in the form of a crab shell (Fig. 1). An advertisement in *The London Evening Post* in October 1731 referred to one of these: 'Lost . . . a Silver Crab-Box chased on the Sides, with a Pebble-Stone Top and Bottom. . . .' This form remained fashionable until about 1750. Another favourite shape of the early years of the century was the cockle-shell, sometimes with its ribs in relief (Fig. 7). These may be what were called *boîtes à coquille*, although it is possible that this refers to real shells mounted as boxes, a conceit inspired by the craze for collecting sea shells.

Exquisite boxes were made from real shells such as the slender conus variety, lined with gold and fastened with lids made from other shells. The lids were attached with delicately crafted gold hinges fashioned as tiny shells forming part of the reeded gold and enamelled decorations of waves, seaweed and coral branches. Rare mother-of-pearl was also admired as a material for gold-mounted

Fig. 2 **En cage box** *bearing an illegible maker's mark, Paris, 1781–83. Gold with inset gouache miniatures by Henri-Joseph van Blarenberghe.*
Painted by one of the most famous of French miniaturists producing gold boxes, these lovely scenes depict the château and park of Romainville, near Paris, the seat of the Marquis de Ségur.
(Wallace Collection.)

Fig. 3 *Enamelled box* by Jean Frémin, Paris, 1756–57. Engine-turned gold with pastoral scenes on each side in basse taille enamel. (Wallace Collection.)

Fig. 4 *Piqué box* by Adrien-Jean-Maximilien Vachette, Paris, 1798–1809. Gold set with piqué panels of exceptional quality. (Wallace Collection.)

Fig. 5 *Box,* probably by Pierre-François Drais, Paris, 1774–75. Basse-taille enamel on an engine-turned ground of gold, set with cameo-like classical miniatures in the style of Joseph de Gault. (Wallace Collection.)

Fig. 6 *En cage box* by Louis Roucel, Paris, 1765–66. Japanese lacquer panels, imported through Holland, set in tooled gold. (Wallace Collection.)

boxes, as well as black pearl and other exotic shells from the Indian Ocean and the East.

The outlines of rectangular boxes began to be made less severe by rounding the corners, and the edges were softened by the use of elaborate mouldings. Occasionally the outline was broken by interrupted curves but, at first, these remained perfectly symmetrical. These early boxes were rather shallow, since snuff was expensive and the box liable to come open and spill the contents. It was in order to prevent this sort of accident that such care was lavished on the construction of the hinge, which on French boxes was almost invariably on one of the longer sides and was a miracle of craftsmanship. Great care was also taken to see that the lid was a tight fit, both to keep the snuff fresh and to prevent the lid from opening accidentally, since there was never a catch of any kind.

By the 1740s there was a return to popularity of the rectangular box, but examples of this period were about one and a half times as deep as earlier ones. From about 1760 they were largely replaced by boxes made with heavily bevelled corners when viewed from above. Boxes of oval plan also became fashionable round about 1740, at first often with *bombé* sides, but after 1750 almost invariably with vertical walls. During the last quarter of the century there was a tendency for boxes to be made longer and narrower than formerly. From about 1745 increasing care was taken to disguise the join of lid and body. There was frequently no external indication of it either in the shape of the box or in the distribution of the decoration. The thumb-piece, usually a major feature of earlier boxes and set with precious stones, was very often entirely absent. After about 1760 the position of the join was usually indicated once more by the decoration, particularly by the architectural treatment of the sides of many Louis XVI boxes.

Cylindrical boxes with lids that lift right off are found occasionally throughout the century. These were probably intended for rouge or powder rather than for snuff, but they were, of course, also made by the craftsmen who made the other boxes. Indeed, these men also made such things as cases for tooth-picks, sewing implements and spectacles, as well as cane-heads and even hilts for dress swords. Daniel Govaers (active 1717–36), one of the earliest box-makers we know anything very much about, also made table plate, but this

4

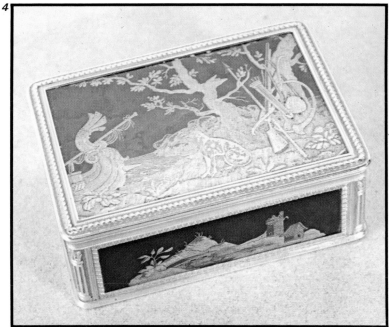

6

7

Fig. 7 **Enamelled box** by Jean Ducrollay, Paris, 1743–44. Gold decorated with white peacock feathers in painted enamel. Cockle-shells were a favourite motif on early French boxes. Sometimes real shells were set into gold mounts, while others, such as this beautiful example, are chased with ribs in relief in imitation of shells. (Wallace Collection.)

Fig. 8 **Designs for gold boxes** by G. Roberday. Engraving published in Paris in 1710. This delightful title-page refers to the designs as being intended for snuff-boxes but, in fact, small gold boxes were used for many other purposes in the eighteenth century. (By kind permission of Mr. A. K. Snowman.)

was probably exceptional.

The variety of decoration and of material employed in the embellishment of gold boxes was enormous. The full repertory of decorative motifs to be found in the applied arts was employed on boxes and they also reflect a good deal of the changing taste in paintings during the century. Early boxes were decorated with typical symmetrical *régence* motifs. Most surviving examples are of plain gold, chiselled and engraved in low relief, the salient features picked out with precious stones. As time went on stones were used more sparingly except on the thumb-piece, but chiselled scenes outlined with tiny stones were still made occasionally in the 1750s. Both the cockle and the crab shapes proved ideal for the asymmetrical, shell-like scrolls of the rococo style but boxes of asymmetrical shape, like those illustrated in the engravings of 1725 by J.-A. Meissonnier, are extremely rare.

One of the most popular methods of decorating boxes, particularly in the first half of the century, was by chiselling all over and accentuating the details by encrusting them with gold of other colours. For instance, red gold was made by alloying with copper, and white gold contained a high proportion of silver. This technique was used not only for boxes largely covered with architectural ornament – pillars, swags, urns, paterae, and so on – but also for

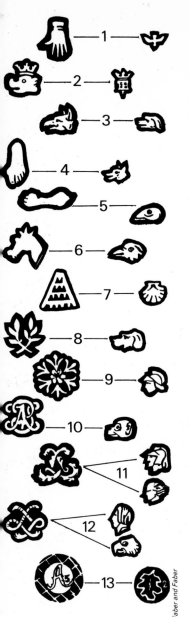

Fig. 9 **Marks struck on gold boxes, Paris, eighteenth century.** *On the left, the charge mark; and on the right the discharge mark or marks.*

1. *Charles Cordier, 1722–27.*
2. *Jacques Cottin, 1727–32.*
3. *Hubert Louvet, 1732–38.*
4. *Louis Robin, 1738–44.*
5. *A. Leschaudel, 1744–50.*
6. *Julien Berthe, 1750–56.*
7. *Eloy Brichard, 1756–62.*
8. *J.-J. Prevost, 1762–68.*
9. *Julien Alaterre, 1768–75.*
10. *J.-B. Fouache, 1775–81.*
11. *Henri Clavel, 1781–83.*
12. *Henri Clavel, 1783–89.*
13. *J.-F. Kalendrin, from Feb., 1789.*

Export marks
(By kind permission of Mr. A. K. Snowman, from his book, Eighteenth Century Gold Boxes of Europe.*)*

the pictorial type in which the surface was almost entirely covered with low relief landscapes, scenes of rustic life, the chase or war, so popular in the years between 1730 and 1760. It seems probable that this sort of work was farmed out to specialist chiseller-engravers like Gerard Debèche, who certainly worked for Govaers. Additional contrast was given by matting the background with a punch and leaving the design bright, or alternatively the ground was chiselled with rays diverging from the centre like a sunburst. In the middle of the century it became fashionable to have the background of the design worked with formal patterns by engine turning. This was done with a special lathe capable of producing an almost infinite variety of repeating patterns, a favourite one reproducing *moiré* silk. In a few cases boxes were decorated solely by this method.

Occasionally, on even the earliest boxes, part of the decoration was picked out in painted enamel in a style seen in the previous century on watch-cases. In the 1740s it was fashionable to have boxes decorated with sprays of flowers painted in enamel against a tooled gold ground. Very often the leaves were enamelled in the *basse taille* technique: the shape of the leaf was cut into the metal and the bottom of the hollow tooled with a pattern. This formed a key for the transparent enamel as well as reflecting light back through it. The enamel was polished flush with the metal unlike the painted enamel which, at this date, was usually raised above the surface.

Boxes bearing the king's portrait were a standard royal present

In the 1750s boxes were very often covered in romantic scenes reserved in the gold in either painted or *basse taille* enamel. Also at this time they began to be painted with similar scenes complete with backgrounds and outlined, as in a picture frame, by rococo scrolls. The subjects chosen were much influenced by the sort of paintings being collected at the time and included still life scenes of flowers, genre scenes after or inspired by David Teniers II, or the classical *putti* of Carle van Loo, and later the works of Boucher, Greuze, and Chardin. A few were actually signed by the enamellers; for instance, Eustache le Sueur and Hamelin.

Since the box had now become a picture gallery, the next step was to make it a frame for actual paintings. The *en cage* box was just this. Externally it consisted of a thin framework of gold round six gouache miniatures under glass. Apart from Boucher-like fantasies and *fêtes champêtres* in the style popularised by Watteau, distant views of the owner's *château* or glimpses of its interior were popular, often carried out by the Van Blarenberghes, father and son (Fig. 2). The *en cage* technique was frequently used to frame hardstone, lacquer (Fig. 6), *piqué* (Fig. 4), or enamel plaques.

Designs in the second half of the century were usually extremely restrained and the chiselling in very low relief. The favourite scheme on both oval and rectangular boxes was for the centre of each panel to contain an oval, often edged with laurel foliage, enclosing a trophy, flowers, an urn, or a scene of tiny figures in either gold or enamel. In the last quarter of the century the centre of the

lid was often decorated with a miniature of a classical scene sometimes painted *en camaïeu*, or of a portrait, sometimes in gouache, more usually in enamel. The spaces on each side of the miniature and the panels of the sides were often enamelled in *basse taille* on an engine-turned ground (Fig. 5). Occasionally, the ground was engraved with sprays of flowers. Alternatively, these areas were enamelled in imitation of hardstone – malachite, lapis lazuli and moss agate – or even set with panels of the genuine material.

Although portrait boxes were typical of this period, they were made all through the century. A very rich box set with diamonds and bearing the king's portrait was the standard royal present to an ambassador or a visiting prince from about 1668. As they were sometimes sold back to the jeweller and presented to another visitor almost at once, they were probably regarded as a tactfully disguised monetary reward.

The eighteenth-century taste for the fantastic led to the manufacture of boxes of unusual shape: *boîtes à baignoire*, shaped like a hip bath; *à carrosse*, shaped like a carriage; or *en forme de bahut*, shaped like a travelling trunk. Similarly there was a widespread use of exotic materials, encouraged by the *marchands merciers*, men like Lazare Duvaux who specialised in expensive toys for the very rich. His day-book records the purchase of Sèvres boxes for mounting by goldsmiths, as well as hardstone, lacquer, and so on. The black and gold Japanese lacquer imported by the Dutch was particularly popular, either as a complete box with gold hinge and lining, or cut up and set *en cage*. One of the most successful of those who worked in this way was Adrien-Jean-Maximilien Vachette (*maître* 1779). Lacquer was also imitated in *piqué*, tortoise-shell inlaid with very fine strips or minute pins of silver and gold to form a design. A particularly rich effect was produced when these panels were set in a brilliant vermilion surround. They could be mounted either *en cage* or in frames on the box.

MUSEUMS AND COLLECTIONS
French gold boxes of the eighteenth century may be seen at the following:
FRANCE
Paris: Musée Cognacq-Jay
            Louvre
GREAT BRITAIN
London: Victoria and Albert Museum
            Wallace Collection
HOLLAND
Amsterdam: Rijksmuseum
U.S.A.
Baltimore: Walters Art Gallery
San Marino,
    California: Henry E. Huntingdon Library and
                Art Gallery

FURTHER READING
Eighteenth century Gold Boxes of Europe by A. K. Snowman, London, 1974.
European and American snuff boxes, 1730–1830 by C. le Corbeiller, London, 1966.
Le Poinçon de Paris, 5 vols. by H. Nocq, Paris, 1926–31.
Tabatières, boîtes et étuis . . . des collections du Musée du Louvre by H. Nocq and C. Dreyfus, Paris, 1930.

French Neo-Classical Silver

1

Fig. 1 *Soup-tureen and stand* by *Antoine Boullier, Paris, 1781–82. Each piece signed 'A. Boullier fecit à Paris', but with the marks of Henri Clavel, overall height 14¾ ins.*
Despite the magnificent acanthus leaf decoration and sculpture of a boar and hound, this tureen is sober, almost puritanical, when compared with rococo work.
(Christie, Manson and Woods, London.)

The silversmiths of the Directory had been apprentices under the *ancien régime*, and thus a continuity of style was ensured despite the turmoil caused by the Revolution in France

It is extraordinarily difficult to put oneself in the place of those living in a previous age. It is easy enough to see, nearly two hundred years after the event, that the French Revolution of 1789 was inevitable given the obtuseness of the Establishment during the whole of the century. One can argue also that some sort of dictatorship, thanks to the quarrels of the chief characters of the new government during the 1790s, was no less inevitable.

What is not so easy is to look into the minds of individuals, of ordinary men like silversmiths, many of them possessed of exceptional skills. They were engaged in a luxury trade dependent upon the continued support of a small number of rich people both in France and abroad and one wonders how many of them during the last twenty years or so before the collapse of the monarchy had any fears about the future. To the great majority of these craftsmen – and not only silversmiths but all the others, cabinet-makers, jewellers and the rest – the French monarchy probably seemed immutable. When the crash came many had to give up their work; others, whether by luck or good judgement or a combination of both, survived to add lustre to the reign of Napoleon.

356

Fig. 2 **Sauce-boat and stand** by Henry Auguste, Paris, 1786. Length of stand 11¾ ins., height of sauce-boat 7 ins. This classically simple piece, in the style termed 'à la grecque' in France, was made by one of the most distinguished French silversmiths of both pre- and post-Revolutionary periods. The easy flow of line from lip to handle is characteristic of his mastery of the neo-classical style. (Firestone Collection, U.S.A.)

Fig. 3 **Soup-tureen,** maker's mark 'L.F.D', fleur-de-lis and crescent below, Paris, 1787. Width 13½ ins. This restrained design, with its swelling form and foliate feet, harks back to an earlier style. It provides a good contrast to the extravagance of the tureen in Figure 1, showing the simpler treatment of a more everyday piece. (Sotheby and Co., London.)

Fig. 4 **Verrière (monteith)** one of a pair by Henry Auguste, Paris, 1789. Length 15⅞ ins. This is an early example of the Empire style which was to dominate French silver for the next thirty years. Despite its dryness, it was an elegant style, well suited to larger pieces of this sort. (Firestone Collection.)

It is tempting, until one looks a little closer, to write of these rather severe works produced at the time of the Directory and the First Empire as if they were in a special style, having no roots in the past. It is worth pointing out that the majority of the men who are remembered as the outstanding silversmiths of those years had all learned their skills under the long and rigid apprenticeship system of pre-Revolution days and, what is more, were already making fine things during the reign of Louis XVI which clearly point the way to the more severe style we loosely classify as 'Empire' The admirable sauce-boat and stand from the Firestone Collection in America (Fig. 2) is an object of classic simplicity (*à la grecque*) and it illustrates this point. The date is 1786, and the maker Henry Auguste, who was destined eighteen years later, having survived the turmoil of the Revolution, to be commissioned by the City of Paris to supply the famous silver-gilt service which the City presented to Napoleon on the occasion of his coronation in 1804. In the tureens of that service he employs a motif which he had already used before 1789. In short, there is no sudden break in style; new ideas are gradually evolved and become fashionable. Silversmiths, almost by definition, are conservative and, while anxious to supply what their customers want, are continually looking over their shoulders to the style of the previous generation.

This is what Henry Auguste's no less distinguished father was doing when he made a famous silver-gilt tureen in 1784, now in the Musée Nissim de Camondo, Paris. It has a boar's head on the cover which, from its style alone, could have been designed by the younger Germain in, say, 1760. This also is what Antoine Boullier was doing in 1781 (Fig. 1). The cover of this tureen is chased with acanthus leaves, its centre surmounted by a boar attacking a hound, while the bowl rests on eagle's claws, and the handles are in the form of a double cornucopia of flowers with eagles' heads between; yet, when compared with some of the more luxurious pieces of the mid-eighteenth century, the decoration seems almost puritanical.

Lest one should jump to the conclusion that the immense production of this extravagant decade was confined to elaborate work of this nature, a distinguished but far less exceptional tureen made in Paris in 1787 by an unknown maker, 'L.F.D.', provides a contrast (Fig. 3). This is a quiet work with a minimum of acanthus decoration, but it too, with its swelling form and four foliate feet, harks back a trifle nostalgically to an earlier style.

During the troubled years immediately before and after the Revolution and during the reign of Napoleon I, the three best-known French silversmiths were Henry Auguste (1759–1816), Jean-Baptiste-Claude Odiot (1763–1850) and Martin-Guillaume Biennais (1754–1843). It is the first whose work appeals most to modern taste, for he seems to retain something of the gaiety of the past amid the decidedly solemn ideals of the early years of the nineteenth century.

His father, retiring in 1785, handed over his business to his son who, thirty years old when the cataclysm overwhelmed the monarchy, had already executed many notable commissions both in France and abroad. He married a member of the Coustou family of sculptors, and a charming sketch by Gérard shows him with his wife and their two

children; the younger one, destined to be well-known as a traveller, was a friend of Géricault and Delacroix. The picture must have been painted before 1795 for in that year Madame Auguste died two weeks after the birth of a daughter. Auguste seems to have remained in business throughout the Terror and the Directory, although it is doubtful whether any silversmith did much more than mark time and husband his resources. His great chance came when the First Consul promoted himself to Emperor. He was entrusted with the chasing of the crown at the Coronation in 1804; with the silver-gilt service presented to the Emperor by the City of Paris; and with the golden tiara given by Napoleon to Pope Pius VII. This last is still in the Vatican, but bereft of its original emeralds and the reliefs,

Connaissance des Arts: Photo Schnapp

Fig. 5 **Jean-Baptiste-Claude Odiot** (1763–1850) by Robert Lefèbvre, 1822. Oil on canvas. This fine portrait shows the great smith Odiot pointing to several of his finest pieces, including a tea-urn which he made to the order of the Emperor Napoleon. (Odiot Collection.)

Fig. 6 **Ewer and basin** from a toilet-service of twenty-nine pieces by J.-B.-C. Odiot (see Fig. 5), Paris, 1812. Silver-gilt, overall height 15¾ ins. Created for the Empress Josephine for use at Malmaison, this magnificent toilet set was made by one of the three greatest silversmiths of Revolutionary and post-Revolutionary France. (Stavros S. Niarchos Collection.)

commemorating recent events, which were removed after 1815.

Auguste also began to work on the altar candlesticks and crucifix which Napoleon intended to present to the Abbey of St. Denis and which were used at the Emperor's second marriage to Marie-Louise of Austria, but he was compelled to abandon this commission and it was completed by Biennais. His last years were tragic, for, like the younger Germain of a previous generation, in spite of his great reputation and innumerable commissions, he went bankrupt. His creditors seemed to have behaved very sensibly, indeed liberally, for they suggested that he remain as head of his business with eight years' grace in which to recover. Instead, he lost his head, abandoned his children and tried, in 1809, to send his silver and stock of precious stones from Dieppe to England. The State promptly seized the cases, sold their contents and deprived him of his rights as a citizen. He reached England but did not remain there; finally, after six years of poverty-stricken wanderings, he died in 1816 at Port-au-Prince, Haiti.

The other two great silversmiths of this time were no less gifted, more fortunate and less foolish. J.-B.-C. Odiot came of a family whose members had been silversmiths since the seventeenth century; like Auguste, he succeeded his father in 1785. He volunteered for the army in 1792, leaving his wife in charge of the business; he was promoted to lieutenant, returned home with a

reputation as a good soldier to add to that which he had already acquired as a pre-Revolution silversmith. He shared with Henry Auguste a remarkable success in the Industrial Exhibition of 1802, the jury being unable to decide between them and so making them joint winners of the gold medal. They were of course rivals and it is possible that Odiot was not too displeased by Auguste's foolish behaviour. At the latter's sale following his bankruptcy, Odiot bought his models, his tools and his designs which still remain in the firm's possession.

In 1814, before the Allies reached Paris, he rejoined the army and was promoted to colonel; a romantic painting by Horace Vernet records him in uniform and a more revealing portrait by the less well-known Robert Lefèbvre of 1822 (Fig. 5) shows him as the fifty-nine year old craftsman proud of his work and pointing to several of his best pieces, among them a famous tea-urn he made to the order of the Emperor. Louis XVIII gave him the Legion of Honour 'for services to the fatherland'. Among his many splendid pieces, the toilet-service he made for the ex-Empress Josephine, which she used at Malmaison, is probably the best known. Its date is 1812 and it includes a mirror supported by a pair of standing figures and the ewer and basin illustrated here (Fig. 6); in all, there are twenty-nine pieces in this princely service. At Josephine's death in 1814, the service passed to her son, Eugène de Beauharnais, and is now in the Niarchos collection.

Odiot was also involved in many other no less extravagant projects, all devised to bring to the Imperial and somewhat parvenu court something of the mystique which had sanctified the *ancien régime*. It was the old snobbery in a new dress, but nevertheless a dress of great dignity and splendour, as witness the fabulous cradle for the King of Rome, L'Aiglon, who was the son of Napoleon and Marie-Louise, and was better known as the Duke of Reichstadt. This cradle was designed by the painter Prud'hon and executed by Odiot (using two hundred and eighty kilos of silver) in collaboration with the ormolu worker Thomire. The cradle was taken to Vienna after the Emperor's eclipse.

It is the opinion of some that the third member of this trio, Biennais, is even more distinguished. That is a matter of personal taste, for his style is rather dry compared with the other two, but there can be no argument about his craftsmanship. Biennais was the notable exception to the rule that nearly all the men who came to the front under Napoleon had undergone the discipline of the apprenticeship system of pre-Revolution days. He seems to have begun his career as a maker of toys, but soon became a silversmith, thanks to the abolition of the *Corporations* (the Guilds which governed the various crafts) by the Decree of March 1791, and speedily proved that he was no man's inferior. His great specialities were the *nécessaire*, the travelling canteen, and other boxes in which all kinds of tea equipment, sewing kit or both could be neatly packed. He provided all the table-services for the Imperial household, and in one year alone (1811) delivered several hundred plates, forty-six dishes, sixty-two dish-covers, ten tureens and thirty-eight candelabra. He employed six hundred people, and, like his predecessors of a century earlier, was no less in demand abroad than he was in France.

He is said to have first obtained the confidence of Napoleon by granting him a very large credit when

Fig. 7 *Detail of a nef by Henry Auguste, Paris, 1804. Silver-gilt. This magnificent piece was made on the occasion of Napoleon's coronation, to the order of the City of Paris. It was a ceremonial nef of the sort reserved by tradition for royal use, as Napoleon wished to restore the old customs and all the old silver had long since been melted down. (Musée de Malmaison, Paris.)*

Fig. 8 *Cadenas (ceremonial platter) by Henry Auguste, Paris, 1804. Silver-gilt, length 14½ ins. This elaborate piece, along with the nef in Figure 7, was part of the royal service used by Napoleon at the banquet held three days after his coronation in 1804. On it were placed his cutlery and bread, while the locked jars held salt, pepper and spices. After the fall of Napoleon, the cadenas was altered under Louis XVIII and restored in the 1850s by Napoleon III. (Musée de Malmaison.)*

the young General Bonaparte returned from Egypt, and by not pressing for payment. That may well be true and shows that Biennais was a far-sighted (or lucky) businessman who could hitch his wagon to a star. When he was accused of selling short weight, he immediately insisted upon an investigation which showed that his deliveries were above, not under, specification. Whatever the truth about the original reason for the marked favour shown him by the Emperor, there can be no question as to his honourable conduct throughout his career nor about the high standard of the innumerable products of his workshops. He retired in 1819.

How secure the regime must have seemed throughout these years of victory, at least until 1812; and how appalling the future must have seemed when the Emperor abdicated, then returned and was finally exiled. An odd clue to the impermanence of all human affairs is provided by the *cadenas* (ceremonial platter) which, with the great nef and other pieces, Henry Auguste made in 1804 to the order of the City of Paris for the coronation (Figs. 7 and 8). Both nef and *cadenas* had been reserved for royal ceremonial use since the time of Charles V, and Napoleon wished to restore the old customs. Those of the past had all disappeared, sent to be melted down at one time or another. Since it was made, the *cadenas* has been altered on two separate occasions. The first was at the Restoration after the fall of Napoleon, when the dim-witted Louis XVIII replaced the Imperial arms

with the fleur-de-lis, the second in the 1850s, when Napoleon III had the fleur-de-lis taken away and the *cadenas* restored to their original form.

MUSEUMS AND COLLECTIONS

French Empire silver may be seen at the following:

FRANCE
Paris: Louvre
       Musée National du Château de Malmaison
       Musée Nissim de Camondo

GREAT BRITAIN
London: British Museum
       Victoria and Albert Museum

PORTUGAL
Lisbon: Museu de Artes Decorativas
U.S.A.
Detroit: Detroit Institute of Arts
New York: Metropolitan Museum of Art
U.S.S.R.
Leningrad: Hermitage

FURTHER READING

Early Neo-Classicism in France by Sven Eriksen, London, 1974.
French Silver, 1450–1825 by Frank Davis, London, 1970.
Les Grands Orfèvres, Connaissance des Arts, Paris, 1965.
L'Orfèvrerie du XIXe Siècle en Europe by Serge Grandjean, Paris, 1962.

Sheffield Plate

Fig. 1 Wine-cooler, *heavily ornamented with fruiting vines, 1825–50.*
(Private Collection.)

Fig. 2 Soup-tureen *in the form of a turtle, 1790s. Length 22 ins., width 17 ins.*
The shell hinges upwards from the neck. This tureen has a capacity of ten pints.
(City Museum, Sheffield)

Fig. 3 Coffee-pot, *c.1760.*
Pot made from single-sided plate, the lid and foot worked from two pieces of fused plate placed copper to copper, the upper layer of silver turned over to conceal the copper edges, height 11 ins.
(City Museum, Sheffield.)

Fig. 4 Tea and coffee machine with spirit-lamp.
The large globular urn swivels to fill the two smaller ones with hot water. These and the drip-bowl may be removed and used separately.
(Private Collection.)

For one hundred years Sheffield plate enjoyed widespread success among the middle classes as a cheap substitute for sterling silver

Sheffield plating is one of several crafts recognised as entirely English in origin. The discovery that silver and copper could be fused under heat was made in 1742 by Thomas Bolsover, a Sheffield cutler garret-master, who was experimenting with foil and rolled copper plate. With Joseph Wilson as partner, and £170 of borrowed capital, he manufactured silver-plated buttons, buckles and small boxes with pull-off lids. The venture was immediately successful. Subsequently, tableware was manufactured by an apprentice of Bolsover; it was intended for the rising middle classes envious of the sterling silver which graced the homes of the gentry.

Associated though it is with Sheffield, the craft soon became established in Birmingham. By 1756 John Taylor was making buttons, boxes and similar light articles, and by 1762 Matthew Boulton and his partner, John Fothergill, had established plating workshops at Soho.

The plated coating of silver had to be more than a mere film in order to avoid discoloration through contact with the charcoal-heated soldering iron. Until the early 1780s the copper sheet was heavily plated, twenty-four ounces of silver to eight pounds of copper. The silver on the standard quality plate that later came into use for tableware was reduced to ten or twelve ounces. Until the early 1770s copper plate could be silvered on one side only, the interiors of hollow-ware being either tinned or gilded.

The concealment of the raw edges was accomplished in several ways, and it is possible for the collector to distinguish several forms of edge and mount treatment, and thus to date the piece approximately.

With the sheared edge (1743–58), the dark reddish copper edges were concealed beneath a film of silver solder or tin. This proved too insubstantial for everyday objects.

The single-lapped copper edge (1758–80s) was introduced by Joseph Hancock. A layer of silver, thicker than formerly, was extended beyond the edge of the copper to overlap and conceal the raw edge, but this, too, offered little resistance to heavy wear.

The double-lapped copper edge (1768 to the early nineteenth century) was the earliest method of applying separately formed concealment to sheared edges. Copper wire was silver plated and then drawn into a fine thread that could be flattened and soldered to the edge of the silvered plate. So skilfully was this done that after burnishing it was virtually impossible to detect the join.

Pure silver was used for minute details, even on common ware

The silver-lapped edge (1775–1815) was formed by a fine U-shaped wire of sterling silver fitted over the edge of the plate, soldered on both surfaces and the joins burnished until invisible.

Silver stamped mounts (from the early 1790s), patterned in relief by die-stamping, were struck in lengths of four to five inches and filled with lead-tin alloy. Silver mounts of the eighteenth century were in bead and thread patterns and the straight and slanting gadroons of the period. Sterling quality was used for fine work; pure silver mounts decorated common ware, as the plate could be rolled much thinner and stamped without the hazard of splitting in the tool.

Silver stamped mounts during the first fifteen years of the nineteenth century were struck from thick metal so that each section could be fixed without filling the back hollows. By 1805 the scope of design had been widened to include festoon-and-bead, leaf-and-scroll, egg-and-dart, laurel leaf, scallop shell, scroll and other motifs.

Samuel Roberts of Sheffield patented improved silver stamped mounts in 1824. By this method, he and his licensees were enabled to reproduce

the ornate scrolling type of border which had first appeared on silver plate around the mid-eighteenth century. The edge of the ware was first filed to follow the indentations of the mount, the bare copper edge being concealed with drawn silver wire hard-soldered into position and hammered flat until it extended a little beyond the ornamental silver mount which was then applied. Vigorous burnishing of the edges completed the process.

Electrotype mounts date from the mid-1840s. These were made by the electro-deposit process evolved by Elkington of Birmingham; lighter in hue than the sterling silver fused to copper or German silver, a silver-coloured metal that contained no silver at all, they are recognisable for this reason.

Ornamental piercing came in with double-plating

Uncommon designs in Sheffield plate were constructed from silvered wires. This followed George Whateley's invention, patented in 1768, by which slender copper rods, round, flat, square and triangular in section, could be silver plated. Not until an improvement was made after the expiry of the patent in 1782 was wire used extensively. Catalogues illustrate table-baskets, toast-racks and epergnes constructed from plated wires until the 1820s.

Ornamental piercing dates from the introduction of double-plating in the early 1770s; it was used for decorating such articles as cake- and sweetmeat-baskets, epergnes, dish-rings, coasters, sugar-baskets, mustard-pots, salts, mazarines and fish-servers. Saw-cutting proved useless as it exposed the underlying copper. Hand-operated fly-presses were fitted with punches of hard tool-steel so that one layer of silver remained protruding slightly beyond the sheared copper, enabling it to be lapped over and burnished, thus concealing the tell-tale streaks of red. With vigorous burnishing the laps became invisible. At first each motif was

361

pressed individually; from the early 1790s they were struck in small groups. The collector will easily detect this work.

Articles associated with domestic illumination were in great demand in both the eighteenth and nineteenth centuries; the manufacture of candlesticks and candelabra became a specialised branch of the trade. Pillar candlesticks were made by Hancock from 1758, crudely but clearly constructed. Later candlesticks consist of six stamped units soldered together. Die-stamping was used consistently. Until the early 1790s much of this was touched up by hand chasing. As a result, fluting or reeding sometimes appears irregular and care

being used only for the hoops, pans and bezels of the nozzles. This silver was not hallmarked as it did not conform to assay office standards.

Teapots were made in shapes constructed of units easy to assemble, with handles of ivory, ebony, horn or hardwood. Sheffield plate catalogues of the 1790s illustrate forms that had been in use for at least twenty years. Some were corrugated vertically and an attractive, now rare, serpentine series was composed of a variety of concave and convex curves. In another pattern the urn-shaped body tapered to a narrow stem rising from a round tapering foot. By about 1790 the cape teapot had become fashionable in Sheffield plate – a rim or

Fig. 6 **Soup-tureen**, c.1820. Silver mounts and gadrooned borders with turned over edges, height 10 ins. (Victoria and Albert Museum, London.)

Fig. 7 **Cheese-toaster** with hot water compartment, c.1805. Pans 2½ ins. square. (City Museum, Sheffield.)

Fig. 8 **Epergne**, with octagonal mirror plateau, late eighteenth century. Height 20 ins. (Victoria and Albert Museum.)

Fig. 9 **Tea-urn**, with green ivory handles and spigot to the dolphin spout, 1770s. Capacity four quarts. (Victoria and Albert Museum.)

Fig. 5 **Soy frame**, hung with crescent-shaped silver labels for 'Cayon', 'Elder' and 'Lemon', hallmarked 1800. (City Museum, Sheffield.)

is needed not to confuse it with the earlier hand-raised fluting.

Candlesticks in the form of composite architectural pillars date from the early 1770s, the lower section fluted as on the Corinthian form, the upper part cylindrical and decorated in low relief with entwined leaves. Fashionable candlesticks of the 1780s and '90s were designed with circular pillars tapering downward to spreading circular feet; the taper was less acute in later examples. Spiral fluting was an ornamental feature of pillars and feet during the 1780s. Motifs derived from ancient Egypt, such as lotus flowers, decorated a series of cylindrical pillars during the final decade of the century.

Candlestick patterns of the eighteenth century continued for more than a hundred years because of the vast accumulation in Sheffield and Birmingham of steel dies for stamping and pressing various units, many of them ornate adaptations of early Georgian rococo styles in silver. The pattern-books of one firm of manufacturers alone carried nearly two thousand designs for candlesticks.

Between 1815 and the early 1830s it was found profitable to stamp the units from which candlesticks were constructed in paper-thin silver and fill them with lead-tin alloy, plated copper

gallery encircling its lid opening. The lozenge-shaped teapot with a pierced gallery encircling the top of the body and a hingeless cover dates from about 1795.

Argyles (gravy-warmers), which commonly go unrecognised, are collectors' treasures; they date from about 1770. The body resembles that of a small teapot with an excessively long, slender, tubular, swan-neck spout. Four methods were used for keeping the gravy hot within the argyle: a simple hot-water jacket; a central hot-water container; a central box-iron; a hot-water compartment in the base.

During the years of the Regency, Sheffield plate is characterised by expansive representations of winged lions, lion masks and sphinxes against backgrounds of leaf- and wicker-work with much of the convex fluting known as reeding. Shells, dolphins and oak-leaves interspersed with gadroons made fashionable edgings. After 1815 patterns were elaborate but difficult to classify as the range was so extensive. There was much pierced work. During the 1820s much Sheffield plate was decorated with applied work, including the ever-popular fruiting vine, flower bouquets and fruit (Fig. 1).

A special copper was evolved for plating in about

1815, alloyed with a little zinc and lead to lighten its colour and make it softer than the normal quality, yet capable of withstanding the fusing process. This metal, plated with silver, was shaped into attractive hollow-ware by spinning a flat disc against a block of hardwood of the desired shape in a fast-running lathe. The operator forced down the metal with a long shaft of hard wood held in the right hand and extending under the arm, gradually working the metal down until it attained the shape of the block. Puckering was prevented with a wooden tool held in the left hand. Close inspection of a spun piece will often reveal faint concentric circles, although these might have been removed by burnishing. Hollow-ware spun from this metal during the 1820s included large tea- and coffee-urns, wine-coolers and venison-dishes.

In July 1830 Samuel Roberts revolutionised the trade in plated ware by patenting a process in which 'a layer of german silver or other white coloured metal was introduced between the silver and copper.'

This was superseded in 1836 by Anthony Merry's patent in which the copper was omitted entirely, the silver being fused directly to the German silver. This was known as 'British plate' and possessed the attributes of Sheffield plate, including silver mounts, but was harder, more durable, virtually

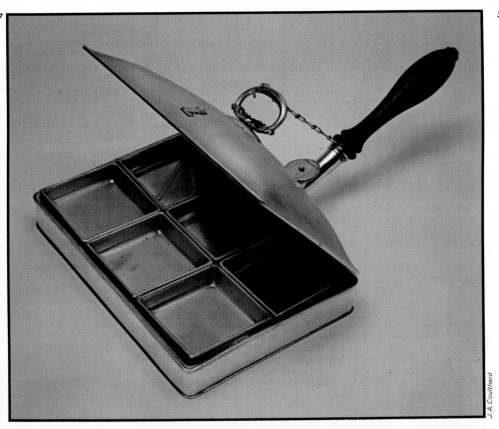

the colour of sterling silver and did not show pink when worn. Among the advantages of British plate was the fact that units could be assembled with hard solder, much less costly than hand-working the seams. Another cost-reducing factor was the small amount of silver required for plating: on copper the silver tended to tinge unless a coating of substantial thickness was applied.

MUSEUMS AND COLLECTIONS
Eighteenth- and nineteenth-century Sheffield Plate may be seen at the following:

Birmingham: Assay Office (by appointment)
City Museum and Art Gallery
London: British Museum
Victoria and Albert Museum
Sheffield: Cutlers' Company
City Museum
York: Castle Museum

FURTHER READING
Antique Sheffield Plate by G. Bernard Hughes, London, 1970.
Old Sheffield Plate by H. Raymond Singleton, Sheffield, 1966.

363

Paul Storr

Fig. 1 **Tea-urn** by Paul Storr, London, 1809–10. Silver with ivory tap-handle. (Victoria and Albert Museum.)

Fig. 2 **Trafalgar Vase** designed by John Flaxman (1755–1826), made by Digby Scott and Benjamin Smith, London, 1805–6. Silver with figures of Britannia Triumphant and a warrior slaying a serpent, inscribed 'Britons Strike Home'. This magnificent classical vase was commissioned by Lloyds Patriotic Fund. (Victoria and Albert Museum.)

Led by the genius of Paul Storr, Regency silversmiths produced magnificent plate that reflected the extravagance of the period

Paul Storr is one of the outstanding figures in the history of English silver, and acclaimed as the greatest silversmith of that extravagant period, the Regency. During his long career, Storr produced a vast quantity of plate for a wide range of patrons, including the Prince Regent, and there is a comprehensive collection of his work at Windsor Castle and Buckingham Palace today. Although he made a lot of simple domestic plate, Storr is best remembered for his ceremonial, classical works, many of them commissioned to mark British naval and military victories. These pieces were often on a monumental scale, and it is greatly to Storr's credit that he managed to keep a perfect balance between form and ornament, especially when one realises that he was working to the designs of distinguished artists and sculptors who appear to have been totally unaware of the limitations of the material.

Storr was born in London in 1771 and apprenticed at the age of fourteen to an Anglo-Swedish silversmith, Andrew Fogelberg of Soho. Here he would have been trained in a style derived from the architect-designer Robert Adam. Fogelberg worked in a delicate and refinedly classical vein. He made great use of the urn-shape, decorating it with swags, garlands and beading, and with a classical medallion relief similar to decoration on contemporary Wedgwood pottery.

Although Storr was working in the manner of his

Fig. 3 **Tureen and cover** *by Paul Storr (1771–1844), London, 1819–20. Silver.*
This handsome tureen in the rococo style has a fluted body decorated with applied foliage and rests on scrolling feet. The massive effect of this small piece is characteristic of Regency silver, particularly that of Storr. (Victoria and Albert Museum, London.)

Fig. 4 **Teapot,** *maker's mark S.H., London, 1812–13. Silver with wooden handle and ivory and wood finial.*
Made in one of the most popular Regency shapes, this simple pot has a matching milk-jug and sugar-bowl. (Victoria and Albert Museum.)

Fig. 5 *Regency silver marks: three variants of the marks of Paul Storr, registered 1792, 1794 and 1833; the mark of Rundell, Bridge and Rundell; of Philip Rundell; and of Digby Scott and Benjamin Smith.*

Fig. 6 **Double-branched candelabrum,** *one of a pair, marked J.A., 1819/20. (Victoria and Albert Museum.)*

master shortly after he finished his apprenticeship in 1792, he rapidly developed his own sturdier interpretation of Classicism. From 1792–96 he worked with William Frisbee in the City of London, and in that year he took over the premises of the silversmith Thomas Pitts in Air Street, Piccadilly. It was here – now working on his own – that Storr made his reputation. His superb craftsmanship attracted a large clientele and he began to produce work for the important firm of Rundell, Bridge and Rundell, as well as making his first contributions to the royal dinner-service.

In 1807 he moved to Dean Street, Soho, probably as the manager of a Rundell workshop there. Although he appears to have been working almost exclusively for Rundells' at this period – he became a partner in 1811 – it is difficult to assess his exact position in the firm, as he continued to call himself 'Storr and Co.' It appears that he valued his independence highly and it was probably due to an infringement upon this that he decided to leave Rundells' in 1819. From that year he worked in Harrison Street, and in 1822 he went into business with John Mortimer of Bond Street, in order to have additional retail premises. This venture was not very successful at the outset – due no doubt to the incompetence of Mortimer – and it was saved only by a substantial loan from John Hunt, who joined the partnership in 1826. From then on the firm flourished, even after Storr's retirement in 1838, eventually becoming Hunt and Roskell, one of the most important silver firms of the Victorian age.

This is not the only link between Paul Storr and the High Victorian period. In 1814 he made a cup to a design by Flaxman and electro-gilded it. This is an isolated example of the early use of an electrical technique which was to revolutionise silver-making after its 'discovery' by the Elkingtons in 1840. Thus Storr, whose work was so firmly rooted in the eighteenth-century tradition, anticipated an important Victorian technical advance by twenty-six years.

He and his fellow silversmiths foreshadowed another Victorian characteristic. In their accurate reproduction of classical ornament, and in the variety of styles they used, they looked forward to the obsessive eclecticism of the mid-nineteenth century. Some of Storr's work is in the rococo style of sixty years before. There was a renewed interest in mid-eighteenth-century art in Regency England,

largely as a result of the French Revolution. Those refugees who had settled in London sold their few salvaged belongings, and there were also important sales abroad, at which there came on the market works of such famous eighteenth-century silversmiths as Meissonnier and the Germains. The silversmiths enthusiastically copied the *rocaille* motifs (Fig. 3) and the *Chinoiseries* which had previously enjoyed such popularity in both England and France. During these years a large amount of plain silver of an earlier date was sent to the silversmiths to be decorated in the revived-rococo manner, a fashion which was to persist throughout the nineteenth century.

Storr could also produce plate in a gothic vein, as some of his ecclesiastical works illustrate. But the style most in demand, the style in which Storr excelled, was the neo-classical.

A. C. Cooper

Fig. 7 **Wine-cooler,** one of a set of four by Paul Storr, London, early nineteenth century. Silver-gilt. (Sotheby and Co., London.)

Fig. 8 **Vase,** designed by Flaxman in the Greek krater shape, made by Paul Storr, London, 1812–13. Silver. Designed in imitation of the cup mentioned in the Idyll of Theocritus, this vase was given by Queen Charlotte to the Prince Regent. (By gracious permission of H.M. the Queen.)

Fig. 9 **Fruit-bowl and stand,** one of a pair by Paul Storr, London, 1810–11. Silver-gilt with glass liner, inscribed 'Rundell Bridge et Rundell Aurifices Regis et Principis Walliae Londini', height 13¾ ins. This piece was part of the ambassadorial silver used by the first Duke of Wellington in Paris. (Wellington Museum, London.)

Fig. 10 **Cake-basket** by Paul Storr, London, early nineteenth century. Silver-gilt; there would probably once have been a glass liner. (Sotheby's.)

366

The successful excavations of Pompeii and Herculaneum in the mid-eighteenth century had been followed by work in Greece, and further excavations revealed fresh discoveries in Egypt. A flood of publications fed the imagination of the designers, silversmiths and their patrons, and silver aped the grandeur of Imperial Rome, the purity of Grecian styles and the exoticism of Egypt. Among the most influential books were Thomas Hope's *Household Furniture* of 1807, Stuart and Revett's *Antiquities of Athens* appearing from 1762, and Denson's *Voyages dans la Basse et Haute Egypte* of 1804. Engravings by Piranesi and etchings by Tatham were also important sources of inspiration, as were the Elgin Marbles, sold to the nation by Lord Elgin in 1816, and Sir William Hamilton's famous collection of classical vases.

'Massiveness . . . the principal characteristic of good plate'

Perhaps the favourite model for silversmiths was the Warwick Vase, discovered at Hadrian's Villa, near Tivoli, in 1770. This immense second-century urn, which was bought by the Earl of Warwick in 1774, was copiously reproduced in ice-pails, centre-pieces, fruit-bowls and presentation cups, especially after Piranesi included it in his *Vasi, Candelabri, Cippi . . .* of 1778. Many other classical urn-shapes were imitated, such as the Greek *krater* (Fig. 8). The Roman lamp reappeared, converted into a spirit-burner beneath hot-water-jugs or plate-warmers. Caryatid figures formed the shafts of candlesticks or the supports of bowls (Fig. 9), and a wealth of classical detailing enveloped silver: the anthemion,

the lion's mask and paw, the Greek key pattern, the Egyptian lotus-flower, the laurel wreath, the acanthus-leaf 'scroll, the rosette, the classical mask, gadrooning and reeding were all liberally employed (Fig. 1).

Embossing and heavy casting were favoured, lending a sculptural, weighty feeling to the designs. This had been advocated by Tatham in his *Designs for Ornamental Plate* of 1806, in which he wrote: 'Massiveness [is] the principal characteristic of good plate'; he had also stressed the importance of a good finish achieved through fine chasing, and his words had been effective. Any piece by Storr – or indeed by his distinguished contemporaries such as Benjamin Smith or Digby Scott – will bear up well under close examination, as a result of this superb surface detailing.

Benjamin Smith and Digby Scott both worked for the great firm of Rundell, Bridge and Rundell, which played such a vital part in the development of Regency plate. Although Storr was an exceptional silversmith and had made a good name for himself in the Air Street days, it is unlikely that he would have enjoyed such extensive royal patronage had he not been in the employ of Rundells'.

Philip Rundell of Bath was apprenticed to the firm of Theed and Pickett of Ludgate Hill, London. In 1772 he became a partner and in 1785 he gained control of the business. John Bridge had, by then, already joined the firm, and he became a partner in 1788. According to an account later written by an employee, Rundell was ambitious and unpleasant, and Bridge was the affable diplomatist who secured the patronage of George III in 1789. The King brought the firm to the attention of his son, who was to become their chief patron. Indeed, the

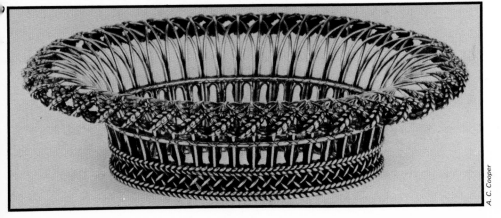

A. C. Cooper

A. C. Cooper

Prince Regent commissioned such lavish quantities from Rundells' that he was roundly accused of unnecessary extravagance by the Whig opposition. His expenditure seems enormous, even today; for example a pair of large candelabra of classical inspiration, commissioned from Storr in 1809, cost him £4,003 15s (Fig. 12).

Agents at Constantinople, St. Petersburg, Smyrna and Baghdad

In 1803 the Prince of Wales, soon to become Regent, commissioned the royal dinner-service from Rundells'. This was the work of Paul Storr, Digby Scott and Benjamin Smith, who worked together between 1802 and 1810, and James Smith (who was later to work jointly with Benjamin Smith, see Fig. 11). By 1807, enough of this was completed to be put on exhibition in the Ludgate Hill showrooms. This must have fired the enthusiasm of many new patrons; no doubt a large number of courtiers followed the Prince's lead, and soon Rundells' were inundated with orders. The workshops were expanded, and agents and correspondents established in Paris, Vienna, St. Petersburg, Constantinople, Smyrna, Baghdad, Calcutta, Bombay and South America. The firm searched for fresh inspiration and new ideas with which to meet the pressing demand. They began to invite a number of distinguished artists, including John Flaxman (Figs. 2, 8 and 12) and Thomas Stothard, to submit designs. Many of these were used for the grandiose presentation pieces which formed their chief output during these years. Appropriate classical themes were re-used; battle-scenes were reproduced from classical sculpture, and the winged figure of Victory was frequently depicted. Although the subject-matter was clearly apt, the results often appear sadly lifeless to us today.

Sixty-six Trafalgar vases valued at £300 each

Lloyds Patriotic Fund commissioned Digby Scott and Benjamin Smith to make sixty-six Trafalgar vases for presentation to those who had played an important part in the battle. They were made in 1805-6, and they were valued at £300 each (Fig. 2). Nelson and Wellington were both presented with numerous trophies. Among the most spectacular were the silver-gilt candelabra and shield commissioned by the Merchants and Bankers of the City of London for Wellington. Stothard designed them and Green, Ward and Green – rivals of Rundells' – employed Benjamin Smith to make them. The candelabra, which are on exhibition at the Wellington Museum, are approximately four feet high, and the shield measures forty inches in diameter.

Despite the huge scale of these ceremonial pieces, the general tendency in the field of domestic plate during the Regency and reign of George IV was towards squatter proportions. This is reflected in the tea-service which became an important feature in every upper- and middle-class household as the price of tea fell. The teapot, often of oval shape, became lower and wider (Fig. 4). Its decoration of lobing or fluting emphasised this, as did the stumpy spout and low-domed lid often set within

Fig. 11 **Pair of sugar-vases** by
Benjamin and James Smith,
London, 1810–11. Silver-gilt.
Like the fruit-bowl and stand in
Figure 9, these magnificent
silver-gilt pieces were part of the
Wellington ambassadorial
service.
(Wellington Museum.)

Fig. 12 **Candelabrum,** one of a
pair designed by Flaxman and
made by Paul Storr, London,
1809–11. Silver, height 51 ins.
Bought by the Prince Regent in
1811, this astonishing creation
depicts the guarding of the
apples of the Hesperides. The
pair was bought for £4,003 15s.
(By gracious permission of
H.M. the Queen.)

a wide, everted rim. The other objects on the tea-
tray followed suit: milk-jug and sugar-bowl were
often made *en suite* with the teapot; even the hot-
water-jug, although much higher, was given a
bottom-heavy appearance. Dinner-services followed the same pattern, with low, wide entrée-dishes
and tureens, and heavy baskets for fruit and bread
(Fig. 10). The quantity of Regency silver dinner-
plates, sauce-boats, salvers, salt-cellars, wine-
coolers (Fig. 7), coasters, coffee-pots and numerous
other household goods, bears witness to the widespread vogue for plate which swept England during
these years. Silver was admired not only for its
intrinsic beauty, but also for the prestige it brought.
It became a status symbol of a growing middle class
to whom, with the development of Sheffield plate
and cheap mass-production, it was now readily
available.

MUSEUMS AND COLLECTIONS

Silver by Paul Storr may be seen at the following:
GREAT BRITAIN
Leeds:	Harewood House
London:	Victoria and Albert Museum
	Wellington Museum

FURTHER READING

**The William and Morrie Moss Collection of
Paul Storr Silver** by Morrie A. Moss, Florida,
1972.
Paul Storr: The Last of the Goldsmiths by
Norman M. Penzer, London, 1971.
An Introduction to Old English Silver by Judith
Banister, London, 1965.

Tea & Coffee Services

Fig. 1 **Teapot** by Edward Farrell, London, 1833–34. Silver. Best remembered for his tea- and coffee-sets on which he set bucolic figures taken from paintings by Teniers, Farrell brought to the human figure a good-humoured naivety and lack of classical sophistication which had a great influence on other silversmiths of his day. (Victoria and Albert Museum, London.)

A microcosm of the changing world of art and artisans, Victorian tea- and coffee-sets help us to understand the design, artistry, manufacture, social demands, taste and art philosophy of the age

A. C. Cooper

Fig. 2 **Milk-jug** *by Mackay, Cunningham and Co., Edinburgh, 1879. Silver-gilt. Inspired by the hitherto unseen Japanese exports which began to arrive in Europe during the 1850s, Japonaiserie silver was in vogue for about thirty years, reaching its peak of excellence in the 1870s. (Mrs. V. J. Hawkins Collection.)*

Fig. 3 **Coffee-pot** *by John Watson, Sheffield, 1818. Silver. This ornate coffee-pot is an early example of the naturalistic style. (Sotheby and Co., London.)*

Fig. 4 **Teapot** *by Edward Farrell, London, 1832. By comparison to Figure 1, this teapot is of unusually plain design. It is probably based on an early eighteenth century Dutch example. (Sotheby's.)*

Fig. 5 **Tea-set** *by Messrs. Hunt and Roskell, London, 1874–75. Silver with chased decoration signed by Aristide Barré. (Thomas Lumley Ltd., London.)*

Fig. 6 **Tea-set** *of registered design, by Messrs. Elkington and Co., Birmingham, 1875. Silver, parcel-gilt engraved in the Japanese manner.*
Pairs of cups and saucers en suite, *Royal Worcester, 1877. Porcelain with tooled gold decoration. (Michael Parkington Collection.)*

Fig. 7 **Tea- and coffee-set,** *probably designed by E. H. Baily, made by Messrs. Storr, Mortimer and Hunt, London, 1849. Silver. (Sotheby's.)*

Fig. 8 **Design for a teapot** *by Christopher Dresser for Messrs. Elkington and Co., 1899. (Messrs. Elkington and Co., London.)*

It is probably fair to say that tea- and coffee-sets formed a major part of the nineteenth-century silversmiths' output. For this reason they are of particular relevance as a study of different forms and fashions and mixtures of styles. This was an age of great prosperity, when the general rule was one of display and when many considered the ownership of such items to be a necessity rather than a mere luxury, either through self-conscious knowledge of good taste or in imitation of it.

So, when George Eliot likens an attitude of Eppie's kitten in *Silas Marner* to a 'design for a jug-handle', she points rather to the mood of the age than to any specific item, although it was in fact used on a milk-jug in the shape of a dairy churn made by George Angell, and registered as a patent design, just eight years later, in 1868 (Fig. 9). This is not to say that Angell adapted the novelist's ideas into reality, but it is good proof of the popularity of those whimsical designs which were in part the predictable outgrowth of the strict naturalistic forms beloved by designers such as E. H. Baily, who worked for Rundell, Bridge and Rundell, and subsequently for Hunt and Roskell, in the days of its widest acceptance around 1840.

From the severe lines of late eighteenth-century styles, and the more classical feeling of the following fifteen years, the naturalistic manner evolved, not so much as a progression from that style, but more as a rebellion against it. Perhaps the first recognisable glimmerings of this are reflected in the work of Edward Farrell.

Farrell, working from premises in Covent Garden, was a silversmith with decidedly novel ideas who, quite early on, produced elaborate pieces of silver and silver-gilt in defiance of the accepted norm (Fig. 4). His designs usually incorporated human figures, with a total lack of the classical sophistication exploited by Paul Storr. He instilled a freeness into the treatment of both human forms and vegetation, thus providing a natural bridge between classical and naturalistic forms (Fig. 3). The latter eventually slid into rococo scrolls, Louis XIV shapes and the Moorish, gothic, Elizabethan, Renaissance and other styles, and the mixtures thereof, that flourished alongside one another by the time of the Great Exhibition in 1851.

Perhaps one of Farrell's happiest notions was the design, in 1824, for a pair of silver-gilt cream-spoons, the bowls of which were scallop shells, the apple-tree handles raided by mischievous cherubs. Now, however, he is best remembered for the manufacture of those bulbous tea- and coffee-sets upon which he set bucolic figures taken from

paintings by Teniers (Fig. 1). Similar sets, proof of the demand for his work, were made in various sizes by several firms throughout the remainder of the century. One, by George Angell, was shown at the International Exhibition of 1862; others, made by Messrs. Hands and Son, and Hunt and Roskell, have been recorded as late as the mid-1890s.

The naturalistic style was reflected in revivals of popular designs from the eighteenth century such as the exuberant forms of rococo and the streamlined elegance of neo-classicism. The lines of the basic style were contorted with wavy rims, scrolled handles and elaborate ornamentation in the form of leaves, flowers and fruiting vines. The acanthus leaf and the grapevine were particularly admired, with heavily veined leaves and generous bunches of grapes clinging to every surface.

A fluted, gourd-shaped body supported by four flowering plants

Natural forms, used on silver and plated wares, promoted the arrival of gourd-shapes, which appeared with or without flutes, plain or embellished (Fig. 12). The variations of expression that manifest themselves round this basic shape were seemingly endless. One is apt to agree with Ralph N. Wornum, in his essay on the Great Exhibition, that 'it is a morbid taste to hunt after variety for variety's sake'. However, a recently noted teapot made by John Angell at a slightly earlier date had a fluted, gourd-shaped body, held up by four flowering plants, the stems of which extended downwards to form the feet. Furthermore, a suggested design for a teapot by J. Strudwick published in the *Art-Journal* in 1849 reveals a body of similar form but with a pedestal foot wreathed in leaves, while the handle and spout represent the twisted stalks of a plant also partially wrapped in foliage.

At about this time, 'the one thing wanted', wrote one critic, was 'GOOD DESIGN; that is', he continued, 'the "all in all" required by so many of our manufacturers'.

Unfortunately, the manufacturers often lacked artistic inspiration, while the artists were usually completely ignorant of the difficulties of translating a design on paper into the article in silver. This situation was somewhat relieved by firms like Elkington and Co., who employed the artists L. Morel Ladeuil, A. A. Willms and others, to oversee their art departments.

An early case of ornament unfitted to the shape and surface upon which it appeared was the well-known Anthia pattern tea- and coffee-service. This

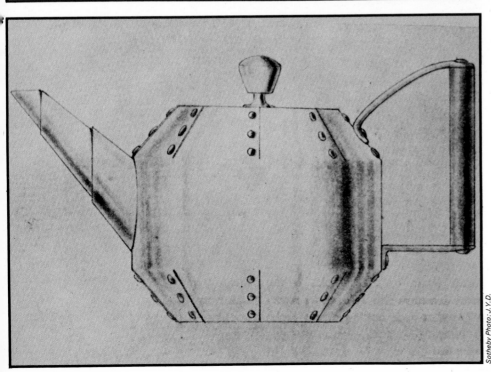

was electro-plated, made by Messrs. Broadhead & Atkin of Sheffield. The designs were by the sculptor John Bell, who was roundly criticised in his efforts to imitate nature for allowing it to assert its own supremacy. Clearly, then, natural designs were to be used with care and discretion if they were not to overwhelm the objects.

Perhaps a better design inspired by nature, though rather more outrageous, was the massive tea- and coffee-set which appeared at Sotheby's in 1967 (Fig. 7). This, made by Messrs. Storr, Mortimer and Hunt in 1849, was probably the work of E. H. Baily, who made full use of large and various shell-forms and the natural grey effects of chased silver, the handles and feet simulating coral.

In contrast to this there is the electro-plated tea-kettle displayed by F. H. Thompson, of Glasgow, at the Great Exhibition. Of this piece, the *Art-Journal* wryly commented: '. . . it is something to find manufacturers forsaking the worn out paths of their predecessors for new ones . . .'. Indeed, the kettle, yet another variation of the gourd form, is surprising in its absurdity, for its large, compressed circular body dwindles down to a point on the head of a figure of Time who strides, scythe in hand, apparently unaware of the unwieldy object that he supports.

Convolvulus blooms and miniature Chinamen seated upon tea-chests

By the late 1840s, one firm in London, Messrs. A. B. Savory and Son, in Cornhill, were offering for sale tea- and coffee-sets of silver in fifty different designs. Prices were £35.12.6d. for a complete Uxbridge pattern tea- and coffee-set, while the Thalia pattern sets were a little more expensive, at £42.10s. Today, similar sets might realize £300 to £400.

It is difficult to distinguish one firm's output from another's. Favourite features appeared again and again, such as tea- and coffee-pot finials modelled as convolvulus blooms, or miniature Chinamen seated upon tea-chests. As in former times, however, manufacturing areas such as Dublin or Sheffield tended to adapt designs to a peculiar local fashion. This was broken by the tendency of the larger firms to supply designs reflecting London styles through their provincial offices.

Joseph Angell and Sons, of Panton Street,

Haymarket, however, had a more or less distinguishable house style, inasmuch as many of their productions displayed more angular and audacious forms than their rivals. For instance, the set they supplied for presentation in 1846 to a retiring Glasgow auctioneer, Alexander Skirving, was of a fluted cylindrical shape, with strange flared bases and foliate handles. Reports of the actual presentation of many such articles can be traced in journals and newspapers of the time, often with interesting results.

The tendency later was towards classical forms of ornament

The Great Exhibition was a turning-point away from the accepted ideas of the preceding thirty years. Succeeding years saw the revival of classical forms, which, in spite of the artists' mistaken

Designs were not limited to those in imitation of antiquity, however. There are many extant examples, in both silver and electro-plate, which give us some idea of the variety of Victorian novelty. Some were made with textured surfaces simulating basket-weave; some, such as those from C. S. Harris, held a firmer grip on the more traditional styles of the eighteenth century; others were chased in the Indian manner with a profusion of tight leafage and mysterious multi-limbed deities; and there is at least one three-piece tea-set modelled as fortified medieval towers, with castellated upper borders and bodies decorated with brickwork dotted with ornamental arrow-slits.

At the same period, Continental designers and craftsmen were given greater opportunities by firms of artistic integrity.

At the time when Japanese prints were having a profound impact on the world of the Impres-

Fig. 9 *Milk-jug by George Angell, London, 1868. Silver. Of registered design, this delightful jug is in the shape of a dairy churn. The kitten handle suggests a passage from George Eliot's* Silas Marner *in which she likens an attitude of Eppie's kitten to a 'design for a jug handle'. Such designs were a predictable outgrowth of the naturalistic forms of the 1840s. (Sotheby's.)*

Fig. 10 *The family at tea, English, c.1875. Photograph. The tea-party came into its own as a social occasion during the Victorian era. It was an age of great prosperity when the general rule was one of display; many people who chose with a certain self-conscious knowledge of good taste, or more often, in imitation of that same inspired selectivity, considered the ownership of elaborate tea- and coffee-sets to be a necessity rather than a mere luxury. Here the tea-table is laden not only with fine porcelain, but also with a silver teapot, cream-jug, cake- and sugar-baskets and cutlery of all descriptions. (Rev. John G. Strang Collection.)*

Sotheby Photo: J.Y.D.

intentions, were hardly a serious effort to reproduce the purer Greek ornament which had caused so much excitement during the dotage of George III. It was during this period, from about 1850 to 1880, that the facility for artistic eclecticism of the nineteenth-century silversmith is perhaps seen at its best. A coffee-pot, registered as a patent design by Messrs. Cartwright and Woodward in 1876, is a good example, for below a band of Vitruvian scrolls the body is decorated with stylised vultures' wings and other motifs of the Near East. This feeling was probably influenced by the political situation and the growing success of excavators of early remains along the Nile. A design for a milk-jug, also in the same flavour, from the workshops of J. B. Hennell, of Charlotte Street, Fitzroy Square, is in the form of a grotesque female figure. Neither harpy nor sphinx, she nestles comfortably, arms folded, on three truncated supports (Fig. 11).

sionists, a Japanese influence was felt in the more domestic world of tea-sets. Elkingtons were quick to realise the potential of the style for the popular market and produced several tea-sets with matching fan-shaped trays, decorated with bamboo, fans and sprays of cherry blossom.

On the other hand, something more profound, perhaps even prophetic, appeared in the work of Christopher Dresser. Understanding the elemental nature of Japanese design, as opposed merely to its decorative qualities, he produced work of a sophisticated nature. His style, unmistakable in its ruthless utilitarian appearance, seems to be remote from the world of over-ripe, fancy-dress silver (Fig. 8). Finding a sustained thread of acceptance, it had to weave its way through all the vagaries of Art Nouveau, all the shoddiness of steam-pressed goods, before finally reasserting itself in the sunburst effects of Art Deco. It is with

Fig. 11 **Milk-jug** *by J. B. Hennell, London, 1877. Cast and chased silver.*
Made in the Egyptian manner, this grotesque female figure, neither harpy nor sphinx, nestles comfortably with folded arms on three truncated supports. (Private Collection.)

Fig. 12 **Tea-kettle and lampstand with burner** *by Messrs. Barnard, London, c.1852. Silver. (Major D. S. B. Skene Collection.)*

Christopher Dresser that the tea-set essentially arrives in the twentieth century, reflecting a design, and a philosophy of design, which intrinsically rejected the banality and whimsicality of so much High Victorian art.

In the 'nineties, however, popular demand for silver tea- and coffee-sets was abating. Changing social conditions and the economic recessions decreased the demand for silver, and accordingly the enthusiasm of designer and manufacturer alike was dampened. Consequently, silver tea-set production was reduced to a shadow of its former status, styles tending to be repetitions rather than creations. With the tedium of its own mannerism, silver design quickly became almost a caricature of itself except within the circles of the Arts and Crafts Movement. The boldness of the 1850s and 1860s developed into the aridity of the 1880s and 1890s. Apart from the work of Christopher

Dresser, good productions, often Continental in design, are by comparison very few.

MUSEUMS AND COLLECTIONS

A selection of Victorian silver and plate tea- and coffee-sets may be seen at the Victoria and Albert Museum, London.

FURTHER READING

Coffee-pots and Tea-pots for the Collector by Henry Sandon, Edinburgh, 1973.
Victorian Electroplate by Shirley Bury, London, 1971.
Modern Silver Throughout the World, 1880–1967 by Graham Hughes, London, 1967.
Victorian Silver and Silver-Plate by Patricia Wardle, London, 1963.

Arts and Decoration

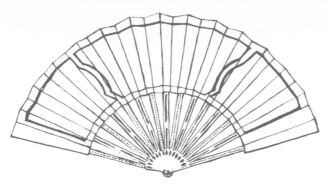

The recurring themes of this book have been style and craftsmanship, continuously reflected in the furnishings and ornaments with which men and women have surrounded themselves for centuries. It has only been possible to provide an outline of the rich world of antiques and the decorative arts. This final section presents a sampling of the many creative traditions which did not fit precisely into the basic categories of the book, but which were too interesting and too important in their own right to be overlooked.

For hundreds of years the Western world has had a passionate interest in things from the Orient such as silks, porcelain, bronzes, all manner of ornaments and paintings. Ornamental jade, carved and polished to silken smoothness, was fashioned by Chinese craftsmen since antiquity. Jade, which is obtained from the minerals jadeite and hephrite, is extremely hard and therefore the skill required to cut and carve it is all the more amazing. Valued more highly than gold, Emperors delighted in ornamental jade and court patronage of the jade carvers enabled the craft to flourish. In addition to the popular animals and birds of legend, they made delicate ornamental table screens, goldfish bowls, dragon vases and miniature objects such as buckles and snuff bottles.

From Japan came carvings of another kind – the highly individual kimono fastenings – *netsuke* – and the exquisitely detailed lacquer seal cases – *inro* – which were suspended from the *netsuke* by cords and a sliding bead – the *ojime*. Originally made of shells and small pieces of wood, the *netsuke* gradually became decorative as well as useful. They were fashioned from ivory, metal, rare woods and other natural materials into delightful mythological figures, sea monsters and favourite saints.

Soft furnishings and fabrics have played an important part in arts and decorations since antiquity. The most beautiful carpets in the world are generally considered to be those from Persia, made of wool and silk in rich colours and intricately knotted by hand. Magnificent hunting carpets featured animals and scenes of the chase, while vase and garden carpets strewn with bright flowers and garlands made them acceptable substitutes for the real thing.

Russian women produced sumptuous embroideries in the centuries following the adoption of Christianity. The subjects were mainly religious and the altar cloths, icons and funerary palls were made of rich velvets, silks and brocades lavishly covered with fine gold and silver stitchery and precious stones.

Tapestry weaving flourished in Europe from the Middle Ages and by the late seventeenth century, French tapestries were rating among the finest wall hangings being produced in Europe. The handsome silk and woollen masterpieces of the Gobelins and Beauvais factories – the Gobelins made royal tapestries and Beauvais those for the court and French society – were gracing the walls of palaces and great houses in France and abroad. Paintings by famous artists of the day were favourite subjects and the overall design included a woven frame. By the 1730s, the Beauvais tapestries were reflecting the rococo vogue for pastoral and romantic paintings in the manner of François Boucher. The tapestries woven at Aubusson were of coarser weave and materials, making them less expensive to produce and very suitable for popular landscapes, pastorals and hunting scenes. Furniture was frequently upholstered in tapestry to match the wall hangings and furniture coverings were produced at both Beauvais and Aubusson.

American quilts and coverlets are a stitched record of the nation's history in the nineteenth century. Woven coverlets were made by itinerant craftsmen who often incorporated simple motifs and initials into the design. Quilts were pieced together from scraps of fabric to form colourful patchwork patterns, and stitched to a warm backing. The finest were those of appliqué and the plain ones that depended for their beauty on the design of the finely executed padded stitching, the trapunto quilts.

Miniature objects have always held a fascination because of the skill and fastidious workmanship required to produce them. Such details can be found on the tiny enamelled boxes and trinkets produced in eighteenth-century Battersea and Birmingham, or in the exquisite decorations painted on French fans of the same period. Jewel-like miniature paintings produced in Persia were made by the book illustrators who executed the poems and legends of ancient Persia in brilliant colours and gold leaf.

The combined skills of scientists and craftsmen were utilised in clock and watchmaking. Together they produced useful mechanical instruments which were often works of art. An early clock for the home was the English long-case or grandfather clock with a weight-driven movement protected inside a wooden case and the mechanism inside a hood. The long-case clock with its brass dial and fine cabinetwork was an important piece of furniture and many distinguished cabinet-makers produced them. Late eighteenth-century French clocks were magnificent in bronze d'or or marble and of rare shapes and mechanical ingenuity.

American clock-making, which did not come into its own until the nineteenth century, was concerned with mass-production techniques and many unusually shaped and relatively inexpensive shelf clocks were produced. The pillar and scroll and banjo clocks were the first purely American designs, but later styles included Gothic, ogee, steeple and acorn clocks. Watchmaking suffered too much competition from the finely crafted English watches of the day, but eventually cheap, accurate 'dollar watches' made it possible for everyone to own a personal timepiece.

The Victorian home was a treasure trove of small ornaments, decorative knick-knacks, novelties, useful boxes and elaborate furniture. Fitted boxes were beautifully made of figured woods inlaid with brass and ivory or of Tunbridge Ware, a unique type of marquetry developed in Tunbridge Wells. No home was complete without ornate papier-mâché tray sets, letter racks or pipe boxes all made of specially treated moulded paper, painted and varnished to look like Oriental lacquer.

Jewellery, which typifies personal style, is a fitting conclusion to the section. The perfection of diamond-cutting techniques in the middle of the eighteenth century led to the creation of spectacular earrings, brooches, necklaces and hair ornaments in an age when men and women were indulging in elaborate self-adornment. The colours of rubies, sapphires and other precious stones were intensified by the aid of foil backings and enclosed mounts. By the end of the nineteenth century, the decorative trend was the restless mood of Art Nouveau and this was perfectly reflected in the jewellery of the period with its dragonfly corsages, pearl and ivory pendants, cloisonné enamel and moonstone butterfly brooches and flowing, jewelled hair ornaments.

Ornamental Jade

Ornamental
Jade

Fig. 1 **Table screen**, *Chinese,
eighteenth century. White jade
with an agate tree, a narrow
green jade frame incised with
gilt rectangular designs and
inlaid with small bats in pink
coral, on an ivory stand, height
without stand 10 ins.,
width 7¾ ins.
Table screens were used by
scholars as they wrote their
scrolls. They protected the
unrolled scroll from the splash
of ink, and steadied the
manuscript.
(Spink and Son Ltd., London.)*

For thousands of years, Chinese
craftsmen have been shaping jade
into useful and ornamental objects
of great textural quality and beauty
which still delight us today

Some three thousand years ago, the Chinese were
shaping pebbles of jade into mystic symbols
associated with their religious rituals. Today,
jade, or *wu*, is still cherished as being more
estimable than jewels, more precious than gold.
The Chinese turn a piece of jade about in their
hands, revelling in its surface texture, and
strike it to enjoy the sonorous ring. This subtle
appreciation is virtually unknown by western
collectors of jade.

Jade is the conventional name given to two
colourful minerals, aggregates of microscopically
small crystals, similar externally, and so hard that
they cannot be scratched with a steel blade. These
semi-precious stones, jadeite and nephrite, are
chemically quite distinct substances and both vary
in colour from nearly white to very dark green, and
from reddish-grey to black. When cut and highly
polished they range from the translucent to the
almost opaque, and glow with a rich sheen.

Originally, jade was found in the river beds and
soil of China itself in the neighbourhood of
Peking. For the past seven centuries, jadeite has
been obtained mainly from quarries sunk in the
peaks of the Kachin country of Upper Burma, near
the Chindwin River. It is quarried in the open by the
primitive method of fire-setting. Large fires are
lit in deep natural cavities of the rock and allowed to
burn throughout the day. At nightfall the fires are
extinguished; the intense cold of the night then
causes the rock to split into portable lumps.
Nephrite is quarried principally to the south of
Yarkand, towards the borders of Kashmir in the
Kun Lun Mountains of Chinese Turkestan.

The very hardness of these minerals is responsible
for the rainbow surface-lustre of carved jade,
the compactness of its closely inter-woven fibres
making the jade carver's craft one of vast effort
and painstaking care. Long tedious months could
be spent by jade-workers in converting a crude
stone or pebble into a work of art.

Ancient jade displays a wider variety of colours
than does that quarried in recent centuries, often
presenting a combination of three, four or five hues.
The more distinct colours a piece displays, the
greater its appeal to collectors. Jade carved later
than the middle of the Ming period is found in
few colours, the more common being milky-white,
both semi-transparent and the opaque type
termed 'mutton-fat'; white opaque; very light,
semi-transparent yellow; semi-transparent or
mottled green; opaque grey and black.

The precise dating of jade carved during these
periods is difficult, although geologists can
analyse the mineral itself and deduce its date and
original source. The dates of the first and
final workings of individual quarries have been
tabulated. Jade worked since the late sixteenth
century lacks the patina of age which distinguishes
carvings of the previous geometrical and naturalistic
periods. Baroque designs for the European
market date from after the middle of the sixteenth
century.

Treadle-operated cutting machinery was used
from this period until the end of the Ch'ien-lung
era (1736–95). Jade so worked may be recognised,
on close examination, by the almost invisible marks
left by the cutting tool. In openwork and lavish
carving, the tools leave irregular tell-tale tracks
revealing their method of application. Sawing and
drilling by treadle power leave surface pittings,
usually imperceptible except under a glass. Cavities
can never be entirely symmetrical.

Jade attained a rare perfection in the Ming dynasty

Collectors of carved jade are seldom able to
acquire examples made earlier than the Ming
dynasty (1368–1644), when jade attained a rarely
equalled perfection. Carefully balanced shapes,
colours and carving make them pure marvels of
craftsmanship, yet give an impression of simplicity.
Decorations include dragons, cranes, peacocks,
lotus flowers, foliage and animals, standing out from
the surfaces of flower vases and water dishes in
naturalistic relief. Models might be adapted from
ancient bronzes – rhomboid, quadrangular or oval –
with indented outlines and carving invariably
corresponding with that of the period copied.

Fig. 2 *Buffalo*, Chinese, *seventeenth century. Green jade, length about 5 ins.*
Buffalos were a popular subject for carvers; they were considered to be river gods.
(Victoria and Albert Museum, London.)

Fig. 3 *Circular table screen*, *one of a pair, Chinese, eighteenth century. Dark green spinach jade with lighter green flecking, diameter 9¾ ins. Superbly carved on each side in low relief with flowers and rocks, butterflies, bats and other insects, these beautiful screens would have been placed in windows as ornaments. (Spink's.)*

Chinese jade carved after the accession of K'ang-hsi in 1662 was robustly modelled with floral work and intended solely for decorative purposes. The Emperor delighted in jade ornaments; his grandson Ch'ien-lung encouraged jade sculpture in the round. Nobles and rich merchants naturally followed his example and patronised the jade-carvers. K'ang-hsi's successor, Yung-cheng (1723–35), preferred designs of extreme elegance, with flamboyant craftsmanship, usually lacking the strength required for practical use. Decorations, carved in low relief or engraved, are of symbolical interest, unlike floral patterns. Ch'ien-lung (1736–95) jade-carvers reached a peak of technical perfection approaching the miraculous.

Men and animals were carved in the round from late in the Ming era until early in the nineteenth century. These pieces were larger and heavier than formerly, many displaying a marvellous sense of motion, thus marking the passing of the static symbolical work. Statuettes and figures in relief in the main represent illustrious divinities and other celestial dignitaries. Figures of the Pa-seen, or Eight Taoist Immortals, supposed to render assistance to those in distress, were in continual demand. The majority were carved as single subjects and exhibited upright on low pedestals of carved wood. More precious were the groups, each of the eight figures succeeding the other in the ascent to the blissful regions, and placed on a pedestal carved to represent clouds. Pedestals for supporting decorative jades from the late seventeenth century were carved from single blocks of eagle-wood from Ceylon (now Sri Lanka). This rare wood, highly valued in China, is heavy, close-grained and pale yellow in hue, with the heart and isolated elongated patches in intense black.

Animal carvings in jade include monsters from early Chinese mythology; these were less massive and more elegant in design than early in the K'ang-hsi period. For instance, in accordance with Chinese court etiquette, the fearsome five-clawed

·Fig. 4 *Kuan-yin, Goddess of Mercy, Ch'ien-lung (1736–95). Green jade with ruby eyes. Although Kuan-yin is often portrayed as a phoenix, she is here seen as a parrot (Peh-ying wu) standing on a rock. (By gracious permission of H.M. The Queen.)*

Fig. 5 *Bowl and cover, Chinese, eighteenth century. Palest celadon jade, diameter over. rim 6¼ ins. The turned-down rim is carved in open-work with lambrequin panels containing Buddhist emblems of Happy Augury. (Spink's.)*

dragon was restricted to the exclusive use of the emperor and his sons, princes of the first and second ranks; the four-clawed dragon was the prerogative of the princes of the third and fourth ranks; the three-clawed dragon was reserved for the nobility.

Variations of type are numerous, such as hornless dragons, those with one or two horns resembling deer's antlers, and winged dragons. Some dragons have tigers' claws and their bodies covered with scales which resemble those of a carp. Dragons and tigers represent the God of Wealth. The phoenix omen of prosperity and harmony, until early in the eighteenth century was usually perched on a tree; in the Ch'ien-lung period it was largely associated with Kuan-Yin, the Goddess of Mercy, and other immortals.

The horse, one of the signs of the zodiac, was an important Taoist emblem, not widely carved in jade until the Ch'ien-lung period. Group carvings, with riders, are found; others are

seen in the 'flying gallop', with four legs outstretched. Other animals included deer, elephants, bears, goats, monkeys, badgers, boars, cats, foxes and the lion or dog of Fo, the latter held to be the defender of law and order and guardian of sacred buildings. Buffalos are considered to be river gods and are usually represented recumbent as though bathing (Fig. 2).

Goldfish found a place in the home of every well-to-do Chinaman. The Emperor Ch'ien-lung apparently possessed a gigantic goldfish bowl of jade, six feet in circumference, cut from a single boulder. Goldfish bowls were usually encircled with carvings of carp, the fabled king of fish capable of changing into a dragon. The Chinese regarded the carp or goldfish as the symbol of vigour and endurance. The carved fish is often shown swimming upstream against the current. Twin fish in a single carving represent happy wedded bliss; goldfish bowls so decorated were very popular as wedding gifts.

Incense burners of three, four or five tiers were used as fumigators in temples and for private use. The lowest tier, supported on three short legs, was a solid bowl in which the incense was burned. Each separate tier, fitting exactly into the one below, was ornately carved and skilfully pierced to permit the emission of the fragrant fumes. The unpierced surfaces of Ch'ien-lung incense burners were carved to display as much symbolism as possible: peaches, bats, lotus flowers, fungi and swastikas were widely used.

Musical jades, resonant carvings associated with the worship of the deities of heaven and earth, had been made for a thousand years before the Ch'ien-lung period, when they were widely reproduced. A single sonorous jade might be placed on the Moon Terrace of a Confucian temple. It was struck with

6

Fig. 6 *Pouring-vessel and cover, Chinese, eighteenth century. Jade encrusted with gilt metal and precious stones.*
In 1741, a group of expert Indian jade-carvers and jewel-setters came to Peking, where they initiated Chinese craftsmen into the arts of inlaying fine tracery in gold and setting jewels against gold foil. The school they founded was called the Hsi Fan Tsi, *or Indian School of jade-carvers.*
(Victoria and Albert Museum.)

a mallet at the end of each verse to assist the choir leader. A set of sixteen stones of different sizes and thicknesses formed the stone chime, a continuation of the custom of the emperor wearing a jade hat with nine strings of jade beads which emitted a range of notes by hitting one another as he walked.

Elaborate sets of equipment for a scholar's table were made. These included the palette, an oval slab of jade with a depression in one end; the ink jar and water-pot; the hand rest; the shallow oblong pen-box; the paperweight, usually a river pebble carved in the form of a mountain with fearsome dragons, lions and mythical monsters; and the table screen (Fig. 1), which was a square tablet of jade carved with an all-over mythical scene, set vertically in a stand. It protected the unrolled scroll from the splash of ink and steadied the manuscript. Similar circular or oblong screens, carved on both sides, were placed in windows as ornaments (Fig. 3).

The Mogul emperors of Hindustan (1526–1707) were fascinated by the splendour of Chinese jade carvings. Imperial workshops devoted solely to this work were established in Delhi, sage-green and white jadeites being imported from Burma. Native jewellers immediately seized upon this

mineral as a perfect background against which to mount precious stones and gems. Jades, resplendently set with rubies, emeralds, lapis lazuli, amethysts and other quartzes, quickly became desirable Mogul luxuries.

Stones were set individually into the solid jade, fixed with gold foil – pure gold beaten into paper-thin sheets – which defined their outlines and created a rich background for their display. Gems and delicate lines of inlaid gold might be set into formal floral patterns. Following the Chinese conquest of Eastern Turkestan, many jewel-encrusted jades were presented to the Imperial Court at Peking as tokens of good will. These superb carvings created a sensation at the Court of Ch'ien-lung, with the result that, in 1741, a group of expert jade-carvers and jewel-setters were attracted to Peking where they established the *Hsi Fan Tsi*, or Indian School of jade-cutters. They initiated Chinese craftsmen into the arts of inlaying fine tracery in gold and setting jewels against gold foil. Within ten years a prosperous trade had been established, the Chinese carvers producing jade which was purely Indian in form and design (Fig. 6). Indo-Chinese jades might be incised with verses in Chinese lauding their divine origin. The finest were inscribed with the square seal of Emperor Ch'ien-lung and retained in the palace. Thus the widespread belief that jewelled jades are invariably of Indian origin is entirely unfounded.

Jewelled jades were also carved and set in China to the commission of the Mogul Court at Delhi, and in the workshops attached to Tibetan and other monasteries in the Buddhist areas of north-eastern India. Religious deities such as Buddha and Tsongkaps, were also carved in the round.

Jades mounted in solid gold or gilt bronze, intended for presents or personal adornment, were made during the Ch'ien-lung period. Also at this time, composite creations representing flowers and fruit were modelled in jade for display on the altars of sacrifice in temples or on tables in homes.

The *Dictionarium Polygraphicum*, 1735, records that jade handles for hunting-knives were imported and that the Turks and Eastern Europeans valued jade-handled sabres. Small articles of eighteenth-century jade include sceptres in shapes adapted from those of a thousand years earlier, household altars, snuff-bottles, ceremonial axes and buckles.

MUSEUMS AND COLLECTIONS

Chinese jade carvings may be seen at the following:
GREAT BRITAIN
London:	British Museum
	Victoria and Albert Museum

U.S.A.
Flint, Michigan:	Flint Institute of Arts
Minneapolis,	Walker Art Center,
Minnesota:	T. B. Walker Collection of Jade
Springfield, Mass.:	George Walter Vincent Smith Art Museum
Washington D.C.:	Freer Gallery of Art

FURTHER READING

Chinese Jade of Five Centuries by Joan M. Hartman, Rutland, Vermont, 1969.
Jade and Other Hardstone Carvings by John Bedford, London, 1969.
Chinese Carved Jades by S. Howard Hansford, London, 1968.
Chinese Jade: A Concise Introduction by George Savage, New York, 1965.

Netsuke and Inro

Fig. 1 *Brown lacquer inro with gold and shell inlay depicting water fowl rising from a bed of rushes, mid-nineteenth century. Cornelian* ojime *(sliding) bead. Ivory* netsuke *depicting a man and boy scattering beans at New Year.*
(Victoria and Albert Museum, London.)

Netsuke and inro were designed for everyday use but the craftsmen of Tokugawa Japan fashioned them as works of art

The *netsuke* provided an easy way for the Japanese wearing a kimono, which has no pockets, to carry at his girdle such objects as an *inro* (seal-case), later often used for medicines, a purse, a tinder-box, a drinking gourd, or a tobacco-pouch (Fig. 9). The *netsuke* (pronounced *nětskĭ*) was a toggle on the girdle from which, at the end of two cords, with its

R. Todd-White

several compartments held together by the *ojime* (sliding bead), hung the *inro*.

The kind of *netsuke* used would depend on the rank and needs of the wearer, and sometimes more than one would be worn at a time. *Samurai* (members of the warrior class) did not smoke in public as this would have been beneath their dignity. Their *netsuke* were usually finely carved for use with the lacquered *inro*, which perhaps contained the family seal, some pills or a herbal remedy. A large *netsuke* would be worn to support heavy objects or to match the figure of a large man such as a *sumo* wrestler. Gamblers often wore *netsuke* of skulls or snakes to bring them luck (Fig. 2). In the Tokugawa hierarchy the merchant ranked beneath the *samurai*, artisan and peasant; members of the merchant class were therefore quite happy to be seen carrying at their side pipes in cases, tobacco-pouches and all the paraphernalia of smoking. Some *netsuke* were even designed to serve as ashtrays *(sui-gara-ake)* as well as toggles.

The origin of the *netsuke* is obscure, as are the dates of its development as an art form. Although now considered among the finest and most characteristic of Japan's minor arts, early *netsuke* were merely shells, gourds or tree roots; the word *netsuke* is a compound of *ne* (a root), and *tsuke* (to fasten). There are few illustrations of *netsuke* in use until the eighteenth century and it is hard to identify seventeenth-century examples with any certainty. Not many were signed before the mid-eighteenth century. Some authorities believe that use was first made of *netsuke* in the late sixteenth century, though toggles were certainly worn in China before that date.

Until the Meiji restoration and the Revolution of 1868 there were a large number of ceremonies at which the *inro* could be worn to advantage. The Japanese lacquerer practised his trade to perfection so that even in China his work was highly praised. The Chinese Emperor K'ang-hsi (1662–1722) attributed the superior quality of Japanese lacquer to the damper climate, which allowed it to dry more slowly and a harder finish to be achieved. The particular qualities of the Japanese *rhus verniciferus*, the tree from which the lacquer gum comes, also contributed to the high standard of Japanese lacquer-work.

Smoking was a major factor in the development of the *netsuke*. Though tobacco was introduced by the Portuguese in the sixteenth century, the habit only slowly became fashionable. In the seventeenth century, tobacco-boxes or pouches became a prerequisite for successful merchants and fashionable men of all but the *samurai* class. More and better *netsuke* were demanded. Gradually the *netsuke* ceased to be a purely utilitarian object to

be worn, worn out and eventually to be discarded.

The Portuguese brought not only tobacco and trade, but also the Christian faith, which proved so popular that the Shogun felt his position to be threatened. In 1614 an edict was promulgated banning Christianity. In 1639, after a two-year rebellion, Japan was closed completely to the Portuguese. The handful of Dutch allowed to trade from the island of Deshima off Nagasaki were virtually Japan's only contact with the outside world until the coming of Commodore Perry's 'black ships' in 1853. The fables, fashions and fancies of the unique and inward-looking society which developed during Japan's seclusion were mirrored in the subjects chosen by the makers of *netsuke*.

Folklore, religion and the legendary history of China and Japan provided some of the most popular early subjects. There were often many stories about a single character and many versions of one story. The great artist and *netsuke*-maker Hogen Shuzan loved to carve figures from the *Sankaikyo* (a classical legend of the Mountain and the Ocean) or from the *Ressenden* (Lives of the *Rishi*). *Rishi*, or *Sennin*, were popular figures in Buddhist and Taoist mythology; resting for thousands of years from the cycle of transmigration, they would emerge from solitude in the mountains to perform miracles. The crane, a symbol of longevity, was depicted as a messenger or as a tireless mount. Shiei, one of the Taoist Immortals, rode to heaven on a large carp, a symbol of perseverance. Kinko, another Immortal, was translated on his carp either to the heavens or to the realm of fishes, depending on the version of the story. Gama *Sennin* (Fig. 3), a frequent subject, is portrayed with a toad into which his astral body is once said to have strayed. The *Ho-o* bird and the

Fig. 2 (Left) *Cow and calf,* netsuke *by Tomotada, late eighteenth century. Carved ivory. This maker is best known for his recumbent oxen made of ivory.*
(Right) *Skull and snake netsuke, unsigned, mid-nineteenth century.*
(British Museum, London.)

Fig. 3 *Gama Sennin. Ivory netsuke, c.1800. This Immortal is portrayed with a toad into which his astral body was said to have strayed. (British Museum.)*

Fig. 4 *Baku, netsuke, unsigned, c.1800. This popular mythical beast, which ate nightmares, is a rare subject in netsuke. (Victoria and Albert Museum.)*

6

7

8

9

Fig. 5 **Goshisho**, *a Chinese general (c.500 B.C.), with heavy kettle and writing-brush, winning his place as the King of Wu's counsellor. Netsuke. (D. J. K. Wright Ltd., London.)*

Fig. 6 **Shojo** *(a drunken sprite) sleeping off the after-effects of sake, netsuke signed by Ikkwan, mid-nineteenth century. (Victoria and Albert Museum.)*

Fig. 7 **Uzume**, *Goddess of Fun and Folly, fondling the nose of a Konoha Tengu, okimono made by Umpo for the western market, mid-nineteenth century. (British Museum.)*

Fig. 8 **Octopus and Kappa**, *netsuke. Octopuses were thought to be lascivious and are usually shown making advances to mermaids. The Kappa was less expansive. (British Museum.)*

Fig. 9 **Flirting at the waterfall** *by Suzuki Harunobu, eighteenth century. Woodcut. Detail showing a tobacco pouch held in place by a netsuke. (British Museum.)*

Fig. 10 **Karasu Tengu**, *netsuke by Shumin. (Victoria and Albert Museum.)*

10

Kirin were sacred hybrids. Born of the conjunction of two stars or of a cow and a dragon, the *Kirin* symbolises elegance, virtue and, in Japan today, a popular make of beer.

The *Baku* (Fig. 4), another popular mythical beast though not a sacred one, is a surprisingly rare subject in *netsuke*. Its function is to eat nightmares. The *Kappa*, with its strange tonsure, is more common but less benevolent (Fig. 8). Sometimes shown with a turtle-shell back, sometimes only with scales, it is a creature of the rivers with a taste for the entrails of children and young women, whom it first abuses before drowning and eating. It also has a taste for cucumbers, but the more usual way of appeasing it is to bow low in Japanese style. Being a well-mannered monster it will bow low in reply and spill from the top of its head the precious liquid from which comes its strength and aggression.

The *Karasu Tengu* (crow sprite) is more frequently seen than the long-nosed *Konoha Tengu* (Fig. 7). Many wooden *netsuke* depict a crow sprite hatching (Fig. 10), a subject which not only appealed to the imagination but could be carved in a robust shape for everyday use.

The *Shojo* (a drunken sprite) is an example of the wit of the *netsuke*-carver (Fig. 6). The creature is a pun on *Shojo* (young girl) and *Shojo* (orang-utan, an animal of Borneo and Sumatra, with long reddish-brown hair, which was reputed to have a liking for alcohol). The *netsuke* therefore showed a long-haired girl inordinately fond of *sake*, either holding out an empty cup or, as portrayed by the great carver Ikkwan, sleeping off the after-effects.

Netsuke of the zodiac animals, symbolising different periods of time, were outstandingly popular. The rat, ox, tiger, hare, dragon, serpent, horse, goat, monkey, cock, dog and boar were each assigned a year and an hour of the day.

Gradually there was a change in fashion from subjects drawn from Chinese mythology and history to native Japanese subjects; and later to natural subjects, for example animals, plants and fruit, which were so popular in the nineteenth century. The researches of such men as Motoori (1730–1801) into Japan's early Imperial history gave new vigour to Shintoism, a religion combining the worship of nature with fanatical loyalty to the reigning dynasty. Shintoism in turn invigorated the opposition to Tokugawa which culminated in the Meiji restoration. Instead of *Sennin*, Confucian paragons, heroes of the Han dynasty or figures like Goshisho (Fig. 5), there were Uzume (Fig. 7), Goddess of Fun and Folly, and the Treasure Ship of the Seven Gods of Good Luck (Fig. 11). In addition, there were Buddhist subjects such as Emma-O, King of Hell and Judge of the Dead, and very often Daruma, the founder of Zen, was represented.

Daruma in particular is a good example of the scant respect the *netsuke*-carver accorded even to semi-sacred and religious subjects. Since tradition had it that his nine years of silent, seated meditation had withered his legs, he is often made in the form of a self-righting doll. There were ghosts, goblins (*bakemono*) and demons (*oni*), usually getting the better of Shoki, the demon-queller, and in the first half of the nineteenth century a profusion of natural subjects, each with some symbolism or story.

There were also *netsuke* of musical instruments like the *koto*, *biwa* and *samisen*; of dances like the New Year Lion Dance or the peasants' *bon odori*;

Hamlyn Group Library

A. C. Cooper

Fig. 11 *The Treasure Ship of the Seven Gods of Good Luck,* netsuke, *signed by Masahiro, nineteenth century.*
The cargo of this mythical ship included the Inexhaustible Purse, the Hammer of Chaos, the Hat of Invisibility and the Lucky Raincoat to ward off evil. Hotei was the most popular god; he could sleep in the snow and predict the future, loved children but hated washing.
(Victoria and Albert Museum.)

Fig. 12 *Inro of five compartments signed in gold characters by the Kajikawa family (active c.1750– c.1850), early nineteenth century. Lacquer with gold and mother of pearl inlay. The* netsuke *is a miniature mask from the classical No theatre.*
(Spink and Sons, London.)

Fig. 13 *Dutchman with cockerel, unsigned* netsuke, *eighteenth century.*
(D. J. K. Wright Ltd.)

of ceremonies like the *cha-no-yu* (tea ceremony); of sports like *sumo* wrestling and *judo*; of games like *kakurembo* (hide-and-seek), or *go*; and in particular there were miniature masks from the classical *No* plays (Fig. 12). Deme Yeiman of Edo and his descendants were mask-carvers by profession and noted for this form of *netsuke*. There were courtiers and monkey showmen (*sarumawashi*), acrobats, blind masseurs (*amma*) and nightwatchmen. Household articles were depicted and mechanical objects such as tinder-boxes or the Dutch traders' compasses and matchlock guns. Nor were the Dutchmen themselves neglected (Fig. 13).

There was great variety in the forms and materials of *netsuke*: the early seal forms, the miniature masks, the *sashi* (rod) form, the *hyotan* (gourd), the coloured dolls called 'Nara-ningyo' (a form originated by Hogen Shuzan), the *ichiraku* (woven wire) form, the simple hunters' trophies or the clever trick *netsuke* of goblins with sliding necks, skulls with moving jaws and loose seeds rattling in a lotus pod. Delicate scenes were carved in clamshells or figures inside a walnut, but the most common forms were the compact statuette or *katabori* group of figures, designed for everyday use, and the *manju*, a disc in the shape of a rice-cake.

A variation on the *manju* was the *kagamibuta* (mirror lid) *netsuke*, a decorated metal disc set in ivory or wood. Metalworkers were most active in this form in the second half of the nineteenth century when *samurai* no longer required their traditional output of swords and sword fittings.

The majority of *netsuke* were made of wood or ivory. Shuzan and other carvers of the early period preferred *hinoki* (Japanese cypress), but it was too light a wood to wear well. Boxwood was most frequently used because of its hardness and fine grain, but *netsuke* of cherry, ebony and other woods are also found. In ivory there is a wide variation in quality; Kwaigyoku Masatsugu was one carver who insisted on using only the best. In Iwami province by the sea, marine ivory was very popular: the tusk of the walrus, the horn of the narwhal and the tooth of the sperm whale. Staghorn was quite a common material while metal, bone, amber, crystal, jet, hornbill, mother of pearl and porcelain were among materials used occasionally. Sometimes *netsuke* were lacquered and painted; sometimes materials were combined. Shibayama and his school are famous for inlay.

Inro were mainly of lacquered wood, since porcelain and other materials were too heavy or too fragile for everyday use. In general, they were made in oblong box forms, with four or five neatly interlocking compartments (Fig. 1). *Inro* in the shape of a tortoise, cicada or some other animal are unusual. There is considerable variety in the kinds of lacquer and the methods in which they were applied for decoration. Blue and green are very rare colours, black, gold and red being the most common. The Kajikawa family and Zeshin are perhaps the most famous names in *inro* (Fig. 12).

Not enough is known about the lives of the makers of *inro* and *netsuke*. Since the signing of works became general only in the nineteenth century, the hand of a master must usually be deduced from the known facts about his materials, forms, style and the quality of the workmanship. A signature may mean no more than that a work is by a pupil or in the style of a master. Kwaigyoku Masatsugu used several signatures.

Moreover there are many forgeries and false signatures; even an expert may not always be able to date and identify a work with certainty. At best, he may be able to show that a particular claim for a piece's authenticity is unsubstantiated. Over two thousand signatures of *netsuke*-makers are recorded, four times as many as for makers of *inro*, the skill of the lacquerer being more difficult to acquire. Some of the greatest makers of *inro*, such as Zeshin (1806–91) also produced a few *netsuke*.

Some makers of *netsuke* and *inro* became especially known for one subject, which was so popular that it was widely copied within their lifetime: Tomotada for the recumbent ox (Fig. 2), the first Masanao for the *fukura suzume* (inflated sparrow), Ikkwan of Nagoya for the sleeping *Shojo*, and later for the rat.

Most of the makers of *netsuke* and *inro* naturally lived in the large towns of Osaka, Kyoto and Edo, where they could best make a livelihood from their carving. By 1750 Edo's population was about one million. Another important centre was Nagoya, close to the forests of Gifu, whose output seems in consequence to have consisted entirely of wooden *netsuke*. Issai and other fine carvers came from other small centres,

After the ending of Japan's seclusion and with the Meiji restoration, the production of *netsuke* and *inro* declined. Many of the patrons from the ruling classes were dispossessed, the *samurai* lost their status, and Western-style clothes with pockets came into fashion. The smoking of cigarettes, also in fashion at this time, was another factor.

The demand for *netsuke* came instead from the influx of foreign collectors and tourists looking for something typically Japanese. *Okimono* (ornaments) were turned out in large numbers, sometimes finely carved but without the simple beauty of the genuine *netsuke* (Fig. 7). The *himotoshi* (cord-holes) were either missing or bored in the wrong place for wearing so that the carving showed to its best advantage. However, at this time also, a few perceptive foreigners built up the great collections of *netsuke* and *inro* which have led to these art forms being so appreciated in the West.

MUSEUMS AND COLLECTIONS

Japanese *netsuke* may be seen at the following:

GREAT BRITAIN
Aberystwyth: University Museum
London: British Museum
JAPAN
Tokyo: National Museum
U.S.A.
Boise, Idaho: Boise Gallery of Art
Boston, Mass.: Museum of Fine Arts
Fort Lauderdale, Fort Lauderdale Museum
Florida: of the Arts
Washington D.C.: Freer Gallery of Art

FURTHER READING

Masterpieces of Netsuke Art: One Thousand Favorites of Leading Collectors by Bernard Hurtig, New York, Tokyo, 1973.
Inro and Other Miniature Forms of Japanese Lacquer Art by Melvin and Betty Jahss, London, 1972.

Russian Embroidery

Velvets, silks and fine brocades imported from all over the world were among the materials used by Russian women embroiderers in the manufacture of some of the most rich and sumptuous needlework ever produced

Fig. 1 **Pall of St. Sergii of Radonezh**, *Stroganov School, 1671 (detail). Embroidered in gold and silver thread on coloured silk, outlined in pearls and studded with precious stones. The pall (pokrov) which was laid over the coffin often bore a life-size effigy. (History and Art Museum, Zagorsk, U.S.S.R.)*

Fig. 2 **Part of an icon cloth**, *Godunov workshop, 1599. Moss green damask decorated with silver plaques and pearls. (Zagorsk.)*

Fig. 3 **Embroidery** *(detail) ordered by Elena of Moldavia, 1498. This forms part of the famous embroidery which was ordered to commemorate the proclamation of Elena's son as heir to Tsar Ivan III. (Zagorsk.)*

Fig. 4 **Pall of St. Sergii of Radonezh**, *1420s. St. Sergii was the founder of the Troitsa Lavra (Trinity Monastery) and several palls bearing his effigy are now kept there (see Fig. 1). (Zagorsk.)*

386

Christianity, introduced from Byzantium in the tenth century, brought to Russia church utensils, crosses, chalices, gospels and elaborate embroideries. This was the first instance of sophisticated needlework in Russia. Though a strong pagan tradition had existed previously, due to the frequent destruction of cities by fire and the Tartar Invasion, none of these early examples is extant. However, a chronicler of the period mentions in his annals that there was a school of embroidery in the Monastery of Ianchin in the eleventh century whose works were considered so fine that they were sent to the sacrosanct Mount Athos.

Who were the Russian women who executed these embroideries? Until the Tartar invasion, women had been entitled to dispose of their own property and mix freely with masculine company, but thereafter they led a secluded life, confined to the *Svetlitsa* (women's quarters) and were concerned only with their households and children. They filled the long hours making church embroideries and teaching their daughters and female household staff to do the same.

Their works were mainly of religious subjects: the Crucifixion, Lamentation and Descent from the Cross, the Virgin and Child and feast days and saints. They used home-woven and -spun materials, coarse flaxen linen and a kind of bunting made and dyed at home, which was used as a lining for fine quality materials. These elaborate and expensive materials came to Russia from East and West: Theodosia, Damascus, Florence, Spain, Arabia and Turkey; Venetian velvet, silk, and gold and silver brocades from Persia and China. The latter were used for the Tsar's and High Clergy's vestments, cuffs, mitres, *aer* (veil to cover paten and chalice), *inditia* (altar-cloth) and chasubles, and were heavily adorned with pearls, precious stones, and gold and silver threads. The Armoury Palace's books quote as many as 160,580 pearls weighing

fifty pounds, to be used for one vestment. Works such as these for tsars and patriarchs were hung on golden cords and displayed in the churches.

In order to execute these lavish embroideries, at least three workers were needed: one to design the pattern on paper; this, if approved, was executed in colour on the *kholst* (bunting) which was used as lining for the silk material or velvet on which the embroidery itself was to be done. The second worker embroidered with coloured silk threads and gold and silver (according to the taste and the financial position of the donor), a task that sometimes took several years. The third worker, the calligrapher, was entrusted with drawing an intricate design of lettering around the border – generally a prayer appropriate to the embroidery, or the name of the donor. This lettering, skilfully interwoven and executed in golden thread, involved an incredible variety of seams and stitches.

A very important factor, both religious and political, in the fourteenth century was the foundation of *Troitsa Lavra* (Trinity Monastery) by St. Sergii at what is now Zagorsk, near Moscow. He gave his blessing to the struggle against the Tartars and gathered monks around him, attracting princes, *boiars* (noblemen), patriarchs and influential people who made donations to his monastery. His popularity was so great that when he died 'all Moscow wept', and his coffin was covered with a *pokrov* (shroud) bearing his full-size effigy embroidered with great refinement and beauty (Figs. 1 and 4).

Two other interesting embroideries are kept in Zagorsk. They do not represent the usual embroidery subjects and are exceptional in that they commemorate two important royal events relating to the line of succession. Tsar Ivan III lost his first wife at an early age; his son, married to Elena of Moldavia, died soon afterwards, leaving a male who was proclaimed heir. The Tsar himself, who was still fairly young, married Sophia Paleologue, a scion of the Imperial Byzantine family. Though Constantinople had been devastated by the Turks, and the Paleologues were in exile, Russia was still infatuated with the idea of the former glory of the Byzantine Empire. Sophia realised this, and forcibly so, when she bore the Tsar a son. Both his wife and his daughter-in-law considered their respective sons to be the Tsar's lawful heir; so the struggle began. The Tsar was easily influenced by the one, and then by the other; one was in favour today, to

be disgraced tomorrow. Elena finally got the upper hand and her son, after a church service of great pomp, was again proclaimed heir.

She immediately ordered an embroidery to commemorate this event (Fig. 3). A long procession of High Church dignitaries carry the Icon of Our Lady; the Tsar, the newly proclaimed heir and his mother, Elena of Moldavia, form a group in the centre; Sophia Paleologue, though wearing the Imperial Byzantine Insignia, stands near the choir singers. Research has now established the exact date of this event: it was between nine in the morning and three in the afternoon that the procession moved from the Cathedral of the Ascension to the Cathedral of the Dormition; the day was Palm Sunday, 8 April, 1498.

Elena's victory was short-lived, however, for the very next year she and her son were sent to prison where they subsequently died. Soon afterwards, Sophia Paleologue's son was proclaimed Prince of Novgorod and heir to the Moscow throne. Sophia responded to this event by bequeathing a *pelena* (embroidered icon) to the *Troitsa Lavra*, with a suitable inscription in which she is referred to firstly as 'Tsarina of Tsargrad' (Empress of Constantinople) and only afterwards as 'Grand Duchess of Moscow'.

The epoch of the renowned mural and icon painter Dionisii and his two sons, who were second only to Rublev, inspired an embroidery executed in 1500 which is now in the Tretiakov Gallery, Moscow. It was found in the Volokolamsk Monastery and depicts in meticulous detail rarely illustrated scenes from the life of the Virgin, taken from the Apocrypha. The figures of the women who surround the resting St. Anne are slender, elongated and almost Hellenistic in their elegant movement.

The *omophorion* (clerical vestment) of the Patriarch Nikon, dated 1672, now in the State Art History Museum, Novgorod, is important because the name of the artist who executed the sketch for this embroidery is known: he was Mikhail Novgorodets and his work here, showing a panoramic view executed in silver and gold threads, faithfully depicts the architecture of the Novgorod Detinets and Moscow's Kremlin as they then were.

After Ivan the Terrible cruelly suppressed the Free City of Novgorod, which was a member of the Hanseatic League (a political and commercial league of Germanic towns), all the political power centred around the Tsar and the Patriarch in Moscow, and one or two rich families. One such family, the Stroganovs, left the conquered Novgorod and Sol'vychegodsk, where they had amassed fame and fortune, and moved to Moscow, becoming the Tsar's bankers. They brought with them their icon painters and embroiderers. So far, forty-eight donations made by this family have been discovered and attributed to their workshops. A peculiarity of the Stroganov family workshops was that their craftsmen signed their works, giving the date and the name of the donor, which now helps in the reconstruction of the Stroganov family-tree.

The Stroganov workshops flourished in the sixteenth century. One *pelena* dedicated to the memory of the murdered Tsarevich Dimitrii, possibly killed on the instruction of Boris Godunov, shows the moment when Dimitrii is falling, stabbed by the assassin's dagger. Another shroud, a

387

Fig. 5 **Embroidered icon,** worked by the first wife of Ivan the Terrible, Anastasia Romanovna, sixteenth century. (Suzdal Museum.)

Fig. 6 **The Lamentation** (detail), Staritskii School, 1561. Embroidered in coloured silks, gold and silver. (Zagorsk.)

Fig. 7 **Inditia,** or **altar-cloth,** Godunov School, 1601. Monastery legend ascribes this work to Ksenia, Boris Godunov's daughter. (Zagorsk.)

Fig. 8 **Sapega's Banner** (detail), Tsar's workshop, sixteenth century.
The Tsar's embroiderers produced not only liturgical and commemorative embroideries but also battle-dresses and war-banners. This banner represents the Archangel Michael appearing to Joshua before the Battle of Jericho. (Tretiakov Gallery, Moscow.)

388

full-size effigy of St. Sergii dated 1671, in the History and Art Museum, Zagorsk, is embroidered with silver and gold threads, the finest quality pearls marking the outlines (Fig. 1). It gives an almost colourless impression, relating it to the gold or silver *oklad* (metal used to cover an icon). This was something new in embroidery.

The Tsar's workshops only worked to orders given by the Tsar and his family. They produced battle-dresses, church donations, vestments and war-banners. One sixteenth-century example known as the Sapega's Banner, now in the Tretiakov Gallery, shows the Archangel Michael appearing to Joshua before the Battle of Jericho (Fig. 8).

An unusual portable *iconostasis* (icon screen), not painted but embroidered, is kept in the State Russian Museum, Leningrad. It was ordered in 1592 by the devout Tsar Fëdor and his wife Irina,

to be taken on their pilgrimages. In later years it travelled with Tsar Aleksei Mikhailovich on his journeys and even later with Peter the Great. In Alexander I's days it was given to the Winter Palace Church and then to the Pensioner Soldiers' Home in St. Petersburg, where it was badly damaged by fire. What was left was transferred on to green velvet (the previous base had been scarlet). At this stage the faces of the saints were overpainted with oil colours. It is now in the Moscow Restoration Workshop, where attempts are being made to salvage as much of the original work as possible.

The Armoury Palace, Moscow, has a special Equestrian Department with a remarkable collection of the Tsar's boots, quivers, saddles, caparisons (horses' trappings) and bridles – all of which are lavishly embroidered with gold threads

and precious stones on leather (Fig. 9).

We have mentioned two embroidery workshops already, those of the Tsar and the Stroganov family. Who could compete with them in terms of finance and sophisticated taste?

Recently in Moscow it was discovered that a technique used by Andronikos Paleologue in 1300 for an embroidery in the church of St. Clement in Okhrida, was adopted by the Staritskii workshop. It consisted of the insertion of beige silk between the lining and the tissue on which the embroidery was to be executed corresponding to the areas where faces, hands and bodies were to be worked.

The Princess Staritskii's family, related to the Tsar Ivan the Terrible, was extremely rich and very ambitious. The Princess's mother even wanted

sonally ordered a *pelena* to be worked on red silk, decorated with pearls and golden plaques engraved with the faces of saints, to be hung under the famous icon of Rublev's *Trinity*. His daughter Ksenia is said to have executed an *inditia* (altar-cloth) in 1601 on silvery brocade with black velvet arabesques (Fig. 7), representing Christ enthroned, with his Mother and St. John standing beside, and two kneeling monks, St. Sergii and St. Nikon of Radonezh. Recent research has shown that the brocade for this altar-cloth was brought from either Spain or Florence and came from the same workshops as the material for the robe worn by Eleanora of Toledo (wife of Cosimo I de' Medici) in 1553, in the two portraits of her by Bronzino, (now in the Uffizi, Florence, and the Wallace Collection, London), and in which she was found buried when her coffin was opened in 1857. It is an example of the very high quality materials used four hundred years ago in Spain, Italy and in some Russian workshops.

One should not wonder that robes worn by people of high rank in Russia, attracted the attention of ambassadors or visiting foreign dignitaries; their chroniclers never forgot to mention the elaborate robes and vestments that they saw, or the profusion of pearls, brocades, gold sequins, stones, diamonds and furs of the Russian Court.

But what about the Russian peasantry? Could they develop a creative folk art? For the sixteenth- or seventeenth-century Russian, Moscow was the metropolis, but there was little connection between the capital and provincial towns, villages and hamlets. The peasant population used home-made, cheap, primitive materials and patterns which had been passed down from generation to generation. Unfortunately, wear and tear have denied us knowledge of all but a handful of the early examples of their work, but in the last few decades great and successful efforts have been made to revive this craft as folk art.

Fig. 9 **Quiver** by Prokofii Andreev, 1673. Gold and silver embroidery on red morocco leather.
Various of the Tsar's family emblems are depicted here and in the centre is an embroidered view of the Kremlin.
(Armoury Museum, Moscow.)

Fig. 10 **Pelena, or embroidered icon**, Godunov workshop, 1593. Given by a member of the Godunov family to the Ipat'ev Monastery, the icon depicts three angels and biblical scenes.
(Boris-Gleb Monastery, Moscow.)

to poison Ivan and proclaim her own son tsar. The plot was discovered and both she and her son were executed. Looking at some of the Staritskii's very fine works, such as *The Lamentation* with the tragic expression on the faces of Mary Magdalen and the Virgin, one feels that the Princess's mother had a premonition of what would happen to her (Fig. 6); but as long as she lived, she did her best to provide her workshop with rare samples, materials and embroideries.

She undoubtedly had contacts with the West. A sixteenth-century shroud which she bequeathed to the Pskov Pecherskii Cloister, employed Italian material. On another, dated 1540, the Mother of God is seated on a carved gothic bench, a style unknown at that date in Russia.

Another workshop belonged to the family of Boris Godunov during his short reign as Tsar. He per-

MUSEUMS AND COLLECTIONS

Russian embroidery may be seen at the following:

GREAT BRITAIN
London: Victoria and Albert Museum

RUSSIA
Leningrad: State Russian Museum
Novgorod: State Art History Museum
Moscow: State Tretiakov Gallery
Zagorsk: History and Art Museum

U.S.A.
New York: Metropolitan Museum of Art
Washington   University of Washington Costume
D.C.:   and Textile Study Centre

FURTHER READING

Art Treasures of Russia by M. V. Alpatov, London, 1968.
Drevnerusskoe shit'e by A. N. Svirin, Moscow, 1963.
'Old Russian Embroideries' by E. Tolmachoff in **The Needle and Bobbin Club Bulletin**, New York, 1947.
'Russian Ecclesiastical Embroidery' by Cyril Blunt in **The Connoisseur** Vol. 98, London, 1936.

Persian Carpets

Persian carpets cover the floors of homes throughout the world. Their owner may know nothing else about Persian art, yet the delicate design and warm colours of Persian carpets will immediately delight him

It is in carpets that the Persians achieved artistic supremacy. Persian pottery, despite the magnificence of its lustre and colours, may have to contend with China. Western architecture may be preferred to that of Persia. Persian miniatures are within their self-imposed limitations unsurpassed but again the delicate brush-work of the Chinese or Japanese masters or early fourteenth century French miniatures may have just as much appeal.

Persian carpets, on the other hand, have no real rivals and world opinion has rightly awarded supremacy to them.

The origin of carpet-making goes back far into early history. The oldest existing carpet was found in 1949 by the Russian archaeologist, Rudenko, in one of the burial mounds of the Pazyryk valley of the Altai mountains. This carpet, which is in the Hermitage in Leningrad, is knotted and is believed to have been made in the fourth or fifth century B.C. Its intricate and elaborate design presupposes a long tradition of carpet-making. The design is strongly influenced by the style of the Achaemenid dynasty which ruled over Persia from the sixth to the fourth century B.C.

This particular carpet has been preserved because of exceptional climatic circumstances – the relentless frost of the Altai mountains – for carpets are by their very nature perishable. Consequently, we have no substantial knowledge of any Persian carpets made before the beginning of the sixteenth century, although from miniature illustrations it would seem that the patterns in the fourteenth and fifteenth centuries were geometrical.

In one of the most celebrated Persian manuscripts, the *Khwaju Kimani* (dated 1396) which is now preserved in the British Museum, there are several miniatures showing carpets. These are decorated with a geometrical pattern consisting of star shapes and octagonal compartments. The borders of most of these carpets have stylised *Kufic* writings. In another famous manuscript, the *Shah-nama Book of the Kings of Firdausi* (copied about 1375) known as the *Demotte Shah Name* after its original owner, an animal which looks like a dragon is depicted. This design may have originated in China, whence Persian artists of the great period of carpets – the sixteenth and seventeenth centuries – often borrowed motifs.

Apart from miniature paintings, we also have the evidence of travellers who mention carpets. Ruy Gonzales de Clavijo, ambassador of the King of Castile to Timur, or Tamburlaine, describes in his account of 1404, the beautiful carpets he saw in Timur's capital of Samarkand. Another ambassador, Barbaro, who was sent by the Republic of Venice to the 'White Sheep' Prince Uzun Hasan (1466–78) in 1471 to Tabriz, is more explicit: 'The ground was covered with most beautiful carpets between which carpets and those of Cairo and Borsa (in my judgment) there is as much difference as between the cloth made of English wool and those of Saint Matthew's'. By 'Borsa', Barbaro refers to the ancient Turkish capital of Bursa, which was celebrated for its carpets.

This testimonial is one of the earliest confirming the supremacy of Persian carpets over the Turkish and Cairene carpets.

As we do not know of any surviving Persian carpets from this period, we can only observe from the representation of Persian miniature paintings that a change of carpet design took place towards the end of the fifteenth century. In the miniatures of the famous Persian painter, Bihzad and his pupils, we see new types of carpets decorated with arabesques and floral scrolls, medallions and compartments. These changes may be attributed to the Timurid Sultan Husayn Mirza (1468–1506) who, like his Florentine contemporary Lorenzo de' Medici, gathered the best artists and poets to his Court. The carpets shown in the miniatures of this period became the prototype of the great period of the subsequent two centuries.

In 1502, Shah Isma'il established the Safawid dynasty. He reunited the country, and under him and his son, Shah Tahmasp (1524–76), Persia enjoyed a period of great prosperity in which the arts and crafts flourished.

In the sixteenth century Persian carpets made of wool and silk were produced by first-class craftsmen, often from cotton prototypes designed by famous artists. There was close co-operation between the painters and weavers, and the magnificent result is not surprising. The Court itself

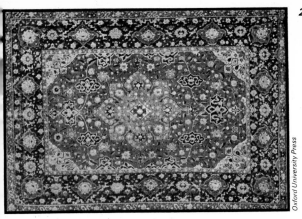

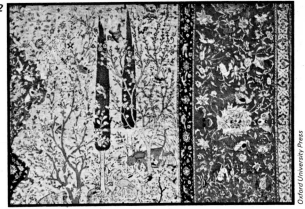

2

Fig. 1 **Medallion carpet,** c.1600.
Silk.
(Collection of J. Widener.)

Fig. 2 **Medallion carpet** *(detail),*
sixteenth century.
Decorated with trees in blossom,
birds and animals on a yellow
ground which contrasts with the
red border and medallion, this is
one of the most beautiful wool
carpets of the period.
(Musée des Arts Décoratifs,
Paris.)

4

Fig. 3 **Silk carpet,** *possibly from*
Kashan, c.1600.
(Metropolitan Museum of Art,
New York. Bequest of
Benjamin Altman.)

Fig. 4 **Vase carpet,** *seventeenth*
century. Wool.
Amongst the flowers which form
the major part of the decoration
are three vases which give the
carpet its name.
(Keir Collection, London.)

Scala

Fig. 5 *'Herat' or 'Isfahan'
carpet,* seventeenth century.
*Wool. Some of these carpets
could have been made in India.
(Museo Bardini, Florence.)*

played an important part by establishing royal looms which were supported by large orders.

The Persian carpet designers' great achievement was, above all, harmony. The different motifs, such as scrolls and palmettes, were ingeniously moulded into a unity; the colours are subtle, often subdued, but always delicate. Persian carpets of the sixteenth century are well balanced and never overcrowded.

The seventeenth century in Persia started with the great Shah 'Abbas (1588–1628), a grandson of Shah Tahmasp. He transferred the capital in 1598 from Qazwin to near Isfahan where some of the mosques and palaces built by him still evoke our admiration and give us an idea of the splendour of his reign.

Unfortunately, from the point of view of carpets, this period was already one of decline. The majority are still splendid, but compared with the products of the sixteenth century they lack the strength and simplicity of earlier designs. The motifs become more and more elaborate and repetitive and sometimes even ostentatious. Even so, this period produced the magnificent 'Polonaise' carpets.

Under the successors of Shah 'Abbas, the manufacture of carpets continued, and we have the testimony of many European travellers such as Chardin and Piero de Valla who were struck by the beauty of Persian carpets.

In 1722 Isfahan was overrun by the Afghans and the Safawid dynasty came to an end. Carpet-making continued on a village and tribal basis, but without the Court's patronage. The great age of Persian carpets was over.

When examining the carpets of the sixteenth and seventeenth centuries, we have to bear in mind that comparatively few examples have survived. Another point to remember is that, even among those which have survived, they have suffered the wear and tear and neglect of centuries. Only a few are really first class and these can without any doubt be attributed to royal patronage.

The classification of Persian carpets of this period is not without difficulty. We assume that there were royal looms in great cities like Tabriz, Qazwin and Kashan, but with the exception of Isfahan, we have no documentary evidence of this. Nor do we know which type of carpets were made in which towns. Therefore it seems safest to classify carpets by their design and decoration rather than by their assumed place of origin.

The dating of carpets is equally difficult. We have only a few examples which are authoritatively dated, such as the 'Ardabil' carpet, which is dated 1539, and the hunting carpet in the Poldi Pezzoli Museum in Milan, dated 1521. Other carpets were documented by the date of arrival of a Persian ambassador bringing them as presents. Again, the representation of carpets of the sixteenth and seventeenth centuries on Persian or Indian miniatures or on contemporary European paintings can be a useful guide.

Broadly speaking, the carpets of the sixteenth and seventeenth centuries can be classified in the following way: hunting carpets, animal carpets, medallion carpets with flower or scroll decoration, vase carpets, garden carpets, prayer carpets and the so-called 'Polonaise' carpets.

Hunting carpets are truly the most magnificent carpets in the world. Among them, one of the finest and most famous is in the Museum of Applied Arts in Vienna. It belonged to the former Imperial House and is reputed to have been a present from Peter the

Great of Russia (1672–1725) to the Emperor Leopold I (1640–1705). In fact, it was probably a present made to the Russian Court by an earlier Shah in the sixteenth century. In its centre field, Persian riders chase antelopes, boars, gazelles, foxes and other animals. The superb border consists of *peris* (angels) surrounded by parrots and Chinese cloudbands. The entire colour scheme is salmon pink, the material silk. The cartoon of this carpet may have been designed by the famous miniature painter, Sultan Muhammad. The size of the carpet is one hundred and twenty-six inches by two hundred and sixty-seven inches and it must have taken fifteen to twenty years to make.

There is a similar though not quite so sumptuous carpet which is now in the Boston Museum of Fine Arts. This belonged formerly to the Torrigiani family in Florence, who, not realising its value or beauty, covered the floor of their hot-house with it. A smaller but very beautiful carpet is preserved in the Royal Palace at Stockholm. The hunting carpet in the Poldi Pezzoli Museum in Milan is dated but its design is not as spontaneous as that of the one in Vienna. Probably it is a provincial copy of a court carpet.

Successful collaboration between painters and weavers

Animal carpets follow hunting carpets most closely. Among these, perhaps the finest is a fragment (Fig. 7) which depicts in its medallion a court scene in a pavilion. The colour of the medallion is light blue and in the background there are bay trees. The whole scene bears a close resemblance to Persian miniatures of the mid-sixteenth century and this fragment is a striking proof of the successful collaboration between painters and weavers; the result is a stupendous scene in wool. The size of this unique fragment is seventy-seven inches by eighty-two inches. It belonged to Baron F. Hatvani in Budapest and was seized during the siege of Budapest in 1945. Its present location is unknown.

Another superb carpet designed with a central medallion and animals is in the Musée des Arts Décoratifs in Paris (Fig. 2). The colouring of the border and medallion is red and the field is a delicate yellow, decorated with beautifully shaped trees, some of them in blossom, birds and animals. The border contains Chinese cloudbands, and pheasants, which in a different way figure on the Vienna hunting carpet.

One of the most famous carpets designed with a medallion and plants is the so-called 'Ardabil' carpet, which is today preserved in the Victoria and Albert Museum, London. Originally it was in Ardabil (North West Persia) where it decorated the shrine of Shaykh Safi, the ancestor of the Safawid dynasty. It is dated 1539, and was sold in 1893 in order to raise money to restore the dilapidated shrine. The size of the carpet is two hundred and eight inches by four hundred and thirty-seven inches, which renders it the largest surviving carpet from the sixteenth century. It has three hundred and forty knots in every square inch. Two mosque lamps appear to hang from the centre medallion and the colours of the field are mainly different shades of blue. The centre medallion is mainly in shades of yellow, and is so delicately designed that it recalls the beautiful luminous stained glass

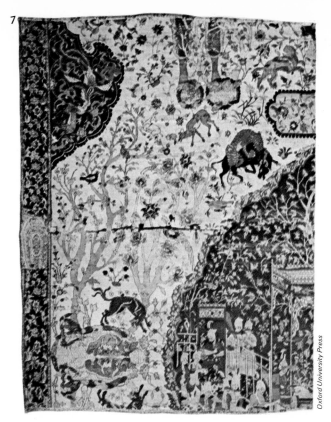

Fig. 7 *Medallion carpet (fragment), 1550.*
Wool, 77 x 82 ins.
(Formerly in the collection of Baron F. Hatvani,
Budapest.)

Oxford University Press

Fig. 6 *Diagram showing metal*
threads cloth-woven over two
and under two warps in the
manner characteristic of many
'Polonaise' carpets.

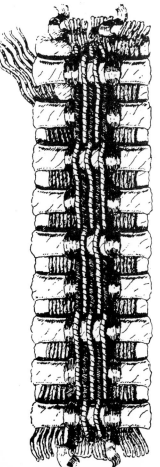

Oxford University Press

rosette windows of early French gothic cathedrals.

Figure 1 shows an extremely fine silk carpet which belongs to a small group of which perhaps not more than ten have survived. The interplay of the rich colours, the restraint in design and the perfect proportions make this an exceptional carpet.

For the Persians, many carpets not only represented, but also provided substitutes for, gardens. In the severity of Persian winters, and from the aridity of the deserts, they could be admired, and the brief spell of spring could be recalled and compared with the Paradise so beautifully described by the Prophet in the Koran.

A beautiful example of a garden carpet which is a perfect reproduction of a sixteenth-century Persian garden is in the collection of the Museum of Applied Arts, Vienna. Formerly it belonged to the celebrated Dr. A. Figdor, one of the greatest collectors of the century, who found it in a farmhouse in Upper Austria. The field is divided into six compartments which are separated by water canals, in which fishes swim. Each compartment represents a section of the garden, full of trees, birds and animals. The colour is red and the carpet is composed of nineteen thousand knots, eight hundred to every square inch. Among the few surviving sixteenth- to eighteenth-century garden carpets, this one takes a special place. The most celebrated garden carpet, however, is in the Prince of Wales Museum in Jaipur, India.

The nostalgic feeling for gardens and nature is expressed in the so-called 'vase' carpets (Fig. 4). These are longish, narrow carpets with flower decoration, and among them can be discerned one or two hidden vases. The colours used are usually blues or reds and the design of flowers is often most effective. Truly, these carpets are good substitutes for a garden.

'Polonaise' carpets were typical products of the period of Shah 'Abbas. During his reign, European art began to influence Persia and the 'Polonaise' carpets have a certain 'baroque' feeling. The name of these carpets originates from the 1878 Paris Exhibition when quite a few of those exhibited came from Poland. Beyond any doubt, they are Persian and most of them were produced between 1600 and 1660. Perhaps they were the results of the Persians' attempts to export more silk products to the West for they are made entirely of silk, inlaid with gold and silver threads. The colouring is delicate, subtle pastel shades and when in good condition they are incredibly beautiful.

In the seventeenth century, Polonaise carpets were presented by the Shah to European rulers and princes. In Venice, at the San Marco Treasury, several are preserved which can be related to the Persian Ambassador's gifts between 1607 and 1622. The most famous 'Polonaise' carpet is perhaps the 'coronation' carpet in Denmark which has been used for the coronations of the Kings of Denmark since the seventeenth century.

Another carpet of the seventeenth century which is seen quite frequently is the so-called 'Herat' or 'Isfahan' carpet. These are often large and their fields contain elaborate, almost over-elaborate, designs with cloudbands, scrolls, palmettes and other plants. Their colouring is usually red and their border often in greens or blues. The knotting is rather coarse and there is no evidence that these carpets were in fact produced in either Herat or Isfahan. On the contrary, some of them were probably made in India, whence they were exported to Europe in fairly large quantities. Standing alone, these carpets are quite attractive; but putting a 'Herat' or 'Isfahan' side by side with a sixteenth-century Persian carpet, one cannot fail to notice the great difference between the two (Fig. 5).

MUSEUMS AND COLLECTIONS

Persian carpets and rugs may be seen at the following:

EGYPT
Cairo: Museum of Islamic Art
FRANCE
Paris: Musée des Arts Décoratifs
GERMANY
Berlin: Islamisches Museum
GREAT BRITAIN
London: Victoria and Albert Museum
HUNGARY
Budapest: Museum of Applied Art
IRAN
Teheran: National Museum
U.S.A.
New York: Metropolitan Museum of Art
Washington, D.C.: The Textile Museum

FURTHER READING

Carpets of Central Asia by A. Bogolyubov, 1973.
Oriental Rugs: A Comprehensive Guide by Murray L. Eiland, Greenwich, Conn., 1973.
Antique Rugs from the Near East by Bode and Kühnel (translated by Charles Grant Ellis), Berlin, 1958.
Survey of Persian Art ed. by A. Upham Pope, London, 1939.

French Tapestries

Fig. 1 *The Chinese Hangings: Return from Fishing* (detail) *from a set of six designs by Boucher, woven at Beauvais many times between 1745 and c.1775.*
(Amelienborg, Copenhagen.)

The French Court in the eighteenth century derived much of its reputation for luxurious elegance from the tapestries made in French workshops

Finance Minister Colbert had created the Gobelins and Beauvais manufactories in 1662 and 1664 to make expensive Flemish imports unnecessary. The impressive tapestries which resulted – woven with richly dyed wools and silks, embellished with gold and silver thread in the seventeenth century – besides satisfying French society were in great demand abroad.

The Gobelins, state-financed to produce tapestries for the Crown, used private commissions merely as supplementary income. The tapestry industry at Aubusson, existing before Colbert's regulations, produced cheaper tapestry for a wider market. Beauvais, with fewer potential customers

for costly products and no regular income from the Crown until Louis XV gave annual orders for diplomatic presents, was financially unstable until the later 1730s. Its first director, Hinard, went bankrupt. The second, Philippe Behagle (1684–1711), managed to keep the looms working during the ruinous wars of Louis XIV at the end of the seventeenth century; but commissions for tapestries, on which he made about one third profit, barely covered the cost of production of tapestries because of those unsold, or those sold at a loss in order to pay the workers. This was still the case in the eighteenth century, when the country's finances had improved, but Beauvais suffered under the inefficient direction of the Frères Filleul (1711–22) and De Mérou (1722–34). In 1732 over ninety tapestries were in store, unsold, the equivalent of more than two years' work, as records of 1722–24 show, from a staff of forty-two weavers, thirty apprentices, five dyers and some three hundred spinners employed in the surrounding countryside.

Making the tapestries was expensive and it was more economical to make several sets from the same cartoons

Making a set of tapestries was expensive. First, the original designs had to be bought: six paintings for the *Isle of Cythera* by Duplessis were valued at 4,870 *livres* in 1732 and Rolly's designs for borders for the set at 500 *livres*. Next, full-size cartoons had to be made, stocks of good quality wools and silks maintained for the weavers to use, and all the employees paid during the lengthy weaving. De Mérou claimed that the one set of the *Isle of Cythera* cost 28,766 *livres* to make and realised only 13,755 *livres* when sold to the King of Poland.

Obviously it was more economical when, as was usual, several sets were woven from the same cartoons; but even this could prove expensive unless a commission stated which pieces of the set were needed, for a whole set might not fit the buyer's room or suit his taste. Later records of Beauvais sales show that Prince Esterhazy purchased four tapestries from Boucher's nine designs for the *Loves of the Gods* (Fig. 4), and Louis XV's many orders for this set included six pieces of *Bacchus and Ariadne* compared with only one of *The Rape of Proserpina*.

The fortunes of Beauvais, although affected by wars and maladministration, depended mainly on the popularity of its designs. Under Behagle, prestige pieces were woven, such as the *Conquests of Louis XIV* or the grand battle scenes of the *Conquests of the King of Sweden*, which were made

Fig. 2 *Daphnis and Chloë: The Vintage*, after a design by Etienne Jeaurat, Aubusson, eighteenth century. This design was originally commissioned by Audran at the Gobelins and woven there between 1738 and 1741. It was apparently pirated by Aubusson. (Victoria and Albert Museum, London.)

2

Museum Photo

Fig. 3 *Pastoral with blue draperies*, from a set of ten pieces designed by Jean-Baptiste Huet, signed in the galloon D. M. Beauvais *for De Menou, Director 1780–93. This design was frequently copied and adapted at Beauvais and Aubusson. (Mobilier National, Paris.)*

Fig. 4 *The Loves of the Gods: Apollo and Clytie*, bearing the royal arms of France and Navarre, probably from one of the sets made for Louis XV, Beauvais, 1756, 1757 or 1761. These tapestries designed by Boucher were woven many times at Beauvais between 1749 and 1772. (Fitzwilliam Museum, Cambridge.)

3

Allo Photo

4

Museum Photo

in collaboration with the Gobelins; Behagle used designs more suited to multiple sales. The *Verdures with Birds* and *Children Playing* of Hinard's time were still woven, with new designs after Flemish and French painters. The *Chinese Hangings*, exotic, flamboyant tapestries designed by 'four illustrious painters' gratified the fashion for *chinoiserie*. Even more popular were the *Grotesques* on a yellow ground, inspired by the engravings of Jean Berain (Fig. 7). These con-

dyes that had to be used if they were to achieve the more painterly results which Oudry as their inspector demanded; but at Beauvais there seems to have been no opposition. Voltaire aptly called Beauvais '*la royaume d'Oudry*'.

Complete success came with Oudry's employment of François Boucher. Between 1736 and 1756, Boucher designed six sets of tapestries: the *Fêtes Italiennes*, the *Story of Psyche*, a new *Chinese Hangings* (Fig. 1), the *Loves of the Gods, Scenes*

Fig. 5 ***Noble Pastoral: the Luncheon** (detail), from a set of six tapestries designed by Boucher, signed on the galloon with the initials of André-Charlemagne Charron, Director at Beauvais, 1753–80.*
The arms in the border show that it was made for Louis XV. Although the earliest recorded set made for the King dates from 1758, the date 1756 with Boucher's name woven in reverse in the lower left corner probably refers to the weaving, as the design was finished in 1755. (Museum of Fine Arts, Boston.)

Fig. 6 ***Chair upholstered in Beauvais tapestries of 1737.*** *(Louvre, Paris.)*

tinued to be made well into the eighteenth century under the brothers Filleul and De Mérou.

The appointment of Jean-Baptiste Oudry as designer in 1726 was a turning-point for Beauvais. His designs were worthy successors to the old favourites of the seventeenth century. He was chiefly famed for his paintings of animals, which were seen in tapestry in his *New Hunts* (1727) (Fig. 8), *Metamorphoses* (1734), *Verdures* (1736), and above all in the *Fables of La Fontaine* which were repeatedly rewoven from 1736 to 1777. Together with his elegant, courtly figures in *Country Sports* (1730) and the *Comedies of Molière* (1732), they provided a challenge to the Beauvais weavers, calling for their finest weave and subtleties of tone. Backed by a sound administrator, Nicholas Besnier, from 1734, Oudry became joint director with him and until 1755 exacted a closer correspondence between tapestry and the original painting than had been known before. The weavers of the Gobelins had protested against the fugitive

from the Opera and the *Noble Pastoral* (Fig. 5). From first to last, the figures of alluring, provocative women, cherubic children, effeminate youths and hoary old men, thinly disguised as the inhabitants of Italy, China, Olympus or the stage, were unchanging. Woven with most delicate flesh tones, with exquisite detail of silken draperies, fripperies and flowers, set in an idyllic landscape, this formula clearly expressed the decorative taste of the age. Commissions abounded and occupied the looms for over forty years. Boucher was the favourite painter of Madame de Pompadour, yet strangely she owned none of his Beauvais tapestries at her death. Louis XV, however, purchased several sets, and monarchs abroad placed orders to grace their courts.

Beauvais was now the fashion. Under directors Charron (1754–80) and De Menou (1780–93), the traditions of Boucher were maintained by the tapestries of the *Iliad* designed by Deshays (1761), by the charming *Russian Sports* (1769) of Le Prince and by Jean-Baptiste Huet's pretty pastoral scenes framed by trees linked with flowers and draperies, woven with many variations from 1780 (Fig. 3). A new note of realism was introduced by the work of François Casanova in his genre scenes, *Country Sports* (1772), *Gypsies* (1777) and *Military Convoys* (1787); and neo-Classicism in both subject and style was well represented by the *Arts and Sciences* of Lagrenée (1788), the *Four Quarters of the World* (1790) and the *History of Alexander* (1797) by Lavallée Poussin, Desoria's *Achilles* (1797) and two

tapestries with superb classical freizes for the borders by Monsiau (1793).

Tapestry borders in the eighteenth century were generally narrower and less imposing than those of the preceding century. At Beauvais more than at Aubusson, the swags of flowers, trophies and grotesques with strap-work and floral scrolls were gradually outnumbered by borders in shaded yellow imitating carved, gilt frames. Sometimes tapestries were designed to fit into the

Fig. 7 ***Grotesque on a yellow ground,*** *one of a set of four after Jean Bérain, Beauvais, first quarter of the eighteenth century. These highly decorative tapestries with plain coloured grounds have a minimum of complicated weaving. (Victoria and Albert Museum.)*

Fig. 8 ***New Hunts: the Wild Boar*** *(detail), from a set of six designed by Jean-Baptiste Oudry, signed* Mérou à Beauvais *(Director 1722–34) and dated 1727. The woven date may refer to the original painting rather than the weaving, which could have been in 1727–29 or 1734. (Residenzmuseum, Munich.)*

panelling of a room and had no borders. This practice of making tapestries an integral part of a particular room's decoration was emphasised by having furniture, screens and upholstered sofas and chairs designed *en suite* with the tapestries (Figs. 6 and 9). The manufacture of these furnishings formed an important part of the industries of Beauvais and Aubusson.

Elected in 1664 to speak for his fellow merchants of Aubusson, Jacques Bertrand, tapestry-weaver to the Royal Wardrobe, reported to Colbert that 'the inhabitants of the place seem born to this work' and requested a dyer and a designer to supply the basic needs of the weavers. Colbert's regulations promised these and arranged for regular inspection of material, workshops and finished tapestries, the latter to be sealed with lead as a mark of approval. These tapestries were to be made having a blue surround with AUBUSSON and the initials of the maker woven into it, and the workshops could put up signs announcing a *Manufacture royale de tapisseries*. But the regulations proved abortive. Not until 1731 did the designer and dyer reach Aubusson, and Letters Patent of 1732 had to confirm those of 1665. The large number of existing unsigned Aubusson tapestries throws doubt on the efficiency of the system of inspection through which the quality of the independent family workshops' output was controlled; but many tapestries proudly bear names of those families, Picon, Grellet, Tabard, Finet, Dumonteil, Barraband, and many others, which, despite losses by war and emigration following the revocation of the Edict of Nantes in 1685, continued weaving at Aubusson.

Their tapestries are, on the whole, neatly and firmly woven. Aubusson frequently augmented the working strengths of the Gobelins and Beauvais, and expatriates staffed workshops for the rulers of

9

cartoons made from engravings of popular paintings, such as the harbour scenes of Vernet, or from tapestries already manufactured elsewhere. Throughout the first half of the eighteenth century new versions were made of Lebrun's monumental *History of Alexander*, designed for the Gobelins in 1663. The Aubusson cartoons began with somewhat simplified designs on a smaller scale, and as features in the designs became increasingly unrecognisable with wear, so the tapestries deteriorated in design. Other Gobelins tapestries were copied, and some very successful versions survive to show the skill of the weavers, among them a charming *Daphnis and Chloë* after Etienne Jeaurat, designed by 1738 (Fig. 2). Beauvais designs were also freely copied. Oudry's famous *Fables of La Fontaine* were being woven at Aubusson before 1764, when the inventory of Madame de Pompadour's goods noted a settee and six chairs covered in Aubusson *Fables*. Oudry's designs for the *Country Sports*, *Comedies of Molière* and *Metamorphoses* came to the town legitimately in 1761, when it benefited from the cast-off cartoons thought to be in too poor condition for continued use at Beauvais, and marked, in the hand of the Marquis de Marigny, the Pompadour's brother, 'Bon pour Aubusson'.

Beauvais provided tapestries for the nobility and Aubusson for the wealthy middle classes in France

Until the Revolution, Beauvais provided the nobility and court officials of France with the majority of their more expensive tapestries, while Aubusson supplied their cheaper ones and catered for the wealthy middle classes. Most of the Aubusson workshops were forced to close through lack of demand in the years of the First Republic. Although Beauvais continued to receive some orders and in the third year of the Republic was formally taken over by the State, its output dwindled until only small panels and furnishings were produced. So, sadly, ended this century of superb tapestry-weaving.

Germany, Switzerland and Portugal. The lower quality of Aubusson tapestries lay largely in the use of a thicker woollen warp and weft, which, with the convenience of the horizontal loom at which a weaver could manipulate the warp with treadles and have both hands free to insert the weft, made their weaving faster and cheaper at the sacrifice of fine detail. This was of real consequence only when producing figure subjects, needing detail for facial expression or a precise rendering of rich garments.

The sturdy, vigorous weave was particularly suited to making the verdure tapestries which formed a large part of Aubusson's production. These were woodland scenes, sometimes including a pond or stream inhabited by waterfowl, with birds in the trees and animals hunting in the undergrowth, sometimes opening out in middle distance to display a palace, a temple or a pagoda. As infinite combinations of these elements could be woven to create any size of tapestry without much additional design cost, they were relatively cheap and proportionately popular.

For more elaborate tapestries, lacking original designs the weavers of Aubusson had many of their

MUSEUMS AND COLLECTIONS

The Mobilier National in Paris has the finest collection of French tapestries, but they are not usually available to the public unless they are on special display at a museum.

Both Beauvais and Aubusson tapestries are to be found in museums, castles and churches, too numerous to list, throughout France.

In Great Britain and the United States, examples of the work of both factories may be seen at most major museums.

FURTHER READING

World Tapestry by M. Jarry, London, 1969. (Translation of *La Tapisserie des Origines à nos Jours*, Paris, 1968.)
French Tapestry by R. A. Weigert, London, 1962. (Translation of *La Tapisserie Française*, Paris, 1956.)
François Boucher and the Beauvais Tapestries by Maurice Block, Boston, 1933.
A History of Tapestry by W. G. Thomson, London, 1930.

American Coverlets

Fig. 1 *Quilted patchwork coverlet*, Baltimore, c.1850. Printed calico with diamond-quilted background, 10ft. 6 ins. x 10 ft. 6 ins. Quilting was functional as well as decorative, for it was a means of distributing evenly the filling of a coverlet and keeping it in place. The filling was carded wool, cotton or down. (American Museum in Britain.)

Derek Balmer

The quilted coverlets of America are not only finely worked objects of great beauty, but also mute witnesses to a hard, simple way of life

The chair of the chairman or the bed of the aristocrat's levee were the objects of considerable embellishment not only in Europe but also in her colonies in North America. Because of the prestigious social position of these two articles of furniture in great houses, they were treated as status symbols in lesser ones. Curtains, bedspreads and valances all formed a considerable part of such embellishment on beds. It is a curious twist of history that today the household craft of making elaborate patchwork quilts has all but died out in the Old World but persists in the countries of the New, such as Australia, Canada and the United States. For these historical reasons it is therefore not possible to discuss American patchwork quilts without some reference to Europe and, in addition, some observations upon the textile industry.

When medieval inventories allude to beds it is the hangings, the coverlets, the bolsters and the mattresses that are described in great detail, not the framework of the bed itself. This was not only due to a proper sense of the priorities of comfort, but also reflected the high cost of textiles in the age before the industrial revolution. This attitude, rooted in cost, persisted well into the eighteenth century and longer. A sale-catalogue of 1747 of the contents 'of the House and Gardens at Chelsea and all thereunto belonging to the Most Noble Robert, Earl of Orford, d'ceased' reads: 'A sacking bottom bedstead with green and straw worsted damask furniture: £2 2s. 0d., a feather bed, bolster and two pillows: £2 0s. 0d.' This contrasts noticeably with, in the same bedchamber 'A walnut tree dressing table, and an India picture: £0 10s 0d.' In view of the great value of textiles, and the feeling of opulence that they therefore imparted, it is small wonder that great ladies like Mary, Queen of Scots, and Bess of Hardwick regarded the art of crewel embroidery as an appropriately aristocratic pastime.

This, then, was the situation in Europe before industrialisation. In British America textiles were even rarer and more expensive. North America was colonised by people of many different European nationalities, including the British, French, Dutch, Spanish, Germans and Scandinavians. All were eventually to come under the political or cultural sway of England, or both.

In general it was the policy of the British government to encourage the production of raw materials but to discourage industrial development in its colonies, and this policy was as true of the textile industry as of any other (though there was little or no legislation against domestic production of textiles for personal use). Wool had long been the basis of England's wealth and in 1699 the Wool Act was passed to prevent the American colonies from competing with the mother country.

The attitude of the British government was well summed up in 1743 when the Board of Trade wrote to Governor Wentworth of New Hampshire as follows: 'It is our express Will and Pleasure that you do not upon any Pretence whatever – give your consent to a Law or Laws for setting up manufactures – which are hurtful or prejudicial to this kingdom'. On the other hand, encouragement was offered to the colonies for the production of those textiles that would not compete with the British Industry. James II, for example, encouraged Huguenots to settle in Virginia at his own expense to develop silk-weaving, and in fact the King was reputed to have worn Virginia silk on the occasion of his coronation. This political background imposed a frugal attitude, and American housewives of the eighteenth century became weavers of homespun and sewers of patchwork quilts.

Though it is true that a textile factory was established at Rowley, Massachusetts, as early as 1638, weaving remained largely a cottage industry in America not only during British rule but also after it ceased. America's industrial revolution was to need the horrors of the Civil War to provide the stimulus for manufactured goods.

Most of the developments in the weaving industry took place in Europe, notably in France and England. The British government of the eighteenth century did all in its power to contain the secrets of these developments; American agents working in England did all in their power to smuggle these secrets across the Atlantic, and eventually and inevitably they were to succeed. During the first quarter of the nineteenth century the American textile industry was using many of these new techniques.

Simple designs woven in blue and white

Plain woven coverlets were obviously much in use, such as the simple linsey-wolsey (coarse stuff of linen and wool mixed, or inferior wool with cotton). Sometimes plain woven coverlets were embellished with stencilled or printed designs and these were often further elaborated with quilting (Fig. 3).

The earliest decorative weaving produced in America appears to have been the simple four harness overshot weave. Many of these coverlet designs, often woven in blue (from indigo grown in the South) and white, possess delightful names, including Bonaparte's March, Dog Tracks, Fox's Chase, Lovers' Knot, Rose of Sharon (also known as Indian War), Sunrise and Whig Rose (clearly of English origin). Various checked patterns in four harness overshot weave were also made of two and five colours with browns and yellows predominating.

From about 1725 to 1825 the double weave, also known as 'double face' and 'summer and winter' weave, was popular (Fig. 6). Designs include Eight-pointed Star, Lisbon Star, Lovers' Knot, Wheel and Star, Snowball and Wheel of Fortune. Many of these were surrounded by a pine-tree border. Much of this weaving was produced in Pennsylvania and, as this state included powerful Welsh communities, the similarity with much weaving from the Principality may well prove to be far from fortuitous.

Coverlets made in America and woven on looms using a Jacquard or similar attachment were always the work of professional weavers (Fig. 7). Jacquard, a native of Lyon, made his invention in 1801 and Jacquard coverlets were being woven in America by

Fig. 2 *The Quilting Party,*
American, c.1858. Oil on
cardboard.
This shows quilting as a central
feature of American domestic life.
Sometimes known as a 'quilting
bee', it was a traditional activity.
In the seventeenth century
Charles I had permitted the
import of quilts from China, and
in seventeenth-century Virginia
armour was made from quilted
fabric.
(Abby Aldrich Rockefeller
Folk Art Collection,
Williamsburg, Va.)

Fig. 3 *Stencilled coverlet,*
Connecticut, c.1830.
This room is from the Joshua La
Salle house, Windham. The
stencilled decoration was
probably executed by a travelling
artist in exchange for board and
lodging and a small wage.
(American Museum in Britain,
Claverton Manor, Bath.)

the end of the first quarter of the nineteenth century. The early examples, and these are rare, were woven in two halves that were eventually sewn together down the middle. The fly shuttle was invented in England by John Kay of Lancashire as early as 1733, but was not in general use in America until the 1860s to '70s, and it was the introduction of this and similar mechanisms that eventually enabled these coverlets to be woven in the full width.

It is usually held that patchwork evolved as the result of sewing together a series of otherwise useless pieces of material to form one 'crazy quilt', creating a possession not only of beauty and utility, but also one provided at little extra cost at a time when textiles were extremely valuable, especially in America. In England at a fairly early date, cloth was frequently bought for the purpose of making quilts, resulting in a greater mobility of aesthetic choice. This threw the responsibility for design squarely upon the needlewoman. No longer did the conditions of frugality impose a discipline for design, and this resulted in patchwork coverlets of either a much higher or a much lower standard. The perfecting of the sewing-machine in the U.S.A. in the third quarter of the nineteenth century also had its effect.

Unmarried girls produced thirteen patchwork quilts

In America it was the custom for an unmarried girl to produce thirteen patchwork coverlets, often with the assistance of her family and friends. These coverlets would eventually form part of her dowry. The thirteenth coverlet was not usually made until she was engaged, and the remaining twelve were not quilted until that time. The thirteenth quilt was expected to be the finest in the series; it was often made in sections by different people and then assembled to form one large quilt.

Pieced coverlets are common to both America and Europe, though appliqué quilts are rare in Europe. Among many examples of geometric, pieced patchwork designs, the star is a recurrent

theme, often alluding to a particular state of the Union. Pieced coverlets and their quilting display a joy in geometry which is somewhat akin to the medieval mason's similar preoccupation, as manifested in tracery. This observation may sound somewhat far fetched, but it is worthy of note that the 1584 inventory of the Earl of Leicester includes 'a faire quilte of crymson sattin vi breadths iij yards 3 quarters naile deep [a nail measuring two and a half inches] all lozenged over with silken twists, in the midst a cinque-foil....'

The quilting bee was an important social event ·

In Ante-Bellum days, the 'quilting bee' was as important socially as the 'sewing circle' was to become during and after the American Civil War (Fig. 2). Many letters, poems and songs have survived which point to the importance of the quilting bee. The following reference evokes the period and character of life with the strength of simplicity: 'Ohio, February 7th, 1841: We have had deep snow. No teams passed for three weeks, but as soon as the drifts could be broken through Mary Scott sent her boy Frank around to say she was going to have a quilting....'

The different designs of American patchwork quilts were known by rather attractive names, although many of these names were interchangeable and some confusion has resulted. Some evoked unpopular images and so were changed; the Wandering Foot design was never made for a dower chest until its name was changed to Turkey Tracks. Other examples include: Crazy Patchwork, Beggars' Blocks, Robbing Peter to Pay Paul, Star of Bethlehem, Meadow Lily, Tulips, Rose of Sharon, Death's Black Darts (yet another name for Wandering Foot), Oak Leaf, Baseballs, Cactus Rose, Tumbling Blocks, Log Cabin, Sunburst, Cakestand, Lotus Flower, Dresden Plate, Princess Feather and Geometric Snowballs.

Apart from the influence of English patchwork design on American examples, mention should be made of the strong significance of the German

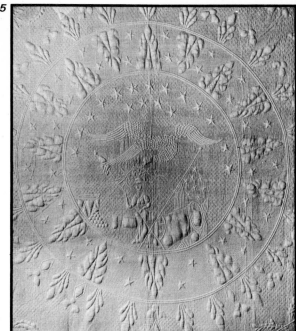

Fig. 4 *Coverlet, American, mid-eighteenth century. Crewel embroidery on a quilted background, 10 ft. x 10 ft. 6 ins. (American Museum in Britain.)*

Fig. 5 **Quilt,** *made by Mrs. Alexander Thompson, c.1821. Trapunto, or Italian, quilting, 7 ft. 5 ins. x 8 ft. 10 ins. (American Museum in Britain.)*

Fig. 6 *Reversible coverlet, Pennsylvania, 1840. Double-woven wool, 7 ft. x 8 ft. (Mr. and Mrs. A. J. J. Ayres Collection.)*

Fig. 7 *Coverlet, woven on a loom using a Jacquard attachment by Harry Tyler, of Jefferson County, New York, first half of the nineteenth century. Wool, 3 ft. 5½ ins. x 7 ft. 11 ins. (John Judkyn Memorial, Bath.)*

communities of Pennsylvania, known as the 'Pennsylvania Dutch'. Religion regulated the lives of these people and preserved their traditions and their domestic arts. Their designs include one of the favourite motifs of the Pennsylvania Dutch, the tulip.

Quilting was a means by which the coverlet top lining and filling (of carded wool, cotton, or sometimes down) could be kept in place, though this could also be achieved by tying. This utilitarian necessity was customarily used to decorative effect. Elaborate quilting designs were drawn with the help of templates of sized paper or textile. Princess Feather, Star and Crown, Peacock Fan, Oak Leaf, Daisy, Swirl, Acanthus, Day-Lily, Starfish, Tea-cup (overlapping circles), Running Vine, Pineapple (the pineapple is often used as a symbol of hospitality) and Spider-web are just some of the many designs used. Simpler quilting designs that did not require templates include: Crossbar, Double Crossbar and Diamonds (Fig. 1).

Sometimes quilting was used to emphasise a pieced or appliqué design but it was also used in a quite arbitrary way. The finest examples of quilting are usually to be found where quilting forms the only decoration and this Italian, or Trapunto, quilt-

ing is of the very best quality as seen in Figure 5.

Quilts with a cotton filling sometimes give a clue to their age. In 1793, Eli Whitney (1765–1825) invented the cotton gin which enables a worker to clean fifty pounds of cotton a day. Exports of cotton in 1795 were forty times higher because of his invention. If a quilt with a cotton filling reveals, when held to the light, a number of impurities, this would indicate an eighteenth-century specimen from before the introduction of the cotton-gin, if clues regarding materials and design agree.

MUSEUMS AND COLLECTIONS
American quilts and bedspreads may be seen at the following:
U.S.A.
Stamford, Connecticut: Stamford Historical Society
Washington, D.C.: The Textile Museum

FURTHER READING
America's Quilts and Coverlets by Carleton L. Safford, New York, 1972.
Old Patchwork Quilts by Ruth E. Finley, 1971.
American Coverlets by James E. Ayres, Newton Abbot, 1968.

Persian Miniatures

Jewel-like miniatures of exceptionally high quality characterise Persian painting in the sixteenth and seventeenth centuries

Fig. 1 *'She would and she would not'* by Muhammadi, Qazwin school, c.1575. $7\frac{1}{4} \times 3\frac{1}{2}$ ins. Muhammadi is said to have been the son of the Sultan Muhammad. (Museum of Fine Arts, Boston, Massachusetts.)

Below: **Map of Persia** showing the main centres of miniature painting during the sixteenth and seventeenth centuries.

During the sixteenth and seventeenth centuries, the king of Persia was known to Europe as the Grand Sophy, a slightly distorted echo of the family name of Safawi, borne by the ruling house throughout that period. The dynasty was founded by Isma'il who was swept to power by a wave of nationalist revival at the beginning of the sixteenth century. He had the great advantage of being able to trace his ancestry not only to the Prophet Muhammad's family, but also to the pre-Islamic Persian dynasty of the Sassanians; for after the overthrow of the latter by the Arabs in the middle of the seventh century, Shahr-banu, daughter of the last Sassanian monarch, is said to have married Husayn, Muhammad's grandson, and from this union the Safawid family boasted its descent.

From the Arab conquest to the enthronement of Shah Isma'il – a period of 850 years – Persia had been in a fragmented state and under the domination of a succession of foreign invaders, Arabs,

Turks, Mongols and Tartars. However, it was under the Mongol rulers in the fourteenth century that a truly Persian style of painting was first developed, and in the following century, under the Tartar Timurids (the family of Timur, or Tamburlaine), it achieved heights it was never to surpass, despite the increased elaboration and magnificence of Safawid Court painting in the period we are to consider.

It must be remembered that classical Persian painting was an art of book-illustration; some murals were produced, it is true, but only a few have survived, in a very damaged state, and they are, in effect, simply enlarged miniatures. The painter's status was relatively humble. He was just one among the body of craftsmen upon whose varied skills the production of a fine book depended, a body that included the calligrapher or scribe, the paper-makers, colour-men and grinders of gold, the illuminator, the ruler of margins and column-lines, and the binder.

The scribe, whose craft gave him the privilege of inscribing the Word of God, enjoyed considerably higher standing than the others; the painter, on the contrary, was always under something of a cloud,

A. C. Cooper

Fig. 2 **Suicide of Shirin on the corpse of the murdered Khusraw,** *possibly by Sultan Muhammad, Tabriz, c.1505.*
11¾ x 8¾ ins.
Sultan Muhammad's style evolved in the Turkman court where he began his career. This final episode in the love story of Khusraw shows Shirin killing herself on the corpse of her murdered husband.
(Keir Collection, London.)

Fig. 3 **Bahram Gur Hunting** *by Sultan Muhammad, Tabriz, c.1540.*
Bahram Gur ruled Persia from 420 to 438 A.D. He is commemorated by Omar Khayyam as 'The Great Hunter'. Sultan Muhammad's style at this stage in his career was less exuberant and more academic than his earlier work illustrated in Fig. 2.
(British Museum, London.)

as his profession was abhorred by strict Muslims who shared the Semitic horror of idolatry embodied in the Second Commandment, and were taught to believe that in portraying human beings and animals the painter was usurping the functions of the Creator. This explains why, in many Persian paintings, the faces and figures have been wilfully defaced. Nevertheless, the tradition of pictorial art in Persia had remained so firmly embedded in the national character for two thousand years that painting was not only tolerated, but actively encouraged and patronised by the great majority of Persian rulers.

If we superimpose a large capital T on the map of Persia, it will give us a rough idea of the relative positions of the three main centres of painting on the eve of Shah Isma'il's accession. The right-hand end of the horizontal will rest on Herat, now within the borders of Afghanistan, but then capital of the great province of Khurasan. Fine manuscripts and miniatures had been produced there throughout the fifteenth century under the Timurid rulers, the last of whom, Sultan Husayn Mirza (1468–1506), was the patron of Bihzad, the most celebrated of all Persian painters. The Herat style was exquisite, precise, and slightly academic.

The left-hand end of the horizontal of the giant T rests on Tabriz. During the latter half of the fifteenth century this city had been the capital of

the Turkman princes who, taking advantage of the increasingly confused state of the Timurid empire, had gradually moved in from the West and established their power over the whole of Persia, excepting only Khurasan. Painting under the later Turkman rulers was brilliant in colour, sometimes uneven in execution, and often markedly original.

The base of our capital T rests on Shiraz. This most Persian of all Persian cities had been under Turkman rule since the middle of the fifteenth century, by which time it seems already to have assumed the role of purveyor of illustrated manuscripts on a commercial scale to those who could not afford to maintain a library staff of their own. For this purpose a fairly simple but generally satisfactory style had been evolved from a blend of Turkman court painting with elements of the Shiraz style as practised earlier under the Timurids. This 'utility' style was broad and effective, though without much refinement or elaboration, and is found in countless illustrated volumes of the works of Firdausi, Nizami and other favourite authors during the last quarter of the fifteenth century.

It was from Herat and Tabriz that Shah Isma'il recruited his library staff, which eventually included the aging Bihzad. The traditions of the two cities are separately recognisable in many of the paintings executed in his reign and in the early years of his son Tahmasp, who succeeded him in 1524,

Fig. 4 **Rustam in battle** from the
Shahnama (Book of Kings) by
Firdausi, Shiraz school, 1566.
14 x 8 ins. (Private Collection.)

Author's Photo

Fig. 5 **Bahram Gur hunting**
from the Shahnama of Firdausi
by Mu'in, 1693.
(Metropolitan Museum of Art,
New York.)

Museum Photo

Author's Photo

Museum Photo

A. C. Cooper

Fig. 6 **The Vizier pleads for the
life of a boy bandit**, Bokhara
school, 1548. 8 x 5 ins.
*This miniature is an illustration
to the Gulistan (Rose Garden) by
Sa'di.*
(Private Collection.)

Fig. 7 **Two Lovers** by Riza-i-
'Abbasi, Isfahan school, 1629.
7 x 4½ ins.
(Metropolitan Museum of Art,
Francis M. Weld Fund, 1950.)

Fig. 8 **Lovers in a garden
pavilion**, Meshed school,
c.1560. 18½ x 12¾ ins.
(Keir Collection.)

and are personified, as it were, in the work of
Shaykhzada and of Sultan Muhammad. Shaykhzada was a pupil of Bihzad and a native of Khurasan;
his work is exquisitely fine and often expressive.
He had all his master's perfection of technique, but
lacked the vital spark of genius (Fig. 11). Sultan
Muhammad, a Tabrizi, may well have begun his
career under the Turkman princes before taking
service with the conquering Isma'il, and his work
at this stage exemplifies the Turkman strain in the
evolving Safawid court style (Fig. 2). He brought
to it a feeling for fantasy, a fertile imagination,
and a bubbling sense of humour. His brilliant and
exuberant paintings are in strong contrast to the
meticulous academic style of Shaykhzada.

Tahmasp (1524–1576), the second Safawid king,
was a keen patron of painting in the earlier part of
his reign, and actually took lessons from Sultan
Muhammad. From his accession until about 1550 he
maintained a library staff of unequalled brilliance,
and during this period the court style of painting
was 'ironed out', so that by the late 1530s even
Sultan Muhammad had been persuaded, or driven,
to drop his exuberant idiosyncrasies and conform to
the smooth and resplendent academic norm, as can
be seen from his work in the famous British Museum
Nizami manuscript of 1539–43.

In the latter part of Tahmasp's reign, the capital
was moved from Tabriz (uncomfortably near the
Turkish frontier) to Qazwin, further to the east.
But the king had by now become a religious bigot,
and had ceased to take any interest in painting,
and though a certain amount of work was done in
the new capital under the patronage of the nobility,
the best painters seem to have transferred their
services to the able and cultured young prince
Ibrahim Mirza, who held his court at Meshed
(Fig. 8). The style was becoming harder in outline,
and the human figures slimmer and more supple,
with longer necks and rounder faces.

Meanwhile at Shiraz and at Bokhara, distinct
styles of painting flourished. As we have seen, Shiraz
was the centre, at the end of the fifteenth century, of
the simplified 'commercial' Turkman style, and
during the first years of Safawid rule this style
continued virtually unchanged except for the
incorporation of the characteristic Safawid turban
with its slender baton, usually coloured red,
rising from the centre. By the middle of the sixteenth century Shiraz painting had approached the
metropolitan style more closely, but its colouring
remained paler and the general effect is often
rather flat and provincial (Fig. 4).

Bokhara, in the land of the Uzbeks, was the
capital of the Shaybanid dynasty during the sixteenth century. The founder of the dynasty,
Shaybani Khan, sacked Herat in 1507, abducting a
number of painters and other craftsmen who were

405

9

10

*Fig. 9 **Picnic scene** by Riza-i-'Abbasi, Isfahan school, 1629.*
8½ x 5½ ins.
This miniature is one of a group which has played an important part in the reconstruction of the career of Riza-i-'Abbasi, the most distinguished painter of the seventeenth century Persian school.
(Keir Collection.)

*Fig. 10 **Combat of the Lion and the Ox** by Sadiqi Beg, Qazwin school, 1591. 11¾ x 8¼ ins.*
This miniature is taken from a manuscript of the Anwar i Suhayli (Lights of Canopus), a book of popular fables.
(Library of the Marquess of Bute.)

*Fig. 11 **Khusraw killing the lion** by Shaykhzada, Tabriz school, c.1525. 12¾ x 8¾ ins.*
This miniature is an illustration to a poem by Nizami which celebrates the life of Khusraw, the last great king of the Sassanian (pre-Islamic) dynasty. In this miniature he is seen killing a lion with his fist outside Shirin's tent.
(Chester Beatty Library, Dublin.)
406

set to work for their new masters. Although Shaybani Khan was defeated and killed by Shah Isma'il in 1510, the Uzbeks continued to give trouble on the north-eastern frontier, and in 1535 they again raided Herat, transporting a further body of artists and craftsmen across the Oxus. Bokhara painting thus began as almost indistinguishable from the Herat style of Bihzad and his school, and this style continued to be its model till well after the middle of the sixteenth century. Sultan 'Abd al-'Aziz (1540–50) was the greatest patron of the arts of the book among the Shaybanid rulers (Fig. 6). But soon after this, Bokhara painting became lifeless and sterile; the imported Herat artists were dead, and their Uzbek pupils do not seem to have had the ability to keep the style alive, far less to develop it.

Returning to the metropolitan style of Qazwin and Meshed, we find the slim and exquisite youths and girls of Muhammadi and his followers throughout the 1570s and 1580s, disporting themselves elegantly at picnics and hunting parties, as well as in the inevitable court scenes. One or two distinguished new artists, such as Sadiqi Beg (Fig. 10) and Siyawush the Georgian, made their appearance at this time. A simplified form of Muhammadi's style is also found in the illustrations of a number of manuscripts from Khurasan, and it seems likely that they were produced in much the same commercial manner as were the Shiraz manuscripts already mentioned.

In 1598 Shah 'Abbas the Great established his capital at Isfahan, in the very centre of Persia, and at that time a very distinguished painter was coming into prominence under whose influence Persian painting underwent a gradual but profound change. This was Riza, whose work under the patronage of Shah 'Abbas earned him the epithet of 'Abbasi. Ever since Persian painting was first seriously studied in the West, some sixty years ago, he has been the centre of controversy. The nub of the problem is this: are the exquisite drawings and miniatures bearing the signature or attribution 'Riza' or 'Aqa Riza' and dating from the 1590s and early 1600s by the same hand as the rather different, coarser, but still masterly works signed 'Riza-i-'Abbasi' between about 1620 and 1635, or are these two groups the work of two different men of the same name? This is no place to rake over the embers of this old dispute; suffice it to say that many who, like the present writer, were formerly 'dualists' have been converted to the view that Aqa Riza and Riza-i-'Abbasi are one and the same painter at different stages of his career. This has been brought about partly by the discovery and publication of several important 'bridge' works (Fig. 9), and partly by the forceful and scholarly writings of Dr. Ivan Stchoukine of Beirut, perhaps the foremost living authority on Persian painting.

In Riza's work, then, we can trace the transition from the slim figures, fluent draughtsmanship, and pure colours of Muhammadi to the distinctly plumper young men and women (often, indeed, with a discreet indication of a double-chin), rapidly sketched with nervous calligraphic strokes, or strongly coloured with purples, yellows and browns. These youths have more than a hint of decadence in their languid postures, curling whiskers and affected gestures. Indeed, after the death of Shah 'Abbas the Great (1628), the

Safawid dynasty rapidly sank into a state of weakness and corruption under a succession of ineffectual or dissipated monarchs.

The style of Riza-i-'Abbasi had many followers in the middle and later years of the seventeenth century, amongst whom Muhammed Qasim was one of the most noteworthy, but the best of the master's successors was probably his pupil Mu'in whose exceptionally long working life stretched from about 1635–1707 (Fig. 5). At first he followed Riza very closely – indeed, he was not above forging his master's signature – but as the century progressed he evolved a fluent and effective style of his own and remained the last great master of the traditional Persian style.

In about 1675, when Mu'in was still in his prime, a younger painter, Muhammed Zaman, was sent to study painting in Italy. The late seventeenth century was not, of course, by any standards the golden age of Italian painting, but Muhammed Zaman conscientiously absorbed the canons of perspective, modelling, and chiaroscuro, and on his return to Persia produced a number of highly finished miniatures in an Italianate style. These immediately 'caught on', and by the end of the century had determined the course of Persian painting for the next two hundred years. But by 1700 the glorious Safawid dynasty was all but played out. In 1722 a comparatively small band of Afghan marauders was able to invade the country, rout the vastly superior Persian army, besiege and sack Isfahan, the capital, and bring the dynasty to an ignominious end.

MUSEUMS AND COLLECTIONS

Persian miniatures are kept in most major and national libraries but are not generally on view. Anyone wishing to examine miniatures from these collections should write to the appropriate library for permission well in advance of their intended visit.
Persian miniatures are, however, on permanent exhibition at the following:

GREAT BRITAIN
Cambridge: Fitzwilliam Museum
Edinburgh: The Royal Scottish Museum
London: British Museum
Victoria and Albert Museum

FRANCE
Paris: Musée Guimet
IRAN
Teheran: Golestan Palace Museum
Archaeological Museum

TURKEY
Istanbul: Topkapi Saray Museum
U.S.A.
Chicago, Ill.: Oriental Institute, University of Chicago
New York: Metropolitan Museum of Art
San Diego, Calif.: Fine Arts Gallery
Washington D.C.: Freer Gallery of Art

FURTHER READING

Miniature Antiques by Jean Latham, London, 1972.
Painting in Islam by Sir T. W. Arnold, reprinted New York, 1965.
Persian Painting by Basil Gray, Geneva, 1961.
Persian Miniature Painting by Laurence Binyon, J. V. D. Wilkinson and Basil Gray, London, 1933.

French Fans

To the eighteenth-century French-woman the fan was the most exquisite of weapons, the most favoured toy, expressing every emotion with graceful virtuosity

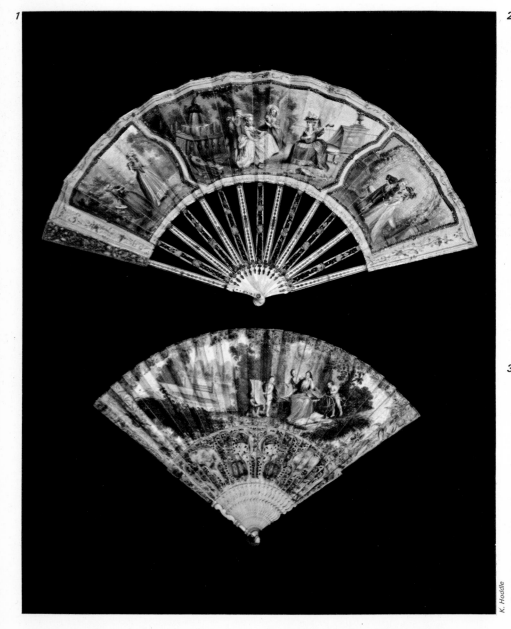

Fig. 2 Above: **Fan,** c.1780, *with scenes from* Monument de Costume *by Moreau le Jeune.* Below: **Fan with herring-bone background.** (*Victoria and Albert Museum.*)

Fig. 1 Above: **Fan,** c.1785. *The mount is of silk painted by Binet.* Below: **Fan depicting Astronomy,** *mid-eighteenth century.* (*Victoria and Albert Museum, London.*)

Fig. 3 Above: **Fan** *with wooden sticks,* c.1780. Below: **Fan** *of the Vernis-Martin type.* (*Victoria and Albert Museum.*)

Fig. 4 *Fashion plate from* Le Galerie des Modes et Costumes Français *by Desracis, 1778.*

Time and again one may note the deft handling of fans in paintings. Most often it is held closed to emphasise a gesture or suggest a pensive mood, as in Watteau's *Champs Elysées* or *Fête in a Park*, Boucher's *Marquise de Pompadour* in the Wallace Collection (Fig. 6), or Nattier's *Marie Josèphe of Saxony*. But, occasionally, the artist could not resist the gay flutter of fans in full display, perfectly recorded in the *fêtes galantes* and pastoral scenes by Lancret, Pater (Fig. 5), Vernet and the like. Although such paintings frequently were the inspiration for innumerable artisan fan painters, it is doubtful whether the famous eighteenth-century artists themselves ever painted fans.

Today, this painting of the mount, or leaf, is likely to be the first detail to attract attention to an antique fan. But, throughout its eighteenth-century heyday, in ever changing mood and style, this symbol of delicious idleness embodied extremely skilful work from a series of widely different provincial craftsmen whose work was co-ordinated by a master fan-maker in Paris.

Briefly, the folding fan is composed of a pliant, folding mount, or leaf, supported by a frame, or *pied*, which consists of a dozen or more flat ribs, flanked by stouter end sticks called *panaches*, or guards. These are held together by a rivet at the base, which, to the French fan-maker, was the head. The upper halves of the sticks away from the rivet are usually plain wisps of wood, because they are concealed under the pasted-on mount; but the lower parts, or *brins*, near the rivet, being visible, are frequently of lavishly decorated ivory, tortoise-shell or mother of pearl.

Sticks of carved ivory, tortoise-shell, sandalwood or painted bone

Sticks overlapping and decorated throughout their length replace the mount in the surprisingly resilient *brisé* fan. These sticks may be of carved and fretted ivory, *piqué* tortoise-shell, sandalwood or painted bone, usually about six or eight inches long and linked around the perimeter with ribbons. Some, from the early years of the century, were richly coloured in varnish imitating lacquer, but the greater number date from the last years of the century and are pale and fragile in the mood of contemporary dress, and neo-classical theme of the period.

For the rest, the mount and its supporting sticks alternated in pre-eminence. Often both were mediocre, created for a few hours' frivolity and to be tossed aside in favour of more topical successors; guests at an assembly might be invited to help themselves from great bowls of perfumes, gloves and fans. Cheap leaves were easily replaced and beautiful eighteenth-century sticks may now be found bearing a chromolithograph of Victorian days. But there were also great master fan-makers assembling magnificent work. Because this tended to be conventional and elaborately pictorial on both mount and sticks, it is still possible for the collector to trace the chronological history of the fan throughout the century by its close association with society as it revolved around its all-dominant monarchy.

At the same time, the ephemeral fan proved the most sensitive expression of the changing tastes that affected all French artists and craftsmen throughout the century, from porcelain-makers to portrait painters. Indeed, it is known that fan-painters decorated the famous porcelain of Sèvres. Some of their fan work then fell to professional embroiderers and lace-women, while the decoration of more work-a-day mounts spread to engravers and printers accustomed to the cut and thrust of topical broadsheets.

In general terms, early fans are dark, with the massive richness of the early eighteenth-century Baroque. This became lighter through the 1730s to 1750s, in the gay frivolity of the Rococo: all asymmetrical scrolls, flowers, shells and waterfalls, as naturalistic yet contrived as the *fêtes* in sunlit woodland glades that delighted Louis XV and his gay courtiers. This, in its turn, gave way to the mellow, graceful neo-classical mood of the 1770s and 1780s before the onslaughts of the troubled 1790s.

Current designs in dress were echoed by fans

In size and extent of opening, the fan reflected the dress fashions of its day, as witnessed, for example, by the huge fans of the mid-century, so confusingly repeated a century later. But it is easy to recognise more than an association between the slender, colour-drained silhouette and the subdued little fans of the century's end.

The eighteenth century opened with the Sun King, Louis XIV, still on the throne of a France which continued to enjoy the opulent magnificence of the Baroque. The folding fan tended to be small, the colours dark, the painted scene of a familiar classical story spread large over a deep mount that rendered the sticks insignificant. Already courtiers expected their fan-makers to associate them with royal occasions, supplying fans on which were laboriously depicted the scenes that absorbed their etiquette-ruled days. The exotic wedding in 1697 of Louis XIV's fifteen-year-old grandson Louis, Duke of Bourgogne, to the twelve-year-old Marie Adélaïde of Savoy, was recorded in minutely detailed scenes of dignified revellers against dark backgrounds, pencilled with marriage trophies.

But Louis XIV died in 1715, and the Court relaxed under the feast-loving Regent and the child he represented, still only thirteen when in 1723 he was crowned Louis XV. When, in 1725, the young King married Marie Leczinska, even a fan could be painted in a gayer, more casual manner, with the young bride and groom at Hymen's altar against faint suggestions of the country landscapes that Louis loved.

Four years later, more fans in this mood commemorated the fun and fireworks that marked the birth of their son; what a century it was for fireworks and masked balls!

In the 1730s and '40s, this light-hearted air was superbly expressed in small scenes of contrived informality. It is interesting to note in these fans the change of atmosphere between the evocative Watteau-esque charm of the early *fêtes champêtres* and the more sophisticated pastorals prompted by Boucher's paintings for Madame de Pompadour (Fig. 11).

Some master fan-makers long continued to commission immensely elaborate *brins* enriched with gold or coloured foil, carved and painted with

scenes such as Venus and Mars within cartouches of asymmetrical scrolls. *Piqué* work scintillated in gold on tortoise-shell and silver on ivory. *Brins* became longer in proportion to the mount and were square-shouldered, overlapping to offer the largest area for ornament (a point to contrast with the round-shouldered Victorian fan *brins*). But huge fans opening to a full half-circle towards the mid-century were in danger of becoming unwieldy. The somewhat shortened mount was then given longer sticks, narrower and more widely spaced.

Sometimes in a particularly ornate fan a proportion of the *brins* – perhaps six out of twelve – were spoon- or spade-shaped, each with one or two swellings for rounded medallion ornaments. This style was sometimes known as *battoir* (Fig. 9), or *Pompadour*, from some imagined association with 'La Pom-pom'. This design required the guards, too, to be swelling in silhouette.

Fans associated with the years around the mid-century include marriage fans again, to commemorate the courtship of the Dauphin, son of Louis XV, and his marriages, first to Marie Thérèse, Infanta of Spain, in 1745, and, after her death, to Marie Josèphe of Saxony in 1747. A less conventional style, which also may be dated, was the cabriolet fan (Fig. 9), named after the small, two-wheeled carriage that became popular in 1754. The special feature was the introduction of two, sometimes three, narrow mounts with a short length of the *brins* exposed between them. The fan with an opera glass attached was noted in 1759, 'for ladies to oppose to the indiscreet opera glasses of our *petits-maîtres*'. Another notion then was the cockade fan with a ribbon in its handle, which could be pulled when the fan was closed so as to form a bouquet of the pliant mount. Fans introducing *chinoiserie* motifs may also be attributed to this restless period.

A Royal wedding – an occasion for magnificent commemorative fans

By this date, additional sparkle might be contrived with tiny gilt sequins sewn to the skin mount. Sequins (Fig. 8), gold-thread embroidery and tambour work (embroidered on a frame) were in and out of fashion throughout the rest of the century and might be matched by tiny metal discs inlaid into the ivory *brins*.

In the 1760s, however, black fans were carried all too often by court ladies while the future Louis XVI had to go through the detested ceremonial of royal grief for brother, father, mother and grandmother. But more celebrations, more music, a huge congregation of courtiers, cavalry and musketeers sparkled around the great assembly of the royal family in the May sunshine of 1770, in Louis' adored forest near Versailles when he met his fiancée, the Austrian Archduchess Marie Antoinette. Here, yet again, was occasion for magnificent bridal fans (Fig. 9), so that every court lady could associate herself with the giant masquerade expressing French civilisation at its most magnificent, albeit that some tradesmen were going unpaid.

Now the neo-classical mood was pre-eminent. Fans had lost their rococo nonsense in smaller, more discreet designs. Detailed figure ornament was usually restricted to three round or oval medallions, in clear bright colours. These were

Fig. 5 *Watching the Dance*
(detail) by J. B. Pater (1695–
1736), early eighteenth century.
This detail shows a young French
girl reclining with a fan.
(Wallace Collection, London.)

Fig. 6 *La Marquise de
Pompadour* (detail) by François
Boucher (1703–70). Oil on canvas.
The fan was so widely used
as an accessory that many
portraits of eighteenth-century
ladies show them holding fine
examples.
(Wallace Collection.)

Fig. 7 *Fan mount*, first half of the
eighteenth century. Gouache
on parchment.
(Victoria and Albert Museum.)

surrounded by extremely delicate pencillings of the ever-recurrent neo-classical motifs: urns, swags of drapery or flower-heads, pendulent bell-flowers and the like. These might fill the blank spaces between medallions portraying, for example, the fifteen-year-old Archduchess in the clouds among Graces and Cupids, with Hymen hovering above and Fame's trumpet banishing Midas and Discordia. Or the whole scene might be symbolised in the marriage of Peleus and Thetis.

It is usually a mistake to imagine that commemorative fans represent actual scenes, since of necessity they were prepared in advance for distribution to favoured guests. Fans for occasions of mourning were kept in readiness, too. When Louis XV died of smallpox in 1774, black was *de rigueur* for the court ladies' formal condolences, from coifs to stockings, with black-gloved hands holding black fans.

By the 1770s, fan sticks were straight, narrow, widely separated, and their ornament usually restricted to delicate formal patterns. Some in elaborate silhouette contained more personal details, however; for example, a fan marking the birth of the Dauphin, 1781, has shell sticks carved with portraits of the King and Queen and Dauphin, with Providence and other emblematic figures.

The printed fan is a subject in itself, offering many a fascinating glimpse of matters attracting public approval or concern, such as the balloon exploits of the Montgolfier brothers in 1783, the Assembly of Notables in 1787, the taking of the Bastille and many interpretations of *La Liberté*.

Inevitably, even after the fatal January 1793, portraits of the King and other members of the royal family continued to appear on fans. Most interesting is the 'secret' portrait with a piece of thin paper pasted on the mount concealing the figure of Louis until the fan is held against the light.

By then, however, many a bright little fan was paying tribute to Napoleon Bonaparte who was shown with figures of Fame and Victory, or with Peace flanked by Commerce and Agriculture among rejoicing peasants instead of nymphs and shepherds, the whole fan surrounded by the red, white and blue of the Tricolor and sewn with cockades. But politics of such bitterness were no province for the idler's fan, which diminished to a wispy toy worn at the waist (hence the introduction of the rivet loop) and was known as *l'Imperceptible*.

Fan-making sheds interesting light on the ways that costs were cut and supplies increased during the eighteenth century. Throughout the century the mount ranged from the extremely fine kid or

Fig. 8 **Fan mount**, c.1780.
Painted and sequinned silk.
(Victoria and Albert Museum.)

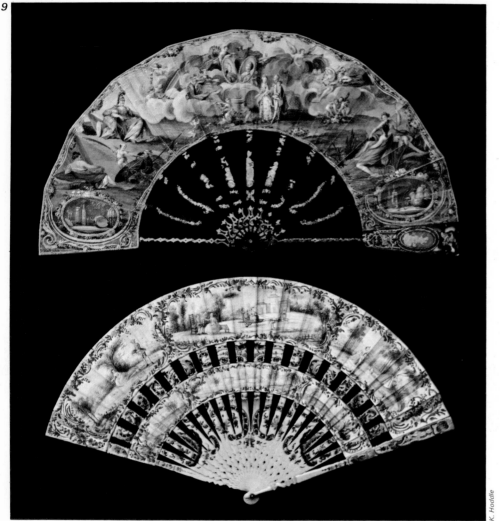

Fig. 9 Above: **Battoir type fan**,
1770, depicting an allegory of the
wedding between the Dauphin,
later Louis XVI, and Marie
*Antoinette. Below: **Cabriolet***
***type fan**, c.1755.*
(Victoria and Albert Museum.)

Fig. 10 **Fan mount**, c.1750. *Pink*
paper with gilt lace and four
flower sprigs in water-colour.
(Victoria and Albert Museum.)

Fig. 11 **Fan mount**, c.1750.
Water-colour on parchment
depicting a pastoral idyll.
(Victoria and Albert Museum.)

lambskin, known to collectors as chicken skin, through parchment to soft hand-made paper. In later years, silk and satin were alternatives for painted ornament as well as for embroidery and sequin patterns in gilt-metal and end-of-the-century steel. The painting was by skilled copyists and their assistants rather than by named artists, using paints mixed with gum to avoid cracking. Heat-hardened varnish paints, popular in England as 'japan', brought rich, vivid colours and a lacquer gloss to some early *brisé* fans; these mostly appear to pre-date the patents of 1730 and 1744 granted to the Martin brothers for their famous *Vernis-Martin* (Fig. 3). Around the mid-century, painting *en camaïeu* was popular, a single colour such as blue or rose pink being used in a range of tones. Other colouring was enriched by a silver ground or by fine parallel zig-zag pencillings glinting in gold and echoed in ivory *brins*, where motifs carved in extremely low relief were set off by background perforations of narrow slits.

The sticks were most usually of thin wood under the mount, secured to *brins* of ivory, tortoise-shell, mother of pearl or bone. Even straw-work has been noted during an end-of-century vogue. The guards harmonised with the *brins* but could be more deeply carved. The *brins* had to be prepared individually, and extraordinarily clever work was required, for example, to build up small pieces of extremely thin mother of pearl, sometimes introducing colour contrasts, just as ivory might be discreetly tinted to emphasise almost flat carved detail.

Fan-makers cut their costs by distributing the *brins* among a series of specialist craftsmen working at home in the provinces, especially in the *département* of the Oise. The town of Dieppe, which had a long tradition of ivory-carving, presented Marie Antoinette with an exquisite ivory *brisé* fan in 1785 to celebrate the birth of the future Louis XVII. Filers, polishers, piecers, carvers, gilders, and even perhaps men to fix spangles or pins of gold, silver or steel, prepared the fan frames for mounts that were painted or printed and hand-coloured in Paris. Only such final details in the fan's manufacture as the jewel-mounted rivet would then be added in the establishment of the master fan-maker whose name inside the fan's carefully shaped and lined box was the assurance of Parisian quality.

MUSEUMS AND COLLECTIONS

French fans of the eighteenth-century may be seen at the following:

FRANCE

Paris: Louvre

GREAT BRITAIN

Bath: Museum of Costume, Assembly Rooms

London: Victoria and Albert Museum

U.S.A.

Pasadena, Calif.: Historical Society Museum

FURTHER READING

A Collector's Guide to Fans Over the Ages by Bertha de Vere Green, 1975.
The Fan Book by MacIver Percival, London, 1920.
History of the Fan by G. Wooliscroft Rhead, London, 1910.
Fans and Fan Leaves: Foreign by Lady Charlotte Schreiber, London, 1888.
The Fan by O. Uzanne, translated from the French, London, 1884.

English Enamels

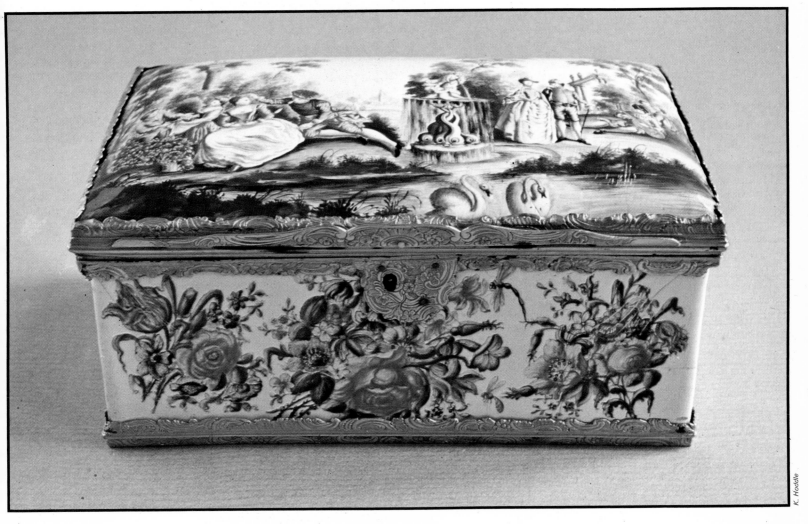

K. Haddle

Fig. 1 *Casket, probably Battersea, 1753–56. Printed in red and painted in colours with subjects from the works of Antoine Watteau. Mounted with chased gilt metal, length 7½ ins., width 5 ins. (Victoria and Albert Museum, London.)*

Birmingham, Bilston and Battersea were among the eighteenth-century centres producing small objects exquisitely decorated with jewel-like enamels

During September 1751, an announcement in *Aris's Birmingham Gazette* stated that: 'Abraham Seeman, Enamelling Painter, at Mrs. Weston's in Freeman Street, Birmingham, makes and sells all sorts of enamelling colours, especially the Rose Colours, likewise all sorts for China Painters. N.B. Most of the eminent Painters of Birmingham, Wednesbury and Bilston have made use of the above colours to their satisfaction'.

From the last sentence it is clear that enamelling was a flourishing trade at that time in a number of Midland towns. In the very same month an Irish-born engraver named John Brooks, then described as 'of Birmingham, in the county of Warwick', applied to patent 'a method of printing, impressing, and reversing upon enamel and china from engraved, etched and mezzotinto plates, and from cuttings on wood and mettle . . .'.

Birmingham had for several decades maintained a reputation as a centre for the production of large quantities of well-made small metal articles, such as buttons, shoe-buckles, and boxes for snuff, patches, bodkins and much else. The fact that the city was free of any guilds to regulate its workers and employers, and was well situated for the supply of metal, fuel and water, attracted to it men of ingenuity who were able to exploit their ideas more easily than in other parts of the country. Before

413

Fig. 2 *Six patch-boxes bearing legends, probably Bilston, early nineteenth century. One box is painted with a view of St. Michael's Mount. The lids are lined either with polished thin steel plates or with looking-glass. Widest width 1 11/16 ins. (Private Collection.)*

Fig. 3 *Snuff-box in the form of a bird, probably Bilston, c.1770. Length 2 ins. (Private Collection.)*

Fig. 4 *Plaque, possibly Birmingham, c.1755–60. Printed in crimson and painted in colours, showing Venus mourning Adonis. Width 3 7/8 ins. (Victoria and Albert Museum.)*

Fig. 5 *'Bottle ticket with a Chain' for cider, possibly Battersea, c.1755. Printed in crimson from an engraving by Simon François Ravenet (1706–74) and painted in brown. Width 2 3/4 ins. (Victoria and Albert Museum.)*

the century was out, Edmund Burke, the statesman, referred to Birmingham as 'The great toyshop of Europe', using the word 'toy' in the sense of a fashionable trifle.

At first, many of the objects were made of gilt-metal in combination with horn, tortoise-shell and other suitable materials, but by at least 1750, plaques of enamel were being used (Fig. 4). The latter were formed from thin sheet copper, cut to size and slightly domed, then coated with a layer of opaque white or coloured glass. In the heat of a small furnace the glass melted and became fused to the metal. The decoration was hand-painted, in a manner similar to that employed for pottery and porcelain, the colours being made fast by further applications of heat. The temperature for the latter purpose was lower than that used for the basic coating in order to melt only the painted work and allow it to combine with the ground.

Such work demanded considerable skill and artistic talent on the part of the painter. On the other hand, printing called for a minimum of such requirements as it could be done successfully by the comparatively untrained and was therefore much cheaper. The process was seen in use and described by Lady Shelburne, who visited the largest manufactory in Birmingham, that of John Taylor, in 1766, and wrote in her diary: 'The method of doing it is this: a stamping instrument managed only by one woman first impressed the picture on paper, which paper is then laid even upon a piece of white enamel and rubbed hard with a knife, or

instrument like it, till it is marked upon the box. Then there is spread over it with a brush some metallic colour reduced to a fine powder which adheres to the moist part, and by putting it afterwards into an oven for a few minutes, the whole is completed by fixing the colour'.

The last reference is to the colour of the transferred print, which was most frequently black. Alternatively, it was sometimes lilac, brick-red or brown and was then sometimes left untouched, but more often these paler tints provided a guide for subsequent painting; thus, the fact that a printed outline has been used occasionally passes undetected. Very rarely printing was executed in gold.

By 1753, Brooks had moved south and joined in partnership with Stephen Theodore Janssen, a City merchant, and a man named Delamain; possibly the Henry Delamain who owned a pottery in Dublin. At York House, Battersea, the three men established an enamel manufactory that was destined to operate for a bare three years, but duly acquired a fame out of all proportion to the size of its output. At one time, until not so very long ago, Battersea was popularly accredited with the making of any piece of English-looking enamel dating between about 1750 and 1900.

Research, however, has revealed that the Thames-side venture was started in order to exploit printed decoration, and that this is what it did. On 18 September, 1755, Horace Walpole wrote to a friend: 'I shall send you a trifling snuff-box, only as a sample of the new manufacture at Battersea,

414

which is done with copper-plates'. Further, when the concern became bankrupt in 1756, the advertisements of the sales of the stock at the factory and of Janssen's personal possessions reveal information about what was made. The latter's house in St. Paul's Churchyard was announced as containing, among much else: '. . . a Quantity of beautiful Enamels, colour'd and uncolour'd, of the new Manufactory carried on at York-House at Battersea, and never yet exhibited to publick View, consisting of Snuff-boxes, of all Sizes of great Variety of Patterns, of square and oval Pictures of the Royal Family, History and other pleasing Subjects, . . . Watch-Cases, Toothpick-Cases, Coat and Sleeve Buttons, Crosses, and other Curiosities, mostly mounted in Metal, double gilt'. At York House there were similar articles, and in addition 'a great Number of Copper Plates beautifully engraved by the best Hands'.

There seems to be no evidence as to whether the printing at Battersea was carried out by a process different from that described above in the words of Lady Shelburne. Certainly the clarity of examples now accepted as having been made there is considerably greater than that of others. John Brooks applied for two further patents for a 'new method' in 1754 and 1755, but as with the earlier one, they were not granted and no details of them survive.

Articles like those once belonging to Janssen have been identified, but in view of the short life of the manufactory they could never have been plentiful and are now scarce. Typical of them are the 'Bottle Tickets with Chains', now better known as wine-labels, which are decorated appropriately with cupids performing such actions as treading grapes, distilling brandy and drawing wine from a large cask (Fig. 5).

Fragile, fascinating and pretty 'toys'

The labels were printed from engravings made by a French-born artist, Simon François Ravenet, who came to London some time prior to 1745, when he engraved two of Hogarth's paintings. His distinctive work for Battersea included a range of portraits of royal and other personages as well as some mythological scenes. The English engraver, Robert Hancock, was at one time given the credit for most of the Battersea output, but it is now thought that he remained in the Midlands, working for one or more firms in the area, until the end of the century.

Identification of the pre-Battersea Birmingham enamels has taken place recently, and followed the discovery of John Brooks' 1751 patent application. He had hitherto been thought to have had a connection only with the London establishment, and it was completely unsuspected that printing had been practised anywhere prior to 1753.

The group of enamels now assigned to the Midlands includes a number with printed ornamentation, but the work is not sufficiently flawless to stand on its own and is invariably touched up or

Fig. 6 *Pair of candlesticks, South Staffordshire, c.1765. Printed, painted and gilt decoration. (Victoria and Albert Museum.)*

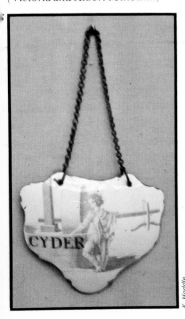

7

Author's Photo

Fig. 7 **Plaque,** *Battersea,
1753–56. Printed in purplish-
black with a portrait of
Elizabeth Gunning, Duchess of
Hamilton, later Duchess
of Argyll, possibly engraved by
John Brooks. Height 3⅜ ins.
(Victoria and Albert Museum.)*

Fig. 8 **Plaque** *signed 'J. Sadler,
Liverp: Enaml:', Liverpool,
c.1758. Printed in black with a
portrait of Frederick the Great,
King of Prussia, height 5·5/16 ins.
(Victoria and Albert Museum.)*

Fig. 9 **Three salt-cellars,**
*probably South Staffordshire,
c.1765. Enamelled with different
patterns, average width 2¼ ins.
(Private Collection.)*

Fig. 10 **Casket,** *Birmingham,
c.1755. The top painted with
subjects from the works of
Antoine Watteau and the front
with painted transfer-prints of
exotic birds after engravings by
Robert Hancock. Width 7¾ ins.
(Sotheby and Co., London.)*

covered over to compensate for the lack of definition and the faulty places in the transfer. Others are entirely hand-painted but reveal their origin because the body of each box is gilt metal or silver on copper (Sheffield plate) with engine-turned or stamped decoration, and only the top of the lid is enamel. Such boxes were typical Birmingham products, and a study of the enamels on them has enabled other similarly painted non-metal-based boxes to be classified. One or more of the many anonymous artists made a speciality of carefully-rendered moss roses, usually with oversize insects crawling on them and a butterfly hovering or at rest. It is a style of decoration found on Chelsea porcelain prior to 1750, doubtless fashionable and pointing strongly to the boxes having been made at that time.

Also attributed to Birmingham are plaques and box-tops painted with Venetian scenes and a plaque in the Victoria and Albert Museum bearing a coloured print of English and Dutch fishermen and the legend 'Success to the British Fishery'. As Janssen was from 1750 vice-president of the newly-formed Free British Fishery Society, this piece was for long considered to have been made in his factory, but it has characteristics that point to its having been made prior to the opening of York House and can only have come from the Midlands. There is, in fact, positive evidence that Birmingham was a highly important enamelling centre from at least 1750 until quite late in the century.

Farther north, at Liverpool, a number of well-printed plaques were also produced. As most of them are signed by their maker, John Sadler, who was active from about 1757 in printing pottery and porcelain, attribution presents fewer difficulties (Fig. 8).

Later enamels, those made after the closure of York House, have generally been classified as 'South Staffordshire' in the belief that all of them emanated from the Bilston area. Once again, there has been a change of thought and a proportion must be allocated to the Midlands.

It is known that there was at least one enameller working in Bilston, a town situated a few miles outside Wolverhampton, as early as 1748, but his work is unidentified. The articles most widely accepted as coming from there are the circular and oval small boxes, for patches or snuff, inscribed with sentimental or moral legends or printed with named views and the wording: 'A trifle from . . .' (Fig. 2).

Wednesbury, not far from Bilston, was also the home of some enamellers, and the writer of a guide to the district noted in 1801 that 'Enamel paintings are done here in the highest perfection and beauty'. A late nineteenth-century author recorded that the place was famed for its pink enamel, discovered by a man named James Ross, and said: '[It] was the envy of all other manufacturers, but the secret of its production was well kept, until at last it was obtained from Mrs. Ross in the hunting field by means of the most unscrupulous that can be conceived'.

This, and many other stories, invite careful investigation, like the enamels themselves. In time, perhaps, the full story of these fragile, fascinating and pretty 'toys' will finally be unravelled.

MUSEUMS AND COLLECTIONS

English Enamels may be seen at the following:

Bilston, Staffs: Museum and Art Gallery
London: Victoria and Albert Museum

FURTHER READING

'Battersea, Bilston – or Birmingham?' by R. J. Charleston in the **Victoria and Albert Museum Bulletin,** Vol. III, No. 1, London, 1967.
'Talks on English Enamels' by R. J. Charleston and Bernard Watney in **Transactions of the English Ceramic Circle,** Vol. 6, Part 2, London, 1966.
'English Enamels in the Eighteenth Century' by Bernard Watney in **Antiques International,** London, 1966.

417

French
Clocks

Connaissance des Arts : Millet

Fig. 1 *Elephant clock, late eighteenth century. Gilt-bronze set with precious stones. (Private Collection.)*

Fig. 2 *Cartel (wall clock), mid-eighteenth century. Gilt-bronze. With its elaborate rococo mounts and Chinese figure, this clock is entirely in the Louis XV style. (Private Collection.)*

Fig. 3 *Boat clock, mid-eighteenth century. Gilt-bronze and porcelain. The support of this clock is simply an excuse for a delightful rococo fantasy. (Château de Thoiry.)*

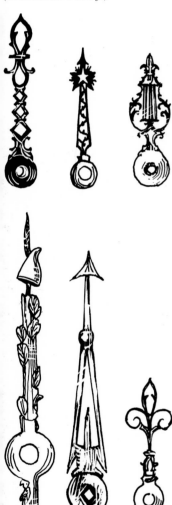

Fig. 4 *Changing styles in hands.*
Top row, from the left: Louis XV hand, with two sides of the fleur-de-lis motif cut off during the Revolution. Late Louis XVI hand. Rare Louis XVI hand for musical or lyre clock.
Bottom row, from the left: Revolutionary hand topped with a Phrygian helmet; the smaller hand represents a lictor's fasces. Consulate hand of simple lines heralding the Empire style. Delicate early Louis XVI hand with fleur-de-lis motif.

Some of the finest scientific and artistic achievements in clockmaking were carried out in late eighteenth-century France

To the casual onlooker all antique French clocks appear ornate, rich, even gaudy. While this may be true of clocks from the Renaissance through the hundred and twenty-five year period from Henri IV to Louis XIV, there are marked changes between those of Louis XV (1715–1774) and Louis XVI (1774–1792).

With the coming of the Revolution, thousands of wealthy patrons – and some royal clockmakers – fled into exile, and it is remarkable that France saw so rapid a resurgence of craftsmanship after the end of the holocaust.

The first marked change was *le style Directoire*, known to contemporary French historians as '*le style Messidor*'. The name comes from the *Directoire*, an executive body of five 'directors' which controlled France after the fall of Robespierre. It was a time of powerful transitions from austerity to extravagance. The French horological historian, Tardy, commented that it was a transitional style with a clear orientation towards classical art. But this period led to new extremes. In clocks, as in other domestic items, a stark simplicity of line became fashionable, wholly in contrast with the florid Rococo of the Louis XV era, and plain frames and cases housed complex scientific mechanisms.

It is against a background of artistic and scientific ferment that one must see the three distinct phases of French horological work. These definite styles are the Louis XVI, the *Directoire*, and the beginnings of *le style empire*, as positive in its period as the *Code Napoléon* itself.

There was little change in the business of clock-making; the workshops of the Royal horologers continued working through many generations for successive monarchs. For example, Alexandre le Faucheur was clock-maker to Louis XV, and his son Jean-Ignace was clock-maker to Louis XVI. Also in the transitional period there are mantel clocks where the theme of the decoration has a Louis XV derivation (in bronze *doré* or *ciselé*) but the ornamentation is in the Louis XVI style.

By 1774, wood for clock cases was considered old-fashioned, and bronze, marble and stone took its place. Porcelain was favoured and, in particular, figures of white biscuit. One naturally does not find the Sun King's gilt rays on pendulum bobs at this time, but the medallion of Louis XVI, usually in an oval plate without raised edges and surrounded by engraved garlands. A French record relates that the whole Louis XVI style was characterized 'by a simplicity and purity of line, a pronounced tendency towards the symmetrical, the whole accentuated by a refined and seductive decoration which removed every trace of blandness'. Outside France it was at first not so easy to distinguish this purity of line, this symmetry; it was not appreciated that designers such as Delafosse, Blondel and Forty were aiming for a seductive and refined style, beautiful though formal.

Around 1780 Demosthène Dugourc, a designer attached to the *Mobilier de la Couronne*, was making clocks and other domestic items in the neo-Grecian style; less distinguished clocks were adorned with bronze and gilt-metal castings representing musical instruments or other attributes of the arts or symbols of the seasons such as baskets of corn and wreaths of flowers, and even attributes of Love including the inevitable arrow, the quiver, the pierced heart and the crown of roses.

This was the zenith of French clock-making; among the great horologers were Ferdinand Berthoud (1727–1807), Jean André Lepaute (1709–60) and his brother Jean Baptiste, Robert Robin (1742–1809), Pierre le Roy (1717–85), the distinguished son of Julien (1686–1759), Abraham Louis Breguet (1747–1823) and many others. Berthoud and Breguet both left their native Switzerland to set up in business in Paris. It is difficult to trace all the makers, since the guild regulations did not restrict the number of sons and nephews in the craft shops as did the London guilds. Thus, in the eighteenth century there were five horologers named Dubois, and five named Amant. Le Roy was and is a common surname, and the number of clock-makers so named is legion – as also is the total of clocks reputed to have been made for Louis XVI's Queen, Marie Antoinette.

Throughout this period the basic circular form of clock movement did not change much, but there were striking changes in dial-plates, and in the introduction of what today are termed 'vase' clocks or 'band' clocks. Here, the hours are indicated on an enamel band rotated against a pointer by the movement in the centre, where might also be placed a lamp or night-light shining through the translucent porcelain near the band.

Designs were published for elaborate frames

Perhaps more than any other, these clocks (known in France as '*cercles tournants*') illustrate the changing value of fashion. One fine marble specimen, an urn supported by the Three Graces, was sold after the Revolution for 1,500 *francs*, and was bought nearly a century later (in 1881) by Baron Double for 7,000 *francs*. Shown in 1900 at the Petit-Palais Exposition, it was then said to be worth three million *francs*.

Very few of these rotating-band clocks carried their maker's name. Louis XVI's designer, Forty, published several plates illustrating '*projets des pendules à cercle tournant*', so he may have been responsible for the general form. Dumont, Lepaute, Boucher and Lepine gave their names to a few of this type but the rest are anonymous.

As the *cartel* (wall clock) went out of fashion the elegant table or mantel lyre clock took its place, and here there was little anonymity. Coteau, Boisard, Roggen and Charles le Roy, all of Paris, were among the leading makers, and again Forty published plates illustrating designs for the jewelled lyre frames. In some types, the movement and dial formed the pendulum which swayed in the lyre frame.

Elegance was giving way to scientific utility, but if the two could be combined, then so much the better. With lyre clocks, for example, the gridiron pendulum, devised by the London maker John Harrison (1693–1776), was used. This consisted of

Fig. 5 *Types of figures used on dials.* *Above: Louis XVI classical dial, using Roman numerals for the hours but not for the minutes. Below: Louis XVI dial using Arabic numerals, with or without decorative festoons.*

Fig. 6 *Table clock, French, early nineteenth century. This typically Empire scene shows Napoleon and Diogenes. (Private Collection.)*

5

an assembly of parallel steel and brass rods supporting the movement, the theory being that in a pendulum so constructed, the distance between the suspension spring at the top and the true centre of oscillation would remain constant, winter and summer. Breguet devised a different type of compensating laminae for watch escapements.

With the lyre clock, for the first time in French clock-making, the movement itself began to be appreciated and displayed as a thing of beauty. In some lyre clocks, the enamel dial was cut away in the centre to show the movement. This was known then as the *mouvement squelette* (skeleton frame), but the true *squelette* as we know it today – an open-frame mantel movement under a glass dome – did not come into fashion until the middle of the nineteenth century.

Robert Robin, Ferdinand Berthoud and others produced high-precision movements in austere frames, of the type known as '*régulateur à remontoir*'. There is a fine example in the apartments of Napoleon I at the Grand Trianon, but it was the passion of Louis XVI for all mechanical novelties which inspired automata as well as regulator, calendar and musical clocks.

As might be expected, the remarkable Breguet capped the theme with his synchroniser, designed towards the end of the eighteenth century. This was a chronometer in table-clock form with a watch-holder at the top of the handsome gilt case. The wearer placed his watch in this holder at night, and by morning it was wound and corrected from the clock. Breguet made one of the last of these to the special order of the Prince Regent in London, in 1814.

The closing years of the eighteenth century saw the general use of small glass-panelled clocks carried in leather cases, now known as

carriage clocks but called in those days '*pendules d'officier*'.

Although France lost in the eighteenth century much of the empire she had acquired in the time of Louis XIV, nevertheless French officers travelled the globe and told the time by their *pendules d'officier*. Generally, these became accepted as utilitarian clocks and consequently were not valued highly.

With few exceptions, the best complex carriage clocks were produced by London makers a century later. During the whole of the Louis XVI period, clocks were produced in enormous numbers, and some makers devised methods of semi-mass-production. To keep the standard high, Berthoud, Lepaute and others obtained State support for a school of watch and clock-making under government control, and a medal was awarded to prize pupils. Unfortunately, the revolution put an end to this high-minded plan.

The contribution of French makers of the late eighteenth century to the pool of horological knowledge is enormous. Present-day horologists still argue about the great advances made in watch and chronometer escapements by the Le Roys. Antide Janvier wrote his exhaustive *Essai sur les Horloges* in Paris during the closing years of the century, which he published in 1811, while among Berthoud's many titles were the *Histoire de la Mesure du Temps*, and *Essai sur l'Horlogerie*. Of the great Breguet, he said contemptuously: 'He has published nothing'.

Breguet survived the Revolution and was as active after it as before. Born in Neuchâtel, Switzerland, in 1747, he was left fatherless at the age of eleven. His uncles worked in Paris, so, on his mother's remarriage, the young Breguet joined them. It is said that he was apprenticed at Versailles, but it is not known for certain where he worked at the outset. It is most probable that he met or worked with Berthoud, his celebrated compatriot who was a few years his senior and was watch- and clock-maker to the French Navy. Breguet attended mathematics classes given by Father Marie, tutor to the children of the Comte d'Artois at the Collège Mazarin. They extolled his work in court circles, and thus he was introduced to the King.

At the age of twenty-eight, Breguet married Cécile, daughter of a Parisian family of good standing and her dowry helped to establish Breguet at No. 39, quai de l'Horloge, in the famous horological quarter by the Pont Neuf.

Better known now as a watch-maker, Breguet worked for Marie Antoinette; the second self-winding *montre perpetuel* was made to her command. The King also bought Breguet watches, although his warranted makers were Lepine and Robin.

His fame spread throughout Europe, and the London House of Breguet and Company was established before 1791, thanks to the Duc d'Orléans and to Breguet's own association with London clock-makers such as Arnold. When the riots were at their worst in Paris, in 1793, Marat told Breguet: 'I warn you that you are on the list to be guillotined, and you must get away'. The Committee of Public Safety granted Breguet a safe-custody pass on 24 June, 1793, and the family sought refuge in Geneva. In Paris, his workshops and machinery were destroyed.

6

Bulloz

Fig. 7 **Design for a vase clock** of
the Empire style, early
nineteenth century.
Although many vase clocks of this
period were made with a rotating
band to tell the time, called a
'cercle tournant', others were
made with conventional faces
and hands. As with much Empire
design, the form is derived
directly from a classical source.

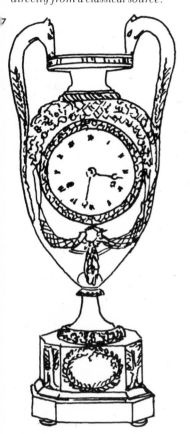

Fig. 8 **Clock**, French, mid-
eighteenth century. The
movement by Etienne le Noir,
the mounts of gilt-bronze set
with Meissen porcelain figures
and flowers.
(Schloss Wilhelmstal.)

Fig. 9 **Clock,** the case by
Prud'hon, c.1810. Bronze.
This lavish neo-classical
sculpture represents an allegory
of the marriage of Napoleon I to
Marie Louise of Austria in 1810.
(Palais de Còmpiègne.)

8

9

Fig. 10 *Design for a small clock in the Empire style by Percier and Fontaine, early nineteenth century.*

Fig. 11 *Lyre clock by Kinable, eighteenth century. Bleu du Roi Sèvres porcelain and ormolu. (Victoria and Albert Museum, London.)*

Fig. 12 *Exotic clock, French, late eighteenth century. Gilt. (Private Collection.)*

10

12

Giraudon

11

Museum Photo

By 20 April, 1795, the Terror had subsided for almost a year. With the support of the government, Breguet was invited to return to France, together with many other distinguished clock- and watchmakers. He was given State aid to re-equip his workshops and he subsequently gathered together some of the finest craftsmen in Europe; the Exhibition of 1798, the first French international industrial exhibition, was his triumph. The House of Breguet exists to this day, and fortunately so do a very large number of examples by many of the Parisian makers whose work spans the age of elegance and the precise austerity of the *Directoire*.

The revolutionaries wished to banish all memory of the monarchy and started a new calendar in 1792, 'Year One of the Republic'. French clocks with calendar mechanisms starting at Year One are extremely rare.

In keeping with the scientific spirit of the *Directoire*, Breguet experimented with decimal time. A few clocks by him and by other Parisian makers of the late eighteenth century have a dial with only ten numerals, not twelve. As the world moves nearer to complete decimalisation, this experiment has special relevance.

MUSEUMS AND COLLECTIONS

French clocks of the later eighteenth century may be seen at the following:

FRANCE
Paris: House of Breguet
          Louvre
          Musée des Arts Décoratifs
Versailles: Château de Versailles
          Grand Trianon

GREAT BRITAIN
London: Guildhall Museum (Worshipful Company of Clock-makers' Collection)
          Science Museum
          Wallace Collection

GERMANY
Wuppertal: Historisches Uhren-Museum

FURTHER READING

Clocks and Watches by K. Ullyett, London, 1971.
French Clocks by Edey Winthrop, London, 1967.
A. L. Breguet, Horologer by C. Breguet, trans. Enfield, 1962.
Old Clocks and Watches and their Makers by F. J. Britten, London, 1956.

English Clocks

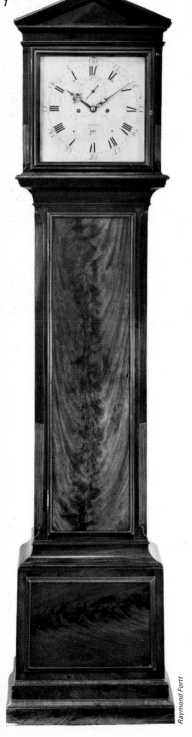

Fig. 1 **Long-case clock** by Justin Vulliamy (1712–97), London, c.1775. Veneered with figured mahogany and decorated with finely worked mouldings, this clock has the simplicity and good proportions lacking in many Chippendale-style clocks. (Private Collection.)

Raymond Fortt

Plain, good quality clocks for the general public; highly decorative and elaborate clocks inspired by a demand from the East; and regulator clocks achieving precision and accuracy; these were three distinct types produced in a memorable century for clock-making

It is possible to divide the London clock-makers working during the reigns of George II and George III (1727–1820) into groups with quite opposing ambitions, catering for clienteles with widely differing tastes.

The first group comprises those who were making good quality and reliable long-case and table-clocks to meet public demand and, by the number still in existence, it seems that production was considerable.

Long-case clocks ('grandfather' was a later American name) were made in simple styles, as in Figure 1, which illustrates a very fine example by Justin Vulliamy of a severe but very well-proportioned clock veneered with figured mahogany, with finely worked mouldings. This would have cost between twelve and fifteen pounds when made in about 1775. More elaborate mahogany clocks were made, mostly in the north of England, in the Chippendale style and, though some were quite handsome, many were ill-proportioned and over-elaborate.

The best London makers included Mudge, the Duttons, Ellicott, Holmes, Dwerrihouse, Lindsey and Justin and Benjamin Vulliamy. These makers also produced table-, bracket- and mantel-clocks in the same traditions as their long-case clocks and a typical example, illustrated in Figure 4, is by Matthew and Thomas Dutton of London. This clock has an enamel dial and a subsidiary dial in the arch for regulation. These fine quality enamel dials must not be confused with the painted dials of the cheaper type of clocks of the period, although even these at times contained moderately good movements.

Figure 2 illustrates another type of table- or bracket-clock which was most popular; this particular example is more elaborate than most and contains a very sophisticated movement by Thomas Colley, successor to the eminent George Graham. The mounts on the case are extremely highly finished and the clock is fitted with very good silver spandrels, making it a piece of outstanding importance.

The long-case clock in Figure 9 is simple and even severe in design, and the case-maker has achieved a splendid balance and proportions. William Dutton was the maker of the movement and this must be recognised as his masterpiece as, although he was inspired by the Graham-Mudge design for the equation movement, the finish to his work is most commendable.

These four preceding clocks illustrate the most popular types produced in the latter half of the eighteenth century.

The second group of clocks may be regarded as of the fantastic or highly decorative type. These were really inspired by a demand from Turkey and other Middle Eastern countries, and also from the Far East, where the Emperor of China amassed a vast collection at the Summer Palace in Peking. The particular style that proved most popular in Turkey were those made by Markwick Markham, Perigal and George Prior with cases veneered in tortoise-shell and elaborately chased gilt-metal mounts (Fig. 7). The movements usually had a third or even fourth train for quarter-striking and musical repeats, which take place every three hours or so, playing jigs, minuets and gavottes. The chapter rings on these clocks usually have Turkish numerals.

The clocks supplied to the Chinese Emperor were elaborate in their design: sometimes they had waterfalls of revolving twisted glass, often enamelled in brilliant colours, sometimes there were scenes in which a moving figure vaguely kept time with the music, and the cases were usually embellished with paste jewels. Many of these clocks were unsigned but the principal maker of these fantasies was James Cox, who carried on a business in Shoe Lane, London.

Cox was described as a toy-maker as well as clock-maker, but his so-called 'toys' were extraordinarily sophisticated and in most cases, if they did not contain a clock movement, they at

Raymond Fortt

Fig. 2 **Table- or bracket-clock** by
*Thomas Colley, London, c.1765.
The fittings and spandrels are of
silver.*
*This elaborate version of a
popular form of clock contains a
sophisticated movement by
Colley, who proudly states on the
face that he was 'Graham's
succ[esso]r'. George Graham
(?1673–1751) was an eminent
London maker, of whom Colley
was a worthy follower
continuing in his best tradition.
(Private Collection.)*

Fig. 3 **'Fabulous' clock** by *James
Cox (died 1788), London, the key
signed and dated 1766. Chased
gilt-metal case with agate
background and paste flowers as
finials; the small clock movement
is connected with a mechanism
below showing the phases of the
moon.*
*James Cox was the foremost
'toy-maker' of his day. Working
in Shoe Lane, London, he
produced elaborate fantasies
usually incorporating a clock or
watch. The example illustrated
is similar to the clocks supplied
to the Emperor of China for the
Summer Palace in Peking.
(Private Collection.)*

Fig. 4 *Mantel- or table-clock by Matthew and Thomas Dutton, London, c.1775. Enamel dial. This handsome clock is of a standard design for the period, but has an enamel dial, which was the easiest to read.*

Fig. 5 *Urn-clock by Vulliamy, London, c.1775. The enamel dials at the top of the urn rotate to show the time.*

Fig. 6 *'Temple' clock, Number 304 by Vulliamy, London, White marble and gilt metal. (Private Collection.)*

Fig. 7 *Table-clock probably made by Markwick Markham, London, c.1750. Tortoise-shell veneer with elaborate metal mounts, chased and gilt. (Private Collection.)*

least had a watch movement included in their design. Figure 3 illustrates a typical example of the workmanship and imagination of James Cox. The metalwork is finely chased and gilt, and the background is of agate with paste flowers as finials. The small clock movement is connected with a mechanism below showing the phases of the moon. Pieces of this type are often elaborately fitted with scent-bottles, scissors, files and other small objects necessary to everyday life. The key is signed and dated 1766.

After producing a number of these astonishing works of art, Cox formed a museum in Spring Gardens which was open to the public for a number of years. He eventually achieved the passing of an Act of Parliament allowing him to sell the contents of this museum by lottery, and an office was opened in Shoe Lane where subscribers could buy tickets. He was obviously a man of substance as he bound himself to give £5,000 in cash to each of the first and second prize-winners if they preferred this sum in lieu of the prize.

It seems that the majority of the museum pieces eventually found their way to China and were purchased for the Emperor. During the Boxer Rebellion at the beginning of the twentieth century, looting took place and many of these works of art are now in museums and private collections in various parts of the world.

In this decorative group, but showing more restraint, should be included the marble, gilt and bronze clocks of Justin and Benjamin Vulliamy. These are fine quality productions and, as part of the Vulliamy sale records exist showing details of the workmen involved and the costs and dates of delivery to named persons of the time, they make an extremely interesting study. These records do not cover the entire sequence of numbering, but from No. 296 to 469 there is much useful information.

The Emperor of China was a keen collector of clocks

The white marble and gilt 'Temple' clock illustrated in Figure 6, which as Number 304 is fortunately in this group, was delivered on 9 February, 1805, to a Captain Johnstone of the Coldstream Guards. This information is followed in the records by a list of all the craftsmen concerned in the making of the separate parts of this clock and it shows that the most Benjamin Vulliamy could have done towards its manufacture was to assemble it: 'Bullock the movement £5 15s 6d; Culver engraving the hands 5s 0d; Amedroz the backplate engraving £2 10s 0d; ditto engraving the frieze 15s 0d; ditto engraving the scroll 3s 6d; Haas the ring 2s 6d; Crockett the gilding £8 18s 0d; Huguenin the brass work £7 0s 0d; Long & Drew the dial 16s 0d; Day the marble £6 0s 0d; Duesburg the figure £4 10s 0d'.

Many well-known figures of the period are mentioned in these accounts: William Beckford bought a kitchen dial in 1799 for £4 10s. A long-case clock was supplied to the Marquess of Blandford in 1801 for £10 5s 6d which was later repaired and sent to a Mr. Thomson in New South Wales. 'Delivered to the King', in January 1805, 'A spring dial for the kitchen at the Queen's House', costing £19 12s 0d, which was obviously far superior to Mr. Beckford's purchase.

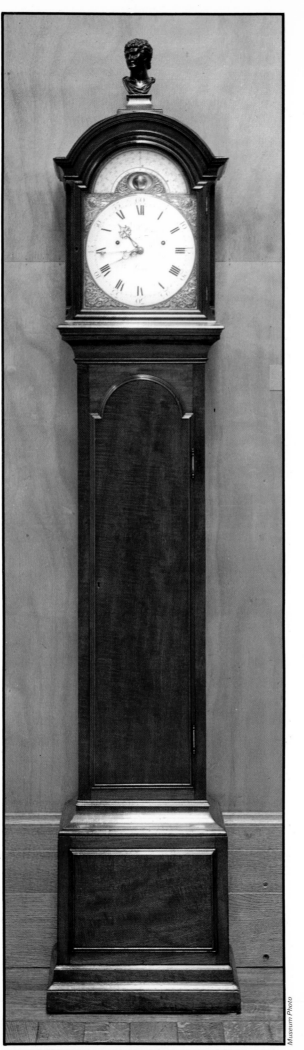

Angelo Hornak

Fig. 8 **Regulator clock** by
Barraud, London, c.1810.
Mahogany.
(Private Collection.)

Fig. 9 **Long-case clock** by
William Dutton, London, c.1765.
Equation timepiece with enamel
dials and silver spandrels.
(Fitzwilliam Museum,
Cambridge.)

Museum Photo

Vulliamy supplied several firms engaged in the export trade, in particular Messrs. Binhacock who, in 1804, had three silver-cased clocks delivered costing over £400 each – a considerable sum at this time. Unfortunately there is no mention of the country to which they were sent and no clocks are recorded which fit their description.

Figure 5 illustrates a very attractive urn-clock by Vulliamy decorated with an enamelled miniature of Frederick, Prince of Wales, by Christian Zincke. The gilt metalwork is finely finished and the general design is architecturally well balanced. This is a clock which may well have been supplied to a member of the Royal Family.

The third group of clock-makers who practised during the period under discussion were the makers of precision clocks who aimed at achieving accuracy. This was really the continuation of the work of George Graham embracing the use of various types of compensated pendulums, the use of jewels as endstones and pallets, and micrometer adjustments on all parts where levelling and the taking up of play would improve timekeeping. They were known as regulator clocks and were usually of severe design and excellent quality.

Figure 8 illustrates a very neat and fine quality regulator by Barraud, an instance where the casemaker has taken much pride in selecting the finest veneers for the surfaces and the mouldings and special care with the fitting of the doors and the hood in order to keep it dust-proof.

The most famous makers of such clocks were Arnold, Mudge, Emery, Grant, Barwise and the Vulliamys. In the nineteenth and early part of the twentieth centuries, many of these regulator clocks were in the possession of clock repairers and clients could check their watches by them. It is not uncommon to find that the signature has been changed to that of its later owner and it is usually the style of the engraving which gives the clue to its further history.

These ninety years or so of clock-making covered a period when many unusual types of clocks were made. Of the types which have not been touched upon are the cartel-clocks of approximately 1765, with their elaborately carved and gilt Chippendale-style cases, the balloon-shaped clocks of the Sheraton period, the lacquer-cased clocks which were made throughout the eighteenth century and those attractive small mantel-clocks made during the Regency period.

MUSEUMS AND COLLECTIONS
English clocks of the eighteenth century may be seen at the following:

GREAT BRITAIN
Cambridge: Fitzwilliam Museum
London: British Museum
Syon House
Victoria and Albert Museum
Oxford: Ashmolean Museum
Sussex: Uppark

FURTHER READING
Clocks by Cedric Jagger, London, 1973.
English House Clocks: 1600–1850: An Historical Survey and Guide for Collectors and Dealers by Anthony Bird, Newton Abbot, 1973.
A History of English Clocks by R. W. Symonds, London, 1947.

Early American Clocks

Fig. 1 *Shelf clocks* by *Chauncey Jerome, New Haven, Connecticut, first half of the nineteenth century. The centre four of these clocks are of the type known as 'steeple clocks'* (*Private Collection.*)

The earliest clocks in America were imported by the first settlers; by the nineteenth century shelf clocks were being made in increasing numbers

The first mechanical clock came to North America with the first settlers, the Dutch and the English, in the early seventeenth century. The more wealthy of the English brought brass lantern clocks, the Dutch brought metal table clocks. On rare occasions in the last quarter of the century, a family travelled across the ocean with the awkward but very valuable possession of a long-case clock.

It is likely that the ownership of a clock had more prestige than practical value because most families would have spent all the daylight hours building a homestead, tilling the soil and tending livestock. Both English and Dutch communities were strongly religious, which might be relevant as accurate timekeeping had its origin in religious needs.

The few clocks owned by the earlier colonists had been imported individually, mostly from England. The earliest American-made clocks still extant are long-case, called 'tall' clocks by the colonists. The first immigrant clockmakers who practised their craft probably arrived a few years before 1700. They certainly came after Peter Stuyvesant surrendered New Amsterdam to the English, when it was renamed New York, for that was in 1664, and it was not until about 1670 that the long-case clock

with a long pendulum was invented in London.

Clockmakers – mainly English, but also Dutch, and German from the Black Forest, and even a few Swedes – followed the national styles that they had learned while apprentices, and there is nothing at first sight to distinguish the Colonial long-case clock from its progenitor in Europe.

It was not easy for a clockmaker to succeed financially by making every part of his clocks. In England, he would have depended to some extent on specialist makers of pinion wire, on brass-casters, hand-piercers, on dial-engravers, and certainly on case-makers. Clockmakers in the Colonies therefore tended to settle in areas where there were others, each gradually finding it more profitable to concentrate on his own special skill.

From quite early days, two distinct communities emerged, one centred on Philadelphia and the other on Boston. Each developed its recognisable style, although the basic designs were European. Makers of the Philadelphia School spread from New York up the Delaware Valley to Virginia and Carolina. Makers of the Boston School were scattered all over New England. In retrospect, although the two groups were probably of about the same importance at the time, Philadelphia was the home of the finer makers and finer clocks. English styles predominated, although clockmakers of German origin had some influence in the Pennsylvanian hills.

Weight-driven pendulum clocks were the main production, as they were accurate and did not demand the particular materials and skills of the spring-maker, which were essential for the portable

427

A. C. Cooper

clock. The simplest and cheapest models were wall clocks with the weights and pendulum hanging below, generally known as 'the wag on the wall'. Better clocks were in tall cases and were sometimes grimly known as 'coffin clocks'. The name 'grandfather clock' did not appear until Henry Clay Work wrote the song of that name in 1876, very much later. The song has particular significance in the history of American clocks because of its lyric: 'My grandfather's clock was too tall for the shelf so it stood twenty years on the floor . . .'. The first truly indigenous American clock was the 'shelf clock'.

The most common style of American long-case clock was very similar to the English provincial style after 1750, with swan-neck pediments on the hoods. A cresting on the hood known locally as 'whales' tails' became typical of the clockmakers in Connecticut, however, having been developed by Thomas Harland, who moved there from Boston; makers in Massachusetts were fond of pierced fretwork cresting. These features are guides to origin.

The most famous maker of this era was David Rittenhouse of Philadelphia, who had established himself as a clock-maker in 1749 at the early age of seventeen. He later specialised in astronomical clocks, some of which worked orreries showing the motions of the planets. He was a man of great ability and far-ranging interests. As a surveyor, he was partly responsible for the Mason-Dixon Line. With John Winthrop and Benjamin Franklin (also a clockmaker and inventor of an accurate one-handed dial), he became famous as a Father of the American Revolution.

Museum Photo

Museum Photo

Museum Photo

Fig. 2 **Banjo clock** by Simon
Willard, Massachusetts, c.1810.
Simon Willard was interested in
the balloon shape and devoted
his energies to his 'patent
timepiece'.
(Old Sturbridge Village,
Sturbridge, Massachusetts.)

Fig. 3 **Girandole clock** by
Lemuel Curtis (1790–1851),
early nineteenth century. Height
39 ins.
(Christie, Manson and Woods
Ltd., London.)

Fig. 4 **Acorn clock** by the
Forestville Manufacturing
Company, 1830. Height about
24 ins.
(British Museum, London.
Ilbert Collection.)

Fig. 5 **Wagon-spring clock** of the
type invented by Joseph Ives in
c.1825 and made throughout
the rest of the century. Height
over 24 ins.
(British Museum. Ilbert
Collection.)

After the Declaration of Independence in 1776,
the Colonists found themselves increasingly short
of raw materials on which they had previously
depended, including copper and zinc which comprised the brass of the clock movement. Makers
therefore began to turn to wood for the plates and
the toothed wheels of clocks, in the same manner
as the clockmakers of the Black Forest of Germany
in the eighteenth century. From this time until
about 1810, almost all American clocks were made
by hand by clockmaker-carpenters.

The situation was changed largely through the
vision and ingenuity of a clockmaker named
Eli Terry, who was primarily responsible for changing the industry from a craft to a factory system.
Terry was also the main catalyst for the shift of
clockmaking to Connecticut. Having served his
apprenticeship from the age of fourteen to Daniel
Burnap, a maker from East Windsor, Connecticut,
who batch-produced clocks, Terry went to work
with Benjamin and Timothy Cheney in a nearby
village. By the age of twenty-one, he had established himself as a maker, in his own right, of wooden
clocks with brass wheels. At some time, he became
fascinated by the problem of producing clocks in
big quantities, probably inspired by the mass-
production pioneer Eli Whitney, who had accepted
what seemed to be an impossible contract to supply
100,000 government muskets in under two years.

Terry's chance came when, owing to an acute

shortage of metal because of Napoleon's blockade
of the British Isles, he was given an order for four
thousand tall clock movements to be made of wood
and delivered within three years. Terry sold his
water-mill-operated factory and bought a larger
mill. He spent a year setting up new works, then
completed the order on time. Despite the huge risk
he took, he was successful not only in producing
good clocks but in making a profit, for he retired
and sold the business to two young clockmaker-
carpenters with whom he had formed partnerships.
They were Silas Hoadley and Seth Thomas, both of
whom became famous on their own accounts.

Terry did not remain idle for long, however. He
became interested in the shelf clock that had
emerged in Massachusetts, and was an original conception. Two farmer's sons, Simon and Aaron
Willard, in Massachusetts, were at the idea's source.
Simon began making clocks while still living on the
farm. One wall clock, made about 1780, had a box
below it that concealed the pendulum and driving
weights. The clock part was in a box with a glass
front shaped and waisted in imitation of the then
popular English balloon clock inspired by the Montgolfier hot air balloons. Later, Willard designed
standing models of similar clocks. Copyists combined the upper and lower parts from Willard's
version and incorporated another glass below that
covering the dial, reverse painting it, and thus
creating the Massachusetts shelf clock.

429

6

Author's Photo

7

Author's Photo

Aaron Willard abandoned the long-case clocks he
was specialising in and turned to shelf clocks, while
Simon, more obsessed with the balloon shape,
devoted his energies to what he called his 'patent
timepiece'. The design later acquired the name
'banjo clock' and is accepted as one of the most
original American designs (Figs. 2 and 6). The
theme was followed by other makers and, in its most
elaborate form – the girandole, developed by
Lemuel Curtis of Concord, Massachusetts – has
today become the most sought after American
antique clock (Fig. 3). The girandole acquired its
name from the elaborate girandole mirrors of the
time, both mirror-frames and clock-cases being
decorated all over with gold leaf.

The shelf clock, nevertheless, became the best-
known and most typical American clock because it
was taken up and developed by the infant manufacturing industry in Connecticut. Terry's first
production model was in a box case with a plain
glass door, on the inside of which the hour numerals
and simple corner spandrel decorations were
painted. The wooden movement could be seen
through the glass, with an hour bell below it, a
pendulum in front of it, and a weight each side.
Seth Thomas also made such clocks under licence
from Terry.

Well before 1820, Terry had refined the case,
adding free-standing pillars at the sides, scroll
decoration with three urn finials at the top and four
feet and a skirt at the bottom (Fig. 7). In other words,
he had taken some ideas from the hood of the long-
case clock, made it rather larger but much narrower,
and given it feet to stand on a shelf. A painted dial
was added behind the glass front door through
which the pendulum and escape wheel on the front
of the movement could be seen. In the lower part
of the door was another panel of glass, the back
painted with decoration with a clear oval shape left
in the centre through which the pendulum-bob
could be seen – another simplification of a traditional long-case theme.

Shelf clocks were made in very large numbers
and, as always seems to happen, the earlier delicate design became debased; later examples
were cruder and heavier in form as the popularity
and number of makers grew. The original Terry
design, called the 'pillar and scroll', was eventually driven out of fashion by a relatively simple
design by another Connecticut clockmaker,

MUSEUMS AND COLLECTIONS

American clocks may be seen at the following:

GREAT BRITAIN
Bath: The American Museum in
                        Britain
U.S.A.
Bristol, Conn.:   American Clock and Watch
                        Museum
Gautier, Miss.:   Gautier Plantation Home
Grafton, Mass.:   Willard House and Clock Shop
New York: University Museum of Clocks
                        and Watches
Washington D.C.:   Smithsonian Institution

FURTHER READING

Antique American Clocks and Watches by
Richard Thomson, Princeton, 1968.
English and American Watches, by George
Daniels, London, 1967.

Victorian Pocket Watches

Fig. 1 **Large silver two-train watch**
by Charles and Hollister, 1850.
The second gear-train drives an
independent central second hand.
(Guildhall, London. Collection of the
Worshipful Company of
Clockmakers.)

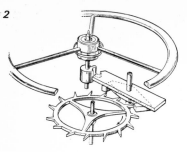

Fig. 2 *Crank roller escapement.*
Edward Massey's crank roller
lever of 1814 was one of the
designs leading to the
development of the English lever
escapement which was
introduced in about 1825.
(From Correspondence Course in
Technical Horology, *Intermediate Grade,* British
Horological Institute, London.*)*

Fig. 3 Left: *Gold minute-*
repeating lever watch in a half-
hunter case, by Edward Ashley of
Clerkenwell, 1890.
Right: *Gold watch by French,*
Royal Exchange, London, 1880.
This watch has an 'up and down'
dial which indicates when the
watch needs rewinding.
(British Horological Institute.)

Fig. 4 Above left: *'Decimal'*
watch by Dover Statter,
Liverpool, No. 1, 1862.
This experimental watch
followed closely on the
publication by the maker in
1856 of a pamphlet entitled The
Decimal System as a Whole in
its Relation to Time, Measure,
Weight, Capacity and Money in
Unison with Each Other.
Above right: *Gold Watch by*
James Ferguson Cole, 1848.
The inscription 'Inv.', from the
Latin invenit, *after Cole's name*
on the dial refers to one of his
own escapement designs, in this
case a 'resilient' lever.
Below: *Gold eight-day, quarter-*
striking, minute-repeating,
lever clockwatch by Alexander
Watkins, 1851.
Exhibited at the Great Exhibition
of 1851, this watch is noted for
its highly complicated
mechanism. The multi-coloured
gold dial was a fashion favoured
by some early Victorian
watchmakers, although shortly
after this time the white enamel
dial became universal.
(Guildhall. Clockmakers'
Company Collection.)

The mechanical genius of the Victorian age found its perfect expression in the clean, functional lines and precise craftsmanship of pocket-watches

The reign of Queen Victoria has come to be regarded as the period in which the mechanical arts reached their zenith; and undoubtedly the skilled craftsmen of those days exhibited an ingenuity and a standard of workmanship such as may never be seen again. It may be that, from today's aesthetic and technological viewpoints, much of this massive endeavour was misapplied. But this cannot disguise the reality that, for instance, a trained man using tools largely of his own making – an exercise which he will have undertaken during his apprenticeship – could fashion complex multi-component objects with a greater degree of precision and to smaller tolerances than at any previous time in history (Fig. 6).

Nowhere is this genius of the Victorians seen to better advantage than in watchmaking, and indeed, had it not reflected the general tenor of the times, it might have been predicted as a logical extension of the craft's already long heritage. Seventeenth-century invention ensured that a watch mechanism would keep going, even if with only haphazard accuracy as a timekeeper. The eighteenth century – and particularly the latter half of it – saw prodigious efforts to improve this last characteristic, and to make a mechanism that would perform consistently even under adverse conditions. This trend continued throughout the nineteenth century, accompanied by efforts to simplify unnecessary complexity, and with a great deal of attention being paid to the convenience of the user in such comparatively unimportant details as the means of winding up the watch and setting its hands, as well as actuating any additional mechanism such as chronograph and repeating work.

Probably the single most important development of the nineteenth century was the gradual perfecting of the detached lever escapement, such as is used to this day in mechanical watches to allow the stored up energy of the mainspring to be released – in fact, to 'escape' – at a consistent rate, and commensurate with the passage of time. The escapement is veritably the heart of a watch – you can hear it 'beating', which is the watchmaker's term for ticking – and many have been designed over the years, although rather fewer actually made.

The lever escapement itself has a very chequered history. In its original form it was devised by the famous English watchmaker Thomas Mudge, and applied by him to a minute number of timekeepers in the mid-eighteenth century; it was discarded for twenty-odd years, and then adopted – in a modified form but still on broadly the same principles – by a handful of London makers for a small number of special watches in the last two decades of the century. It then seems to have been abandoned for a second time, to reappear, modified once again, after about 1815.

At that time, the principal development leading up to the conventional English detached lever escapement was Edward Massey's crank-roller

lever of 1814 (Fig. 2); the rack lever, an intermediate invention, is not a detached escapement – that is to say, at no point in its motion is it free of contact with the gear train powered by the mainspring – and therefore it cannot rank as a true ancestor of the English lever, even though there are similarities. Another significant step forward was George Savage's two-pin lever, which, chronologically, followed closely on Massey's invention. By about 1825, the table-roller lever had been introduced – the English lever escapement in its essential form – and modifications later, notably a double roller in the latter half of the nineteenth century, did not affect the action of this mechanism.

Even when the lever escapement had reached this stage of perfection, however, there were still one or two brilliant makers who continued to experiment with its design in order to make an even more sophisticated product, the most notable of these being James Ferguson Cole. Born in the last decade of the eighteenth century and living to a ripe old age – he died in 1880 – Cole patented his first detached escapement in 1821, and in 1830 invented a so-called 'resilient lever' escapement, following this up with further escapement inventions in 1840 and 1859. What is more, his inventions worked well – unlike many that less able contemporary designers produced – and since Cole was himself a craftsman of the finest calibre, his work is nowadays among the most highly prized by collectors of mid-Victorian watches (Figs. 4 and 5).

'Keyless' winding seemed impossible to achieve

So, when Queen Victoria ascended the throne, the English detached lever escapement was already well established as the essential controller of a really precise watch, and by 1860 the two other escapements with claims to precision timekeeping, the duplex and the detent, had virtually disappeared. These, together with another obsolescent escapement, the cylinder, had their roots in the eighteenth century; yet strangely an even earlier one, the verge, continued – probably on account of its robust nature – to be made in the provinces until about 1880, for those who could not afford the more sophisticated and therefore expensive product.

Throughout most of the last century, therefore, it was possible to own a watch that would perform with consistent accuracy, that was not too bulky, and that posed no special inconveniences for the user except one – the need to wind it with a key.

Part of the reason for this defect, if such it was, was English insistence on the fusee watch as indispensable to accuracy – the fusee was a component intermediate between the mainspring and the gear train, the function of which was to even out the power of the former so that it did not exert more driving force when fully wound, and commensurately less as it ran out. Various forms of so-called 'keyless' winding were tried with the fusee watch, but without great success, so that, eventually, the fusee was abandoned towards the end of the century in favour of the going-barrel – that is, direct drive off the mainspring – which had long been used by foreign manufacturers.

Nevertheless, attempts to perfect keyless winding occupied the energies of many watchmakers during

the period, starting with Thomas Prest in 1820. His system, although it operated through a winding button on the end of the pendant of the watch as in present-day usage, could only be applied to going-barrel watches, and remained relatively undeveloped during Prest's lifetime. A more successful approach for fusee watches employed a pump action, that is a push-pull applied usually to a knob on the pendant. A slightly different version of this was the one patented by A. Burdess of Coventry in 1869 (Fig. 7), in which a lever projecting from the edge of the movement and pumped up and down acts upon a ratchet mounted on the axle of the fusee. English preoccupation with the inconvenience of watch keys probably reached its greatest heights of absurdity as late as 1870, when J. A. Lund, of the firm of Barraud and Lund, marketed watches with detachable keys which were concealed in the pendant of the watch-case when not in use, and were topped by a button exactly similar to that used for winding up keyless watches, which the product then appeared to be.

Throughout Queen Victoria's reign horological inventiveness knew no bounds, although it is doubtful whether some of the more fanciful proposals, especially in the design of escapements, were ever tried out in practice. The mainstream of ideas, as we have seen, was concerned with the lever escapement and ways of winding up the watch. Chronograph work – that is to say, an ordinary watch with added stop-watch facility – also manifested

433

itself in a variety of designs. Repeating work – in which the time could be made to sound, either on a bell or on wire gongs inside the watch-case when the mechanism was set off – had been common-place in the eighteenth century, but not until the nineteenth was this sufficiently refined to repeat the time to the nearest minute. The means of actuating repeating work was improved, in addition, so that, instead of depressing the pendant, it was only necessary to push a slide located in the band of the watch case. Right at the end of the century, a few watches were made – by Nicole Nielsen in London, and Bonniksen of Coventry – incorporating the principle of the travelling escapement. Two designs of this device – the *tourbillon* and the *karrusel* – both had the effect of mounting the escapement in a carriage or cage, which itself revolved inside the movement of the watch. By this means, frictional errors in the

Fig. 5 *James Ferguson Cole,* *photograph taken shortly before* *his death in 1880.* *J. F. Cole was one of the most* *inventive and celebrated of* *Victorian watchmakers. During* *his long working life he devoted* *much time to improvements and* *modifications to the lever* *escapement.* *(British Horological Institute.)*

Fig. 6 *Watchmakers' hand tools* *These were as beautifully made* *as the watches themselves, as* *may be seen by this group* *comprising a* douzième *gauge* (top left), *a slide-gauge* (top right) *and a depthing-tool* (below). *(British Horological Institute.)*

running of the watch due to its position could be largely corrected, making for yet greater accuracy in performance.

As watches gradually became more functional, any tendency towards superfluous decoration died out and, in the main, Victorian watches tend to be plain both outside and in, a considerable contrast with those made even as late as 1820. The exception to this can be found in some of the provincial output, where old fashions died hard. Some early Victorian makers favoured metal dials decorated with multi-coloured gold embellishments, while a little engine-turning on dial and case was not considered out of place (Fig. 4). Soon after 1850, however, the enamel dial became as universal as it had been a hundred years earlier. The so-called hunting and half-hunting cases – in the former, a solid cover protects the dial while in the latter, a central glazed hole in this cover permits the time to be estimated without any need to open it – first appeared around 1802 and examples are found dating from then into the present century (Fig. 3). Presentation watches, popular throughout the nineteenth century, are revealed only by the inscriptions

outside or inside the back cover of the case.

Continental watches differed considerably

So far, we have dealt only with English-made – and principally London-made – watches of the period, and it is important to note that the development of Continental watches followed substantially different lines. In other European countries, for instance, decoration continued to be important throughout the nineteenth century and products from the principal centres of manufacture, mainly in France and Switzerland, are often embellished with engraving or enamelling, sometimes in the form of niello.

On the mechanical side, it is interesting to note that the lever escapement seems to have been

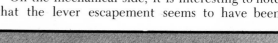
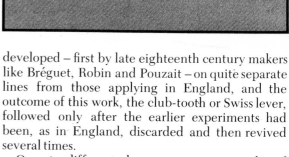

developed – first by late eighteenth century makers like Bréguet, Robin and Pouzait – on quite separate lines from those applying in England, and the outcome of this work, the club-tooth or Swiss lever, followed only after the earlier experiments had been, as in England, discarded and then revived several times.

On yet a different plane, an enormous number of watches, mainly cheap, were imported into England as a result of the great advances made in mass-production methods, mainly by the Swiss, from the middle of the century onwards. London makers, whose endeavours had traditionally been directed towards making a better rather than a cheaper watch, were resentful of this intrusion and the whole English craft suffered a period of upheaval as it adapted itself to the new circum-stances. Only one English firm had exhibited watches made by machine tools driven by steam power in the Great Exhibition of 1851, while an attempt by a Swiss manufacturer to introduce mass-production methods a few years earlier had encountered so much opposition from the tradi-tional craft that it was stifled. Right to the end of the

Fig. 7 *Group of Victorian watch-movements.*
Above: *The lever winding-mechanism operating on the axle of the fusee was patented by Burdess of Coventry in 1869.*
Centre left: *This under-dial view of a minute-repeating watch signed 'Dent – Watchmaker to the Queen' shows the complexity and small scale of the mechanism.*
Centre right: *An early example of mass production, this movement is engraved 'Russell's Machine-Made Lever'.*
Below: *Prior to the establishment of the National Physical Laboratory, the performance of high quality watches and chronometers was tested at Kew Observatory. This watch movement was graded 'A' by the Observatory and, although it bears the signature 'W. B. Pidduck, Manchester', it was almost certainly made by a London craftsman.*
(Author's Collection.)

A. C. Cooper

century the argument of quality versus quantity still raged; and indeed, the death throes of the English hand-finished watch continued down to our own times, when the Depression of the 1930s saw its final disappearance.

Sadly, too, well-dispersed factories have replaced such centres as Clerkenwell, in London, where watch- and clock-making had thrived in Victorian times and earlier, and where – certainly up to the 1880s – the large majority of the local population had been engaged in one or another branch of the craft. There still remains in this area, however, one outstanding and appropriate memorial to those old-time craftsmen in the form of the British Horological Institute, in Northampton Square. Founded in the 1850s, and with its red brick building planned by the man who designed Big Ben, the British Horological Institute is the trade association of the modern industry in England; yet it contrives, at the same time, to preserve a sense of continuity of the best traditions of the past – probably the most effective way of ensuring the maintenance of standards in a craft where they have always been of supreme importance.

MUSEUMS AND COLLECTIONS
Victorian pocket-watches may be seen at the following:
GREAT BRITAIN
London: British Horological Institute
             British Museum (Ilbert Collection)
             Guildhall (Clockmakers' Company
             Collection)
             Science Museum

FURTHER READING
Clock and Watch Escapements by W. J. Gazeley, London, 1975.
The Country Life Book of Watches by T. P. Camerer Cuss, London, 1967.
Watches by Cecil Clutton and George Daniels, London, 1965.
Britten's Old Clocks and Watches and Their Makers, edited by G. H. Baillie C. Clutton and C. A. Ilbert, seventh edition, London, 1956.
Watches – Their History, Decoration and Mechanism by G. H. Baillie, London, 1929.

Later American Clocks and Watches

Fig. 1 *Drop octagon wall clock*, with *Whiting wagon spring movement, by Atkins, c.1865.*
The steeple clock was the most popular form of shelf clock at this period, but the octagon wall clock, such as this example, the hour-glass and the skeleton clock were also made.
(Henry Ford Museum.)

Museum Photo

Pillar-and-scroll clocks, ogee clocks, steeple, American square, gothic, beehive, novelty and ticket clocks – these were some of the types which made America unrivalled in the nineteenth-century production of clocks

The 1830s saw great changes in the American clock industry, which began mass producing and exporting brass clocks in such numbers that the pattern of world production was radically altered. During the same period a new kind of watch industry emerged, based on principles that every watch-manufacturer anywhere subsequently had to adopt.

The pillar-and-scroll shelf clock, Connecticut's most important contribution to American clock design, reached the peak of its popularity a few years before 1830, when it was challenged by a smaller and cheaper version that still had a wooden movement, since cast brass was expensive and used only for eight-day clocks.

The most successful challenge to the pillar-and-scroll design was devised by Chauncey Jerome. It was a shelf clock with a single door and bronzed looking-glass instead of a painted glass panel in the lower part of the door. The Jerome design was heavier than the earlier ones and the top cresting very basic. It was truly a debasement of, rather than an improvement in, design. It appealed to the public, though, with the result that many other makers followed the style, some reverting to scenic panels instead of using mirrors, and introducing thick, carved pillars at the sides and heavily carved cresting in the Empire style on the top.

By the 1830s, a heavy case with a flat top and thick, plain pillars at the sides was in greatest favour. From about 1844, there was a reversion to the simpler case with an undecorated moulding all round, rather like a picture-frame. Such clocks are known as 'ogee', after the ogee form of moulding which shows in section a double continuous curve: concave passing into convex.

The great depression of 1837 forced most makers of wooden clock movements into bankruptcy and almost destroyed the industry. Chauncey Jerome was one of those seriously affected. His customers would not pay bills, so he decided to set out himself on a debt-collecting trip. One night in Richmond, Virginia, lying awake in bed (as he wrote later), it suddenly struck him that all the American brass clocks had been eight-day clocks and that there should be a market for thirty-hour brass clocks.

Fig. 2 **American square clock** by Jerome and Company, c.1860. Ogee case of finely figured walnut veneer. (Strike One.)

Fig. 3 **Eight-day shelf calendar clock** by the Ithaca Clock Company, New York, c.1870. (Henry Ford Museum, Dearborn, Michigan.)

Fig. 4 **Columned clock** by Seth Thomas, Thomaston, c.1860. Rosewood case with ringed gilt columns, panel of flowers and a game bird. (Strike One, London N.1.)

The high quality image of the brass clock should ensure sales at a low price, and, at the same time, trouble through dampness and the fragility of the wooden clock movement would be avoided.

Jerome designed a clock movement out of the factory-made, rolled brass that had recently become available, instead of cast brass. It was small, spring-driven and to be wound daily, and he set up a factory to make it in large quantities. Spring-driven clocks were still a relative novelty. Elisha Brewster was the first to make springs of tempered brass for American clocks. They were superseded in about 1830, when imported steel springs became available.

Jerome's cheap, brass clocks were fitted into simple, wooden cases of gothic form; this was the time of the Gothic Revival in Europe. With his brother he made so many cheap clocks from about 1838 that he nearly forced the Connecticut mass-production pioneers, Terry and Co., out of business. Seth Thomas, the other big manufacturer of wooden clock movements, quickly assessed the future and converted his own factory to the production of brass clocks, and the handful of other Connecticut clockmakers who had survived the recession followed suit.

In the 1840s the Jerome and Seth Thomas production was so vast that they were selling clocks in the traditional clock-producing countries of Europe at such low prices that they caused severe damage to the English industry, which recovered only temporarily by concentrating on better quality, and to the German Black Forest industry, which, by adopting American methods, recovered completely in the 1850s.

Many of Jerome's brass clocks were fitted into ogee cases and were known in this form as 'American square' clocks (Fig. 2). Chauncey Jerome did not succeed financially, despite his brilliance. He went into partnership with the famous showman P. T. Barnum, and lost everything in a spectacular bankruptcy. The Seth Thomas company became one of the world's biggest companies, incorporated today in the General Time Corporation which still manufactures under his name (Fig. 4).

Gothic influences on style persisted for many years. Shelf clocks were made with tops of inverted V form and conical steeples at each side, and in this form they became known as 'steeple clocks'. The gothic arch form, favoured by clockmakers in many countries and called the 'lancet', was named the 'beehive' in America. It appeared in the late 1840s in a form about eighteen inches high, and it persisted into this century. Jerome even offered for sale a version which incorporated his cherished mirror panel.

The most extraordinary spring-clock was invented by Joseph Ives; for its motive power it had a leaf-spring identical to those used on carts and wagons. The spring was mounted in the base: one end operated the timekeeping mechanism, the other the striking mechanism. The first was made in about 1825 and most were produced after 1850, the best known being by Birge and Fuller in the steeple style. There were, however, other forms of shelf clock: the octagon wall clock (Fig. 1), the hour-glass and the skeleton-clock forms. Most went for eight days, and a few for thirty days.

From about 1860, one of the most favoured domestic clocks had a second dial below, about the same size as, or even larger than, the clock dial.

This indicated the date by a hand, and often the day of the week and the month (Fig. 3). There were many standing and wall models, some later ones combining the clock and calendar dials.

As the nineteenth century ran on, many makers had to find novelties to stay in business. Some turned their attention to the Augsburg 'blinking-eye' clocks of the seventeenth century for inspiration and made cast-iron clocks in the shape of dogs and lions, the eyes of which moved with the beat of the pendulum. One novelty clock of brightly-coloured cast iron in the form of Black Sambo reflects a social attitude of the period.

The Ansonia Clock Company was very active at this time and devised many strange shapes of clock. Some were taken from earlier European ideas, such as a pendulum in the form of a child on a swing, patented in the 1880s. The same company made quite accurate copies of French ormolu cases that were themselves copies of French eighteenth-century cases (Fig. 6).

A more important American contribution that became more than just a novelty was the ticket clock, showing the time in numbers – digitally – instead of by hands. The first version was known as the 'Plato time indicator' and was patented in 1902. Within about four years, the Ansonia

Fig. 5 *Shelf clock by the Forestville Manufacturing Company, Bristol, Connecticut, c.1840.*
This rounded gothic shape is more unusual than the steeple shelf clock.
(Henry Ford Museum.)

Fig. 6 *Ormolu clock by the Ansonia Clock Company, Ansonia, New York, c.1890, inspired by a mid-eighteenth-century French clock.*
Towards the end of the century, makers had to devise many sorts of novelty clocks and cases in order to stay in business.
(Henry Ford Museum.)

Fig. 7 *Ogee shelf clock with alarm movement, by the Waterbury Clock Company, Waterbury, Connecticut, c.1870.*
(Henry Ford Museum.)

Boston, where he learned mass production methods.

Howard's contribution to watchmaking was that he joined Aaron Dennison and Samuel Curtis, both from Boston, in buying a business which had been started by four brothers named Pitkin, and which had made the first serious attempt to mass-produce watches. The first watch was made in 1834. It was a lever watch with a going barrel like today's watches, instead of the English fusee and chain drive. Unfortunately the brothers quarrelled and finally one of them, after losing his mind and destroying many watches, committed suicide in 1846. About eight hundred watches were made, of which only about three hundred were sold.

Aaron Dennison – 'Father of the American Watch Industry'

Dennison was the driving force in the group of three and the final achievement that founded the industry was due to him. Curiously, Dennison, although known as the 'Father of the American Watch Industry', was largely unsuccessful in his financial affairs. He set up the American Horloge Company, which eventually became the Waltham Watch Company and spawned most of the other American watchmaking companies.

Dennison himself emigrated to England in order to set up a watch factory. That failed, but in 1874 he founded a company for the manufacture of watch-cases that survived until 1967.

For many years collectors had not bothered much about American watches, but now they are considered important as examples of pioneer methods of mass production. Probably the most interesting are the rotary watches, made sometime after 1876, and the Waterbury 'Long Wind', both of which had movements that revolved in the case to reduce timekeeping positional errors. The Waterbury had a mainspring that was eight feet long or more, and there were many contemporary jokes based on the time the owner took to wind the watch.

Wallace Heaton Photo

Fig. 8 **Briggs Rotary Pendulum Clock,** *Bristol, Connecticut, c.1870.*
Under a glass dome instead of in a wooden or other case, this strange novelty clock has a pendulum which swings in a small circle rather than oscillating.
(Wallace Heaton Collection.)

Company had made forty thousand of them.

Electric battery clocks were new in the very early twentieth century. One produced in New York, the 'Tiffany Never-wind', had a torsion pendulum that oscillated slowly beneath the dial and was under a glass dome instead of in a case. A mechanical clock of about the same time was similarly cased and had a more unusual time-base, a conical pendulum that was mounted in front of the dial and swung in a small circle (Fig. 8).

Towards the end of the nineteenth century, alarm and domestic clocks became more and more like their European equivalents, the two streams continuing to merge until the present day.

The infant American watch industry first tried to make English-style verge watches in quantity but, despite an embargo on the import of English watches, without much success. In the 1830s the embargo was lifted, for by then the English were producing the new and much more accurate lever pocket-watch, which became so popular that it put an end to early watchmaking efforts in America.

Success eventually came partly through the efforts of a clockmaker named Edward Howard, who had been apprenticed to Aaron Willard in

MUSEUMS AND COLLECTIONS

American clocks and watches of the nineteenth century may be seen at the following:

GREAT BRITAIN
Bath: American Museum in
                     Britain, Claverton Manor
U.S.A.
Bristol, Conn.:   American Clock and Watch
                     Museum
New York, N.Y.:   New York University
                     Museum of Clocks and
                     Watches
Washington D.C.:   Smithsonian Institution

FURTHER READING

Antique American Clocks and Watches by Richard Thomson, Princeton, 1968.
A Treasury of American Clocks by Brooks Palmer, New York, 1967.

Papier Mâché

Fig. 1 **Sofa**, *English, mid-nineteenth century. Papier-mâché, gilt and painted in colours on black, with mother of pearl inlay, height 3½ ft., length 5 ft. Because of their great size, few sofas were made entirely of papier mâché, and only a very small number of these has survived.* (*Victoria and Albert Museum, London.*)

Fig. 2 **Nest of tables**, *English, c.1860. Papier-mâché, hand painted with rustic scenes and inlaid with a mother of pearl chess board.* (*De Havilland Antiques Ltd., London.*)

From Queen Victoria downwards, nineteenth-century society found papier-mâché boxes, trays and other furniture an indispensable part of everyday life

Although small papier-mâché articles were made in England from the early eighteenth century, it was not until the end of the century that they became important products of the industrial towns of Birmingham and Wolverhampton. This growth in the industry was largely due to Henry Clay's invention of a heat-proof panel of laminated paper which he patented in 1772. The finer and more costly products were made from this material, although pulp continued to be used as well. Both these basic materials were known as 'papier-mâché'.

By the time Queen Victoria came to the throne in 1837, japanned, painted and pearled papier-mâché wares were being mass produced in every con-

ceivable form, from the smallest button to a piano. In the intermediary range, there were boxes of all kinds, trays, bread-baskets, tea-caddies, letter-holders, snuffer-trays, vases, picture-frames, furniture and many other items.

Improved transportation made it possible to export these products to the Americas, Portugal, Spain and India. High production continued until the 1860s, when the demand tapered off. After this time, the firms still in business had a large stock to draw on, sufficient to satisfy the demand for japanned wares which declined steadily until its demise at the turn of the century.

The small box for snuff, patches or comfits was the earliest and most important product made of papier-mâché, but it was surpassed in production by the growing demand for waiters and trays. It became *de rigueur* for wealthy households to possess a set of costly trays.

The great interest in trays resulted in the creation of new shapes and a great variety of elaborate designs. In shape, the trays were rectangular,

octagonal, oval and a form called 'Gothic'; some were made in nests of five. One variation of the Gothic was the parlourmaid's tray, which had one side curved to fit the waist for support when the tray was heavily laden. Another popular tray was designed by George Wallis of the Old Hall Works at Wolverhampton. This was an oval tray with a scalloped edge which he named the 'Victoria' in honour of the young Queen.

In 1840, when Victoria married Albert, the well-known firm of Jennens and Bettridge of Birmingham presented her with a set of three papier-mâché trays decorated with such 'elegancies as plashing fountains, formal foliage and exotic birds on a green ground'. The daughter of the firm's partner, T. H. Bettridge, was also married

sizes with felt glued to the base to protect the surface of the table.

Snuffer-trays were also made at the end of the eighteenth century and remained in production as long as the industry was active.

Letter-writing was of great social importance and a complete set of writing-materials were provided in the guest-rooms and boudoirs of fine houses. There were lap-desks, or 'escritoirs', that had a velvet-covered writing-surface under the lid, which lifted up to reveal ink-bottles, a wafer-box and a slot for pens. There were also inkstands that stood on flat, round feet or on in-turned scrolls; they usually had a wafer-box placed between two crystal bottles with a slot for pens in front.

3

4

A. C. Cooper

Fig. 3 *Canterbury, English, c.1860. Papier-mâché with elaborate painting, gilding and inlay of mother of pearl, height 1 ft. 7 ins.*
Created at the end of the eighteenth century, when it was made in mahogany or walnut, the canterbury was intended to hold sheet music.
(Victoria and Albert Museum.)

Fig. 4 *Chair, English, mid-nineteenth century. Wood and japanned papier-mâché with gilding, mother of pearl inlay and caned seat.*
While some furniture was made entirely of papier-mâché, the makers found that it was in fact far more durable if combined with wood or metal. This superb chair combines a wooden frame with a decorative panel of papier-mâché.
(Victoria and A   1useum.)

in that year and a duplicate set of trays was made for her. The design was then cancelled. Nevertheless, many trays were made thereafter with designs similar to those of the wedding gifts.

In 1850, workmen at the Old Hall Works learned that the Queen was going to pass through Wolverhampton, and they decided to present her with a papier-mâché tray. Edwin Haseler, the flower-painter, was directed to ornament the tray with roses. The Queen stopped for only three minutes and the tray, laden with fine hothouse grapes, was passed into the carriage. 'Forthwith the grapes were swept onto a table and the tray handed back through the window of the moving train': a bitter disappointment for Haseler.

In 1847, Richard Redgrave .A.R.A. designed a most unusual tray for Jennens and Bettridge. This wine- or supper-tray resembled the parlourmaid's tray but had shallow wells in the two lower corners for bottles or decanters, and space above and between them for a place-setting. A variation of this tray, made in the 1850s, was rectangular in shape with a shallow well at each corner.

Bottle-stands or wine-coasters were made in the 1790s by Henry Clay of Birmingham, later of London, and by others in the nineteenth century. They were made in pairs and in pint and quart

Cabinets, made to hold writing- and sewing-materials, opened on top to disclose a satin-lined interior in which ivory or mother of pearl sewing-accessories were kept. Two doors in front of the cabinet covered small drawers meant to contain stationery, seals and other necessities of letter-writing. In 1849 Jenny Lind, the famous Swedish opera singer, visited the shop of Jennens and Bettridge, where she was presented with a maroon cabinet ornamented with 'mother of pearl figures in the Watteau style'.

The mantelpieces in Victorian rooms were often decorated with a pair of hand-screens or fans. They were made of panels mounted on turned ebony, ivory or gilt-wood sticks. These attractively decorated fans, 'intended becoming to shade the face', were roughly oval, square or helmet-shaped with scalloped or gadrooned edges. Before the fireplace there was often a cheval- or pole-screen.

One article, little known today, was called a 'voider'. This was a japanned basket into which dirty plates and cutlery were deposited after each dinner course. In *Great Expectations*, when Mr. Jaggers entertained Pip at dinner, he had two of these baskets on the floor by his chair into which he placed the dirty dishes. On the table there might well have been a round, handsomely japanned papier-mâché condiment stand complete with bottles and jars for sauces and spices.

Everyone loved boxes, and japanners made them in all sizes and for many uses. There were boxes for jewellery, handkerchiefs, gloves, fans, knitting-needles, sewing and one called 'The Ladies' Companion', which was used for toilet or travelling. Boxes were lined with satin, velvet or finely patterned papers, and decorated round the keyhole with pearl, ivory or silver escutcheons. The locks on some were impressed with a crown and 'V.R.', indicating that the locksmith held a royal patent.

Visiting-card cases, made as early as 1826, became more popular as the century advanced. Some were in the folio style and others had a hinged lid; all were lined with silk or plush to keep the embossed

Fig. 5 *Bedroom suite, English, late nineteenth century. Painted and gilt papier-mâché with mother of pearl inlay. Beds of papier-mâché were rare even in the nineteenth century, and few complete bedroom suites were made. Most are thought to be quite late in date. (Temple Newsam House, Leeds.)*

cards clean and smooth. There was at the time a recommended procedure for correctly using a card case. The lady was instructed to hold the case in full view while opening it to extract a card. It was also suggested that a fancy handkerchief be carried, to form an appropriate back-drop to the case. A caller's card was left in a handsomely ornamented tray, which usually had a heavy, gilt-metal, bale handle.

When Prince Albert died, japanners produced a number of pieces decorated in a subdued manner, using mauve and grey paint with mother of pearl. Since that day, however, this form of decoration has been overlooked.

During her long period of mourning, Queen Victoria expected her ladies-in-waiting to trim their purple and black dresses and hats with jet and this shiny black material became fashionable. An enterprising manufacturer devised an imitation and less costly jet made of black paper, cut and carefully japanned a shiny black to imitate the real thing. The demand for this product hardly survived the century.

Many Victorian homes boasted a loo- or chess-table (Fig. 2). The game of loo could be played by any number of people, but three-handed loo was the game usually played. For loo and other games

requiring counters or tokens, used to represent actual coins, there were round fish-shaped pearl chips. The 'fish' were kept in attractive counter-trays, the majority only four inches in length.

Round or oval table-tops of die-pressed paper panels had moulded bulbous pedestals set into square or round bases with three or four splayed scroll feet. A sturdier type of paper table had a pedestal of wood on tripod feet.

While some furniture was made entirely of papier-mâché (Fig. 1), Jennens and Bettridge discovered that furniture had a better chance of survival if it was combined with wood or iron (Fig. 4). It was also found that a piano-case made of paper panel had no resonance. Consequently, many pieces of furniture made of wood or iron only had japanned panels set in the frames. It is not unusual today for furniture made entirely of wood to be mislabelled 'papier-mâché' because of its elaborately painted and pearled decoration.

Japanned papier-mâché wares can be found with coloured backgrounds, imitation graining or marbling. In general, black was the standard colour used under the 'excessive fullness' of leaf gold, paint colours and pearl shell designs. The lack of restraint in the decoration of the Victorian period was sometimes criticised in contemporary writing; for example, in 1847 *The Birmingham and General Advertiser* said that japanned wares had 'upon their varied productions ornament of some kind or other. Quality was hardly considered'. This point of view did not generally prevail, for the taste of one hundred and twenty-five years ago was less restrained than that of today; 'show and glitter' was a trade-mark of the period. Whether or not one admires the designs, the majority were well executed with good brush-strokes, well-applied bronze powders and finely cut shell, for the better manufacturers saw to it that their artists were well trained and their products of a high standard.

Quantities of papier-mâché products have survived for our interest and pleasure. Many of the articles that were necessary or useful at the time of their manufacture are now only curiosities admired by collectors for their ornamentation, and they are good reminders of a past style and taste. ✠

MUSEUMS AND COLLECTIONS
English papier-mâché wares of the nineteenth century may be seen at the following:

GREAT BRITAIN

Birmingham:	City Museum and Art Gallery
	Blakesley Hall
Cardiff:	The National Museum of Wales
London:	Victoria and Albert Museum
Wolverhampton:	Municipal Art Gallery
	Bantock House

U.S.A.

Cooperstown, N.Y.:	Farmer's Museum
Litchfield, Conn:	Litchfield Historical Society

FURTHER READING
English Papier-Mâché of the Georgian and Victorian Periods by Shirley Spaulding De Voe, London, 1971.
Papier-Mâché Artistry by Dona Z. Meilach, London, 1971.
Papier-Mâché in Great Britain and America by Jane Toller, London, 1962.

Stevengraphs

Fig. 1 *Portrait of the cricketer* **W. G. Grace** *by Thomas Stevens, probably 1895. Woven silk.*
This Stevengraph is reputed to depict 'W.G.' on the occasion of his century of centuries in 1895.
(Author's Collection.)

Sold originally for only a few pence, the colourful silk pictures known as 'Stevengraphs' have recently enjoyed a well-deserved revival of popularity

In recent years several new collecting subjects have become fashionable and that with which we are concerned has devotees, not only in Great Britain, but in North America, Australia and on the Continent. These silk pictures, or 'Stevengraphs', were mere late Victorian, mass-produced novelties, sold for a few pence – novelties that now have a period charm.

The story commences in 1801 after the invention in France of the Jacquard loom. Silk-woven designs could be mass produced on this loom by means of a set of pierced cards which were automatically fed into the machine. Hundreds of miles of decorative ribbons were produced and soon very detailed ribbons were issued by the French manufacturers. Figure 4 is an example from the 1840s, and the all-important Jacquard loom with the set of pierced cards can be clearly seen.

These looms soon came into general use in Great Britain, particularly in the silk-weaving centre of Coventry, where some fifty per cent of the population (including women and children) were employed in the industry. However, in 1860, as a result of the Cobden Treaty, one clause of which permitted the duty-free entry into Great Britain of French silks, Coventry silk-workers suffered mass unemployment.

This distress was overcome by the simple expedient of adapting the machines to weave an upright design rather than a horizontal, continuous one, the new strips being cut into short lengths and finished with silk tassels for use as book-markers. The widely read *Art-Journal* gave publicity to the new products, '. . . the artisans engaged in the silk factories of Coventry are suffering very greatly from a general stagnation of business. An attempt is being made to give employment to these latter by the production of woven book-marks – many of which that have come before us are exceedingly elegant in design and beautiful in workmanship; quite works of illuminated art. A large demand for these cheap and pretty ornaments would tend to alleviate much distress'.

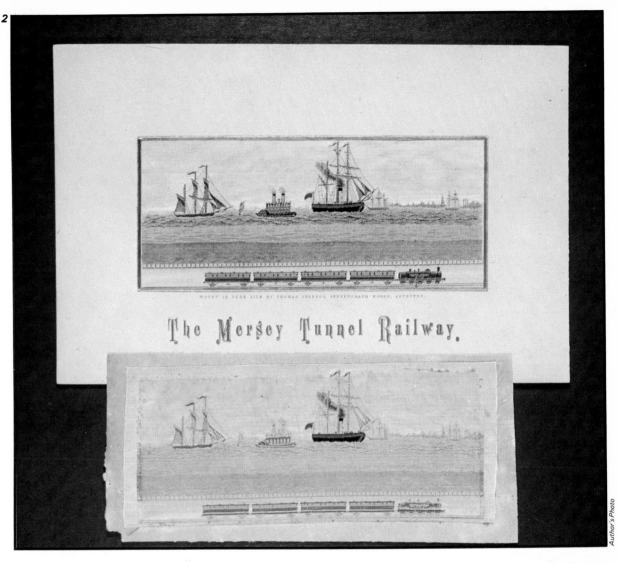

Fig. 2 *The Mersey Tunnel Railway,* *two silk examples. That above is a superb silk in mint state and in its original card mount, whereas the silk below is faded, stained and unmounted. Examples in bad condition are of little value and spoil a collection. (Author's Collection.)*

A large demand was certainly soon built up, thanks to very wide publicity in newspapers and journals engendered by the samples sent to editors by the enterprising Thomas Stevens. Stevens is traditionally credited with the introduction of these book-markers, and certainly his firm produced by far the largest number and led the field in its publicity of the silk-woven novelties. It was Stevens who introduced the trade-name 'Stevengraphs', a name now generally associated with all Coventry woven pictures, although he had many competitors, in particular W. H. Grant.

Thousands of silk-woven novelties were used as greetings cards

An attractive Stevens double-ended book-marker is shown in Figure 5. This, like many other designs, was intended as a Christmas gift. Thousands of such silk-woven novelties were used as we would a Christmas card or calendar, for these book-markers were originally mounted on a paper backing on which the donor could write an appropriate message. Stevens claimed to have introduced over nine hundred different designs, and many of these were linked to special events to ensure a steady annual sale. There are messages relating to birthdays, the New Year and weddings, while many of 'Forget-me-not' type were made as Valentines. A further series was intended as gifts to a mother, father, sister or brother, and a lengthy series of Bible-markers were woven with religious motifs. Many special designs were made for the Continental market or for the United States of America. These Stevens book-markers were made in the present century, together with a rather neglected series of Valentine cards, silk-fringed, coloured greetings cards and even silk jewellery.

In 1879 Thomas Stevens introduced a new idea, one which quickly caught the public fancy and which is the main concern of present-day collectors – the silk-woven pictures framed in a card mount. These Stevengraphs were introduced to the public at the little-known York Exhibition, which opened on 7 May, 1879. Here the Stevens loom wove two scenes of local interest – the London and York Stage Coach and Dick Turpin's Ride to York (Fig. 3). The public could buy these charming pictures 'hot from the loom' at a shilling each, and the *Yorkshire Gazette* reported: 'Doubtless many hundreds will avail themselves of the opportunity of securing, at the small price asked, one of the textileographs, or, as they have been called in honour of their originator, "Stevengraphs", as a souvenir of the Exhibition'.

These souvenirs certainly caught on and before the Exhibition closed on 31 October, 1879, two more designs had been introduced, and sale of the new silk pictures was extended to the whole county.

A Stevens advertisement issued in November, 1879, as shown in Figure 8, features the standard book-markers, Christmas cards and Valentines, as well as the first four Stevengraph pictures. That listed as *The Good Old Days* is the London York Coach, renamed, its pair being a charming railway

445

DICK TURPIN'S RIDE TO YORK,
ON HIS BONNIE BLACK BESS.
1739.

REGISTERED.

Here's a health to her memory ; shirk it who dare—
If you love what is noble, pledge Turpin's brave mare ;
And the draught will be welcome, the wine will be good ;
If it have half the spirit and strength of her blood.
May the steed that comes nigh her in courage and fire ;
Carry rider more worthy to make her heart tire ;
Though she saved him, and died to prove what she could do,
Yet *her* life was most precious by far of the two.

WOVEN IN THE
YORK EXHIBITION,
1879.

THOMAS STEVENS,
Inventor & Manufacturer,
Coventry & London.

Fig. 3 **Dick Turpin**, 1879, a very rare early version of this Stevengraph without a signpost, added in subsequent issues. (Author's Collection.)

Fig. 4 **The Jacquard Loom** from a painting by C. Bonnefond, drawn and put on the card by A. Manin, woven by Carquillat, 1840s. Finely woven silk. This superb French silk picture shows the loom with strings of the pierced cards which controlled the machine. (Kettering Museum and Art Gallery, Northamptonshire.)

Fig. 5 **Double-ended bookmarker**, 1870s. Woven silk. (Author's Collection.)

Fig. 6 **The re-enactment of the Lady Godiva Procession through the streets of Coventry.** Woven silk. (Author's Collection.)

Fig. 7 **The First Set**, a rather rare Stevengraph introduced in 1881. Woven silk. (Author's Collection.)

scene entitled *The Present Time*, while a race-scene, *The Struggle* (later called *The Finish*), had been added to pair with *Turpin's Ride to York*. The early examples of these have a credit printed on the card mount, stating that they were woven at the York Exhibition (Fig. 3). Various amendments were made to the early pictures and printed card mounts before the ideal was achieved. These variations were issued only for a brief period and some consequently are very rare – in some cases only two or three examples are at present known.

Completely new pictures were issued, initially at the rate of approximately one a month, and at least seventy subjects occur, ranging from battle-ships to a fine series of sporting pictures. They were often sold from travellers' sample books, in which they were set four to the double page.

In 1866 a series of portraits was introduced, selling at the reduced price of sixpence. These silks, of which about eighty different subjects are known, featured royalty, heads of state, politicians, historical personages and sportsmen of the period. Not only were British personages represented, but also Continental, Russian and American. Many of these portrait silks are now surprisingly rare, and some are only known in an unmounted state.

A further innovation was introduced early in the present century when W. H. Grant and the Stevens firm introduced postcards incorporating silk-woven panels. These novelties (which were also made on the Continent) have recently come into favour with collectors and represent a good, relatively inexpensive, facet of collecting. Some

446

WOVEN IN PURE SILK.

WOVEN IN SILK BY THOMAS STEVENS, INVENTOR AND MANUFACTURER, COVENTRY AND LONDON.   (REGISTERED.)

Fig. 8 *Stevens advertisement from* The Bookseller, *5 November, 1879. The standard products are listed, as well as the first four silk-woven pictures.*

prefer those cards which have been used and which bear a message relating to the card or to the exhibition where it was woven and purchased, but many silk-panelled cards can still be found in a mint state, as they were purchased at the height of the post-card craze, to be mounted in an album. The Stevens firm also produced cards depicting famous passenger liners, to be sold aboard ship.

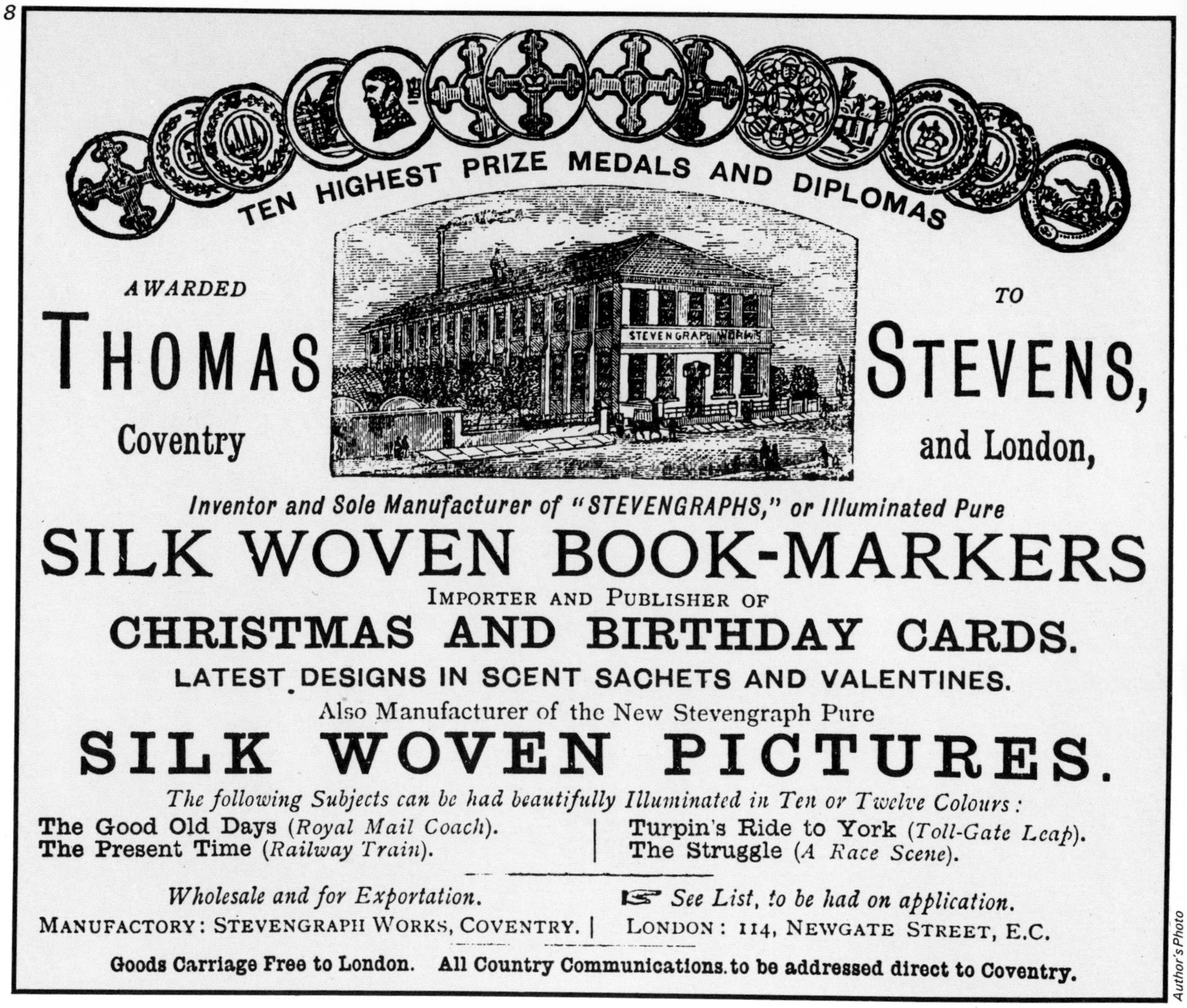

HINTS TO COLLECTORS

The serious collector should consider only those examples in first-rate condition, with brightly coloured silks and with an unstained, perfect, original card mount. The extremes of condition are well illustrated in Figure 2, where an almost mint mounted *Mersey Tunnel Railway* picture (purchased in the original protective envelope in which it left the factory) is seen with an unmounted silk of the same subject, showing bad staining and a general fading of the coloured silks.

These Victorian silk-woven pictures and their card mounts are very prone to damage, which will affect the market value considerably. The coloured silks will fade when exposed to strong sunlight. Dampness will cause staining or running of the colours, while the mounts become brittle with age and should be treated with extreme care.

Much research needs to be carried out on this relatively new subject – especially on the work of Stevens' competitors. The many Stevens products – other than the well-known and quite plentiful book-markers, silk-pictures and postcards – offer the collector seeking a new field of study ample opportunity to make his mark.

COLLECTORS' ASSOCIATION

Many Stevengraph collectors belong to the international Stevengraph Collectors' Association and benefit from the information that is exchanged and the knowledge of fellow-collectors. The address of the Association is Irvington-on-Hudson, New York 10533, U.S.A.

MUSEUMS AND COLLECTIONS

Although most Stevengraphs are in private hands, examples of Coventry silks may be seen at the following:

GREAT BRITAIN
Coventry: Herbert Art Gallery and Museum
London: Victoria and Albert Museum

FURTHER READING

Stevengraphs and other Victorian Silk Pictures by G. A. Godden, London, 1971.
Stevengraphs Price Guide by Austin Sprake, Guernsey, 1971.
Stevengraphs by Austin Sprake and Michael Darby, Guernsey, 1968.
Thomas Stevens and his Silk Ribbon Pictures by Alice Lynes, Coventry, 1959.
The Silk Pictures of Thomas Stevens by Wilma Sinclair Le Van Baker, New York, 1957.

Tunbridge Ware

Using up to one hundred and fifty different sorts of wood, the craftsmen of Tunbridge Wells, in Kent, created a uniquely English art with their boxes, trinkets and souvenirs

There is some dispute about precisely what can be called Tunbridge ware. The fine jewel-cabinet illustrated in Figure 4 is accepted as an example of good, late nineteenth-century work, but early forms of the ware often go unrecognised.

Tunbridge ware developed in the late eighteenth century, and it existed in a rudimentary form a century and a half before that. In 1606, the discovery at Tunbridge Wells of the health-giving chalybeate waters converted a small village into a fashionable spa and there existed, according to John Evelyn, 'extravagant turnings and insinuations'. In 1699, Celia Fiennes recorded 'shopps full of all sorts of curious wooden ware which this place is noted for, the delicate neate and thin ware of wood both white and lignum vitae wood'.

By 1699, John Jackson, a dealer in Cheapside, London, was advertising Tunbridge ware. This ware in plain wood or variegated lignum vitae was no doubt turned on a lathe to produce drinking-vessels, ladles and pestles and mortars. The area was rich in woods of many varieties, but there is no reason to suppose that the work was markedly different from that of other resorts and spas. Furthermore, none of the nineteenth-century makers, energetic in their assertions of the early origins of their trade, claim anything as early as the seventeenth century. The Wise family of Tunbridge was the only exception; they claimed to have been established as turners by 1685.

In the nineteenth century many makers claimed to have been the founders of Tunbridge ware. Thomas Barton and the Burrows family asserted that their forebears, professional or ancestral, were already making genuine Tunbridge ware in 1720, while William Fenner contented himself with the year 1730. This may refer to the first adoption of

Fig. 1 *Tea-caddy,* an unusually ambitious piece of early geometric work. Maple, length 12½ ins. Fine sticks of coloured woods were glued together in bundles and then sliced across to form mosaics.
(Author's Collection.)

Fig. 2 *Dressing-table box* with scent-bottles, labelled by Edmund Nye. Length 9 ins. Note how the floral motif is let into the ebony surround with no bordering pattern.
(Author's Collection.)

the technique stimulated by the cabinet-maker's use of marquetry after Charles II returned from exile in Holland. Different coloured woods in geometrical, floral and, later, shell patterns were cut out and veneered on to plain wooden boxes, tea-caddies, dressing-boxes and voiders. It seems likely that the Tunbridge manufacturers supplied marquetry motifs to cabinet-makers, which would explain the mention in advertisements of 'wholesale' supply.

Marquetry work was certainly available in Tunbridge by 1762. Samuel Derrick, a friend of Dr. Johnson, describes motifs of, 'highly polished yew, cherry, holly and other woods', and *The History of Tunbridge Wells*, published in 1766 by Benge Burr, records 'a prodigious variety of the prettiest ornamental inlays that can be imagined, some of which are so excellent in their kind that it is hard to believe that they are not assisted by the pencil. But besides holly, they used no small quantity of cherry-tree, plum-tree, yew and sycamore; the yew, especially, is of late become very fashionable, and the woods vineered with it are certainly excessively pretty'.

This account reveals the degree of elaboration that had developed, and helps to explain the relatively high price of £1 4s. paid for a work-box in that year. The demand must have been considerable by the decade 1768–78, when Fanny Burney wrote her diary. She relates how whole shops on one side of the Pantiles were devoted to the selling of Tunbridge ware and Benge Burr states that, by 1766, among society visiting the Wells for their health, 'it was customary to take Tunbridge fairings to their friends at home'. On the other hand, Derrick felt that it was much underrated: 'Were this smuggled abroad and then imported as a foreign commodity, I am persuaded that people would run after it, but alas! – everyone knows it is English and the encouragement is therefore poor'.

Some of the finest Tunbridge ware was made in the early years

Towards the end of the eighteenth century, the pennant-shaped design known as the 'vandyke pattern' began to appear, possibly as a development from the backgammon boards which, like cribbage and Pope Joan boards, were popular at this period (Fig. 5). The emergence of the illusionistic cube pattern characteristic of Tunbridge ware must date from the late eighteenth century. It is found on boxes and on small pieces of furniture.

This style prevailed until about 1830, when the end-grain technique superseded it; some of the finest work was done during this earlier period. The excellent shapes of the boxes, the fine balance between the cube pattern and the narrow bandings of beadings along the edges and the overall simplicity achieves an effect which is often preferred to the later, more intricate work.

There is rich variety of colour and texture in the woods, which were primarily local; later, imported woods were also used, until a total of one hundred and fifty different types were employed. Herein lies a distinguishing feature of Tunbridge ware. There is an enormous feeling for the actual quality of the wood, and in the cubes one can observe that great care has been taken to explore the decorative possibilities of the wood by cutting across the grain, with

Fig. 3 **Group of stickwork items,** *including a stiletto used for sewing, an ointment-pot and a barrel-shaped container with end-grain work. Height of barrel 1 in.* (Author's Collection.)

Fig. 4 **Jewel-cabinet** *with a scene of the ruins of Bayham Abbey and imitation Berlin wool floral patterns, using two slices off the same block, one reversed. Height $6\frac{1}{2}$ ins.* (Author's Collection.)

Fig. 5 **Cribbage box** *with cube and vandyke patterns, early nineteenth century. Length $9\frac{1}{2}$ ins.* (Author's Collection.)

Fig. 6 **Photograph-album.** *An unusual Tunbridge ware item, displaying green wood in the star pattern, which is surrounded by bird's eye maple, tinted greenish yellow by the chalybeate waters of the area. $9\frac{1}{2}$ ins. x $7\frac{3}{4}$ ins.* (Author's Collection.)

Fig. 7 **Teapoy,** *possibly by G. and J. Burrows, c.1830. Height 31 ins. This example of early geometric work is beautifully displayed on the eight facets of the tapering stem. It was probably made by Burrows, the first firm to depict birds and butterflies. Beetles are the rarest feature in this work.* (Author's Collection.)

6

7

A. C. Cooper

A. C. Cooper

the grain or across a knot to reveal a circular pattern. Additionally appealing is the fact that work of this period is usually in excellent condition.

The high point of this technique was marked by the making of a combined reading-, writing- and work-table for Princess Victoria in 1826. Colbran, in the *New Guide to Tunbridge Wells*, in 1840, records how William Fenner, Edmund Nye, Messrs. Sharp and James Friend drew lots to decide who should have the honour of making it. Fenner won, and made 'A table formed with kingwood beautifully veneered with party-coloured woods from every part of the globe . . . it was considered a unique specimen of the taste and ingenuity of Tunbridge Ware manufacturers'.

The cube pattern was one of the constant features of Tunbridge ware, even after the introduction of the end-grain principle. At first the cubes were seen alone with fine banding of alternating light and dark woods; these bands were later replaced by wider bands in end-grain surrounding a central motif of cubes including one piece of green wood. A maker in Rye by the name of Green, who used the cube pattern as late as the 1930s, perfected a variation by further reducing in size the cubes and increasing the number of colours, always using one or two pieces of green wood and employing the end-grain method for what was originally a marquetry system.

The lack of recognition given to the early cube pattern reflects the general uncertainty about the origins of the work. Besides marquetry, plain wooden boxes painted with thin bands of colour, usually red, black and green, and transfer prints of views of Tunbridge Wells and other resorts, seem to have been produced by the Tunbridge ware makers. The looseness with which the term was applied is reflected in the fact that between 1765 and 1825 seven London dealers announced: 'Tunbridge Toys', 'Tunbridge Ware and all other Turnery Wares', 'ivory turner and Tunbridge Ware manufacturer', 'Tunbridge Ware, print seller and perfumer' and 'Lignum Vitae and Tunbridge Ware'. It seems likely that the phrase 'Tunbridge

ware' was being used to describe objects made in Tunbridge Wells as distinct from its use as a term describing a particular craft. The real beginning of Tunbridge ware as a distinct craft should be identified with the emergence, in the cube and vandyke patterns, of a highly sensitive use of woods.

The next development must have occurred some time in the 1820s, when the characteristic end-grain technique emerged. In 1840, Colbran indicated that the system was by then well established. The *New Guide to Tunbridge Wells* contains an advertisement by George and James Burrows in which they claim to be the inventors of this mosaic work and, since there are no other claimants, this is very probably the truth. Fenner and Company announced 'Mosaic and Inlaid wood Work selling at very reduced prices owing to the introduction of new Machinery'. This is undoubtedly a euphemism for the discovery of the end-grain principle; the company was perhaps reluctant to advertise it as a form of mass production.

Briefly, the system relies on the grouping together of fine sticks, sometimes thinner than a match-stick, and between six and ten inches long, into bundles. These were glued together down the long side in such a way that the pattern, visible at each end, ran the length of the block. Slices were taken from across the block and stuck on to a brown paper backing. They were then veneered on to the box. There should thus exist at least ten identical versions of a design. Although the veneer was only one-sixteenth of an inch thick when sanded down, the use of crude saws led to enormous wastage. These blocks were assembled according to a chart which would list '2 Holly, 1 Green, 3 Beech', and so on, and the design could be checked against a water-colour pattern on squared paper. The process was slow, due to the slow-drying glue, and only small amounts could be stuck at one time. Nevertheless, it did enable a certain speeding up in manufacture and encouraged the appearance of an unprecedented variety of patterns. Once the blocks were made up, any combination of border pattern and central motif could be used on one box, and,

451

although this would seem to lead to uniformity, identical combinations of patterns were never made. Every piece is unique.

The teapoy in Figure 7 is an excellent example of this new mosaic inlay in its early phase when the small geometrical patterns were used. This piece also contains birds and butterflies and exceptionally also bees or beetles, marking the first departure from the geometrical pattern, which may well be by Burrows; Colbran records, 'Mr. Burrows was the first to introduce butterflies and birds'.

The end-grain principle had another application called 'stickwork' (Fig. 3). The blocks could be turned on the lathe instead of sliced across the grain, revealing pretty, longitudinal patterns. Stickwork was confined to the geometrical pattern and used for small pieces only.

In the nineteenth century we know of more makers by name. The problem of distinguishing the work of one maker from another, however, is considerable, since very few makers' labels survive. The issue is further confused by the fact that whole families, such as the four Burrows brothers, were in the business, and it passed from father to son for generations. The Wise family, mostly by the name of George, from Tonbridge, were in the business from 1885 to 1899. Some of the earliest labels are those 'Published by Geo. Wise, Tunbridge, Apr. I, 1807', for example, on a box with a transfer view, but this may well refer to the publication of the print used for the transfer. It was not uncommon for Tunbridge ware shops to be print-sellers, too.

Edmund Nye and Thomas Barton used labels more extensively than any other makers (Fig. 2), although labels do also exist on pieces by G. Wise Jnr., T. Burrows, J. Friend, A. Talbot, R. License, R. Russell, J. Medhurst, W. Upton, H. Hollamby (only on thermometers) and Boyce, Brown and Kemp, who were later known as the Tunbridge Ware Manufacturing Company. Usually the existence of a label denoted the work of a maker rather than that of his workshop. Latterly, however, a small, oval, indelible ink stamp was used in place of the paper labels, and seems to have been used at random, more often on small and poor quality pieces. Care should be taken to distinguish between manufacturers and dealers. Many dealers – 'fancy repositories', in London, the South coast and other resorts – took to putting their labels on, like W. Childs of Brighton.

Some pieces were sent to France to be mounted in ormolu

Tunbridge ware was obviously sold very widely across the country and examples exist of ambitious work apparently sent to France for mounting in ormolu. At the other end of the scale the humbler pieces – sewing- and writing-accessories, for instance – could be bought from a pedlar, as Mayhew records in *London Labour and the London Poor* of 1851. One such lived by selling 'small articles of Tunbridge Ware and perfumery, etc., etc., by munging [begging] over them'.

By 1843, and very likely a little earlier, the sophisticated Berlin wool pattern made its appearance. The floral pattern on the jewel-cabinet in Figure 4 is a fine example of the tiny wood tesserae echoing Berlin wool embroidery patterns. The elaborate and dense masses of flowers, oak-leaves and ferns, achieving a remarkably three-dimensional effect, are typical of this style. Both Barton and Nye employed this type of work extensively, the designs becoming increasingly more naturalistic and enhanced by the use of coloured woods, especially green. This green wood is usually oak which has been attacked by the fungus *chlorosplenium aeruginosum*, making it change colour. The photograph-album in Figure 6 is an excellent example of the green set off against a range of rich colours.

The more elaborate technique leads to the development of architectural ruins, of castles, priories, cathedrals, ruined abbeys (Fig. 4), country mansions and some street views. Of over twenty designs, with many variants, the most common of all is Eridge Castle. An example of Bayham Abbey was exhibited by Nye at the Great Exhibition of 1851.

A high point in the history of Tunbridge ware is marked by the large number of makers exhibiting at the Great Exhibition, dominated by the ambitious work of Edmund Nye and his apprentice, Thomas Barton, later his partner and perhaps the greatest manufacturer of all. They exhibited a table with a 'representation of a vessel sailing on the ocean, which, viewed at a distance, is a perfect imitation of Nature'; another, made from 129,540 pieces, depicted the grosbeak and the Baltimore oriole.

A piece by Nye with a magnificent Vanessa Juliana butterfly adorning the top of an elaborately inlaid work-table is to be seen in the Tunbridge Wells Museum. Nye made a feature of birds and butterflies in both end-grain and marquetry.

Thomas Barton continued the high quality of Nye's craftsmanship until his death in 1902. Barton used richly coloured woods extensively, especially the green, and set them dramatically in very dark woods, often ebony. The attention to detail can be seen in the careful corner-mitring, the fine interior papers and silks and the leatherised and marbled papers on the bottom of the boxes, set into the recessed panel characteristic of the ware. His sense of proportion and balance of design are constant features of his work. Although Boyce, Brown and Kemp and Green of Rye were working as late as the 1930s, their work does not approach the intricacy, the use of rich woods and the attention to detail. Thomas Barton, whether working on the scale of a pin cushion or of a tea-caddy, achieved a standard of craftsmanship which is unique and English.

MUSEUMS AND COLLECTIONS

Tunbridge ware may be seen at the following:

GREAT BRITAIN
Birmingham: City Museum and Art Gallery
                     (Pinto Collection)
London: Bethnal Green Museum
Maidstone: Borough Museum and
                     Art Gallery
Tunbridge Wells: Municipal Museum

FURTHER READING

Tunbridge and Scottish Souvenir Woodware by Edward and Eva Pinto, London, 1970.
Treen and Other Wooden Bygones by Edward Pinto, London, 1969.
Mansions, Men and Tunbridge Ware by Ethel Younghusband, Slough, 1949.

Fitted Boxes

Fig. 1 *Needlework-cabinet, English, mid-nineteenth century. Rosewood inlaid with mother of pearl, the interior lined with blue silk and gold-tooled red leather. Miniature chests of drawers were a favourite type of work-box in the Victorian era. This example has numerous silver and mother of pearl needlework-requisites in the well, while the bottom drawer is fitted for writing. (Brown Collection.)*

Made of polished woods, veneered or inlaid with mother of pearl and brass, elaborate fitted boxes for jewels, cosmetics, sewing, writing, games, picnics and medicines, drawing, painting and smoking equipment — all these were popular with well-to-do Victorians

The Victorians had a great liking for fitted boxes and caskets. The needs which brought them into being had mostly existed, and had been met in some degree, long before Queen Victoria's sixty-four-year reign commenced. The Victorians' achievement was to combine numerous small cases of necessities into larger ones; to lower costs by a degree of mechanisation, making them available to a greater proportion of the population; and, finally, to bring them into line with the taste of their age.

The most popular materials for the different boxes were varieties of hardwood, frequently veneered and sometimes handsomely inlaid with contrasting woods, mother of pearl or brass, or decorated with ormolu mounts which might act as settings for semi-precious stones. Many of these receptacles originally had outer cases of leather or cloth for protection when travelling. Weight was not important, for not only did servants travel with their masters and mistresses on coaches and trains, but there were plenty of porters waiting to pick up a threepence or sixpence, or perhaps even a shilling, at railway stations. Some fitted cases were made entirely of leather or shagreen; others, essentially for use at home rather than for travel, were of silver, enamel, lacquer, and papier-mâché. Some of the most attractive wooden fitted boxes available to collectors are decorated with Tunbridge wood mosaic.

Excluding tea-caddies and tea-chests, which represent a subject on their own, domestic fitted boxes include jewel-boxes; fitted dressing- or beauty-boxes; work-boxes; writing-boxes; games-boxes; picnic-boxes; travelling medicine-boxes; smokers' compendia; painting- and drawing-boxes. The dividing-line between these nine varieties of fitted boxes was by no means clear cut; a fitted dressing-case, in particular, frequently contained a section for jewellery, and it might also incorporate a writing-box, a needlework section and occasionally basic tea-making or picnic equipment.

Some of the most attractive Victorian jewel-caskets are quite simple in form, with tops of curved 'trunk' form, leather covered and lined with padded velvet or satin. They nearly all include a well and a tray or trays fitted for a watch, rings, bracelets, necklaces or pendants. A variant is the Swiss or Tyrolean peasant-carved casket in Figure 3, which has fabric-lined, swing-out trays above a well, which is padded and fitted for a watch and jewellery; this was made in about 1840–45.

Some of the most elaborate and over-decorated mid-nineteenth-century jewellery-boxes were made for the 1851 and 1862 Exhibitions. The majority are based on medieval caskets in the form of truncated domes. Some are in the form of gothic, ecclesiastic buildings and resemble reliquaries, complete with statues of saints in niches; others are Renaissance-inspired. These unrepresentative

R. Todd-White

Fig. 2 **Writing-box,** *English, mid-nineteenth century. Figured walnut inlaid with Grecian key pattern bandings, with ebony decorated borders.*
When opened out, this box has a tooled-leather writing-slope with compartments for pens and ink and wells for stationery.
(Antique Supermarket, London.)

Fig. 3 **Peasant jewel-casket,**
Swiss or Tyrolean, c.1845. Carved wood with swing-out trays lined with purple fabric above a well fitted for a watch and jewellery. This is a variant of the ordinary tray-fitted Victorian jewel-casket. (Birmingham Museum and Art Gallery, Pinto Collection.)

Fig. 4 **Double-lidded work-box,**
English, 1820–30. Painted wood decorated with coloured prints of Brighton Pavilion and the sea-front.
This box dates from the Regency, but the type continued to be made in Victorian times. (Victoria and Albert Museum, London.)

3

4

exhibition pieces are of the most beautiful quality, and while their purchase had status value at the time, to modern eyes they appear as overdone in their ornament as was the fulsome praise lavished on them in the contemporary *Art-Journal* catalogues.

Victorian fitted dressing-cases were ingeniously designed and often included much more than the normal dressing-table set of hand-mirror, brushes, combs and various silver-topped, cut-glass bottles and pots. A jewel-tray was a frequent feature, sometimes contained in a secret drawer, and manicure- and sewing-implements, and occasionally tea-making equipment, were also included. A dressing-case shown by Asprey's at the 1862 Exhibition was of polished walnut with gilt-engraved corners and locks, escutcheons and handles. The silver-gilt and cut-glass interior fittings included all the usual toilet requisites, a tray of manicure- and sewing-implements, a magnifying-glass, a stationery-drawer, a blotter and a pair of candlesticks. Such a case, ideal for travelling, would originally have had a protective outer case of leather.

Less luxurious, but nevertheless a high-class product, is the dressing-case illustrated in Figure 5. The exterior of this example is veneered with figured coromandel wood, inlaid with brass and mother of pearl. A mother of pearl plaque in the centre of the lid is engraved 'G.E. to J.E.E. January 1855'. The interior is lined with gold-tooled cerise leather, matching satin and crushed velvet. The fittings in the tray are of engraved silver and cut glass with matching silver lids. The velvet-cushioned panel held in the lid by a spring is reversible, and the other side contains a dressing-mirror; this removable panel forms the lid of a recess to hold papers. In addition to a well for holding brushes and combs, the case contains two spring-controlled secret drawers. One opens out of the left-hand side, and the other, velvet-lined and fitted for jewellery, opens in front. A case of this pattern was awarded a gold medal in the 1851 Exhibition. This basic design was very popular and many cases of similar layout, plain veneered but with plated fittings, were made in the 1850s.

Also shown in Figure 5 is a lady's dressing-table casket, the design of which originated in France in the 1820–30 period. Of hexagonal form, it is veneered with thuya-wood and has ebonised and gilt mounts. It holds, on four of its doors, glass bottles engraved with gilt lines and stars, in pierced gilt-metal holders of gothic outline; the other two doors are lined with blue *moiré* silk pads, with pockets for small implements. The gilt-metal knob on the top, connected to a central spindle, actuates cog-wheels which control the opening and closing mechanism and also operate the small musical-box in the base. Caskets of this type were made with gilt-metal fitments for many other purposes, particularly for holding cheroots, with a piercer and match-holder included.

Another Victorian fitted case was made in the form of a miniature grand piano; when the lid is raised, it discloses a velvet-lined tray fitted with manicure- and sewing-implements and, at the same time, motivates a musical-box in the base.

Attractive Victorian fitted inkstands, some with stationery-cabinets incorporated, were also made as miniature grand or upright pianos. The fitted writing-box which opened out to form a sloping surface, popular in Georgian times, continued to be

Fig. 5 Left: ***Dressing-case***, *English, 1850–60. Figured coromandel inlaid with brass and mother of pearl, with engraved silver and cut-glass interior fittings, cerise satin, velvet and leather linings; and including two jewel-drawers. In this photograph, the case is seen with the mirror reversed and the left-hand secret drawer exposed; 12 ins. x 9 ins. x 7¼ ins. A case of this pattern was awarded a gold medal in the 1851 Exhibition. Right:* ***Toilet-casket****, English, mid-nineteenth century. Thuya-wood, partially ebonised, fitted with bottles and manicure-implements. (Birmingham Museum and Art Gallery, Pinto Collection.)*

Fig. 6 ***Gentleman's travelling-case****, English, c.1840. Mahogany, length 8¼ ins., diameter 2⅜ ins. Cleverly designed to hold the maximum in the minimum space, this early Victorian case is of a type which originated in the 1820–30 period. It has a well concealed beneath the mirror for storage and a tray for two razors and scissors. Under the tray are compartments for a shaving-brush, tooth- and ear-picks, tweezers, corkscrew and toothbrush. The circular pewter box at the end is for tooth-powder. Gentlemen's hair-brushes always had their own separate cases at this time. (Birmingham Museum and Art Gallery, Pinto Collection.)*

5

Reilly and Constantine

6

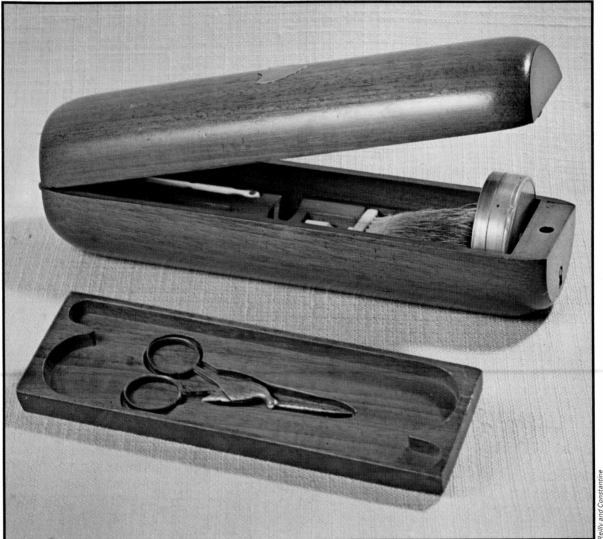

Reilly and Constantine

made throughout Victoria's reign (Fig. 2), although towards 1900 it was largely superseded by fitted travelling writing-cases in leather.

Victorian artists' and draughtsmen's combined fitted boxes are rare and their value largely depends on how complete their interior equipment is and whether it is all original. The same applies to Victorian medicine-cabinets. Invariably well made, these are the direct descendants of the Georgian apothecary's case and they should contain, in addition to the original bottles, such items as scales, pestle and mortar, beakers and measuring-glasses.

Gentlemen's toilet needs were well catered for but the cases were usually small, because it was general for a pair of hair-brushes with comb to have a leather case of their own. An ingenious *multum in parvo* for travelling is shown in Figure 6. It originated in the 1820–30 period, but continued in production throughout Victorian times. It is a neat and cleverly designed mahogany cylinder, which holds a surprising amount. A mirror in the lid conceals a well (original contents unknown); the tray, shown alongside, holds two razors with a recess below them for scissors. Under the tray are compartments for a shaving-brush, tooth- and ear-picks, tweezers, corkscrew and toothbrush; at the end is a circular pewter box for tooth-powder.

The most popular Victorian containers used for picnics were waterproof-lined, wickerwork hampers, with wicker handles, fastening-loops, eyes and sharpened willow bolts. Some were unfitted, general-purpose hampers; others had loops and pockets for everything which is still needed on a picnic, with one notable exception – the thermos flask, a blessing which did not appear until 1907. Instead, there was a folding spirit-stove and bottle of methylated spirits, a small saucepan and one or two beverage-bottles encased in a wooden flask and with a glass in the screw-on wooden cap. These are now collectors' finds.

For luncheon *en route*, the container might vary from the hiker's handkerchief to the elaborately fitted box carried by the traveller in horse-carriages or first-class railway compartments. Coming under the latter heading is the oak box which was made for the Reverend William Cashel Stuart in about 1870 (Fig. 7). Externally it is veneered with ivory; inside it is lined with blue velvet. Carved in ivory on the lid, and engraved on the silver fittings within,

Fig. 7 *The Rev. William Cashel Stuart's travelling luncheon-box,* English, c.1870. Oak, veneered with ivory and carved with the Stuart family coat of arms, lined with blue velvet.
This useful box contains a silver flask and sandwich-box, silver-mounted horn beaker, and a silver-lidded finger-bowl. There is also a small, ivory-framed mirror, and the original napkin with drawn-thread fringe. (Formerly in the author's collection.)

7

Sydney W. Newberry

are the arms of Mr. Stuart, who was the fourth son of the second Earl of Castle Stewart. Centred in the velvet-lined lid is a small, circular, ivory-framed mirror, and in separate compartments in the box are the original engraved silver flask, sandwich-box, silver-topped finger-bowl, silver-mounted horn beaker and napkin with drawn-thread fringe.

The completely fitted work-box and work-table evolved only in the late eighteenth century and did not come into popular use until the nineteenth century. As many of the finest early boxes are of Chinese lacquer and contain elaborately carved Chinese ivory spools and silk-winders, it seems probable that the fully fitted work-box originated in the Far East. There are a number of reasons for the late arrival of this useful object. The eighteenth-century lady, when working, wore an apron with capacious sewing-pockets. She also usually had separate cases fitted for scissors, crochet-hooks, thimbles, needles and pins. Additionally, she had a variety of winders, because she had to wind her own threads from skeins and hanks; ready-reeled cotton and thread were early nineteenth-century inventions, while silk on reels followed a little later. Work-boxes in great variety were made in Victorian times, but far and away the most popular receptacle throughout the period was the woven work-basket, lined with buttoned, padded silk or satin.

Another popular type of Victorian work-box was the miniature chest of drawers, with a fitted compartment under the lid and the drawers below enclosed by a pair of doors or a fall flap. An attractive specimen in rosewood, inlaid with mother of pearl, is shown in Figure 1. Regency double-lidded work-boxes, as shown in Figure 4, had eighteenth-century ancestry, but continued to be made in the Victorian era.

The Victorian games-compendium, like the work-box, evolved from the grouping together of a number of smaller fitted boxes or cases. The most popular of the simple compendia, and one with a long pre-Victorian history, was the chess and draughts outfit formed as two 'book volumes', hinged together. The interior box, which held chessmen, draughts, dice and dice-cups, opened out to form the backgammon board and, when turned over, the flat surface produced the chess- and draughts-board. A *de luxe* compendium usually had in its lid a folding draughts/chess-board, the reverse marked out for backgammon, and in the box itself were separate compartments for chessmen, draughts, bezique-cards and markers, whist-cards and markers, piquet-cards, dice-cups, dominoes and, occasionally, a cribbage board.

MUSEUMS AND COLLECTIONS

Victorian fitted boxes may be seen in many museums in Great Britain, notably the following:

Brighton: Brighton Museum and Art Gallery
London: Bethnal Green Museum
London Museum
Victoria and Albert Museum
York: York Castle Museum

FURTHER READING

The Collector's Book of Boxes by Marian Klamkin, Newton Abbot, 1972.
Objects of Vertu by Howard Ricketts, London, 1971.
Treen and Other Wooden Bygones by Edward H. Pinto, London, 1969.

Smoking Accessories

*Fig. 1 **Eighteenth-century pipe-cases.** From the left: probably Dutch; end-hinged, boxwood. Probably Austrian; end-hinged, boxwood. Dutch or German; end-hinged, brass-mounted ebony with a combination lock. English black clay pipe with its side-hinged fitted case, c.1800. (Pinto Collection.)*

Introduced to Europe in the sixteenth century as a cure for disease, tobacco occasioned the invention of a bewildering variety of attractive smoking accessories

Many contradictory statements are recorded as to who first brought tobacco to Europe, who first smoked it, where and when; probably the truth will never be established. What remains undisputed is that it first reached Europe from America, but we do not know for certain tobacco's precise origin.

There are at least three European contenders for this honour: Frère André Thevet visited Brazil in 1555 and published a book on his travels in 1558. In his book he accurately describes tobacco and states that in his garden in Angoulême he was growing it from the seeds he had brought back with him. Then there is Francisco Hernandez, who introduced the plant to Spain in 1559. The most famous name in the story, however, is Jean Nicot, who gave his name to nicotine. Nicot was French Ambassador to Portugal from 1559 to 1561; he sent seeds to Catherine de 'Medicis, Queen of France, and for a time, tobacco was known in France as the

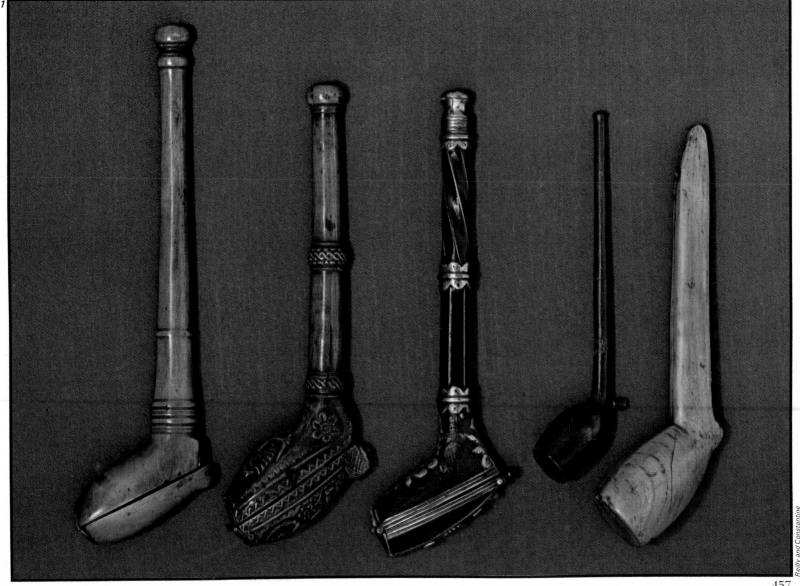

'Queen's Herb'. It is ironical that the introduction of tobacco to Europe was as a medicinal specific and that one of the claims made for it was as a cure for malignant growths.

The introduction of tobacco to the British Isles is generally credited, or debited, to any one of the following: Sir Walter Raleigh, Sir Francis Drake, Sir John Hawkins or Sir Ralph Lane. Bearing in mind the close ties between France and Scotland, it would not be surprising if tobacco came to Scotland before England, but there is no proof. Although there is a chimney-piece at Cawdor Castle, Scotland, dated 1510, depicting a fox smoking a pipe, the date appears to be too early for tobacco, but he may have been smoking medicinal herbs, which were probably introduced to Europe somewhat earlier.

Raleigh taught his friends to smoke, presenting them with pipes

The first reliable date for the introduction of tobacco to England is 1565. William Harrison, the Elizabethan chronicler, who in the 1570s commenced his *Description of England*, says, 'Tobacco was first brought, and made knowne in England by Sir John Hawkins, about the yeere one thousand five hundred sixty-five, but not used by most englishmen in many yeers after, though at this day commonly used by most men and many women...'. This seems good evidence in favour of Hawkins as

the introducer, but in the 1631 edition of Harrison's work this note is added: 'Sir Walter Raleigh was the first that brought tobacco into use, when all men wondered what it meant'. The answer seems to be that Hawkins introduced tobacco and Raleigh cultivated it on his estate in Ireland from seeds given to him from America by Ralph Lane. Raleigh is also known to have taught his friends to smoke and to have presented them with silver pipes. The legend of the servant, throwing a bucket of water over his master when he first saw him smoking, is now firmly attached to Raleigh but in earlier times it was as frequently associated with Drake, Hawkins or Lane and was alternatively a flagon of wine or a tankard of ale.

James I, who loathed Raleigh and judicially murdered him in 1618 after a travesty of a trial, wrote an arrogant and bombastic treatise in 1603 entitled *Counterblaste to Tobacco*, in which, by innuendo, he denounced Raleigh as the instigator of the tobacco habit. James' *Counterblaste* did not decrease tobacco addiction, so he raised the duty from 2d. to the then penal figure of 6s. 10d. per pound – of course diverting the taxation to himself! He also sold a monopoly to the Worshipful Company of Pipe-Makers. By 1614 there were upwards of seven thousand shops selling tobacco in and near London, so the King's finances must have benefited considerably. Since the time of James, penalties on tobacco addicts in Great Britain have all been pecuniary, but in some parts of seventeenth-century Europe they varied from whipping and mutilation to death. The plague of 1665 gave tobacco a further impetus, smokers and chewers being considered immune, and even children were encouraged to smoke.

When first introduced, Elizabethan tobacco cost the then enormous sum of 3s. per ounce, coming by way of Spain and the Spanish colonies. This was reduced some fifty years later to about 8d., as imports from Virginia increased. In 1651 the Duke of Bedford, a heavy smoker, paid 3s. 4d. per pound for Virginia tobacco, but 10s. per pound for Spanish. In the 1750–70s period, Sir John Filmer paid 1s. 6d. per pound for Virginia tobacco, but by 1794 Parson Woodforde was paying 2s. 8d. There are six main groups of interesting small objects available for the collector of bygones of smoking – pipes, pipe-cases, tobacco-jars, tobacco-boxes, pipe-trays, racks and stands and tobacco-stoppers.

Clay pipes were not generally smoked by women of fashion

Although, as already mentioned, literary references to silver pipes exist, it is extremely doubtful that many were made; it is believed that so far only one early seventeenth-century example has come to light. They would have been expensive and much hotter to smoke than clay pipes.

For over two hundred and fifty years, the clay pipe ruled almost supreme, with little challenge from other materials. The clay was smoked all over Europe by both men and women, although generally not among women of fashion. Men and women smoked pipes of similar shape and size. The fragility of clay pipes and their disadvantage of fouling quickly did not matter much because they were so cheap. In most inns and coffee-houses, it

Fig. 2 *Pipe-case*, English, seventeenth or very early eighteenth century. Elaborately carved walnut with sliding shutter. (Pinto Collection. Birmingham City Museum and Art Gallery.)

Fig. 3 *English wooden tobacco-boxes.* Top left: Cedarwood box inlaid with bone, engraved 'For you the best is not too good', 1706. Top right: Wooden box, 1664; one of the earliest dated examples. Bottom: Carved boxwood box, c.1780, showing a haberdasher measuring out ribbon for his customer. (Pinto Collection.)

2

3

Reilly and Constantine

was usual to present customers with long, clean, clay pipes for smoking on the premises and these, after use, were placed in an openwork iron cradle known as a pipe-roaster; this was suspended by an iron ring over a charcoal fire, and the pipes were roasted clean. It is doubtful, however, if such a device was considered worthwhile in private houses, owing to the cheapness of clays. In 1651, the Duke of Bedford paid 18s. 6d. per gross for them, but by 1665, the year of the plague, he paid 22s. 6d. for twelve gross lots. Around 1695, he was paying between 24s. and 36s. for twelve gross lots; other recorded accounts corroborate these figures. Fairholt, in 1859, relates that clays then cost 1s. 4d. per gross wholesale and retailed at 4 for 1d. – theoretically a good profit, but breakages were great.

Clay pipes were moulded in iron or, more rarely, wooden moulds made in two halves. Owing to the high cost of early tobacco, the bowls of Elizabethan and James I clay pipes were minute. They were barrel-shaped, pitched far forward from the stem and very shallow. During the seventeenth century, bowls gradually increased in diameter, became considerably deeper and the forward tilt lessened. After 1700, the top rim of the bowl tended to be parallel to the stem, instead of being at right angles to the sides of the bowl.

Decoratively moulded clay pipes were made from early in the seventeenth century; their bowls, which include images of Sir Walter Raleigh, seem to be mostly Dutch. English designs from after the Restoration may be floral, geometric or armorial. In the nineteenth century, notabilities, inventions and events were commemorated on the bowls of clays. Early centres of clay pipe manufacture were at Bristol and London; in the eighteenth century, Broseley in Shropshire came very much to the fore, but there were many other provincial centres.

Despite the fact that old clays were commonly ground down to make moth-balls for putting in woollens, their bowls, often with part of the stem remaining, are dug up from nearly every excavated site in Britain, inhabited from the seventeenth century onwards. The foundations of a James I hunting-lodge, excavated in 1964 in Hertfordshire, yielded a considerable quantity of clays.

Short pipes were made to be used when travelling

There is a mistaken belief that all long clay pipes belong to the eighteenth century. Actually, long and short clays have been smoked in all periods, but as clays are so fragile and must be protected in the pocket, short ones were mostly used for travelling. They were also used by the poor.

Very short 'cutties' were often carried in oval or oblong pocket boxes with the tobacco, but gentlemen used pipe-cases for medium length clays. Most of these cases are of wood, some elaborately carved. The seventeenth- and eighteenth-century

Fig. 4 *English tobacco-jars.*
Top row from the left: *Yew-wood jar, mid-eighteenth century. Mosaic inlaid jar, eighteenth century (not Tunbridge ware). Ring-turned jar, seventeenth century.* Lignum vitae *jar, mid-eighteenth century.*
Bottom row from the left: *Coffin tobacco-box, the sort of macabre jest which delighted the Georgians. Staved jar, Dutch or Scottish, c.1800. Ebony jar, early eighteenth century.*
(Pinto Collection.)

Fig. 5 *Hardwood pipes, European, eighteenth century. Left: Austrian, c.1790. Cherrywood stem with horn mouthpiece. The silver-lidded and mounted bowl, inscribed Johan Gölner, is carved with miniature scenes after Teniers, depicting wine-making and peasants drinking in a garden. Centre: Italian bowl, silver-lidded and carved with the Holy Family. Austrian bowl, mid-eighteenth century. Silver-lined, carved with a hunting scene, and delicately pierced with rococo scrolls for weight reduction and cool touch. Probably a German bowl, late eighteenth century. Silver-mounted and -lidded, depicting Mercury spreading his benediction over a sailing ship leaving a bale- and barrel-loaded quay. Right: probably a Viennese pipe, eighteenth century, brass-lidded with a horn stem, carved with flowers and foliage. Austrian 'documentary' bowl, late eighteenth century. Boxwood carved with trading scenes. (Pinto Collection.)*

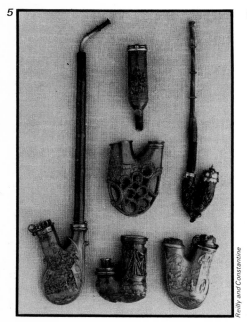

5

6

Reilly and Constantine

Reilly and Constantine

Fig. 6 *Pipe storage, showing the various different methods used to hold pipes. Back row: pipe-rack with candle-holder, eighteenth century. Mahogany, of a fairly sophisticated design. Pipe-rack, provincial, eighteenth century. Oak, with spaces for 'church-wardens' at top and holes for short 'cutties' below. Front row: Mahogany pipe-cradle, eighteenth century. Mahogany pipe-tray with tinder-box, eighteenth century. (Pinto Collection.)*

cases in Figures 1 and 2 exemplify the difference which was usual, although not invariable, between the clays of these two centuries. Cases for seventeenth-century clays are enclosed at both ends and have sliding shutters; eighteenth-century cases are open at the mouthpiece end and have hinged lids over the bowl ends. The reason for the change is that eighteenth-century pipes developed 'spurs' on the bases of their bowls, and the shutter could not slide over them.

A selection of seventeenth- and eighteenth-century wooden pocket tobacco-boxes is shown in Figure 3, but very similar designs to some of them were moulded in horn, by Obrisset, and also in brass, copper and silver. Some of the oval boxes were intended to accommodate a short clay pipe with the tobacco.

For home use, an important essential was the tobacco-jar, which had to be carefully made of a material that would not absorb the tobacco moisture and allow it to become dry. Lead was probably the earliest choice. Although it could be moulded decoratively, it was easily damaged; also, lead being re-usable, the majority of these early jars have been destroyed. Wooden tobacco-jars, lined with lead or foil, were lighter, less easily damaged and quite as efficient, although challenged to a small extent in the eighteenth century by silver, and in the nineteenth century, much more formidably, by glazed earthenware. Wooden jars were made in a considerable variety of shapes and woods for home use, but most of the large specimens of barrel outline were used on the shelves of tobacconists' shops. A selection of domestic wooden jars of the seventeenth and eighteenth centuries is shown in Figure 4.

Ever since tobacco was introduced, there have been differences of opinion as to the best way of storing pipes when not in use. Consequently, eighteenth-century and earlier makers of racks and trays had to provide for pipes horizontal, and pipes vertical with bowls downwards (Fig. 6). In the nineteenth century, with the advent of briars, racks were made to hold pipes vertically with bowls uppermost.

Additional to clays, and long before the introduction of briars, wooden pipes were smoked commonly in north-west Europe – Russia, Finland and Scandinavia, the lands of wood. In England, cherrywood, and in America, corn cobs, had their devotees. All these cost more than clays, fouled just as quickly and, although cool in smoking, were not long-lasting.

Elaborate silver lids were made to cover pipes for outdoor use

There were also other pre-briar, hardwood pipes which have considerable interest for collectors. Although usually described as German, nineteenth-century, their provenance and usage included Austria, Hungary, Switzerland, Holland, Italy and other countries and some undoubtedly date from the eighteenth century. They were made from a variety of close-grained, hardwood roots and must have provided cool smoking but, because the woods used char easily, they usually had iron or silver linings. The bowls (as Fig. 5 shows) are mostly of mid-European shape, curving back and forming a U-shape with the long stems, which might be of cherrywood – said to improve flavour – or, later, of flexible woven tubing connected to a stag-horn mouthpiece. The bowls of the best specimens are frequently silver-mounted and provided with elaborately pierced and moulded, hinged, silver lids, for smoking out of doors. The large wooden bowls are often skilfully carved with hunting, religious or mythological subjects, or historical scenes which convert them into veritable miniature documentaries.

Meerschaum pipes, some most artistically carved, were probably not made before the nineteenth century. Collectors should beware of earlier-dated meerschaum specimens because, in the late nineteenth century, a Viennese firm collected waste meerschaum, ground it into powder, added glue and moulded it decoratively, with earlier dates included.

MUSEUMS AND COLLECTIONS

Smoking accessories may be seen at the following:

FRANCE
Paris: Musée Carnavalet
GREAT BRITAIN
Birmingham: City Museum and Art Gallery,
                     Pinto Collection
London: Astley's, Jermyn Street
                     Guildhall Museum
U.S.A.
Grafton, Vermont: Grafton Historical Society

FURTHER READING

'The Clay Pipe, its Place in English Ceramics' by Adrian Oswald in Transactions of the English Ceramic Circle, Vol. 7, Pt. 3, London, 1970.
Treen and Other Wooden Bygones by Edward H. Pinto, London, 1969.
The Pipe Book by Alfred Dunhill, London, revised edition, 1969.
Nicotiana Tabacum by Georg A. Brongers, Amsterdam, 1964.
'Tobacco Pipes' by Adrian Oswald in The Concise Encyclopedia of Antiques, Vol. 4, London, 1959.

Early Jewellery

Fig. 1 **Diamond flower**, c.1775. *The larger diamonds are in openwork settings. (Harvey and Gore, London.)*

Fig. 2 **Initialled pendant**, c1785. *Bristol glass and diamonds. Initialled pendants were often worn as mourning jewellery, and were popular as gifts. (Harvey and Gore.)*

Technical advances and changing fashions in the eighteenth century gave both men and women the opportunity to revel in lavish self-adornment with jewels of great brilliance and intricacy

At the end of the seventeenth century the magnificently worked gold and enamels which had in the preceding centuries enhanced the rich costume brocades of courtiers and well-to-do gentlefolk were eclipsed by the art of the jeweller. By the nineteenth century the jeweller, in his turn, suffered in the cross-fire between the impractical artist-designer and the industrial manufacturer. In the intervening years of the eighteenth century both men and women revelled in the ever-increasing opportunity to pursue the fashionable vogue for jewellery and adorned themselves lavishly with a multitude of gems.

Men in their embroidered coats and waistcoats might be restricted to jewelled watches, watch-cases and chains, snuff-boxes, rings, seals and a plethora of buttons and buckles, increasingly favoured by the fashionable tailor. But there were for women many important hair ornaments (aigrettes), necklaces and bracelets such as multiple rows of pearls with diamond-studded clasps, increasingly ornate ear-rings and finger rings, brooches, including the massive stomacher *sévigné*, and sentimental lockets and cameos. There were jewelled stay-hooks for hanging watches, or more expensive gold or pinchbeck chatelaines (Fig. 13) from which to suspend a multiplicity of minor needs such as etuis of agate or painted enamel and, at the end of the century, thimble-boxes and vinaigrettes. For court dress, in particular, the jewelled parure—a matching set comprising necklace and bracelet, brooches and ear-rings – could add surface patterns of light and flashing fire to rich fabrics which were often gold-embroidered and festooned with strings of pearls.

The jeweller tried to ensure that the light which fell on his stone was reflected off again as its fire. This involved backing the stones with bright silver or copper foil which would intensify the colour of a simply cut sapphire or ruby. It would also cause paste 'jewels' to sparkle. To prevent the foil from tarnishing, an enclosed setting was necessary. This was achieved in an infinitely more individual manner than the shallow hollows of later stamped or cast mounts.

Even the diamond, hardest of all stones, was close-mounted when presented in the flat-based, faceted dome known as the rose cut, a popular cut for cluster setting. But someone late in the seventeenth century (no longer positively identified as the Venetian Peruzzi) worked out for the diamond the immensely difficult brilliant cut with a flat 'table' top (smaller than today's) and so cunningly faceted that it held within itself an unrivalled fire. This meant that jewellers from about the 1740s could give it an open claw setting.

This was the period of the diamond spectacular. Mrs. Delany in 1756 described Mrs. Spencer's first appearance at Court: 'her ear-rings three drops, all diamonds, no paltry scrolls of silver. Her necklace most perfect brilliants, the middle stone worth a thousand pounds set at the edge with small brilliants. Her cap all brilliants . . . (made in the fashion of a small butterfly skeleton) had a very good effect with a pompon; and behind . . . a knot of diamonds with two little puffs of diamonds where the lappets fastened, and two shaking sprigs of brilliants for her hair; six roses all brilliants for her stays. . . . Her watch and etui suited to the rest and a seal of a Mercury cut in a very fine turquoise . . .'.

Seven huge diamonds sparkled from each ear

Queen Charlotte's jewellery is illustrated in many portraits (Fig. 11), usually including a high necklace of either chunky diamonds or rows of pearls, with more pearls as shoulder loops, girdle and bracelets. Hoppner picked out the diamonds and sapphires of a high head-dress and Thomas Frye the massive aigrette above her forehead and the seven huge diamonds in each girandole ear-ring.

This was the century that witnessed the change in style from the florid Baroque to the scrolling asymmetrical Rococo of the 1730s, '40s and '50s,

Fig. 3 *Diamond Maltese Cross pendant*, c.1790.
(*Harvey and Gore.*)

Fig. 4 *Portrait of Susannah Hope by Joseph Wright of Derby (1734–97), c.1760. Oil on canvas. Pearls were highly popular throughout the eighteenth century. They were worn in the hair, round the neck and wrists or, as here, could be strewn over the bodice of a dress to set off the fabric.*

Fig. 5 *Pendant, eighteenth century. Rose diamonds, enamel, seed pearls, hair and ivory. Human hair was frequently used in jewellery, and such pieces were favourite gifts to a loved one.* (*N. Bloom and Sons, London.*)

Fig. 6 *Pendant in the shape of a cross, c.1780. Diamonds and turquoises.* (*N. Bloom and Sons.*)

Fig. 7 *Necklace, c.1760. Diamonds in a stylised flower and leaf motif.* (*S. J. Phillips, Ltd., London.*)

Fig. 8 *Ribbon brooch, c.1760. Diamonds with a suspended pearl.* (*S. J. Phillips, Ltd.*)

Fig. 9 *Brooch, c.1780. Pink topazes and diamonds in the shape of a flower.* (*S. J. Phillips, Ltd.*)

followed by the suave, flowing lines and conventional detail of the neo-classical mood with its love of the pointed oval such as can be seen in navette brooches and marquise rings. The ellipse shape broadened into a blunter oblong by the end of the century. This fairly plain shape was, however, contrasted to a variety of decorative alternatives including the Maltese Cross (Fig. 3), plume and wheatear motifs.

Only briefly around the 1720s and '30s did the white fire of diamonds drive coloured jewels out of the limelight. Before the mid-century, sapphires, rubies and emeralds became popular with the fashion for naturalistic flower designs.

It is important to remember, however, that costly jewels were largely limited to a number of conventional motifs that could be taken apart and worn in a variety of ways, such as mounted on black for the endless occasions of mourning, as noted by Lady Grizel Baillie in 1702. It is in the less costly work intended for a wider public that the collector may trace in detail the course of eighteenth-century fashion.

'Steel embroidery was introduced this season and very generally worn'

One has only to look at trade-cards with their many references to 'false stone work', such as those in the Heal Collection, to appreciate the endless demand for smaller, more everyday jewellery. Joseph Lowe, for example, offered in 1748: 'Variety of stayhooks, ear-rings, necklaces, sleeve buttons set with stones. Plain and enamelled gold rings, diamond and other stone rings, great choice of silver gilt, pearl, tortoiseshell and other buttons'.

Illustrations to such advertisements give a vivid picture of changing tastes, widely expressed in golden topazes, foil-enriched red garnets, amethysts, rock crystals and other forms of quartz, agate, amber and turquoise. It was a century that still regarded such stones as worthy of the best craftsmanship. Even the finest paste, such as that manufactured by G. F. Stras (1701–73), was a glass infinitely softer and less brilliant than the diamond but, close-set against bright metal foils, it achieved wonderful effects of shimmering light and, at times, was more vivid than any opal or aventurine.

An important alternative to the diamond was the hard, bright, iron pyrites usually called 'marcasite'. But even more widely popular was facet-cut steel. In 1785 Mrs. Papendick wrote: 'It was a brilliant Court. The dresses were very showy, as steel embroidery was introduced this season and very generally worn'.

Eighteenth-century jewels were usually simply mounted in silver, but the gold used for watches and chatelaines was brilliantly imitated in a special quality of copper and zinc alloy evolved by Christopher Pinchbeck (d. 1732) (Fig. 13). This was soon followed by other brass alloys under the general term of 'gilt metal'. Enamel painting on gold, such as the heavy figures on baroque watch-cases, was superseded in the 1760s by pastoral idylls, delicately painted on white enamel enclosing a core of copper and mounted in gilt-metal for small objects such as chatelaines (Fig. 12) and etuis.

Some exclusive, jewel-studded lockets enclosed portrait miniatures, and others used rock crystal to protect decorative motifs fashioned by a specialist craftsman in 'human hair jewellery' (Fig. 5). Throughout much of the century, both day and evening wear were enhanced by the clever use of pearls. On the Continent these were often imitations, but in Scotland, Wales and Shropshire river pearls proved a profitable harvest. Sir Richard Steele, the essayist, noted in 1710 a new fashion for bracelets of braided hair, pomanders and seed pearls, and these threads of tiny pearls, individually weighing less than half a grain, were applied in vast quantities to cover buttons or to serve as twisted cords and tassels among the larger pearls at the neck and waist and over the cap or coiffure. Thomas Pennant in 1771 observed that between 1761 and '64 more than £10,000 worth were sent to London from the Tay and Isla rivers alone (Fig. 4).

Hair ornaments included not only gold and silver pins but the pompon (an ornamental bunch of flowers or ribbons named after Madame de Pompadour), which was in vogue around the middle of the century. The Duchess of Portland's daughter, Betty, in 1754 had a 'very fine sprig of pearl, diamonds and turquoise for her hair by way of a pompon'. Hair was frizzed and worn higher from the 1760s. By the 1770s the extreme head-dresses for formal occasions offered every opportunity for the jeweller to devise lively patterns based on flower and star motifs. Even in the 1790s there was a wide use of jewelled combs and hairpins.

Ear-rings had to harmonise. The brilliant-cut drop, or *pendeloque*, or the rose-cut *briolette* was elaborated into the most imposing broad girandole ear-ring composed of three pendant drops or pearls hanging from a large stone.

Necklaces were often constructed from many rows of pearls in a choker design but there were alternatives such as the *rivière* (unbroken line) of graduated single stones that especially suited the square cut of eighteenth-century diamonds and the surface-covering setting expected of well-handled, easily shaped paste.

'Some by a snip of woven hair In posied lockets bribe the fair'

Brooches, bracelets and rings offered opportunities for the sentimental, especially in the second half of the century. John Gay, the poet, in 1720 referred to the donors of such gifts:

'Some by a snip of woven hair,
In posied lockets bribe the fair'.

Early in the century a jewelled brooch might carry an oval pendant locket, hinged at the top and fronted with coloured stones, edged with pearls. From around the middle of the century the locket might be fronted with a glazed miniature, a hinged opening at the back enclosing the sitter's hair 'formed in a curious manner'. Mrs. Papendick described in 1761 a pair of bracelets given by George III to his bride, Queen Charlotte, which appear in several portraits. These consisted of 'six rows of picked pearls as large as a full pea; the clasps – one his picture, the other his hair and cypher, both set around with diamonds'.

Late in the century the locket was small and often circular, splendidly jewelled on the front and bearing a cipher or monogram in diamonds on the back, which opened to disclose a miniature portrait opposite a lock of hair or other memento.

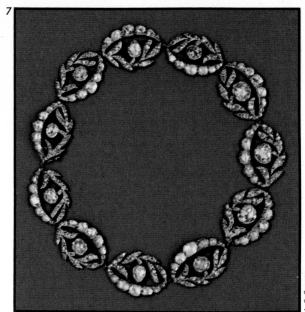

Fig. 10 **Ring**, c.1760. Rubies and diamonds in the shape of a bow. (N. Bloom and Sons.)

Fig. 11 *Portrait of Queen Charlotte* (detail) by Sir Thomas Lawrence (1769–1830). Oil on canvas. Queen Charlotte's jewellery has become famous through portraits. Here she is shown wearing a single row of pearls, beautifully complemented by bracelets and rings. (National Gallery, London.)

A. C. Cooper

Museum Photo

Pendants, brooches, bracelet clasps and rings remind us of the period's enjoyable melancholy; frequently the shuttle outline encloses a picture of a woman prostrate beside a funeral urn under a willow tree which weeps seed pearl tears. The impact of Greek ornament came only at the very end of the century but must be mentioned as it inspired the great vogue for cameos showing classical heads rather than human portraits.

Queen Charlotte had a diamond hoop as the customary guard to her wedding ring and on her right little finger a medallion portrait of the King. But 'fingers cramped with rings' seem mainly to have been the delight of the *nouveau riche*.

Jewellers carried out a brisk trade in mourning rings

Memorial rings were important. Samuel Pepys willed that one hundred and twenty-nine mourning rings should be given away at his funeral in 1709, and throughout the century advertising goldsmith-jewellers continued to stress that mourning rings could be made 'with the greatest expedition'. Early in the century they tended to have narrow hoops concealing the initials, but by the 1740s the fashion was for the hoop to display the name and date on an enamelled ground, black for the married and white for the unmarried, either undecorated or in a pattern of rococo scrolls. On the plainer hoop of the 1760s, the date and age of the deceased were set around in gold letters. This was soon joined by the marquise design, covering about half the finger, with its urn and weeping willow painted in grisaille or with a tiny painted silhouette, followed by the oval and rectangle of the 1790s which bore initials edged with jet or pearls.

The collector has a wonderful and seldom explored field among buckles. Joseph Lowe offered 'All sorts of hat, stock, stay, girdle, knee and shoe buckles'. For the coronation of William III, the Earl of Bedford hired suitable buckles for two shillings. And in 1786 Sophia von la Roche commented on 'the coming fashion for tying shoes with laces'. But through the buckle's eighteenth-century hey-day a man might require a silver, jewel-set buckle even to fix his stock cravat at the back of his neck under his wig.

MUSEUMS AND COLLECTIONS

Eighteenth-century English jewellery may be seen at the following:

Birmingham:	City Museum and Art Gallery
Cambridge:	Fitzwilliam Museum
London:	London Museum
	Victoria and Albert Museum
Nottingham:	City Art Gallery and Museum
Bury St. Edmunds:	J. G. Parkinson Memorial Collection

FURTHER READING

Antique Paste Jewellery by M. D. S. Lewis, London, 1970.
'Lockets' in **More Small Decorative Antiques** by Therle Hughes, London, 1962.
A History of Jewellery by Joan Evans, London, 1953.
English Jewellery from the Fifth Century to 1800 by Joan Evans, London, 1921.

K. Hoddle

13

K. Hoddle

Fig. 12 **Watch and chatelaine en suite** by Chapman, London, 1781. Gold and enamel.
Pastoral scenes incorporating portraits were often used for the decoration of chatelaines.
(London Museum.)

Fig. 13 **Chatelaine** with a pincase, thimble and etui, late eighteenth century. Pinchbeck.
Decorative gold watches and chatelaines were imitated in pinchbeck, a copper and zinc alloy.
(London Museum.)

465

Art Nouveau Jewellery

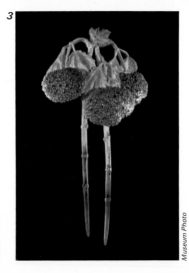

The Art Nouveau style is perhaps best expressed in the delicate, imaginative and colourful jewellery of the period

Jewels may be the finest expression of Art Nouveau; their small scale, their fragility and their infinite variations of size, colour and shape made them ideal vehicles for the prevailing mood.

The dreamy character of Art Nouveau was too inconsistent to sustain major works. Charles Rennie Mackintosh's Glasgow School of Art, the quarter-built church of the Sagrada Familia by Gaudí in Barcelona, the Castel Béranger block of flats by Guimard in Paris, and the large town houses commissioned by the Solvay family from Victor Horta and by the Stoclets from Josef Hoffmann in Brussels: these are some of the very few large-scale Art Nouveau monuments. In reading about Parisian life towards the end of the last century – in Proust, in Jean Renoir's biography of his father the painter, or indeed in the histories of the early years of the other great painters of the period, Braque, Matisse or Picasso – there is no mention of Art Nouveau. Cubism, which followed it, and the various stylistic revivals, gothic, classical and Egyptian, which preceded it, are better known.

So, in terms of quantity, Art Nouveau jewellery

Fig. 1 Butterfly woman by Eugène Feuillâtre, c.1900. Gold, enamel and moonstones. (Private Collection, Paris.)

Fig. 2 Tiara by R. Lalique, c.1900. Gold, horn and mother of pearl. (John Jesse Collection, London.)

Fig. 3 Comb by René Lalique, c.1900. Gold, horn and enamel. (Gulbenkian Foundation, Lisbon.)

Fig. 4 Tiara by an unknown French maker, c.1900. Gold, silver, enamel and fire opals. Snakes were suited to both the mood and the linear style of the period. (Private Collection.)

Fig. 5 Comb, Falize Frères, Paris, 1900. Gold, horn and enamel. (Museum für Kunst and Gewerbe, Hamburg.)

Fig. 6 Belt-buckle by René Lalique, c.1899. Gold, enamel and chrysoprase. (Gulbenkian Foundation.)

was unimportant. But in quality it is memorable, and it was extremely inventive and well made – rare qualities alone, rarer still together.

Although nobody can explain quite why the new style originated, two contemporary books written by leading practitioners throw considerable light on this period. Vever, the distinguished jeweller, in 1908 published a massive three-volume survey of French nineteenth-century jewels, the last volume focusing almost entirely on Art Nouveau; and Henri Bouilhet, of the successful silver factory Christofle, performed a similar service for silver in 1900. Their accounts are profusely illustrated with dated work.

It is surprising that the manager of a medium-sized silver or jewellery workshop should deliberately set out to publicise the products of his friends

and competitors as well as his own, yet this is exactly what Vever and Bouilhet did. One explanation must be that they enjoyed a sense of commercial security; they both represented old family firms. Eighty years ago, when there were thousands of private patrons, Vever must have felt confident that his own would continue to appreciate his work.

Fashion magazines and the lavish art papers *Art et Décoration* in Paris and *L'Art Moderne* in Brussels, started in 1881; *Studio* in London, founded in 1893, also provides source material on the Art Nouveau movement.

The largest public collection of Art Nouveau jewels is in the Musée des Arts Décoratifs in Paris, where, however, the jewels are kept principally in the vaults, for security reasons. When newly created as a semi-private foundation in the Pavillon Marsan, a wing of the Louvre, the Museum showed foresight and extravagance by buying Art Nouveau jewellery from the leading producers, notably from those exhibiting at the huge Paris Exhibition of 1900; so on a very modest scale did London's Victoria and Albert Museum and museums in Copenhagen, Hamburg, Berlin and Brussels.

In 1965 the Dutch crown jeweller, Karel Citroen, exhibited widely the remarkable collection of smaller Art Nouveau jewels which he had himself assembled and sold it to the Hessisches Landesmuseum at Darmstadt, which now has many good French pieces on display. Special exhibitions at Goldsmiths' Hall, London, in 1961; the exhibition *Le Bijou 1900*, showing superb French work, at the Hôtel Solvay, Brussels, in 1965; *Werke um 1900* at Berlin's Kunstgewerbe Museum in 1966, and *Gold & Silber, Schmuck & Gerät*, which formed part of the Dürer celebrations in Nuremberg in 1971, have all contributed to knowledge of the subject.

Other evidence is of course provided by jewels still in circulation. These are scarce; surprisingly, since at least some of the workshops were large: René Lalique, for instance, was employing thirty craftsmen at the turn of the century. In all there were probably three or four dozen artist-jewellers working in the Art Nouveau style in France.

Most old jewellery is eventually melted down, but with Art Nouveau pieces this would hardly have been worth while as they usually had very little intrinsic value. Perhaps they were so much disliked when fashion changed that they were simply destroyed or lost. Queen Victoria bought two pieces by Lalique from the Paris 1900 Exhibition; Agnew's, the British art dealers, had a Lalique show in 1905, but most of the pieces are now untraceable. Whatever the reason, these pieces are extremely rare today.

The pieces, even when found, often remain a mystery. Most French artists defied the French hallmark laws and omitted to have their jewels marked, frightened perhaps of the risk of damage in the scraping and punching process. Some artists even omitted to sign their names (Lalique is here exceptional – he seems always to have given his whole name), and in most cases a pair of initials was considered adequate. If these initials do not correspond to a name in Vever's book, they are often impossible to trace, although sometimes the leather boxes provide a clue. Although Art Nouveau seems so close to us in spirit and time, it has retained a characteristic remoteness – the facts are few and far between.

Probably the most spectacular Art Nouveau

James Mortimer

Fig. 7 **Pendant** by René Lalique, c.1898. Gold, enamel, carved ivory and a baroque pearl. Dreamy faces and long hair were commonly used to express the unworldliness of Art Nouveau. (Gulbenkian Foundation.)

Fig. 8 **Dragonfly corsage ornament** by René Lalique, c.1898. Gold, enamel and chrysoprase. The wings and tail of this superb ornament are flexible – an amazing feat of craftsmanship – and the enamelling is of the highest quality. Its exceptional size (the wing-span is over 10 ins.) and delicacy give the piece a ceremonial quality. (Gulbenkian Foundation.)

Fig. 9 **Belt-buckle** by René Lalique, c.1903. Gold, translucent enamel and aquamarine with glass fruits. In this fine piece, Lalique shows his mastery of static pattern; much of his other work (Figs. 3, 4, 7 and 8) has more emphasis on a flowing line. (Gulbenkian Foundation.)

Fig. 10 **Brooch** by Marcel Bing, c.1900. Gilt copper, cloisonné enamel and a cabochon garnet. The head-dress of this characteristic woman with flowing hair is medieval in inspiration. A version of the brooch of the same design but with the head and neck of the woman carved in ivory was exhibited in 1900 at L'Art Nouveau, the Paris shop run by Samuel Bing, brother of Marcel. (Musée des Arts Décoratifs.)

display in any medium, anywhere, is in the new Gulbenkian Museum at Lisbon. Against a dark background are over a hundred large, dazzling pieces by René Lalique; everything about them is unexpected and brilliant. There are designs of extraordinary grace and originality, craftsmanship of unbelievable intricacy, including the most difficult types of enamelling and stone-carving, materials of compelling strangeness – glass mixed with diamonds, platinum and gold mixed with horn and aluminium (Figs. 3, 6, 7, 8 and 9).

Calouste Gulbenkian, Armenian by birth, oil millionaire by his own creation, lived in Paris and London most of his life; he was introduced to Lalique by Sarah Bernhardt, the jeweller's first great patron. He always bought the best – hence this magnificent series of commissions, without parallel in the history of twentieth-century jewellery.

René Lalique (1860–1945) was indeed the genius of the Movement. He was born at Ay (Marne). He always wanted to draw, and when his merchant father died in 1876, his mother sensibly apprenticed him to the distinguished conventional jeweller Louis Aucoc. He abandoned the Ecole des Arts Décoratifs for lack of time and, from 1878, studied at Sydenham, returning in 1881 to work for several Paris firms making wallpaper, fabrics and prints for jewellers. The firms he worked for as freelance designer and craftsman included Jacta, Aucoc, Cartier, Boucheron, Renn, Gariod, Hamelin and, most important, Destape, whose business he finally inherited in 1886. From 1890 he studied glass techniques in his rue Thérèse workshop.

He attracted Sarah Bernhardt's notice and she commissioned two groups of jewels for *Iseyl et Gismonda*. In 1895, Lalique won third prize on his first appearance at the Salon, the same year as his first recorded use of the female nude in jewellery. In 1896 he first used horn – an important innovation; in 1897 he was made a Chevalier of the Légion d'Honneur; in 1903 he designed and built a shop at 40, Cour Albert I, where his son and granddaughter now live; in 1905 he opened a shop in the Place Vendôme. In 1909 he leased, and the next year bought, a glass factory at Combes la Ville, glass becoming ever more prominent in his jewels, until in 1914 he finally abandoned jewellery. It is sad that his firm, which continues today under his son's direction in rue Royale, makes only glass, having lost contact with the early jewellery inspiration.

Lalique was a technical, as well as a stylistic, innovator. He used machinery to reduce his large prototypes to actual working size, and he employed Eugène Feuillâtre (1870–1916) to investigate enamelling techniques on silver. Platinum was used, not because of its value, but because he liked the colour, and, with similar detachment, he made frequent use of glass, horn and occasionally aluminium. His pieces, more than any other jeweller's, show the artist's impatience with the mystique of the precious stone.

If Lalique's style tended to be sweet, and derived from natural objects such as birds and flowers, the other really inspired French Art Nouveau jeweller, Georges Fouquet (1862–1957), had a somewhat harsher vision, preferring thistles and nightmare insects. Son of Alphonse Fouquet, jeweller in the Avenue de l'Opéra, he inherited the business in 1895 and turned to a new style, co-operating with

artists such as Tauret, Desroziers, Grasset and the graphic designer Alphonse Mucha. He won prizes at the Exhibitions of 1900 and 1901 and built a new shop at 6, rue Royale, designed by Mucha and demolished in 1920. At the Paris Exhibitions of 1925 and 1937 he was president of the jewellers. He executed many of Mucha's designs, through him no doubt meeting Sarah Bernhardt and many personalities in the theatrical world.

Henri Vever (1854–1942) was another jeweller of standing; with his brother, Paul (1851–1915), he inherited his firm in 1874 from their father, Ernest. He attended evening classes at the Ecole des Arts Décoratifs and worked by day with various jewellers – Loguet, Hallet and Dufong. In 1889 the brothers won two prizes at their first exhibition and in 1891 the Croix de la Légion d'Honneur at the French Exhibition in Moscow. In 1893 Henri was commissioner at the Chicago World's Fair, and he won prizes at Bordeaux in 1895, Brussels in 1897 and Paris in 1900. Vever may eventually be better remembered for his book than for his jewels, which were often too heavy and massive to suit the linear feeling of Art Nouveau.

Other prominent names were Lucien Gaillard (b.1861), Eugène Grasset (1841–1917), Victor Prouvé (1858–1943), Emile Gallé (1846–1904), Paul Liénard (1849–1900), Georges de Ribaucourt (1881–1907), L. Gautrait and Henri Dubret. Perhaps they did not produce enough jewellery to establish a clear identity, but they all shared in the creation of this exotic new style.

Their most important achievement was the release of jewellery from commercial interests; the artist-jeweller was born again after his extinction by large retail firms and precious stones during the nineteenth century. Then there was the integration of the several arts: Art Nouveau jewels were often given the names of specific symbolist poems by Mallarmé, Apollinaire or Baudelaire.

The Art Nouveau movement was played out by 1910, and many of the jeweller-craftsmen and patrons were killed in the First World War. Its achievement is still with us today; we think of jewels no longer just as business and money – they are art and inspiration, too.

MUSEUMS AND COLLECTIONS

French Art Nouveau jewellery may be seen at the following:

DENMARK
Copenhagen: Kunstindustrimuseet
FRANCE
Paris: Musée des Arts Décoratifs
GREAT BRITAIN
London: Bethnal Green Museum
PORTUGAL
Lisbon: Gulbenkian Foundation Museum
WEST GERMANY
Darmstadt: Hessisches Landesmuseum

FURTHER READING

The Art of Jewelry: A Survey of Craft and Creation by Graham Hughes, London, 1972.
The Renaissance of the Artist-Jeweller by Graham Hughes, London, 1970.
Modern Jewellery, an International Survey 1890–1967 by Graham Hughes, London, 1967.

Index

Italics indicate illustrations

Abaquesne, Masséot 35, 36
  work 38, *39*
'Abbas the Great, Shah 21, 392, 406
'Abd al-'Aziz 406
Absalom of Yarmouth 252
Ackermann, Rudolph 210, 224
Adam, Elias 319
Adam, Robert 117, 177–8, 181, 187, 200
  design of, copied in pottery 82–3
  work of 178, *179*
Adams, John, 2nd U.S. President 101
Adams, John Quincy, 6th US President 102
Adams, Nehemiah 197
  work of *198*
agate ware 81, 305
Agricola, Georgius: *De Re Metallica* 242, *246*
Aitken, John 198
  work of *196*, 197
albarello 31, *32*, 33
Alcora pottery 47, *47*, *48*, *48*, 49
Aloncle, F.: work of *67*
altar-cloth: Russian *388*
altar-table 128, *129*
Altenburg stoneware 28
American clocks 375, 427–30, 436–9
  coverlets and quilts 375, 399–402
  furniture: Chippendale style 182–5
    Colonial 156–60
    early 146–50
    Federal 196–204
    Gothic 225
  glass: Art 296–300
    Colonial 254–8
    19th century 274–7
  porcelain 99–103
  redware 50–4
  silver: early 313–17
    Colonial 332–5
    Revere, Paul 346–50
  watches 439
American Horloge Company 439
Amsterdam pottery 43
andiron *320*
Andreev, Prokofii: work of *389*
Andreoli, Giorgio: work of *30*, 31
Angell, George 370
  work of *372*
Angell, John 326
Angell, Joseph, & Sons 371–2
animals: cups modelled as 319
Ansonia Clock Company 438–9
  work of *438*
Antonio de San Simone 239
Ao-Kutani wares 18, 19
apothecaries' jars, *see* drug jars
'apple pie' plate *52*
Aranda, Don Bonaventura Pedro de Alcántara, Count of 48
Archambo, Peter 340
'Ardabil' carpet 392
Argenson, Marquis d' 66
argyles: Sheffield plate 362
Argy-Rousseau, G. 295
Arita porcelain 11, 17, *17*, 18, 19
armadio 122, *123*
armchairs, *see* chairs
armoire: French 172, *172*
Arnold, John 426
Art glass: American 237, 296–300
Artigues, Gabriel D' 284, 286
Art Nouveau: furniture 117, 232–5
  glass 237
    French 286, 292–5
  jewellery 375, 466–9
Arts and Crafts Exhibition Society 229
Arts and Crafts Movement 117
  furniture 228–31
  pottery 108–11
Art Workers' Guild 229

Ashbee, C. R.: 229, 230–1
Ashley, Edward: work of 432, *433*
ashtrays: French glass 295
athéniennes 207, *207*, 209
Atkins (clockmaker): work of *436*
Aubusson tapestry 375, 394, *395*, 397–8, *398*
Aucoc, Louis 468
Auguste, Henry 357–8
  work of *357*, *359*
Augustus the Strong 55–6, 319
Augsburg silver *318*, *319*, 320, *320*, 322, *322*
aumbry 119
Austin, Jesse 97
Austrian furniture 214, *215*, 216
Avelli, Francesco Xanto: work of *32*, 33
aventurine glaze 113
Avril, Etienne 206

Baccarat glass 237, 264, *278*, 279, *279*–80, *281*, 282, 284, 285, *286*
Bacchus, George, & Sons: work of *273*
Bailey, C. J. C. 111
  work of, *110*, *111*
Bailey, Joseph 113
Bailly, Leon 302
Baily, E. H. 370, 371
  work of 370, *371*
Baker, Constance A.: work of *114*
Bakewell, Benjamin 275
Ball, William 86
  work of *88*
Ballin, Claude 322
Baltimore furniture 198, 203, *203*
Bancker, Adrian: work of *334*
band clocks 419
banjo clock *428*, 429, 430, *430*
banner: Russian *388*
baptismal ewer: German silver 322
Barbe, Jules 291
Barbin, François 62
Barlow family 110
Barnap, Daniel 429
Barnard, Messrs: work of *373*
Barnsley, Ernest 229, 230
Barnsley, Sidney 229–30
  work of *230*
Barnum, P. T. 438
barometer cases 140
Baroque furniture 117
  English 142–5
Barr, Martin 79
Barraband family 398
Barraud (clockmaker): work of 426, *426*
Barraud & Lund 433
Barry, Sir Charles 227
Barry, Joseph B. 203
barter 50
Barton, Thomas 449, 452
Barum ware 110, *110*, 111
Barwise, John 426
basalt *80*, *81*, 83
basins: English silver *340*
  redware *54*
baskets: French glass *284*
  Wedgwood *83*
bath: pottery for use in 24
bat-printing 98
Battersea enamels 375, *413*, 414–15, *415*, 416
Baumgartner, J. J. 320
beakers: American silver *313*, 314, *316*, 316–17
  Bohemian glass 264, *265*, *266*, 267
  French glass *285*
  German and Bohemian glass 243, *244*
  German silver *319*, 320, *320*
  Venetian enamelled glass 239

Beauvais tapestry 375, *394*, 394–7, *395*, *396*, 398
Beckford, William 213
bedroom: Empire 209
  renaissance 124
bedroom suites: papier-mâché *443*
beds: Biedermeier *214*
  Elizabethan 117
  Empire 209
  four-poster 119, 120, *121*, 123, 135, *201*
  French provincial 172, *175*
  Great Bed of Ware 120, *121*
  Italian 122, 123, *123*
  Josephine's *205*
  Napoleon's *206*
  Shaker 222
  sleigh-bed 202
  state-bed *145*
  testers on 120
  Tudor 119
  Victorian Gothic *223*
  William and Mary 142, *143*
Behagle, Philippe 394, 396
Beham, Hans Sebald 26
Beilby family 252
Beitler, Mathias 323
Belfast glass 259, 261
Belgium: Art Nouveau furniture 232–5
Bell, John 371
bellarmines 27, *27*
Bellarmino, Cardinal Roberto 27
Bell family 53
bells: church 350
benches: American 149
  backed 124
Beneman, Guillaume 166, 206
Bentley, Benjamin: work of *329*, *331*
Bentley, Thomas 83, 90
Bérain, Jean 138, 142, 396
Bérain, Jean, father and son 48
Bergé, Henry 295
Bernhardt, Sarah 468
Berthoud, Ferdinand 419, 420
Bertrand, Jacques 397
Besnier, Nicholas 396
Bewick, Thomas 252
Beyer, Melchior 319
Bible-box 150
bidet dressing table *195*
Biedermeier furniture 213, 214–17, *214–217*
  glass 267
Biemann, Dominik 264–6
Biennais, Martin-Guillaume 357, 358–9
Bigaglia, Pietro 279
Bihzad 390, 404–5
Biller, Johann Ludwig 319–20
Biller, Lorenz II 319
Bilston enamels *414*, *415*, 416
Binet (painter): work of *408*
Bing, Marcel: work of 468, *469*
Bing, Samuel 302, 304, 305
Binge and Fuller 438
Birmingham 413–14
  enamels 375, *415*, 415–16, *417*
  plate 360
  silver *371*
Black, Adam 193
blanc de Chine porcelain 11, *15*, 16
Blanck, Jurian: work of *316*
Blaue, Wilhelm Jansson 319
Blondel (clockmaker) 419
blue and white porcelain 11, 17, *17*, 21, 84–8, 101
blue and white pottery 21
Bohemian glass: early 237, 242–6
  19th century 264–8
Bokhara 405–6
  paintings from *405*
Boisard (clockmaker) 419
Bologna glass 239
Bolsover, Thomas 360
Bolton, Thomas: work of 342, *343*,

344
Bonaparte, Joseph 203
bone ash 74
bone china 11, 77
bonheur du jour 208
Bonneford, C.: painting by *446*
Bonniksen (watchmaker) 434
Bonnin, Gouse, 101
Bonnin & Morris wares *101*
Bontemps, Georges 284–5, 286
  work of *284*
bookcases: by Boulle 140
  English 213, *213*
  French 209
  Samuel Pepys types *133*, 134
  Sheraton *193*
book-markers 445, *447*
Booths of Tunstall 77
Boston, Massachusetts: Mint 314
Boston & Sandwich Glass Company: work of *276*, *277*, 300
Botticelli, Alessandro 123
Bott, Thomas 289
Böttger, J. F. 71
bottle ticket, *see* wine-label
bottles: American glass *256*, 298, *299*
  Italian glass *241*
  Persian lustreware *23*
  Persian pottery 22, *24*
  pocket-: American glass 257
Boucault (furniture maker) 172
Boucher (clockmaker) 419
Boucher, François 325, 355, 375, 409
  work of *394*, *395*, *396*, *411*
boudoir furniture 164
Bouilhet, Henri 467
Boulle, André-Charles 117, 136–41, 162
Boullier, Antoine 357
  work of *356*
Boulton, Matthew 360
Bowes, Sir Martin 312
bowls: American glass *296*, *297*
  American silver 348, *349*
  celadon *14*
  Chelsea 72, *73*
  Chinese porcelain *101*
  English glass *271*, *272*, *291*
  French glass *285*, 295
  Irish glass *263*
  jade *379*
  Persian pottery *24*
  redware 53, *54*
  Sunderland *93*
  'turnover' (serving): Irish glass 262, *262*
Bow porcelain 11, 85–6, *87*
boxes: enamel *414*, *415*
  fitted: Victorian 375, 453–6
  gold 351–5, *351–5*
  papier-mâché 440, *443*
Boyce, Brown & Kemp 452
Boynton, Dr Lindsay 179
Brannan, C. H. 111
  work of *110*
breakfast service: Sèvres *67*
Bréguet, Abraham Louis 419, 420–2, 434
Brehon, Collins 342
Brewster, Elisha 438
Brewster, William 148
Bridge, John 366
Bristol porcelain 76, 86
Bristol/Worcester porcelain 76
Britannia standard 307, 327, 328
British Horological Institute 435
British plate 363
Broadhead & Atkin 371
Brocard, Joseph 294
  work of *294*, 295
Bromwich, Thomas 178
bronzes: applied to furniture 207
Brooks, John 95, 413, 414, 415
Brown, Ford Madox 109
Brown, John 91–3

Brown, Richard 213
Brühl, Count Heinrich von 56
Bruns, Jean-Antoine 208
Buck, Jonathan: work of *341*
buckles 464, 467, 468, *469*
buffalo: jade *378*
buffet: French 174
Bunzlau stoneware *26, 27, 28*
Buquoy, Count George 266
Burdess, A. 433, 435
bureau-cabinet 144
   Queen Anne *151,* 155
bureau plat 140
bureaux: American 184, *185*
   block-front 184, *185*
   English 134, 144
   French 140, 208
   Queen Anne 151, *154*
   roll-top 165
Burgkmair, Hans: work of *246*
Burke, Edmund 414
Burmese glass 298, *299*
Burney, Fanny 450
Burr, Benge 450
Burrows, George & James 449, 451
   work of *451*
Burrows, T. 452
Burton, William 89
Butin (potter) 39
Butler, Dr William 312
butter-dish: Irish silver *342*

cabinets: American 148
   Arts and Crafts *230,* 231
   Chinese 129
   Chippendale *176*
   collector's *217*
   English *133,* 134, *135*
     mirrored *248*
   filing *209*
   French *138,* 140, *171*
   Gothic *227, 227*
   'Indian' 133
   Japanese *129,* 130
   papier-mâché *442*
   pedestal *207*
   Queen Anne 151
   Sheraton *192*
   William and Mary 142, *143*
Cabirol, Barthélémy 172
caddy, *see* tea caddies
Cadenas: French *359,* 359
Cafaggiolo maiolica *30,* 31, 33
Caines, Thomas 274
cake-baskets: Irish silver 342, *343*
   Regency silver 366, *367*
Calderwood, Robert: work of *344,* 345
calendar dials 438
Callot, Jacques 244
Cambridge, Richard 178
cameo carving: imitations 268
cameo glass: American 300
   English 287–91
   French 294
canapé: Art Nouveau 232
candelabra: English gilt *212,* 213
   Regency silver *365, 367, 368*
candleholder: American glass 298, *299*
candle-stands: American 148, 160
   Chippendale *180*
candlesticks:
   altar: French silver 358
   American glass *255, 275, 277*
   American silver *315,* 332, *332*
   blue and white porcelain *88*
   Dutch delft *43*
   enamel *415*
   English silver *328, 329, 331, 337*
   St Porchaire ware *36, 37*
   Sheffield plate 362

canister, *see* tea-caddies
Canot (furniture maker): work of *173*
cans: silver 330
canterbury *442*
caquetoire 119, *119*
carafe: English glass *269,* 272
Caranza, Duc A. de 295
Carlton House 225
carpet-bowls 93
carpets: oldest 390
   Persian 375, 390–3
Carr, John 177, 178
carriage clocks 420
cartel *418,* 419
cartonnier: Louis XIV *164*
Cartwright & Woodward 372
Carver, John 148
Casanova, François 397
caskets: enamel *413, 416, 417*
   Venetian glass *240, 241*
cassapanca 124
cassone 117, *122, 123,* 123–4
Castel Durante maiolica *29, 31, 33*
Castel Durante pottery *47*
Castiglione, Baldassare 124
castors: American silver *215, 317*
   English silver *337*
   faience *34, 35*
   Irish silver *345*
Catalonia pottery *45, 46–7, 47, 47*
Catherine de Medici 127
Catherine the Great 82
caudle cup: American silver *315*
Caughley 86, 88, 95
causeuse *209*
Cazin, J. C. 111
celadon *14,* 14
   silver-mounted 312
celery-vase: American glass *275*
centrepieces: English silver *336,* 340
Century Guild 228–9
ceramics. See also porcelain, pottery, etc.
   transfer-printed 94–8
Chaffers' factory 86
chairs: American *147,* 148–9, *149, 150, 159, 182, 184, 203*
   Art Nouveau *232, 234, 235*
   Arts & Crafts *228,* 229
   back stool 120
   'bended back' 144, *153,* 153
   Biedermeier *215, 215*
   brewster 148–9
   cane *133, 134*
   carvers 148–9, *150,* 225, 227
   Charles II *133, 134*
   Chippendale 178, *179*
   construction 184–5
   conversation chair 119, *119*
   dining *152, 153,* 219, 225, *226,* 227
   Elizabethan *118, 120*
   English: 17th century *133*
     19th century *442*
   factory-made 219
   features introduced by Jacob 207
   Federal 201
   folding: Chinese *129, 130*
     x-shaped *124, 124*
   French *173, 175*
     Directory *209*
     Hepplewhite *188*
   Glastonbury 120
   Gothic 223, *223, 225*
   Hepplewhite *187, 196,* 197
   high-backed 142–3
   Italian *124, 124*
   ladder-back (slat-back) *147,* 149, *149,* 201, 219, *219*
   leg designs 117, 144, 153–5
   Martha Washington (Lolling') 201, *204*
   oval-back *196,* 197, 198
   painted *189, 203*
   panel-back 119–20
   Queen Anne 144, *152, 153,* 153

   159–160
   Regency *210, 212,* 213
   'ribband-back' *179*
   rocking- 219–20
   roundabout, or corner 160, *160*
   shepherd-crook arms *153*
   shield-back 188, 190
   side-chairs 159
     three-slat 219
   sleeping-chair *132*
   square-back 200
   tassel-back *182*
   throne chair *206*
   turned ('thrown') 120
   upholstered 120, 134, 143, *145,* 158
     in tapestry *396, 398*
   vase- or urn-backed 201
   Windsor 160
   wing chairs 134, *144, 182*
   x-frame 120
chaise-longue, *see* day-bed
chalices: French 347
   Irish 341, 343–4
Chamberlain, Robert 79
Chambers, Sir William 178
champagne glasses: English *273*
Channon, John: work of *248,* 249
Chantilly porcelain 60–4, *61, 63*
Chapman of London: work of *465*
Chardin, Jean-Baptiste-Siméon 355
Charles I 248
Charles II furniture 117, 131–5
Charles & Hollister: work of *431*
Charlotte, Queen 461, *464*
Charron, André-Charlemagne: work of 396, *396*
chauffeuse 209
Chebsey, Thomas and John 261
cheese-dish 98
cheese-toaster: Sheffield plate 362, *363*
Chelsea-Derby 74
Chelsea porcelain 11, 71–4, 85, 416
Cheney, Benjamin and Timothy 429
Chéret, Joseph 295
chest of drawers: American *146,* 147, *149, 150,* 158–9, *196,* 197
   English 133
   evolution of 123
   table à la Bourgogne 165
chest-on-chest 153, 184
chests: American *147,* 148, *148*
   bachelors' 153
     cassone (marriage) 117, *122, 123,* 123–4
   Hadley 148
   'hope' (dower, marriage) 117, *122, 123,* 123–4, 148
   medieval 124
   miniature, Japanese *126,* 127
   'Nonsuch' 120
   Shaker 220–2
chiffonier 208
Chinese Chippendale *182, 183,* 185
   furniture, lacquered 126–30
     differences between Japanese and 128–9
   jade 376–80
   porcelain: American imports 100, *100–1,* 102, *103*
     Ming 12–16
   silver *325*
Ch'ing dynasty 323
Ching-te chen 14
chinoiserie 11, 117
   silver 323–6
chipolin 162
Chippendale, Thomas 117, 176–81, 182, 223
   Gentleman and Cabinet-Maker's Director 179, 181, *181,* 184, 224
   work of 176–81
chocolate-pots: English silver 328–9, *329*
Choisy-le-Roi glass *284,* 284–5

Chou dynasty 13
Christian II of Saxony 245
Christian's factory 86
Christmas cards 445
Christy, J. F.: work of *269,* 272
chronograph 433–4
Cirou, Cicaire (Ciquaire) 61, 62
Citroen, Karel 467
Clark, John 150
Clay, Henry 440, 442
Clerkenwell, London 435
Clichy glass 264, *278, 279, 280–2, 281*
clock-cases: Chelsea 72, *73*
   French 17th century 140, *140*
   materials for 419
clock-piece: Staffordshire 106, *106*
clocks: American 375, 427–30, 436–9
   battery 439
   decimal time 422
   dials *420,* 423
   digital 438–9
   elaborate 423–6
   English 423–6
   French, from 1720 375, 418–22
   hands *419*
   mass-production 438
   movements 438
   novelties 438
   pendulums 419–20
   precision 426
   spring-driven 438
   wall *418,* 419
   weight-driven pendulum 427–8
cobalt blue 11, 13, 17, 36, 76, 90, 95
Cobb, John 178
coconut shell: silver-mounted 310–11
coffee pots: American silver 334, *335,* 349–50
   Bow 86, *87*
   English silver *324,* 328–9
   Irish silver *344*
   Sheffield plate 360, *361*
   silver 307
   Victorian silver *370*
   Wedgwood *81*
   Worcester 78
coffee services: Mennecy *63*
   Victorian silver 369–73, *371*
coffee-urn: American silver *348*
cofferer 119
coffin clocks 428
Colbert, Jean-Baptiste 39, 394
Cole, Henry 272
Cole, James Ferguson 432, *434*
   work of 432, *433*
Collaert, Adrian 26
Colley, Thomas 423
   work of *424*
Collins, Richard: painting by *330*
Collins, William: work of *212,* 213
Colman, Samuel 302
Cologne stoneware 27, *28*
colours: ground 66–67, 77
   over-glaze 95
   under-glaze 16, 20, 95
commodes: American 198, *199*
   English 193, 213, *213*
   French *139,* 140, *161, 162, 163,* 167, *169, 170, 174, 175, 206,* 208
companion figure: Stuart *132*
comport: American glass *276*
Condé, Louis Henri de Bourbon, Prince de 61
Condés (furniture makers) 172
condiment set: Irish glass and silver 260
Coney, John 314
   work of 313, *315*
Connecticut clocks 427, 429, *430*
Connecticut furniture 148
Conrado, Antoine 36
Conrado, Augustin 36
Conrado, Domenico 36
consoles 209
Consulate furniture 205–9, 210

Copland, H. 179
Copley, J. S.: painting by *347*
copper: for plating 362–3
copper oxide 51, 244
copperwork 350
Corillet (glassmaker) 295
Cork glass 259, *261*, 262, 263
Cork silver *341*, 342, *343*, 344–5
Corning Glassworks 277
Coronation Cup 312
Corsali, Andrea 14
Coteau, Jean 419
Cottingham, L. N. A.: work of *227*
couches: American 200, *201*
　　English 144
Courtauld, Louisa: work of *324*
Courtauld, Samuel: work of *326*
coverlets: American 375, *399–402*
Cowell, William: work of *316*
Cowles, G.: work of *324*
Cox, James 423–5
　　work of *424*
crab-box 352, *352*
Crace, J. G. & Sons 226
　　work of *227*
crackle-glass 241
cradle: silver 358
Cranch, Edward P. 113
creamers: American glass 255
　　English glass 255
creamware 81–2, 85, 95, 100
Cressent, Charles 162
Cresy, Edward 110
cribbage box *450*, 451
cristallo 237, 239–41, 243
crizzling 246
Cros, Henri 295
crucifix: silver 358
crystal: cameo work 289
　　silver-mounted *308*, 309, *309*, 312, *312*, 319
cullet 239
cupboards: American 148
　　corner cupboard 162, *163*, *164*, *169*
　　court cupboard 120
　　evolution 123
　　German 216
　　housekeeper's *224*, 227
　　Italian 122, *123*
　　Queen Anne 151
　　Tudor 119
cup-plates: glass 276
cups: American silver *313*, *316*, 317, 334, *334*, *346*
　　animal models 319
　　Bohemian glass 266, *267*
　　English silver 329, *329*, 337
　　German silver 318–19
　　German silver-mounted *319*, 320
　　ostrich egg mounted *310*
　　redware 50, *51*
　　Venetian glass *240*, 241
Curtis, Lemuel 430
　　work of *428*
Curtis, Samuel 439
Custode family 36
cut glass 243, 245–6
　　method of cutting 262–3
　　thickness required for cutting 271
cyma curve 159
Cypriote ware 305

Dammouse, Albert 295
Danhauser 215
Daniel, Henry 91–3
Daniel & Brown 90
Darker, William: work of *331*
Daum, August and Jean 295
　　work of *292*, *293*
Davis, Alexander Jackson 225
Davis, William 76, 79
day-beds: English 133–4, *135*, 144, *145*

French 209, *209*
　　Queen Anne *151*
Debaufre, Joseph 340
Debèche, Gerard 355
decanters: American *258*
　　Bohemian *264*
　　English 271
　　French *285*
　　Irish *261*
decimal time 422
decimal watch 432, *433*
Décorchement, François 295
Delafosse (clockmaker) 419
Delamain, Henry 414
De Lamerie, Paul 307, 326, 336–40, work of *336–40*
delft 11
　　in America 100
　　English 40
　　Dutch 40–4
Della-Robbia Company Ltd 108–9
Demay, Jean-Baptiste-Bernard 208
Deming Parlour *182*, *183*
De Moedler 323
De Morgan, William 89, 108
　　work of *109*
Demoulin (furniture maker) 172
Dennis, Thomas 148
　　work of *146*
Dennison, Aaron 439
Denon, Baron Dominique Vivant 207, 366
Denyemon, Yoshidaya 19
Derby, Elias Hasket 11, 198
Derby-Chelsea 74
Derby porcelain 11, 86
Derrick, Samuel 450
Deruta lustreware 89
Deruta maiolica 29, *29*, 31, *32*
Deruta pottery 47
Deshays (tapestry designer) 396
desks:
　　Bureau du Roi 166, *167*, *167*
　　fall-front 156, *156*
　　kneehole *136*
　　lap-desks 442
　　Queen Anne *151*
　　roll-top 165, *169*, 170
　　slope-top (slant top) 158, *159*
　　tambour *200*, *201*, 202, 204
　　writing: Arts and Crafts 228, 229
　　　English *144*
　　　fall-front 151
　　　French *169*, 170
　　　German 216, *217*
Desoria (painter) 397
Despret, Georges 295
Desprey (glassmaker) 267
Desracis: painting by *409*
dessert-basket: Worcester 75
Devon pottery 98, 111
De Vries, Vredeman 118
diamonds 461–2
　　cutting 375, *461*
Diderot, Denis:
　　Encyclopédie 172, *174*, 175
digital clocks 438–9
Dillway, Hiram 276
Dillwyn, Lewis Weston 93
Dinglinger, Georg Christoph 319
Dinglinger, Georg Friedrich 319
Dinglinger, Johann Melchior 319
Dining Parlour: English 18th century 189–90
dinner services:
　　Regency silver 367, 368
　　Swan Service: Meissen 56, 57, 58, 59
　　Wedgwood *82*
Directorie design 205–6
Disbrowe, Nicholas 148
dishes: Dutch delft *41*
　　English silver *339*
　　faience *36*
　　Japanese porcelain *17*, *19*

maiolica *32*, *33*
　　Ming porcelain *12*, *13*, *15*
　　redware 50, *51*
　　Spanish *45*, *46*
dish-rings: Irish silver 342, *343*
D'Olier, Isaac 342
doll's house: Chippendale *178*
Donaldson, John 74
Doulton's of Lambeth 109–10, *111*
dower chests ('hope', marriage) 117, *122*, *123*, 123–4, 148
Downing, Andrew Jackson 225
Drais, Pierre-François: work of *353*
Drake, Sir Francis 458
dram cups 314
Drausch, Valentin 245
Drentwett, Abraham 319
Drentwett, Emmanuel 322
Drentwett, Philip Jacob: work of *320*
Dresser, Christopher 372–3
　　work of *371*
dressers: Arts and Crafts 229
　　French 174
dressing-cases: Victorian 454, *455*
dressing-suite 248
dressing-tables: bidet table *195*
　　Chippendale *180*
　　English 188, *189*
　　French 209
　　knee-hole 153
　　Louis XIV 165
dressing-table box: Tunbridge ware *449*
dressing-table casket, *see* toilet-casket
drinking glasses: development 241
drug jars: Dutch delft *41*
　　French 35
　　Italian 31, *32*, *33*
　　Spanish *46*, *48*, *49*
Dublin glass 259, 261
Dublin Goldsmiths' Company 342
Dublin silver *341*, 341, 342, *343*, 344, 345
Dubois, Jacques: work of 162, *163*
Dubret, Henri 468
Dubut, Jean-François: work of 162, *163*
Duché, Andrew 53
Ducrollay, Jean: work of *354*
Duesbury, William 72, 74
　　work of *74*
Duesbury-Chelsea 74
Dugourc, Demosthène 419
Dugourc, Jean-Demosthène 207
dumb waiter 165
Dummer, Jeremiah 314
　　work of *315*
Dumont (clockmaker) 419
Dumonteil family 36
Dundas, Sir Lawrence 178
Duplessis (bronze modeller) 165
Dutch delft 40–4
Dutton, Matthew and Thomas 423
　　work of *425*
Dutton, William 423
　　work of *426*
Duvaux, Lazare 141, 162, 355
Duvivier, William 72
Dwerrihouse, Thomas 423
Dwight, Timothy 314
Dyce, William 110

earthenware: in America 100
　　earliest 11
　　glazes 81
　　tin-glazed 34–9, 40–4, 46, 89
easie-chair 144
Eastlake, C. L. 228
Eaton Hall, Cheshire 225, *225*
ébéniste 162
Eberlein, Johann Friedrich: work of 57, *57*

écuelle: German silver 322, *322*
Edict of Nantes 142
Edinburgh silver *370*
Edkins, Michael 252
Edward, John 326
Edwards, Benjamin 261
Edwards, G. 72
Edwards, John 314
Eenhoorn family 43, 44
Egan of Cork 345
Egerton, Friedrich 266–7
　　work of *268*
egg cups: pottery 96, *97*
Egypt: influences from 210
Egyptian lustreware 46, 89
Eichbaum, William Peter 275
Eissler, Caspar Gottlieb 322
electro-plating 307
Elfe, Thomas 185
Elgin Marbles 366
Elgin vase 288
Eliot, George 370
Elizabeth I furniture 118–21
Elkington & Company 361, 370, 372
　　work of *371*
Ellicott, John 423
Elliott, John 185
elm 153
Elton, Sir Edmund 111
embroidery: Russian 375, 386–9
Emens, Jan 26, 28
Emery, Josiah 426
Empire furniture 117, 205–9
enamel: manufacture 414
　　over-glaze application 77
enamelling: English 413–16
　　on glass 239, 243–4, 245, 258
　　on gold *353*, *354*, 355
　　on porcelain 14, 18–19
　　first examples 14
Engelbrecht, Martin 322
English clocks 423–6
　　enamels 413–16
　　furniture: Arts and Crafts Movement 228–31
　　　Chippendale 176–81
　　　Elizabethan oak 118–21
　　　Hepplewhite 186–90
　　　Queen Anne 151–5
　　　Regency 210–13
　　　Victorian Gothic 223–7
　　　walnut 131–5
　　　William and Mary 142–5
　　glass: cameo 287–91
　　　18th century wineglasses 250–3, *250–3*
　　　looking-glasses 247–9
　　silver: Queen Anne 327–31
　　　Regency 364–8
　　　rococo 336–40
engraved glass 245–6
engraving on glass 243, 244–6
Ensell, Edward 275
épergne: English silver *336*, 340
　　Sheffield plate 362, *363*
escapements:
　　crank roller 432, *432*
　　detent 432
　　duplex 432
　　lever 432
　　travelling 434
escritoires 442
Evans, Edward 156
　　work of *156*
Evelyn, John 131, 247, 248, *449*
ewers:
　　English silver *340*
　　faience *34*
　　French glass *285*
　　German silver 320
　　Ming porcelain *16*
　　mother-of-pearl mounted 310
　　Persian pottery *23*
　　Rookwood *112*
　　silver-mounted crystal *312*

silver-mounted porcelain *308*, *309*
Venetian glass *240*, 241
Eyck, Konraet ten 316
Eysler, Johann Leonhard 319

Fabergé, P. C.: work of *302*
Face, Jacob: work of *291*
Faenza maiolica 29, *32*, 33, *33*
faience 11, 34–9
  painting 42
  Turkish 13–14
fakes and forgeries:
  Chinese view of 14
  of redware 54
  of Sèvres 66
  of Staffordshire figures 107
  of Worcester 77
Falconet (Sèvres modeller) 68
Falize Frères: work of *467*
famille colours 11
fans: French 408–12, *408–12*
Farrell, Edward 370
  work of *369*, *370*
Fawkener, Sir Everard 71
Fearon, Henry Bradshaw 275
Federal furniture: early 196–9
  later 200–4
felspar 11
Fenner, William 449, 451
Fereday, J. T. 291
  work of *287*
Ferrara glass 239
Ferrer, Vincente 48
Feuillâtre, Eugène 468
  work of *466*
Fiennes, Celia 449
Figdor, Dr A. 393
figures: Arts and Crafts 110, 111
  Chantilly *63*, 64
  Chelsea *70*, *71*, *73*, *74*
  glass *294*, 295
  jade 378–9, *378*, *379*
  Japanese porcelain *18*, *20*
  Meissen porcelain 55, *55*, 57, *57*, *58*,
    59
  Mennecy porcelain *62*, 64
  Ming porcelain *15*
  Staffordshire 104–7, *104–7*
Filleul, Frères 394, *396*
Findlay, John and Hugh 203
  work of *203*
Finet family 398
fire-screens: American 160
fish: jade 379
fishbowl: Ming porcelain *13*, 16
fish-slice: English silver 338
Fitzgerald, C. P. 14
FitzGerald, Desmond 177
Flach family 26
Flaxman, John: work of *364*, *368*
Flight, Thomas 79
flint-glass 271, 276
Fogelberg, Andrew 364
folklore: China 382–4
  Japan 382–4
Fontaine, Pierre François Léonard
  207, 210
  work of *422*
Fontana maiolica 33
Fordham, Elias Pym 275
forest glass 243
Forestville Manufacturing Company:
  work of *437*
forgeries, *see* fakes and forgeries
Forty (clockmaker) 419
Fothergill, John 360
Fouquet, Alphonse 468
Fouquet, Georges 468
Fournier, Louis 64
Franklin, Benjamin 428
Frechen potteries 27
Frederick the Great 59, 320–1

Frederick William Elector of
  Brandenburg 246
Frederick William I, King of Prussia
  320
Frémin, Jean: work of *353*
French (watchmaker): work of 432,
  433
French clocks from 1720 *375*, 418–22
  faience 34–9
  fans 408–12
  furniture: Boulle 136–41
    Consulate and Empire 205–9
    Louis XIV 161–5
    provincial 171–5
  glass: Art Nouveau 292–5
    coloured 283–6
  gold boxes 351–5
  Hepplewhite *188*
  silver, Neo-classical 356–9
  tapestry *375*, 394–8
  watches 434
Friend, James 451, 452
Frisbee, William 365
Fritsche, William 291
Froydeveau (furniture maker) 174
fruit-bowl: Regency silver 366, *367*
Fry, Laura A. 113
Fulham pottery 108, *109*, *110*, 111
Fuller, Loie: glass model of *294*, 295
furniture:
  American Chippendale 182–5
    Colonial 156–60
    early 146–50
    Federal 196–204
  Art Nouveau 232–5
  Arts and Crafts Movement 228–31
  Biedermeier 213, 214–17
  Chippendale 176–81
  construction 158, 184–5
    dowel and tenon *185*
    panel and frame 118
  differences between American and
    European 203
  Egyptian influences 210
  Elizabethan oak 118–21
  English baroque 142–5
  French: Boulle 136–41
    Consulate and Empire 201, 205–9
    provincial 171–5
  gesso 155, *155*
  Hepplewhite 186–90
  Italian, early 122–5
  lacquered 126–30
  Louis XIV 161–5
  mass-produced 117
  metal 206
  mirror-faced 249
  painted 203
  Queen Anne 151–5
  Regency 201, 210–13
  Shaker 218–22
  Style Directoire 205–6
  Victorian Gothic 223–7
  wood for 119
fusee 432

Gabriel, Jacques 172
gadrooning 120, 314
Gaillard, Lucien 468
Gallé, Emile 237, 286, 287, 294–5, 468
  work of *292*, *294*
Gambini, Giulio 36
Gamble, Elias 338
games-compendium: Victorian 456
Gatchell, Jonathan 261
Gaudé 467
Gaudreau, Antoine 162
  work of 162, *163*
Gauron (sculptor) 64
Gautrait, L. 468
Gay, John 462
General Time Corporation 438

German furniture 214, *215*, 216
  glass, early 242–6
  porcelain exports 102
  silver 318–22
  stoneware 25–8
gesso furniture 155, *155*
Ghiselin, Cesar 317
Gibbons, Grinling 145, 248
Gibbs, James 184
Gilbody, Samuel 86
gilding: banning 62, 64
  on glass 252
  honey- 67
  on porcelain 67
Giles, James 74
Giles of London 252
Gilliland, John L. 277
gilt furniture 142
gilt metal 462
Gimson, Ernest 229
  work of *229*, 230, *231*
giraffe 210, *211*
girandole clock *428*, 430
Girard, Francis 341
Girls' Festival 126, 127
glass:
  American Art 237, 296–300
    Colonial 254–8
    19th century 274–7
  Art Nouveau 237, 286, 292–5
  Biedermeier 267
  Bohemian 237, 242–6, 264–8
  colour 237, 267, 304
  components 237, 242
  cristallo 237, 239–41, 243
  cutting 243, 262–3, 271
  earliest 278
  enamelled 258
  enamelling 239, 243–4, 245
  English: cameo 287–91
    18th century wineglasses 250–3
  engraving 243, 244–6
  flint- 271, 276
  forest glass 243
  French coloured 283–6
  German, early 242–6
  gilding 252
  gold-ruby 246
  hyalith 265, *265*, 266–7
  ice-glass (crackle-) 241
  iridescent 268, 304
  Irish 259–63
  lace-glass 237, *240*, 241, 277
  lime soda 277
  lithyalin 265, *265*, 266–7, *268*
  lustre 304, 305
  mounted 311–12
  opal-decorated 296
  opaline 286
  ornament 272
  overlay (cased) 267
  overshot (ice) 298–300
  painting 266
  potash-lime 245
  pressing 276–7
  ruby 267
  shaded 298–300, *299*
  silvered (mercury) 296
  soda 237, 238, 278
  stained 267
  threaded 298–300
  Venetian 238–41
  Victorian 269–72
  Zwischengoldglas 264
glass-blowing:
  development 237
  method 237
  16th century *246*
glass-hawker 242
glassmaking: 14th century 238
glass-pressing machine 237, 276
glazes: aventurine 113
  coloured 23, 51
  cracked 13
  crackled 23

crazing 97
  early 13, 14
  eggshell 14
  felspar 11
  green 81
  lead 25, 31, 50, 51, 54, 62
  manganese 51
  matt 115
  pooled 14
  on soft-paste porcelain 66
  tin 11, 46, 61
Gobelins tapestry *375*, 394, 395, 396,
  398
Goble, Robert 344
  work of *341*, 342, *343*
goblets:
  American glass *296*
  American silver 348
  Bohemian glass 246, 266, *267*, *268*
  English glass *269*, 272, *273*
  French glass *284*
  German glass 242, 243, 244, 245
  Venetian glass 239
Goddard family 184
Godunov, Boris 389
Godwin, E. W. 231
  work of *228*, 229
gold: boxes 351–5
  hallmarks 342, *355*
  melting down 307
  Gold-rubin (gold-ruby) glass 246
goldsmiths 307
Gonzaga, Duke Luigi, of Mantua 36
Gonzales de Clavijo, Ruy 390
Gorely, Mrs Jean 91
Gorham Manufacturing Company 114
Gostelowe, George 184
Gostelowe, Jonathan 185
Gothic furniture 117
  Victorian 223–7
Gourdin (furniture maker) 172
Gouyn, Charles 72
Govaers, Daniel 353–4
Grace, W. G.: silk portrait of *444*
Grainger and Company 77
grandfather clock, *see* long-case clocks
Grant (clockmaker) 426
Grant, W. H. 445, 446
Grasset, Eugène 468
Grattan, Henry 260
gravy-warmers: Sheffield plate 362
Gray, A. E. & Company 93
Great Fire of London 131
Green family 119
Green, Ward and Green 367
Grellet family 398
Grendey, Giles: work of *151*
Grenzan stoneware 27
Grenzhausen stoneware 27–8
grès de Flandres 110
Greuze, Jean Baptiste 355
Griffo 35
Grignon, René 315
Gubbio lustreware 89
Gubbio maiolica 30, 31
guéridon 140, 206, 208–9
Guilds: French 172
  for glass workers 246
Guild Statutes of 1743 162
Guimard 467
Gulbenkian, Calouste 468
Gumley, John 142
Gwynn, Nell 248

Haarlem pottery 43
Hache family 174
  work of *172*
Hadley chests 148
Haig, Thomas 180–1
hair ornaments 462
half-hunting cases 434
Hallett, William 178

Hall-in-Tyrol glass 244–5
Halter, Casper 255
Halton, John Martin 255
Hamelin (enameller) 355
Hamilton, Sir William 83, 366
hampers : Victorian 456
Hampton Court Palace: King's
  Presence Chamber 144
Hancock, John 90, 91–3
Hancock, Joseph 360, 362
Hancock, Robert 77, 95, 415
  copy of work 416, 417
Hankar, Paul 235
hard-paste porcelain 11, 71
Harland, Thomas 428
Harris, C. S. 372
Harrison, William 118, 310, 458
Hartshorne, Albert 261
Harunobu, Suzuki: work of 383
Haseler, Edwin 442
Hawkes, Thomas: work of 271, 272
Hawkins, Sir John 458
Hayman, Francis 178
Haynes, George 93
Heal, Sir Ambrose 187, 231
Heinrich, Franz 215
Heitze, J. G.: work of 56
Henglin, Johann Erhard II 319
  work of 319
Hennell, J. B. 372
  work of 373
Henri II ware 34, 37
Henry VIII 247
Hepplewhite, Alice 186–7
Hepplewhite, George 117, 186–90,
  200
  Cabinet-Maker's London Book of
    Prices 197
  Cabinet-maker & Upholsterer's
    Guide 186, 187, 189, 190, 197
Herat 404–5
  carpet 392, 393
Herbert, Thomas 21
Hernandez, Francisco 457
Hertaut, Nicolas 172
Hervieu (bronze caster) 165
Hess, Jan 245
highboy: American 157, 158, 159
  160, 183, 184
Hill, John 261
Hinard 394
Hirado porcelain 20
Hirschmann, W. 268
Hispano-Moresque lustreware 45–7
Hoadley, Silas 429
Hobbs-Brockunier & Company: work
  of 296, 298, 298
Hobe, Georges 235
Hodgetts, Joshua 289
  work of 290
Hoffmann, Josef 467
Hogarth, William 332–3, 338
Höhr stoneware 27, 28
Holdship, Richard 77
Hollamby, H. 452
Holland: delft 40–4
hollow-ware: German 67
Holmes (clockmaker) 423
honey-gilding 67
hookah 21, 22
Hope, Susannah 462, 463
Hope, Thomas 201, 210, 366
hope chests (dower, marriage) 117,
  122, 123, 123–4, 148
Hopper, Thomas 225
horn : silver-mounted 319, 319, 320
Höroldt, J. G. 56
horse: jade 379
Horta, Victor 234, 467
  work of 232–3, 232, 235
houses : standard scheme in 17th
  century 131–2
Houses of Parliament, Westminster
  227
Howard, Edward 439

Howard, Thomas 314
Hsi Fan Tsi 380
Huet, Jean-Baptiste 396–7
  work of 395
Huguenots 142, 307
Hull, John 314
  work of 313
Humpen: glass 243, 244, 245
Hunt, John 365
Hunt and Roskell 365
  work of 370, 371
hunting cases 434
Hurd, Jacob 333–4
  work of 333, 334, 335
Hurst, Henry: work of 315
Husayn Mirza, Sultan 390, 404
hyalith glass 265, 265, 266–7

ice glass 241, 298–300
icon: embroidered 388, 388, 389
icon cloth 386, 387
Ikkwan 385
  work of 383
Iles, Frank 108
Illsach, Ringel D' 295
Imari wares 11, 17, 18, 18, 19
incense burners: jade 380
  Japanese porcelain 20
inkstands:
  American glass 276
  maiolica 31
  marquetry 141
  papier-mâché 442
  Sèvres 65, 68
  silver chinoiserie 326
  stoneware 25, 28
inlay 118
  illusionistic 124
  woods for 204
Inness, George 302
Innsbruck glass 243, 244–5
inro 375, 381, 381, 384, 385
intarsia work 120
Irish glass 259–63
  silver 341–5
iron red 13, 17, 19
Isfahan carpet 392, 393
  paintings 406
Isma'il, Shah 390, 404
Isnik pottery 22
Issai 385
Italian furniture, early 122–5
  maiolica, 16th century 29–33
Ivan III, Tsar 386–7
Ives, Joseph 429, 438
ivory:
  Japanese netsuke 382
  silver-mounted 310, 311

Jackson, Sir Charles 314
Jackson, John 449
Jacob (Desmalter), François Honoré
  Georges 208
  work of 206, 208
Jacob, Georges 207–8
  work of 206
Jacobs, Lazarus 252
Jacquard, Joseph-Marie 400–1
Jacquard loom 444, 446
Jacques, Symphorien 62
jade:
  cutting 376
  musical 380
  ornamental 375, 376–80
jadeite 376
James I 458
James II 142, 400
Janssen, Stephen Theodore 414, 416
Janvier, Antide 420

Japanese:
  furniture, lacquered 126–30
    difference between Chinese and
      128–9
  netsuke and inro 381–5
  porcelain 17–20
japanned wares 440–3
japanning 133, 144, 155
japonaisserie 11
jars:
  Dutch delft 41
  maiolica 32, 33
  Ming porcelain 13, 14, 15
  Rookwood 114
  Spanish 47, 47
Jardelle (glass cutter) 275
jardinières 208
  Chantilly porcelain 63
  Louis XIV 165
  Sèvres 68
Jarves, Deming 276
Jeaurat, Etienne 398
  work of 395
Jennens and Betteridge 442, 443
Jensen, Gerreit 142
Jerome, Chauncey 436–8
  work of 427, 437
jet: imitation 443
jewel boxes: Victorian 453–4
jewel cabinets:
  French 170, 170
  Tunbridge ware 450, 451
jewel caskets:
  French 17th century 141
  Swiss or Tyrolean 453, 454
  Victorian 453
jewellery 375
  Art Nouveau 375, 466–9
  early 461–5
Jones, E. Alfred 347
Jones, Owen 291
Jordaens, Jacob: painting by 26
Josephine, Empress 358
  bedroom 205
Joubert, Gilles 165, 166
jugs:
  American porcelain 99, 100
  American silver 334, 346, 347
  blue and white 85, 88
  Bohemian glass 243, 268
  English glass 269, 271, 272
  glass mounted in silver 311–12
  Goat and Bee 71, 71
  Irish glass 260
  Irish silver 344
  lustreware 90, 91, 92, 93
  Philadelphia porcelain 102, 103
  redware 52
  silver-mounted glass 308, 309
  stoneware 25, 26, 27
  tigerware, mounted 311, 312
  Victorian silver 370, 372, 373
  Worcester 79
Jullien, Joseph 62
Jury of Art Manufacturers 205
Juster, Joe: work of 108, 109

Kaendler, Johann Joachim 55–9
  work of 55, 57, 58
Kajikawa family: work of 384, 385
Kakiemon wares 11, 18, 20
Kännerbackerland 27
Kay, John 401
keeping-room : American 147
keg: redware 52
Kent, William 93
Kenton & Company 229
Kersting, Georg 215
kettle: English silver 327, 371, 373
kettle stand: silver 328
Kingsley, Rose G. 115
kingwood 134

Kinsky, Count Johann 246
Kip, Jesse 316
Kirchner, Johann Gottlieb 56
Kirman pottery 21–2
Kizai-emon, Sakaida 18
knobs:
  pressed-glass 276
  silvered glass 296
Knütgen family 26, 27
Ko-Kutani wares 18–19, 18
Korea: influence on Japanese
  porcelain 17
Kothgasser, Anton 266
Kraak porselyn 15, 16
Kreismeier, Simon 255
Kreussen stoneware 28, 28
Kreybich, Georg Francis 242
Krüger, Jean Guillaume Georges 320
Kubachi pottery 22, 22–3
Kunckel, Johann 246
Kutani wares 18–19

lace-glass 237, 240, 241, 277
lacquer:
  Chinese and Japanese used on
    furniture 162
  Japanese 381, 381
  making 127
  panels mounted in gold 353
lacquered furniture 126–30
lacquering: of furniture 127–30
Ladeuil, L. Morel 370
Lalique, René 295, 467–8
  work of 292, 293, 466, 467, 468, 469
Lambeth pottery 44
Lamerie, Paul de, see De Lamerie,
  Paul
lamps:
  American glass 275, 276, 277, 300,
    301, 302
  French glass 294
  leaded shades, American 302, 305
lamp-standard: English 212, 213
Lancret, Nicolas 409
Lane, Arthur 23
Lane, Sir Ralph 458
Lannuier, Charles-Honoré 202–3
  work of 203
lanterns: celadon ware 14
lap-desks 442
Lapierre (furniture maker) 174
Lascelles family 177, 179
Launay, Hautin et Cie 384
Laune, Etienne de 26
lava glass 305
Lazarus and Rosenfeld 267
'lazy Susan' 263
Leach, Bernard 111
lead crystal 246
lead oxide 237
lead glaze 31, 50, 51, 54, 62
Lebrun, Charles 136, 138, 398
Lecheverell, Alphonse Eugène 288
Leeds Pottery 81
Le Faucheur, Alexandre 419
Le Faucheur, Jean-Ignace 419
Lefebvre, Daniel 36
Lefèbvre, Robert: painting by 358,
  358
Le Gaigneur (cabinet maker) 141
legends:
  China 382–4
  Japan 382–4
Legras, Auguste 295
Lehman, Caspar 245
  work of 244
Leighton, John H. 276
Leighton, William 277, 296
Leighton, William Jr 298
Lemon, William: work of 196, 197,
  198, 198
Le Noir, Etienne: work of 421

Lepaute, Jean André 419
Lepaute, Jean Baptiste 419, 420
Lepautre, Jean 142, 319
Lepine, Jean Antoine 419, 420
Leplat, Raymond 319
Le Prince 396
Le Roux family 316
Le Roy, Charles 419
Le Roy, Julien 419
Le Roy, Pierre 419
Le Sueur, Eustache 355
Letablère, John 342
Lethaby, W. R. 231
    work of 229
Levasseur (cabinet maker) 141
Levavasseur (potter) 39
Leveillé, E. 292–4
Libbey, William 296
Libbey Glass Company 377
License, R. 452
Liénard, Paul 468
Limerick silver 341, 342
Lind, Jenny 442
Lindsey (clockmaker) 423
line of beauty 333
linsey-wolsey 400
Litchdon Pottery 111
lithography: use on ceramics 97–8
lithyalin glass 265, 265, 266–7, 268
Liverpool enamels 416, 416
    porcelain 85, 86, 100, 102
Lloyd, John (porcelain): work of 104
Lloyd, John (silver): work of 342, 343
Lobmeyr, Louis 268
Lock, Matthias 179, 184
Locke, Joseph 298
    work of 290
long-case clocks 375, 423, 423, 426, 427, 428
Longport lustreware 92
Longton Hall porcelain 86, 87
Longworth, Joseph 113
looking glass, see mirror
Lorenzo the Magnificent 124
Lötz, J. 268
Loudin, Germain 165
Loudon, J. C. 224
Louis XIV 136–41
    furniture 161–5
Louis XV furniture 117
Louis XVI 166–70
Louis, Victor 172
lowboys: American 158, 159, 159, 184
Lowe, Joseph 462, 464
Lowestoft porcelain 84, 85, 86, 88
Lücke, J. C. L. 56
luncheon-boxes 456, 456
Lund, J. A. 433
lustre:
    application 46
    on maiolica 31
lustre glass 304, 305
lustreware 23–4, 23
    Egyptian 89
    English 89–93, 108
    Hispano-Moresque 89
    Mesopotamian 23, 89
    Persian 23
    resist ware 90
    Spanish 45–7
    Welsh 90, 91
Lutma, Johannes 319
Lutz, Nicholas 277
lyre clock 419–20, 422

McDonald, W. P.: work of 112
Macé, Jean 136
mace: Irish silver 344
McIntire, Samuel 197–8, 201–2, 204
Mackay, Cunningham & Company: work of 370
Mackintosh, Charles Rennie 467

Mackmurdo, A. H. 228–9
    work of 228, 229
mahogany 156
    types 184
Mahony, Kean 345
maiolica 11, 40, 89
    glaze 31
    painting 31, 33
    16th century 29–33
Malaga pottery 46
Maling, William 93
Malmaison, Château de 207
    bedrooms 205, 206
Maltese silver 344
Manchu dynasty 323
manganese 36
manganese glaze 51
Manises lustreware 89
Manises pottery 46
Mansell, Sir Robert 247
Mansfield, John 314
Manwaring, Robert 187
maple 147
marblized ware 305
marcasite 462
Marchand (furniture maker) 162
Marie Antoinette 166, 170
Markham, Markwick 423
    work of 425
Marot, Daniel 142, 155
    work of 145, 155
marquetry 117, 118, 450
    in brass and tortoise shell 138–40
    English 131, 132, 145, 153
    French 162, 166, 167
    woods for 131
marriage chest (dower, 'hope') 117, 122, 123, 123–4
Marshall, Mark V. 110
Martabani 14
Martin, Robert Wallace 111
    work of 108, 109
Martin brothers 162
Martinware 111
'Mary Gregory' glass 288
Masahiro: work of 384, 385
Masanao 385
Masatsugu, Kwaigyoku 385
mask jug: Worcester 79
masks: glass 295
Massey, Edward: work of 432
Mattoni of Carlsbad 266
Maus, Octave 233
Mayer, Thomas 96
Mazarin, Jules (Giulio) 127
mazers 147
Medhurst, J. 452
Mayhew, Henry 452
Medici porcelain 71
medicine-cabinets: Victorian 456
Meissen porcelain 11, 55–9, 55–9
Meissonnier, Juste-Aurèle 162, 322, 338, 354
Mennecy porcelain 60–4, 60, 61, 62, 63, 64
Mennicken family 26, 27–8
méridienne 209
Mérou, de 394, 396
Merry, Anthony 363
Meshed 405
    paintings from 405, 406
    pottery 21–2, 21, 24
Mesopotamian lustreware 46, 89
metal furniture 206
Metz, Christian: work of 319
Meyer, Friedrich Elias 59
    work of 55
Migeon, Pierre II 165
    work of 162, 163
Mildner, Johann Josef 264
millefiori glass 237, 278–9
Ming dynasty 376
Ming porcelain 11, 12–16, 21
    mounted in silver 308, 309, 312
miniatures:

French 352
Persian 375, 403–6, 403–6
Minors, Thomas 336
Minton, Thomas 95
mirror back: by Boulle 136
mirror-frames: by Boulle 141
mirrors:
    Chinese Chippendale 182
    dressing mirror 151, 153
    English 145, 210, 211, 247–9
    French 209
    pier-glass 190
    Queen Anne 155
    Sheraton 195
Mohn, Gottlöb 266
Mohn, Samuel 266
Molitor, Bernard 208
Monot, M. 285
Monsiau 397
monteiths:
    American silver 315
    English silver 331, 331
    French silver 357
    Irish silver 342, 343
Montgeoffroy, Château de 172
Montgomery, Charles 197
Montmorency, Duc de 35
Moore, Edward C. 302
Moore, George 142
Moore, John 342
Moreau le Jeune, Jean-Michel: work of 408
Morris, George 100
Morris, William 108, 117, 228, 229
Morris, Marshall, Faulkner & Company 228
Morse, Nathaniel: work of 332
Mortimer, John 365
Moser family 266
mosque-lamps: French glass 294
moth-balls 459
mother-of-pearl: silver-mounted 310, 319, 319, 320
Mount Washington Glass Company: work of 296, 298, 299, 300
mourning rings 464
Mucha, Alphonse 468
Mudge, Thomas 423, 426, 432
muffle-kiln 14, 42
mugs:
    American glass 257
    Bohemian glass 265
    Chinese porcelain 100
    English pottery 96
    English silver 330–1, 331
Muhammad, Sultan 392, 405
    work of 404
Muhammadi: work of 403, 406
Mulvaney, Charles 261
Murano 238
    glass 237, 286
musical jades 380
mustard-pots:
    English silver 323
    Worcester 79

Nabeshima porcelain 19–20, 19
Nailsea glass 272
Nancy School of glassmaking 294–5
Nanking ware 95
Napoleon Bonaparte 206–7, 357, 358–9
Nash, John 225
Nattier, Jean-Marc 409
needlework-cabinet: Victorian 433, 456
nef:
    French silver 359, 359
    Venetian glass 240, 241
Neo-classicism 187
    silver 307, 356–9
nephrite 376

netsuke 375, 381–5, 381, 382, 383, 384, 385
    woods for 385
Neuber, Johann Christian 320
Neufville, Louis-François de 62
Nevers faience 36, 37, 39
New England Glass Company 276, 277
    work of 297, 298, 299
New England potteries 53
Newton, Clara Chipman 113
Nichols, Mrs Marian Longworth 113
Nicholson, P. and M. A. 213
Nicot, Jean 457
Niculosa, Francisco 47
Niderviller porcelain 101, 101
Nielsen, Nicole 434
Nieuhoff, Johannes 324
night-table bason stand 195
Nîmes faience 35
Nogaret, Pierre 174
Nogaret School 175
Northwood, John: work of 288, 289
Northwood, John II 289
Northwood, Joseph 288
Northwood, William 289
Nostell Priory, Yorkshire: State bedroom 177
Novgorodets, Mikhail 387
Nuremberg glass 244, 245
Nye, Edmund 451, 452
Nys, Johannis 317

oak 147
    Elizabethan furniture in 118–21
Obrisset 460
O'Carryd, Thomas 341
Odiot, Jean-Baptiste-Claude 357, 358, 358
    work of 358, 359
Oeben, Jean-François 165
    work of 167
ogee clocks 436
Oglethorpe, General James 53
Ohlau silver 319
oil-lamp: American glass 275
Olerys, Joseph 48
Omian family 26
O'Neale, Jefferyes Hamett: work of 72, 73
ormolu: use in furniture 170
ostrich egg: mounted in silver 310
Oudry, Jean Baptiste 396, 398

Paddy, Samuel 314
Paine, James 177, 178, 179
painters: Persian attitudes to 403–4
painting:
    on faience 36, 42
    on glass 266
    on maiolica 31, 33
    miniatures, 352, 375, 403–6
    over-glaze 77
    on porcelain 67, 77, 410
    under-glaze 13, 77, 85
Pairpoint Manufacturing Company 300
    work of 300
Paleologue, Andronikos 389
pall: Russian 386, 386, 387
pan: Dutch delft 42
panel and frame furniture 118
paperweights:
    American glass 274, 277
    French 278–82, 278–82
    jade 380
    vases 302, 303, 304–5
papier-mâché 375, 440–3
parlourmaid's tray 442

Pargeter, Philip 288
Paris glass 284–5
  gold: boxes 352, *353*, *354*
    marks on *355*
  silver *356*, *357*, *359*
Parmantier (furniture maker) 174
parquetry 117, 132, 153
Parr, Thomas: work of *105*
Passglas 244
pastille-burner: lustreware 90, *90*
patch-boxes: enamel *414*
patchwork: American 399–402
pâte d'émail 295
pâte-de-verre 294, 295
Pater, J. B. 409
  painting by *411*
Pazaurek, G. E. 276
'peacock-feather' vases 304
pearls 462
pearlware 85, 95
pedestals:
  Biedermeier 215
  English 210, *211*
  French *141*
Peereboom, Georges Antoine 235
Pelham, Henry: engraving by *346*,
  347
Peligot, Eugène 279
Pelikan family 266
Pellatt, Apsley 267, 277, 288
Pelletier, Jean 142
Pellipario, Nicola 33
Penig stoneware 28
Pennant, Thomas 462
Pennington, Seth 86
Penrose, George and William 260–1
Pennsylvania pottery 53, *54*
Pepys, Samuel 134, 464
Percier, Charles 207, 210
  work of *422*
Perigal (clockmaker) 423
Perley Parlour *160*
Persian carpets 375, 390–3
  lustreware 23
  miniatures 375, 403–6
  pottery 21–4
    distinguishing 22
Perugino (Pietro Vannucci) 123
Pete, David: work of *341*
Pfohl, Karl 266
Philadelphia clocks 427
Phillips, John 93
photograph album: Tunbridge ware
  451, *452*
Phyfe, Duncan 201, 204
pianos 215
  boxes in shape of *454*
  'giraffe' 210, *211*
  grand 191, 210
  papier-mâché cases for 443
  'square' 210
Piccolpasso, Cipriano:
  Three Books of the Potter's Art
  29–31, *30–1*, 89
picnic hampers 456
Picon family 398
picture-frames: French *141*
pier-glass: Hepplewhite *190*
Pierre, François 277
Pillement, Jean Baptiste 325
Pillot (furniture maker) 175
Pimon, work of *157*
Pinchbeck, Christopher 462
pine 147
Pineau (furniture maker) 162
pipe-cases *457*, *458*, 459–60
pipe-cradle *460*
pipe-rack *460*
pipe-roaster 459
pipes:
  briars 460
  clay 458–9
  hardwood 460, *460*
  meerschaum 460
  silver 458

wooden 460
pipe tray *460*
Piranesi, Giambattista 366
pitchers:
  American glass *275*, *296*
  American silver *349*
Pitkin brothers 439
plaques:
  enamel 414, *415*, 416, *416*
  Spanish pottery 48, *49*
Platel, Pierre 337–8
plates:
  Chantilly porcelain 62, *63*
  Chelsea 72, *73*
  Dutch delft 42, *44*
  faience *36*, *37*
  lustreware *91*, *92*
  maiolica *30*, *31*, *32*
  Persian pottery 22, *22*
  redware *52*
  Spanish *46*
  transfer-printed *94*, *95*
platinum: for lustring 90
Plato time indicator 438–9
platter, ceremonial: French silver
  359, 359
Poirel, Nicholas 36
Poiriet (furniture maker) 162
poison:
  boiling in celadon 14
  shattering crystal 312, 319
'Polonaise' carpets 393
Pompadour, Madame Antoinette la
  Marquise de 65
porcelain:
  American trade 99–103
  blue and white 17, *17*, 21, 84–8, 101
  Chelsea 70–4
  for clock cases 419
  colours on 61
    ground 66–7, 77
  earliest 11
  enamelling 14, 18–19
  firing: early success at 13
  gilding 62, 64, 67
  hard-paste 11, 71
  ingredients 11
  Japanese 17–20
  Meissen 55–9
  Ming dynasty 12–16, 21
  mounted in silver *308*, *309*, 312
  painting 67, 77, 410
  printing 77
  Sèvres 65–9
  soft-paste 11, 61–4, 66, 71, 76, 86, 101
    preparation 66
  under-glaze blue 20
  under-glaze painting 13, 77, 85
  under-glaze red 16
  use on furniture 162, 164, 165
  Worcester 75–9
porcelain marks 98
  blue and white 88
  Chantilly 62, *64*
  Chelsea 71, *72*
  Japanese 18
  Ming 13, 14
  Mennecy 63, *64*
  Persians imitating Chinese 22
  Worcester 76, *77*
porringers 329
  American silver *313*, 314
Portland vase 288
  copy *290*
postcards 446–8
potato-rings, see dish-rings
Poterat, Edmé 36, 39
Poterat, Louis 39
pot-pourri: Sèvres 66, 68, *69*
Potsdam glass *242*, 246
pottery:
  American 112–15
  Arts and Crafts Movement 108–11
  earliest 11

painting 11, 82
Persian 21–4
  distinguishing 22
  redware 50–4
  Spanish 18th century 45–9
  Staffordshire figures 104–7, *104–7*
  stoneware 25–8
  transfer-printing 93
pottery marks 98
  Dutch delft 44
  Rookwood *115*
pouring-vessel: jade *380*
Poussin, Lavallée 397
Pouzait (watchmaker) 434
Powell, James 268
Powell, James, & Sons: work of *271*,
  272
Prague glass 245
Pratt, F. & R. 96–7
Prest, Thomas 433
Priester, Johann Jakob 319
Prince, Reverend Thomas 347
printing:
  multi-colour 96–7
  on porcelain 77
  transfer- 82, 93, 94–8
Prior, George 423
Prouvé, Victor 295, 468
'Provincial' dish *15*, 16
Prud'hon (clockmaker): work of *421*
Pugin, Augustus Welby Northmore
  225–7
  work of *226*, *227*
punch-bowls:
  American silver *315*
  Dutch delft *40*
  English silver 331, *331*
  Irish silver 342, *343*

qalian 21, *22*
Qasim, Muhammed 406
Qazwin 405
  paintings from *403*, 406, *406*
Queen Anne furniture 117, 151–5,
  159
  mirrors 248
  silver 307, 327–31
Queen's ware 81–2, *81*, *82*, *83*
quilting 399
quilting bee 401
quilts: patchwork 375, 399–402
quiver: embroidered *389*

Raeren stoneware 26, *26*
rafraichissoir 165
Raimondi, Marcantonio 33
Raleigh, Sir Walter 458
Rannie, James 180
Raphaelle ware 33
Ravenet, Simon François 415
  copy of work 414, *415*
Ravenscroft, George 237, 246
Ravensworth Castle, Co. Durham 225
Rawlins, William 314
récamier 209
Redgrave, Richard, A.R.A. 272, 442
  work of *269*
red lead 276
redware 11, 50–4
Regency furniture 210–13
  silver 364–8
regulator clock 426, *426*
Reichsadler glass 246
Reid, William 86
Reinicke, Peter 57
  work of *58*
reliquary: *cristallo* 240, 241
Rémond, Félix 208
Renault, René 172

repeating work 434
resist lustring 90
Revere, Paul II 307, 346–50, *347*
  work of 346–50
Revett, N. 366
Rhee Sambae 17
Ribaucourt, Georges de 468
Ricardo, Halsey 108
Richardson, Benjamin 288
Richardson, Francis 317
Richardson, Joseph Snr: work of *335*
Richardson, W. H. & B.: work of *269*,
  272
Riedel, Joseph 267
Riesener, Henri François 167
Riesener, Jean-Henri 165, 166–70,
  167
  work of *167–70*
rings, mourning 464
Rittenhouse, David 428
Rivoire, Apollos 347
Riza-i-'Abbasi: work of 406, *406*
Roberday, G.: work of *354*
Robert, Joseph-François 284
Roberts, Samuel 360, 363
Robin, Robert 419, 420, 434
Robinson, Enoch 276
rock crystal, *see* crystal
Rockingham porcelain 106
rococo 321–2
  furniture 117
  silver: English 336–40
    German 321–2
Rodmarton Manor 229
Roe, Nathaniel: work of 328
Roggen (clockmaker) 419
Roman glass 238
Rookwood pottery 11, 112–15
Ross, James 416
Roucel, Louis: work of *353*
Rouen faience *34*, *35*, 36, *37*, 38, *39*
Rouen porcelain 61
roundel: Dutch delft *41*
Rouse (Ros), William 314
Rousseau, Eugène 286, 292–4
  work of 292, *293*
Roux, Edouard 48
Royal Dublin Society 260
Royall, Anne 275
Rudolf II 245
Rundell, Philip 366
Rundell, Bridge & Rundell 365, 366–7
Ruskin, John 230, 271
Russell, Sir Gordon 231
Russell, R. 452
Russian embroidery 375, 386–9

Sadiqi Beg 406
  work of *406*
Sadler, John 416
  work of *416*
Sadler & Green 82
Safawid dynasty 390, 392, 403, 406
saggar 42
St Cloud porcelain 61
St Louis glass 237, 264, 278, 279, *279*,
  280, *280*, 282, *283*, 284, *284*, 285,
  285–6
St Porchaire ware 34, *37*
salt: use in glazes 25
salts:
  American glass *255*, 277
  American silver *315*
  enamel 416, *417*
  English silver *339*
  German silver *318*
  Irish glass 259, *262*
  maiolica *30*
  silver mounted crystal *308*, *309*,
    309, *311*, *312*
  stoneware 28
salvers:

American silver 333, 335
  English silver 324, 338, 339, 340
Samson of Paris 77
Samurai 381
Sandeman, George 179
Sanders, Robert 317
Sanderson, Jacob 201–2
Sanderson, Robert 314
  work of 313, 315
sauce-boats:
  American silver 335
  French silver 357, 357
  Irish silver 342, 343, 344, 345
saucer: Sèvres 66
Savage, George 432
Savage, Thomas 314
Savery, William 184
savonarola 124, 124
Savory, A. B. & Son 371
scent-bottles:
  Chelsea 72, 73, 74
  English glass 288, 289, 291
  French glass 295
Schaats, Bartholomew 316
Schaeffler, Daniel 320
Schaper, Johann 244
Schinkel, Karl Friedrich 215–16
  work of 214
Schmidt, Christoph 319
Schneider (glass maker) 295
Schneider, Gaspard 206
Schnelle 26, 26, 27
scholar's equipment: jade 380
Schwanhardt, Georg 245
Schwerdfeger (furniture maker) 170
Scott, Digby 326, 366, 367
  work of 364
Scott, Thomas 189
screens:
  cheval- (pole-) 442
  fire- 160
  glass 302
  hand- 442
  table: jade 376, 377, 378, 379, 380
scribe 403
scriptor (scriptones, scritores) 134, 135, 144
Schürer, Christof 244
secretaire ('secretary') 159
  à abattant (drop-front) 165, 168, 169, 172, 208, 208
  American 182, 197, 198, 198, 199, 202, 204, 204
  English 178, 188
  French 162, 163, 168, 169, 170
'secretary', see secretaire
Seddon, George 188
  work of 189
Seeman, Abraham 413
semainier 208
serpentine 312
serre-papiers 209
Serrurier-Bovy, Gustave 234–5
  work of 232, 233, 235
services:
  American silver 349, 350
  French silver-gilt 357
settees 158
  American 201
  Queen Anne 154
settle 119
Sèvres porcelain 11, 64, 100, 101, 101, 410
  early years 65–9
  use on furniture 162, 164
sewing-machines 401
Seymour, John and Thomas 202
  work of 198, 199, 200
sgabello 124, 124
Shaker furniture 218–22
Shakers 218–19
Shanbally Castle, Co. Tipperary 225
Shang dynasty 13
Sharp, Messrs 451
Shaw, John: work of 198, 199

Shaybani Khan 405–6
Shaykhzada 405
  work of 406, 407
Shearer, Thomas 189, 190
Sheffield plate 307, 360–3
  silver 370
shelf cabinet: Japanese 126, 127
shelf clocks 427, 430, 430, 436, 437, 438
shells: gold-mounted as boxes 352–3
Sheraton, Thomas 117, 191–4, 200, 201
  Cabinet Dictionary 193, 194
  Cabinet-maker and Upholsterer's Drawing Book 190, 191, 192, 193, 193–4, 194, 195, 197
  Cabinet-Maker, Upholsterer and General Artist's Encyclopaedia 193
shield: Regency silver 367
Shintoism 384
Shirayamadani, K.: work of 114
Shiraz 404
  lustreware 23
  paintings from 405, 405
Shirley, Frederick S. 298
sho-dana 126, 127
Shumin: work of 383
Shuzan, Hagen 382
sideboards:
  American 196, 197, 198, 201
  Arts and Crafts 228, 230
  cellaret 190
  French provincial 171
  Sheraton 193
Siegburg stoneware 26, 27
Siena maiolica 31, 32, 33
Sigalon, Antoine 35
  work of 36
Silesian glass 245–6
silk-weaving 143
silver:
  American 313–17, 332–5
  assays 342
  Britannia standard 307, 327, 328
  casting 307
  chinoiserie 323–6
  cut-card work 307
  French Neo-classical 356–9
  German 318–22
  hallmarks 338, 342, 365
    American 314
    Irish 344
  Irish 341–5
  Maltese 344
  melting down 307
  mounted wares 308–12, 319
  Queen Anne 327–31
  Regency 364–8
  town marks: Irish 344
  Victorian tea and coffee sets 369–73
Simms family 266
Siyawush 406
sleeping-chair 132
sleigh-bed 202
slip 50, 51
Slodtz brothers: work of 162, 163
Smith, Benjamin 326, 366, 367
  work of 271, 272, 364
Smith, George 210
  work of 212, 213, 223
Smith, James 367
  work of 328
Smith, John: work of 331
Smith, William 296
Smithin, Samuel 336
smoke: use in lustring 46
smoking:
  in Japan 381–2
  introduction into Europe 457
smoking accessories 457–60
snuff-boxes:
  enamel 415
  French gold 352–5
snuffer-trays 442

Soane, Sir John 225
sofas: 158
  Biedermeier 214, 215, 215
  conversational 227
  French 173
  Italian 124
  papier-mâché 440
sofa-table 201
soft-paste porcelain 11, 61–4, 66, 71, 76, 86, 101
Soumain, Simeon 316, 332, 334
soup-tureen, see tureens
South (New) Jersey glass 255–6, 274
soy frame: Sheffield plate 362
Spain: 18th century pottery 45–9
Sparkes, John 109–10
Spencer, John 177
Spiller, Gottfried 246
spill holder: redware 50
Spode, Josiah II 11
Spode pottery 90, 91, 95
spoons:
  Irish silver 341, 342, 345
  Victorian silver 370
spout-cup: American silver 316
Sprimont, Nicholas 71, 74
spur marks 18
Staffordshire lustreware 89, 90, 91, 92
  porcelain figures 104–7, 104–7
  pottery 80–3, 96
stained glass 267
Stalker and Parker:
  Treatise of Japaning and Varnishing 144
stands: Shaker 220, 221, 222
Staritskii workshop 389
Statter, Dover: work of 432, 433
Stchoukine, Dr Ivan 406
steel: jewellery in 462
Steele, Sir Richard 462
Stevengraphs 444–8, 444–8
Stevens, Thomas 445
  work of 444
Stevens and Williams 288
  work of 290
stickwork 450, 451, 452
Stiegel, Henry William 237, 255, 256–8, 274
Stöckel (cabinet-maker) 166
Stodart, M. & W.: work of 210, 211
stoneware 11, 54, 55
  in America 100
  black 83
  German 25–8
  glazes 25
  salt-glazed 109
stools:
  American 149, 150, 150
  back-stool 120
  Elizabethan 118, 120
  Italian 124, 124
  William and Mary 144, 144
  X-framed 209
Storer, Bellamy 113
Storr, Paul 326, 364–8
  work of 364–8
Storr, Mortimer & Hunt 371
  work of 370, 371
Stothard (silver designer) 367
Stourbridge glass 269, 287, 298
  imitations 268
Stowe, Buckinghamshire 225
strap-work 118
Stras, G. F. 462
Stroganovs 387
Strudwick, J. 370
Stuart, James 'Athenian' 181, 366
Stylen, Wynant 165
  work of 167
sugar bowls:
  American glass 254, 255, 255, 257, 276
  American silver 347
  Chantilly 63
  English silver 328

German glass 254, 255
Irish glass 261
Mennecy 61, 62, 63, 63
Worcester 78
sugar-box: American silver 315
sugar-castor, see castors
sugar-vases: Regency silver 368
Sunderland pottery 91, 93, 93
Sunflower Pottery 111
Sung dynasty 13, 14
Sutton, John: work of 329
Swansea lustreware 91
Swansea pottery 93, 95
Swan Service 56, 57, 58, 59
Swatow porcelain 18
sweetmeat dish: American 101
Swiss watches 434
Symon family 26
Symonds, James: work of 148
synchroniser 420
Syng family 317

Tabard family 398
table à la Bourgogne 165
table cistern: maiolica 36, 37
table en chiffonière 164, 165
tables:
  altar-table 128, 129
  American 149–50
  Art Nouveau 232, 233
  butterfly- 150
  cabinet- and writing- 198, 199
  card- 145, 153, 201, 203
  centre- 212, 213
  console 171
  dining- 201, 220
  double 233
  draw 119, 120
  drawing- 213
  drawing-room 210, 211
  drop-leaf 160
  English walnut 133
  gaming- 160, 443
  gate-legged 132, 134, 150
  Greco-Roman 208
  inlaid, Italian 125, 125
  knee-hole 145
  lacquered, Chinese 129, 130
  leg designs 117
  library 177, 181
  Louis XIV 162, 163
  multi-functional 165, 166
  octagonal 226, 227
  pedestal 148, 207
  Pembroke 182, 186, 190, 201
  pier- 187, 202
  papier-mâché 440, 441
  Queen Anne 155
  reading- 189
  renaissance 124
  side- 145, 154, 209
  small 134–5
  sofa- 201
  tables à transformation 165
  table volante 165
  tea- 160
  toilet-: American 150
  tripod 182
  Tunbridge ware 451
  used on beds 128
  vide poche 164
  wine- 189
  with drawers 140
  work- 208, 215, 216, 217, 456
  writing- 137, 145, 198, 199
table-service: French silver 358
Tabriz 404
  paintings from 404, 406, 407
  pottery 23
Taddel, Heinrich 320
Tahmasp, Shah 390, 405
tailoress' counter 220

Talavera de la Reina pottery 45, 46, 47–8, 49
Talbert, Bruce J. 228
   work of 230
Talbot, A. 452
tallboy: English 153, 184
tankards:
   American silver 315, 316, 349, 350
   Bohemian glass 266, 267
   English silver 329–30, 329
   German silver 319
   Irish silver 342, 343
   silver chinoiserie 324
   stoneware 26, 26, 27, 28
   Worcester 86, 87
Tanqueray, David: work of 328, 329
tansu 126, 127
tapestry: French 375, 394–8
Tardessir, Domenico 36
tassel marks 22
Tatham, C. H. 291, 366
Taylor, John 360, 414
Taylor, William Watts 113–14, 115
tazza: French glass 285
tea and coffee machine: Sheffield plate 360, 361
tea-caddies: (canisters)
   Chinese 326
   Dutch delft 40, 41
   English silver 324, 326, 328, 337, 338
   Irish glass 259
   Spanish pottery 48, 48
   Tunbridge ware 449
tea-party 372, 372
teapots:
   American silver 316, 332, 333, 334, 335, 349, 350
   Chinese silver 325
   English silver 327, 328, 328
   Longton Hall 86, 87
   lustreware 92
   Mennecy 60, 62
   Regency silver 365
   Sèvres 68, 69
   Sheffield plate 362
   silver 307
   Victorian silver 369, 370, 371
   Wedgwood 80, 81
   Worcester 78, 86, 87
teapoy 451, 452
teasets (services):
   American silver 350
   Mennecy 63
   miniature 86, 88
   Regency silver 367–8
   Victorian silver 369–73, 371
tea-urns:
   English silver 323, 364
   Meissen 56
   Sheffield plate 362, 363
Teniers, David II 355
Terry, Carden 345
Terry, Eli 429
   work of 430
Terry & Company 438
textileographs 445
Theed & Pickett 366
thermos flask 456
Thevet, Frère André 457
Thierry de la Ville d'Avray 166–7
Thomae, Benjamin 56
Thomas, Seth 429, 430, 438
   work of 437
Thomire, Pierre-Philippe 208
Thompson, Mrs Alexander: work of 402
Thomson, Hale 296
'Three Friends' motif 18
tiara: golden 357–8
ticket clock 438–9
Tiffany, Louis Comfort 237, 301–5
   work of 301–5
tiffin set 43
'Tiger Eye' 113

tigerware 26
   silver garnished 311, 312
tile-pictures 38, 39, 47, 48
tiles:
   Dutch delft 42, 43, 43
   Persian pottery 23
   pottery 108
   tin-glazed 35
Timbrell, Robert: work of 329, 331
tin-glaze 31, 34–5, 61
tin oxide 11, 34, 46
Tinworth, George 110
tobacco: introduction into Europe 457
tobacco-boxes 458, 460
tobacco-jars 459, 460
toilet- (dressing-table) casket 454, 455
toilet services:
   English silver 323, 338, 339
   French silver 358, 359
   porcelain 69
Tokuyemon, Toshima 18
Tomotada 385
   work of 382
torchères 140, 215, 210, 211
Tournay, Marquis de 172
tou ts'ai enamelling 20
Townsend family 184
trade-marks 98
Trafalgar vase 364, 367
transfer-prints 83, 93, 94–8
trapunto quilts 375, 402
travelling-case, gentleman's 455, 456
trays:
   faience 36, 39
   papier-mâché 440–2
   Persian pottery 22
Tucker, William Ellis 102
Tucker & Hemphill 102
Tucker porcelain 99, 100, 102, 103
tumblers :
   American glass 256
   Bohemian glass 266
Tunbridge ware 375, 449–52
Tunbridge Ware Manufacturing Company 452
tureens:
   French silver 356, 357, 357
   Queen's Ware 82
   Regency silver 365
   Sheffield plate 360, 361, 362
Turkey-work 120
Turkish faience 13–14
Turner, Thomas 95
Tyler, Harry: work of 402

under-glaze colours 16, 20, 95
Upton, W. 452
Urbino maiolica 31, 32, 33
urns: Wedgwood 83

Vachette, Adrien-Jean-Maximilien 355
   work of 353
Valentien, Albert R.: work of 112, 114
Valentine cards 445
Van Blarenberghe, Henri-Joseph 355
   work of 352
Van Briggle, Artus 115
Van Cleynhoven, Quirinus 43
Van der Burgh, Cornelius 316
Vandercruse, Roger (Lacroix or Delacroix) 165
Van der Velde, Henry 234–5
   work of 232, 233, 234, 235
Van Dyck, Peter 316, 332
   work of 317, 335
Van Frijtom, Frederick 43
   painting 41
Van Inburgh, Peter: work of 313

Van Loo, Carle 355
Van Riesenburgh, Bernard 164–5
   work of 161, 162, 163, 164, 165
Van Vianen family 319
vase carpet 391, 393
vase clocks 419, 421
Vasenpokal 243
vases:
   American glass 296, 296–8, 297, 298, 301, 302, 303, 304, 305
   Art Nouveau glass 292, 293
   Arts and Crafts Movement 108, 109, 110, 111
   Bohemian glass 264, 265
   Chinese export 102, 103
   Dutch delft 41, 42
   Elgin 288
   English glass 271, 272, 287, 288, 289, 290, 291
   'Etruscan' 83
   faience 37, 39
   French glass 283, 284, 286
   Irish glass 260
   Japanese porcelain 20
   maiolica 29
   Meissen 57, 58, 59
   paperweight 302, 303, 304–5
   Philadelphia porcelain 102, 103
   Portland 288
      copy 290
   Regency silver 364, 366, 367
   Rookwood 112, 114
   Sèvres 68
   Spanish pottery 48, 49
   Wedgwood 80, 83
   Worcester 76, 77, 77, 78, 86, 87
Vaupel (Vaupal), Louis (Lewis) 276
veneers 131, 132
   end-grain 451–2
   woods for 204
Venetian glass 237, 238–41, 286
Vernet, Claude-Joseph 409
Vernet, Horace 358
vernis Martin 162
verrière: French silver 357
Versailles, Palace of 136
Vestier, Antoine: painting by 167
Vever, Henri 467, 468
Vever, Paul 468
Victoria, Queen 442, 443
Victorian fitted boxes 375, 453–6
   glass 269–72
   Gothic furniture 223–7
   silver tea and coffee services 369–73
vide poche 164
Vile, William 181
Villiers, George 247
Vincennes porcelain 62, 64, 65
Vingt, Les 233
Violette faience 39
visiting-card cases 443
Vivarini 239
voider 442
Voigtland stoneware 28
Vonêche glass 264
Vulliamy, Justin and Benjamin 423, 425–6
   work of 423, 423, 425

Weals, Peter 230
Wakefield, Hugh 271
Waldenburg stoneware 28
Waldglas 243
Walker, Thomas: work of 342, 343
Wall, Dr John 74, 76, 79
wall-cistern: Spanish 47
Wallis, George 442
wall-papers 178
walnut 156, 184
   furniture in 131–5
   types 153

Walpole, Horace 223, 414
Walpole salver 338, 339, 340
Walter, Amalric 295
   work of 294, 295
Waltham Watch Company 439
wardrobes:
   Art Nouveau 235
   French 138, 141, 172, 172
Warwick vase 366
Washington, George 101, 102, 198
watches:
   American 439
   decimal 432, 433
   escapement 432, 432, 434
   history of mechanism 432
   keyless winding 432–3
   mass-production 434–5
   self-winding 420
   Victorian 431–5
   two-train 431
watch-holder: Staffordshire 104
watch-movements 435
watchmakers' hand tools 434
watch-stand: pottery 90
Waterbury Clock Company: work of 438
water-carrier: redware 52
water closets 165
Waterford glass 259, 260, 261–2, 263
Waterhouse, Alfred 225
Waterloo Glass House Company 260, 261
Watkins, Alexander: work of 432, 433
Watson, John: work of 370
Watteau, Antoine 409
   work of 413, 416, 417
Webb, Edward 314
Webb, Philip 272
Webb, Thomas 288, 289, 298
   work of 287, 288, 289, 291
Webb, Thomas, & Sons 271
Wedgwood, John 96
Wedgwood, Josiah 11, 80–3, 89, 95
Wedgwood lustreware 90, 90–1
   pottery 80–3, 96, 97
Wednesbury enamels 416
Wellington, 1st Duke of 366, 368
Welsh lustreware 90, 91
Wentzell, John William 255
Westerwald stoneware 25, 26, 27, 27–8
Westropp, Dudley 261
Whateley, George 361
Wheeler, Candace 302
Whieldon, Thomas 81
Whipham & Wright: work of 323
Whitefriars glass 268
Whitney (glass maker) 276
Whitney, Eli 402, 429
wig-stands 39, 41
Wilcox, H.: work of 114
Wilhelm V of Bavaria 245
Willard, Simon and Aaron 429–30, 439
   work of 428, 429, 430
Willems, Joseph: work of 72, 73
William and Mary furniture 117, 142–5
   mirrors 248
William Henry, Prince 181
Williams, Richard and Company 260
Willms, A. A. 370
willow pattern 95
Wilson, Joseph 360
Windsor Castle 225, 226
wine-bottle 27, 27
wine-coolers:
   glass 270, 271–2
   porcelain 62, 63
   Sheffield plate 360
   silver 366
winecup: silver 314, 329
wineglasses: English 250–3, 250–3, 272, 273
wine-labels (bottle tickets): enamel

479

414, 415, *415*
Winn, Sir Rowland 177, 179–80
Winslow, Edward 314
    work of *315*
Winter, Martin 246
Winthrop, John 428
Wise family 449, 452
Wistar, Caspar 237; 255
Wistar, Richard 255–6
Wollters, Herman 27
Wood, Anthony à 331
Woodall, George 289, 291
    work of 288, *289*
Woodall, Thomas 289, 291
    work of *287*
wood:
    in American furniture 203–4
    18th century varieties 153
    for French provincial furniture
        174–5
    for furniture 119
    for marquetry 131, 132
    for netsuke 385
    for veneers and inlays 204
Worcester porcelain 75–9, 85–6, *87,
    96,* 100, 370, *371*
Work, Henry Clay 428
work-basket: Victorian 456
work-box: English *454,* 456
Wornum, Ralph N. 370
Wright, Joseph: painting by 462, *463*
writing-box: English *454*
writing cabinet :
    Sheraton 192, *193*
    Stuart 134
writing-desks, *see* desks
writing materials: papier-mâché 442
Wyatt, James 225
Wyatville, Sir Jeffry 225
Wynkoop, Benjamin 316

Xavier, Saint Francis 17
Xhrouet 67

Yarmouth, Lord 65
yoshidaya 19

Zaman, Muḥammed 406
Zeitz stoneware 28
Zeshin 385
Zwischengoldglas technique 264